THE SCIENTIFIC STUDY OF
POLITICAL LEADERSHIP

The Scientific Study of Political Leadership

GLENN D. PAIGE

THE FREE PRESS
A Division of Macmillan Publishing Co., Inc.
NEW YORK

Collier Macmillan Publishers
LONDON

The Free Press
A Division of Macmillan Publishing Co., Inc.
866 Third Avenue, New York, N.Y. 10022

Collier Macmillan Canada, Ltd.

Library of Congress Catalog Card Number: 76-50464

Printed in the United States of America

printing number

1 2 3 4 5 6 7 8 9 10

Library of Congress Cataloging in Publication Data

Paige, Glenn D
  The scientific study of political leadership.

  Bibliography: p.
  Includes indexes.
  1. Leadership. 2. Political sociology. I. Title.
HM141.P282   301.15'53   76-50464
ISBN 0-02-923630-4

Excerpts from Jasper B. Shannon, ed., *The Study of Comparative Government* (1969), are reprinted by permission of the reprint publisher, Greenwood Press, Inc. Excerpts from Gabriel A. Almond, "Political Development: Analytical and Normative Perspectives," *Comparative Political Studies* 1, 4 (January 1969), 447–469, are reprinted by permission of the author and the publisher, Sage Publications, Inc. Excerpts from Dankwart A. Rustow, ed., *Philosophers and Kings,* entire issue of *Daedalus* (Summer 1968), are reprinted by permission of the publisher. The excerpt from *On the Death of King George,* Caedmon Record TC 1003, is reprinted by permission of Caedmon Records, Inc. Excerpts from the CBS News Special, "Five Presidents on the Presidency," as broadcast over the CBS Television Network, April 26, 1973, are reprinted by permission of CBS News. Excerpts from Gopinath Dhawan, *The Political Philosophy of Mahatma Gandhi* (1962), are reprinted by permission of the Navajivan Trust. Excerpts from Adolf Hitler, *Mein Kampf,* trans. Ralph Mannheim (1975), are reprinted by permission of the Houghton Mifflin Company and Curtis Brown Ltd. The excerpt from Mary H. Curzan, ed., *Careers and the Study of Political Science* (1976) is reprinted by permission of the American Political Science Association. Titles of doctoral dissertations retrieved from the Datrix II system are reprinted by permission of Xerox University Microfilms.

For
Richard C. and Marjorie L. Snyder
political scientist, teacher, friends

The universe is not given to us as a map or a guide. It is made up by human minds and imaginations out of slight hints which come from acute observations and the profound stratagems of experiments.

ISIDOR I. RABI
Nobel Laureate in Physics

There is an infinite number of factors and relations which influence and determine events in varying degrees, and it is impossible to grasp all of them. Still we can pick out the dominating forces at work and by observing external reality and by experiment and practice, trial and error, grope our way to ever-widening knowledge and truth.

JAWAHARLAL NEHRU
Prime Minister of India

Each generation redefines its own image of political science, with greater insight, one might hope, as our understanding of political life increases.

DAVID A. EASTON
Political Scientist

CONTENTS

LIST OF ILLUSTRATIONS

Tables

Figures

PREFACE

IT IS HOPED THAT this book and an earlier collection of readings, *Political Leadership* (1972),[1] will help advance the scientific study of political leadership in colleges and universities throughout the world. The rise of a nonviolent world community of scholars dedicated to the creation and use of knowledge on this subject is as essential for human well-being as is the cooperation we expect from scientists who study agriculture, demography, medicine, and global ecology.

Those who are prejudiced against "science" and "leadership" may be inclined to dismiss this book on the basis of its title alone. Those willing to devote their attention to the challenges it poses, however, should emerge from their reading with a clearer sense of needed next steps.

My indebtedness to the contributions of political scientists and of scholars in other scientific and humane disciplines will be abundantly apparent. So will be the limitations of a single scholar, in a single discipline, in a single language, in a single cultural setting, at a given point in historical time. That is why this book constitutes a call for scientific collegiality within and across disciplines and nations, aspiring toward convergence in the study of political leadership of the most varied values and skills. Both the complexity and the importance of the subject demand it.

In writing this book I benefited greatly from a joint appointment in the Department of Political Science and in the Social Science Research Institute (now the Social Sciences and Linguistics Institute) of the University of Hawaii, where I have been teaching undergraduate and graduate courses on political leadership since 1968. The encouragement and stimulation of colleagues like Harry J. Friedman and Robert S. Cahill, indeed all of them,* have been exceptionally significant. Among administrators, linguist Guy Kirkendall's rare combination of supportiveness and ability to challenge exploration of unfamiliar

*Belinda Aquino, Theodore L. Becker, Douglas Bwy, Richard W. Chadwick, Michael Haas, Manfred Henningsen, Philip E. Jacob, Henry S. Kariel, George Kent, Benedict J. Kerkvliet, Richard Kosaki, Yasumasa Kuroda, Oliver Lee, Werner Levi, Norman Meller, Michael L. Mezey, Neal A. Milner, Deane E. Neubauer, Lawrence H. Nitz, Richard Pratt, Fred W. Riggs, Ira S. Rohter, Glendon Schubert, Michael J. Shapiro, Robert B. Stauffer, Dae-Sook Suh, John F. Wilson, our graduate assistants, and office staff Jeanette T. Matsuda, Carole K. Moon, and Lynette H. F. Kotake.

terrain has been a cherished contribution to a scholar's journey. With Goethe, he has reminded me, "All theory is grey, my friend, but the precious tree of life is green." To the University of Hawaii Foundation and to former president Harlan Cleveland, I am indebted for a semester of innovative program support that permitted exploration of ideas that could contribute to the creation of a political leadership research center. To the multidisciplinary group of graduate students who contributed to this project, I am grateful: Talmage Day (propositional inventory), Chung-si Ahn (biographical inventory), Sheila Babbie (interactive leader-follower survey research), Stanley Stephenson (experimental design), Sylvia Hirahara (knowledge utilization), and Richard Panter (multimedia resources for research, teaching, and application).

Some of the basic ideas about what needed to be done in the study of political leadership took shape during my previous tenure in Princeton University. Awareness of indebtedness to that institution continues to grow. As this book neared completion, I surprisingly rediscovered that Princeton scholars Richard C. Snyder and Hubert H. Wilson had included an excerpt on "Political Leadership" from a work by Charles E. Merriam in their pioneering introductory textbook, *Roots of Political Behavior* (1949),[2] which they had dedicated "to the students of Politics II at Princeton University in 1947-1948." That is where my own introduction to political science began. Although none of us will ever forget those two master teachers, I had forgotten Merriam's essay among all the readings Snyder and Wilson had piled upon us in the old Chancellor Green Library. They had pointed out the "root" of something that I, and others, had an excited sense of rediscovering decades later. I hope that this book, even if forgotten, will someday make a similar contribution to the chain of human political learning.

The multidisciplinary perspective of this book and its sense of cultural limitation would have been unlikely without enormously stimulating interdisciplinary graduate training in political science at Northwestern University (1957-1959) combined with East Asian language and area study at Harvard University (1955-1957). Insight into the creative potential of political leadership might not have occurred if Northwestern social psychologist Donald T. Campbell had not urged us to be alert for "natural political experiments" and if subsequently I had not immersed myself in the study of divided Korea, partly as a visiting scholar in the Graduate School of Public Administration, Seoul National University, under the auspices of the University of Minnesota (1959-1961). Brief but impressive meetings with North Korean scholars in Moscow (1960) and Paris (1973) helped to deepen comparative perspective as well as to make real the possibility of peaceful scientific interchange.

Involvement with Korea, first as a soldier in 1950, finally brought me to a nonviolent value position. It was clear by the 1970s—sooner for some—that the war fought for peace, freedom, and liberation had led to unprecedented militarization, repression, threats to employ nuclear weapons, and a deadly race for nuclear capabilities. Against this background, it was shocking to discover that the U.S. Department of State was the main obstacle to acceptance by North Korean scholars in 1973-1974 of an invitation for a peaceful visit to the University of Hawaii. That meant no *aloha* for North Koreans. Rooted in twenty-three years of Korea-related thinking and emotions, my reaction to this discovery was intensely personal. My values had to change.

Whatever future orientation is expressed in this book has been greatly influenced by the late Hawaii Governor John A. Burns, who appointed me in 1970 to a group to plan for a Governor's Conference on the Year 2000.[3] This led to my education as program chairman by journalist-scholar George Chaplin, overall conference chairman; political science colleague James A. Dator; leading futurists; and hundreds of Hawaii citizens; as well as by the extraordinarily imaginative international futures research community in meetings held in Kyoto (1970), Bucharest (1972), and continued in the International Conference on Malaysia in the Year 2001, held in Kuala Lumpur (1975).

Since publication of *Political Leadership* (1972), I have benefited by correspondence with a number of colleagues on problems related to the study of political leadership. These include Jose V. Abueva, James D. Barber, Carl Beck, Arnold Beichman, Yehezkel Dror, Richard H. Dekmejian, Lewis J. Edinger, Linton C. Freeman, Alexander L. George, Betty Glad, Bae-Ho Hahn, John Higley, Robert M. Johnstone, Chong-Lim Kim, Thomas W. Milburn, John D. Montgomery, Kinhide Mushakoji, David Roth, S. Lee Seaton, Lester G. Seligman, Richard Stubbs, John E. Tashjean, Robert C. Tucker, Thomas C. Wiegle, and Jerzy J. Wiatr. Such correspondence has been especially meaningful for a mid-Pacific island scholar.

To all these individuals and institutions—colleagues, students, staff—and to all who support our scholarly labors, I am grateful.

For bibliographical assistance I am indebted to former Princeton students Karl D. Jackson and John O. King, Jr., and to Carolyn Kiyabu Ball of the University of Hawaii. My mathematical geography colleague Forrest R. Pitts has been uncommonly generous in providing me with citations on leadership discovered in the course of his wide-ranging search of the social science literature on simulation.

For permission to reprint copyrighted material, grateful acknowledgment is made to the authors, editors, and publishers cited on page iv and in the source lines of tables and figures.

For critical suggestions to improve the manuscript, I am indebted to David H. Y. Chen, Harry J. Friedman, Liane C. Kosaki, Daniel Lerner, and Michael S. Shimoda, as well as to Tita Gillespie and the extraordinarily insightful anonymous colleagues whom she invited to review the manuscript on behalf of The Free Press. For meticulous copy editing, I thank Madeleine Sann Birns. For help at every stage of transition from typescript to printed page, I am grateful to Claude Conyers, who gracefully instructed me in the arts of clarity and accuracy, and to Valerie Klima, who planned and checked myriad bookmaking details with uncommon care. If I had been able to follow through on all the good advice and opportunities these friends gave me, substantially greater progress would have been made.

Finally, *mahalo* and *aloha* is expressed to my wife, Glenda Hatsuko Paige, who patiently typed and retyped the manuscript with skill and understanding. It was she who cheerfully best summed up the meaning of this book for both of us as a product of "love, sweat, and tears."

CHAPTER 1

POLITICAL LEADERSHIP:
CHALLENGE TO POLITICAL SCIENCE

We have really never thought clearly about leader-
ship in a free society.[1]

JOHN W. GARDNER
1961

THE SCIENTIFIC STUDY of political leadership presents a challenge to the entire discipline of political science. Simultaneously it challenges concerned scholars throughout the social sciences, natural sciences, humanities, and professions. The challenge is to recognize the importance of political leadership, to focus scientific attention upon it, and to begin the cumulative process of conceptualization, theory building, empirical research, education, application, and institutionalization that eventually will lead to the creation of a subdisciplinary and potentially *trans*disciplinary scientific field of global significance.

Such a field is needed to dispel myths, to assist understanding of the relevance of political leadership behavior for social life, and to enhance awareness of the enormous creative potential inherent in political leadership for contributing to the realization of more humane conditions of life in all societies.

"Political leadership" is the behavior of persons in positions of political authority, their competitors, and these both in interaction with other members of society as manifested in the past, present, and probable future throughout the world. This means not only the behavior of persons in positions of highest authority but also those at intermediate and lower levels; not only monarchs, presidents, and premiers but governors, provincial chairmen, and mayors, as well as village chiefs, headmen, and leaders of party cells. It means not only single personalities but also the "collective leadership" of aggregate bodies, and those both not in isolation but in interaction with "followers." It means leadership not only in one type of institution (e.g., party, legislature, or bureaucracy) or process (e.g., policy decision, election, or revolution) but across them all. It means not only men but women; not only incumbents but competitors and

1

revolutionaries; not only those who rule by moral suasion and reasoned agreement but those who gain compliance by fear and force; not only the admirable but the despicable; not only the "successful" but those who "fail."

Whether or not we are prepared or permitted to focus scientific attention upon such behavior, its importance is constantly thrust upon our attention by political events. Dictators command sometimes willing nations to military, economic, or cultural ruin. Revolutionaries achieve the seemingly impossible, struggle with one another, and are frequently transformed into enemies of their own ideals. Monarchs vie in setting national tones of elegance or decadence. Electoral candidates compete in mock combat that sometimes turns real. The decisions of all variously delight and depress us. To underscore their importance political leaders are assassinated, arrested, tortured, vilified, impeached, and exiled—as well as lauded, rewarded, respected, and reelected. Always important, emotionally significant, usually powerful, and sometimes dramatic, their behavior constitutes the stuff of which myths are made.

Myths

All societies create myths to disguise the true nature of political leadership within them. These myths serve the interest of both leaders and followers, most often providing plaudible explanations for the dominance of the former and the submissiveness of the latter.

Interestingly, such myths tend to distort reality in either of two ways: either they exaggerate the potency, morality, and efficacy of the leaders or they underrate them. The more authoritarian-coercive the polity, the greater the propensity to exaggerate; the more representational-consensual the society, the more the underestimation. Paradoxically, the greater the societal emphasis upon collective solidarity, the more likely the overstatement of individual leader competence; whereas the more individuality is stressed, the more probable the detraction. The subordination of the individual in the former situation seems to encourage vicarious fulfillment through idealization of leading figures, while the accentuation of competition among individuals in the latter creates a propensity toward anxious denigration. In both cases, the greater the socioeconomic injustice, the greater the expected distortion of leadership reality.

In external relations, societies seem to reverse the direction of domestic distortion. Those that exaggerate their significance at home tend to deemphasize their importance abroad; domestic detractors tend to portray foreign leaders in benevolent or malevolent extremes. The collisions of these myths with political realities give rise to both internal and intersocietal traumas as illustrated in this century by Hitler's Germany, Stalin's Russia, and Nixon's America.

These are, of course, not scientific truths but only provocative plausibilities that challenge scientific imagination, for to measure the extent of mythical distortion, its origins, and outcomes presupposes still-to-be-created scientific knowledge of world political leadership reality. To achieve such knowledge presents a major challenge to contemporary political science. Through scientific inquiry we must learn to overcome the biases of reverence and contempt that lead us at once to expect too much and too little, to view political leaders as so mystical as to elude understanding or as so mundane as to require no special efforts for comprehension. We must overcome not only these inhibitions but external constraints as well. The scientific study of political leadership on a global scale will have to overcome taboos at least as strong as those that once discouraged scientific inquiry into religion and sex. About the subject of political leadership, it can be dangerous to be curious.

Cutting through the myths of omnipotence, omni-competence, and omni-morality versus impotence, incompetence, and venality, we need to combine an unprecedented awareness of reality with an uncommon degree of wisdom in order to survive and prosper with meaning. Although political leadership is neither omnipotent nor omni-competent, it is potentially omni-relevant.

Omni-relevance

The scientific study of political leadership proceeds from a sense of the omni-relevance of what political leaders do, or do not do, in regard to virtually every aspect of global life. This relevance is produced by positional centrality, power capability, and follower expectations. From an all-societal, or global, perspective, political leaders may be viewed at the center of expanding rings of interconnected social networks that link them, directly or indirectly, with every other human being. The linkages may be physical or psychical. Through human beings and the technology created by them, the behavior of political leaders may affect all aspects of the nonhuman natural environment. Examples include military security and the allocation of collective economic resources. The ultimate relevance is possessed by those political leaders who are potentially capable of ordering individuals, groups, villages, towns, cities, and now whole nations to be destroyed. More indirect but pervasive relevance is illustrated by political leadership influences upon the structure and functions of economies and upon the allocation of collective goods. Even if the dominating forces of society are conceived as being external to formal political leaders—such as military establishments, corporate giants, or dictatorial classes—the central significance of these leaders is illustrated by the fact that influences from such external sources characteristically are exerted *through* them.

The choices they make or fail to make seemingly affect everything. By contrast all other occupations appear to be of limited relatedness. This is reflected in societal expectations. Everything may depend upon the farmer, industrial worker, soldier, and scientist, but we customarily hold only political leaders responsible for all conditions affecting agriculture, industry, security, and culture. They stand at the center of our communal expectations.

Political leaders have contributed to the emergence of the most serious problems now confronting the peoples of the world and they are universally expected to contribute to their solutions. A major task for science will be to improve our understanding of this problem-relevant behavior. We need to understand how political leaders have contributed to the production of incredibly destructive military weaponry and what they can do to move whole societies from violent to nonviolent modes of conflict resolution. We need to know how they have contributed to economic injustice and what they can do to remove it. We need to understand how they have affected human rights and what they can do to improve their expression. And we need to know the same for problems affecting population limitation, famine coping, ecological vitality, cultural creativity, and other major human concerns.

If leaders are potentially relevant to everything, and if their behavior relates to the emergence of, and possible solutions to, the most pressing problems facing humankind, what views are we to have of their problem-solving capability? Are we to view political leaders more as the puppets of circumstances or as sources of creative problem-solving behavior?

The principal thesis to be tested in the future scientific study of political leadership is that *political leaders constitute a source of enormous creative potential* that has been inadequately appreciated by modern political science, political leaders themselves, and the citizens of the world for—and with—whom such leaders are expected to make decisions.

Creative Potential

What would be convincing evidence that political leaders, individually and collectively, can have a creative influence upon society akin to that of scientists and artists? By political creativity we mean the capacity for combining ideas and action in such a way as to produce conditions that are, for a given society, different from those previously existing.

Suppose we could divide a whole society into two test groups with all conditions except political leaders equal. Let us assume that each leadership group has a different conception of ends and means. Suppose that the experiment runs from time 1 to time 2 in groups A and B, with political leadership groups PL_a and PL_b acting upon conditions C_a and C_b.

If conditions at time 2 were identical to those at time 1 for both groups we would assume that PL_a and PL_b had no effects beyond condition maintenance. If, however, conditions at time 2 *both* differed from those at time 1 *and* from each other, then we would assume that the different political leadership groups had some effect. We could not be certain that leadership accounted for all the observed variance, but it would be reasonable for us to begin to treat political leadership behavior as a source of potential creativity in influencing societal conditions. Beyond the two leadership groups themselves, we would explicitly also want to call attention to the potentially creative influence of the external experimenter in introducing the different political leadership stimuli into the otherwise similar groups. While the exact details of each case and of the entire experiment as a whole would be of interest, what would be even more important would be the underlying insight into the extraordinary creative potential in political purposiveness.

Mid-twentieth-century politics has provided us with four natural political experiments virtually identical to that described above. These are the emergence of different political leadership groups in the divided nations of China, Germany, Korea, and Vietnam after 1945, exemplified by the competition between Mao Tse-tung and Chiang Kai-shek, Konrad Adenauer and Walter Ulbricht, Kim Il Sung and Syngman Rhee, and Ngo Dinh Diem and Ho Chi Minh, as influenced by external leaders Stalin, Truman, their successors, and allies.

Over three decades, conditions in each part of the previously united nations became strikingly different both from their 1945 base and from each other. The four societies directly influenced by Marxist-Leninist political leadership tended, for example, toward single-party politics, collectivized agriculture, state industry, and cultural homogeneity. The four contrasting leadership groups led their societies variously to military, single-party, or multiparty politics; private agriculture; mixed industry; and differing degrees of cultural heterogeneity from repressive orthodoxy to relative tolerance. This is not to imply that the parts of the divided societies became completely different from each other. Languages, for example, were basically similar, despite some significant differences in content and usage. But in each of the four cases, overall societal differences were undeniably substantial.

The experience of the divided societies is of profound scientific and human significance and merits a massive interdisciplinary effort at understanding. For the experience of divergence in these previously united societies provides a severe test for any theory of society, be it political, economic, social, or cultural. Any hypothesis or proposition must be able to account for observed changes in conditions in *both* parts of each society. The thesis advanced here is that political leadership behavior will be found to be of great importance. Furthermore, it is held that the most extraordinary human significance of these experiences is not that claimed by either revolutionaries or counterrevolutionaries but rather the insight they give into the creative potential inherent in political behavior, and especially in political leadership.

The case for approaching the scientific study of political leadership from the perspective of creative potential, however, need not rest entirely upon the dramatic evidence of the divided nations at midcentury but may ultimately derive from the creative capability of the human brain. This does not mean only the innate qualities of uniquely gifted individuals, as Hitler would have it, but rather the capacity of political leaders and followers to improve upon their inventiveness, to provoke or respond to the creativity of others, and to assist the translation of ideas into social action. As Salomon has written with profound insight, "The mechanical adjustments of social life to economic contingencies cannot be fully understood without realizing the creative power of the human mind."[2]

This hypothesis requires a shift from viewing leaders as being determined largely by socioeconomic circumstances to a perspective that sees them in potentially creative interaction with their followers and with socioeconomic conditions such that purposive political behavior can actually change factors formerly viewed as determining. We underscore here the creative potential of leader and follower brains in interaction, with initiative from either one as precedent to common action. The counterhypothesis that political leadership behavior has no creative effect upon society and cannot be a source of societal creativity also needs to be entertained and tested as one of the checks upon distortions in a growing body of scientific knowledge on this subject.

The natural experiments of the divided societies, and the properties of the human brain, strongly suggest the fruitfulness of approaching the scientific study of political leadership from the hypothesis of creative potential. Enhanced understanding of this potential will markedly assist efforts to design more humanely effective political systems for the future and to assist transition to them from present conditions.

Design and Realization of Alternative Political Futures

At midcentury we are gradually coming to realize that the contemporary automobile is ill designed for human safety and that present rates of energy consumption are rapidly exhausting fossil fuel resources. This realization in both cases is leading, somewhat reluctantly, to efforts to create more desirable alternatives.

Analogously, a major challenge facing students of political leadership is the hypothesis that present patterns of leadership—regardless of type of regime—are ill designed to ensure human survival and that more humanely efficient uses of human and nonhuman energy in political systems need to be achieved. Otherwise, ill-designed institutions and the destructive uses of political energy, combined with leadership errors, may contribute to the occurrence of increasingly dangerous political "accidents." These "accidents" kill and maim, destroy productive economic, social, and cultural life, and destructively alter the physical environment.

This is not to imply that the study of political leadership can depart immediately from an applied prescriptive base with a claim to solve humanity's political problems. The past lack of scientific focus and relative inexperience with applied science under conditions of rigorous evaluative controls belie such a capability. But we should not shrink from such an aspiration: that is, to achieve scientific and humane knowledge of such quality and usefulness that it can be applied to assist the progressive creation and attainment of ever more desirable patterns of political behavior from the smallest to the largest human community.

Nor is this to imply that the study of political leadership needs to depart solely from a perspective of complete pattern change. It needs to proceed also from hypotheses that certain degrees of pattern maintenance and pattern reform may be desirable. Somewhat like political leaders themselves, with respect to any given pattern of leadership behavior, scientists may entertain conservative, reformist, and revolutionary action hypotheses. Nevertheless, the main scientific breakthroughs are likely to come, as in theoretical physics, from "radical" imagination that temporarily outreaches what can be observed and empirically verified at a given stage of scientific development.

To be maximally effective and responsible in making a contribution to future political design, the scientific study of political leadership must be developed in a matrix of time (past, present, and future), empirical potential (actual and possible), and values (the desired and the desirable). It should attempt to assist in solving problems of temporal, empirical, potential, and normative interdeterminacy in social life. This means to study political leadership as it was, is, and will be; as it could have been, can be, and could be; as it should have been and should be.

Therefore, the approach suggested here embraces simultaneously the most conservative and the most radical of perspectives. That is, it is essential to describe, explain, predict, and evaluate political leadership behavior just as it was, is, or will be. Still, at any given stage a fundamental transformation in this behavior may be probable, or preferable, or perhaps inescapable. In seeking knowledge that will be useful in making decisions from these perspectives, students of political leadership will contribute to accomplishing the tasks of the academic discipline of political science.

Political Leadership and the Tasks of Political Science

The principal tasks of the discipline of political science are *to describe, explain, predict, and evaluate political behavior, to apply knowledge of that behavior, and to nurture creative persons who can perform all these tasks.* Accordingly, the scientific study of political leadership must strive to describe leadership behavior, to explain it in the past and present, to predict it in the future, to evaluate it in all circumstances, to affect political leadership performance, and to educate persons who will humanely study and interact with leaders, as well as become leaders themselves.

The study of political leadership is not all of political science; yet, it is of pervasive disciplinary relevance in much the same way that natural political leadership relates to a whole society. There is no major field or subfield of political science to which the study of political leadership cannot contribute and from which it cannot learn. This is implicitly understood by every political scientist. What we need now is to make this point explicit in the establishment of a new subfield with disciplinewide relevance.

Attention needs to be focused upon political leadership in relation to *major fields* such as political theory, national politics, comparative politics, and international relations; to *major paradigms* for political analysis such as power, decision making, cybernetics, structural-functionalism, value allocation, the new political economy, and Marxism-Leninism; to *single polity* studies such as those of China, the Soviet Union, India, the members of the United Nations, and other political communities; to *types of political system* such as monarchies, military dictatorships, and single-, two-, and multiparty systems; to *institutional components* of political systems such as parties, bureaucracies, the military, legislatures, courts, economic institutions, and patterns of citizen participation; and to *political processes* such as policy making, budget making, diplomacy, elections, revolutions, peace, and war.

The call for disciplinary attention to political leadership represented by this book is summarized in Figure 1. Such a focus will facilitate the aggregation of insights from other specialties and the generation of independent insights of its own. Political leadership needs to become a major focus of explicit disciplinary attention from both a science-based human perspective and a humanities-based scientific perspective. Either way, the challenge to scientific imagination is inescapable.

FIGURE 1. Political Science Relevance of Political Leadership

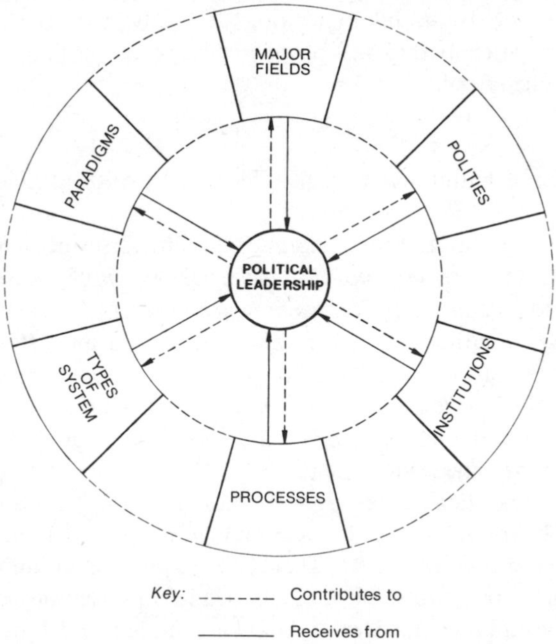

Key: _____ Contributes to

        _____ Receives from

Foundations of an Emerging Field

Among continuing tasks required to establish the study of political leadership as a subfield of political science are (1) to locate it in the context of major theoretical overviews of the nature of politics; (2) to take account of contributions being made to subfield development from diverse disciplinary sources; (3) to inventory alternative conceptual approaches to leadership inside and outside the discipline; (4) to construct integrating frames of reference; (5) to explore research, teaching, and applied needs and capabilities; and (6) to create the institutional arrangements that are required to undergird field development. This book seeks to provide a broad foundation for the accomplishment of all these tasks. No single effort can be adequate; only scientific cooperation can ensure progress.

The intent of this chapter has been to challenge scientific imagination to dispell myths about political leadership, to explore the omni-relevance of political leadership behavior, to examine the hypothesis of extraordinary creative potential inherent in political leader-follower interactions, to suggest the contributions that knowledge of this subject may make to political system design, and to urge the establishment of political leadership studies as a subfield of political science.

Chapter 2 sets forth a brief review of the surprising past inattention of American political scientists to political leadership. Although the behavior of political leaders has long been of widespread disciplinary concern, until the 1960s this concern had been diffuse, and it has still not received the convergent attention that adequate treatment of the subject requires. Chapter 3 complements this disciplinary overview with examples of recent and notable contributions to subfield development. These chapters should interest both those who might question the need for subfield development and those who accept the need but wish to understand further the disciplinary resources that can be drawn upon to fulfill it.

Chapter 4 begins a multidisciplinary exploration of concepts of leadership that may stimulate or guide inquiry in this field. The intent of this chapter is to expand awareness of alternative sources of conceptualization that may enrich future political leadership studies. Those who seek a single satisfying conceptual outcome will be disappointed by this chapter; those who view it as an opportunity for creative response should find it rewarding.

Chapters 5 and 6 present what is termed a "multivariate, multidimensional linkage approach" to the study of political leadership. First, six interacting variables are posited as predictors of political leadership behavior patterns: personality, role, organization, task, values, and setting. Then an attempt is made to link these leadership patterns and variables to eighteen dimensions of political behavior derived principally from contemporary paradigms for political analysis. The approach is conceptual and heuristic, drawing examples mainly from political biographies to illustrate linkages among the variables and dimensions.

This approach serves as a basis for considering needed field foundations in research, teaching, and application, which are explored in Chapters 7, 8, and 9. These chapters present the theses that studies conceived in terms of leader-follower *interaction* provide an unusual challenge to research imagination; that political leadership should be given at least as much educational attention as societies previously have devoted to education for military, business, legal, medical, and administrative leadership; and that the study of political leadership should be developed explicitly as a field of applied social science. Although treated separately and incompletely, problems of research, teaching, and application are interrelated and must be solved conjointly for substantial field development.

Finally, Chapter 10 begins to explore institutional contexts and program activities that will advance the scientific study of political leadership. These range from the work of individual scholars in colleges and universities, through university centers and regional consortia, toward promotion of global scientific cooperation through creation of a world center for the scientific study of political leadership that would operate under international auspices of the highest integrity.

Appendixes call attention to resources that can undergird further field development. These include a bibliography of selected doctoral dissertations with title references to "leadership" in all disciplines from 1925 through 1975; a selected multidisciplinary bibliography that illustrates the range of resources that can be drawn upon for further progress; and a selected list of political leader biographies for teaching and research.

This book thus presents a multifaceted agenda for disciplinary, transdisciplinary, and transnational scholarly consideration and action. It is based upon the assumption that political leadership is of central significance in human affairs and that efforts to understand it, educate for it, and influence it are the most economical and productive investments that can be made for the general welfare of mankind.

We begin by noting the surprising past inattention to political leadership in American political science.

CHAPTER 2

THE SURPRISING LACK OF
DISCIPLINARY FOCUS

*The essence of government is the relationship
between leaders and the led. Oddly enough, no
aspect of political science has received less
objective investigation.* [1]

JASPER B. SHANNON
1949

IT IS NOT SURPRISING that virtually all political scientists, like other members
of society, have appreciated the importance of leaders or dominant figures in
political life. But what is somewhat surprising is that the study of politics as a
social science has not focused attention sharply upon the concept of "political
leadership." One explanation of this lack may be that political leadership is of
such obvious disciplinary importance that no specialized attention need be given
it. As folk wisdom suggests, "A fish is not likely to be the first to discover
water." The discovery or rediscovery of the obvious may take longer and seem
less exciting to some. Thus, it would not be surprising to find political scientists
among the last to appreciate the importance of the idea of "political leadership"
for their discipline.

The American Political Science Review

One indication that the concept of political leadership has not been a focus
of attention since the emergence of the American branch of the postgraduate
discipline after 1880[2] may be found in the titles of articles published in the
American Political Science Review. The computerized keyword index prepared
by Kenneth F. Janda of 2,614 articles that appeared during the initial fifty-
seven-year period, from 1906 to 1963, makes it easy for us to discover that the
words "leader" or "leadership" appeared in such titles only seventeen times.[3]

11

These titles were Arnold Bennett Hall, "The Development of a Method for Investigating Legislative Leadership" (1925);[4] Charles E. Merriam, "Research Problems in the Field of Parties, Elections, and Leadership" (1930); Harold D. Lasswell and Renzo Sereno, "Governmental and Party Leaders in Fascist Italy" (1937); Harold W. Stoke, "Executive Leadership and the Growth of Propaganda" (1941); C. Arnold Anderson, "The Utility of the Proposed Trial and Punishment of Enemy Leaders" (1943); Clarence A. Berdahl, "The Leadership of the United States in the Post-war World" (1944); Lester G. Seligman, "The Study of Political Leadership" (1950)—*to which we shall return with great interest;* Robert T. Holt, "Age as a Factor in the Recruitment of Communist Leadership" (1954); Henry Wells, "Ideology and Leadership in Puerto Rican Politics" (1955); Arthur W. MacMahon, "Woodrow Wilson as Legislative Leader and Administrator" (1956); Lewis J. Edinger, "Post-totalitarian Leadership: Elites in the German Federal Republic" (1960); Fred I. Greenstein, "The Benevolent Leader: Children's Images of Political Authority" (1960); Herbert McClosky, Paul J. Hoffman, and Rosemary Ohara, "Issue Conflict and Consensus among Party Leaders and Followers" (1960); Ralph K. Huitt, "Party Leadership in the Senate" (1961); P. J. Vatikiotis, "Dilemmas of Political Leadership in the Arab Middle East: The Case of the United Arab Republic" (1961); Peter H. Merkl, "Equilibrium, Structure of Interest and Leadership: Adenauer's Survival as Chancellor" (1962); and Lewis J. Edinger, "Military Leaders and Foreign Policy-making" (1963).

When viewed in the context of other *APSR* articles of this period, these titles permit us to make several observations. First of all, while the idea of "leadership" was found useful in executive, party, legislative, foreign policy, and area studies, it was not employed extensively as an analytical concept. By comparison, during the same period, 77 titles mentioned "vote-voter-voters-votes-voting"[5] and 277 titles referred to "legislation-legislative-legislature-legislatures." On the other hand, "leadership" appeared more frequently than the related idea of "elite(s)/elitism," which was found in only 5 titles.[6]

A long-delayed but sudden rise in the frequency of use of the word "leadership" is to be noted. Beginning with Hall, it took nineteen years for a notable mention of "leadership" to be made. If we start with Seligman's 1950 contribution, we can say that forty-four years elapsed before a serious effort was made to conceptualize "political leadership" as a subject for disciplinary attention. Thus, we find one mention in the 1920s, three in the 1930s, two in the 1940s, three in the 1950s, and a marked jump to seven titles in only the first three years of the 1960s. We will consider later some reasons why this may have occurred.

Interestingly, nearly half of these titles (seven out of seventeen titles) employed the idea of leadership in connection with the study of politics outside mainland United States. Therefore, we find the terms "leader" and "leadership" associated with "Fascist Italy," "Enemy," "Communist," "Puerto

Rican Politics," "German Federal Republic," "Arab Middle East," and German Parties."

Among the titles on leadership we also find a unique reference to "followers" by McCloskey et al. (1960), the only mention of this concept in more than a half century.[7] "Followership," of course, is a much broader concept than that of voting, more akin to the idea of "citizenship,"[8] and is a natural complement to the idea of leadership. Thus, it is not surprising to find that the less developed the concept of leadership, the less explicit the idea of followership.[9]

If we turn from titles to contents, the impression of the lack of focus on the concept of leadership is sustained. Such a clustered review, of course, is an artificially imposed one, bringing together articles solely on the basis of the words "leader" or "leadership" in their titles. But we might expect articles thus entitled to reveal more about our professional understanding of leadership as a general political phenomenon than those whose authors made other identifying conceptual choices. In such articles, taken as a whole, we sense the absence of core concepts of leadership, competing or consensual; the lack of cumulativeness; the seeming irrelevance of philosophical tradition; systematic inability to draw upon leadership-related concepts of the past or visions of the future; the important but limited responsiveness to contemporary political events; and inability to make use of the findings of one study to understand another. In a sense, these seventeen articles are virtually unrelated. In another, they can be made so: an order can be induced from, or imposed upon, them—or both. They present a conceptual problem as well as parts of a solution in the same way that the disparate articles of any given volume of the *APSR* challenge us to ask, "What is political science?" and at the same time at least hint at a temporary answer.

Reviewing the seventeen titles with references to leadership, we see that the concept of leadership was not employed for purposes of integration, comparison, or analysis of interactions among leadership positions. Thus, even within the American context we do not find titles explicitly linking presidential, senatorial, congressional, gubernatorial, mayoral, party, and other forms of political behavior with a common integrating concept of "leadership."[10] Nor do we find titles in a comparative mode such as "A Comparison of Presidential, Gubernatorial, and Mayoral Leadership," "A Comparison of Executive, Legislative, and Judicial Leadership," or "A Comparison of Top, Middle, and Lower Level Leadership in Three Types of Political System." Neither are there titles that focused attention upon "Interactions among Presidential, Gubernatorial, Mayoral, Legislative, Party, and Judicial Leaders."[11] Furthermore, we do not encounter many titles that explicitly link the concept of leadership with the analysis of social problems; for example, titles in the mode of "Political Leadership Influences upon War [Peace, Revolution, Economic Welfare, Race Relations, etc.]."[12]

But the absence of a core concept of political leadership that could contribute to, and benefit from, other political science interests did not mean the neglect of certain cóncrete American political leadership positions. However, the largely unrelated and incomplete treatment of these positions only highlighted the absence of an integrating concept of leadership. From 1906 to 1963, sixty-one titles mentioned "presidency-president-presidential-presidents"; twenty-three titles referred to "senate-senator-senatorial-senators"; forty titles mentioned "representation-representative-representatives"; twenty-seven titles referred to "governor-governor's-governors'-gubernatorial." "Candidates" and "legislator-legislators" were each mentioned three times. "Party-activists," "precinct captain," and "precinct committeemen" were each mentioned once. The word "politician," the generic name for a professional political leader in American life, was mentioned only once.[13] "Mayor" was not mentioned at all.[14]

Thus, with the exception of Seligman's "The Study of Political Leadership" (1950), the titles of articles in the first half century of the *American Political Science Review* suggest that while political scientists were aware of the importance of leadership they had not focused major analytical attention upon it. If *APSR* titles are not convincing evidence of disciplinary inattention, then consider the fact that books dealing principally with "political leadership" are *not* likely to be classified under political science but rather under sociology in American libraries that follow the Library of Congress classification system. For example, my book *Political Leadership* (1972) is likely to be classified as HM141: H, "social science"; M, "sociology"; 141, "the great man, leadership, prestige, cf. genius."[15]

Sabine

This same point can be appreciated in an entirely different and perhaps more satisfying way for those who are rightly skeptical about the quality of inference permitted by keywords in the titles of journal articles. Consider, for example, the treatment of the concept of "leadership" in George H. Sabine's highly influential *History of Political Theory*, first published in 1937 and thereafter an indispensable reference for graduate students preparing for their predoctoral general examinations.[16] With respect for the Cornell philosopher's awesome erudition, generations of doctoral candidates have been guided by Sabine through the history of Western political thought.[17] Through him, sometimes for the last time, doctoral candidates have learned of the ideas of Plato, Aristotle, Cicero, Seneca, John of Salisbury, Philip the Fair, Boniface VIII, Marsilio of Padua, William of Occam, Machiavelli, Luther, Knox, Bodin, Grotius, Hooker, Hobbes, Harrington, Milton, Filmer, Sidney, Halifax, Locke, Rousseau, Hume, Burke, Hegel, Bentham, Mill, Marx, and others.

Sabine's index contains only a single four-page reference to "leadership," as follows:

Leadership, in fascism and national
socialism, 883-888, 900-901.[18]

When we examine the text we find that the first reference is to a section entitled "The Folk, the Elite and the Leader." This section is based mainly upon Hitler's *Mein Kampf* and ends with the statement: "The Leader manipulates the people as an artist molds clay."[19] Mussolini and Lenin are also mentioned in this section, as is Max Weber. The word "charismatic" is mentioned, but there is no citation of Weber's works and no exploration of the Weberian concepts of traditional, charismatic, and rational-legal authority. The second reference is to a section on "totalitarianism," in which Sabine describes the Nazi "leadership principle" as "the substitution of personal authority for authority working through regular channels and the substitution of imposed regimentation for self-government."[20]

The explicit image of leadership in Sabine is both scanty and definitely pejorative from a liberal democratic point of view. The idea of "leadership" seems to apply only to German naziism, Italian fascism, and Soviet communism. The treatment of the concept in the history of political thought is explored neither directly nor in terms of functional equivalents. Again, as in the *American Political Science Review,* we find a set of ideas that are highly relevant for a concept of political leadership being treated in a dispersed, largely unrelated manner. Thus, in Sabine's index, we find Plato's "philosopher-king" (nine page references, but no attempt to trace the idea beyond Aristotle), "monarchy" (carefully traced in seventy-three references from Herodotus to Hegel), Machiavelli's *Prince* (five references), "the divine right of kings" (twelve references), "hero worship" (two references), and citations of Lenin (eighty-seven references), Mussolini (fourteen references), and Hitler's *Mein Kampf* (nine references).

By contrast, the major interest that political theorists have had in the concept of "natural law" is exemplified by Sabine's careful examination of its history in two full chapters and 107 page references devoted to its treatment by successive thinkers from the Stoics to Marx. If the idea of "leadership" had been of similar central concern we might have expected a comparable chronological survey. Of course, we would not expect Sabine or any other historian of political thought to do this in a mindless way—that is, to find continuities, functional equivalents, and inventions centered upon a nonexistent core concept, or to impose Plato's philosopher-king upon Hitler's leadership principle, or vice versa. But might there not be a concept that calls attention to relations between leaders and the led under which we might compare "philosopher-king," "prince," and "führer," as well as other images of this kind?

One reason that such a common concept seems not to have arisen in the history of Western political thought might be because a dichotomy opened up between the explorations of ideal forms of political society (after Plato) and the empirical analysis of political institutions (after Aristotle, but especially after Machiavelli); whereas a concept of "leadership," implying the study of leader-follower relations in moving toward or away from valued ideals would have required them to be treated together. And one reason that the schism in political thought arose and continued might well be the continued neglect of a remarkable classical writer in whose principal political works the two perspectives are combined. The name of this major and by no means obscure author can be found neither in Sabine's *History of Political Theory* nor in the keyword index of the *American Political Science Review.*

He is, of course, Plutarch (ca. A.D. 40-120), the Greek writer whose extant biographies of fifty Greek and Roman leaders plus eighteen short comparative essays mark him as the greatest student of political leadership in the history of the Western world.[21] Plutarch's brief comparative evaluations of Greek and Roman leaders, while seemingly of little interest to historians and biographers, are of surpassing interest to political scientists and deserve recognition as a source of insight.

As illustrated and partly influenced by Sabine, the thought of the American political scientist on the subject of political leadership now tends to jump from Plato to Machiavelli and then perhaps to modern contributors of ideas about leadership such as Carlyle, Mosca, Pareto, Weber, Michels, Merriam, and Lasswell, as well as to the writings of actual leaders such as Hitler, Lenin, Mao, and Gandhi. A promising early task of political leadership studies will be to locate Plutarch between Plato and Machiavelli and to search for thinkers like Plutarch in other intellectual traditions.

Major Approaches to Political Analysis

The same professional influences that produced the treatment of "political leadership" in the *APSR* and to which the philosopher Sabine contributed in graduate education may be assumed to have subtly influenced the main approaches to political analysis that have been created by American political scientists. Let us explore six approaches that are currently engaging disciplinary attention: the study of politics through the analysis of power, decision making, cybernetics, authoritative value allocation, probabilistic system-functionalism, and the new political economy. While we will be seeking to discover how these six approaches explicitly deal with the concept of "political leadership," we need to be aware that this implies the need for a similar exploration of the treatment of the idea of "followership."

Power

The concept of "leadership" does not appear in the index of Robert A. Dahl's *Modern Political Analysis* (1963), a highly significant summary statement of an approach to political inquiry in terms of the concepts of influence and power.[22] Despite this omission, Dahl's analysis is rich in leadership-related concepts and examples that promise both to contribute to and benefit from a more explicit focus upon the idea of leadership in political science.

The core point of departure for Dahl's analysis lies in a dyadic influence relationship between two actors, A and B, suggestive of the ideas of leader-follower or leader-leader relations. Influence is defined as "a *relation among actors* in which one actor induces other actors to act in some way they would not otherwise act."[23] Five ways of measuring influence, all focused upon follower behavior, are suggested: "(1) amount of change in the position of the actor influenced, (2) the subjective psychological costs of compliance, (3) the amount of difference in the probability of compliance, (4) differences in the scope of responses, and (5) the number of persons who respond."

The concept of power is not formally defined in this monograph[24] but Dahl calls attention to the "state" as "a peculiarly important source of "power" because it can secure compliance through two types of "coercive influence": "negative coercion," based upon a legitimate monopoly of physical coercion, and "positive coercion," based upon control over great resources.[25] Four ways "to detect and weigh power" are suggested: occupation of formal official position, reputation for influence, participation in decision making, and the one most favored by Dahl, relative influence in initiating or opposing decisional outcomes.

In a chapter on "political man," Dahl identifies four important groups: "the powerful, power seekers, the political strata, and the apolitical strata."[26] This classification implies that political leaders are to be found among the powerful and power seekers. In a subsection on "power seekers and leaders," Dahl asks why people seek power and he critically evaluates three answers: "collective good," "self-interest," and "unconscious motives."[27] In a subsection on "the powerful," he asks why some people gain more power than others and gives as reasons "differences in the amount of resources used" and "differences in the skill or efficiency with which resources are applied." These differences, in turn, are found to be dependent upon situational and motivational factors such as objective availability, opportunities, genetic differences, values, and incentives.[28]

Furthermore, in two diagrams, Dahl succinctly contrasts two answers to the question "How are political ideas related to institutions?" In the first, termed a "rationalist" explanation, the "political theories of rulers" are depicted as producing both "political institutions" and "social and economic institutions."[29] In the alternative model, termed a "materialist explanation," the direction of causal influence is reversed and more conceptual elements are added: thus, "social and economic institutions" produce "status, income, and wealth," which in turn bring "power" that is translated into both "political institutions" and "political theories of rulers (ideologies) and ruled (utopias)."[30]

In brief, Dahl's power approach to political analysis provides a richly suggestive framework within which to pursue the study of political leadership. At the same time, the desirability, opportunities for, and possibly beneficial consequences of, a more explicit concept of political leadership are apparent. The absence of "leadership" from the index of *Modern Political Analysis,* when viewed against the intellectual history of American political science, is only one hint that a finer focus upon the idea of "political leadership" might help to improve understanding in terms of power and other approaches to political analysis.

For example, a concept of political leadership might call more attention to measuring the behavior of the influencer as well as that of the influenced, and then their behavior in interaction. It might contribute to redirecting attention from ecological influentials to direct agents of the state and to their employment of, and responses to, coercive influences. It might return attention to the behavior of persons in, or aspiring to, formal positions of authority as a basis for thinking about the functional redesign of such roles as well as to the nurturing of skills required to perform them in present or altered form. Furthermore, it might make a contribution to advancing beyond the "rational-materialist" argument by calling attention to an intervening pattern of concrete human behaviors of potentially causal influence upon both ideas and objectively given institutions and circumstances. Or, on the other hand, even if the behavior of political leaders is conceived of as that of captive slaves under joint domination by ideas and circumstance, more focused study upon this kind of slave behavior might contribute to the liberation of insight into the nature of politics.

Although Dahl's general analysis does not explicitly focus upon the concept of political leadership, it is interesting to note that when the power approach was applied in a major empirical study of the community power structure of an American city the idea of leadership emerged to greater salience. When Dahl looked at New Haven and asked, "Who rules in a pluralist democracy?" the terms "leaders" and "leadership" appeared more frequently in response. Of the twenty-eight major subsection titles in *Who Governs?* (1961), Dahl's pioneering study of New Haven political history, two explicitly contain the concept of "leadership" ("The Ambiguity of Leadership" and "Five Patterns of Leadership") and five others mention "leaders" or "subleaders."[31] Also, the ideas of "leaders" and "subleaders," but not "leadership," are extensively indexed.

The patterns of community leadership differentiated by Dahl are like multiple arrows pointed in the direction of political leadership, with only a slight but essential adjustment required to produce convergence in the center of the target. The community leadership patterns are described as "(1) covert integration by economic notables, (2) an executive-centered 'grand coalition of coalitions,' (3) a coalition of chieftains, (4) independent sovereignties with spheres of influence, and (5) rival sovereignties fighting it out."[32] Transformed more explicitly into political leadership terms, these five patterns might be characterized as the political leader as puppet; the political leader as dominant influential; political leaders as coalition colleagues with other politicians and community influentials; political leaders as sharers of nonoverlapping spheres of influence with other leaders and community influentials; and political leaders as competitors for power against both other politicians and community influentials. It is but a minor change from the idea of elite, notable, or influential group analysis in community power studies to focus more precisely upon the behavior of political leaders. And to ask, "What influence might purposive actions by political leaders have upon the emergence, maintenance, and change of either monistic or pluralistic decisional patterns within or across political communities?"

In fact, toward the end of *Who Governs?* Dahl concentrates brief attention upon "a small core of professional politicians [who] exert great influence over decisions."[33] The image given by Dahl of the professional politician is one of intense concentration: "He is at it, awake and asleep, talking, negotiating, planning, considering strategies, building alliances, making friends, creating contacts—and increasing his influence." Dahl further explains that the reason the professional politician gains more influence than other persons, given the same resources, is that he or she has more "skill in politics." Dahl hypothesizes that this skill results from higher levels of motivation to learn and greater opportunities (time) to learn. Therefore, he concludes that New Haven mayor Richard C. Lee was a "successful political entrepreneur" who "pyramided his resources" to transform the power structure of the city from a "pattern of petty sovereignties" into an "executive-centered" coalition.[34]

In the final chapter of *Who Governs?* Dahl seeks an answer to the question of why the successful political entrepreneur does not continue to pyramid resources into a dictatorship that subverts the democratic system. He answers that "leaders lead—and often are led" in a context of "widely held beliefs by Americans in a creed of democracy and political equality [that] serve as a critical limit on the ways in which leaders can shape the consensus."[35] But even these beliefs, he concludes, are not immutable "through those complex processes of symbiosis and change that constitute the relations of leaders and citizens in a pluralist democracy."[36] Thus, Dahl ends *Who Governs?* on a theme close to "How They Lead."

Comparison of *Modern Political Analysis* with *Who Governs?* suggests the hypothesis that the more empirical the inquiry, the more likely the salience of the ideas of "leaders" and "leadership" in politics—or of functional equivalents.[37] The truly unusual leadership of Mayor Richard C. Lee of New Haven, during 1953–1969, including the years in which the research on *Who Governs?* was undertaken, made it unlikely that leadership of the "mayor" would be overlooked after the manner of the *APSR* during 1906-1963.

Decision Making

A similar pattern can be seen in Richard C. Snyder's contribution of "A Decision-making Approach to the Study of Political Phenomena" (1958).[38] Both this article and the original statement of the approach in 1954[39] did not explicitly focus attention upon the concept of "leadership." Rather, emphasis was placed upon processes of organizational decision making by authoritative officials in an analytically defined "decisional unit." The interaction over time of three "variable clusters" ("spheres of competence," "communication and information," and "motivation") was viewed as producing "the selection from a socially defined, limited number of problematical, alternative projects [i.e., courses of action] of one project to bring about the particular future state of affairs envisaged by the decision-makers."[40] It was implied that dominant political leaders such as elected politicians might be found among the organizational decision makers, but no special attention was given to explicating their particular roles in terms of a concept of leadership.

However, in the first attempt to apply this conceptual framework in the study of a major American foreign policy decision, Snyder recognized the usefulness of the idea of "leadership" to describe the special influence that the most prominent political power figure had upon the creation of the group, its mode of decision making, its values, and its emotional tone.[41] Wrote Snyder, "Our exposition of the organizational variable (or, indeed, of the other two variables) did not, in its first crude presentation, set forth a leadership function."[42] Thus, the "leadership" of the president and of the secretary of state was subjected to analysis as both independent and dependent variables associated with decisional processes and outcomes. Additionally, "charismatic" (the president) and "idea" (the secretary) leadership roles were distinguished in this case.

As political scientists further develop the idea of decision making to permit cumulative, comparative, and interactive analyses of such subjects as citizen, voter, community, party, legislative, executive, and judicial choices, it is likely that the idea of "political leadership" will help to explain not only who decides but also how they decide, what they decide, how the decisions are implemented, and what responses to them are made.

Thus, just as Dahl's work on power permits recognition of political leaders among the powerful and the seekers after power, so has Snyder's insight into decision making facilitated finding political leaders among the decision makers. But much remains to be done to develop political leadership studies as a contribution to either power or decision-making analysis.

Cybernetics

The concept of "leadership" is explicitly indexed and of pervasive implicit importance in the cybernetic approach to political analysis proposed by Karl W. Deutsch in *The Nerves of Government: Models of Political Communication and Control* (1963).[43] "This book suggests," wrote Deutsch, "that it might be profitable to look upon government somewhat less as a problem of power and somewhat more as a problem of steering; and it tries to show that steering is decisively a matter of communication."[44] He explained more fully, in a definition that combines the ideas of power, decision making, and value allocation with a communications and control approach:

> If we define the core area of politics as the area of enforceable decisions or, more accurately, of all decisions backed by some combination of significant probability of voluntary compliance with a significant probability of enforcement, then politics becomes the method par excellence for securing preferential treatment for messages and commands and for the reallocation of human or material resources. Politics thus appears as a major instrument for either retarding or accelerating social learning and innovation, and it has been used in both functions in the past.[45]

This approach implies an image of leadership as the behavior of a steersman-communicator who decides, controls, allocates, learns, and innovates. However, no formal definition of leadership was offered and thus the image of leadership that emerges falls in the category of what Deutsch has termed "qualitative notions that disclose little detailed structure behind them" such as Carlyle's "great men" and Toynbee's "creative minority."[46]

But despite the lack of formal definitional focus, Deutsch explicitly raised questions that promised to facilitate linkage between the idea of leadership and an approach to politics in terms of communications and control. For example, Deutsch asked how the demands upon leaders of power maintenance tasks detract from the performance of social learning and adaptive tasks;[47] how the abilities of leaders to anticipate the attitudes and reactions of "followers" affect power position maintenance and adaptive steering;[48] how leaders enhance or inhibit a society's creative combinatorial capabilities;[49] what effects leaders have upon the speed, priorities, and rate of information flow in a society;[50] what the "intellectual load" is upon leadership under given conditions;[51] what leadership capabilities are for anticipating and adjusting to future events;[52] how leader emphasis upon short-range goals strengthen or weaken probabilities for achieving long-range goals;[53] and what capabilities leaders have to set limits upon or to brake movement in conflicting group aspirations.[54]

By asking such questions Deutsch has made it easier to link the study of political leadership with cybernetic models of politics.

Authoritative Value Allocation

The concept of "leadership" appears only once in the index to David A. Easton's *The Political System* (1953),[55] in which he sought to shift the primary focus of the discipline from the concept of power to "the idea of the authoritative allocation of values." "The struggle for power," wrote Easton, "does not describe the central phenomenon of political life; rather it refers only to a secondary even if crucial aspect."[56] "We find out how power is used anywhere," he continued, "only the better to know how it is used in relation to social policy." [57] Thus he concluded, "political science is the study of the authoritative allocation of values as it is influenced by the distribution and use of power." [58]

The sole index reference to leadership in this work is a statement that Harold D. Lasswell's inquiry into the power drives of individuals expressed in *Power and Personality* (1948)[59] "broke new ground in the study of political leadership." [60] However, in a closely related discussion of the concept of "political elites" and in a further discussion of types of authority, Easton evidences concern for the kinds of behavior upon which a concept of leadership would focus attention. In a critique of Lasswell's *Politics: Who Gets What, When, How* (1936),[61] Easton argues that the perspective contained therein is too limited to serve as a "vehicle . . . for the investigation of the whole political system." [62] In Easton's view, the political elite approach would lead primarily to the investigation of "the means the elite uses to arrive at and survive in the seat of power." [63] It would show only how a small minority holds power, could not cope adequately with "the antithetical assumption that the masses dominate over policy," [64] and would not adequately treat Lasswell's own interest in "changing value patterns." [65] In explaining that "even in the smallest and simplest society someone must intervene in the name of society, with its authority behind him, to decide how differences over valued things are to be resolved," [66] Easton used an African example to define several types of authority pattern that are predictive of, but not entirely the same as, those later hypothesized by Dahl to be possible in New Haven: formal central political authority; a clanwide council of elders; subclan elders operating in relative independence; warring clan elders in violent conflict; and neutral clan elders seeking arbitration and reconciliation.[67]

The concept of "leadership" does not appear at all in the index of Easton's next exposition of "the political system" in *A Framework for Political Analysis* (1965).[68] But it is employed explicitly in the text itself to describe the "need for a new leadership" in the stressful transition of a "developing nation" from a "tribal form of organization" toward a generalized "national form of political leadership," [69] a process that is accompanied by extremely important changes in the "volume and variety of demands" upon the political system. Next follows a passage that *explicitly* employs the idea of "leadership" to refer to behaviors that both *create* and *build support for* what Easton defines as three basic components of a political system: "political community, regime, and authorities."

> But something more [than changes in the volume and variety of demands] is also at stake in these emerging national units. It is to be found in the need for a new leadership to weld together a group that can offer sufficient support for a new political unit, a new set of structures for getting things done politically, and new political authorities to provide leadership and administrative skills. These are the basic components of a political system which might be labeled the political community, regime, and authorities. The search for rapid economic and social development, combined with political stability, imposes on such systems the need to generate a leadership which can promote and sustain support for these components.[70]

Although this passage portrays "leadership" as the creator and supporter of system components, overall emphasis seems still to be placed upon leadership as a "need" that is "imposed" by general system requirements. Thus, "leadership," like power, is not of central concern.

In *A Systems Analysis of Political Life* (1965),[71] Easton further elaborated his conceptual framework. The index contains one reference to "leadership," which directs attention to a discussion of "personal legitimacy" as a contributor to "diffuse support for authorities and regime."[72] In this section, Easton attempted to distinguish his concept of "personal legitimacy" from Max Weber's idea of "charisma," which is taken to be subsumable under the former. Easton first cited Weber's idea of charisma as based "on devotion to the specific and exceptional sanctity, heroism, or exemplary character of an individual person, and of the normative patterns of order revealed or ordained by him."[73] Pointing out that some "fraudulent" leaders are not genuinely devoted or exemplary in character but succeed by manipulation of fabricated imagery, Easton concluded, "All political leadership, and not the charismatic type alone, if it is effective in winning support at all, carries with it this legitimating potential; hence the concept of personal legitimacy covers a broader range of leadership than charisma, in Weber's original sense, and includes the latter."[74] As the index suggests, and as this passage illustrates, Easton appears still to have considered "leadership" as a personal or at least personality-derived quality, either genuine or spurious, in a way reminiscent of his earlier citation of Lasswell's *Power and Personality* in *The Political System.*[75]

But despite its limited formal treatment of the idea of political leadership, *A Systems Analysis of Political Life* contains many significant references to aspects of political leadership behavior. In introducing the concept of "gate-keeping" as a "structural mechanism" for regulating the conversion of wants into demands and thenceforth into social policy, Easton included political leaders under the broader idea of "gatekeepers."[76] Political leaders are also included among the "authorities" who contribute to want conversion. Easton further drew upon an insight from Lucian W. Pye's *Politics, Personality and Nation Building* (1962) to support the idea that sometimes authorities create demands as well as anticipate, react to, or "abort" the demands of others.[77]

In explaining how demands are "negotiated through to outputs" by "structural means" that produce "decisions, compliance, and implementation," Easton introduced the concept of "authority roles."[78] Whether formally or informally defined, these roles are analytically separable from the "authorities," who are their incumbents, and constitute "more or less stable sets of roles which tend to be complementary and which, as a set, are distinguishable from other roles in the total political structure."[79]

In sum, while Easton's approach to the political system yields many insights into political leadership, the idea of political leadership is not brought into sharp focus. Furthermore, the thrust of the discussion of "authorities," among whom political leaders and their opponents presumably must be placed, is that their behavior is more a product rather than a producer of system influences, a dependent rather than an independent variable. Thus, a full chapter is devoted to a discussion of "authorities" as *"objects* of support" (emphasis added)—but no chapter is fully devoted to exploring them as *creators* of support. And in the diagram that summarizes the entire argument, nineteen arrows are pointed as expressions of influence toward the box marked "authorities," while only a single line, later divided into two arrows, symbolizes outputs to the environment.[80]

Nevertheless, Easton's pioneering framework has made it easier to find political leaders among the "authorities" and to attempt to link their behavior with the allocative patterns of demands and supports that are the key to his analysis of a total political system.

Structural Functionalism

The concept of "leadership" is not of salient concern in Gabriel A. Almond's important introductory essay, "A Functional Approach to the Study of Comparative Politics," in *The Politics of the Developing Areas* (1960),[81] by which the Committee on Comparative Politics of the Social Science Research Council (under Almond's chairmanship) launched a series of studies designed "to compare the political systems of the 'developing areas,' and to compare them systematically according to a common set of categories."[82] Neither "leader(s)" nor "leadership" was indexed in this inaugural volume. Furthermore, no subsequent volume in the series was devoted to the theme of "Political Leadership and Political Development," although attention was focused upon communications,[83] bureaucracy,[84] "political modernization" in Japan and Turkey,[85] education,[86] political culture,[87] political parties,[88] and "crises and sequences."[89]

Almond first defined "the political system" as "the ['more or less'] legitimate, order maintaining or transforming system in the society"[90] and assumed that "the same functions are performed in all political systems, even though these functions may be performed with different frequencies, and by different kinds of structures."[91] He then set forth as the initial focuses of analytical attention four "input functions" ("political socialization and recruitment, interest articulation, interest aggregation, and political communication") and three "output functions" ("rule making, rule application, and rule adjudication").[92]

Describing how these functions were identified, Almond explained, "We derived our functional categories from the political systems in which structural specialization and functional differentiation have taken place to the greatest extent."[93] Thus, asking what functions were performed by political "structures" enabled the derivation of "interest articulation" from interest groups, "interest aggregation" from political parties, "political communication" from "the specialized media of communication in Western countries," and "rule making, application, and adjudication" from the idea of "separation of (legislative, executive, and judicial) powers." The basis for deriving the "recruitment and socialization function" was not so easily found in a differentiated concrete structure; therefore, we find the more vague statement that "the existence in all political systems of methods of political recruitment and training led us to the question 'How are people recruited to and socialized into political roles and orientations in different political systems?' "[94]

Since the ideas of "political leaders" and "political leadership" were not of special concern, Almond did not ask: What functions for a political system are performed by political leaders, either as individuals or as groups? For example, noting that some societies distinguish three key political leadership roles—ceremonial head of state (e.g., monarch or president), chief administrator (e.g., premier), and leader of the principal institution of coercive power (e.g., party, army)—one might derive the functions of affective integration, instrumental innovation, and power position maintenance. A number of other questions might have been raised. Given a conception of the functions of political leaders in a political system, what are the possible variations in the structural distribution of the way in which these functions are performed? And, more basically, how do the behaviors of incumbents in political leadership roles or role sets, combined with the behaviors of significant others who interact with them, contribute to the performance of the functions of a political system, however these functions may be defined? Are these political leadership behaviors to be regarded as subfunctions, the performance of which may strategically affect the functioning of the political system as a whole?

It should be appreciated that there was nothing in the functional approach proposed by Almond that prevented the raising of such questions. As Almond explained, "The functional categories which one employs have to be adapted to the particular aspect of the political system with which one is concerned."[95] And further, "While there is justification for having underplayed the governmental structures in this study, their neglect in the development of the theory and of the functions of the polity represents a serious shortcoming in the present analysis."[96]

Thus, while there is no clear focus upon leadership in this early summary of a functional approach, there are a few explicit indications of concern with the behaviors to which this concept would call attention, and a mood of discontented search for more fruitful categories of structural attention. For example, the functions of "initiation, modification, and vetoing"—so suggestive of political leadership behavior—were mentioned twice in this essay as having grown out of a collaborative effort with Bernard C. Cohen and Princeton graduate students to make an empirical study of "the functions performed by the Executive, the Congress, pressure groups, and the press in the making of foreign policy."[97] The word "leader" frequently was used in this essay in discussions that raised the problem of dualism between formal and informal influence; e.g., the importance of the "opinion leader" as a link between the individual and the mass media of communications;[98] the existence of "informal leaders of party groups" as an example of informal structure within the formal structure of a Western parliament;[99] and the statement that "though a mayor may wear the trappings of his formal office, it may really be a caste leader or a headman who is talking."[100] Thus, where the concept of "leader" emerged, it was likely to suggest informal but compelling influence rather than probably less efficacious formal authority.

One feature of this early statement of a functional approach is the absence of a concept other than that of "political structures" that would call attention to the central processing organ for both inputs and outputs. In the absence of such a concept, a method of structural enumeration was employed; e.g., "legislatures, political executives, bureaucracies, courts, electoral systems, parties, interest groups, and media of communication"[101] and, in the case of British political structures, "interest groups, political parties, parliament, cabinet, and monarchy."[102] Of these, the most prevalent concept used throughout the essay in a way that implied a center of purposeful initiative and effective influence was "interest group" or "pressure group": these words appeared more than ninety times. By contrast, the words "political elite(s)" or "elite(s)" were employed only seven times.

The absence of a concept of a strategically central purposeful actor who behaves in politically significant ways—such as might be implied by the ideas of "leader" and "leadership"—as well as the search for such a concept can be illustrated in Almond's essay. Thus, not unexpectedly for a biologically influenced structural-functional approach, the "heart" was chosen as the central political processing organ in an analogy intended to explain how the "political communication function" works: "One may liken the communication function to the circulation function of the blood. It is not the blood but what it contains that nourishes the system. The blood is the neutral medium carrying claims, protests, and demands through the veins to the heart; and from the heart through the arteries flow the outputs of rules, regulations, and adjudications in response to claims and demands."[103] But in the final portion of the essay, in which Almond suggested alternative research strategies for creating a "probabilistic theory of the polity," both the idea of political leadership and the search for a different kind of organic analogy are implied. "What is a case study, anyway?" Almond asked. "It is an effort at reconstructing, by documentary research and interviewing of informants, a *public policy individual* [emphasis added]. In this public policy individual will be found the specific performances of political and governmental functions by the structures of the polity."[104] Thus, to Dahl's concepts of the "powerful and power seekers," Snyder's concept of "decision makers," and Easton's concept of "authorities," Almond added the idea of the "public policy individual."[105]

In "A Developmental Approach to Political Systems" (1965),[106] Almond further developed his functional approach, partly in response to criticism that the earlier formulation had been "a static theory, not suitable for the analysis and explanation of system change."[107] In terms of its significance for the emergence of something like a concept of political leadership as a principal focus of disciplinary concern, this essay is remarkable in at least three ways. First is the explicit statement that "the political system" ought to be viewed as an independent variable as well as a dependent variable in relation to its environment.

> We explicitly add two more questions to ["Who makes decisions?" and "How are decisions made?"]. The first of these is what impact does the political system have, what does it do, in its domestic and international environments? And the second question is what impact does the society and the international system have on the political system?[108]

A second notable feature of this essay is the introduction of the idea of "conversion functions," which convert "the inputs of demands and supports" into "extractive, regulative, distributive, symbolic, and responsive" outputs.[109] These conversion functions combine what had been treated as input and output functions in the earlier essay:

> (1) the articulation of interests or demands, (2) the aggregation or combination of interests into policy proposals, (3) the conversion of policy proposals into authoritative rules, (4) the application of general rules to particular cases, (5) the adjudication of rules in individual cases, and (6) the transmission of information about these events within the political system from structure to structure and between the political system and its social and international environments.[110]

The introduction of the concept of "conversion functions" into the analysis implies that there might be a strategically central political leadership "structure" that contributes importantly to the process of conversion.

A third significant feature of this essay is the emergence to high salience of the terms "political elite(s)" or "elite(s)," which Almond used more than forty times. No formal definition of the concept of political elite was offered and no references to previous contributors to elite theory were made, such as Mosca, Pareto, Dahl, and Mills. Almond defined political elites at one point by reference to "kings, presidents, ministers, legislators, and judges."[111] At another point he called attention to an important function performed by them: "Political elites both originate innovative flows and respond to innovative flows that originate elsewhere."[112] These responses might be "adaptive, rejective, or substitutive."[113]

Thus, in "A Developmental Approach to Political Systems" (1965), Almond's earlier interest in "interest groups" faded, the image of the "public policy individual" disappeared, and the idea of "political elite" rose to prominence. The words "leader" or "political leadership" did not appear at all. Nor had they appeared in the index to the earlier *The Civic Culture* (1963).[114]

But in Almond and Powell's *Comparative Politics: A Developmental Approach* (1966),[115] "leadership" figured in two index references that call attention to political leadership as both a dependent and an independent variable in the developmental process, as well as raise the question of appropriate education for leadership. Thus, from the dependent perspective Almond and Powell noted that "the gigantic bureaucracy-party organizational complex characteristic of these societies will dominate and shape the responsiveness of the system. This implies that *regardless* of the personal desires and ideological commitments of the political leaders it will be very difficult for such systems to develop a broad responsive capability."[116] With independent emphasis, they wrote:

> Clearly leadership strategies do make a vast difference in the development of many aspects of the political system. An approach to this problem in predictive theory is to view various alternative courses of leadership action, planned or not, as *political investment strategies.* The developmental theory can then suggest the implications for the system of alternative strategies, given the present conditions of the system and the environment.[117]

Thus, in the progressive elaboration of an approach to politics in terms of probabilistic system-functionalism, Almond seemed to move from the idea of a "public policy individual" to a general concern with "political elites," along with a more specific interest in "leadership strategies" as an important contribution to variance in the "structures" hypothesized to perform the functions of a political system. The ideas of "leader" and "leadership," however, continued to remain peripheral and essentially unexplicated.

In 1969, however, in an essay entitled "Political Development: Analytical and Normative Perspectives,"[118] Almond began to discuss "leadership" and "problem-solving" more explicitly in response to criticism of structural-functional theories.

> In recent years the argument has been advanced that political systems theory leaves out the phenomenon of leadership and problem-solving behavior; in other words, it tends to be mechanistic. The general tenor of this criticism both from the economists and political scientists is that the approach to political development via the notion of leadership and problem-solving models is a superior alternative to system-functional approaches. Again I believe that there is much validity in this criticism. But when it suggests an approach to political development theory via the notion of leadership and problem-solving as an *alternative* to system-functional concepts then I would suggest that it has gone too far. For system-functional concepts put us in the position of being able to account for the setting and process within which leaders make choices and seek to solve problems. From a developmental point of view the problem-solving behavior of leaders effects changes in this problem-solving context and process, in other words changes the structure and culture of the system. Thus the development of adequate theory in the field of political modernization has to be able to adopt both of these approaches and strategies.[119]

"Leadership" is not formally defined in this essay, nor are alternative concepts considered, but some indication of meaning is characteristically given by a single reference to "entrepreneurship, or leadership (the party organizer, the demagogue) with skills in mobilizing and organizing large numbers of relatively uneducated electors."[120]

In the concluding portions of this essay Almond seems to be responding to perceived criticism of the "system-functional approach" in two ways: first, by conceiving the "political system" as a reified political actor; second, by conceiving "political elites" as the principal agents for solving system-related problems.

In discussing five "categories of political system performance" ("regulative, extractive, distributive, responsive, and political capital accumulation"), Almond clearly treats the political system as a purposive actor. For example, "every political system engages in some set of purposive activities—i.e., it punishes crime, it compels performance on contracts, and the like."[121] Or, "when a political system legitimates participatory activity on the part of different groups of the population it may said to be responding to these demands."[122] And further, "a successful or effective political system in foreign conquest, in the maintenance of peace, in the maintenance of internal order, in the growth of the economy and/or a favorable distribution of its products, creates loyalty, commitment, and support, on which the political system can draw in times of stress or threat, crop failures, famines, or depressions."[123]

The conception of "political elites" as the principal system problem solvers is illustrated by Almond's call for "the development of an approach to political analysis which will enable us to say something cogent about the problem-solving performance of political elites."

> If we have good measures of the flow of demands and outputs and the magnitudes of the system's political reserves, it should become possible to evaluate decisions made by political elites, using measures of rational choice. Here the analytical procedures involve ascertaining the goals and policy objectives of elites and relating these to the actual performance level of the political system and its potential. Are the policy goals of the political elites attainable given the available resources of the political system and competing demands for the uses of these resources? To what extent are the extractive goals of the political system related to their welfare goals?[124]

This final question suggests that perhaps the concepts of "political elites" and "political system" are being used interchangeably, while further suggesting that the "political system" can be thought of as a goal-oriented political actor.

Furthermore, since the main concluding body of the essay seems to be directed to show how a "system-functional approach" and a "leadership and problem-solving approach" can be combined, it may be that the term "political elite(s)" is also being employed as a synonym for political leaders and political leadership. The term "elite(s)" is employed twenty times in this essay; "leader(s)"/leadership" appear seven times, including five references in the quotation above. Additionally, the terms "decision-makers" and "policy-maker" each appear once. The greater frequency of use of these terms as well as "choice," "problem-solving," and "decisions" tends to remind us of the more purposeful images of Dahl's "professional politician," Snyder's "political decision makers," and Deutsch's cybernetic "leadership," or, as will be seen, Lasswell's "policy scientists."

One sentence of the essay contains what many political scientists will consider as an explicit statement of elitist bias. In discussing problems of the normative evaluation of political system performance, Almond explained, "Broadly speaking, the empirical basis for the evaluation of a political system can be viewed as a set of scores of performance according to standards specified by political elites, social scientists, and philosophers, and corrected for the constraints imposed by conditions in its environments."[125] Implicitly Almond thus raised a sharp, continuing, evaluative challenge to the entire field of leadership studies.

The New Political Economy

The concept of "leadership" does not appear at all in the index of the most recent challenging vision of "a new kind of political science," which has been presented by Warren F. Ilchman and Norman Thomas Uphoff in *The Political Economy of Change* (1971).[126] But the words "leader" and "leadership" appear in the second sentence of the text: "What would a political scientist have advised this young African leader who on the first of August, 1966, accepted leadership of the National Military Government of Nigeria?"[127] Furthermore, the images of political authority figures employed in the book's first chapter, "Why Political Economy," imply that political leadership behavior—if not the concept itself—is to have high salience in this approach. Thus, in the opening chapter alone we find twelve references each to "leader(s)" and "statesman-statesmen," four to "leadership," and three each to "political entrepreneur," "political entrepreneurship," and "politician(s)."

In the second chapter, wherein the principal elements of "the new political economy" are set forth, the image of the "statesman," mentioned sixty-five times, emerges to high prominence. The main tasks of the political economist, in fact, relate importantly to the statesman. They are (1) to understand and accept the "choice-making" ("ordering of choices") perspective of the statesman or antistatesman as a product of "necessity and his values";[128] and (2) "to make the statesman's calculations explicit, so that political economists may assist him in making more productive choices."[129] To fulfill these tasks the political economist "combines the economist's interest in productivity with the political scientist's sensitivity to issues of distribution"[130] —a kind of political engineering—into a form of expert knowledge that serves as the basis of his advice.

The approach is summarized as follows:

The new political economy may be described as the analysis of the political choices that statesmen and other persons make involving the polity's scarce resources. It aims at improving the efficacy of these choices so that desired ends may be better or more economically achieved through political processes. Such analysis must be both projective and evaluative. The political economist attempts to make calculations of the costs and benefits of alternative uses of scarce resources more precise and predictable. By basing his calculations on the objectives and possibilities to be found in a particular political community, he should be able to help statesmen and anti-statesmen to make more productive choices, congruent with their own value commitments and with demands from the political economy.[131]

On the face of it, despite the absence of the concept of "leadership" from the index, the new political economy might seem finally to have focused disciplinary attention squarely upon political leaders and political leadership. Indeed, *The Political Economy of Change* must be viewed as making an important contribution to movement in that direction, as well as making one part of the discipline more formally an applied science. But the long-standing lack of disciplinary clarity about the idea of leadership shows up in the spurious concreteness of the idea of the "statesman." This can be appreciated in several ways.

No formal definition of the "statesman" is given: there is only an index reference to "statesman, political actor as head of regime,"[132] and several textual assurances are offered that the analysis is intended to serve "anti-statesmen" and "revolutionaries" as well. There is no discussion of why the term "statesman" is employed to describe the central political actor, in preference to alternative conceptions of political leadership (e.g., the "powerful," "decision makers," "authorities," "political elites," or even "political entrepreneurs"); presumably, this image was chosen to convey the idea of a dominant political figure (male) who makes wise decisions. Presumably, too, the most wise would be the statesman who accepted the advice offered him by the political economist. This is another place in which difficulties arise. Suppose, as seems more likely than in the case of counsel given by economists on the basis of "strictly economic" models, that political economists disagree in their advice? How and why will the statesman then choose? How can his choice be predicted? How evaluated? How influenced? Thus, to describe, explain, predict, evaluate, and even influence the statesman's decisions, the political scientist must give much more attention to the behavior of the statesman (political leader) and to the process of statesmanship (political leadership) than is called for in the present statement of the political economy approach. The fact that statesmen (statespersons), like political economists, are likely to be in disagreement both within and across polities also belies the implied image of a single rational actor who thinks in the language of the new political economy.

A related problem is contained in the discussion of "three factors" that will "simplify" the statesman's "calculations necessary to assess the productivity of different investments in infrastructure." These are a hierarchy of goals, scarcity of resources, and propensities for different sectoral responses to investment decisions. "First, a statesman is aware of some hierarchy of goals. If he is not, there is nothing the political scientist can do for him."[133] There are some problems with this claim that more focused attention upon political leadership itself might help to solve: the description and explanation of the emergence and change of goals, not all of which may be in hierarchical order or in conscious awareness; the description and explanation of conflicting goal structures that affect aggregate leadership behavior; and the description and explanation of the effects that interacting advisers, such as political economists, may have upon the definition and ordering of leadership goals.

Significantly, the "statesman" or "political entrepreneur" is not listed as one of the twenty-six infrastructure elements to which cost-benefit, input-output analysis of potential investments is to be applied.[134] The elements of the "political infrastructure" are "regime political party, auxiliary organizations, opposition party, elections, local and regional government, ideology, economic development plan, interest groups, legislature, constitution, and legal system." The "administrative infrastructure" includes "public bureaucracy, armed forces, police, and intelligence organization." Additional infrastructure elements under three additional categories are specified: "communications media, education, and economic capital formation."

The "statesman" who is sometimes embedded in one or more of these elements (e.g., regime or opposition party) and whose behavior potentially can affect them all is omitted as an explicit category of analysis. The behavior of the statesman as the principal political entrepreneur is so pervasive and so central to the analysis at systemwide, subsystem, or intersystem levels that it escapes explicit analytical attention. Given scarce resources, for example, might not investment in the "statesman" be the most strategically productive investment? Thus, despite its highly significant advancement of a new model of political economic analysis, and its needed call for an applied orientation by at least part of the discipline, *The Political Economy of Change* reflects the past lack of clear analytical focus upon political leadership in political science. At the same time it offers a new framework within which the importance of the description and analysis of political leadership behavior can be better appreciated.

The approaches we have considered under the headings of power, decision making, cybernetics, value allocation, probabilistic system-functionalism, and the new political economy by no means exhaust contemporary modes of political inquiry. Others that need to be reviewed for their treatment of "political leadership" range from Marxism-Leninism[135] through conflict integration[136] and control[137] models to existentialism[138] and social anarchism.[139] Nor do these foreclose approaches that may arise in the future; for instance, models that deal more explicitly with human emotions and creativity in relation to quality of life. For whatever approaches to general political inquiry we may adopt, however, we may ask, "What image of salient figures is suggested?" (For example, the images we have encountered of "power influencer," "power wielder," "decision maker," "steersman-communicator," "authorities," "political elite," "political entrepreneur," and "statesman.") Whatever images appear, we need to ask about the degrees of freedom of associated behavior, viewed either as independent or dependent variable. If the term "leadership" appears, we need to ask about its defining characteristics and causal connections.

Thus far the approaches examined have revealed relatively little elaboration of a concept of political leadership behavior, but all have indicated some appreciation of its importance. Eventually a similar review needs to be made of the way in which "leadership" has been treated in the political science literature on (1) macroclusters of political institutions—e.g., "totalitarian" and "democratic" polities); (2) institutional segments—e.g., parties, legislatures, executives, bureaucracies, and judiciaries; and (3) major political problem or process areas— e.g., campaigning, budgeting, and conducting foreign relations. This remains a future task for the convergent, cooperative development of political leadership studies within the discipline.

Some Major Overviews of the Discipline

Further indications of a lack of disciplinary focus upon the concept of political leadership—plus abundant signs of the importance of leadership behavior—can be found in several efforts to gain an overview of political science as a discipline and to discern promising directions for future exploration. For example, neither "leadership" nor Plutarch can be found in the index of Bernard Crick's *The American Science of Politics* (1964),[140] a richly insightful interpretation by a British scholar of the intellectual history of American political thought as it influenced the rise of a "science of politics" from the American Revolution to the 1950s. But, not surprisingly, the book begins with quotations from the writings of George Washington in 1796 and Thomas Jefferson in 1826 that illustrate the kind of interest that political leaders everywhere seem to have in the political education available to young persons in their societies. As Jefferson cautioned, "In the selection of our Law Professor we must be rigorously attentive to his political principles."[141] The further influence of political leaders on the development of American political science itself, however, is not explicitly explored.

No essays on political leadership are included in two collections aimed at taking stock and looking ahead edited by Roland Young, *Approaches to the Study of Politics* (1958),[142] and James C. Charlesworth, *Contemporary Political Analysis* (1967),[143] although attention is directed to the major approaches of power, decision making, systems theory, functionalism, and communication; empirical focuses such as the "group" and the "community"; and modes of analysis from political philosophy to mathematics. Plato finds a prominent position in the first of these volumes[144] and does not escape mention in the second.[145] Plutarch is mentioned once by George Kennan, as essential reading for prospective diplomats, in the second volume.

Recognizing that "nothing is more difficult to appraise than the progress of a discipline in the behavioral sciences,"[146] *Political Science* (1969), edited by

Heinz Eulau and James G. March, a survey conducted under the joint auspices of the National Academy of Sciences and the Social Science Research Council, does not focus explicitly upon the concept of "leadership." Among the more manifestly leadership-related papers commissioned by the panel to review significant aspects of the discipline are essays on political elites (Carl Beck), the study of Congress (Heinz Eulau), legislative behavior research in the states (John G. Grumm), candidate selection and leadership recruitment (Lester G. Seligman), the presidency (Aaron Wildavsky), and research on executives in state government (Deil S. Wright).[147] But aside from the implied general orientation of Beck's paper, no essay is directed toward the search for a cross-institutional and cross-polity insight into a locus of purposeful political behavior that would be implied by a concept of "political leadership."

From the scant, three-page index reference to "leadership role" in Harold D. Lasswell's enormously suggestive *The Future of Political Science* (1963),[148] one might have predicted that the study of political leadership did not have much of a future. But the text both expresses and implies a rich and varied interest in leadership.[149] Lasswell's formal definition of leadership alone hints that failure of the discipline to focus squarely upon leadership would mean missing something of central importance: "For present purposes," he explains,

> I distinguish advice and management from each other and I give separate consideration to the role of leadership. This term is intended to designate the public leader, the one who plays an influential conspicuous part in public affairs. Leadership goes beyond advice to commitment; it goes beyond management to goal setting and high-level integration. The full-time public figure or active politician comes in this category.[150]

The principal image that *The Future of Political Science* conjures up is that of the creative political scientist as leader. It is the political scientist who purposefully investigates and potentially facilitates the most fruitful workings of the "decision process" ("intelligence, promotion, prescription, innovation, application, appraisal, and termination"), toward fulfillment of human value aspirations for "power, enlightenment, wealth, well-being, skill, affection, respect, and rectitude."[151] Political scientists are the catalytic persons who create the experiments, prototypes, and micromodels that are needed to define and solve societal problems through the intelligent application of knowledge. Leadership is seen to be a key factor in the power relations, emotional tone, and qualitative productivity among political scientists themselves. Lasswell observed, "It has been fortunate for political science that some departments where intellectual differences are most pronounced have been led by men of integrity and sophistication who have been able to disagree without rancor and to avoid the 'Hobbesian' trap."[152] Sometimes political scientists may intervene directly in political life: "Political scientists typically feel under an obligation to provide civic leadership where leaders are few or weak,"[153] even though "a practicing politician is not necessarily a competent political scientist, and a competent political scientist is not necessarily a [competent] practicing politican."[154]

It is but a slight, subtle, yet necessary shift of emphasis to move from the image of the creative social scientist who studies, interacts with, and much less frequently replaces politicians to focus disciplinary attention squarely upon the behavior of political leaders who study, interact with, and sometimes replace scholarly political scientists. Thus, although *The Future of Political Science* implies the image of the creative political scientist rather than that of the creative political leader as a primary subject for continuing disciplinary concern, it is but a small shift to focus attention upon the creative potential of political leadership as well as that of political science. That this was earlier appreciated by Lasswell himself is evidenced by his remarkable essay "Democratic Leadership and the Policy Sciences" in *Power and Personality* (1948),[155] and this point deserves to be reintroduced in thinking about the future of the academic discipline of political science.

The Teaching of Political Science

The lack of explicit focus upon the concept of "leadership" in the *American Political Science Review,* in Sabine, in major paradigms, and in disciplinary overviews is evident also in the teaching of political science. Until recently, few precollegiate, undergraduate, graduate, or continuing education courses have concentrated upon this subject and few political scientists have regarded the study of political leadership as a field of primary or secondary specialization. Certainly, there have been numerous courses on specific leadership roles, institutions, and processes—such as those devoted to the American presidency, the Congress, political parties, and electoral campaign techniques—plus experiments with internships to give students direct experience with leaders in action, but there has been little core concern with leadership itself that could both benefit from, and contribute to, these other teaching activities.

Thus, even in full-scale efforts by master teachers to survey, improve, and communicate the teaching competence of the discipline such as in *Teaching Political Science: Challenge to Higher Education* (1965),[156] neither index references to "leadership" nor essays specially devoted to questions raised by the idea of political leadership are likely to be found. We do not find analytical focus and debate upon any number of important questions. Should political science prepare some research scholars who are specialists on political leadership behavior? If so, how? Should the discipline give special attention to the educational needs of persons (1) who are already in positions of political leadership; (2) who have strong interest in eventually occupying such positions; (3) who seek to perform unconventional political leadership roles; (4) who have a high probability of working in close association with political leaders; or (5) who are required to respond to, make demands upon, and evaluate the competence of political leaders in their own or other societies throughout their civic life cycle?

The values that would partly explain the lack of a teaching focus upon political leadership are suggested in a summary of American political ideals in Paul Tillet's insightful essay "Teaching and Creative Citizenship" (1966):

> The central American ideal of consent of the governed puts upon our society the obligations of maintaining conditions of equality, achieving full participation in the political process, devising institutions to make the consent of the governed a genuine force in public life, and combining majority rule with respect for the rights of minorities; all the while permitting individuals of exceptional talent full scope for the use of their creativity. Perhaps the basic tenet of American life is to arrange affairs and devise social and political institutions so as to permit the individual to realize his fullest potential.[157]

This statement implies that educationally all Americans are to be treated as political equals and that the later rise of some to dominant leadership positions should be decided as the result of a competitive struggle among exceptionally talented individuals. From this perspective, neither the idea of educating *all* Americans for political leadership nor the idea of nurturing *some* more than others is likely to be acceptable. For the many would lack exceptional talent and attention to the few would violate the norm of equality.

An exception seems to be the explicit attention devoted to the idea of "internships" as a mode of political education. However, the same diffuseness about the nature of leadership in American political life embodied in the "citizenship" approach is characteristic of the important review of this experience by Bernard C. Hennessy in *Political Internships: Theory, Practice, Evaluation* (1970),[158] covering mainly the period 1958–1966. Although evaluative questions included such concerns as postintern candidacy for elected office ("yes" 2.7 percent and 3.7 percent in two different groups) and effects of internship upon later political activity ("yes" 31.1 percent and 39.4 percent in the same two groups),[159] these questions were not clearly focused upon learning to lead or upon evaluating political leadership in an academic-action context.

This lack of attention directed to questions of teaching for and about political leadership may well have been the product of antiauthoritarian values in American political and academic culture, as well as nonegalitarian authoritarian apprehension that education for leadership would be dominated by inimical interests. Interestingly, by comparison, Americans have been willing to focus attention very explicitly on education for military and business leadership. Furthermore, such education has been conceived in terms of core preparation deemed transferable, renewable, and extendable across different business and military roles and organizational contexts. By contrast, Americans seem to have preferred an ad hoc, "muddling through" (but not thereby unpatterned) approach to on-the-job training for political leaders.

Community Service

What are the implications of a lack of focus upon political leadership for other forms of university service to the community in addition to research and teaching? Lacking a needed full-scale overview of the community service contributions of American political science that is comparable to efforts to inventory other aspects of the discipline, I can suggest only two here. First, sophisticated campaign assistance to incumbents in, or aspirants for, elected American political office is beginning to be rendered by private enterprise research, media, and attitude manipulation teams on a largely secret and short-range basis. By choice or by external compulsion, virtually no departments of political science offer public campaign consulting services within a context of long-range concern for the overall performance of political leadership in the community and for broadening the basis of political leadership recruitment. Second, with a few notable exceptions, political scientists have not attempted to be, nor have they been perceived as, serious sources for the provision of advice that might lead to the improvement of community life from the perspective of purposive political leadership initiatives—from the viewpoint of neither incumbent nor conventional aspirant nor revolutionary leader. Thus, whereas political scientists are among the first to know the political defects of a community, they are likely to be among the last to see opportunities for assisting in purposive political leadership efforts to remove them. They seem to prefer an approach based upon broad education of critical citizen intellect, suggestions for structural reform, administrative consultancies, advisory service to more or less established interest groups about how they might influence the outcomes of existing political institutions, ad hoc outraged protests, and sometimes private commitment to the campaign success of incumbent or aspiring candidates for office. These and other complex issues are inadequately treated here, but it seems that the discipline of political science as a whole does not have a clearly defined field of public service activity focused upon improving the performance of political leadership in American society, including assistance to nonleader citizens in ways to effect improvement in leader performance. And this does not imply only mindless service to help dig in an already well entrenched "establishment." Assistance to transitional forms of leadership and to the creation of alternative forms of leadership are also contemplated.

Interpretations of Disciplinary "Neglect"

It is both exciting and somewhat surprising to discover that the concept of "political leadership," although of pervasive latent significance, has not been of long-standing salient concern in American political science. Neither widespread interest in Plato's "philosopher-king," Machiavelli's "prince," and Weber's "charisma" nor interest in "representation" developed into a full-scale field of political leadership studies. Interestingly, also, neither the numerous empirical studies of city "bosses" in the United States[160] nor those of the "presidency" led directly into a more general field of political leadership studies. Viewing "bosses" with somewhat disdainful admiration as a passing phenomenon of urban political sociology and viewing "presidents" with somewhat reverential ambivalence as a growing locus of power, few American political scientists seem to have been prepared to treat them within a common conceptual framework that would also embrace relatively neglected mayors and governors, as well as the more studied legislators.

Perhaps the combined effects of philosophical ideals set too high and perceived reality regarded too low produced massive disciplinary cognitive dissonance reduction by avoidance of direct confrontation with the idea of leadership in politics.

Why has this been so? A first hypothesis is that academic subcultures tend to exhibit some of the same characteristics as their immediate societal contexts. Thus, absence of emphasis in American political science upon "political leadership" can be interpreted in part as a reflection of the characteristic disdain of salient political figures in American political culture. Originating in a revolt against monarchy, American political culture seems to have passed from a period of admiration for "Founding Father" Washington and other men of wealth and talent, through the era of "Common Man" Jackson, in which anybody was as important as everybody else, through rule by self-interested, potentially corrupt political "bosses" in the age of industrialization, to the image of legally trained, sophisticated, white-collar criminals manipulating public policy for selfish corporate interests in postindustrial "Watergate" society. In designing their political institutions, Americans thus seem to have desired to keep their political leaders weak, underpaid, untrained, unstable, and responsive to the most vocal or surreptitiously influential interests. There have been heroes, of course, for some but not all Americans—Washington, Lincoln, Theodore Roosevelt, Woodrow Wilson, Franklin Roosevelt, and John F. Kennedy. But there has been a tendency to see these men as unusual expressions of national virtue rather than as performers of critical societal functions that required cumulative improvement from the county to the Capitol, even in the absence of uncommonly talented figures. Americans proceeded in the not unfounded faith that crises would call forth heroes and that mediocre muddling through was pragmatically preferable to strained striving for unattainable leadership ideals.

On the other hand, when things have gone bad, most often externally but sometimes domestically, Americans have been quick to personify their difficulties in malevolent leaders. Thus, we symbolically killed King George, vilified Lincoln or Jefferson Davis in accord with Civil War sympathies, ridiculed Kaiser Bill in World War I, hung Hoover with the Great Depression, and fought World War II against the triple villains Hitler, Mussolini, and Tojo, while transforming Stalin from slave master to savior to satan as need and plausibility coincided. Overall it has seemed that Americans have wished to take credit themselves for what has gone well for the country but to blame individual leaders, especially foreign ones, for the bad. Interestingly, Americans seem to have been willing to concede greater importance to the impact of foreign leaders upon other societies than to that of American leaders upon our own. This can be seen in the World War II adulation of Churchill, de Gaulle, and Chiang—and the post-1945 prominence accorded to leaders like Mao Tse-tung and Fidel Castro. Americans rightly have "feared" bad leadership—and hesitatingly "admired" good leadership when it appeared, with ambivalence that made it more comfortable to ignore the problem until feelings could be vented in condemnation.

Reflected in American political science, this tendency resulted in the lack of a specialized focus: no sustained competitive, conceptual exposition; no serious attempt to link concepts of leadership with prevalent analytical paradigms; no serious effort to work out evaluative criteria for judging performance that would be appropriate for time and circumstance; no specialized courses and seminars; no cumulative research tradition; no sustained applied effort to make knowledge about leadership socially useful. There was no recognized subfield of political leadership studies within political philosophy, American government, comparative politics, and international relations—and no integrative subfield that would seek to achieve a cross-field disciplinary and transdisciplinary perspective on leadership.

Within the academic tradition of political science it was clear that failure to focus upon "political leadership" was as characteristic of a "traditional" as it was of a "scientific" approach to politics. The lack of conceptual focus cannot be attributed to either philosophy or method, whether verbal or quantitative, empirical or normative. All shared in it to varying degrees; the deficiency was not individual but subcultural.

One explanation lies in European intellectual influences upon American political science during the past century: the evolutionary determinism of Darwin, the psychological determinism of Freud, and the economic determinism of Marx. The image of politics produced by the combined influence of these three thinkers of genius is that it is a pygmy held aloft in the grip of a massive determinist giant. This image accorded well with the colloquial language of American politics: elected representative officials were supposed simply to represent more basic economic, social, and psychological interests. They were not to have an independent, potentially creative, autonomous impact on society. Americans could more readily accord this possibility to generals, business entrepreneurs, and sometimes artists, but not to politicians. By and large, American political science, both "behavioral" and "traditional," agreed with this mode of thinking.

Since revolutionary movements are apt to exhibit some of the same attributes as the establishments against which they are in revolt, neither critics of contemporary American political science nor critics of American politics have tended to think very clearly about problems of past, present, transitional, and possible future forms of political leadership. Even revolutionary thought in the antiauthoritarian political culture that emerged out of the revolt against monarchy was not likely to deal with the subject of political leadership, except to be against whatever leadership there seemed to be and to place faith in individual interest or group muddling through in the traditional manner.

Yet, wherever relatively free social science inquiry is possible, it is likely that the scientific study of political leadership will arise. Despite past neglect, for example, it is now beginning to emerge rapidly in American political science.

CHAPTER 3

CONTRIBUTIONS TO AN EMERGING FIELD

*It was only a small step to the systematic redis-
covery of leadership as a central political process.*[1]

DANKWART A. RUSTOW
1968

AGAINST THE BACKGROUND of widely recognized importance but lack of explicit, concentrated, disciplinary attention, some contributions to the emergence
and future development of political leadership studies stand out with striking
clarity. Two of these, with identical titles, "The Study of Political Leadership,"
were contributed by Jasper B. Shannon (1949)[2] and Lester G. Seligman
(1950).[3]

Merriam's Hope

With the appearance of the Shannon and Seligman essays, it seemed that at
last a call issued by Charles E. Merriam twenty-four years earlier was about to be
answered. Wrote Merriam at the conclusion of *Four American Party Leaders*
(1926):

> In view of the fundamental importance of leadership in any community and
> especially in modern democracy, it is of the greatest consequence that
> studies of the qualities of political leadership be energetically and intelli-
> gently prosecuted. And I venture to express the hope that the necessary
> interest and enterprise for this purpose will be forthcoming in the not
> distant future. We cannot hope to manufacture at our will Lincolns, Roose-
> velts, Wilsons, and Bryans, but we may reasonably look forward to a more
> intelligent view of the whole problem of leadership, to a more intelligent
> training of potential leaders, and to progressively intelligent popular dis-
> crimination in the selection and rejection of the personnel of leadership,
> and in the circumscription of its metes and bounds.[4]

41

It is noteworthy that Merriam's call for the study of political leadership combined normative concern for the quality of leadership in a "democracy," a scientific approach implied by the word "studies," an explicit interest in education both for and about leadership, and a concern for the application of knowledge by both leaders and followers to define the scope of political leadership behavior. These interests reflected Merriam's own remarkable combination of political science and political action in a career that included service as one of the founders and early presidents of the American Political Science Association, as chairman of the pioneering political science department at the University of Chicago, as Chicago alderman (1909-1911 and 1913-1917), and as unsuccessful Republican candidate for mayor (1911 and 1917).[5] Merriam's works, like those of other political scientists or political philosophers who have also been political leaders—Woodrow Wilson,[6] T. V. Smith,[7] and Stephen A. Bailey[8]—may yield special insights into political leadership.[9]

Shannon's Provocative Assertion

Shannon began with a provocative assertion: "The essence of government is the relationship between the leaders and the led. Oddly enough, no aspect of political science has received less objective investigation."[10] He then continued in an essay that was historically imaginative, morally committed to the improvement or redesign of political leadership institutions, and dedicated to the idea of better education both for prospective leaders and for all citizens in the wise choice of leaders.

In Shannon's view, the forces of modern history were producing a downward shift in the social origins of political leaders from hereditary and aristocratic classes through the middle to the lower class. While there were many obstacles to, and distortions of, this process, it would be the result of increasing mass participation in politics. The more the most numerous classes of mankind participated actively in politics, the more would leaders emerge from them.

Such a shift, however, was being accompanied by some dangerous, irrational distortions. Upwardly mobile lower-class leaders, for example, might be excessively deferential to established institutions. Also, while citizens in ordinary times might prefer leaders of average abilities, they were apt to cry out "for strong-men, for supernatural leadership" in the various "crises" that accompanied the era of industrialization. Hitler's Germany provided a recent, clear example. Shannon cautioned:

> Perhaps a more realistic, not to say more scientific age will look upon our belief in leaders who can solve our social ills by political magic as absurd as we regard the divine power attributed to monarchs in the healing of bodily ills. Perhaps it is characteristic in a mass age to expect and hold leadership accountable for more than it can accomplish, which leads leadership to request increasing powers coincident with their responsibility. The abdica-

tion of individual responsibility may lead to the destruction of the polity in which it could be exercised. Confused and baffled, we follow the practice of the ages, we make men into gods and worship or curse them as fortune, fate, or the weather make us alternately comfortable or unhappy. In any case the size and complexity of human problems have become so great that only the inordinately ambitious or the well nigh saintly unselfish will assume the task of political leadership. Institutions need to be constructed for the industrial age which will reduce mass dependence upon charismatic leadership.[11]

Shannon then prescribed what needed to be done:

First of all must come the recognition of the need for the special talents of politics, the ability or art of attaining social cohesion and giving direction to social forces—the recognition of the fact that politics is a calling worthy of the finest brains contemporary society can develop. Along with this selection and training of leadership skills must come a civic education which is aware that far more important than the knowledge of the intricacies of the structure of constitutional or legal government is the ability to distinguish between the shoddy and the genuine in political leadership. The judicious selection of intelligent and public welfare-minded leaders is the essence of effective citizenship. The problem of group cohesion is extremely difficult in the guild socialism of an industrial era with the numerous centrifugal forces developed in the new technology. The gift of attaining unity out of diversity and action out of chaos is a quality more precious than diamonds. If representative government, or man himself, is to survive the age of atomic fission, political invention must discover, encourage, and canalize into positions of social responsibility those rare persons who have an aptitude for persuasive social control.[12]

Although neither Shannon's conclusion that what was needed was more "persuasive social control," nor his other value assumptions need necessarily be accepted, it is clear that he was attempting to focus disciplinary attention much more clearly upon the subject of political leadership. Writing in the early stages of the postwar "behavioral science revolution" in political science. Shannon did not devote great attention to specifying the nature and role of scientific research in relation to his objectives. But this was soon done by another colleague, Lester G. Seligman, entirely independently, in the first article specifically devoted to the general subject of "political leadership" in the forty-four-year history of the *American Political Science Review.*

Seligman's Call for "The Study of Political Leadership"

In his remarkable essay, Seligman noted the social salience and normative importance of the subject of leadership, reviewed the results of relevant research in other disciplines, suggested an approach in terms of "politics by leadership," and pointed out directions for future research.

In Seligman's view, political science ought to focus attention upon the study of leadership for two main reasons. The first was the extraordinary rise in the power of political executives in the twentieth century. This development he regarded as posing a central problem for political analysis much as had been posed by "popular sovereignty and direct democracy" in the eighteenth century and "stratification and group conflict" in the nineteenth century.[13] Second, like Merriam and Shannon, Seligman stressed the importance of political leadership studies for creating and maintaining a democratic society. "Democratic thought has not yet wrestled with the problems of the implications of leadership," he wrote. "Motivated perhaps by its opposition to authority, it has regrettably left to the proponents of authoritarian and aristocratic-conservative politics, the elaboration of a political theory of leadership."[14] This was exactly, of course, the implication of the treatment of "leadership" in Sabine's *History of Political Theory*.

Pointing to interdisciplinary sources of potential insight, Seligman then called attention to approaches that raised questions about leadership "as a social status position" (emergent social background studies); "in types of social structures" (emergent small group studies); "as organizational function and institutional position" (the emergent literature of business and public administration); "as a personality type" (emergent research on political personalities); and as "political biography" (mainly studies by historians). In his review Seligman pointed out limitations in the various approaches and suggested ways in which they might be overcome. He suggested that social background studies ought to be supplemented by case analyses of both successful and unsuccessful leaders so as to facilitate more meaningful interpretations of the significance of these characteristics for actual patterns of political leadership behavior. Moreover, he cautioned against overreliance on the insights from business and public administration studies of leadership: political leadership roles might be different. While noting that "some of the most vibrant and stimulating" studies were being made of the "character structure" of leaders, Seligman called for inquiry into the interaction between personality and social determinants of political leadership behavior. Furthermore, Seligman not only called for renewed interest in political biography but also suggested that the "theoretical insights of social science" ought to be introduced into biographical studies so as to contribute to the advancement of theories of political leadership.

In introducing the concept "politics by leadership," Seligman established his position in the continuing debate over whether personal traits or impersonal circumstances were to be regarded as the more important determinants of political leadership behavior.[15] He took the "synthetic view" that leadership consists of "both traits and functional relationship to group and situation."[16] Then he defined "politics by leadership" as "a conception of politics that finds power factors in society best approachable through the understanding of leader-led and leader-leader relations." Seligman further explained:

A politics by leadership conception would concern itself with generaliza-
tions concerning four types of relations: (1) the relations of leaders to led
within particular structures, (2) the relationship between leaders of political
structures, (3) the relationship between leaders of one structure and the
followers of another, and (4) the relationship between leaders and the
"unorganized" or nonaffiliated.[17]

Next Seligman suggested four areas for "profitable leadership research":

(1) recruitment or developmental studies, i.e., studies concerned with the
social origins and career lines of political leaders, (2) studies of the representational dimension of leadership—the character of acceptance by followers, (3) studies of political leadership techniques, (4) specific case studies
of leadership functions in typologically expressed political situations.[18]

Finally, reflecting upon the entire discussion, Seligman concluded: "The
approach which we find most useful is the one that centers always on the power
and policy context of political leadership behavior."[19] By this he meant to
stress the linkage between leadership behavior and changes in the distribution of
societal "power and influence" as well as to trace the influence of leaders upon
the making of public policy. Thus, although he did not and could not mention
them, since in most cases they had not yet emerged, Seligman foresaw the
possibility of linking leadership studies with various approaches to the study of
politics—power and influence, decision making, cybernetics, value allocation,
structural functionalism, the new political economy, and others still to come. He
also foresaw the possibility of linking political leadership studies with public
policy questions of all kinds.

There was more than seeming coincidence in Merriam's 1926 call for
political leadership studies and Seligman's 1950 response because Seligman had
received his professional training at the University of Chicago, where Merriam's
influence was felt long after his departure; where Lasswell's interests in power,
elites, and leadership were influential; and where there was a remarkable interdisciplinary approach in the social sciences.[20] This was the department that had
taken the city of Chicago as a site for field research and had nurtured such
pioneering works as Harold F. Gosnell's *Negro Politicians* (1935),[21] notable
both for its unusual interest in black leaders and for its employment of the term
"politicians," which had appeared so rarely in titles of articles in the *American
Political Science Review*. Gosnell also had created noteworthy sketches of
political bosses in *Machine Politics: Chicago Model* (1937).[22]

Seligman's essay received relatively little attention until it was reprinted in
Political Behavior: A Reader in Theory and Research (1956), edited by Eulau,
Eldersveld, and Janowitz.[23] Fourteen years later and twenty years after its
initial publication, it was again reprinted in *Micropolitics: Individual and Group
Level Concepts* (1970), edited by Kessel, Cole, and Seddig.[24] Gradually, the
discipline was beginning to focus attention upon the idea of leadership.

By 1975, twenty-five years after Seligman's call for "The Study of Political Leadership," a remarkable number of significant studies had appeared in precisely those areas to which Seligman had called attention. Not all of them, of course, were inspired directly by his essay but they evidenced both his foresight and the direction of professional concern to subjects that would contribute to the emergence of political leadership studies.

Very vigorous development occurred in *social background studies* of political leaders, or political "elites." These were aided by improved survey research methods and multivariate statistical analyses among political scientists, as well as by the revolutionary ease and speed of aggregate data analysis made possible by rapidly improving electronic computer technology. Elite studies in American political science were influenced strongly by political sociology, especially by ideas from Mosca,[25] Pareto,[26] Michels,[27] and Mills.[28] They received special attention after the publication of Lasswell, Lerner, and Rothwell's *The Comparative Study of Elites* (1952);[29] attracted increasing interest after such stock-taking efforts as Matthew's *The Social Background of Political Decision Makers* (1954)[30] and Marvick's *Political Decision Makers* (1961;[31] and benefited both from a massive display of the literature in Beck and McKeckni's *Political Elites: A Select Computerized Bibliography* (1968)[32] and from an insightful qualitative overview of the whole approach by a British scholar, Geraint Parry, in *Political Elites* (1969).[33]

As foretold by Seligman, scholars specializing in social background studies increasingly felt the need to progress beyond the amassing of descriptive socio-economic statistics toward more powerful predictive and causal analyses. As suggested by Donald D. Searing's thoughtful critique in "The Comparative Study of Elite Socialization," (1969),[34] this would require greater precision in three respects: the specification of leadership behaviors that are the object of prediction; the specification of those background characteristics that are hypothesized to predict leadership behavior; and the specification of the theoretical linkages among independent background variables and dependent leadership behaviors. To assist in identifying such linkages Seligman had called for case studies of successful and unsuccessful leaders. While not yet used in the way Seligman had envisioned, both case and aggregative studies of "winners" and "losers" began to appear.[35]

Seligman had called attention to *studies of small groups* that had been made in other social science disciplines, notably sociology and social psychology, that might provide insights into the nature of leadership in larger organizational contexts. As if in response to Seligman's suggestion, Sidney Verba explored the potentialities and limitations of the small group literature in *Small Groups and Political Behavior: A Study in Leadership* (1961).[36]

Seligman had also referred to the potential importance for political leadership studies of *writings on executive leadership* in business and public administration; for example, Chester I. Barnard's *The Functions of the Executive* (1938).[37] Again as if in response to this need there appeared Richard E.

Neustadt's analysis of presidential leadership as "the power to persuade" in *Presidential Power: The Politics of Leadership* (1960)[38] and Harlan Cleveland's *The Future Executive* (1972),[39] which argued for a new style of catalytic, nonhierarchical leadership applicable in both private and public management.

Personality studies had been noted by Seligman as an important source of insight into political leadership behavior, as forecast by Lasswell's *Psychopathology and Politics* (1930)[40] and his *Power and Personality* (1948).[41] As if in response to this need, several major studies were published: Alexander George and Juliette George's analysis of the origins, conditions, and effects of compensatory striving to repair damaged self-esteem—*Woodrow Wilson and Colonel House* (1956);[42] E. Victor Wolfenstein's psychoanalytic interpretation of revolutionary leadership in terms of unresolved oedipal problems—*The Revolutionary Personality: Lenin, Trotsky, Gandhi* (1967);[43] Alex Gottfried's psychosomatic analysis of leader behavior under stress—*Boss Cermak of Chicago* (1962);[44] James D. Barber's effort to predict leader performance on the basis of personality propensities for activity (active-passive) and affect (positive-negative)—*The Lawmakers* (1965),[45] *Power in Committees* (1966),[46] and *The Presidential Character* (1972);[47] and Robert C. Tucker's *Stalin as Revolutionary, 1879–1929* (1973).[48]

The *study of leadership recruitment* had been listed first in Seligman's 1950 statement of research priorities and to that he subsequently turned his own attention in such studies as "Elite Recruitment and Political Development" (1964),[49] *Leadership in a New Nation* (1964),[50] *Recruiting Political Elites* (1971),[51] *and Patterns of Recruitment* (1974).[52] Among important recent contributions to the understanding of recruitment are Joseph A. Schlesinger's description of the "structure of opportunity" provided by turnover rates in the set of elected American political leadership positions in *Ambition and Politics* (1966)[53] and Kenneth Prewitt's analysis of the recruitment of political leaders in terms of the sequential solution of problems characterized as a "Chinese box puzzle" in *The Recruitment of Political Leaders* (1970).[54] Closely related to the study of leadership recruitment were studies of political socialization and political participation; for example, Fred I. Greenstein's *Children and Politics* (1969)[55] and Lester Milbrath's *Political Participation* (1965).[56] Such works made it easier to ask how leaders themselves learned to lead and to give special attention to political leaders as political participants.

Seligman had also called for *studies of representation* that would view leadership in part as a function of acceptance by followers. In the two decades that followed publication of his essay, it seemed that American political science developed separately the two parts of a representational approach and was groping toward ways to combine them into a leader-follower interaction model. On the one hand, there appeared the pioneering demonstration of representational role orientations (e.g., "delegate, trustee, and politico") of elected leaders by Wahlke et al. in *The Legislative System* (1962).[57] On the other hand, there appeared the description, analysis, and prediction of follower (voter) behavior in terms of orientations toward "party, candidate, and issue" in Angus Campbell et al., *The American Voter* (1960).[58] These formulations implied the need for a framework of analysis in which both leader and follower behavioral orientations could be viewed in interaction over time; that is, a framework that could view leadership as a function of followership and followership as a function of leadership.

The *study of leadership techniques* had also been viewed as a future research priority by Seligman. This need was met in part by such works as James MacGregor Burns's *Roosevelt: The Lion and the Fox* (1956),[59] Alexander L. George's *The "Operational Code": A Neglected Approach to the Study of Political Leaders and Decision Making* (1967),[60] and Howard W. Wriggins's inductive prescription of required strategies for leaders in newly developing nations in *The Ruler's Imperative* (1969).[61]

Seligman's call for "*case studies* [emphasis added] of leadership functions in typologically expressed situations" was less clearly met, partly because political typologies themselves were not highly developed despite persistent efforts from Aristotle to the most recent important contribution by David A. Apter in *The Politics of Modernization* (1965).[62] In a sense, however, typological studies of leadership had begun to arise inductively out of inquiries into the nature of community power such as Hunter's *Community Power Structure* (1953),[63] Dahl's *Who Governs?* (1971),[64] and Agger et al.'s *The Rulers and Ruled* (1964).[65] Studies such as these began to suggest that communities could vary in terms of what kinds of leaders were influential in deciding community issues. Studies of political variation within postcolonial nations and small group studies both had made the same point: there could be either relative concentration or dispersal of decision-making functions. It remained a challenge for students of political leadership to describe and explain political leader behavior under these different conditions.

One of the important needs stressed in Seligman's essay, although it had not been included in his final list of four research priorities, was to develop the *study of political biography*, in part by introducing insights from the other social sciences. This enhances appreciation of the appearance of Burns's biography of Roosevelt, with its pioneering "A Note on the Study of Political Leadership,"[66] and of two remarkable essays by Lewis J. Edinger that sought to focus disciplinary attention more sharply upon "Political Science and Political Biography" (1964).[67]

Edinger's Call for "Political Biography"

Edinger's essays constituted more than just a plea for the study of political biography, although that was his main concern, because they called the attention of the discipline to the study of political leadership in a general way. The first essay presented a rationale for the study of political leadership, pointed out past neglect, and suggested reasons why American political scientists had not made leadership a central concern in contrast to the approach taken by European colleagues and scholars in other disciplines.

Edinger saw two main reasons for oversight: "the general intellectual and political climate in the profession, and the theoretical and methodological orientation identified with the so-called behavioral approach to the study of politics."[68] Edinger found a "group-oriented" tendency in American political culture "wherein the political boss and the dictator are perceived as aberrations."[69] He next asserted that some political scientists, characterized by "intense personal involvement in left-of-center political activities," demonstrated a "predilection for attributing decisive influence on political developments to social and economic forces rather than to individual leaders."[70] Furthermore, Edinger argued that strict emulation of the physical sciences inhibited the study of individual leadership, which was beset by problems of scanty and unreliable data and difficulties in the measurement of influence and motives. He also thought preoccupation with the present tended to mean the neglect of important influences from the past.

To overcome these difficulties Edinger called for the combination of humanities and social science skills. "In short," he urged, "I propose that we employ conceptual models and—whenever practicable and practical—quantitative analysis in conjunction with the frank but disciplined use of empathy and other forms of imaginative speculation."[71]

In the second essay Edinger presented a conceptual framework for the study of political leadership. He defined "political leader" as "a 'central actor' occupying a *focal position* which relates to various *counter-positions* in a particular role set."[72] "Political leadership," he further explained, "is thus a position—or in the language of the cognitive approach to role analysis—the location of an actor or actors in a group, characterized by the ability of the incumbent to guide the collective behavior of the group in the direction of the desired authoritative distribution of values in a community."[73] For this approach Edinger drew heavily upon Gross, Mason, and McEachern's *Explorations in Role Analysis* (1958),[74] thus contributing to the interdisciplinary enrichment of political leadership studies urged by Seligman in 1950.

Edinger's framework for the analysis of political biography directed attention to the political leader as a purposive actor and thus contributed toward filling the conceptual void that had characterized the first half century of the discipline. He intended his formulation to have general utility; it was applicable not only to a single role such as that of the American presidency.[75] It also attempted to link the idea of "leadership" with a major paradigm for political analysis, in this case Easton's formulation of "the authoritative allocation of values," which was another way of expressing Lasswell's "who gets what, when, how." Edinger's approach was presented at the same time that he was writing his biography (1965) of the German Social Democratic leader Kurt Schumacher[76] and was followed soon by an edited collection of essays, *Political Leadership in*

Industrialized Societies (1967),[77] by which he sought further to focus attention upon the subject.

In "The Comparative Analysis of Political Leadership" (1975),[78] Edinger proceeded to raise a series of questions that comparative research should seek to answer, calling special attention to variations in "efforts to obtain control," "the exercise of control," and "the impact of control." "To put it another way," he explained, "comparative inquiry focuses on differences as well as similarities, in the acquisition, performance and consequences of control."[79] Although neither Dahl's work on "power"[80] nor March's on "influence"[81] was explicitly cited, Edinger questioned the criteria that might be employed to argue that leader behavior "caused" changes in follower behavior and, by implication, vice versa.[82] Also, Edinger significantly began to raise questions about standards by which to judge the quality of leadership, distinguishing between "analytically intrinsic" and "analytically extrinsic" criteria to judge leadership ends and means.[83] These criteria were reminiscent of, but not completely identical with, the distinctions between "actor" and "observer" viewpoints that had been introduced into political science most recently by the decision-making approach. Plutarch's contribution to comparative leadership evaluation remained to be rediscovered. Overall, Edinger's essay implied, but did not explicitly state, that it might be possible to link political leadership studies with existing paradigms of the nature of politics—or possibly to integrate them into a new configuration. This latter, bolder assertion had been made in 1968 by Edinger's Columbia colleague Dankwart A. Rustow.

Rustow's Anticipation of "A New Theoretical View"

Philosophers and Kings: Studies in Leadership (1968),[84] a collection of essays by scholars in five disciplines, conceived and edited by Rustow, advanced the interdisciplinary approach espoused by Merriam and by Seligman and Edinger. The purpose was to examine "leadership as a process of innovation and leadership as the recurrent interplay between private personality and public performance."[85] The volume thus sought to enhance understanding of both political and intellectual innovators. Among the political leaders discussed were Gandhi, Lenin, Hitler, Mussolini, Nkrumah, Atatürk, de Gaulle, Bismarck, and Andrew Johnson. Intellectual leaders included Newton, Merriam, James Mill, and William James. The important idea of treating political and intellectual innovators in the same framework of analysis was reminiscent of the approach implied by Lasswell's *The Future of Political Science* in 1963. It also preceded the inclusion of Lenin's "theory of one-party organization and revolution," his "Soviet type of one-party state," Gandhi's "large-scale nonviolent political action," and Mao's "peasant and guerrilla organization and government" among sixty-two major advances in social science from 1900 to 1965 identified by Deutsch, Platt, and Senghaas in 1971.[86]

In his introductory essay, Rustow, like Edinger but unlike Merriam, Shannon, and Seligman, did not make an explicit case for the study of leadership on the normative ground that it would improve democratic politics. It was simply an important and challenging subject for analysis that was being simultaneously rediscovered by many scholars who often seemed unaware of each other's efforts. "His eyes fixed firmly ahead," observed Rustow, "not every scholar has recognized how many others are engaged in similar feats of pioneering" [87]—and even then Seligman's "The Study of Political Leadership" was not mentioned.

For Rustow, a "meaningful question" to guide political leadership studies was "Who is leading whom from where to where?" [88] Like Edinger, he thought that an explanation for the past absence of disciplinary focus upon this question could be found in the scientific orientation of the discipline. "In the growing body of systematic social science," he explained, "there remained less and less room for explicit attention to leadership."

> But as the older institutional-legal approach to the study of government came to be considered less and less adequate, [political scientists] began to adopt a new vocabulary of structure and function from cultural anthropology and a new technique of survey research from social psychology. Amid the verbal abstractions of the one and the quantitative correlations of the other, the political animal—be he citizen or ruler—was in danger of disappearing from the political scientist's view. [89]

As observed in Chapter 2, "leadership" was not a central concept in several major contemporary approaches to political science; yet, it is too simple to attribute this lack to a preoccupation with science and scientific method. For one thing, failure to focus upon leadership tended to characterize the discipline as a whole, not just the self-consciously "scientific" parts of it, and predated the rise of the "behavioral" approach to politics. For another, a broader view of what is meant by behavioral science was required. The comparatively great attention given explicitly to the study of "leadership" in psychology and social psychology, for example, fields that preceded political science in emphasis upon quantification and scientific rigor, showed that the methods of sociobehavioral sciences themselves did not impede the study of leadership in politics. [90] In political science this assertion was confirmed by the pioneering survey research studies of legislators by Wahlke and Eulau in *The Legislative System* (1962) [91] and of party leaders in the Detroit area by Samuel Eldersveld in *Political Parties: A Behavioral Analysis* (1964). [92] True, too, there is nothing inherent in nonquantitative methods of political analysis that would prevent their application to the study of political leadership. The discovery or neglect of political leadership as a subject for political inquiry could not be attributed primarily to the presence or absence of a commitment to quantitative scientific methods.

Like Seligman and Edinger, Rustow pointed to the historical milieu of American political science in the mid-twentieth century as an explanation for rising interest in the study of political leadership. "By the 1950's," he explained,

both the more secluded setting of the scholar's study and the more turbu-
lent environment outside became increasingly favorable to a new intellectual
attack on a long-neglected problem. A half-century of revolutions, economic
crisis, and war had undermined traditional institutions, challenged accepted
ideas, and dramatized the role of individual leaders such as Hitler, Roosevelt, Stalin, Churchill, Nehru, and de Gaulle.[93]

Similarly, Edinger had referred to influences represented by the "names of
de Gaulle and Castro, Nasser and Nehru, Ho Chi Minh and Ngo Dinh Diem,
which daily crowd the headlines."[94]

A passage devoted to the influence upon American political science of the
experience of the new nations that emerged out of the breakdown of the world
colonial system after World War II takes on special significance. This is because
Rustow was a member of the Committee on Comparative Politics of the
Social Science Research Council, which originally had not planned a volume
of essays specifically devoted to "political leadership" in its series on "political development."

> The new theorizing about political development and political modernization
> led to the rediscovery of broad historical questions of change in the social
> world and broad philosophical questions about the range and limitations of
> deliberate human control over such change. From either kind of question *it
> was only a small step to the systematic rediscovery of leadership as a central
> political process* [emphasis added].[95]

Rustow's rediscovery of the centrality of leadership may be compared with Max
Weber's definition of politics in terms of leadership that appears in the second
paragraph of his seminal essay "Politics as a Vocation." "We wish to understand
by politics," Weber explained, "only the *leadership* or the influencing of the
leadership, of a political association, hence today, of a state" (emphasis added to
"leadership" and removed from Weber's original stress upon "political" and
"state").[96] It may also be compared with Talcott Parsons's view that "the goal
of the polity is the production or generation of effective *leadership* and, on a less
general level, of binding decisions" (emphasis added).[97]

Near the conclusion of the introductory essay to *Philosophers and Kings,*
Rustow made an unprecedented claim for the potential significance of political
leadership studies. "In a field like political science," he wrote, with obvious
reference to the major approaches then current in the discipline,

> a focus on leadership may help to resolve some current methodological
> dilemmas. The generation that participated in the "successful revolt" against
> the older institutional-legal approach in favor of behavioralism has been
> engaged ever since in a wide search for a new basic unit of analysis. Some
> have sought it in a "functional" vocabulary, too abstruse to be applied in
> political research, some in the making of "decisions" that have proved
> difficult to isolate from the stream of reality, some in an elusive quantitative
> measure of power, and some in messages of communication so numerous as

to defy inquiry. The leader as the figure omnipresent in any political process, as the maker of decisions, originator and recipient of messages, performer of functions, wielder of power, and creator or operator of institutions can bring these disparate elements into a single visible focus. The study of leadership, moreover, can readily be supplemented with an examination of the social and political organization that he founds and transforms, with an analysis of the psychological appeals and political sanctions that give leader and organization a hold on their mass following. *In short, there may be the elements of a new theoretical view, both comprehensive and dynamic, of the political process as a whole* [emphasis added] .[98]

With Rustow's 1968 suggestion that the study of political leadership might provide a new theoretical focus for the entire discipline of political science, we have come a long way from the minimal treatment of "leadership" that we noted in the first six decades of the *APSR*, in Sabine, in major theoretical approaches, and in disciplinary overviews. The radical nature of Rustow's suggestion lies in the fact that it does not merely imply that the idea of leadership might be developed as a auxiliary concept to enhance present approaches but that this study might be able to integrate or supersede them all in an entirely new configuration of elements. Although the case for the study of political leadership need not rest upon such an all-embracing claim—there is abundant need for, and promise in, adding a leadership perspective to existing paradigms and disciplinary subfields—Rustow's insight creates awareness of a distinct possibility that stands as a challenge to political scientists.

Increasing Disciplinary Interest

By the mid-1970s there were abundant indications that the study of "political leadership" was rapidly becoming a central disciplinary concern. A striking symbol of the new awareness was Jeffery L. Pressman's "Preconditions of Mayoral Leadership." This essay, published in the *American Political Science Review* in 1972,[99] is notable both for the first title mention of the word "mayor" in sixty-six years of *APSR* history and for its rare linkage with the concept of "leadership." Another sure sign of growing interest was the publication of an annotated bibliography entitled *Theory and Research in the Study of Political Leadership,* first compiled by George T. Force and Jack R. Van Der Slik in 1967, later revised and expanded by them and Charles Dewitt Dunn in 1972.[100]

An especially important indicator was a pioneering panel discussion, "The Concept of Political Leadership," chaired by Betty Glad during the 1973 annual meeting of the American Political Science Association.[101] Attention was focused upon a paper by James MacGregor Burns, "Toward the Conceptualization of Political Leadership," that added to the earlier conceptualizing efforts of colleagues such as Kenneth F. Janda, "Toward the Explication of the Concept of Leadership in Terms of the Concept of Power" (1960);[102] Sidney Verba, "The Concept of Leadership" (1961);[103] James C. Davies, "Leaders and Followers" (1963);[104] Carl J. Friedrich, "Power and Leadership" (1963);[105] Dankwart A. Rustow, "The Nature of Political Leadership" (1967);[106] Léon Dion, "The Concept of Political Leadership: An Analysis" (1968);[107] Ann Ruth Wilner, *Charismatic Political Leadership: A Theory* (1968);[108] Donald D. Searing, "Models and Images of Man and Society in Leadership Theory" (1969);[109] and James V. Downton, "Leadership in Social Systems" and "Functions of Leadership" (1973)[110]—as well as other pioneers such as Merriam, Shannon, Seligman, and Edinger.

Further evidence of heightened interest at the 1973 APSA meeting was provided in a demonstration by Dorothy Guyot of her initial efforts to create an effective multimedia approach to teaching an undergraduate course in political leadership. Other papers read at the 1973 meeting illustrated the diversity of disciplinary resources available for political leadership studies.[111] Concomitantly, departments such as those at Stanford and Princeton began to add courses—undergraduate, graduate, or both—explicitly devoted to "political leadership."

Another noticeable trend was for greater salience of the term "leadership" in book titles, articles, subheadings, indices, and research proposals, as disciplinary attention became more focused upon this subject. For example, a pioneering interdisciplinary essay, "Patterns of Leadership," by social psychologist Daniel Katz appeared in the inaugural *Handbook of Political Psychology* (1973), edited by Jeanne N. Knutson.[112] At Ohio State University the interdisciplinary Mershon Center for the Study of Leadership and Public Policy emerged under the scholarly inspiration of Richard C. Snyder and his colleagues. Based at the same center, a multiuniversity research program designed to compare the usefulness of alternative approaches to the understanding of international relations, pioneered by Charles F. Hermann and associates, began to explore the effects of personal characteristics of political leaders as one source of explanation.[113]

Incipient Paradigmatic Linkages

As the idea of political leadership grew in importance, there were initial efforts to explore how it might be treated in relation to the analytical paradigms then current in the discipline. Most notable was Almond's attempt to account for leadership. In "Approaches to Development Causation," an essay introducing *Crisis, Choice and Change* (1973),[114] co-edited with Flanagan and Mundt, he discussed the subject of leadership in greater detail than at any time since *The Politics of the Developing Areas* (1960).

The tone of the essay was set in the first sentence of a three-page section, entitled "Leadership and Development Causation," in which Almond explained:

"The most recent contender in the political development literature is the leadership approach; its principal protagonist is Dankwart Rustow."[115] The idea of leadership was thus perceived in a spirit of contention. There was a "protagonist," with an implied antagonist. There was now a "leadership school" to be defended against and criticized.

Among Almond's principal criticisms was a repetition of his 1969 insistence that "leadership" should rightly be conceived as a subordinate but not a competing paradigm for political analysis, thus rejecting Rustow's bold 1968 hypothetical insight.[116] He further pointed out that "despite the obvious importance of the leadership variable in developmental explanation and its growing literature, no systematic effort has been made to place it in a broader strategy of developmental explanation."[117] "Dramatic" leadership (nothing is said of the possibility of an undramatic variety) does not always appear: "It is quite evident that in many significant historical episodes leadership in its more dramatic manifestations simply doesn't appear."[118] The "leadership school" should consider analysis in terms of leadership behavior as a dependent variable rather than allegedly always as an independent variable.[119] Leadership should perhaps be treated under another analytical category, decision making, for instance. "Clearly, then," Almond wrote, "leadership as an aspect of development causation is a species of a larger category of causation that may appropriately be called 'decision-making.'"[120] Further, "Thus the leadership school can be criticized for its failure to place high salience under a larger category of choice phenomena that includes the collective and individual, the rational and the non-rational, as subcategories."[121] In defending against the "leadership school," Almond seemed to be discovering or reaffirming decision making as an approach to the study of politics.

Interestingly, the term "elites" is not employed at all in this short discussion of leadership, nor does it appear as an index category of the total volume. By contrast, eight pages of the book are indexed under the concept of "leadership style." The index, however, does not adequately reflect the larger textual content in both cases. The idea of "leadership" is not defined in Almond's discussion of "Leadership and Development Causation"; yet, apparently, he understood and criticized it in terms of the behavior of single individuals of extraordinary influence upon events. He concluded: "The unusual and innovative leader is the individual who discovers or creates new options, mobilizes and combines new and old resources in creative ways, or arrives at policy formulations that change the issue distances among the competing political actors."[122] In this formulation, Almond seemed to be rediscovering his own long abandoned concept of the "public policy individual." In any case, by 1973 the ideas of "leadership theory," "leadership properties," and "leadership linkages" (all *not* subsumed under "decision making") had become salient parts of diagrams in which Almond suggested new understandings of the antecedents, processes, and consequences of historical change in political systems.[123]

In addition to Almond's contribution, other noteworthy efforts to link "political leadership" to more general modes of analysis began to be made. In *Rebel Leadership* (1973), Downton began to build upon Almond's work by analyzing leadership in structural-functional terms.[124] So did Tsurutani in *The Politics of National Development* (1973) by linking leadership to the performance of Almond's "regulative," "extractive," and "distributive" functions.[125] Viewing political leadership as a central factor in "modernization" or "development," Tsurutani further created, operationalized, and explicated a typology of leadership based upon three variables: "commitment," "intelligence and skill," and "dominance."[126]

Similarly concerned with political development, Dettman (1974), in six case studies, began to explore the possibility that Riggs's concepts of "fuzed," "prismatic," and "diffracted" social structures might serve as partial predictors of the emergence, success, and failure of national leaders who exemplified Weber's three claims to legitimacy: "traditional," "charismatic," and "rational-legal."[127] Also, Byars (1973) suggestively began to ask whether processes of emergence, tension, and change of affective and instrumental tasks observed at the small group level by Bales and others might provide insight into leadership behavior in seven types of macropolitical system.[128]

The work of Almond, Downton, Tsurutani, Dettman, and Byars collectively constituted a seminal foundation for adding a political leadership perspective to the field of "political development" and suggested that the proponents of other approaches to political inquiry might take similar account of the idea of "political leadership," or something like it, in their future conceptual, empirical, and normative theory-building efforts.

American Societal Context

What are some possible reasons for growing disciplinary interest in the study of political leadership in the 1970s? Can we discover some clues in contemporary world historical experience, the nature of American society, the character of recent political science disciplinary development, the interdisciplinary social science context, and the qualities of certain teacher-scholars?

Certainly, political scientists who were over forty-five years of age in 1975 had personally experienced some great international events for which political leaders had been at least dramatic symbols. They would recall, for example, that World War II appeared in part as a global struggle in which the efforts of Churchill, Chiang, de Gaulle, Roosevelt, Stalin, and others were pitted against those of Hitler, Mussolini, Tojo, and their allies. In the dramatic revolutionary postwar breakdown of the world colonial system they had also experienced the meteoric rise and sometimes tragic or well-deserved demise of such leaders as Nehru, Gandhi, Sukarno, Nasser, Nkrumah, Castro, and Mao. Furthermore, in the relentless postwar political conflict that marked the divided nations committed to competitive communist and anticommunist modes of development (a struggle in which Americans became deeply involved), they could appreciate that this was in part a struggle between Mao and Chiang, Kim and Rhee, Ho and Diem, Ulbricht and Adenauer, as influenced by the competition between Soviet leaders Stalin-Malenkov-Khrushchev-Brezhnev and American leaders Truman-Eisenhower-Kennedy-Johnson-Nixon-Ford-Carter. Additionally, as Americans watched competitive party experiments collapse around the world, they observed, and often assisted in, the emergence of military officers as "strong leaders" to "save" nations and ensure economic development.

Within American society itself, this group had experienced the dramatic campaigns of the crusading Roosevelt of the inspiring voice, the surprising pugnacity of presidency-made Truman, the remarkable lack of bellicosity and the surprising military-industrial skepticism of Eisenhower, the call to Camelot by tragic hero Kennedy, the unintended manipulation of the "Great Society" into great defeat by Johnson, the demoralizing influence of near-impeached Nixon, interim coaching by Ford, and revival by Carter. They also had heard the voices of those who had tried but failed, creating a sense of alternative directions: Willkie, Dewey, Stevenson, Goldwater, McGovern, and others. Additionally, the assassinations of the Kennedys, Martin Luther King, Jr., George Lincoln Rockwell, Malcolm X, and others created a sense of loss and dismay, an awareness of differences.

By the mid-1970s, Americans faced but hoped personally not to have to solve a cumulative set of military, economic, racial, environmental, energy, sexual, and other "crises." They also began to talk explicitly about a "leadership crisis" and to attempt to identify persons who might solve it.[129] But the era was certainly not one of adulation of politicians or of authority figures in general. It would be a mistake to interpret the rise of American scientific interest in political leadership studies in such terms. It was a time of challenge from the bottom up: from the poor to the rich, from racial minorities to racial majorities, from women to men, from voters to politicians, from consumers to corporations, from patients to doctors, from students to teachers, from the counterculture to the establishment, and so forth. Still, the time was not one of linear revolutionary movement. By the 1970s there were signs of counterchallenges from the top down. It was, rather, a period of social psychic pendulum swings between a militant sense of conservative righteousness and a passion for fundamental reform, moderated midway by apathetic inertia.[130] Yet almost all who experienced the three post-1945 decades had a sense of deepening crisis, from military victory to defeat, from atomic monopoly to oligarchy, from economic upsurge to decline, from faith to doubt.

But what of the link between these events and the rise of political leadership studies in American political science? Those familiar with Bernard Crick's historical interpretation of American political science might well attribute the emergence of interest in this subject to his hypothesis that political science is a product of social crisis. As Crick explained:

The study of politics is everywhere a response to the belief that there is a crisis. The difficulty besetting American political thought is that perhaps that while there has never been a crisis deep enough for a rethinking of the original beliefs to take place, yet there has always been, underlying the massive surface confidence, enough frictions of adjustment and growth to make a formal political science seem needed, and needed on a uniformly large scale. But because these crises have been regarded as marginal or as problems to be clearly solved so as to maintain the validity of the old beliefs in new circumstances, this political science did not take the form of political theory or philosophy, but citizenship training or education; and it mostly grew up not as a "learned science" as [John W.] Burgess mainly wished, but as a "technological science" as [Carroll D.] Wright entirely wished.[131]

But why was the post-1945 "crisis" of American society in its global context apparently producing marked interest in the scientific study of political leadership; whereas objectively more severe crises such as the American Revolution, the Civil War, and the Great Depression had not? These earlier crises had not focused attention upon leadership in a "technological" or "learned" or "training" or "philosophical" manner. Why now? Also, since most other contemporary societies had recently experienced leadership crises amidst tumultuous post–World War II global development—e.g., Soviet or Chinese seizure with problems related to the presence or absence of Stalin or Mao Tse-tung—why was it that the interest in leadership seemed to arise predominantly in American political science?

More definitive answers must come eventually from those future scholars who will write a global intellectual and sociological history of the emergence of world political science, but at least some hints can presently be given. First of all, American political science enjoyed a measure of autonomy vis-à-vis the political figures who ruled the society. The ideal tradition was one of academic independence in thinking about alternatives to present American institutions, derived either from study of the past, or from inquiry into other contemporary societies, or from contemplation of the future. Second, American political science had experienced a determined, post-1945 movement to make inquiry more "scientific" by emulating natural science, social science, and behavioral science models. One often forgotten impetus behind this so-called behavioral science revolution in American political science, characterizing especially the work of those scholars who introduced behavioral science approaches into the study of international relations, was to find scientific knowledge that would permit mankind to eliminate war. One of the most significant features of the behavioral science revolution was not that it sought to hypothesize, measure, quantify, and theorize but that it demanded direct empirical understanding of men and women in politics. It summoned political scientists out of the libraries. Thus, it was natural that the idea of the scientific study of political behavior should eventually come to focus squarely upon the behavior of political leaders in interaction with the led, as Shannon had hoped to see in 1949. And it was natural that in an antiauthoritarian political culture, scientific thought should eventually focus upon the behavior of dominant or revolutionary political figures, following upon the scientific breakthroughs it had achieved in formerly taboo areas such as sex and religion. Furthermore, those political scientists who objected most to the effort to apply the methods of science in political inquiry—in favor of philosophical and humanist appeals—contributed further to the discovery of political leadership behavior as a source of potentially creative humanist initiative in politics. For the scientific discovery of political leadership in part was a product of the effort to recover a sense of creative, purposive, meaningful, and expressive individual and group life under the impersonal, automated, and often unjust conditions of postindustrial, mass American society.

But it is too simple, of course, to view the emergence of political leadership studies as a purely domestic disciplinary development. The scientific study of political leadership seems recently to have arisen primarily out of three convergent trends: the study of American leaders, as illustrated by the work of James D. Barber, Herbert McCloskey, and Alexander and Juliette George; the study of leaders abroad, as in the contributions of Lewis J. Edinger and Dankwart A. Rustow; in the conceptualizing efforts of scholars whose work spans both of the foregoing, such as Lester G. Seligman; and in cross-polity comparative contributions such as those of E. Victor Wolfenstein, Gordon DiRenzo,[132] and Robert D. Putnam.[133]

Political Science Context

In fact, as we view the emergence of scientific political leadership studies within the broad context of disciplinary development since 1945, it is apparent how much of great potential relevance for the future development of this field has been accomplished. Paradoxically, the more clear we become about the neglect of, and the need for, concepts of political leadership, the more conscious we become of resources of possible disciplinary relevance, ranging from paradigmatic overviews, through institutional studies, to studies that emphasize social background and personality. An outline of current disciplinary resources is presented in Figure 2 (p. 60). Scholars familiar with the post–World War II development of American political science will appreciate the massive bibliography that would be required adequately to reflect the scope and depth of the resources to which attention is symbolically directed here.

Multidisciplinary Context

The emergence of political leadership studies in political science has been preceded and paralleled by the growth of leadership studies in other social science disciplines and applied professions. The context of this development was

FIGURE 2.   **Political Science Context of Emerging Political Leadership Studies**

MAJOR ANALYTICAL APPROACHES TO POLITICAL SCIENCE

Power	Decision Making	Cybernetics	Value Allocation	Structural Functionalism	New Political Economy

ARENAS AND INSTITUTIONS

International politics; national politics; community power (urban, rural); traditional, transitional, and modernizing political systems

CONCEPTS OF POLITICAL LEADERSHIP

The philosopher-king, Machiavellian prince, political elites, charisma, and other images from classical and modern theorists

PROBLEM-SOLVING STRATEGIES

Operational codes, ruling imperatives, campaigning, revolution

PERSONALITIES	*ROLES*	*VALUES*
Biography	Executive	Ideologies
Political styles	Representational	Law
	Judicial	

ORGANIZATIONS

Parties, legislatures, bureaucracies, military, judiciary

RECRUITMENT, MOBILITY, SOCIALIZATION

Career patterns, opportunity structure, social learning

FOLLOWER VALIDATION

Voting, public opinion, interest groups, participation

SOCIAL BACKGROUNDS

Class, ethnicity, sex, occupation, education, religion

---

thus one with rich potential for interdisciplinary borrowing of concepts, theories, and methods that would advance understanding of leadership in politics. While political scientists, for example, could discover the wealth of psychological studies of leadership reviewed in Stogdill's indispensable *Handbook of Leadership* (1973);[134] psychologists such as Hermann and her colleagues could strikingly show how their discipline might address itself directly to the study of political leadership in *A Psychological Examination of Political Leaders* (1977);[135] and two professors of business administration, Kotter and Lawrence, could brilliantly demonstrate how creative transdisciplinary imagination could illuminate the neglected subject of mayoral leadership in *Mayors in Action* (1974).[136]

We have been reviewing here signs and possible interpretations of the rapidly emerging field of political leadership studies in American political science. This phenomenon provides a worthy challenge to the sociologist of knowledge and the historian of science. Understanding of field development would benefit greatly from an effort to share the experiences of the many scientists who are beginning to view the study of political leadership as an extraordinarily important subject for inquiry, education, and action.

While I have not attempted to examine the history of scientific political leadership studies in other contemporary political cultures, this remains an important scholarly task. Have others preceded the American discovery of the neglect of, and need for, the independent, academic, scientific study of political leadership? Are scientific political leadership studies apt to originate in, and to diffuse from, the less authoritarian, more academically independent societies? Are more authoritarian polities likely to develop political leadership studies as a directly controlled applied science designed to strengthen existing authority? Are some societies with idealized, even sacrosanct, forms of political leadership and virtually deified ruling individuals likely to repress entirely the idea of the scientific study of leadership? I hope that these kinds of question and others of scientific importance can be addressed in a truly global future community of scientists whose attention will be sharply focused upon the study of political leadership.

Past neglect. Present emergence. Future potential. Now we need to ask, "What is meant by 'political leadership'?"

CHAPTER 4

ALTERNATIVE SOURCES OF CONCEPTUALIZATION

The precise nature of political leadership is one of the most difficult problems in the domain of politics, or indeed, in social action, yet it is one of the most real phenomena in political and social behavior. [1]

CHARLES E. MERRIAM
1945

THE CONTEMPORARY RISE of interest in the study of political leadership presents the discipline of political science with a clear and continuing conceptual, theoretical, research, evaluative, and action challenge. What is political leadership? What alternative conceptions of it seem promising for comparative exploration? What are the mutual implications of these in relation to varying conceptions of a political system? What factors explain political leadership? What causal influences does it have upon political institutions and vice versa? What inquiries promise most new understanding of it? What are its likely future forms? How is political leadership to be evaluated? And what purposive interventions are possible in relation to it?

After long disciplinary inattention it is unlikely that initial conceptual efforts will be entirely adequate or gain widespread acceptance, but it is important that such efforts be made as a step toward more adequate treatment of this subject in the future. The very term "political leadership" immediately presents a problem of compound indeterminacy: political scientists are by no means agreed upon the meaning of "political" and other social scientists have suggested a wide variety of images of "leadership." This kind of diversity can be regarded as a source of both confusion and enrichment. Confusion arises mainly when no two alternative images are persistently developed and applied so that their relative scientific usefulness can be comparatively evaluated. Enrichment comes from the contributions of multiple perspectives to fuller understanding.

Diversity in conceptualizing political leadership is thus expected, useful, and unfortunately potentially dangerous. It is expectable partly because "for any concrete social object, there is an infinite number of analytical aspects."[2] This is because the human brain is capable of creating alternative descriptions, explanations, and evaluations of social reality. Social reality itself, of course, also varies. Diversity is useful because comparison of similarities and differences among studies of the same social object from different approaches is the best method that social scientists have for improving confidence in the validity[3] and comprehensiveness of knowledge. Maurice Duverger has explained that combining different images of politics (e.g., "Marxist," "liberal," "conservative," and "fascist" images) facilitates more complete understanding and greater critical awareness "in the same way we can arrange photographs of the same object taken from different points of view so as to obtain a more complete image of the object than would be possible from any direct perspective."[4] Diversity can sometimes be dangerous because human history unfortunately reveals a series of bloody conflicts over conceptions of the legitimacy, rights, and obligations of powerful political figures. Even today there are few communities in which political leaders welcome efforts to conceptualize their work in ways that differ from convention. Thus, where "political power grows out of the barrel of a gun,"[5] as Mao Tse-tung observed, a scientific effort to conceptualize political leadership can mean looking straight down muzzles at people who pull triggers.

Sources of Conceptual Insight

The purpose of this chapter is to call attention to some alternative sources of insight that may be useful now and in future efforts to conceptualize political leadership. Five basic sources will be explored: the natural language ideas of experienced political leaders themselves; leadership images suggested by studies of the social behavior of animals; insights from the humanities; concepts being developed in other social and behavioral sciences; and images of leadership found in the various subfields of political science.

This effort at conceptual exploration cannot be regarded as definitive or exhaustive. Experts in the specialties examined will better appreciate all the potentialities and nuances of interpretation possible therein. Furthermore, no effort has been made to explore other possible sources of important conceptual insight that eventually may enrich the scientific study of political leadership. Among these are natural sciences such as biology and chemistry (especially studies of the brain), applied technologies such as the electronic computer,[6] and the leader-follower rationales that underly professions such as teaching (the nurturing of capabilities), medicine (the prevention and cure of suffering), law (the normative regulation of behavior), and the military (command and obedience). The conceptual potentialities of two kinds of language have also not been explored: natural verbal languages other than English[7] and mathematical languages. All of these and others that will come to mind may contribute to conceptual progress. Undoubtedly, future scientific advancement will be greatly facilitated by the creation of finely articulated mathematical models of political leadership that are retranslatable into—although not necessarily limited to—the full richness of human experience.[8]

Experienced Political Leaders

One place to begin creating scientifically useful and socially significant concepts of political leadership is to ask how experienced leaders themselves view what it is that they and other leaders do. This means a wide-ranging inquiry across time, levels, and space into how leaders have thought about leadership of the past, present, and future. These insights may be cognitively simple or complex and morally lovable or detestable. An adequate study of any particular leader's conceptions and their evolution should range over the entire record left by a historical leader and should be supplemented by direct exploratory discussions with living leaders, active or retired.[9]

Even though fragmentary, some of the following images hint at the rich diversity of insight that may be obtained by asking about conceptions of political leadership that are held by experienced leaders.

Leadership as Decision and Persuasion. "Leadership is the ability to decide what is to be done, and then to get others to want to do it"—Dwight D. Eisenhower.[10] "A leader is a man who has the ability to get other people to do what they don't want to do, and like it"—Harry S Truman.[11]

Leadership as the Implementation of Creative Imagination. "A political leader is a person with the ability to imagine non-existing states of affairs combined with the ability to influence other people to bring them about"—Puerto Rico governor Luis Mùnoz Marín.[12]

Leadership as Biological, Collective, or Class Dominance. "Any organized society must have a leader and men are divinely destined to fulfill that role"—Utah state representative Eldon H. Barlow.[13] Some Micronesians are "born to rule"; others are "born to serve"—Ponapean leader Heinrich Iriarte.[14] "The working class leads everything"—Mao Tse-tung.[15] "The city inescapably *leads* the village. . . . The village inevitably *follows the city*. The only question is *which class* of the 'city' classes can lead the village"—Lenin.[16]

Leadership as Influence by Example. "What a few will do, others will copy";[17] "clean examples have a curious method of multiplying themselves"[18]—Gandhi. "The essence is to be more revolutionary and set the example"—Ché Guevara.[19]

Leadership as the Skillful Management of Social Relations. "A free government is a government by politicians. And a politician is a public relations man who knows how to get along with people. I think that the most honorable title that can be given a man is to say he is a politician. I've always said that the great statesmen you read about were all politicians. They became statesmen after they are in their graves"—Harry S Truman.[20]

Leadership as Creative Brutality Based upon Hostilities against Out-group Enemies. "The art of leadership consists of consolidating the attention of the people against a single adversary and taking care that nothing will split up their attention. . . . The leader of genius must have the ability to make different opponents appear as if they belonged in the same category."[21] "Whatever goal man has reached is due to his originality plus his brutality."[22] "To be a leader means to be able to move masses"[23]—Adolf Hitler.

Leadership as the Revolutionary Expression and Consolidation of Class Interests. "The art of the politician and the correct understanding by the communist of his own tasks, consists in the correct appraisal of the conditions and the moment when the vanguard of the proletariat can successfully seize power; when it will be able, during and after this, to obtain sufficient support from sufficiently broad sections of the working class and the non-proletarian working masses; when he will, after that, be able to support, strengthen, and broaden his rule, educating, teaching, and attracting wider and wider masses of the laboring population"—Lenin.[24]

Leadership as Satisfaction of Follower Needs. "Serve the people"—Mao Tse-tung.[25] "Leadership means service to others"—Hawaii governor John A. Burns.[26]

Leadership as Task Performance. "We talk too much about leadership in the abstract. The essence of leadership is the successful resolution of problems and the successful attainment of objectives which impress themselves as being important to those whom one is called upon to lead"—U.S. State Department Policy Planning Staff director Paul H. Nitze.[27]

Leadership as Slave or Master of Circumstance. "It is fatally stupid to attribute to public men the changes of fortune which the unfolding of events produces in states. . . . Man is the weak toy of fortune, which he may often predict quite well but never be sure of. . . . To assume that politics and war will go according to our plans, unfolding blindly by the mere strength of our desires and encouraged by the limited means at our disposal, is to wish by humane means to emulate divine power"—Simón Bolívar.[28] "If we do not win, we will blame neither heaven nor earth but only ourselves"—Mao Tse-tung.[29]

Taken as a whole these concepts suggest that political leadership comprises decisional initiative, pacific and coercive persuasion, the exacerbation or reduction of conflict, follower need satisfaction as related to task accomplishment, and action within an influencing but partly influenceable situational context. More systematic comparative inquiry across different political systems, levels of leadership, and socioeconomic settings will need to be conducted in order to achieve greater understanding of similarities and differences in the ways active leaders think about what they do. These natural language insights need to be supplemented also by the views of close associates and observers of active leaders, both supportive and critical.

Social Behavior of Animals

Another potential source of insight into the nature of human political leadership lies in the study of nonhuman animal behavior. This was earlier appreciated by Merriam, who included three references to animal studies among the twenty-nine references for further research that he appended to *Four American Party Leaders* (1926).[30] Somit,[31] among others, has recently called for greater attention by political scientists to the study of animal behavior, the potentialities and limitations of which have for long been a subject of discussion by psychologists[32] and anthropologists.[33]

As yet, political scientists have not systematically reviewed the animal studies literature specifically for insights into or hypotheses about human political leadership behavior.[34] This remains a task for the emerging field of political leadership studies. Among other things, political scientists have much to learn from animal scientists about observational research methods. Since animal scientists cannot "interview" their subjects, they have to be exceptionally inventive in devising observational modes of inquiry.[35] Thus, the exploration of leadership images here is intended to be but an initial reconnaissance.

Leadership as Coercive Dominance. The most salient image of social precedence to emerge from animal studies is that of the "dominant animal." Dominance is defined in terms of a status hierarchy, or "peck order," that is established by the exercise of coercive or threatening behaviors. Peck orders take several forms, such as "peck right," wherein the dominant animals are not attacked in return, and "peck dominance," wherein reciprocal attacks are asymmetrical. Dominance is associated variously with control over food, territory, and sex.

Although actual or threatened physical coercion is sometimes correlated with the establishment of a dominance relationship, an image of animal leadership based solely upon coercion is not adequate. As Tiger and Fox have pointed out, dominance is associated with achieved centrality of attention;[36] both dominance and deference are partly learned behaviors;[37] deference persists even after the brute strength capabilities of dominant animals diminish;[38] some dominant animals retire from their salient positions to become "solitaries";[39] and status hierarchies can be changed "if attention can be taken away from the dominant animals."[40] Furthermore, physical dominance does not explain all of animal leadership behavior. For example, male red deer physically dominate their harems in the rutting season. But when alarmed, females immediately reassert their greater influence over the herd's movement, and male sexual domination gives way to female initiative in ensuring group survival.[41] As Kolata concluded after a review of controversies in animal dominance studies, "It now seems likely that no one kind of social behavior is associated with dominance and that not all groups of primates even have dominance hierarchies."[42]

Leadership as the Initiation of Uncoerced Following Responses. Many students of animal behavior have preferred to reserve the term "leadership" only for initiatives that induce uncoerced following responses in others. They wish to distinguish this case both from coercive dominance and from the machinelike patterns of biologically programmed relations that seem to characterize some insect societies such as termites.[43]

The experimental operationalization of leadership as precedent initiative as distinguished from coerced subordination is illustrated by a goat study by Stewart and Scott.[44] They measured dominance by greater degrees of butting and pushing behaviors when a handful of food was placed upon a small surface between pairs of animals. Leadership was measured by observing which goat in a pair of known dominance relations initiated joint flight (as contrasted with uncoordinated escape behaviors) when standing pairs placed a few feet apart were threatened with separation by a person's attempt to walk between them. The principal findings of this study were that dominance and leadership were not correlated and that "these two phenomena are the result of two separate learning processes which are not associated."[45] Interestingly, Greenberg discovered that dominant sunfish also tended to be leaders in a task of maze running.[46] These contrasting findings suggest that coercive dominance and noncoercive initiatives are different analytical dimensions of leadership that may characterize the same or different individuals across species and possibly across tasks within species.

Leadership as the Elicitation of Involuntary Following Responses (Imprinting). An image of leadership as the elicitation of biologically determined following responses was suggested in Lorenz's pioneering studies of "imprinting" in certain species of birds,[47] as critically evaluated and extended by Moltz from a learning theory perspective.[48] In imprinting, humans and even inanimate objects can elicit following responses similar to those elicited by the natural mothers of young birds.

The basic assertions of imprinting theory are that following responses can be established only during a limited period early in an animal's life, that they are not learned through reinforcement by rewards and punishments, that once learned they tend to persist with remarkable strength throughout life, that other response capabilities acquired later in life will tend to be directed toward the earlier imprinted (leading) object, and that responses to an imprinted object will tend to be generalized to all members of its class.

The idea that there is an involuntary biological mechanism that determines following responses in some species under certain circumstances naturally raises the question of whether there may not be a similar biological determinant of leading initiatives. That is, is there a biological determinant underlying the behavior of mother ducks and human experimenters such as Lorenz that "causes" them to lead the behavior of inexperienced ducklings? Or, simply, are there biological bases to *both* leader initiatives and follower responses?

Such questions will interest students of political leadership who will seek to explore further the thesis advanced by Tiger and Fox, who have asserted: "The paying of attention to a dominant animal is both the basis of political society and the major mode of its dynamics. Millions of years of biopolitical evolution have programmed the primate to pay attention to dominant animals, providing the right cues are given."[49]

Leadership as Emotional Exchange. An extraordinary recent experimental study by Menzel of leader-follower relations among a group of chimpanzees within the boundaries of a one-acre field provides evidence for what I interpret to be mutual emotional needs for each other by *both* leaders and followers. Seeking explicitly to answer the question "Do leaders need followers?" Menzel set up an experiment wherein an established chimpanzee "leader" alone was introduced to food hidden across the field from a point where "followers" were caged. Next the leader was returned to the group in the cage. Under control conditions, both leader and followers were released simultaneously from the cage; the leader guided the others to the food; "and on more than 80% of the trials the food was gone within 2½ min." Under the experimental conditions, however, after being shown the food and returned to the cage, only the leader was released, with the following observed results:

> The leader whimpered, defecated, begged toward the experimenters, or tried to open the release cage door to get to his companions. Bandit [a leader] subsequently threw a tantrum in which he screamed, rolled on the ground, tearing his hair, and then ran and clung to a tree. . . . Once the door of the cage opened and the followers emerged, the behavior of the leader changed rapidly. The leader ran to a follower, screamed and embraced him, and within 5 sec. was off and running for the food.[50]

On the other hand, Menzel reported a series of experiments in which the animals were given a choice of obtaining clearly visible food across the field (interpreted here as a choice of directly instrumental behavior) or of following the leader to a hidden source of food (interpreted as power or emotional responsiveness). He noted, "On 88% of all trials involving leaders, more animals followed the leader than went to visible food."[51]

Leadership as Information Giving. Although not explicitly discussed in terms of "leadership," von Frisch's classic inquiry into bee communication[52] suggested another image of it: the giving of information. Von Frisch demonstrated that returning "finder" bees who had discovered food outside the hive communicated the direction, distance, and nature of this food to other bees by body language ("dancing"), sound (variation in buzzing), and smell (flower scents carried on their bodies). Thus, as the result of information given by the discoverer bee, other bees knew the direction, distance, and kind of food available outside the hive without direct experience of it. They then "followed" the directions given by the finders.

The importance of communications for leadership behavior among primates, when combined with higher status position, is further illustrated by Carpenter's observation of howler monkeys. "The communicative postures, movements, and vocalizations of the principal male have an observable, different, and stronger effect on group members than do the same gross behavior patterns produced by a low-order male, such as one that has recently joined the group."[53]

These indications of the importance of communication in animal behavior recall the sociological insight of Charles H. Cooley, who wrote in 1902: "All leadership takes place through the communication of ideas to the minds of others, and unless the ideas are so presented as to be congenial to those other minds, they will evidently be rejected."[54]

Leadership as Mutual Mimicry (Allelomimesis). Allelomimesis, "mutual mimicking," was defined by Scott as "behavior in which two or more animals *do the same thing* with some degree of mutual stimulation."[55] Such behavior is characteristic of flocks of birds, herds of mammals, and schools of fish when they are acting in concert and in which no single animal or group of animals seems to be the initiator, dominator, or model of group behavior. An example is a V-shaped flock of geese in flight.

"In true leader-follower relationships," Scott explained, "the behavior concerned is allelomimetic with both animals responding to each other but to an unequal degree."[56] Followers may be rewarded by the reduction of anxiety about undefended attack and by the provision of food.

The degree of mutual mimicry versus dominance behaviors may vary within and across species. Carpenter reported, for example, that among male howler monkeys as compared with male rhesus monkeys or male baboons, there is relatively less dominance behavior; however, the male howler monkeys tend to dominate female howler monkeys as a group.[57] This is reminiscent of the human situation in which there may be a good deal of egalitarian behavior among party cadres or members of legislative bodies, combined with high degrees of dominance behavior by them in relation to outsiders.

Leadership as Group Centrality. The concept of a political leader as a "central actor" might well have been derived from observation of the central position of the dominant male in a baboon troop on the march[58] or the position of the master cock among sage grouse during the mating season.[59]

A human parallel might be suggested by an aerial photograph of a Zambian cattle herding village that shows a thousand huts encircling the chief's compound, which is itself composed of a circle of huts for his wives.[60] The idea of centrality is found in the concept of the leader as a "central person" for group emotions advanced by Redl[61] and by Bavelas, Leavitt, and other students of small group leadership conceived in terms of informational centrality.[62] Subsequently, Gross and others introduced the concept of "central actor" to sociological role analysis[63] and this notion was introduced to political science by Edinger in his definition of leadership as the behavior of a *"central actor* occupying a *focal position* which relates to various *counter positions* in a particular *role set."*[64]

This is not, of course, the way in which an image of political leadership defined in terms of positional, emotional, informational, or interactional centrality entered political science from an animal studies origin, but it might have happened that way—and something similar might happen in the future if animal studies are given concentrated attention by students of political leadership.

Arts and Humanities

Whereas animal studies offer the possibility of approaching the study of human political leadership from a relatively detached perspective, the arts and humanities offer exactly the opposite opportunity: to view political leadership through the creative work of those who seek to express the keenest sensibility of being human.[65] Thus, images of political leadership may be expressed in sculpture,[66] painting,[67] architecture,[68] music,[69] dance,[70] drama,[71] cinema,[72] opera,[73] musical comedy,[74] poetry,[75] comic impersonation,[76] and literature.[77] Such images may arise out of the creations of the large urban centers or from the folk traditions of the hinterlands. They may represent an outpouring of love and adulation, an anguished cry of revolutionary hatred, the cold incisiveness of cynical detachment, an urge to laugh at the ridiculousness of leader behavior, or the need to cry. Such works may be commissioned, coerced, or spontaneously produced. Some may be fictionalized portrayals of actual political leaders, written by highly informed, close observers who otherwise have no way to express their knowledge and feelings. Verdi's opera *Rigoletto,* for example, was banned as subversive by French censors and had to be rewritten to downgrade the main political figure to an Italian duke because it portrayed the follies of Francis I of France with embarrassing intimacy.[78] The "fictionalization" of political leadership reality is also illustrated by novels and short stories recently written by American journalists[79] and political leaders themselves.[80]

Another source of humanistic insight into the nature of political leadership, as well as into the personalities of the leaders themselves, is artistic behavior, ranging from amateur efforts to those of professional quality. Thus, students of political leadership will be unusually interested in such things as Napoleon's fiction,[81] the novels of Disraeli[82] and José Rizal,[83] the paintings of Churchill,[84] the architecture of Hitler,[85] the poetry of Mao Tse-tung[86] and Leopold Senghor,[87] the songs of King Kalakaua,[88] the big band dance music of Prince Sihanouk,[89] the symphonic conducting of British prime minister Edward Heath,[90] and the musical comedy of Philippine senator Raul S. Manglapus.[91]

In addition to noting the artistic endeavors of political leaders, of course, we need to be aware of the cases in which professional artists have sought political leadership roles; e.g., some writers, actors, and actresses.

Leadership as a Creative Art. One image of leadership that emerges from the humanities is not only that some political leaders are portrayed by artistic works—or that some leaders are creative artists—but also that political leadership itself is a creative art in which the basic materials are human and in which the scale varies from individuals to vast populations. This thesis has been advanced by Roskill.

> I do not think it is generally realized how intimate a connection exists between leadership and the Arts. It seems to me that some of the greatest leaders have discovered and developed in their work a means of self-expression akin to what the painter finds in painting, the musician in the composing or playing of music, and the writer in the expression of his thoughts and feelings on paper. To such men, leadership was, in my view, a work of creation analogous to that of inspired painters, musicians, and writers. They were in fact artists in the broadest sense of the word. Other successful leaders, probably far greater in number, have shown themselves sensitive to and appreciative of the Arts; and that category overlaps with many leaders who have been gifted amateurs of the Arts, and who have found in them the mental relaxation needed by every man who carries heavy responsibilities.[92]

Even given Roskill's insight, it is still striking to find clear confirmation of it in the words of the Cuban revolutionary leader Fidel Castro.

> We love the Revolution as a labor. We love it just as a painter, a sculptor, or a writer may love his work. And, like him, we want our work to have perennial value. . . . Revolution is an art. And politics is also an art. The most important one, I think.[93]

We find a similar image in a poem written in prison by the Vietnamese revolutionary leader Ho Chi Minh.

> The ancients used to like to sing about natural beauty:
> Snow and flowers, moon and wind, mists, mountains and rivers.
> Today we should make poems including iron and steel,
> And the poet should also know [how] to lead an attack.[94]

Ho has also spoken about "using people" as an artist would use the materials of his craft: "To use people is like using wood. A skilled worker can make use of all kinds of wood whether it is big or small, straight or curved."[95]

It is not unthinkable that in a future nonviolent society, or as a contribution to its emergence, political leadership may come to be defined as a creative art in which questions of creativity, medium, and design[96] will receive as much attention as the "death-dealing power of the state" has received in the past.[97]

Leadership as Surrogate Parentage. A humanist approach is apt to portray leader-follower relations in terms of parent-child relationships. Its ancient origins are illustrated by the patricidal imagery of Sophocles' play *Oedipus the King* (ca. 430–411 B.C.) and the reciprocal obligations of filial piety so basic to the Confucian mode of classical Chinese thought.[98]

When a leader dies or is assassinated, the family imagery is apt to emerge in the ensuing upsurge of emotions. An eloquent example of this pattern is contained in a eulogy composed and spoken by the British actor Laurence Olivier upon the death of George VI in 1952.[99]

What does it mean to have a king? And how is it possible for whole nations to feel a personal sense of grief in the passing of one who must be for all, except for a very few, no more than a symbol—a symbol, moreover, which is immediately carried on interrupted by death.

I think I can express what is felt. The idea of a representative personage with the constitutional rights to advise, born to his task and therefore entirely beyond the reach of party political influences, is very attractive and comfortable to us—and invites us to believe in the possible ideal of a man in authority.

To express a little more warmly our feelings for the monarchy, one could say that it is for us as though we had two families—our own and our royal family. And our royal family unites all our nations in a way that is dear and comfortable for us.

The king is our father, the queen, our mother, and their children, our royal brothers and sisters. [Emphasis added]. In the death of our king we feel the dumb strangeness of a father gone. Expressed in such perfect simplicity by our poet, "He was a man, take him for all and all, I shall not look upon his like again."

In grateful comfort we now turn with love and comfort to our gentle young mother, to whom we shall cry out loud, "God save Queen Elizabeth! Long live Queen Elizabeth! May the queen live forever!"

The relative youth of President John F. Kennedy apparently lessened the explicit father imagery in the responses by poets to his assassination on November 22, 1963. Still, Robert Hazel wrote of the president "I love as my grandfather loved Lincoln."[100] Both these examples, of course, emphasize the loving side of parent-child relationships, but the total relationship holds potential for hatred and ambivalence as well.[101] Accordingly, the responses of artists to the death of hated as well as loved leaders merit comparative examination. Furthermore, the parental political leadership imagery needs to be explored not only from the child's or sibling's perspective but also from the paternal and the maternal viewpoint.

Leadership as Emotional Interaction. Overall the arts call attention to the emotional aspects of leader-follower relationships. A good example of this is provided by the theme of the modern ballet *Le Leader* [102] created and danced by the French artist Janine Charrat and her company in New York in 1957. Charrat has written, in verbal explanation of her nonverbal artistic intent:

> L'argument de mon ballet comportait surtout l'étude de l'enthousiasme et du pouvoir magnétique du conducteur d'hommes, avec tout ce que cela entraîne de ferveur et en même temps d'extravagances, tous les dangers du mauvais conducteur ou de celui qui se laisse entraîner par ses passions et son orgueil; je faisais du même coup l'apologie de la ferveur de la foule vis à vis du bon conducteur.[103]

> (The argument of my ballet comprises above all a study of the enthusiasm and magnetic power of the leader of men, with all that this entails of fervor and excesses, all the dangers of the bad leader or one who lets himself be

carried away by his passions and pride; at the same time I present a justification of the crowd's devotion to a good leader.)

In this conception, we find some of the elements that would be required in a fully developed emotional portrayal of leadership: "enthusiasm," "magnetic power," "fervor," "passions," "pride," and "devotion."

Social and Behavioral Sciences

In looking toward animal studies and the humanities for insights into political leadership, we have been pursuing a strategy of understanding akin to that employed by Plato in seeking to define the concept of "statesmanship" in 362 B.C. "Well, then," Plato asked, "what example is there . . . which we can take and set beside statesmanship, and which, because it constitutes an activity similar to statesmanship, can be of real help to us in finding what we are looking for?"[104] In the same spirit, political scientists will wish to explore images of leadership emerging from other behavioral and social sciences, where important reviews of the literature recently have been conducted in psychology,[105] anthropology,[106] sociology,[107] and economics.[108]

Leadership as Salient Initiative. A ubiquitous image of leadership in natural language concepts, ethology, the humanities, and the social sciences is that leadership involves some kind of outstanding initiative in group activities. The sociologist Charles H. Cooley, for example, unvexed by the complexities that later disturbed Merriam as cited at the beginning of this chapter, wrote simply in 1902: "Leadership is only salient initiative."[109] A similar perspective was offered by Cowley, who added the idea of follower responsiveness: "A leader is an individual who is moving in a particular direction and who succeeds in inducing others to follow after him."[110]

A seminal contribution to the pioneering interdisciplinary project to study leadership carried on at Ohio State University in the 1950s was subsequently made by the social psychologist John K. Hemphill, who introduced the idea of "initiation of structure" as one definition of leadership. "To lead," explained Hemphill, "is to engage in an act which initiates a structure in the interaction of others as part of the process of solving a mutual problem."[111] Hemphill later differentiated among "attempted," "successful," and "effective" leadership on the basis of whether the initiatives were tried, were accepted by other group members, and actually contributed to the solution of group problems.[112] In later experimental research, members of the Ohio State University group and others identified a second factor in leadership, termed "consideration," defined as the showing of concern for followers. "Consideration" and "initiation of structure" were shown to vary in relative importance according to the situation. As reported by Stogdill, recent experimental researchers have not been completely satisfied with this two-factor approach to leadership and are searching for a more adequate, multifactor solution.[113]

The Universality of Leadership in Human Societies. One consequence of adopting the idea of initiative as a defining characteristic of leadership is that it opens up a vast perspective upon the potential for an actual expression of such initiative in groups of all sizes and cultural settings. After reviewing the anthropological literature on leadership, Lewis concluded: "Whether or not a society has institutionalized chiefs, rulers, or elected officials, there are always in any society, leaders who initiate action and play central roles in group decision-making."[114] He further explained, "There are no known societies without leadership of at least some aspects of their social life, even though there are many that lack a single overall leader to enforce his decisions."[115] An example of this kind of leading initiative under conditions of minimal differentiation of formal authority structure is given by Mair:

> No Nuer [a cattle-herding people in the Sudan] will let any other address an order to him. The leadership of the "bull" is recognized only in the sense that people wait for him to give a lead. Moving with the cattle from camp to camp in the dry season may be compared with the Tindiga band in search of food. The people in a Nuer camp do not discuss and reach a decision. They wait until the leading man moves and then follow when it suits them.[116]

Note that this may be an example of cross-species social learning from animal (cattle) to human behavior.

Sources of Leader Initiative. Recent economic studies of "entrepreneurship" seem to have gone somewhat further than political science in raising and seeking alternative answers to the question "Why do some persons engage in salient leadership initiatives?" Four different but not necessarily mutually exclusive sources of explanation have been suggested for which political analogs can readily be identified:[117] (1) the *personality* of the entrepreneur, e.g., persons with high need for achievement;[118] (2) the *social background* of the entrepreneur,[119] e.g., persons from families with declining social status;[120] (3) the *"purely economic incentives"* provided by the market system itself;[121] and (4) the *system of cultural values* that legitimates or inhibits entrepreneurial activity. Like political scientists, economists are faced with the theoretical task of linking entrepreneurial leadership or behavior with the structure and functioning of an economic or political system as both independent and dependent variables. Clearly, the future development of leadership studies in politics and entrepreneurship studies in economics should be mutually enriching.

Leadership as Concentrated or Dispersed Performance of Related Functions. Since one of the age-old questions of fundamental importance to political science has been the degree to which "power" is concentrated in, or diffused among, various constituent elements of a political system (e.g., persons, factions, parties, legislatures, courts, classes, ethnic groups, regions, or nations), the results of a leadership experiment directly on this problem by social psychologists Havron and McGrath should be of exceptional interest.[122]

With the cooperation of United States Army authorities, they divided a training unit into two parts, each of which was trained in a different concept of leadership. In one part, twenty-four squads were trained in the traditional conception of military leadership: the person with the insignia of higher rank (i.e., the sergeant at the squad level) is the leader and must be obeyed. In contrast, however, they trained the second half of the unit (twenty-four squads) in the idea that leadership is a set of group functions channeled through a salient member and requiring the initiative and cooperation of all group (squad) members. They explained further that one of the reasons for high levels of combat deaths is the inability of unassisted formal authority figures adequately to process combat-relevant information.

The two groups of differently trained squads were then sent through a simulated combat exercise. At the point of departure, formal leaders (sergeants and corporals) were "killed" (removed from the squad) and the now "leaderless" squads were required to complete the exercise.

The results were startling, even to the experimenters: no traditionally trained squad scored as high as any squad trained in the idea of leadership as a set of group functions. There was complete nonoverlap of scores between the two groups. In the traditionally trained squads, "the members depended entirely on the leader to take initiative." In the experimentally trained squads "someone inevitably took over and the unit's performance on the mission was almost as good as the performance of those same squads when the leaders were present."[123]

If we leave aside questions of performance criteria, the military task situation, and more precise specification of functions, this example suggests that leadership can be conceived in terms of both a concentration and a dispersal of associated functions within and across groups, institutions, and political communities. It further suggests that purposive political leadership itself, defined as initiative plus coercive or consensual persuasion, can influence the degree of concentration or dispersal in a social unit.

Leadership as "Group Syntality." The psychologist Raymond B. Cattell suggested that leadership be measured in terms of "group syntality," defined as the performance of the group as a whole.[124] In Cattell's view, variation in syntality is associated with change in two other variables: "personnel" (group membership) and "structure" (relationships among members). Cattell proposed a subtractive method for measuring leadership: each member of the group is removed from it in turn and the consequent variations in group output associated with the absence of each member are taken as measures of the relative contribution to "leadership" of that person. The idea of group syntality seems related to the concept of "social facilitation," defined by W. C. Allee, a student of comparative animal and human sociology, as "any increment in frequency, intensity or complexity of behavior of one individual resulting from the presence of the other."[125]

The basic idea of measuring leadership in terms of group performance on some criterion task is central also to the "contingency theory" of leadership that has been advanced through the experimental work of Fred E. Fiedler.[126]

Interestingly similar to, although not identical with, the idea of leadership as variation in total group performance is Lenin's view that "the whole art of conspiratorial organization must consist in utilizing everybody and everything . . . and at the same time maintaining *leadership* over the entire movement."[127]

Leadership as the Provision of Models for Emulative Behavior. The idea that man is an "imitative animal" derives at least from the time of Aristotle and has its parallel in the ancient Confucian idea that the best government, as the best family, is that based upon the influence of moral example. Sources of social science insight that can be drawn upon to create an image of leadership as suasion by example include Gabriel Tarde's *The Laws of Imitation* (1903)[128] and the more recent contributions of social learning theorists such as Miller and Dollard's *Social Learning and Imitation* (1941)[129] and Bandura and Walters's *Social Learning and Personality Development* (1963).[130] Important additional insights can be found in Bloomfield's discussion of language borrowing[131] and in theories related to the diffusion of innovations[132] and epidemiology.[133] While Stogdill's review of the experimental literature does not stress a social learning concept of leadership, his discussion of social norms and reference groups is closely related.[134]

The basic idea of an emulative behavior approach is that leadership behavior consists in setting examples that are followed by others who are reinforced for this behavior by rewards or punishments. In the Miller and Dollard formulation, for example, leaders provide "cues" that elicit imitative responses that bring "rewards" and consequent "drive" reductions or satisfactions for followers.[135]

Not all imitative behavior, of course, is affectively positive: the imitation of political leaders by comedians, caricaturists, critics, and opponents may be rooted in aggressive hostility or at least in emotional ambivalence. Ernst Kris suggested, for example, that "when we are imitated, we feel threatened in our individuality, superseded and dismissed."[136] Ngo Dinh Diem, for example, was known as a "master mimic"; his renditions of local French notables and American ambassadors were famous among his close associates.[137] Some leaders seem to imitate each other in this way, especially among friends in relaxed moments. Negative or avoidant models also seem to be important as stimuli for the development of different qualities among competitors and the provision of support for alternative leaders. As one successful, upwardly mobile business executive commented in an interview about positive and negative models, "I made up my mind that should I ever be president, I would do exactly the opposite of X, and I could not lose!"[138]

A most interesting discussion of the limits of leadership by example as related to organizational scale was offered by a Chinese Communist party member who described his transition from leader of a small agricultural production unit to leader of a larger one. He explained, "The way I'd led the small 16-household co-op, was to take part in farm work myself and set a good example on every job we did. . . . But this method didn't work at all after we turned into a large co-op. . . . Nobody could get 300 members of 130 households moving in this way."[139] Thus, he found that he had to lead indirectly by assisting subordinate leaders in solving problems; through visits to all the fields he gained an overall grasp of the production situation. He found it impossible to lead simply by setting a personal example of field work. This report of practical experience suggests that fruitful insights may emerge from further exploration of a modeling behavior approach to leadership.

Power, Task, and Affective Dimensions of Leadership. There is abundant indication in the literature of the behavioral and social sciences that it is useful to think of leadership in terms of three analytical aspects: a power dimension, a task or instrumental dimension, and an emotional, expressive, or affective dimension.

Social scientists first identified two leadership requirements in small groups: a need for guidance in technical task accomplishment, often referred to as "instrumental" or "task" leadership, and a need for emotionally satisfying behaviors that will contribute to harmonious relations among group members, often termed "social-emotional" leadership.[140] The need for the one sometimes clashes with the need for the other. As Gibb explained, "Leaders find their instrumental leadership incompatible with popularity, while followers find themselves needing the leader but hating him because of this."[141]

Robert F. Bales added a third dimension to the initial two. Relying partly upon the results of his "interaction processes analysis" of small group behavior, Bales determined that "there are at least three fundamental dimensions of social evaluation involved as one person views another in a group setting."[142] Who has the most power and authority? Who has the most competence to assist solution of group problems? And who is best liked? These dimensions might be termed "powerability," "taskability," and "likability."

Bales's three-dimensional conceptualization has received powerful support from the convergent perspectives of several social science disciplines and subfields. Contemporary psychology seeks to understand human behavior primarily through theories of reinforcement, cognition, and emotion. Atkinson, McClelland, and others, for example, have developed a method for describing persons in terms of needs for power, achievement, and affiliation.[143] Bass has suggested that leaders can be described in terms of whether they are self-oriented, task oriented, or interaction oriented.[144] In sociology, Amitai Etzioni has found it useful to distinguish institutions as being predominantly coercive, utilitarian, or identitive.[145] Additionally, linguists have found it convenient to analyze language in terms of its "effective," "cognitive," and "affective" aspects.[146]

Political scientists will observe in nature many things that seem to confirm the importance of these general dimensions of human behavior more specifically for political leadership. Some societies, for example, seem to have approximated a three-way functional leadership role differentiation as in the presence of general party secretary (power), premier (task), and president (affect) in the Soviet Union. At the other extreme, the American practice seems to have concentrated all three dimensions in the office of the president. In between are the dichotomizing tendencies of modern Japan and England, where power and task capabilities are concentrated in a prime minister while affective and symbolic unity is provided by a constitutional monarch. At a subsocietal level, advisers to the governor of Hawaii, without reference to the social science literature, counseled him in 1969 to add a third staff person specializing in social and religious organization affairs (affect) to the two already responsible for political patronage (power) and state administration (task). Additionally, Honolulu mayor Frank F. Fasi, a Democratic primary candidate for governor in 1974, customarily began his campaign "coffee hours" by introducing his wife, who spoke of her love and respect for him (affect), then the city administrative director, who spoke of the mayor's executive excellence (task); finally, the candidate-mayor himself appeared, exhibiting the confidence and aggressiveness of a victorious political veteran (power).[147]

Leader-oriented, Follower-oriented, and Interaction-oriented Perspectives. Empirical leadership studies may focus upon what leaders do, what followers do, or upon what both do in interaction. Examples of the first two from political science are studies of the leadership styles in legislatures[148] and the behavior of voters in American presidential elections.[149] It is more difficult to cite a basic political science paradigm for leader-follower interaction analysis over time. Industrial sociology seems to provide more clear-cut examples. Studies in that field customarily examine the supervision, attitudes, and behaviors of factory foremen and the related perceptions and behaviors of workers under their supervision; subject the results to comparative analysis; proceed to prescribe changes in the behavior of one or both parties to the interaction in terms of expected increase in performance criteria; and sometimes follow up with restudy of the success or failure of the changed interaction system.[150] This approach will be important in future political leadership studies.[151]

Some of the most famous "leadership" studies in social science, however, were not interactive in nature. An example is the study of *follower* reactions to the experimental manipulation of three leadership "styles" ("authoritarian," "democratic," and "laissez-faire") by social psychologists White and Lippitt.[152] A *leader*-oriented version of this study would focus attention upon the productivity and satisfactions of leaders when confronted by experimental manipulations of the same three follower styles. A higher order study would then look at the reciprocal effects and changes over time of interactions among the three styles as measured by the behavior of both leaders and followers.

An interaction approach to leadership analysis is beginning to enter political science partly from anthropology, economics, and psychotherapy. Variously termed "exchange theory" or "transaction theory," the basic idea as stated by Lewis involves "a series of reciprocal exchanges in which leaders donate to followers and followers reciprocate in kind or with other items of value."[153] Scott proposed a "patron-client" model for political analysis as follows:

> The patron-client relationship—an exchange relationship between roles—may be defined as a special case of dyadic (two-person) ties involving largely

instrumental friendship in which an individual of higher socioeconomic status (position) uses his own influence and resources to provide protection or benefits or both, for a person of lower status (client) who, for his part, reciprocates by offering general support and assistance, including personal services, to the patron.[154]

It is likely that exchange and transactional approaches to leadership will attract considerable attention in political science since they are compatible with an economic conception of politics as a process of "value allocation." Insofar as such exchange theories omit or deemphasize emotional or affective exchanges or identifications, in favor of theories that are more material or utilitarian in nature, however, they may be overlooking an important insight from both animal studies and social anthropology.[155]

Leadership as Goal-directed Interpersonal Influence through Communication. Another model of leadership likely to be of special interest to political scientists was proposed by Tannenbaum and Massarik in 1957.

> We define leadership as *interpersonal influence, exercised in situation and directed through the communication process, toward the attainment of a specified goal or goals.* Leadership always involves attempts on the part of the *leader* (influencer) to affect (influence) the behavior of a *follower* (influencee) or followers in *situation.*[156]

This model provides links with theories of influence and communication.

Leadership as Human Agriculture. An unusual approach to leadership in terms of what he calls an "agricultural model" has been contributed by the organizational behavior theorist Warren G. Bennis. The agricultural metaphor came to mind as Bennis tried to think of a concept of leadership that would be more "organic" than the traditional, "mechanical" concepts of hierarchical bureaucracy, which he viewed as becoming increasingly inappropriate for contemporary American society. Bennis suggested that by leadership he meant *"an active method for producing conditions where people and ideas and resources can be seeded, cultivated, and integrated to optimum effectiveness and growth."* For Bennis such an image implied the need for acquiring "four sets of competencies": knowledge of large, complex systems; practical theories of intervention and guidance; interpersonal competence, especially understanding the effects of personality on self and others; and "a set of values and competencies which enables one to know when to confront and attack, if necessary, and when to provide the psychological safety so necessary to growth."[157]

Leadership as an Increasingly Differentiated Set of Interacting Variables. A major lesson to be learned from the voluminous behavioral and social science literature on leadership published over the past two decades is that leadership needs to be conceptualized in terms of a complex set of interacting variables. The trend toward more explicit differentiation can be seen in two successive summaries of the leadership literature presented by Gibb in 1954 and in 1969. In the earlier statement, although he mentioned such additional concepts as group, role, and task, Gibb concluded, "In general it may be said that leadership is a function of personality and of the social situation, and of these two in interaction."[158] In 1969, he wrote:

> Any comprehensive theory of leadership must incorporate and integrate all the major variables which are now known to be involved, namely, (1) the personality of the leader, (2) the followers with their attitudes, needs and problems, (3) the group itself, as regards both (a) structure of interpersonal relations and (b) syntality characteristics, (4) the situation as determined by physical setting, nature of task, etc. Furthermore, any satisfactory theory must recognize that it is not these variables *per se* that enter into the leadership situation, but rather the perception of the leader by himself and by others of the group and the situation. . . . What is needed is a conception in which the complex interactions of these factors can be incorporated.[159]

Looking further back, over at least a century of modern social science thinking, it appears that social scientists have been probing the various component elements of an ancient question: are humans the creators or products of their environment?[160] While some social scientists in the age of industrialization have seemed to place greater emphasis upon objective socioeconomic factors, others have probed more deeply than ever before into the role of personal qualities. The crude conclusion that both dimensions are important impels us to seek increasingly precise specification of more satisfying sets of explanatory factors.

One example of an experimental search for a multivariate theory of leadership is provided by the work of social psychologist Fred E. Fiedler. Fiedler developed a set of five variables (four independent, one dependent) that have proved unusually useful for the research problems chosen for the development of what he has termed a "contingency model of leadership effectiveness."[161] These comprise a measure of *personality* ("least preferred coworker" score, high or low); a *role*-related measure ("position power," high or low); a measure of the quality of the leader's relations with other *group* members ("group relations," good, moderate, or poor); and a measure of *task* clarity ("task," structured or unstructured). The four independent variables are taken as predictors of levels of group productivity on assigned tasks.

The importance of task as a variable, either objectively given or subjectively chosen, emerges frequently in the social science literature on leadership and undoubtedly deserves closer attention by students of political leadership. A sociometric study of children in a summer camp, for example, showed that different children were chosen by their peers to lead them in different activities (tasks)—e.g., swimming, arts and crafts, rest.[162] This finding implies that in a relatively unstructured social system leadership will vary with task in relation to the task-related competence of group members, assuming completely shared information about relative task competence. Thus, a task-dependent model of leadership salience is suggested. When leadership positions are formally fixed, variations in task qualities are found to require different leadership styles for effective performance by position incumbents.[163] This suggests a task-dependent model of leadership style.

A tendency for leadership success in one task to create a propensity for leader initiative and follower acceptance in other tasks has been noted in many studies, despite experimental findings by Fiedler that "leadership performances over different tasks are uncorrelated."[164] An implication that much of present human political leadership is the result of the generalization of leader-follower responses in coping with the tasks of war can be drawn from the anthropological observation by Lewis that "where hostilities are frequent or constant, the war leader may tend to become a dominant figure in the community, something that has to be considered a major element in the development of states from previously stateless societies."[165] Thus, the concept of "task" should be of special interest for political leadership studies, even though this concept has not been rigorously explicated for general social science use. As the psychologist Shneidman has noted, in the standard stimulus-organism-response model of behavioral science "there has generally been too little systematic study of the stimulus."[166]

Political Science

We now turn to an exploration of the conceptual resources of political science itself for insight into the nature of political leadership. Like the foregoing surveys, this is a vast and complicated task that can only be begun here: virtually every aspect of the discipline has some relevance for this topic and only a large-scale cooperative survey effort focused upon the idea of "leadership" could adequately reveal the full scope of disciplinary resources. But we can briefly call attention to several areas of inquiry that seem to have special importance for the task of conceptualizing "political leadership" and for developing it as a subfield for research, teaching, and public service. Others will occur to readers and those that seem most promising should be explored in depth as a contribution to the continuing scientific process of progressing from the known to the unknown by the "revolutionary" overthrow of prevailing "paradigms"[167] or by the juxtaposition of "images."[168]

Images from Classical Political Thought and Theories of Statecraft. The rise of interest in the study of political leadership provides an opportunity to reexamine the history of political thought on a global basis for more specific insights into the nature of "leadership." As was shown by our review of Sabine in Chapter 2 this is a necessary undertaking.

Although virtually all Western-trained political scientists are aware of Plato's "philosopher-king" as an authority figure whose rule is based on the exercise of pure reason—an ideal generally regarded as unrealistic and probably totalitarian in implication—this image deserves fresh examination and comparison with the much less well known "realistic" Platonic images of leadership. These include images of "timocratic" leadership (rule by pride and honor), "plutocratic" leadership (rule by wealth), "democratic" leadership (rule by popular consent on the basis of equality), and "tyrannical" leadership (rule by coercion).[169] It will be rediscovered that Plato discussed the emergence, functioning, decline, and transformation of these forms of leadership, or "rule," in terms of such variables as family political socialization, socioeconomic structure, types of political institutions, and follower responsiveness.

Leadership images may be inferred from classical formulations of types of polities. In the *Statesman,* for example, Plato articulates seven types of constitution, each of which implies some concept of leadership.[170] The first is the ideal or "genuine" constitution, which involves the "rule of the true statesman." Then there are three "imitative constitutions," each dichotomized into a law-abiding and a law-flouting form. Thus, for *one-man rule,* there is monarchy and tyranny; for *rule by the few,* there is aristocracy and oligarchy; and for *rule by the many,* there is lawful and unlawful democracy. In the *Statesman,* Plato also discusses various images of, and analogs for, statesmanship or leadership—e.g., images of the shepherd, ship's captain, ship's pilot, and physician—while developing a preferred conception of the ideal leader as a "weaver" who skillfully combines the contributory "arts" of other social roles into the "kingly art of ruling the state."[171] Modern social science discussions of the integrative functions of leadership undoubtedly echo this ancient Platonic idea as well as respond to contemporary needs for cohesion and catalytic systemwide action.

Another Western image that deserves fresh examination is Machiavelli's complex characterization of the "prince."[172] Among his well-known admonitions are those that urge the ruler to be constantly ready for war; to be prepared to be "not good" when this approach appears advantageous; to suffer the disgrace of being thought miserly rather than the hatred of rapacious generosity; to rely more on being feared than loved; to be ready to imitate the behavior of the fox, who can "recognize traps," and the lion, who can "frighten wolves"; to appear to be "merciful, faithful, humane, sincere, and religious"; to avoid being despised and hated; to avoid neutrality; and to uphold "the majesty of his dignity, which must never be allowed to fail in anything whatever." Machiavelli's image of the prince may have many uses, including stimulation of the creation of alternative images of leadership more suitable for other times and circumstances, *as well as the creation of contra-Machiavellian techniques of followership.*

Images of "leadership" can also be found outside Western thought that may contribute to the emergence of a "global Sabine" with a culturally varied index on this subject. The Chinese historical legacy, for example, provides three modal images of leadership with a rich tradition of interpretation.[173] These are the Confucian image of leadership by moral example, the legalist image of leadership by the manipulation of rewards and punishments, and the Taoist image of leadership by nonleadership, exemplified in the phrase "the greatest conqueror wins without joining issue."[174] We also need to rediscover the "leadership" images of the Islamic tradition: the ideally desired caliphate (based upon religious law), the next best, mixed caliphate (combining religious and secular law), and *mulk* (secular kingship).[175] Note that the Platonic, Chinese, and Islamic images of leadership all state or imply that there is a preexisting ideal form of leadership of which all existing examples are relatively corrupt versions. This suggests that efforts to conceptualize political leadership are connected with deep, unsatisfied yearnings of the human personality.

John E. Tashjean has called for the rediscovery and reinterpretation of works that he has termed "statecraft theory" as a source of insight into political leadership.[176] The distinguishing features of such works are that they are written by experienced politicians or by advisers to such leaders—"winners"— rather than by inexperienced philosophers or defeated contestants for political power—"losers."[177] The distinction sometimes may not be easily made, and experienced losers may provide valuable perspectives on leadership,[178] but the emphasis upon an active, operationally relevant perspective as a complement to more detached, speculative viewpoints is an important one to have in the study of political leadership. Additional insights into leadership may come from the writings of professionals such as diplomats, who are required to interact with political leaders in an intimate way.[179]

After a remarkable survey of ancient and medieval writers in the Greco-Roman tradition, from the sixth through the sixteenth century, Lester K. Born has given us a composite image of the "perfect prince" as inductively derived from the literature of tutelary advice.

> In summary we may say that the perfect prince of these ten centuries must be wise, self-restrained, just, devoted to the welfare of his people; a pattern of virtue for his subjects; immune from flattery; interested in economic developments, an educational program, and the true religion of God; surrounded by efficient ministers and able advisers; opposed to aggressive warfare; and, in the realization that even he is subject to law and that the need of the prince and his subjects is mutual, zealous for the attainment of peace and unity.[180]

Similar surveys in other cultures, comparisons, and analyses in terms of the action implications of ideal cultural images of this sort present important conceptual challenges to students of political leadership.

Charismatic, Traditional, and Rational-Legal Leadership. In contemporary political science the idea of "charisma" is one of the most widely employed concepts related to leadership. By contrast, the term "charismatic" does not even appear in the index of Stogdill's massive review of the experimental social psychology literature on leadership.[181]

The term "charisma" is of Greek origin and means "gift." Max Weber adopted it from Christian scholarship to describe one of three bases of "belief in the legitimacy" of a "system of imperative coordination." He defined imperative coordination as "the probability that certain specific commands (or all commands) from a given source will be obeyed by a given group of persons."[182]

Weber took "belief in legitimacy" as one of five explanations for subordinates' obedience to superiors; the others he identified as "custom," "affectual ties," "material calculation of advantage," and "ideal (wertrational) motives."[183] All five were taken to be essential for a stable superior-subordinate (leader-follower) relationship. Thus, the idea of "charismatic leadership" represents only one aspect of a much fuller concept of political leadership stated or implied in Weber's writings.

Charismatic leadership, in essence, means "gifted" leadership. Thus, attention is called to the nature of the gifted quality, the responsiveness of others to it, and the conditions under which it emerges and declines. Weber himself offered two principal definitions of charisma. The first emphasizes charisma as a personal attribute of a leader, i.e., "a certain quality of an individual personality by virtue of which he is set apart by ordinary men and treated as endowed with supernatural, superhuman, or at least specifically exceptional powers and qualities."[184] The second stresses the responsiveness of followers as "devotion to the specific and exceptional sanctity, heroism or exemplary character of an individual person, and of the normative patterns or order revealed or ordained by him."[185] Taken together, the two definitions comprise a necessary perspective upon a leader-follower relationship. Charismatic leadership involves *both* a leader quality *and* a follower response. In calling attention to them both Weber was neither confused nor confusing about the locus of charisma, as has often been suggested.

Wilner, who has made a major contribution toward making the concept of charismatic leadership operationally useful for political science, specified that the defining characteristic is "the absolute emotional and cognitive identification of a following with the leader and his descriptive [what is], normative [what should be], and prescriptive [what should be done] orientations, i.e., the unqualified belief in the man and his mission."[186] She has characterized the intense emotional quality of charismatic followership in terms of "devotion, awe, reverence, and blind faith" as contrasted with more common feelings of "affection, admiration, respect, and trust."[187]

Weber suggested in addition to "charisma" two other bases of belief in legitimacy from which additional types of leadership[188] can be inferred. These are *rational-legal* ("resting on a belief in the 'legality' of patterns of normative rules and the right of those elevated to authority under such rules to issue commands")[189] and *traditional* leadership ("resting on an established belief in the sanctity of immemorial traditions and the legitimacy of the status of those exercising authority under them").[190] From the leader's perspective Wallerstein has summarized the three types of leadership in terms of claims upon follower obedience: "Do it because I, your leader, say so"; "Do it because it has always been done this way"; and "Do it because it is the rationally agreed-upon law."[191]

Weber, Wilner, Wallerstein, and others have discussed possible patterns of transformation and change among these three types of leadership: charismatic leadership, for example, might help to create either of the other forms, facilitate transition between them, or decline in response to changes in other political, economic, or social variables.[192]

The Idea of a "Political Elite." In Western thought related to political leadership, after Plato's "philosopher-king," Machiavelli's "prince," and Weber's "charisma," the idea of a "political elite" very frequently appears. The literature of contemporary political science shows that interest in the study of political elites has preceded, paralleled, and frequently interlocked with emerging concern for the study of political leadership.

The idea of a political elite entered American political science mainly through the work of Harold Lasswell;[193] the notion grew out of the earlier insights of Mosca and Pareto, two European thinkers,[194] and found expression in pioneering single case studies,[195] comparative studies,[196] methodological critiques,[197] and subfield overviews.[198] The word "elite(s)/elitism" appeared only five times in titles of articles in the *APSR* from 1906 to 1963, six times from 1964 to 1968, and three times in the period 1969–1975.[199] In 1967, however, Beck and McKechnie were able to compile a bibliography containing some 15,000 relevant items.[200] In 1969, articles mentioning "elite(s)" in titles began to be cross-listed in the keyword index to the *APSR* under the concept of "leadership."[201]

The word "elite" is derived from the French verb *élire,* which means "to choose" or "to elect." Thus, political elites are the chosen or elected ones. In French usage, the term tends to carry the connotation of high moral or cultural worth, reminiscent of Greek ideals of virtuous "kingship" or "aristocracy." By contrast, in English language social science usage, the term has come to refer to persons of high political, economic, and social status, with an underlying assumption that they are able to wield coercive power to defend their interests— an image closer to the Greek ideas of "tyranny" and "oligarchy."

In political science there has been a tendency to employ the term broadly to refer to all high status influentials in politics; however, empirical studies have concentrated attention upon holders of formal political positions such as executives, legislators, bureaucrats, and party officials. Thus, in introduction to his masterful survey of the elite literature, Parry explains that he is concerned with "elites in politics ... not merely 'politicians' to whom the term political elite is sometimes confined. ... Business interests, unions, the military, the bureaucrats are all to be regarded as 'political elites' for the present purpose."[202]

"Political elite" thus tends to serve as a collective term for those persons of high status, skill, wealth, and coercive capability who influence politics, as in C. Wright Mills's conception of "the power elite."[203] It implies inequality and high position on a ladder of social stratification. Although theories of elites contain provisions for change such as when "tough-minded lions" displace "soft-minded foxes" in Pareto's view of "the circulation of elites," which is reminiscent of the views of Plato, Polybius,[204] and Hertzler,[205] these are but variations on a basic theme of static structural dominance. The main direction of implied influence is from the top down, not from the bottom up; elites are expected primarily to dominate not to be responsive. As defined by the political sociologist Wiatr, the term "political elite" refers to those cases in which "(a) distribution of power is markedly unequal, a minority having much greater power than the rest of the community; and (b) access to the leadership group is restricted in such a way that leaders and followers do not easily change roles."[206] A further implication is that political elites are determined by the socioeconomic structure of society; they do not determine or change it.[207]

The universal applicability of the concept of elites for political studies has recently been challenged by Wiatr himself.

> Leadership and leaders can be defined without the use of the category of *elite* or *political elite*. . . . Elites exist where and when the distribution of valued resources is so markedly unequal that some minorities differ considerably from the rest of the group by the high concentration of one or more of these resources. [But] there is no economic elite among small farmers in a village where nobody has markedly more than others. There is no intellectual elite among a tribe of equally uneducated people. . . . Whether there is a *political elite* depends, therefore, not on the existence of the leadership group, which is universal in all political communities, but on the way in which access to the group that performs the function of leadership is distributed. All political communities perform the function of leadership and, therefore, all of them have political leaders.[208]

Support for Wiatr's view has come from Lewis's review of the anthropological literature on "leadership."[209] Both argue that "leadership" defined in terms of salient initiative is the more universal pattern of behavior.

Interestingly and perhaps significantly, the term "eliteship" is not employed with "elite" in common English usage[210] in the same way that "leader" and "leadership" are used to differentiate actor and action. Whereas "leadership" tends to imply initiative, directional movement, and interaction with followers, the idea of "elite" evokes more an image of a dominant collective. Whereas the leader "leads," the elite "rules." To use "revolutionary elite" to mean not yet successful revolutionary leadership is a contradiction in terms; whereas this contradiction is not inherent in the idea of revolutionary leadership.

Positional, Reputational, and Participational Leadership in a Monistic or Pluralistic Leadership Structure. Political science studies of "community power" or "community decision making" have explored two major questions that are important to consider in efforts to formulate appropriate concepts of political leadership. How are community leaders to be most validly identified? And do these leaders, however identified, constitute a single decisional unit or a plurality of units in relation to the various decisions made in a community?

Three principal methods of identification have been considered: position, reputation, and participation, depending upon whether the person holds a salient formal office, is reputed to be influential in community affairs, or is found by case methods to be effectively involved in making community choices. In practice, all three methods are usually combined. Dahl, for example, first employed positional criteria to show that the elected mayors of New Haven came successively from "patrician," "entrepreneurial," and "ex-plebe" backgrounds from 1784 to 1953.[211] He similarly employed positional criteria to identify economic and social notables.[212] Then he examined three areas for community decision—political nominations, urban redevelopment, and public education—to argue that "individuals who are influential in one sector of public activity tend not to be influential in another sector and, what is probably more significant, the social strata from which individuals in one sector tend to come are different from the social strata from which individuals in other sectors are drawn."[213]

Agger and associates employed a very strict definition of political leadership in terms of participation in decision making. *"Political leaders,"* they wrote, "are political participants who have contributed to a decisional outcome and hence are accorded a share in political power, and, moreover, who contributed in at least the authoritative consideration stage of a decision process."[214] They further explained that "political leaders are analogous to the managers in a business organization,"[215] that they may be "private citizens or government officials,"[216] that leaders of component organizations may or may not be leaders of the more encompassing community power structure,[217] and that voters technically may be considered political leaders under the definition but usually are not.[218] In identifying leaders to be interviewed, as well as in selecting the decisional issues to be analyzed, the Agger group employed a combination of positional and reputational techniques, constantly tested against an emerging analytical sense of significant decisional issues. For example, "two randomly and independently selected samples of officers of formally organized voluntary associations and elective and appointive officials of local government provided information about each community's policy problems."[219] Then the first panel was asked to identify persons of reputed influence.

> In most cities, certain persons are said to be influential "behind the scenes" and to have a lot to say about programs that are planned, and projects and issues that come up around town. What persons in [this community] are influential in this way or are influential in being able to stop particular community policies? Are there any other people with whom these leaders work that have not been named so far and should be included in a list of community leaders?[220]

The second panel was asked to review and to supplement the list. Persons on the list were then asked about their participation in a set of community decisions that had been identified by a combination of interview and documentary methods. The strict criterion of participation in decisions that had desired outcomes was then applied to identify the "manifest [political] leaders" of four communities: "Farmdale," fourteen persons; "Metroville," forty-one; "Petropolis," fifty-nine; and "Oretown," forty-one.[221] These people were later interviewed to discover reputed cliques among the leadership groups. Agger and associates expressed keen awareness of the varied results that might be achieved from even this combination of identification methods. "Given the fact that the universe is bounded by informants' perceptions or conceptions, any change in the identity or number of informants, or in the standard of consensus or agreement used to include or exclude nominees, means a potentially different universe and a different set of Manifest Leaders."[222]

A striking feature of Dahl's and Agger and associates' studies was the recurrent salience of formally elected officials even though the two approaches did not explicitly seek to focus *primary* analytical attention upon them. Wrote Dahl of urban redevelopment, "Perhaps the most significant event in the modern history of city planning in New Haven is that very little happened until redevelopment became attached to the political fortunes of an ambitious politician [Mayor Richard Lee]."[223] Agger and associates reported, "In all four communities, the elected political leaders were actual political leaders."[224] Additionally, mayors were members of the "inner cliques" in three of the four communities, while a councilman was such a member in the black segment of the fourth.[225] This recurrent salience is not surprising in light of the findings of Douglas Fox, who compared five studies that employed all three methods of leader identification and found that from 22 percent to 56 percent of positional leaders were identified by both the reputational and the decisional method, with higher identifications possible when one of these methods was employed alone. While we do not know from Fox's data how many positional leaders were formally elected officials, such as mayors and councilpersons, the results of his comparison are noteworthy (see Table 1).

Despite these hints of the possible importance of elected political officials, community power studies seem not to have focused explicitly upon the formal and informal relationships among the mayor, council members, party leaders, governor, lieutenant governor, state legislators, president, vice-president, and national legislators—including aspirants for these positions—as they influence community decisions. The narrow decision participation concept of political

TABLE 1. **Percentage of Positional Leaders Identified by the Reputational and Decisional Methods in Two Southern and Three New England Communities**

| | Southern Communities | | New England Communities | | |
	A	B	C	D	E
Reputational Method	56	59	36	27	23
Decisional Method	81	94	27	22	23

Source: Combined data from Douglas M. Fox, "The Identification of Community Leaders by the Reputational and Decisional Methods: Three Case Studies and an Empirical Analysis of the Literature," *Sociology and Social Research* 54, 1 (October 1969), 95, 98.

leadership, of course, would also obviate attending to the functions of aspiring and opposition leaders in American politics, to say nothing of revolutionary and protest political leadership throughout the world.

With respect to the issue of whether American communities have either monistic or pluralistic power structures, the evidence thus far seems to be that both are possible in a single community across historical time and across communities in a given period. The question of future directions within and across political cultures remains a testable hypothesis. Dahl has argued, "In the course of the past two centuries, New Haven has gradually changed from oligarchy to pluralism."[226] Agger found that two of the American communities studied during 1946 to 1961 had predominantly "competitive mass" power structures (Petropolis and Oretown) while two were of the "consensual elite" type (Farmdale and Metroville),[227] with variations occurring within each community across time.[228] These were defined in terms of "ideological convergence-divergence" and "breadth-narrowness of the distribution of political power" measured in terms of citizen participation. Methodological comparisons by Fox have further suggested that the existence of a monistic or a pluralistic power structure is not an artifact of research techniques. After examining fifteen community power studies he concluded, "There is not a single study in which reputational and decisional methods discover different types of power structures. . . . This is incontrovertibly true if we group the studies into [those] which discover pyramidal structures, on the one hand, and non-pyramidal structures, on the other."[229] This means that students of political leadership need not make a priori assessments of what kinds of power structures they are likely to find. This caution applies especially in cross-societal, historical, and futures-oriented inquiry.

Before leaving the community power literature, it is important to note that both Dahl and Agger and associates evidenced explicit interest in the concept of a "professional politician."[230] This image hovers in the background of American political science, calling up the idea of a boss, broker, or manipulator who specializes in winning electoral campaigns and influencing governmental decisions in the interests of future victories, patronage, and community or subcommunity welfare. Within the broader concept of a socioeconomic elite or of all who influence community decisions, such a person would play a specialized political role seeking to maximize (or minimize) direct or indirect influence exercised by subsocietal components upon general societal decisions. A more narrowly defined "political leader," for whom the "professional politician" might serve as a prototype, may eventually emerge as a specialist in the general process of making community decisions.[231]

Images of Political Leadership in Role Orientations. Studies of styles of role performance, especially of formal positions in the American political system, are another rich source of political leadership imagery. Such studies typically describe the basic characteristics of a formal leadership position and then proceed to demonstrate that incumbents tend to vary in their styles of role performance, in terms of either reported beliefs or other forms of behavior.

Thus, the American presidency was described by Rossiter as a position characterized by convergent requirements for action as: "Chief of state, chief executive, commander-in-chief, chief diplomat, chief legislator, chief of party, voice of the people, protector of the peace, manager of prosperity, and world leader."[232] In a widely appreciated study Neustadt argued that presidential power is the "power to persuade," thus suggesting the idea of "persuasion" as a principal characteristic[233] of American presidential leadership. Hargrove constructed a typology of presidential styles in terms of "action" and "restraint."[234] This typology was further developed by Barber, who suggested that different styles of presidential leadership can be described in terms of two interacting personality variables: activity-passivity and positive-negative affect.[235] Additionally, Barber suggested that presidential leadership styles can be described in terms of emphasis upon "rhetoric" (verbal dramatization), "business" (attention to administrative detail), or "interpersonal relations" (interpersonal persuasion, especially in an intimate, face-to-face context).[236]

In legislative studies, Matthews identified four types of senator in terms of social background and nature of occupational achievement: "patricians" (high social status and high political accomplishment), "amateurs" (low status and low political accomplishment but high business or other professional achievement), "professional politicians" (low status but high political accomplishment), and "agitators" (low status, low political or other professional accomplishment but precocious political rise).[237] Clapp dichotomized members of Congress as primarily "constituency-oriented" or "legislation-oriented."[238] Employing activity and affect variables, Barber described Connecticut state legislators as "lawmakers" (active-positive), "advertisers" (active-negative), "spectators" (passive-positive), and "reluctants" (passive-negative).[239] Additionally, Barber characterized legislators in terms of party cohesion as "automatic partisans," "persuadables," and "neutrals."[240] The pioneering studies of representational role orientations by Wahlke, Eulau, Buchanan, and Ferguson have provided a rich variety of images of representational roles ("trustee, delegate, politico"), purposive roles ("inventor, broker, tribune"), areal roles ("state oriented, district oriented, district-state oriented), and pressure group roles ("facilitator, resistor, neutral").[241]

Similarly, Eldersveld described Republican and Democratic precinct leaders in terms of whether they considered themselves to be primarily "vote mobilizers," "ideological mentors," or "social-economic welfare promoters" or to have "no role at all."[242] Additionally, Wilson compared Democratic party leaders in terms of whether they were "amateurs" (motivated mainly by issues and general principles) or "professionals" (seeking mainly patronage and power maintenance).[243] Interestingly, Wilson also identified three types of party organization, each of which implies a corresponding style of leadership:

"utilitarian" (based on control over patronage), "solidary" (based on need for social interaction), and "purposive" (based on devotion to a "cause").[244]

Other generic images of American politicians include three described in 1908 by Arthur F. Bentley: the "boss," who leads by "pulling wires" of a tightly knit machine; the "demagogue," who leads a broad, heterogeneous, and unstable coalition by means of emotional appeals buttressed by biased reasoning; and the "broker-mediator," who restrains parties in conflict and assists them in making mutually tolerable decisions on the basis of potential ability to invoke more powerful support than that available to the parties in conflict.[245] Additionally, Schlesinger described elected American political leaders in terms of whether their ambition levels were "discrete" (seek only one term in a single office), "static" (seek to remain in the same office), or "progressive" (aspire to higher office).[246] Significantly, Ladd's study of leadership in a suffering racial minority focused attention sharply upon "conservative," "moderate," and "militant" styles.[247]

The absence of a general analytical focus upon "leadership" throughout the discipline has meant that role orientation and style studies such as the above have tended to be pursued in a compartmentalized fashion. For example, executive roles tend not to be studied with legislative or party role concepts— and vice versa. Furthermore, not all formal leadership roles in American politics have been systematically described for comparison. Finally, the question of whether leadership role orientations discovered by political scientists can be related to the principal analytical dimensions of leadership suggested in other behavioral sciences remains to be explored (e.g., "self-oriented, task-oriented, and interaction-oriented" leadership; "power, task, and affective" leadership dimensions).

Political versus Administrative Leadership. The search for appropriate concepts to guide the emerging field of political leadership studies needs also to be informed by awareness of the lively controversy over the nature of administrative leadership that has animated American students of public administration in the twentieth century.[248] The controversy can be understood partly in terms of the American constitutional system of separation of powers among legislative, executive, and judicial branches of government, suggestive of the political functions defined by Almond as "rule making, rule application, and rule adjudication." It can be understood also in terms of the past century of American domestic political history, which has been marked by reform efforts to create a professional civil service removed from the corrupting influences of electoral politics, as well as by popular reluctance to accept the feasibility or desirability of entrusting fully either the determination or the execution of public policy to administrative science technocrats. The professional and social status claims of public administrators versus those of politicians also have been an influence; members of either group can claim or deny that they partake of the qualities of the other, as expedience dictates.

Viewed as an ideal-type dichotomy, political leadership means setting general policy, mobilizing support, and supervising implementation, including the appointment and firing of at least top public officials. Administrative leadership in an ideal form is the faithful execution of the laws and achievement of the general goals specified by the elected officials. Ideally, politicians lead—partly by creating and resolving conflicts—while administrators serve as technical followers. In military terms, political leaders are the invading shock troops; public administrators are the housekeeping camp followers.

These images are sometimes reversed so that elected American officials are portrayed as mere robots manipulated by technical administrative expertise. The standoff image is mixed: both groups interact to make public policy, to ensure public support, and to implement policy, with varying degrees of objective adequacy. The same can be said of judicial officials, who frequently are appointed and confirmed by elected politicians and who often are ex-politicians themselves.

As expressed by Gulick, the present status of the administrative versus political leadership controversy is that " 'politics' and 'administration' cannot be separated into mutually exclusive categories"[249] and that "the administrator is a leader par excellence,"[250] but that the administrator must not "rush into partisan politics or usurp the functions of the professional political leader."[251] This challenges students of political leadership to define a field of inquiry that adequately treats the area of nonoverlap with the political functions of administrative leadership.

Initial Efforts at Conceptual Overviews. Finally, efforts to conceptualize political leadership—and thus to fill the disciplinary gap of the past fifty years—can draw upon some pioneering efforts to link the idea of leadership with other concepts of broad political science interest: (1) "power," (2) "system," and (3) "function."

(1) Leadership as a Form of Power. A contemporary effort to define "leadership" in terms of power has been made by Janda, who has noted that "studies of leadership and studies of power have been conducted almost independently of each other."[252] For Janda, "leadership" is to be defined as consensual follower response to legitimate leader initiative. It is a form of consensual, but not coercive, power. A coerced response would not be an indicator of leadership. Janda has explained that leadership is "a particular type of power relationship characterized by a group member's perception that another group member has the right to prescribe behavior patterns for the former regarding his behavior as a member of a perticular group."[253] Thus, he attempts to differentiate leadership from coercive domination in a way reminiscent of the animal studies literature,[254] the psychological literature,[255] and early Greco-Roman thought.

As Polybius (ca. 204–120 B.C.) wrote in *The Histories,* "We must by no means apply the title of kingship, without scrutiny, to every monarchy, but must reserve it for one agreed to by willing subjects and ruled by good judgment rather than by terror and violence."[256] Or, as Plato explained in about 362 B.C., "Tendance of human herds by enforced control is the tyrant's art; tendance freely accepted by herds of free bipeds we call statesmanship."[257]

For Friedrich, who also has discussed leadership in terms of power, leadership can be either coercive or consensual.[258] Power itself is partly "a possession" and partly "a relation" among men that manifests itself in the behavior of followers.[259] Coercive power may be "physical," "economic," or "psychic"; these sources may underlie consensual power as well. In Friedrich's view, leaders are "power-holders," "power-spenders," and "power-makers."[260] Leadership has three primary roles—"initiating, maintaining, and protecting"; followers have three corresponding patterns of behavior—"imitating, obeying, and acclaiming."[261] The types of power and the types of leadership are all related and sometimes change into one another. Friedrich further differentiated "rule" ("institutionalized political power")[262] and "rulership." A leader becomes a "ruler" when followers "conform habitually to the preferences, expressed or implied, of the leader."[263] "Rulership" is not formally defined, but thirteen types of political order are described as "patterns of rulership":

> anarchy-fragmented type; tribal rule of the king-priest type; despotic monarchy (rule over extended territories); oligarchy of the nobility (either by birth or cooption); oligarchy of the wealthy; oligarchy by priesthood— theocracy; direct democratic rule; tyranny; bureaucratic rule; parliamentary-cabinet rule (government by elected representatives), aristocratic—nobility and wealth predominating—or democratic—all classes included; presidential-congressional rule (government by an elected president and an elected assembly); military dictatorship (including pretorian rule); and totalitarian dictatorship.[264]

It is implied that the power behavior of leaders or rulers contributes to the creation, operation, and transformation of these institutional orders.

Besides encountering problems of definition, these political science efforts to link the idea of leadership with the concept of power seem to have suffered from two additional sources of difficulty. First, Max Weber, preoccupied with the bases of "legitimacy," did not include *coercive* power as a fourth type of reason why men obey: do it because you'll be tortured, mutilated, or killed if you don't. This type of compliance claim need not be inspirational, habitual, or legal. Thus, political scientists are faced with the unfinished task of describing and explaining coercive and other behaviors of actual political leaders. Second, political science, like political societies themselves, is groping toward a concept of power that will enable the realistic understanding of both coercive and consensual aspects in the past and present as well as transition toward an almost universally desired diminution of coercive power in the future.

(2) *Leadership and the Idea of a Political System.* Although not talking explicitly in terms of a political system, Searing proposed two contrasting ideal

types of leadership that might apply equally to the understanding of political systems as a whole and the relation of leaders to them. These he termed "organismic" and "mechanistic" models of leadership. In the organismic model leadership is characterized by "interdependent parts," "evolutionary change," and "system-dominant" factors. In contrast, the mechanistic model portrays leadership as having "atomistic parts," "conflict relationships," and "subsystem-dominant" factors.[265] The organismic-mechanistic imagery is reminiscent of, although conceptually more complex than, the leadership dichotomy proposed by Hook in terms of the "eventful man," whose actions are determined largely by historical forces upon which he has little creative influence, and the "event-making man," without whose initiatives and actions a given historical outcome would be unlikely.[266] Hook pointed to Neville Chamberlain as an example of the former; Lenin, as an example of the latter.[267]

Searing's and Hook's images thus imply that a political leader can be understood both as a creator and as a captive of political institutions; that leadership behavior can produce incremental or quantum change; and that it can act upon the system through relations of diffuse interdependence or compartmentalized autonomy. It is likely that historical references, parallel or sequential, can be found for both images and that a more precisely articulated concept of political leadership will be developed to assist explanation of the emergence, operation, and transformation of both types of circumstances.

(3) Leadership and the Performance of Political System Functions. Downton made an early effort to link the idea of leadership with a structural-functional approach to political analysis.[268] "By assuming that social systems are self-regulating," he explained, "structural functionalists have been led generally to overlook the contributions that leadership makes in the adjustment process."[269] Defining "leadership" broadly as "the chief coordinating structure of social systems,"[270] Downton further explained:

> Through goal setting and attainment, leadership coordinates the activities of other structures in order to increase the [extractive, regulative, distributive, symbolic, and responsive] capabilities of the system. By increasing capabilities, leadership contributes in a positive way to the service capacity of the system, which enhances its ability to persist.[271]

More specifically, "leadership" is defined as something "assumed" when a group member "successfully initiates action for the group. . . . Consequently, leaders must be identified in terms of the relative volume of successful initiatives achieved by each member."[272] A "function" is taken as "a *task* that is relevant to the system's performance of services."[273] These are dichotomized as instrumental functions ("goal setting, communicating, and mobilizing") and expressive functions ("ego-support"). Revolutionary leadership "emerges when ruling leaders perform their functions inadequately."[274] Thus, the rise of rebel leadership is a response to the inadequate performance of functions by ruling leaders that brings a decline in system capabilities and loss of popular support.

Downton's effort to link a concept of leadership as coordinating initiative with a structural-functional approach should stimulate further attempts to relate leadership to this and other principal paradigms in contemporary political science.

The foregoing brief survey does not exhaust the disciplinary and transdisciplinary resources that can be drawn upon to create concepts of political leadership that will advance the scientific study of politics. Future students of political leadership will be faced with the exciting challenge of searching out promising insights from experienced leaders and from followers, from animal studies, from the humanities, from the sociobehavioral sciences, from other professional disciplines, and from the various subfields of the discipline of political science itself, both within given political-academic cultures and comparatively across cultures, in past, present, and future perspectives. Conceptual advances will depend greatly upon cumulative progress in developing overall scientific paradigms of "politics," such as those reviewed in Chapter 2, combined with careful efforts to explicate the political leadership correlates of each new paradigm.

Because of past neglect within political science of the concept of political leadership no single image is dominant; existing resources do not constitute much more than a mélange of images such as "philosopher-king," "prince," "charisma," "elite," "patron-client," "statesman," "dictator," "boss," "president," "representative," and "revolutionary." Therefore, paradoxically, the potentials for pluralism and parochialism are both great: intradisciplinary diversity combined with transdisciplinary isolation.

Somehow, future students of political leadership will have to reach beyond the limitations of past and present conceptualizations toward more parsimonious and penetrating images that will markedly advance scientific understanding. We must proceed beyond Lenin's curtly insightful "Kto kovo?" (Who [does what to] whom?) through Rustow's equally insightful "Who leads whom from where to where?" toward formulations that will increase our understanding of who leads whom, with respect to what, under what circumstances, how, why, with what costs and benefits, and with what effects upon institutions, individuals, political systems, and human society as a whole.

First, political science must recognize the conceptualizing task. Then, with awareness of potential resources, the discipline must strive to accomplish this task. Chapter 5 contributes to that undertaking.

CHAPTER 5

A MULTIVARIATE, MULTIDIMENSIONAL
LINKAGE APPROACH: VARIABLES

I use the office of mayor to attain my goal of getting jobs and resources for my people.

JOHNNY L. FORD, SR.
Mayor of Tuskegee, Alabama
1973

GIVEN PAST NEGLECT, present rapid emergence, and great diversity of conceptual resources, what needs to be done now to advance the scientific study of political leadership? The principal conceptual tasks now before us are to articulate more fully a set of assumptions concerning the nature of leadership, to establish rules for the identification of leaders, to describe patterns of leadership behavior to be explained, to explore explanatory variables by which these patterns may be predicted, and to specify linkages between leadership behavior and general political paradigms, concrete political institutions, and specific political processes. All these tasks, of course, interact; progress in one may assist advancement in another.

The present chapter will concentrate upon specifying a set of anticipatory variables and illustrating linkages among them. The following chapter will pursue the problem of political linkages by means of a hypothesized set of dimensions of political behavior. Overall, this perspective constitutes a multivariate, multidimensional linkage approach. Patterns of political leadership behavior are viewed as the product of a set of interacting variables, which in turn are regarded as being related to the diverse dimensions of a system of political behavior. The multivariate idea emerges directly parallel to the experience of social psychological studies of leadership as summarized by Gibb in Chapter 4.[1] The notion of dimensions is suggested by the existence of partly competing paradigms in contemporary American political science.

Assumptions

In the assumption of omni-relevant creative potential that was suggested in Chapter 1 as a lesson of the experience of the divided nations, and in realization that leadership must be approached in multivariate, multidimensional terms, we need to underscore the assumed importance of salience, initiative, and inter-action as characteristic features of political leadership. Lack of concentrated awareness of the importance of all of these may have inhibited political leader-ship studies in the past. The exploration, critical evaluation, and revision of these assumptions are likely to assist progress in political leadership studies of the future.

Salience. Durkheim advised social scientists to "approach the social realm where it offers the easiest access to scientific investigation."[2] From this perspec-tive, the prominence of political leaders is striking. In Chapter 4 we saw signs of this salience in political assertions of class dominance, in the positional promi-nence of animal influentials (ahead, amidst, behind), in the artistic portrayal of the "magnetic power" of a lead dancer, and in the importance of the model in emulative diffusion of social learning. Furthermore, we observed it in classical definitions of polities in terms of number of rulers, in typologies of community political systems based upon prominence of participation in making decisions, and in the many studies of the behavior of persons in formally prominent political leadership "roles."

Despite criticisms that "real" leaders may be hidden behind formal role incumbents, that leaders conceal or express class power, and that there is no such thing as leadership in a complex society, no study has as yet been unable to identify salient persons in politics or in other areas of social life.

Initiative. The idea of initiative is close to, but not identical with, the idea of combinatorial creativity. Initiative implies precedence in movement and direction setting. As Cooley would have it, "Leadership is only salient initia-tive."[3] In Chapter 4, we saw signs of the importance of initiative in such things as the flight of a frightened goat, the initiation of movement among the Nuer by the "bull," the impact upon economic development of the entrepreneur, and the potential contribution of "charismatic" leadership in political change.

Interaction. Political leaders cannot not interact.[4] There can be neither leadership nor followership without both leaders and followers in interaction. This interaction has been observed in the political idea of leadership as service to others, in the frustration of a chimpanzee leader when deprived of followers, in the efforts of some leaders to communicate to others through the arts, in Cattell's conception of leadership as "group syntality," in the idea of political leadership as a form of patron-client relationship, and in demonstrations of different patterns by which political leadership role incumbents relate to other members of society.

This interaction may be viewed as either leader dominated or follower dominated or as the product of reciprocal cooperation. To Michels's idea of the

"technical indispensability" of leaders as always beyond the control of followers[5] and to Bentley's concept of leaders as a product of group creation,[6] we
must add a third perspective: leaders are in part the followers of those they are
leading; followers are partly the leaders of those whom they follow. Creators are
in part the creatures of their own creation.[7] Or, from a somewhat different
viewpoint, as folk wisdom cautions, "We become like our adversaries, whether
we will it or not."

General Orientation

Against this background, the general orientation toward political leadership
that is suggested here may be summarized as follows: the concept of political
leadership directs attention to the potentially creative behavior of salient persons
in interaction with significant others of similar potential as they engage in
initiatives of pervasive societal relevance. This behavior is ultimately predictable
on the basis of a set of interacting explanatory variables. It can further be related
to emerging general conceptions of the nature of politics, or of a political
system, by positing dimensional linkages in terms of those conceptions. This
crude formulation requires clarification and illustration. Its present purpose is
merely to consolidate and underscore some basic ideas that need to be accounted for at this stage in developing an approach to the scientific study of
political leaders.

Identification

An important task in the scientific study of political leadership will be to
establish rules for the identification of political leaders and followers in interaction. Given the controversy in community power studies over whether decision makers are best identified by reputation, position, or participation in the
determination of policy outcomes, it is likely that different approaches to
identifying patterns of political leader-follower interaction will emerge for critical evaluation and testing. It is essential, therefore, that each study of political
leadership make clear the identificational criteria being employed so that cumulative, comparative field advancement will be assisted.

The approach taken here is to combine sequentially position-centered and
task-related identifications of leaders and followers from a perspective that
additionally encompasses both manifest and latent behaviors. Let us begin with a
position-centered mode of identification: that is, political leaders are taken to be
persons in positions of formal political salience, conventional competitors for
such positions, and persons who seek revolutionary displacement of incumbents
and possible radical transformation of the positions themselves. Followers are
taken to be all other members of society who interact either directly or

indirectly with the leaders as identified above. Followers may range from an inner "affective core" group, through persons who actively participate in deciding the outcomes of position-related leader behavior, to all other persons whose relative passivity contributes to validating the outcomes of incumbent, competitive, and revolutionary political leadership behavior. For analytical purposes, leaders and followers may be identified singly; they may be identified by sampling; and they may be identified as aggregates in relation to the positions that constitute a given political leadership system.

This position-centered approach has been chosen as a point of departure for several reasons: to focus attention more sharply upon the total set of formal political authority positions in a society; to make variations in the powers of these positions a leadership variable itself in the form of "role"; and to provide a focus for deliberate efforts to improve political leader behavior for the common good. Where abuses of formal positions are found, for example, this may lead to such things as redesign of position powers, change in rules of recruitment and incumbency, and redesign of follower interactions.

In the American political system, a position-centered mode of identifying leaders would require attention at least to the behavior of persons in the following categories: president, vice-president, senator, representative, governor, lieutenant governor, state legislator, mayor, councilperson, party chairpersons at national, state, and local levels, candidates for all the foregoing positions, and salient figures of political movements that would radically alter this formal position set. Attention would be directed to patterns of interaction among all persons in these positions as well as their interaction with followers. Followers in this case would be defined as core staff and campaign supporters; validating voters and active constituents; institutional influentials—business, labor, and media; bureaucracies over which the elected leaders have some influence such as through budgets and appointments to executive and judicial departments—or to which they respond; and the main body of formally politically passive citizenry. In other societies, functionally equivalent position sets and follower relationships would be sought.

Two objections to this approach may immediately arise. Is it not a "reactionary" return to formal institutional analysis? The answer is "yes"—from a viewpoint that seeks to predict concrete variations from general behavioral principles rather than to deemphasize the specific in search for the general, or to neglect the "political" in politics while searching for the political in everything else. A second objection is that some societies may not have functionally differentiated political leadership roles. We have noted this among the Nuer of Sudan and F. G. Bailey has explained this situation among the Konds, a hill tribe of Orissia, India, as follows: "The Konds had no political leaders because they had no specialized political groups to be led."[8]

This possibility requires us to be prepared to employ a second mode of political leader identification when the primary mode does not suffice. It requires us to be prepared to identify persons who take salient initiatives in interaction with others in relation to matters we define as "political." In fact, this is really not so different from the criteria employed in the positional mode of leadership identification since it depends upon the identification of *political* positions. Both are dependent upon the meaning given to the concept "political": this is not something peculiar to political leadership studies but is a common conceptual problem underlying identification and analysis in all other fields of specialization in *political* science. Task-relevant identification of leaders therefore requires us to look for salient persons whose initiatives and counter-initiatives evoke supportive and countervailing responses in other members of society in matters considered political.

The distinction made here between positional and task methods of leader-follower identification helps to clarify why political leadership studies, however central and necessary, are not all of political science. An overall conception of the political both underlies and transcends the position- and task-related approaches to leadership. This is what the discipline of political science as a whole, with its various fields of specialization, strives to comprehend.[9]

At an advanced stage of political leader-follower identification it will enormously enrich analysis if both manifest and latent behaviors are taken into consideration. That is, we want to know not only who leads and who follows at any given time but also who might lead and who might follow. Latent leadership identification thus means assigning probabilities to individuals and groups within societies as to who will become incumbents, conventional competitors, and revolutionaries and who will follow them. Overarching both manifest and latent identification, of course, is normative identification. We should always be prepared to ask not only who should lead but also who should follow.

Having identified who leads and who follows, it remains to specify the patterns of political leadership behavior that are to be described, explained, predicted, evaluated, and affected.

Political Leadership Patterns

Patterns of political leadership behavior may be regarded both as the products of predictor variables and as predictors themselves of political system outcomes. That is, they may be treated for analytical purposes as independent, dependent, or intervening variables. These patterns are a core concern of political leadership studies. They may be specified in advance on the basis of theoretical anticipations, or they may be derived ex post facto after careful study of leadership behavior. In either instance, an ideal goal is to measure these leadership patterns independently of the variables that anticipate them and independently of the effects they are hypothesized to have upon the political system, although all may be linked in a relationship of circular causality.

As reviewed in Chapter 4, various patterns of leadership behavior have been described in the literature. These patterns challenge us to explain their emergence and political effects. They include, it will be recalled, such images as "charismatic," "traditional," and "rational-legal" types; "delegate," "trustee," and "politico" styles; and self-oriented, task-oriented, and interaction-oriented leadership patterns. Further images may be created in terms of any one of the dimensions of political leadership behavior to be explored in Chapter 6.

An excellent example of the combination of a priori and ex post facto conceptual techniques to focus attention upon a limited set of theoretically significant leadership patterns is provided by Kotter and Lawrence in a study of mayoral leadership in twenty American cities.[10] They began with ten images of mayoral leadership drawn from the literature ("power broker," "public entrepreneur," "public executive," "policy expert," "coalition builder," "muddler," "multi-hat role," "formal structure," "personality," and "community power") and ended up with five patterns of mayoral behavior ("ceremonial," "caretaker," "personality/individualist," "executive," and "program entrepreneur"). The five patterns were derived from empirical observations made in terms of three variable clusters: "agenda setting," "network building," and "task accomplishment,"[11] as summarized in Table 2.

Another approach to specifying patterns of leadership behavior that is likely to be of fundamental importance in the advancement of political leadership studies is to define them in terms of the concept of change. This change may be

TABLE 2. Kotter-Lawrence Typology of Mayoral Leadership

	CHARACTERISTIC BEHAVIORS		
MAYORAL TYPE	*Agenda Setting*	*Network Building*	*Task Accomplishment*
1. "Ceremonial"	Small scope Short run	Personal appeal No modification No staff	Individualistic
2. "Caretaker"	Large scope Short run	Discrete exchange Limited modification Loyal staff	Moderate bureaucratic
3. "Personality"/ individualist	Moderate scope Midrange	Personal appeal Little modification No staff	Individualistic
4. "Executive"	Large scope Midrange	Mixed appeals Some modification Some staff	Bureaucratic
5. "Program entrepreneur"	Very large scope Short-medium-long range	Extensive mixed appeals Some modification Staff resources	Entrepreneurial

Source: Based on John Kotter and Paul R. Lawrence, *Mayors in Action* (New York: Wiley, 1974), pp. 105–121.

minimal, moderate, or maximum, corresponding roughly to the natural language concepts of "conservative/reactionary," "reformist," and "revolutionary" political leadership. Politically significant change may be further differentiated into structural change, procedural change, and policy change, emphasizing variously decision making, organization, process, or outcome.

For analytical purposes, therefore, we can posit the following three patterns of political leadership behavior that need to be described, explained, predicted, and evaluated and the effects of which upon a political system need to be understood:

> *minimal change ("conservative") leadership;* tending toward maintenance of existing political institutions and policies;
>
> *moderate change ("reformist") leadership;* tending toward moderate change in given institutions and policies; and
>
> *maximal change ("revolutionary") leadership;* tending toward fundamental transformation of existing institutions and policies.

The characterization of political leadership in terms of these three patterns must be recognized as being a complex but nevertheless essential task if the overall purposive influences of individual and aggregate political leadership are to be better understood. For example, consider the frequent occurrence of domestic institutional conservatism combined with radical foreign policy change. What is needed is an overall change-propensity score, a measure of the predominant direction of behavior, that will be a composite of, and therefore decomposable into, diverse propensities toward structural, procedural, and policy change. The same complexity can be expected to characterize all efforts to specify and measure ideal types of political leadership behavior.

Whatever patterns of leadership behavior are posited, it is important that the scientific study of political leadership begin to explore systematically the hypothesis that political leaders, as individuals and as aggregates, act in patterned ways that affect the creation, maintenance, and change of institutions as well as the processes and policy outcomes of institutional behavior.

Anticipatory Variables

Having specified patterns of political leadership behavior, the next conceptual task is to identify a set of "anticipatory variables" that will facilitate analysis of the emergence and effects of these patterns. These anticipatory variables simply alert attention to things that may help to describe, explain, predict, evaluate, and intervene. Anticipatory variables thus serve multiple functions. Stated more narrowly, we need to identify a set of explanatory variables to be explored as possible predictors of patterns of political leadership behavior. As the scientific study of political leadership progresses, diverse explanatory factors are likely to be explored and, to the extent that we are able to develop a more adequate scientific memory through electronic information storage and retrieval, we should become progressively more confident in our understanding of which variables are most important in what contexts.

As a reasonable point of departure for political leadership studies, six explanatory variables, very broad in scope and requiring subvariable differentiation, are suggested. There are two explanations for their choice. First, although some of them are used here in a slightly different way from the customary, they are all widely employed concepts in the contemporary social and behavioral sciences. Each of them is potentially rich in transdisciplinary social science conceptualizations and empirical findings. The second reason for their choice is simply that they appear to call attention to important correlates of political leadership behavior. This is, of course, a simple, "face validity" argument and is ultimately based upon a combination of intuition and empirical plausibility. In the latter aspect some confidence has been gained through the study of political leader biographies.

Some may object that the variables chosen are of such a general nature that they apply not only to leadership in politics but also to any kind of social leadership—in fact, to any kind of social behavior. I hope that this is true. We need to see political behavior as a form of human behavior and we need to employ all the behavioral science and humanist insights we can muster to understand it. Whether such behavior is "political" or not depends, of course, upon paradigmatic efforts to conceptualize the nature of politics. The term "political leadership behavior" is simply one of conceptual and empirical indeterminacy: the task of political science in this instance is simply to create temporary resolutions of this indeterminacy that will facilitate scientific progress.

The six variables chosen as a point of departure here are *personality, role, organization, task, values,* and *setting.* They are posited as sources of explanation for the emergence, functioning, change, and decline of whatever patterns of political leadership behavior are taken as the focus of analytical attention. Although these are all common concepts in the contemporary sociobehavioral sciences, none is unambiguous and each needs to be operationalized in ways most appropriate to a given empirical inquiry. Thus, they are to be taken as variable concepts, at a high level of abstraction, that require further definition and measurement.

These six variables are conceived to be in interaction. Each "selects," "is selected by," "shapes," and "is shaped by" every one of the others. Thus, we can have personality-dominant *or* setting-dominant leadership. Both sides of the great man *versus* situation debate on occasion can be "right." Why not adopt a conceptual framework that permits this possibility to be recognized? Taken as an aggregate cluster that permits variations in the relative weight of component variables and thus anticipates variations in "explanation," these six variables are seen as mutually influencing elements that produce the behavior patterns of incumbent and contending political leaders. Stated somewhat more formally,

Patterns of political leadership behavior are a function of personality, role, organization, task, values, and setting factors in reciprocal interaction, plus error variance for which these variables do not account

or

$$PLB_{i-k} = f(P,R,O,T,V,S) + e$$

where *PLB* refers to political leadership behavior, $i\text{-}k$ indicates the range of identifiable patterns, *P, R, O, T, V, S* refer to the six anticipatory variables introduced above, and *e* is an error term, a surrogate variable for those determinants of political leadership behavior that are *not* appreciated in this formulation.

Predictive and Applied Models

Following the distinction between *econometric* (predictive) and *program* (goal attainment) models in business decision making,[12] we may envision the parallel development of closely related predictive and applied models of political leadership. In terms of the present formulation, a predictive model can be stated as follows:

Predictive model. If *persons* of characteristic P_{i-k} are incumbent in, or aspiring to, *roles* R_{i-k}, within a context of amplifying and restraining *organizational* influences O_{i-k}, and are confronted with *tasks* of the type T_{i-k}, with evoked *values* V_{i-k}, in physical-technological-social-economic-cultural *settings* S_{i-k}—then *political leadership behaviors* PLB_{i-k} are likely to occur with *political institutional consequences and political system consequences of* the type PI_{i-k} and PS_{i-k}.

An applied model may be created from the same set of variables in the following way:

Applied model. If change in *PLB* is desired, then changes in one or more *personality* P_{i-k}, *role* R_{i-k}, *organization* O_{i-k}, *task* T_{i-k}, *value* V_{i-k}, and *setting* S_{i-k} variables should be accomplished—or changes in *political institutions* PI_{i-k} or *political system variables* PS_{i-k}, insofar as the latter are not analytical constructs without direct empirical referents.

Let us now consider each of the suggested anticipatory variables in turn and examine linkages among them in greater detail.

Linkages, Hypotheses, Propositions, and Laws

In the sections to follow, statements of relationships among the six variables will be termed "linkages." Since the idea of a "linkage statement" is not in common use, a brief explanation is in order. Linkage statements are initial assertions of association among variables of a conceptual framework that aim to orient thought to possible relationships. They may be simply descriptive or they may suggest causal influences. Linkage statements are to be distinguished from *hypotheses*, which are taken to be anticipatory statements of relationships that are being tested through specifically designed research efforts to explore their validity; *propositions*, statements of hypotheses that have been tested outside the original bounds of their creation and found to have at least some degree of significant support; and *laws*, propositions with extraordinarily high degrees of certainty. A conceptual framework is a set of linkages; a hypothetical pre-theory is a set of hypotheses; an empirical pre-theory is a set of propositions; a hypothetico-propositional pre-theory is a mixed set of propositions and hypotheses; and a theory is a set of laws. One challenge to scientific imagination is to proceed from conceptual frameworks to laws. This requires constant interactions among verbal formulations, empirical research, and mathematical expression.[13] The progression of development, of course, need not be linear; the physical law of entropy, for example, has stimulated conceptual and pre-theoretic efforts in communications approaches to social science analysis.

1. PERSONALITY

Personality is taken to be the aggregate characteristics that define a unique human individual. Included are biological, physiological, and psychological factors. Where more than a single leader is involved we may speak of shared personality characteristics. Personality is viewed as subject to change from birth to death and as the product of past learning, present influences, and future expectations. The principal task connected with personality in political leadership studies is not to show that personalities of leaders differ from those of nonleaders. Rather, it is to describe, explain, predict, evaluate, and influence whatever personalities leaders do have. Since the study of personality is a recognized subfield of the scientific discipline of psychology, is a main concern of other social sciences such as cultural anthropology, and is a growing field of interest in political science, pioneered by Lasswell and many others,[14] students of political leadership can draw upon a wide range of personality concepts, theories, and operational measures. At the same time they can challenge scientific students of personality with problems and puzzles that arise from political leadership studies themselves.

Several hypotheses about the influence of personality upon political leadership behavior have already been explored. Six are sketched here. (1) *Compensatory striving hypothesis:* If the self-esteem of a potential leader is damaged in early childhood socialization, then this person will strive to gain a sense of self-worth by maximizing one or more compensatory values;[15] this striving does not take place in all situations but only under conditions in which the sense of self-esteem is especially threatened.[16] (2) *First independent success hypothesis:* If a potential political leader achieves first success in attracting follower support by means of one of three modes of influence (rhetorical expressiveness, businesslike management of details, interpersonal dealing), then this person will tend to exhibit prominently the same style in subsequent leadership behavior.[17] (3) *The needs for power, achievement, and affiliation hypothesis:* If a potential leader personality is characterized predominantly by a high need for power, achievement, or affiliation, then leadership positions sought, campaign style, and subsequent role performance are likely to demonstrate the corresponding characteristic.[18] (4) *The revolutionary personality hypothesis:* The revolutionary political leader is a person characterized by unresolved oedipal conflict and a person "who escapes from the burden of Oedipal guilt and ambivalence by carrying his conflict with authority into the political realm."[19] (5) *The sex differentiation hypothesis:* In a given cultural setting it is likely that female leaders will differ from male leaders on certain measures of personality, holding type of leadership position constant.[20] (6) *The birth order hypothesis:* Firstborns are more likely to rise to leadership in times of crisis; middle children are more likely to lead in periods of calm; and last-born persons are likely to predominate among revolutionaries.[21]

Despite these and other important insights much remains to be done to clarify the nature and effects of personality on political leadership behavior. Among such tasks are to describe political leadership behavior in precise detail so that personality patterns can be more readily identified, to inventory theories of personality in order to formulate a wider range of explanatory hypotheses, to contrive laboratory and field experiments to test the effects of personality in political leadership, and to challenge personality specialists with political leadership puzzles. Among other needs are to explore the intuitive or nonformal personality theories employed by experienced political leaders themselves to interpret associates' or opponents' behavior; to avoid entrapment in concern for personality pathology; to seek life-cycle, developmental views of political leadership personalities, not just ad hoc insights; to study the interactions of leader and follower personalities; to seek multidisciplinary perspectives on personality development; and finally to proceed beyond the construction of personality typologies to show how personality influences other aspects of political leadership behavior.

The following section presents a set of linkage statements that relate "personality" to each of the other five components of the suggested conceptual framework. Each statement will be illustrated by examples drawn from biographical or other leadership studies.

Personality may be linked to other anticipatory leadership variables in several ways. *Linkage 1.2.1: The more assertive the personality, the more the propensity to expand role potentials.* Wrote Sorensen of Kennedy, "He was a strong President primarily because he was a strong person."[22] To give another example, in pre-Marcos Philippines, tenure for the president normally was limited to four years (one term). After declaration of martial law in 1972, the presidential term of office became indefinite. *Linkage 1.3.1: Personality affects the creation and viability of organizations.* Tarn, for example, explained that the personality of Alexander the Great was an important factor in the creation and demise of his empire: "Up to Alexander's death the Empire was held together solely by himself and his (mixed) army . . . and a further source of weakness was that the ultimate care of everything—the army, administration, law—fell upon himself personally, entailing a stupendous amount of work; probably only his habit of occasionally sleeping for 36 hours kept him going; certainly toward the end he was growing more impatient and irritable."[23] Or, as Fischer observed, "Trotsky . . . was primarily a mass appeal man. Lenin primarily an organization man. Trotsky needed a stage, Lenin an office."[24] *Linkage 1.4.1: Personality affects task selection and the choice of means in task accomplishment.* Two examples from the career of John F. Kennedy provide illustrations. First, on task selection, Sorensen noted that in the 1960 presidential election campaign, "Unlike Mr. Nixon, the Senator attempted to tackle a new subject or combination of subjects in almost every speech."[25] Second, taking the use of polls as a means for accomplishing the task of electoral victory, we can see that American leaders have differed in their use. Ithiel de Sola Pool noted, "President Truman never liked the pollers and has lambasted them with juicy epithets. Eisenhower neither used nor understood them well. Neither did Stevenson who read research reports but tended to act in utter disregard of them. The same thing cannot be said of any of the top political figures of 1960. Nixon, Rockefeller, and Kennedy all relied on polls, read them carefully and understood them."[26] *Linkage 1.5.1: Personality relates to the kind of values sought and to the intensity of commitment to them.* Fidel Castro explained, "With my ideas and temperament, even in my school and university days, I could not have been a capitalist, a democrat, a liberal. I always had it in me to be a radical, a revolutionary, a reformer, and through that instinctive preparation it was easy for me to move into Marxism-Leninism."[27] *Linkage 1.6.1: Personalities select and shape settings.* As the research on state legislators by Wahlke and others suggests, there are "state-oriented," "district-oriented," and "district-state"-oriented legislators. This means that the personalities of leaders in similar roles tend to orient them toward different geographical, technological, and sociocultural constituencies. Leaders can also contribute to changes in physical settings. According to Gallagher, Tunisia's President Habib Bourguiba sought to replace conservative country hedgerows with open rows of trees and to transform core city cemeteries into open parks in order "to alter the attitudes of the individual by transforming his life habits."[28]

Personality may also be viewed as subject to influences from each of the other five variables of the conceptual framework. *Linkage 2.1.1: Role attracts and affects personality.* Commenting upon the unexpectedly "good" performance as president by former senator and vice-president Harry S Truman, socialist leader Norman Thomas remarked, "Power educates as well as corrupts."[29] Some personalities, of course, learn less. Sorensen suggested that former mayor Celebrezze of Cleveland seemed to learn little after his appointment to the Kennedy cabinet. "After a year of Cabinet meetings . . . in which Celebrezze at some length analyzed every world and national problem in terms of his experiences in Cleveland, the President was more amused than admiring."[30] Tiger reported from animal studies that when a formerly subdominant male monkey with a low level of testosterone was experimentally manipulated into the role of monkey leader, his hormonal level rose to that characteristic of a dominant animal.[31] *Linkage 3.1.1: Organizational characteristics influence the kinds of personalities that are acceptable in leadership roles and the degrees of latitude afforded them in role performance.* As summarized by Gibb, experimental studies of small groups have shown that "authoritarian personalities preferred status-laden leadership, accepted strongly directive leadership, and regarded the authoritarian leader as 'better' than his more democratic counterpart."[32] And as Key observed, "leaders are apt to be captives of their followers, who will follow them just so far and no further."[33] Experienced leaders are sensitive to the effects of organization on leader personalities. Of his first impression of Soviet premier Khrushchev, President Kennedy recalled, "I expected him to be smart and tough. He would have to be smart and tough to work his way to the top of a government like that one."[34] *Linkage 4.1.1: Tasks impose objective demands upon leader personalities for effective task accomplishment.* For example, Hargrove has written that the task of coping with the American Depression in the 1930s required capacities for "dramatization" not possessed by Herbert Hoover,[35] that the tasks of "fast-moving, unstructured situations" posed difficulties for Dwight Eisenhower's slower moving "logical orderly mind,"[36] and that the multiple tasks of national leadership were found uncomfortable by Woodrow Wilson, who was described by Colonel House as having a "one-track mind."[37] *Linkage 5.1.1: Values attract congruent personalities and contribute to possible cognitive dissonance in them.* It is probable, for example, that authoritarian and violent creeds attract personalities with special needs for them. When reality diverges, it is likely that the personality responds to what Festinger and others have conceptualized as "cognitive dissonance."[38] For example, a letter from Hitler to Mussolini shows that Hitler was deeply disturbed by the necessity for concluding a nonaggression pact with the hated "Jewish-Bolsheviks" in 1939 and greatly relieved by his decision to invade the Soviet Union in 1941.[39] *Linkage 6.1.1: Cultural settings nurture contrasting personalities who compete for societal influence and mutually influence each other.* Indian culture, for example, produced the nonviolent personality of Gandhi and the violent personality of Subhas Chandra Bose.[40] Puerto Rico produced leader personalities who became identified with three different solutions to the problem of the form of relationship the island should have with the United States: Luis Ferré (statehood), Luis Muñoz Marín (commonwealth status), and Albizu Campos (independence).[41]

2. ROLE

Like personality, role is one of the most complex concepts in social science but it is constantly found to be of analytical usefulness. Definitions range from the sweeping formulation of Linton ("the sum total of culture patterns associated with a particular status")[42] through the expectation-based measure of Gross ("a set of expectations applied to the incumbent of a position"),[43] to the more limited conception of Banton ("sets of rights and obligations").[44] For political leadership studies a Banton-like concept of role defined in Fiedler-like terms of "position power," plus a Gross-like operational definition as incumbent-other expectation to which has been added objective analysis, seems well worth exploration. The important thing is to separate the concept of "role" from that of "personality," with which it has been confounded frequently in political research. Rossi, sharply stating the case for an independent conception of role, explained, "It seems likely that the most important source of variation among decision-makers lies in their roles rather in the personal qualities they bring to their offices."[45] Similarly, March illustrated the utility of keeping the concept of "role" (position) analytically separate from other aspects of incumbent behavior in the measurement of political leader influence.[46]

It is important to understand that political leadership roles do vary and that their structure can either amplify or diminish the effects of incumbent personalities. One of the best ways to appreciate variation in leadership roles is through the experience of persons who have been in several of them. A former governor who moved to the United States Senate told Matthews, "I moved from one world to another. . . . Back home everything revolved, or seemed to revolve, around the Governor. I had a part in practically everything that happened. There was administration. There was policy making. But down here there was just a seat at the end of the table."[47] Former New York City mayor John Lindsay once contrasted his experience as mayor ("where the action is") and congressman ("the biggest kibbitzer in the world") in much the same terms.[48] Similarly, John F. Kennedy observed, "It is a tremendous change to go from being a senator to being a President. In the first few months it is very difficult."[49] And Lenin once told Trotsky, "The transition from the state of legality, being driven in every direction, to power—is too rough. It makes one dizzy."[50] While cross-role differences may be the more striking, within-role variations that occur abruptly or over long periods of time[51] need to be recognized, too. Also aggregate clusters of roles as well as single roles need to be studied as sources of political leadership influence upon a political system.

Among future role-related tasks in political leadership studies are the need to clarify the concept of role and devise appropriate operational measures; to conduct comparative role studies across levels, institutions, and cultures; to map systems of roles within a given political context, including both formal and nonformal aspirant positions; and to demonstrate relationships between role and other aspects of political leadership behavior. Greater analytical attention to role may assist education of potential incumbents as well as appreciation of when a change in role may be more significant in improving performance of a political system than a change in incumbent personality.

Among role properties that will be found especially important for political leadership analysis are rights to command coercive, military, and police power;

veto power over decisions by others; age, social background, tenure, and other restrictions on incumbency; imperative responsiveness, obligations to account to others; value systems to which incumbency requires commitment; and connectivity with roles of greater, equal, or lesser significance.

The main empirical finding to date in political science role studies related to political leadership is that *for any given formal institutional role, different styles of incumbent performance are possible.* An example is the role of legislator, which has been shown to permit "delegate," "trustee," or "politico" styles of performance.

As an independent variable, role may be related illustratively to other variables of the conceptual framework in the following ways. *Linkage 2.1.2: Roles tend to attract personalities with related characteristics (these may be eufunctional and sometimes pathologically dysfunctional).* On the basis of a comparative study of elected politicians in two local settings (Eastern City and Louisiana parishes), Browning and Jacob discovered that "offices with high potential for power and achievement are occupied by men who are more strongly power- and achievement-motivated than politicians in low-potential offices."[52] *Linkage 2.3.1: The more the role power, the greater the leader influence upon overall organizational behavior.* An example of this was the domination of the House of Representatives prior to 1910 by Speaker "Uncle Joe" Cannon, who had the power to appoint members of all committees, to control the agenda as concurrent chairman of the House Rules Committee, and to withhold recognition from any member wishing to speak. The "revolution" against him in that year subsequently made the House less dependent upon the authority of the Speaker.[53] The differential attraction to higher offices of money, services, and other forms of electoral or revolutionary campaign support also illustrates the organizational effect of potential role power. *Linkage 2.4.1: Roles are characterized by an associated set of tasks that tend to stimulate the task engagement behaviors of aspiring incumbents.* The role of the American president, for example, is characterized by what Lasswell has called needs for "high level integration" and what Parsons has termed requirements for "goal-setting" and "goal implementation."[54] These require a president to engage in a highly diverse set of tasks as described by Rossiter[55] and others. Thus, it is not surprising that Matthews reported that senators who aspired to be president "gave more floor speeches than the average senator and pursued a wider range of legislative interests."[56] *Linkage 2.5.1: Roles are connected with the affirmation of certain values.* This is exemplified by the inaugural oath required of all American presidents that they will "preserve, protect and defend the Constitution of the United States of America." It is also illustrated by the reply of a subarctic Cree Indian to an anthropologist's question as to whether he would like to be chief: "I am not good enough. A chief has to be a good man—one who doesn't do anything bad."[57] *Linkage 2.6.1: Roles shape the scope and impact of incumbent influences upon the setting.* In discussing the role of American political leaders on architectural design, for example, Edward J. Logue, of New

Haven redevelopment fame, an experienced administrator and politician, explained that the president has a seldom used great potential for influence,[58] that "the governor of a state has a very crucial role in the matter of design,"[59] and that "of all our political figures the mayor is in the position to do the most good or the most harm in the matter of design. He is also the last person anybody ever thinks of talking to seriously on this subject." "Regardless of what city charters and ordinances say," Logue further advised, "the mayor usually has effective control over the selection of architects."[60]

Alternatively, role may be seen as the product of other influences. *Linkage 1.2.2: The nature and intensity of affective investments by incumbent or aspiring personalities influence the emotional characteristics of leadership roles.* Such emotional investments may be positive or negative and may produce similar or opposite reactions in others. Wrote White of Lyndon Johnson in the early years, "Openly and unashamedly he values, respects, and enjoys high public office, and openly and unashamedly he enjoys its perquisites while bearing its burdens."[61] *Linkage 3.2.1: The more egalitarian the organization, the greater the emphasis upon "persuasion" as a leadership role expectation.* Both the Chinese Communist party's ideal emphasis upon the ideological re-education of deviant party members versus their physical imprisonment or liquidation and the portrayal of presidential authority as the "power to persuade" in the ideal American system of checkmating powers and egalitarian citizenship seem consistent with this view. *Linkage 4.2.1: The more crucial the tasks for societal survival, the more likely their attachment to high level leadership roles.* This kind of role-task linkage is illustrated by a reminiscence of former president Johnson's:

> President Nixon said to me, "How did you feel when you weren't President any more?" And I said: "I don't know whether you'll understand this now or not but you certainly will later. I sat there on that platform and waited for you to stand up and raise your right hand and take the oath of office and the—I think that the most pleasant words that ever—that ever came into my ears were "So help me God," that you repeated after that oath. Because at that time I no longer had the fear that I was the man that could make the mistake of involving the world in wars, that I was no longer the man that would have to carry the terrifying responsibility of protecting the lives of this country and maybe the entire world, unleashing the horrors of some of our great power if I felt that was required; but that now I could ride back down that avenue, being concerned about what happened, being alarmed about what might happen, but just really knowing that I wasn't going to be the cause of it, that that went over to some other man.[62]

This kind of task assignment is, of course, a product of both leader willingness and follower concurrence. Combat bomber crews, for example, have been found to prefer that the aircraft commander make survival decisions rather than reach such decisions by egalitarian voting. *Linkage 5.2.1: Values influence expansive or restrictive role definitions by incumbents and significant others.* "Shocking as this may sound in the ears of many people who have come to accept quite a different picture of the presidency," explained former presidential assistant Arthur Larson, "President Eisenhower simply did not believe that he should be leading crusades of a moral, humanitarian, or civil rights nature. He believed that his job was to operate exclusively within the governmental powers of his office."[63] *Linkage 6.2.1: Settings enhance or diminish role power.* As Saddam Hussein, vice-chairman of the ruling Revolutionary Command Council of Iraq, explained to a reporter during the international "energy crisis" of 1973, "No leader can come in the way of oil in the battle of destiny."[64] This implies that physical resources affect the authority of political leadership roles, strengthening some and weakening others, regardless of the personalities of incumbent leaders.

3. ORGANIZATION

Another important source of variation in political leadership behavior is what might be termed "organization," used here in the broad sense of social interaction among dyads, small groups, formal organizations, institutions, ad hoc collectivities, horizontal social strata, vertical societal segments, and whole political communities.[65] Under this variable can be considered followers, opponents, and in fact all other members of a society whose behavior influences or is significantly influenced by political leaders, either directly or indirectly.

The study of political leadership will benefit from future efforts to combine the insights of pioneering studies of organizational behavior in the social sciences[66] with similarly innovative inquiries into organizational aspects of political behavior. Among outstanding examples of the latter are the Georges' analysis of the dyadic relation between Woodrow Wilson and Colonel House,[67] the small group influences implied in Fenno's study of the cabinet[68] and in Cronin and Greenberg's study of the presidential advisory system,[69] the major effort by Janda to devise a universally applicable method for the description and analysis of political parties,[70] the extension of the pioneering legislative studies of Wahlke, Eulau, and others,[71] the richly suggestive effort by Kothari and Roy to compare the mutual perceptions of elected politicians and members of an administrative bureaucracy,[72] the effort by Milbrath to clarify private business and other pressures on elected officials,[73] the insight into the societal support bases of political leaders provided by the pioneering studies of voting behavior by Campbell, Miller, and others,[74] and the important effort to probe the interaction between political leadership and changing public opinion by Cornwell.[75] Difficult though it may be, the study of political leadership presents the challenge of understanding the influences of political leadership behavior both within and across these kinds of social interaction contexts as they vary with personality, role, tasks, and other significant variables. Here, the interstitial, pivotal, integrative importance of attempting to develop for political science a concept of political leadership is apparent.

Among current social science propositions that link leadership with organizational behavior are Lipset, Trow, and Coleman's hypothesis that *organizations created from the bottom up are characterized by more member controls over leader behavior than those organized from the top down,*[76] Hollander's "idiosyncrasy credit" hypothesis that *the more an aspiring leader initially conforms to organizational norms and expectations, the greater the accumulation of confidence credits that later may be drawn upon for support of the nonconforming initiatives that are expected at higher leadership levels as contributions to organizational success,*[77] and Milgram's extraordinarily interesting "small world hypothesis" that *"only 5.5 intermediaries will, on the average, suffice to link randomly chosen individuals, no matter where each lives in the United States."*[78]

In general, leader personality and role in relation to organization may be viewed on a continuum between polar types of domination and subjection. Domination is illustrated by the position of Peter the Great versus the Russian senate. "The Senate was a body for transmitting the autocrat's will and had no independent will of its own; its powers were those of an agent and not of a principal; it had no sovereign powers, and was merely responsible for carrying out instructions; it was an administrative instrument and not a political force."[79] The defeat of President Woodrow Wilson by seven votes in the Senate on the issue of American participation in the League of Nations in 1920 illustrates the reverse relationship.

A richly suggestive idea for the future development of political leadership studies is that for any given conception of leadership that is asserted ("type," "style," "orientation," etc.), one or more corresponding conceptions of "followership" are implied that may or may not be eufunctionally congruent. For example, follower images implied by the representational roles "trustee," "delegate," and "politico" might be "beneficiary," "boss," and "partner." The reverse approach to the appreciation of organizational effects upon leadership needs also to be explored. For example, if voters are found to be "personality oriented," "party oriented," or "issue oriented," then we might expect campaigning leaders to exhibit styles correspondingly oriented. Two recent contributions to this perspective are of potentially great significance. Pigors has importantly suggested four generic types of followers: "constructive," "routine," "impulsive," and "subversive,"[80] while Barber has reminded us of the basic calculus of followership that is so influential in leadership behavior in terms of "automatic partisans" (supporters or opponents), "persuadables" (independents), and "neutrals" (the purposefully uncommitted).[81]

Among indicators of the general concept of organization are such variables as size, sociopersonal attributes of participants, patterns of interunit relationships, resources, and power-influence outputs. Thus, organizations may be large or small, homogeneous or heterogeneous, tightly or loosely structured, armed or unarmed, supportive or resistant. Admittedly, the calculation of a matrix of multiorganizational influences upon leader behavior is a complex task, requiring attention to both those of a relatively stable, supportive, oppositional, destructive, or benign nature and those of an ad hoc quality present only when certain tasks and values are salient.

Some possible linkages between organization and other variables of the framework include *Linkage 3.1.2: Positive, negative, and neutral influences from organizational sources relate to variance in the emotional tone of leader personalities.* "On a popular tour," wrote Davies, "[Woodrow] Wilson was at first shocked and then braced by hearing a voice from the crowd yell 'Atta boy, Woody,' an appellation no intimate of his would dream using."[82] By contrast, Bullock reported that the apathetic response of Berlin citizens to the movement of a mechanized division through the city on the eve of the invasion of Czechoslovakia in 1938 made a "singularly deep impression" upon Hitler.[83] These examples are also to recall that political personalities have emotional as well as power-related and instrumental task–related aspects.[84] *Linkage 3.2.2: Organizational size affects the scope of leadership role specialization.* It is likely that the larger an organization composed of leaders, the more narrowly specialized the role expectations within it. Students of the U.S. Congress, for example, have noted that members of the House (435 members) are expected to be more specialized in legislative interests and to be more team oriented than members of the smaller Senate (100 members). On the other hand, if the number of leadership roles is held constant, then the larger and more heterogeneous the validational followership, the broader the role expectations; e.g., the American presidency. Leadership roles need to be conceived as subject to conflicting expectations related to size and other organizational variables. *Linkage 3.4.1: The more diverse the organization in the technical competence of members, the greater the expected variation in task definitions and prescribed coping strategies and the greater the salience of the task of intraorganizational social-emotional problem solving.* Torrance and Aliotti, for example, showed experimentally that social-emotional problem solvers tend to arise within five-person groups when they contain two experts rather than one, at least when the groups are characterized by negative versus positive affective relations.[85] The assemblage of private and governmental economists by President Ford in September 1974 to advise him on how to cope with inflation was thus expectably accompanied by both diversity and conflict. *Linkage 3.5.1: Organizations are sources of value salience and conflict.* In the introduction to *Profiles in Courage,* John F. Kennedy referred to three organizational sources of "terrible pressures" that have tended to discourage acts of moral courage by elected American political leaders.[86] These are family needs, the expectations and actions of fellow political leaders, and the expectations and influences of constituents, including interest groups, economic blocs, organized letter writers, and ordinary voters. At crucial moments these fiercely interact with the leader's desire to be liked and to be reelected. *Linkage 3.6.1: Organizations affect setting characteristics.* An example is the agricultural collectivization policy pursued by the Korean Workers party from 1953 to 1958: the physical size of tilled fields was expanded; the social base of agricultural labor was changed from the single family to the multifamily cooperative; the economic basis was changed from private property to communal property; and marked technological changes were made in the direction of mechanization of labor.[87]

Organizations are also affected by influences coming from the other variables. For example, *Linkage 1.3.2: Personalities tend to create distinctive patterns of organizational behavior in immediate associates that express their felt needs.* President (former general) Eisenhower found it comfortable to organize his immediate White House staff in a hierarchical pattern similar to a military headquarters'; all subordinate staff work had to clear through his "chief of staff," former New Hampshire governor Sherman Adams.[88] By contrast, President Kennedy conceived himself at the center of a wheellike structure of staff relationships and encouraged direct access by peripheral staff members. As Sorensen recalled, "Not one staff meeting was ever held, with or without the President."[89] Personality influences on staffing seemed so salient to Matthews during his study of U.S. senators that he suggested that personality characteristics of leaders might be indirectly inferred from the composition and behavior of staff members.[90] *Linkage 2.3.2: Role affects the scope of organizational interactions.* The greater the role power, the more diverse organizational sources of influence upon, and responsiveness to, it. As President Kennedy explained about the different organizational concerns related to the roles of senator and president, "The big difference [about making speeches as president rather than as senator] is all the different audiences that hear every word. In the senate and campaign we didn't have to worry so much about how Khrushchev and Adenauer and Nehru and Dirksen would react."[91] *Linkage 4.3.1: Tasks are related to organizational differentiation.* In his effort to seize power in Germany, Hitler organized the Nazi party into two task-related branches: the first was designed to attack the existing government and included foreign, press, and infiltration divisions; the second aimed at preparing cadres for the future Nazi regime and had divisions devoted to agriculture, economics, race and culture, ministry of interior, legal questions, technical questions, and labor services. Propaganda was controlled by Hitler as a separate department.[92] For the task of collectivizing food grains from the Russian countryside in 1918, Lenin and the Bolshevik party organized special urban worker squads to enter the villages and bring out the grain: "They were to comb the countryside for grains, split the village between poor peasants and kulaks, organize the former into Committees of the Poor, get information from them on hoards, bootleggers, and so forth."[93] Tasks may also be seen as variables influencing the differential of American executive departments, legislative committees, and electoral campaign organizations. It is not assumed, however, that such differentiations are optimal for effective task accomplishment. *Linkage 5.3.1: Values affect organizational functioning.* Matthews, for example, showed how the "folkways" of the U.S. Senate influence organizational performance; these include "apprenticeship, legislative accomplishment versus selfish publicity, specialization, personal courtesy, reciprocity, and institutional patriotism."[94] *Linkage 6.3.1:Settings affect the scope of organizational interaction.* An example of an expanded scope of interaction is provided by the major United Nations–sponsored international conferences on the physical environment (Stockholm, 1972), population (Bucharest, 1974), and the law of the sea (Caracas, 1974). In each case there was an objective characteristic of the physical environment that caused concern (pollution, high rate of population growth, limited resources), combined with technological potential for problem solving (antipollution, contraceptive, and ocean mining devices), that led to attempts to coordinate organized human behavior effectively to reduce cause for concern.

4. TASK

A task is taken to be a problem to be solved, an occasion for decision, or a discrepancy between actual and desirable states of affairs. Tasks need to be viewed both as perceived by political leaders and as objectively given.

An example of objectively given tasks that emerge to leader consciousness is provided by the remarkably similar experiences of New York mayor Lindsay and British prime minister Wilson, who discovered immediately after election that the problems facing them were greater than they had expected. Explained Lindsay, "I do not believe there is anything more shocking to one who has just waged a campaign for office than to find out that things were even worse than he said they were. But that is precisely the state in which we found ourselves. . . . We had made campaign promises without a proper knowledge of what we would find, once elected."[95] Similarly, Wilson found on the very day he took office in 1964 that Britain's international balance of payments deficit was twice that which he had expected (£800 million versus £400 million). He explained, "It was this inheritance that was to dominate almost every action of the Government for five years of the five years eight months we were in office."[96]

The usefulness of a concept of task in leadership research has been demonstrated by the experimental studies of Fiedler, who employed a single dichotomy of tasks as being "structured" or "unstructured."[97] It is also suggested by Hermann's research on crisis decisions, which he has defined as responses to tasks having three characteristics: "short decision time," "high threat to values," and "surprise."[98] Tasks may also be defined in terms of the dimensions of political behavior that will be explored in Chapter 6. For example, we may find it useful to analyze tasks in terms of whether they are self-defined or other imposed, coercive or consensual, high or low in cost, distributive or monopolistic, complex or simple, routine or ad hoc, positive or negative in affect, short or long in range, change promoting or change resistant, and independent of, or relatively connected with, other tasks.

The main challenges now facing the study of political leadership are to conceptualize task in theoretically useful ways, to perfect methods that are appropriate for task research, and to relate increased task-related knowledge to educational and applied activities.

Some ways in which tasks relate to other variables in the conceptual framework are suggested in the following linkages. *Linkage 4.1.2: Tasks affect personality.* The task of electoral campaigning in American politics, for example, requires that candidate leaders shake hands with as many potential voters as possible. This can lead, among other things, to a crushed, mangled, painful hand. The discomfort of extensive handshaking was important enough to be mentioned in Sorensen's biography of Kennedy.[99] A more severe example is the exacerbation of Ché Guevara's asthma by the tough revolutionary campaign in Bolivia.[100] Tasks can affect body chemistry as well: a candidate for the Hawaii state legislature in 1972 told me, for example, that for image purposes he gave up two of his favorite indulgences for the course of the campaign—drinking beer and smoking cigars. *Linkage 4.2.2: Tasks affect the expansion or contraction of role rights and obligations.* Students of the American presidency have noted that tasks related to fighting two world wars and to the growing pressures of international relations have markedly strengthened the role of the presidency. This expanded capacity, they suggest, has then been extended into domestic tasks. As explained by Rossiter, "the more deeply a nation becomes involved in the affairs of other nations, the more powerful becomes its executive branch."[101] As a further illustration, Lewis reported that among Alaskan Eskimo the task of hunting places the hunt leader in a "more or less long-term position as leader in other contexts"; whereas among Plains Indians, "who are evidently loath to take orders, the authority of the hunt leader is clearly limited to the summer hunt."[102] *Linkage 4.3.2: Tasks affect the scope of organizational involvement.* Campaigning American politicians appreciate this relationship well and seek to associate themselves with tasks-issues having broad appeal rather than those that do not. Jerome Kretchmer, environmental protection administrator for New York City, said in 1971, for example, that "he would not mind riding a garbage truck all the way to City Hall." He further explained, "[Pollution control is] not as difficult to deal with as schools, welfare, drugs. . . . It really affects everybody, so it lends itself to solution because of its universality."[103] *Linkage 4.5.1: Tasks evoke related values.* Studies of international crises have suggested that crisis clarifies values and makes latent values manifest. It is probable that this process was involved in 1962, when Robert F. Kennedy "passionately" resisted a recommendation that the United States launch a surprise "surgical" air attack to remove Soviet missiles from Cuba, with the declaration that there should be no American "Pearl Harbor": "My brother is not going to be the Tojo of the 1960's."[104] *Linkage 4.6.1: Tasks shape setting characteristics.* The tasks of industrialization and preparation for industrial warfare, for example, have been related to depletion of energy and other natural resources and to pollution of the natural environment. The tasks of fund raising in the American competitive electoral system have been related to the structure of the economic system and to the position of large political donors within it. And military needs for communication and mobility have resulted in perfecting such politically useful technologies as walkie-talkies (small, portable, two-way radios) and helicopters. Tasks of mass, secret, accurate balloting have led to the invention of voting machines and the development of computer programs to ensure fast, accurate counts.

A reversal of influences upon task as a dependent variable is also to be expected. This is illustrated by *Linkage 1.4.2: Personality variation even within the same leader tends to influence task definition and engagement.* Three examples suggest the influence of aging upon task selection. Hitler reportedly told British ambassador Henderson in 1939 that "he was now fifty; therefore if war had to come, it was better that it should come now than when he was fifty-five or even sixty years old."[105] Ché Guevara wrote in his diary in 1967, "I have reached thirty-nine, and inexorably the age is approaching which forces me to think of my future as a guerrilla fighter; however, for the time being, I am sound."[106] A U.S. senator told Matthews, "I'll be perfectly frank with you. Being active on as wide a range of issues as I have been is a man-killing job. In a few years I suspect that I will be active on many fewer issues. I came down here as a young man and I'm gradually petering out."[107] *Linkage 2.4.2: Role properties influence the adequacy with which certain types of tasks can be pursued.* It is often argued, for example, that the short two-, four-, or six-year tenure of most elected American political leaders has two effects upon incumbent task engagement: it directs incumbent energies toward reelection and position maintenance tasks and away from constructive problem-solving tasks; also, it leads to short-range versus long-range planning and action.[108] *Linkage 3.4.2: The more the functional differentiation of organizations to correspond with salient task characteristics, the more the task-coping success.* In 1972, Joseph Napolitan, an experienced professional adviser to candidates for major elected offices in the United States, suggested that the following organization would enhance electoral success: a campaign manager, a television producer, a radio producer, a radio announcer, a graphics specialist, a media time buyer, a television coach, a polling firm, an issues group, a press-media staff, an advance team, a scheduling secretary, an office manager, a finance manager, a constituencywide director of organization with a network of local chairpersons, troubleshooters, a private secretary, a receptionist and/or switchboard operator, and liaison persons with special interest groups.[109] The usefulness of a professional campaign consultant, of course, was taken for granted. *Linkage 5.4.1: Values can inhibit task identification and engagement.* An example is provided by the inability of British governments under prime ministers Sir Robert Peal and Lord John Russell to define and implement appropriate measures to cope with the Irish potato famine of 1845–1849. The historian Cecil Woodham-Smith attributed much of their ineffectiveness to "the fanatical faith of mid-nineteenth century British politicians in the economic doctrine of laissez faire, no interference by government, no meddling with the operation of natural causes."[110] A contemporary example was Chicago mayor Daley's "bootstrap theory" of self-advancement of ethnic minorities, which he based on past upward mobility of certain ethnic groups and which has inhibited more positive action to help Chicago's black population.[111] *Linkage 6.4.1: Variations in setting factors create propensities for some tasks rather than others to be more salient.* For example, lack of natural resources creates exceptional tasks of managing societal interdependence; burgeoning urban populations create extraordinarily pressing tasks of providing water, food, housing, sanitation, police, fire, and other services; polluting industrial technology makes imperative the task of modifying or abandoning such technology; and the division of formerly united nations makes salient the tasks of reintegration or mutually tolerable coexistence.

5. VALUES

As Alfred G. Meyer succinctly reminded us, "All political action demands choice, which is based on a system of values."[112] Values are taken to be standards that influence choices among, and commitments to, "modes of conduct" and "end-states of existence." As explained by Rokeach:

> To say that a person "has a value" is to say that he [or she] has an enduring belief that a specific mode of conduct or end-state of existence is personally and socially preferable to alternative modes of conduct or end-states of existence. Once a value is internalized it becomes, consciously or unconsciously, a standard or criterion for guiding action, for developing and maintaining attitudes toward relevant objects, and situations, for justifying one's own and others' actions and attitudes, for morally judging self and others and for comparing oneself with others. Finally, a value is a standard employed to influence the values, attitudes, and actions of at least some others; for example, our children's.[113]

Rokeach, after other contemporary social scientists, has distinguished two types of values: *instrumental values* (stated as "I believe that such-and-such a mode of conduct [e.g., honesty, courage] is personally and socially preferable in all situations with respect to all objects") and *terminal values* (expressed in the form "I believe that such-and-such an end-state of existence [e.g., salvation, a world at peace] is personally and socially worth striving for").[114] I should like to add a third type of value—the idea of an *intrinsic value*. This is defined by the statement that "I believe that such a social or physical object or condition is good, beautiful, just (or bad, ugly, unjust, etc.) regardless of whether it is a means or an end and without prejudging the permanence or ephemerality of either the object or this evaluation.

In a value content analysis of the writings of four political leaders—Norman Thomas, Lenin, Goldwater, and Hitler—Rokeach showed that they expressed distinctively different patterns of reference to the values of "freedom" and "equality." For Thomas (socialist), the values of "freedom" and "equality" were both highly salient. For Hitler (fascist), they were both found to be low. Lenin (communist) cited equality over freedom. Goldwater (conservative) emphasized freedom over equality.[115] To this very suggestive beginning we need to add other values of special political relevance; for example, value orientations toward *violence* or *nonviolence*.

Challenging the thesis that the late twentieth century is witnessing the "end of ideology," Rokeach has provided evidence that even a single value may be a good predictor of other behavior. For example, he found rank ordering of belief in "salvation" to be a good predictor of church attendance.[116] The apparent lack of explicit value commitments by elites in modern industrial societies, the decline of traditional values, should not blind social scientists in those societies to their importance, historically or in other societies. No "end of ideology" is implied by Fidel Castro's declaration "I prefer to die riddled with bullets than to live humiliated"[117] or Ho Chi Minh's adoption of the French revolutionary slogan "I'd rather die as a free man than live as a slave."[118]

Following the pioneering political science studies of values by McCloskey and associates,[119] Jacob and colleagues,[120] Putnam,[121] and others, a principal task of political leadership studies should be to focus sharply upon the nature of, and effect of values upon, political leadership behavior. We will wish to gain penetrating insight into values that are intimately operative in leader behavior as well as those that are of a more remote, ex post facto rationalizing quality. Hoping to reduce conflict we should not ignore values that imply sharp, even deadly, contention; or being fascinated with conflict, we should not be blind to values that imply opportunities for consensus and peaceful cooperation. We will have to be prepared to view leaders as value creators as well as consumers, actively engaged in value controversies as well as neutral, patrons as well as persecutors, critics as well as confirmers, and consistent as well as committed to the value of inconsistency. Among analytical aspects of political leadership values that will require investigation will be substance, salience, direction, intensity, scope, interconnectedness, compatibility, conflict, change and stability. Values operative at different stages of a leader's career will be of special interest: aspiration, ascendancy, decline, and disengagement.

We will also wish to investigate if and how leader values influence their behavior in relation to such questions as control of the leadership position, concentration versus dispersal of leadership functions, survival of politically significant entities, tolerance of criticism and competition, centralization versus decentralization, conservation versus change, scope of follower participation, equality versus inequality, violence versus nonviolence, and autonomy versus interdependence. We need not only to foresee such value relevancies in advance but also to be open to their discovery in the course of empirical inquiry. Overall, students of political leadership should be aware that explicit concern with the concept of "values" will provide them with a potential linkage of importance with such general overviews of politics as Easton's "authoritative allocation of values" and Ilchman's "new political economy."[122] In addition, the concept of values provides an explicit opportunity to link political leadership studies with law, religion, philosophy, and esthetics, as well as with more conventional political science interests in political theories, philosophies, and ideologies.

Linkages between values and other variables include *Linkage 5.1.2: Values sometimes cause behavior that is incongruent with that predicted from socioeconomic status characteristics of a personality.* Sorensen wrote of Senator John F. Kennedy, "He consistently voted—on oil and gas interests, for example—against his own (and his father's) pocketbook."[123] A more radical example is provided by the revolutionary Fidel Castro, whose father was "a *latifundista,* a wealthy landowner, who exploited the peasants."[124] Still another striking example is provided by Nobutaka Ike's observation that in the purposive "modernization" of Japan after 1868, "the new [Meiji] regime, although controlled by men of samurai origin, decided to liquidate the samurai class."[125]

Linkage 5.2.2: Deeply held values in other sectors of society may influence definitions of rights and obligations of political leadership roles. A common source of definition has been the means-ends values associated with the image of the military commander. As Bullock explained, "It was from the Army that [Hitler] took the *Führerprinzip;* the Leadership principle, upon which first the Nazi Party, and later the National Socialist State, were built."[126] As defined by Reichstag law:

> The Führer must have all the rights demanded by him to achieve victory. Therefore—without being bound by existing legal regulations—in his capacity as Leader of the Nation, Supreme Commander of the Armed Forces, Head of Government and supreme executive chief, as Supreme Justice and Leader of the Party—the Führer must be in a position to force with all the means at his disposal, every German, if necessary, whether he be common soldier or officer, low or high official, or judge, leading or subordinate official of the Party, worker or employer, to fulfil his duties. In case of violation of these duties the Führer is entitled, regardless of rights, to mete out punishment and remove the offender from his post, rank, and position without introducing prescribed procedures.[127]

Other potential sources historically have been those of religious chief, senior farmer, industrial manager, or even, as in the classical Chinese ideal, scholar.

Linkage 5.3.2: Values influence the membership, structure, and tolerated influence of organizations. Values influence both inclusion and exclusion. Concern for civil rights led Congressman John F. Kennedy to become the first member of Congress from New England to add a black person to his staff.[128] Later, as president, he had a rule, violated at least once, that he would appoint no defeated politician to his cabinet.[129] On structural questions, Lenin, for example, insisted on a "tightly knit party of professional revolutionaries who gave not only their loyalty and sympathy, as the Mensheviks would have preferred, but all their time too to political work and who, therefore, were to function as soldiers and officers in an army under a single command."[130] Analogously, according to Fischer, "Lenin always rejected guerrilla fighting. He preferred tightly organized firmly disciplined military formations under central control."[131] And in deciding not to give Soviet artists an independent potential political influence outside party control, Lenin reflected the value position he had expressed in 1905: "Down with literary supermen!"[132]

Linkage 5.4.2: Terminal values may be employed to justify the application of contrary instrumental values in interim task engagement. In *State and Revolution*, Lenin justified violent means by nonviolent ends.

> We set ourselves the aim of destroying the state, that is every organized and systematic violence, every use of violence against man in general. . . . But striving. for socialism, we are convinced that it will develop into communism; that, side by side with this, there will vanish all need for force, for the *subjection* of one man to another, and of one part of the population to another since people will *grow accustomed* to observing the elementary conditions *without force* and *without subjection.*[133]

On the other hand, some ends-values may be completely compatible with means employed in task execution, as in Hitler's dedication to anti-Semitism and German nationalism.

Linkage 5.6.1: Values influence the scope of perceived setting relevancies. An example is found in the constant polemic between nationalism and internationalism in the history of twentieth-century political thought. For some thinkers, national interests and thus national conditions are paramount. For others, concern for such values as world peace, economic welfare, justice, and ecosurvival lead to global imagination and associated empirical analysis.

Values can also be seen as affected by other variables as in *Linkage 1.5.2: Personalities vary in the intensity of their value commitments and thus in the operative force of such values.* Trotsky, known as a "merciless disciplinarian," once had a regimental commander and a political commissar executed for moving troops without instructions. Other Bolshevik leaders considered this action too severe but were overruled by Lenin, who expressed complete support for Trotsky.[134] In writing of the Cuban Revolution, Matthews recalled that "the most precious of all revolutionary qualities, loyalty, has its inescapable counterpart in treachery."[135] The fate of all political movements in crisis depends in large part upon the personal commitments of adherents. *Linkage 2.5.2: Aspirant roles, as compared with incumbent roles, tend to evoke variation in the quality and/or relative intensity of associated values.* Fischer, for example, compared Lenin as a revolutionary and as later head of state: "As a writer, propagandist, and thinker before the revolution, Lenin was never inductive. He was deductive. He accepted truth as handed down by Marx and selected data and arguments to bolster that truth. . . . As a statesman, Lenin observed, weighed, and reasoned and arrived at decisions on the basis of reality." Fischer further explained that this was because "a revolution denies experience, denies existing conditions."[136]

Linkage 3.5.2: Organizational structures can restrict or expand variations in values. In a discussion with Clara Zetkin of political influences upon the arts,

Lenin once explained that the Soviet state would remove Russian artists from the pernicious influences of the tsarist court and the private market to the protective support of state commissions under party supervision. Lenin further explained that the criteria for support should be that art "must be loved and understood" by workers and peasants. Thus, in order not to allow artistic "chaos," Lenin insisted upon the "partyness" of art and objected to the creation of a cultural commission independent of direct party control.[137]

Linkage 4.5.2: The more crucial the task for the maintenance of position power, the more probable the deviation from positive values and deception to conceal such deviation. In the period prior to the Nazi assault upon Poland in 1939, Hitler told his generals, "I shall give a propagandist reason for starting the war, no matter whether it is plausible or not. The victor will not be asked afterwards whether he told the truth or not. When starting and waging war it is not right that matters, but victory."[138] In July 1918, on the eve of a violent left Social Revolutionary party revolt against Bolshevik rule, Lenin told the Fifth All-Russian Congress of Worker, Peasant, and Red Army Deputies: "For Russia the time is gone, irrevocably gone, I am sure, when people debate socialist programs according to the books."[139] An experienced veteran of Chicago elections told Mike Royko, "A good precinct captain will always find a way to steal votes."[140]

Linkage 6.5.1: Objective-setting conditions create propensities for certain values to become salient in leader behavior. For Lenin's Russia these conditions in 1917 were administrative breakdown, war, hunger, and tenancy that led to the slogans "All Power to the Soviets," and "Peace, Bread, and Land." For Hitler's Germany, these conditions included defeat in war resulting in loss of territories, unemployment, and racial prejudice that led to value emphasis upon re-armament, lebensraum (living space), industrial production, and anti-Semitism. In China, a century of foreign humiliation, peasant suffering, and bureaucratic decline plus warlord upsurgence provided the conditions for Sun Yat Sen's affirmation of the values of "nationalism," "socialism," and "democracy," which were subsequently expressed in revolutionary action by Mao Tse-tung's Communist party under such value slogans as "anti-[Soviet] revisionism," the "people's communes," and the "people's democratic dictatorship."

These considerations lead to a fuller discussion of setting as the last of the primary variables in the conceptual framework.

6. SETTING

Political leadership takes place in, is conditioned by, affects, and is affected by its environment. Thus, a major challenge facing political leadership studies is to determine which partial aspects of an environment or which total configurations of environmental characteristics are causally related to political leadership behavior.

Scholarly interest in setting characteristics as related to leadership behavior has a parallel in the investigations of political leaders themselves. Fischer reported, for example, that Lenin in 1893, exiled in Samara at age twenty-three, commissioned a study of village life along the Volga that required answers to numerous queries on 200–250 questionnaires that provided materials for subsequent analytical articles written the next year in St. Petersburg.[141] Mao Tsetung in 1927 carried out a month-long inquiry into rural life in five counties of his native province of Hunan that contributed to his famous "Report of an Investigation into the Peasant Movement in Hunan."[142] Jomo Kenyatta, later prime minister of Kenya, published in 1938 a study of the tribal life of his native Gikuyu tribe; he conducted the study under the guidance of anthropologist B. Malinowski.[143] Thus, some political leaders have shown themselves to be unusually keen students of setting characteristics.

The term "setting" is being employed as a symbol of the environment; it is taken to have six principal aspects: natural physical aspects, manmade physical and technological aspects, economic aspects, social aspects, cultural aspects, and patterns of associated events. The idea of setting may fruitfully link political leadership studies with relevant aspects of such fields as geography, technology, economics, demography, sociology, and cultural anthropology. In its holistic concern, the concept of setting also provides a linkage with all disciplines, conceptual frameworks, or theoretical efforts that seek to describe and explain total configurations[144] of interrelated elements. Contemporary examples are provided by history, general systems theory,[145] and efforts to study total societies.[146]

Often, setting configurations in Western social science have been hypothesized to unfold in some form of linear progression based upon economic productivity. Examples are the Marxist vision of progression from primitive communism to feudalism, capitalism, socialism, and communism; Organski's portrayal of the "stages of political development" from primitive unification to industrialization, national welfare, and abundance;[147] and the futurist projections of Tateisi and others of societal change from a "primitive" stage through "collective, agricultural, handicraft, industrialized, mechanized, automated, cybernetic, optimized, and autonomous" stages into a "natural" society, spanning the period from 1000 M.B.C. to after A.D. 2033.[148]

A recent sharp challenge to such images, however, is the "world model of limits to growth" developed through computer simulations of conditions in the period 1975–2100 by Meadows, Meadows, Randers, and Behrens.[149] They have argued that unless exponential population growth, capital investment, and resource utilization can be purposively limited to equilibrium conditions, then the world prior to the year 2100 will see disastrous breakdowns produced by the interacting deleterious effects of population explosion, declining food per capita, increased industrial output per capita, increased pollution, and exhaustion of natural resources. These equilibrium conditions are defined as a situation in which births equal deaths, creation of renewable resources equals depletion of nonrenewable resources, and investment equals depreciation.

Another conceptualization of setting that portrays human social inter-actions, or "interfaces," with interdependent aspects of the physical environ-ment has been suggested by Nunn, as shown in Figure 3.

The introduction of setting variables into political leadership studies is thus of exceptional importance. We will want to know how political leadership behavior tends to promote change in setting characteristics and how changes in these variables in turn affect factors related to political leadership.

A major hypothesis to be investigated by students of political leadership is the Marxist insight that *variations in the ownership and modes of production of goods and services produce both characteristic patterns of predominant political leadership behavior and patterns of conventional or revolutionary challenges to that leadership—both within and across societies.* The corpus of Marxist social science writings, plus the extensions of Lenin, Mao, and others need to be systematically reviewed to identify more specific hypotheses about leadership

FIGURE 3. Human Interfaces with the Environment

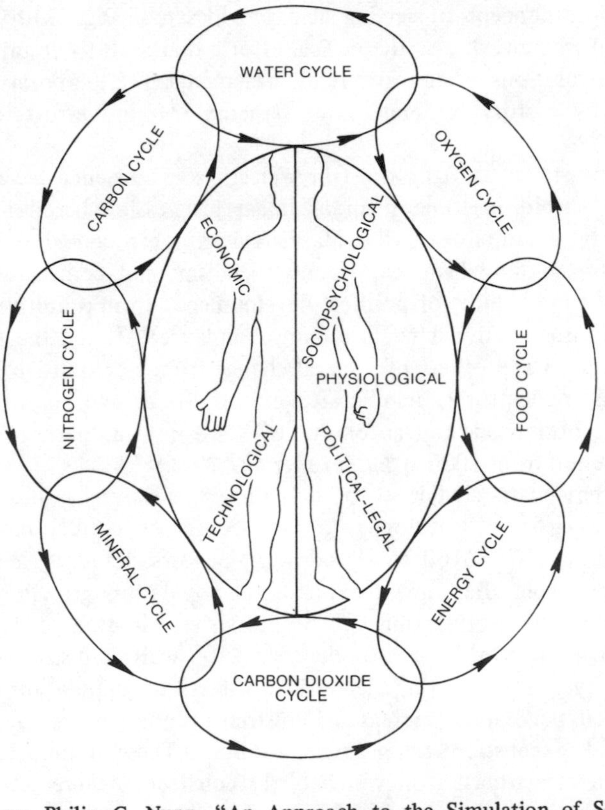

Source: Philip C. Nunn, "An Approach to the Simulation of Social Systems," *Simulation Today*, no. 14 (n.d.), p. 54. Reprinted by permission of the Society for Computer Simulation (Simulation Councils, Inc.).

behavior that can be tested in "precapitalist," "capitalist," "socialist," and other economic settings.[150] We will also wish to explore systematically the reverse hypothesis that *purposive political leadership initiatives make critical contributions to the creation, operation, and change of systems of economic ownership and production.*

As the following brief exploration of setting linkages suggests, however, there are aspects of the environment, sometimes surprising ones, besides economic variables of ownership, production, and distribution, that seem to offer promising lines of investigation. Among these aspects can be included such things as physical "beauty," territorial size, boundedness, natural resource presence-absence, population size-composition-distribution-mobility, economic inequality, urbanization, literacy, communications and transportation technologies, permeable-impermeable caste-class stratification systems, nuclear versus extended kinship systems, ethnic and religious homogeneity-heterogeneity, societal integration-disintegration, structure of relative autonomy versus dependence, conflict characteristics, and relative degrees of societal change.

One conceptual relationship of interest is *Linkage 6.1.2: Physical environments can affect the emotional tone of leader personalities.* Recalling his guerrilla days in the Boconó mountain zone, the Venezuelan revolutionary Teodoro Petkoff noted that "although this is not politically very important [!], it had very majestic mountain scenery, *that uplifted one's spirit* [emphasis added], especially when I compare it with the desolate mountains of Falcón State where we organized the guerrillas in 1962–63."[151] The idea that political leaders are linked to physical terrain is rooted deep in human experience. Lucy Mair wrote, for example: "Whereas Nilotic kings take their origins from rivers, the most conspicuous natural features of their flat country, the legends of a mountainous Ruanda and hilly Buganda depict the first kings as falling from heaven on a hill top."[152] Erasmus, in *The Education of a Christian Prince,* advised, "The prince should love the land over which he rules just as a farmer loves the fields of his ancestors or as a good man feels affection toward his household."[153] Weather, too, may exacerbate revolutionary emotions. After a comparative study of several revolutions, Emilio Casal concluded that "the wildest excesses take place on days on which the weather is particularly unbearable."[154]

Linkage 6.2.2: Under conditions of relative freedom of political expression, variation in socioeconomic and cultural setting characteristics is likely to be expressed in correlated political leadership roles. In a study of the backgrounds of Japanese Diet members, for example, Nishikawa discovered that legislators from different parties differed in their pre-Diet careers. Stated in terms of the most frequent previous career characteristic, conservatives came from "proprietor-manager backgrounds"; socialists had been "labor union officials"; and communists emerged from the ranks of "party officials."[155]

Linkage 6.3.2: Communications and transportation technologies influence the scope, structure, and quality of organizational interaction. Some examples include pioneering political uses of the *telephone* by William McKinley, who used it to undercut local bosses;[156] the *train* by Theodore Roosevelt, who was the first to make a nationwide railroad campaign tour, speaking directly to 3 million persons—and afterward requiring treatment by a throat specialist;[157] the electric *loudspeaker* by Warren G. Harding, who first used it to address inaugural crowds;[158] campaign *films* by Senator Robert M. La Follette and by Adolf Hitler;[159] the *automobile* by Huey Long, who successfully broke a Louisiana political taboo—"Never campaign in a car among country people; they will resent it as a pretense of superiority and vote against you";[160] the *airplane* by Hitler in his Goebbels-inspired "Hitler over Germany" electoral campaign of 1933;[161] the *radio* by Hitler and by Franklin D. Roosevelt to create simultaneous emotional rapport with and among millions of listeners;[162] *television* by John F. Kennedy in campaign debate, news conferences, and special programs designed to strengthen popular support;[163] and the *jet plane* and *helicopter* by Kennedy and by his successor, Lyndon B. Johnson, which extended both range and mobility and created new needs for "advance men" in personal political campaigning.[164] Overall, these technologies have provided opportunities for more widespread and temporally immediate leader-follower interactions, reaching toward a global scale. We need to try to understand what political leadership must have been like when *none* of the above technologies was available as compared with the present era, in which *all* are available. We need also to ask what future leader-technology interactions are desirable and possible.

Linkage 6.4.2: Setting characteristics influence task definition. The Russian famine of 1921–1922, for example, presented Lenin in his role of national leader with the task of obtaining food for his people. Previously he had said of famine, "You capitalists cannot eliminate it, but we can."[165] However, with 35 million people hungry, authenticated cases of cannibalism,[166] and orphans begging and turning to crime, Lenin defined the task as requiring the importation of food and the acceptance of aid from capitalist sources, demonstrating value flexibility quite unlike the rigidity that had impeded British efforts to cope with the Irish famine of 1839–1840. After seizing power in primarily agricultural Cuba, Fidel Castro defined the mastery of agricultural problems, the establishment of government control, and the increasing of production, especially of sugar, as "the central task of the Revolution."[167]

Linkage 6.5.2: Setting characteristics contribute to the definition of salient social values. A striking illustration of this linkage is provided by the symbolism of the national seal and flag of the dry, agricultural, cattle-herding, and newly industrializing black-majority African nation of Botswana (1972 population: 620,000). The seal contains representations of water, agriculture, cattle, and industry, as well as wildlife. The five-striped flag has a wide horizontal black stripe in the middle, symbolizing the black majority, paralleled above and below by narrower white stripes that signify the nation's racial minority;

broad blue stripes at top and bottom stand for sky and water. This drought-plagued nation's motto is "Pula"—"Let There Be Rain."[168]

Setting characteristics can lead to the emergence and reinforcement of countervalues as well as those that are congruent with existing conditions. As explained by Herbert L. Matthews:

> When Fidel Castro and his even younger associates came into power they looked around and then back at their history. They saw the social imbalances—the few wealthy and the many poor, the unending, shameless corruption, the tragic farce that their Cuban variety of democracy and their so-called democratic elections represented; the capitalism that enriched a small minority and left the majority in misery; the domination of their economy and their very system of life by the United States, a foreign power; and they said, "If this is democracy and capitalism, we don't want them."[169]

Again, the other components of the framework can be seen as influencing setting characteristics. *Linkage 1.6.2: Personalities affect setting characteristics.* Indonesian president Sukarno, for example, had little interest in population limitation through family planning; his successor, President Suharto (1967–), however, gave it a high priority, with the result that purposive efforts to slow the rapid rate of Indonesia's population growth began to be made.[170] Analogously, Korean president Syngman Rhee (1948–1960), who had been an anti-Japanese revolutionary exile, refused to regularize diplomatic, trade, and investment relations with Japan; his successor, Chung Hee Park (1961–), who had served as a pre-1945 Japanese imperial army officer, agreed in the mid-1960s to the "normalization" of diplomatic relations with Japan, which was accompanied by marked changes in the Republic of Korea's domestic and international economic relationships. Changes in a single incumbent personality, of course, can be correlated with setting change: Mao Tse-tung, for example, changed from a negative to a positive position on population limitation, which reversed Chinese public policy on this subject.[171]

Linkage 2.6.2: The more the role power to influence economic development decisions, the greater the effects upon the setting. Candidates in Hawaii's 1974 gubernatorial election, for example, debated whether it was better to invest the governor (and legislature) of the state with more authority over statewide land use and other developmental planning or whether it was better to seek decentralized strengthening of the positions of the four mayors (and councils) who lead the state's component counties.[172] This debate called attention to the scope of role power and its structural location in relation to vulnerability to private economic pressures.

Linkage 3.6.2: The greater the organizational size, heterogeneity of composition, functional differentiation of subunits, disciplined structure, and resources, the greater the influence upon the setting. In most contemporary nations, national governments, as the largest formal organization, have the greatest influence upon the physical features, economic system, social structure, and cultural qualities of a society. The influence of political leaders upon the setting is amplified or diminished by these large national bureaucracies. In addition, recently it is being argued that large multinational corporations are both markedly affecting the environment and limiting the ability of national political leaders to control their behavior.

Linkage 4.6.2: Tasks vary in their setting relevancies. The leadership tasks of gaining power and revolutionary transformation of society seem to be the most demanding of total setting knowledge, influence, and responsiveness. In regard to the task of winning a peaceful electoral competition, the importance of gaining detailed knowledge of the constituency is repeatedly emphasized by experienced leaders.[173] In solving the problems of revolutionary guerrilla war, the importance of the setting in all its aspects becomes strikingly evident. As reported by Regis Debray, Fidel Castro gave "meticulous and almost obsessive attention . . . to the smallest concrete detail of preparation for the most minor action [including] the placing of fighters in an ambush operation; the number of bullets issued to each one; the path to be taken; the preparation and testing of mines; the inspection of provisions; etc."[174]

Linkage 5.6.2: Values are connected with the reinforcement or transformation of setting characteristics. The most striking mid-twentieth-century examples are to be found in the divided nations of China, Germany, Korea, and Vietnam, in which divergent physical, economic, social, and cultural conditions have resulted from the purposive pursuit of different ideas about desired ends and acceptable means. In these nations, competitive versions of "capitalist" and "socialist" societies have been constructed.

Leadership as a Complex Set of Interacting Variables

As illustrated by the foregoing linkage statements, political leadership needs to be thought of as the product of a complex set of mutually interdependent factors. But, complex as the above may appear, it is undoubtedly too crude to describe and explain political leadership in a fully satisfactory way. Thus, continuing conceptual efforts are essential both to clarify components of the present framework and to create necessary alternatives to it. Eventually, every single component must be rigorously operationalized, measured, and empirically tested. However crude and undramatic the present conceptual effort may be, it is not clear that it will be less helpful to the future development of political science than our present images of the knowing "king," wily "prince," inspiring "charismatic" figure, deal-making "politician," and dominant "elite." At least it provides an explicit multivariate statement under which the components of these earlier images may be subsumed. At most it will help to stimulate the creation of better concepts and linkages leading ultimately to hypotheses, propositions, and laws.

In addition to the concepts and linkages that have been presented, it is important to underscore the importance of placing the subject of political leadership within a larger framework of societal change. Because political change has been an ancient concern and because high rates of setting change can be expected[175] on a global scale in the foreseeable future, it is imperative that political leadership studies be approached within a framework of imagination that encompasses past change, present change, and alternative future potentials for change.[176] Among cyclical, linear, and dialectical models of leadership change that merit rediscovery and fresh examination are those of Polybius (monarchy / kingship / tyranny / aristocracy / oligarchy / democracy / rule by force and violence / monarchy, etc.),[177] Hertzler (breakdown / rising dictator / coup / conquest / entrenchment / decline / overthrow / restoration or innovation / breakdown, etc.),[178] Pareto (lions / foxes / lions / foxes, etc.)[179] and Marx and Lenin (slave masters / feudal lords / capitalist bourgeoisie / proletarians / communists).[180] We might add observed oscillations in some contemporary nations between military and civilian party rule.

A promising change model yet to be fully articulated and explored is one that might be termed a diffusion-of-example model, whereby innovations in leadership styles, policies, and roles themselves become stimuli for imitative behavior that spreads by processes of cognitive recognition, emotional identification, and material reinforcement both horizontally and vertically across leadership roles within and across polities. Such changes can be viewed as part of a multidimensional macroprocess of social learning within and across total societies.

In summary, it is important to recall that the patterns of interaction described by the six component variables are conceived as producing (1) patterns of leadership behavior capable of typological description, (2) measurable effects upon the functioning of total polities, component institutions, processes, and other subjects of specialized political science concern, and (3) variance in the functioning of political systems conceived at the highest levels of abstraction (or greatest scope of empirical application). Thus, the conceptual problem of political leadership studies is to identify and link primary causal variables with patterns of concrete leadership behavior that are then viewed as linked to each important subject of political science concern.

One way of recalling the anticipatory variables that have been explored here—and one example of their apparent "fit" with social reality—is contained in the brief statement by an experienced political leader that began this chapter. Said Mayor Ford, "I [*personality*] use the office of mayor [*role*] to attain my goal [*task*] of getting jobs and resources [*values*] for my people [*organization*]"—to which we need add only a reference to *setting* (Tuskegee, Alabama, United States of America, 1973), which implies also certain institutional and systemic characteristics.

Having explored some multivariate linkages, we now approach the analysis of leadership in relation to multiple dimensions of political behavior.

CHAPTER 6

A MULTIVARIATE, MULTIDIMENSIONAL LINKAGE APPROACH: DIMENSIONS

A writer almost always presents one aspect of a case, whereas every case can be seen from no less than seven points of view, all of which are probably correct in themselves, but not correct at the same time and in the same circumstances.[1]

MOHANDAS K. GANDHI
1927

THE GROWING EFFORT to concentrate disciplinary attention upon the study of political leadership poses a major challenge to seek ways to relate leadership behavior to general conceptions of the nature of a political system. What are the most significant political attributes to which the study of political leadership should be related? This would be an easy question to answer if there were a single, commonly accepted paradigm for what we mean by a political system, operationally identifiable, and having a verified set of empirical relationships. At present, there is no such paradigm, at least not one fully articulated at the theoretical level, empirically verified, and commonly accepted by political scientists. As explored briefly in Chapter 2, what we do have are a number of major intellectual efforts to explicate such a paradigm. They constitute important advances toward creating a set of concepts and specifying relationships among them that would permit us satisfyingly to describe, explain, predict, evaluate, and affect political behavior. These are the principal political science concerns with power, decision making, cybernetics, value allocation, structural-functionalism, political economy, and other approaches, including Marxism-Leninism.[2] Faced with a problem of political analysis, the political scientist customarily draws eclectically, explicitly or implicitly, from several of these.

Students of political leadership thus simultaneously must grapple with two tasks of enormous difficulty: to clarify a useful approach to the idea of

133

"leadership" and to clarify and relate this approach to a satisfying concept of the "political." Both tasks call for reduction of high levels of ambiguity.

The present chapter seeks to engage disciplinary imagination in the latter task. Its shortcomings will be readily apparent. It will not satisfy all or even most political scientists. As is true for the discipline itself, its aspirations outrun its accomplishments. But even with this special sense of shortcoming it is offered as a stimulus to scientific advancement.

Basic Tasks

The questions to which this chapter seeks to draw attention and to evoke collegial problem-solving contributions are many. What is the minimum set of "dimensions" of political behavior to which the study of political leadership should be related? What criteria should underlie the definition and selection of these dimensions? How are these dimensions to be measured? What relationships exist among them? What theoretical construct unites the analytically created dimensions in the way that natural political behavior free of scientific analysis constitutes an undifferentiated whole? Finally, how are these dimensions to be related to the multivariate determinants and patterns of leadership behavior explored in Chapter 5? Even though these questions are incompletely answered here, they constitute an ongoing challenge to political leadership studies. In trying to answer them, students of political leadership will constantly draw from core scientific understandings about the nature of politics and may gradually contribute to the emergence of an integrated approach to political understanding.

Paradigmatic Indicators of Multidimensionality

We begin and end with the idea that political leadership behavior is multi-dimensional. This is suggested by the emergence of alternative paradigms for political analysis that stress certain aspects of political behavior more than others. It is suggested also by the pragmatic eclecticism of political scientists faced with practical problems of inquiry. Since no approach seems completely satisfying, elements are drawn from other approaches until a greater sense of adequacy is achieved. For example, contemporary definitions customarily link the ideas of "power," "authoritative decision," and "value allocation," while tacitly assuming the effects of cybernetic social learning, structural and functional variation, and deliberate political entrepreneurship under conditions of class or other social conflict.

This suggests that there is nothing inherently "wrong" with the presently existing, partly competing, and partly overlapping paradigms in political science. Political behavior is characterized by coercive and persuasive force (power), public policy and voting choice (decision making), information-based innovation and social learning (cybernetics), conflicts over the distribution of material and symbolic values (value allocation, political economy, and Marxism-Leninism), and organizational variation related to performance of political system needs (structural-functionalism). They are all reasonable portrayals of partial analytical aspects of political behavior as a whole. They suggest that an adequate treatment of political leadership should take account of the things to which they call attention. In short, they suggest that politics is multidimensional.

Political leadership studies may draw upon each paradigm for dimensional insight, may independently pose puzzles for paradigmatic solution, and may contribute through its multidimensional perspective to political science progress.

Idea of a Dimension: Power, Affect, Instrumentality

By dimension is meant an analytical aspect of a variable that is shared across variables; in effect, a dimension is a cross-variable variable. In terms of the present multivariate linkage approach a dimension is an analytical aspect of behavior that cuts across all six variables or that characterizes the patterns of leadership behavior that are hypothesized to be the result of the interactions among those variables.

As examples of dimensions, consider the three aspects of behavior to which behavioral and social scientists have repeatedly called attention in slightly different terms but with a strong sense of convergent validation. For purposes of illustration we may call them the "power," "affective," and "instrumental" dimensions of social behavior. They are suggested by characterizations of personality in terms of needs for power, affiliation, and achievement; portrayals of small group leadership needs for solving problems of authority, emotion, and task accomplishment; characterizations of social structures as predominantly coercive, emotionally expressive, or functionally utilitarian; and analyses of language in terms of imperative, emotive, and cognitive modes of discourse. From these examples we can see that the dimensions of power, affect, and instrumentality cut across the variables/social objects of persons, small groups, larger social structures, and components of cultural systems.

Addressing ourselves to the present multivariate approach, we can inquire into the power, affective, and instrumental aspects of personality, role, organization, task, values, and setting—and of conservative, reformist, and revolutionary patterns of political leadership behavior. The cross-variable correlates of each dimension are heuristically suggested in Figure 4 (p. 136). At the center of the diagram is a point designated "political leadership," which indicates the undifferentiated wholeness to which all analytical distinctions apply.

Interpreting these dimensions in relation to the component variables, we can ask how the power, affective, and instrumental characteristics of personalities interact with those of roles, organizations, tasks, values, and settings. We can ask what the overall power, affective, and instrumental loadings on these variables are as well as question the relative power, affective, and instrumental characteristics of the resulting patterns of conservative, reformist, or revolutionary leadership behavior.

By imagining that each of the seven rings (leadership style plus six predictor variables) can rotate, for each dimension three ideal-type dimensional configurations can be hypothesized: complete congruence, as portrayed in Figure 4, where there is perfect alignment or compatibility across variables on the given dimension; partial congruence, where alignment occurs across two or more variables; and complete incongruence, where no variables on a given dimension are interconnected.

With respect to relationships among the three dimensions, some kind of balance theory (or imbalance theory) of a predictive and potentially prescriptive nature might be employed. For example, predictively it might be hypothesized that the more the congruent alignment within each dimension and the more the loadings are in the direction of high degrees of authority, positive affect, and technical competence—the more the expected pattern of conservative leadership. Alternatively, with declining levels of power, affect, and instrumentality, associated with growing incongruence in alignments, the emergence of reformist leadership would be expected. At low levels of power, affect, and technical

FIGURE 4. Three Illustrative Dimensions: Power, Affect, and Instrumentality

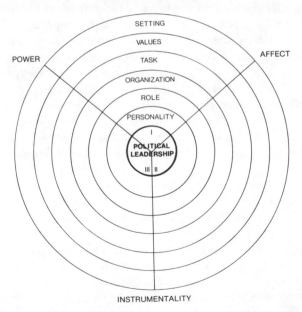

Key: I. Conservative leadership pattern; II. reformist leadership pattern; III. revolutionary leadership pattern.

effectiveness, the emergence of revolutionary leadership would be expected. If successful, a revolutionary effort might be transformed through a growing coalignment of power elements, perhaps accompanied by affective integration and followed by instrumental integration, into a new pattern of conservative leadership.

Across dimensions, regardless of leadership style, it can be anticipated (1) that coercive power is likely to have polarizing effects on affect and dysfunctional effects upon technical competence; (2) that high levels of positive affect will probably reduce coerciveness and promote the development of technical competence; and (3) that technical competence will be conducive to high affect and low coercion. Prescriptively, for example, it can be expected that efforts to reduce coercive power should seek to improve instrumental competence and increase positive affect. These are, of course, only illustrative linkages.

The preceding tridimensional discussion cannot avoid being provocative. As ubiquitous as the three dimensions are in the social sciences, there is still no satisfying cross-disciplinary theory about their determinants and interrelationships. Inability to predict within and across dimensions, like inability to predict processes within and across the proffered political science paradigms, is linked to the lack of a satisfactory causal theory of society, the ambiguity of concepts at high levels of abstraction, the implicit effects of hidden intervening variables, and inadequate understanding of how human values and purposiveness cause variation in concrete circumstances. The frank recognition of these difficulties in the effort to develop the scientific study of political leadership may assist overcoming them. The same problems confront the development of any paradigm in contemporary political science.

Sources of Dimensional Derivation

From this preliminary exploration of the nature of a dimension and of expected problems of analysis, we can proceed to explore further the possibility of transforming existing political science paradigms into a theoretically provocative, multidimensional context in which to advance the study of political leadership. A powerful reason for giving close attention to the relationships between general political science paradigms and concepts of political leadership is that each may be implicit in the other. Eden and Leviatan, for example, have argued that implicit theories of leadership underlay student responses that produced a four-factor profile of leadership: support, work facilitation, interaction facilitation, and goal emphasis.[3] This alerts us to expect to find (1) implicit leadership theories in general formulations of the nature of politics and (2) implicit general paradigms associated with emergent theories of leadership. Thus, a continuing analytical task is to make the implicit in each explicit.

As a point of departure, consider the paradigmatic dimensional configuration suggested in Figure 5.

FIGURE 5. Paradigms as Sources of Dimensional Derivation

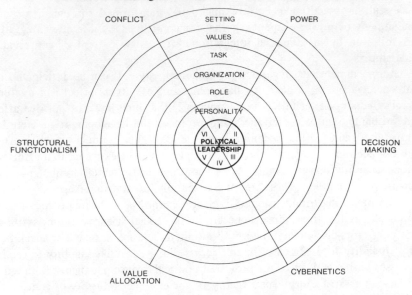

Key: I-VI refer to unspecified types of political leadership behavior.

At the very least we should ask what variations given patterns of political leadership have upon the several paradigmatic dimensions. For example, how do conservative, reformist, or revolutionary leadership behaviors affect power relationships, public policy making, the processing of societal information, the distribution of social values, the performance of political system functions, and the levels and outcomes of social conflict? Furthermore, we should ask what contributions each of the predictor variables makes to variations in the dimensional correlates of leadership behavior. Additionally, we should proceed to ask what configurations of various interdimensional relationships are expectable and what implications these have for both the determinants and the patterns of political leadership behavior within a total social system context.

Proceeding from the idea of viewing major approaches to political analysis as dimensions of political leadership behavior, we now can suggest a promising set of more finely differentiated dimensions for further inquiry. Mainly of paradigmatic origin, and partly expressive of contemporary political science concerns that have not become paradigms, these dimensions represent a priori judgments of significance. No case can be made that these dimensions logically or empirically identify all the important aspects of any political system or that they are conceptually distinct and uniquely monodimensional. It can be argued only that they call attention to major concerns of political science to which the study of leadership should be explicitly related. They appear to be reasonable points of departure toward future conceptual clarifications and empirical discoveries. Subsequent experience will add, modify, and subtract dimensions as well as clarify whether the idea of dimensional analysis itself contributes to scientific progress.

Dimensions of Political Leadership Behavior

At least eighteen dimensions are posited as aspects of any political system to which the analysis of political leadership behavior can be related: (1) violent coercion, (2) nonviolent influence, (3) control, (4) responsiveness, (5) conflict, (6) compromise, (7) consensus, (8) positive affect, (9) negative affect, (10) distribution, (11) association, (12) space, (13) time, (4) communication, (15) technicity, (16) activeness, (17) creativity, and (18) morality. These dimensions may be related to major approaches to contemporary political analysis, as suggested in Table 3 (p. 140).

At first the exploration of eighteen dimensions of political leadership behavior may seem to be a radical departure from repeated social science findings of the usefulness of two leadership dimensions ("showing consideration" and "initiating structure") or three (power, affect, and instrumentality). But this may be more apparent than real. It can be hypothesized that the eighteen dimensions cluster in the following ways: 1 through 6 (power), 7 through 9 (affect), and 10 through 17 (instrumentality), with dimension 18 standing alone but overarching all three of the foregoing as a surrogate for human capacity for moral judgment.

Whether or not political leadership eventually turns out to be duodimensional or tridimensional, there is ample justification for an initial multidimensional approach. We hope to create understanding of political leadership on its own terms. It may be more complex than the leadership that has customarily been studied among college students, business managers, teachers, and even military officers, all of whose concerns political leadership can encompass. As Guilford advised with respect to factor analysis, "the larger the domain [of inquiry], the larger the number of factors to be expected, if coverage is comprehensive in the tests used."[4] Furthermore, Guilford noted that "it is very important to have at least three times as many tests as factors," that it is essential to develop advance hypotheses about factors to be found in investigation, and that eventually "we should aim at one-factor tests."[5]

Dimensional Definitions: Applied to Gandhi and Hitler

In order to clarify what is meant by each dimension, brief definitions will be given, together with an indication of a hypothetical range of variation. For each

TABLE 3.   Dimensions of Political Leadership Behavior

Dimension	Paradigmatic Referent	Almond's Functions	Lasswell's Values*
1. Violent coercion	Power	Regulation	Power Well-being (safety)
2. Nonviolent influence	Power	Regulation	Power
3. Control	Power	Regulation	Power
4. Responsiveness	–	Responsiveness	–
5. Conflict	Marxism-Leninism	Rule adjudication	Power
6. Compromise	–	Rule adjudication	–
7. Consensus	–	Aggregation	–
8. Positive affect	–	Symbolic production	Affection Respect
9. Negative affect	–	Symbolic production	–
10. Distribution	Value allocation/Political economy	Extraction Distribution	Wealth
11. Association	*Structural* functionalism	Aggregation	–
12. Space	–	–	–
13. Time	–	–	–
14. Communication	Cybernetics	Communication	–
15. Technicity	Structural *functionalism*	Rule adjudication	Enlightenment Skill
16. Activeness	–	–	–
17. Creativity	Decision making Cybernetics	Rule making	–
18. Morality	Political philosophy	–	Rectitude Well-being (health)

*It is exceptionally interesting in this connection to discover that Lasswell attempted to link his values with types of "bosses": power ("political boss"), respect ("patriarch"), rectitude ("the-arch"), affection ("favorite"), well-being ("gangster"), wealth ("patron"), skill ("master"), and enlightenment ("pundit"). Harold D. Lasswell and Abraham Kaplan, *Power and Society* (New Haven: Yale University Press, 1965), p. 159.

dimension, it will be useful to distinguish between broad and narrow definitions. For example, defining "communication," Ithiel de Sola Pool explained:

> A broad definition of "communication" is any transmission of signs, signals, or symbols between persons. By a narrow definition, however, "political communication" refers only to the activity of certain specialized institutions that have been set up to disseminate information, ideas, and attitudes about governmental affairs.[6]

This distinction suggests a way to differentiate between and to link effects of political leadership behavior with variations in dimensions of societal behavior that are more or less directly attributable to it. For example, all societies have violence: some of it derives directly from political leadership behavior; some of it is attributable indirectly to political leadership behavior; and the remainder is relatively independent of political leader influences. From this perspective the contribution to be made by political leadership studies to understanding social behavior is clear. Even if the social sciences employed common concepts, theories, and methods, the variations in leader-follower interactions in politics would still be of special interest. The idea of behavioral multidimensionality, like the idea of "system," provides a link through which both disciplinary specialization and integration in the social sciences may be facilitated.

In the following sections, each of the eighteen dimensions is illustrated by references to the leadership behavior of Gandhi and to that of Hitler. This comparison was made after the derivation of the eighteen dimensions in order to test whether empirical referents of the dimensional ideas could be found in the natural discourse or other behaviors of historical leaders. Hitler and Gandhi were selected because of their drastically different orientations toward violence, the acceptance or rejection of which not only is central to political life but also fundamentally affects the character of political science itself. The employment of brief citations from Gandhi and Hitler leaves much to be desired. The statements are not critically evaluated within the entire thought system of the leader involved. They do not systematically show causal influence upon events or the degree of congruence between rhetoric and other forms of reality. But they do suggest the promise of future efforts to carry out multidimensional as well as multivariate analysis of leader behavior.

1. *Violent Coercion.* By violent coercion is meant actual or potential application of physical force leading to death. Violence can mean threats to physical well-being, incarceration, control over all conditions of physical existence, torture and mutilation, and all forms of killing individuals or groups, regardless of whether these behaviors are considered "legitimate" or "illegitimate." Special attention is directed to political leader relations with police, armies, guerrillas, and paramilitary forces as well as the espousal of values and setting conditions that enhance or inhibit violence.

Hitler's leadership promoted violence; Gandhi sought to minimize and eventually to eliminate it. For Hitler, who liked to be called "Wolf" by his intimates,[7] violence was the basis of politics: "War is the most natural, the most ordinary thing. War is a constant; war is everywhere. There is no beginning, there is no conclusion of peace. War is life. All struggle is war. War is the primal condition."[8] For Gandhi, violence was a sign of political failure. When violence was employed to keep order in several Indian provinces in 1940, he wrote, "To the extent that the Congress ministries have been obliged to make use of the police and the military to that extent, in my opinion, we must admit our failure."[9]

2. *Nonviolent Influence.* Nonviolent influence means actual or potential ability to maintain or change desired behavior without violence. This includes all forms of behavior by which A influences the direction and magnitude of B's behavior that do not imply ultimate physical destruction of B. Nonviolent influence ranges from persuasion by words or other symbols, through bargaining of goods and services, to mass withdrawal or positive expressions of human support such as in general strikes, elections, and demonstrations insofar as these do not imply intent to kill.

Gandhi sought to make nonviolence the fundamental principle of politics. For Hitler, it was merely a tactical expedient. "My experience of satyagraha ["insistence on truth," "love-force," nonviolent direct action]," wrote Gandhi, "leads me to believe that it is such a potent force that, once set in motion, it spreads till at last it becomes a dominant force in the community in which it is brought into play, and if it so spreads, no Government can neglect it."[10] Hitler, on the other hand, viewed peaceful political action as meaningless unless backed by physical force: "Any so-called passive resistance has an inner meaning only if it is backed up by determination to continue it if necessary in open struggle or in undercover guerrilla warfare."[11]

3. *Control.* By control is meant A's ability to expand or contract the range of B's responses. Control ranges from totalitarian direction of all aspects of social life, through a mixed state of direction in some areas, with high degrees of freedom in others, to a condition of autonomy of social components. Measures of control include the extent to which individuals, families, groups, and organizations must seek external validation in order to pursue preferred alternatives.

Hitler's leadership tended toward the imposition of total control, based upon a military model, upon a whole society. Fest explained, "National Socialism combined the practice of total control with the doctrine thereof."[12] As Hitler forecast in *Mein Kampf,* "The principle which made the Prussian army of its time into the most wonderful instrument of the German people must some day, in a transferred sense, become the principle of our whole state conception: authority of every leader downward and responsibility upward."[13] For Gandhi, leadership should tend toward the replacement of state control based upon violence by self-control based upon nonviolence. "In such a state," he explained, "everyone is his own ruler. He rules himself in such a way that he is never a hindrance to his neighbor. In the ideal State, therefore, there is no political power because there is no State."[14]

4. *Responsiveness.* Responsiveness indicates the propensity for A to respond supportively to the expressed wishes of B. Responsiveness ranges from refusal to communicate, through efforts to achieve an accurate understanding of needs, to active cooperation in seeking need satisfaction.

For Gandhi leadership should seek to make authority responsive to individuals. For Hitler, the task was to make individuals obedient. Gandhi, too, sought disciplined followers—but a followership based upon voluntary, reasoned compliance with a right to withdraw at any time. "I detest autocracy," he wrote.

"Valuing my freedom and independence, I equally cherish them for others. I have no desire to carry a single soul with me if I cannot appeal to his or her reason."[15] On the other hand, Nazi storm troopers were required to take "an unconditional oath of loyalty to Hitler personally and to pledge, 'To carry out all orders fearlessly and conscientiously since I know that my leaders will require of me nothing illegal.' "[16]

5. *Conflict.* By conflict is meant the degree of opposition evoked in B by the intended or actual behavior of A compounded or discounted by the degree of counteropposition in A evoked by B's actual or intended response. Viewed as mutual opposition, conflict can range from covert resentment, through sporadic eruptions of discontent, to large-scale confrontations of a nonviolent or violent nature such as demonstrations, revolutions, and wars.

For Hitler, conflict was prevalent, violent, and beneficial. According to him, we live in a "world of eternal struggle, throughout which one being feeds on another and the death of the weaker means the life of the stronger."[17] "What mankind has become, it has become through struggle."[18] For Gandhi, "Serious differences among non-violent people will be few and far between and will be adjusted by mutual discussion, persuasion, sometimes by arbitration and rarely, when these methods do not suffice, by self-imposed suffering."[19]

6. *Compromise.* Compromise is defined as agreement to accept less than optimal settlement of issues in conflict. It ranges from complete refusal to temper any demand, through minimal concessions, to mutual acceptance of conditions markedly inferior to those ideally desired by the parties involved.

Gandhi welcomed compromise; Hitler disdained it. "The satyagrahi," explained Gandhi, "whilst he is ever ready for fight, must be equally eager for peace."[20] While seeking opportunities for "voluntary surrender of non-essentials" that would eliminate violence, Gandhi pledged, "My compromises will never be at the cost of the cause or the country."[21] In contrast, Hitler told the military high command at Obersalzberg on the eve of the September 1, 1939, German attack upon Poland, "My only fear is at the last moment some *Schweinhund* [filthy swine] will present me with a mediation plan."[22] "All hope for compromise is foolish; victory or defeat," he told his generals on November 23.[23] But an October 3 diary entry by General Ritter von Leeb suggested that the German people would have been receptive to compromise efforts: "Poor mood of the population, no enthusiasm at all, no flags flying from the houses. Everyone waiting for peace. The people sense the needlessness of war."[24]

7. *Consensus.* Consensus refers to degree of shared agreement. It has a cognitive component measured by shared information about the objective state of affairs, an evaluative component measured by agreement on related values, and a co-active component measured by readiness to cooperate in ways consistent with these shared understandings and normative beliefs. Consensus ranges from complete disagreement on conditions, values, and actions, through partial convergence, to complete agreement.

For Gandhi, the consensual basis of the ideal polity would lie in the widespread acceptance of the principle of nonviolence. The government of a nonviolent state would rule "through its moral authority based upon the greatest goodwill of its people."[25] In Hitler's racist theory, however, the consensual basis of the German "folkish State" lay in "the preservation and advancement of a community of physically and psychically homogeneous creatures."[26] This view of consensus provided the rationale for the barbaric extermination of Jews as "impure" racial elements.

8. *Positive Affect.* By positive affect is meant feelings of approval and supportive attachment to a social object. These range from mild approval through moderate liking to intense love. Political examples include the affective components of loyalty to persons, parties, institutions, polities, and intersocietal movements.

Gandhi stressed love. Hitler appealed to racial and national pride. Wrote Gandhi, prophetically for both his own and Hitler's death by violence, "Though there is repulsion enough in Nature she lives by attraction. Mutual love enables Nature to persist. Man does not live by destruction. Self-love compels love for others. We are all bound by the tie of love. . . . Where there is love there is life; hatred leads to destruction."[27] Appealing to German pride, Hitler urged, "It must be a greater honor to be a street cleaner and citizen of this Reich than a king in a foreign state."[28]

9. *Negative Affect.* Negative affect means feelings of disapproval and aversion related to a social object. These range from mild disapproval through moderate dislike to intense hatred. Political examples include dissatisfaction with prevailing socioeconomic conditions and revolutionary or wartime hatred.

While Hitler welcomed and incited hatred, Gandhi sought to replace it with love. In the early stages of creating the Nazi movement, Hitler urged that its members "should not shun the hatred of the enemies of our nationality and our philosophy and its manifestations; they must long for them."[29] By contrast, Gandhi explained, "My idea of nationalism is that my country may die so that the human race may live. There is no room for race hatred here."[30]

10. *Distribution.* By distribution is meant the degree of concentration-dispersion and equality-inequality of socially valued objects. These objects include natural resources, material goods, generalized media of exchange, and non-zero-sum elements like information. The distribution of noxious elements as well as positively valued ones is also a matter of concern. Distribution ranges from narrow concentration to wide distribution among shareholders and from inequality to equality in the amount of their holdings.

With respect to the economy, Gandhi remarked, "My ideal is equal distribution, but so far as I can see it cannot be realized. I therefore work for equitable distribution."[31] Gandhi favored equality but worked for relative equity. Hitler espoused a certain degree of equity, but his whole belief system was based upon the assumption of human inequality and acceptance of an inequitable distribution of status, goods, and services as justly emerging out of competitive struggle. He wrote in *Mein Kampf:*

> Anyone who believes today that a folkish National Socialist State must distinguish itself from other states only in a purely mechanical sense, by a superior construction of economic life—that is by a better balance between rich and poor, or giving broad sections of the population more right to influence the economic process, or by fairer wages by elimination of excessive wage differentials—has not gone beyond the most superficial aspects of the matter and has not the faintest idea of what we call a philosophy.[32]

11. *Association.* By association, or structure, is meant patterns of interaction among members of a society. Interest is directed from the smallest social unit to global society. Association ranges from isolation through semiengagement to high levels of interactive integration. Overall patterns of association include subcomponents that are centralized or decentralized, hierarchical or horizontal. Political examples include the political structure of society as expressed in constitutions that partly define institutions and specify rules of participation in, and relationships among, them.

Gandhi's conception of associational structure was concentric; that of Hitler, hierarchical. The nonviolent society envisioned by Gandhi would be based upon "groups settled in villages in which voluntary co-operation is the condition of dignified and peaceful existence." He further explained:

> In this structure composed of villages . . . life would not be a pyramid with the apex sustained by the bottom. But it will be an oceanic circle whose centre will be the individual always ready to perish for the village, the latter ready to perish for the circle of villages, till at last the whole becomes one life composed of individuals. . . . The outermost circumference will not wield power to crush the inner circle but will give strength to all within and derive its own strength from it.[33]

This associational structure would expand to global proportions. "For a nonviolent person, the whole world is one family."[34]

Hitler's hierarchical conception envisaged superior individuals over less able individuals, Aryans over Jews, and the German folkish state over other nations. This hierarchy need not have many levels and actually tended toward the establishment of the minimum number of links centered upon the person of Hitler himself. As forecast in *Mein Kampf,* "The best organization is not that which inserts the greatest, but that which inserts the smallest intermediary apparatus between a leader of a movement and its adherents."[35] This notion, as Fest observed, became "one of the fateful weaknesses of the regime" and in the tragic war with the Soviet Union "finally led to a condition approaching total anarchy."[36]

12. *Space.* The spatial dimension calls attention to the relative physical location of social objects, defined in terms of proximity-distance, and to the arenas in which these relationships occur, defined in terms of spaciousness-compactness. Politically this dimension directs attention to such things as territoriality, population density, and social distance.

Hitler's conception of space was expansive; that of Gandhi implied contraction. In a 1930 speech, forecasting his world war for *lebensraum,* Hitler declared, "Every being strives for expansion, and every nation strives for world domination."[37] Wrote Gandhi, "I wholeheartedly detest this mad desire to destroy space and time, to increase animal appetites and to go to the ends of the earth in search of their satisfaction."[38] In a contractive vein, he explained, "*Swadeshi* [belonging to, or made in, one's country] is that spirit in us which restricts us to the use and service of our immediate surroundings to the more remote."[39]

13. *Time.* Time itself is a multidimensional concept, including orientations toward substance (past, present, and future), rate (slow, fast), and supply (scarce, abundant). As a political dimension, time is taken to be mainly a substantive orientation ranging from preoccupation with the past, through concentration upon the present, to far-sighted anticipation of future conditions.

Gandhi, absorbed in what he regarded as experiments to create truth, was preoccupied with neither past nor future. Advancing a one-step-at-a-time doctrine, he explained, "The very nature of the science of *satyagraha* precludes the student from seeing more than the step immediately in front of him."[40] Hitler, however, seemed to exhibit what Fest has termed "temporal anxiety,"[41] caught between the past ignominy of Germany's 1918 defeat and the glorious future envisioned in *Mein Kampf:* "We all sense that in the distant future humanity must be faced by problems which only a highest race, become master people and supported by means and possibilities of an entire globe, will be equipped to overcome."[42] For Hitler's Germany the past and future seemed to compel drastic present action. For Gandhi the present was past and future.

14. *Communication.* Communication refers to the modes by which information is transmitted and received within a society. Communication may be direct or indirect, frequent or infrequent, cheap or costly. In range, communication can vary from isolation to overload in both transmission and reception.

Both Hitler and Gandhi emphasized communication, with stress upon transmission, but they differed in the modes they employed. Hitler used emotional rhetoric in theatrically staged mass meetings with the intent of widespread diffusion through the mass media, radio, press, and film. "The important thing is not what the genius who has created an idea has in mind, but what, in what form, and with what success the prophets of this idea transmit it to the broad masses."[43] Gandhi, who also exhibited magnetic qualities of attraction in mass gatherings, stressed direct personal moral example, diffusing throughout a society by word of mouth. "Non-violent action does mean much silent work and little speech or writing," he explained.[44] His emphasis upon person-to-person communication can be explained partly by the position of the revolutionary, who does not have access to dominant mass media. "Let every one become his own walking newspaper," Gandhi advised, "and carry the good news from mouth to mouth. . . . The idea here is of my telling my neighbour what I have authentically heard. This no government can overtake, or suppress."[45]

15. *Technicity.* Technicity refers to the instrumental or problem-solving characteristic of a society. It ranges from simple to complex, defined in terms of the number of elements involved in problem solution and the diversity of the rules regulating relationships among these elements. Technicity also varies in terms of ambiguity from problem areas of known solutions to those whose solutions are indeterminate. By their decisions, laws, and decrees political leaders help to make societies technically more or less complex and more or less competent in solving the unending chain of problems that are deliberately created or that arise outside the realm of intention. By decisions to try to limit rates of population growth, political leaders have sought to reduce overall technical complexity. By decisions to create ever more destructive weapons and ever more sophisticated delivery systems, they have increased it.

Gandhi's leadership tended toward reduction of the technical complexity of society; Hitler tended to increase it. Gandhi envisioned that "the bewildering multiplicity of functions which the modern state performs will become unnecessary in the non-violent state due to the simplicity of life, decentralization, and the absence of class conflict and militarism."[46] For economic production, Gandhi hoped to limit mechanical complexity to "any machinery which does not deprive the masses of men of the opportunity of labour, but which helps the individual and adds to his efficiency, and which a man can handle at will without being its slave."[47]

"Hitler's dictatorship," as Albert Speer noted in his final speech at Nuremberg, "was the first dictatorship of an industrial state in this age of modern technology, a dictatorship which employed to perfection the instruments of technology to dominate its own people."[48] Although Hitler favored greater industrialization and technological complexity, he did not always pursue this goal. For example, he planned to deindustrialize occupied areas of western Russia in order to weaken communism;[49] he retarded the development of the Messerschmitt Me-262 jet fighter plane;[50] and he failed to order winter equipment for German troops in Russia in 1941[51] —"There will be no winter campaign," he predicted.

16. *Activeness.* By activeness is meant the frequency and vitality (energy level) of participation of members of a society in various societal activities, including political, economic, social, and cultural endeavors. Activeness ranges from passivity, through moderate commitments of time and energy, to highly frequent and energetic efforts. Postcolonial efforts by political leaders to mobilize whole nations for industrial development are illustrative of high activism.

Both Hitler and Gandhi had energizing effects upon their societies, but the objects of activeness differed. Hitler's contribution to German activeness emphasized aggressive linear escalation of both human and industrial effort. "Victory lies eternally and exclusively in attack," he wrote.[52] "It is false to believe that a purely *passive* will, desiring only to preserve itself, can for any length of time resist a will that is no less powerful, but proceeds *actively.*"[53] For Gandhi, the problem of activeness was to redirect the energies of the Indian people from positive cooperation with imperialism to nonviolent revolution, and from subordination to machine industry to human craftsmanship, symbolized by the spinning wheel, which would be the foundation of active efforts to improve village economic and cultural life. "A non-violent revolution," he explained, "is not a programme of 'seizure of power.' It is a programme of transformation of relationships ending in a peaceful transfer of power."[54]

17. *Creativity.* By creativity is meant capacity for societal innovation. This means the degree to which innovative combinations of old and new elements, apprehended either as models for emulative behavior or as discoveries in trial and error learning, are made for the purpose of expressing values and solving societal problems. Fundamental concern with social creativity is implied by contemporary political science interest in decision making, public policy analysis, and cybernetics. Creativity ranges from low to high depending upon the degree of combinatorial invention. At the low end of the scale is repetition of past behavioral patterns; at intermediate levels is emulation of externally derived models; at the high end lies invention. Indicators would include political, economic, social, and cultural innovations such as new public policies, scientific discoveries, and architectural, literary, and artistic creations.

Both Hitler and Gandhi were creative persons, the creativity of the one leading to the destruction of his society, that of the other to the destruction of himself. They present a contrast in violent versus nonviolent creativeness. For Hitler, creativity in individuals and by extension in society was inborn and best evoked by crisis. He wrote, "The hammer-stroke of Fate which throws one man to the ground suddenly strikes steel in another, and when the shell of everyday life is broken, the previously hidden kernel lies open before the eyes of the astonished world. . . . True genius is always inborn and never cultivated, let alone learned."[55]

It was Gandhi's claim that the creativity of nonviolence must be of a higher order than that required by violence. "If intellect plays a large part in the field of violence," he asserted, "I hold that it plays a larger part in the field of non-violence."[56] In his vision, the highly creative culture of nonviolence would eventually spread throughout a society and the world through moral contagion.

18. *Morality.* There is, of course, an underlying "eighteenth dimension" of political behavior, to which political philosophers call attention, that can be made explicit here. Let us call it the moral dimension of political behavior to which leadership relates. The idea of a normative dimension differs from the concept of "values" as predictors of leadership behavior because it calls for an independent assessment of the influence of leader behavior upon the moral qualities and tone of a society. Through the inclusion of a normative dimension

of analysis, political leadership studies can explicitly seek to join moral concern and empirical science in a single analytical framework.

Although morality is itself multidimensional and will be subject to definitional variation greater than that to be expected in other analytical dimensions, let us define it here broadly as meaning justice, goodness, and humaneness. This may be represented on scales ranging from just to unjust, good to evil, humane to inhumane.

Viewed from this perspective, and taking their entire political lives into consideration, Gandhi's leadership promoted the just, good, and humane, whereas that of Hitler contributed to the opposite. The one urged humankind toward love, truth, nonviolence, tolerance, and socioeconomic justice; the other promoted hate, deception, violence, intolerance, and ethnoeconomic oppression.

Moral Dimension

The moral dimension underlies not only the behavior of political leaders but also that of political scientists who study leadership behavior. It affects the selection and treatment of analytical variables in ways both obvious and subtle. The scientific approach to controlling their deleterious effects upon the creation and use of knowledge lies in making values explicit. For political science seeks not only to describe, explain, and predict but also to contribute to the emergence of ever more just societies.

Therefore, with respect to the dimensions of analysis that have been presented here, my own value biases, insofar as I am aware of them, are the following: (1) that political violence, even though empirically prevalent, is immoral and should evoke political science efforts to eliminate it at least as serious as those devoted to eliminating human diseases such as cancer; (2) that nonviolent alternatives require political science developmental efforts at least as substantial as those now devoted by military establishments to war; (3) that control is not unilaterally desirable and that it should not exceed levels needed to achieve nonviolent productive and distributive justice; (4) that greater degrees of responsiveness of existing political institutions to minority and disadvantaged interests need universally to be sought; (5) that useful nonviolent conflict should be promoted with love to achieve more just conditions; (6) that compromise is preferable to conflict that will heighten violence, increase distributive injustice, and repress freedom; (7) that greater degrees of social consensus are desirable, especially on responsibility for common welfare and freedom from oppression; (8) and (9) that more love and less hate are desirable; (10) that there should be more equitable distribution of social and economic values; (11) that ever higher levels of societal integration are not unilaterally superior but that provisions should be made for voluntary withdrawal, compartmentalization, and diversification; (12) that the globe should be regarded as the common human habitat and that neither close nor distant space should be exploited to the disadvantage of the other; (13) that past, present, and future time orientations should be mutually liberating rather than enslaving; (14) that immediacy and extensiveness of communication should be combined through physical presence and technology; (15) that the right to know should be at least as precious as the right to possess; (16) that technical complexity is neither to be worshipped nor feared but to be dealt with in a way that will improve human well-being; (17) that active and passive behavior should be combined for just results; and (18) that creative human potential, expressed, nurtured, and protected by purposive political action is the best hope we have for realization of humane aspirations.

Multidimensionality in a Letter from Lenin

A further illustration of the empirical relevance and analytical utility of the multidimensional approach that has been suggested is provided by a passage in a letter from Lenin to party leaders on the eve of the Bolshevik Revolution.

> In order to treat insurrection in a Marxist way, i.e., as an art, we must, without losing a single moment, organize a *general staff* of the insurrectionary detachments; we must distribute our forces; we must move the loyal regiments to the most strategic points; we must occupy the Fortress of St. Peter and St. Paul; we must arrest the general staff and the government; against the military Cadets and the Savage Division we must move such detachments as will rather die than allow the enemy to approach the centre of the city; we must mobilize the armed workers and call upon them to engage in a last desperate fight; we must occupy the telegraph and telephone stations at once, quarter *our* general staff of the insurrection at the central telephone station, and connect it by telephone with all the factories, regiments, points of armed fighting, etc.[57]

Imagine this passage placed at the center of Figure 6 (p. 153) to exemplify natural political leadership behavior. Then let us proceed in one or both of two ways to examine whether the passage contains indicators of multidimensionality: either beginning with sentence content and recalling relevant dimensions or taking each dimension and scanning for passage referents. In effect, through such a procedure, the multidimensional framework acts as a kind of sensitized screen through which the raw political leadership material is filtered, with the result that some elements stick and stay, while others fall through unattracted. We will be interested in observing which dimensions attract and hold and which dimensions find no referents. And we will ask whether it is reasonable in that context that the dimensions cluster in the way they do.

On encountering this passage I was surprised to discover rather clear referents for thirteen of the eighteen dimensions. Linked to keywords in the natural sequence of the text, they are as follows: "insurrection" (technicity), "art" (creativity), "without losing a single moment" (time), "organize a *general staff*" (association), "distribute our forces" (distribution), "we must move" (activeness), "loyal regiments" (positive affect, responsiveness), "to the most strategic spots" (space), "we must arrest" (control), "such detachments as will rather die" (violence), "last desperate fight" (conflict), and "connect it by telephone" (communication).

One of the missing five dimensions, negative affect, is implied by the revolutionary situation, but it is not detectable by this kind of literal content analysis. Three other dimensions, most reasonably, do not attract referents in this passage since they are the antithesis of hitherto conventional revolutionary political action: nonviolence, compromise, and consensus. The eighteenth dimension, morality, stands apart, demanding independent moral judgment. Views will differ. Facile judgment, even from a nonviolent position, will not be attempted here.

Dimensional Variation and Interdimensional Linkages

In addition to critical evaluation and refinement of the effort at dimensional identification presented here, major future tasks of political leadership studies will be to create linkages between leadership patterns and dimensional variation; to inquire into the multivariate sources of pattern-related dimensional variation; and to explore interdimensional relationships. One approach will be through matrixes that relate each predictor variable with every dimension and relate each dimension with every other dimension.

There are hints in the natural language of political leaders that an exploration of interdimensional linkages is likely to be fruitful. For example, consider the following linkages suggested by Gandhi. *Interdimensional Linkage 1.10.1: Violence relates to inequitable distribution.* "Violence implies exploitation and every State exploits the poor."[58] *Interdimensional Linkage 2.10.1: Nonviolence relates to equitable distribution.* "I shall bring about economic equality through non-violence, by converting the people to my point of view. . . . I will not wait until I have converted the whole society to my view but will straightaway make a beginning with myself. . . . For that I have to reduce myself to the poorest of the poor."[59] *Interdimensional Linkage 8.10.1: Positive affect relates to equitable distribution.* "Love and exclusive possession can never go together. Theoretically, when there is perfect love, there is perfect non-possession."[60]

Or consider *Interdimensional Linkage 1.11.1: Violence promotes centralized associational structure.* "Centralization cannot be sustained and defended without adequate force."[61] *Interdimensional Linkage 2.10.1: Nonviolence promotes more widespread associational participation.* "The weakest can partake in it [nonviolence] without becoming weaker. They can only be the stronger for having been in it."[62] *Interdimensional Linkage 10.3.1: Decentralized associational structure leads to less external control.* "The experience of India clearly shows that the less decentralized a resisting or constructive non-violent organization, the easier it is for the Government to paralyze it."[63] *Interdimensional Linkage 2.3.1: Nonviolence relates to less control.* "The more non-violent a State is, the greater will be the scope for individual freedom."[64]

Examples of how emotions and force affect technical problem solving and creativity include *Interdimensional Linkage 9.15.1: Negative affect impedes technical rationality.* "I have found that more appeal to reason does not answer where prejudices are agelong."[65] "Ultimately one is guided not by the intellect but by the heart. . . . Argument follows conviction. Man finds reason in support of whatever he does or wants to do."[66] *Interdimensional Linkage 1.17.1: Violence impedes creativity.* "Military force interferes with the free growth of the mind. It smothers the soul of man."[67] *Interdimensional Linkage 2.17.1: Nonviolence relates to creativity.* "If intellect plays a large part in the field of violence, I hold it plays a larger part in the field of non-violence."[68]

These are, of course, only illustrative linkages but they do suggest the possibility of systematic interdimensional analysis combining the insights of experienced political leaders, empirical multivariate correlations, and theoretical imagination.

A Multivariate, Multidimensional Linkage Approach: Summary

The overall approach that has been presented in Chapters 5 and 6 is summarized in Figure 6. The image intended is that of six linked predictor variables that produce various patterns of political leadership behavior that affect and are affected by eighteen dimensions of political behavior. These dimensions in turn are linked. Each dimension is further hypothesized to have a potentially identifiable empirical referent in each of the six predictor variables. Although analytically fragmented, the variables and dimensions are connected into an integrated whole in two ways: first, through the idea of linkages; second, through the naturally given wholeness of political leadership behavior as it exists in social reality. Two complementary theory-building tasks are thereby posed: to clarify further the asserted linkages among variables, dimensions, and patterns of political behavior, leading to the advancement and testing of hypotheses, and to confront this emerging analytical and theoretical framework with naturally given political leadership behavior in its holistic form. Cumulative, mutually reinforcing efforts to resolve the tension between these two tasks should lead over a long period of time to the development of a body of theory that is both rigorous in its own terms and comprehensively relevant for the real behavior of leaders in politics.

The analytical model in Figure 6 may now be transposed to the center of Figure 1 (p. 8) as one approach to answering the challenge of political leadership studies. It is not impossible that systematic pursuit of this perspective within the discipline might eventually extend Dahl's definition of political power to mean *capacity to make changes in leadership variables that bring variation in*

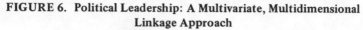

FIGURE 6. Political Leadership: A Multivariate, Multidimensional Linkage Approach

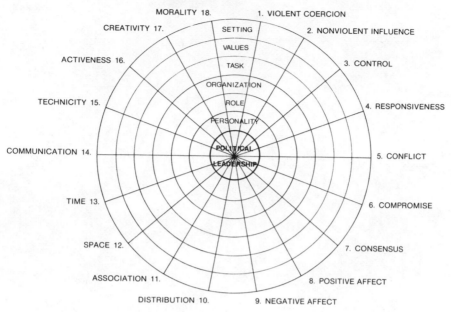

one or more dimensions of political behavior. Since such initiatives might be taken from any societal position, the introduction of a leadership approach to political analysis paradoxically might contribute to the elimination of elite biases in political thought and action.

Advancement from this multivariate, multidimensional perspective, however, will require a multifaceted research effort.

CHAPTER 7

FIELD FOUNDATIONS: RESEARCH

*Awareness of ignorance is itself the result of some
sort of understanding.* [1]

NIKO TINBERGEN
1953

RISING INTEREST in the study of political leadership, and a concomitant search
for appropriate concepts and linkages to guide inquiry, presents a new challenge
to political science research imagination. As we raise new questions and rediscover old ones, we are challenged both to adapt useful methods of inquiry from
the rapidly developing sociobehavioral sciences and to create new methods that
are peculiarly appropriate for political leadership research.

A Pioneer: Woods on Monarchical Influence

A remarkable early research effort that merits rediscovery and advancement
was the attempt in 1913 by Frederick Adams Woods to link the personal
characteristics of monarchical political leaders with the overall "material conditions" of their countries during their reigns.[2] Woods proposed that the personal
characteristics of monarchs—termed "strong (+)," "mediocre (±)," or "weak
(−)"—influence the political and economic conditions of their countries, rated as
"progress (+)," "stagnation (±)," or "decline (−)."

Woods explained that he first formulated the thesis of monarchical influence during study of the emergence and decline of Portugal as a great world
power before and after 1521. "The rise and fall of Portugal follow very closely
the personnel of the monarchs," he noted, "no more so than most nations, but
more noticeably so than some, because here nearly all the early monarchs were
strong while all the later were mediocre or weak."[3] The Portuguese origins of
Woods's thesis are illustrated in Tables 4 and 5. The results of Woods's broader

155

investigation of 354 monarchs in fourteen countries from A.D. 987 to 1811 are summarized in Table 6.

This early effort by Woods intrigues us because of the central importance of the problem to which he addressed himself, the effort he made to combine qualitative and quantitative analysis, the careful thought he gave to arguing the validity of his measures,[4] the ability of his method to produce deviant cases contrary to his hypothesis, and his sense of the limitations of his approach. Woods recognized, for example, that his approach was limited to the period of high monarchical influence and needed to be extended into the comparative study of antimonarchical modern democracies.[5] He also limited inquiry to "material" political and economic conditions as opposed to "spiritual and intellectual" aspects of social life.[6] Both these questions will merit attention in future efforts to improve upon Woods's pioneering work.

If the Woods's research initiative had been systematically extended by political scientists in the decades after 1913 into a fully developed method for measuring the influence of political leaders upon total societies, or subsocietal units, it is likely that far greater understanding of the role of political leadership in societal functioning would have been achieved. Sixty-one years after Woods's suggestive work, for example, Kotter and Lawrence reported that they were

TABLE 4. Portuguese Rise (1097-1521)

MONARCH'S CHARACTERISTICS	MATERIAL CONDITIONS		
	Progress	*Stagnation*	*Decline*
Strong	10	0	1
Mediocre	1	2	1
Weak	1	0	3

Source: Adapted from ratings presented by Frederick Adams Woods, *The Influence of Monarchs: Steps in a New Science of History* (New York: Macmillan, 1912), pp. 333-337.

TABLE 5. Portuguese Decline (1521-1788)

MONARCH'S CHARACTERISTICS	MATERIAL CONDITIONS		
	Progress	*Stagnation*	*Decline*
Strong	0	1	0
Mediocre	1	4	1
Weak	0	2	6

Source: Adapted from ratings presented by Frederick Adams Woods, *The Influence of Monarchs: Steps in a New Science of History* (New York: Macmillan, 1913), pp. 337-340.

unable to rate the performance of twenty American mayors because of lack of value consensus, lack of understanding of causal processes linking the mayor and urban conditions, and lack of empirical indicators that defined what those conditions were before, during, and after a mayor's incumbency.[7] Unless part of political science research is clearly focused upon an effort to understand the causal influences of persons in positions of salient political authority, we will not know much more about this matter in the year 2013 or 2077 than we knew in 1913 or in 1977.

Against the background of Woods's pioneering research effort and the conceptual framework presented in Chapters 5 and 6, we can begin to outline an overall research strategy for the systematic development of political leadership studies. The formulation of such a strategy at the present stage of political science progress requires us to suggest measures for the as yet unmeasurable, to borrow methods broadly from other disciplines, and to try to foresee important subjects of inquiry related to the components of the conceptual framework that has been advanced. In short, we need to mobilize social science imagination and methodological resources to seek answers to the questions of *how political leaders affect societal functioning* and *how variations in societal variables affect political leadership behavior.*

These questions pose an immense disciplinary challenge. For example, they imply that we need to develop macroscopic research methods appropriate for the investigation of any one of the general paradigms for political inquiry that have been suggested, from "power" to "the new political economy." They imply further that once such paradigms can be fully operationalized for total system inquiry they need to be operationally related to empirical referents of images of total societal functioning that are being explored by macrosocietal theorists such as Talcott Parsons and Marion J. Levy, Jr. That is, "the political" needs to be made operationally researchable in relation to any given conception of "the social" or "the economic" or "the cultural" and of all these in interaction. These

TABLE 6. The Influence of Monarchs (987-1811)[*]

MONARCH'S CHARACTERISTICS	MATERIAL CONDITIONS			
	Progress	*Stagnation*	*Decline*	*Total*
Strong	105	27	11	143
Mediocre	26	31	19	76
Weak	30	18	87	135
	161	76	117	354

[*]Countries studied were France, Castile, Aragon, United Spain, Portugal, the Netherlands, Denmark, Sweden, Russia, Prussia, Austria, Turkey, Scotland, and England.

Source: Frederick Adams Woods, *The Influence of Monarchs: Steps in a New Science of History* (New York: Macmillian, 1913), p. 244.

tasks call for large-scale, multimethod, cooperative research designs within and across the social sciences. This will require innovations in graduate training and in transdisciplinary research administration.

At a less abstract level, we need to progress beyond present descriptions of the functioning of concrete polities, the institutional components of polities, and specific political processes, with special emphasis upon description and explanation of political leadership behavior in relation to them.

Furthermore, we will need to explore methods of research appropriate for identifying alternative conceptions of what is meant by "political leadership" and for inquiry into the multivariate, multidimensional mode of analysis that has been suggested here or other approaches that will be created.

Conceptual Research

As suggested in Chapter 4, a recurrent need will be to explore alternative sources of imagery in order to advance scientific political leadership inquiry. These include the natural language concepts of incumbent, retired, defeated, or aspiring leaders; the natural language concepts of followers; the contrasting or convergent ideas of leadership in the animal sciences and humanities; leadership concepts in the sociobehavioral sciences; emergent concepts in the subfields of political science; and, indeed, concepts from any source of creative insight in the academic disciplines, applied professions, or other areas of community life. Comparative conceptual research across disciplines, roles, sexes, classes, and cultures will be essential. Such conceptual inquiry eventually should include psycholinguistic analysis of terms related to the idea of "leadership" in as many of the world's languages as possible, as well as efforts to create a world language for the scientific study of political leadership expressed in mathematical or other globally intelligible symbolic form. In addition to engaging in historical or contemporary conceptual scanning, this kind of research should address itself to futures imagery—asking what future forms of political leadership are conceivable, possible, probable, and desirable; how these relate to past or present imaginings and experiences; and what implications they have for progression from present practices toward more desirable alternatives.[8]

A promising method for describing and analyzing concepts of political leadership is the technique of "cognitive mapping" being developed by Shapiro and Bonham,[9] Axelrod,[10] and others, adapting insights from graph theory[11] and cognitive psychology[12] and often having an interest in bargaining or persuasion.[13] Through interviews and documentary analysis, this technique seeks to identify significant variables as perceived by a social actor in relation to a given subject, to describe perceived causal relations among such variables, and to develop rules for predicting stability and change among elements of such a map. This technique can be adapted readily to the study of the concepts of leadership held by social scientists or others and to the study of relationships among the components of such concepts.

Describing Patterns of Political Leadership Behavior

A recurrent associated need will be the development of methods for describing patterns of leadership behavior conceived as dependent or intervening variables in relation to predictor or outcome variables. That is, we want to describe political leadership behavior independently of those factors taken to be its causes or consequences.

A promising contemporary approach that may stimulate the creation of such methods in the early development of political leadership studies is the "operational code" approach suggested by Leites,[14] reaffirmed and extended by George,[15] and followed up by a number of researchers such as Johnson.[16] As presently employed, the operational code approach, through interviews and content analysis, seeks answers to two broad sets of questions: *philosophical issues* (what is the essential nature of political life, one's opponents, prospects for the future, and control potentialities) and *instrumental issues* (how best can one select goals, pursue them effectively, calculate and control risks, act with proper timing, and conduct cost-benefit analysis of alternative means).

Herbert Yee has suggested a method for quantifying the operational code approach, as shown in Figure 7 (p. 160). Patterns of response to the issues can be taken as independent, dependent, or intervening variables with respect to other aspects of political leadership behavior. While much remains to be done to establish the validity, reliability, qualitative significance, and theoretical usefulness of the proposed scales, Yee's effort should assist in moving the operational code approach to political leadership studies another step forward.

Another approach to describing patterns of leadership behavior that may stimulate the creation of measures more specifically designed for political leadership inquiry is the Ohio State Leader Behavior Description Questionnaire.[17] This instrument, developed by Hemphill,[18] Stogdill, and others, first emphasized the dimensions of "showing consideration" and "initiating structure." Later efforts have been made to give it additional dimensions such as "representation of member interests, tolerance of uncertainty, persuasion, retention of the leadership role, tolerance of member freedom of action, production emphasis, predictive accuracy, and reconciliation of conflicting demands."[19] Items constituting these ten subscales are measured in terms of five responses—"always, often, occasionally, seldom, or never"—each of which is given a score from 5 to 1 (or 1 to 5 for negatively stated items).

Research on Anticipatory Variables

In Chapter 5 six variables were suggested as sources of variation in observed patterns of political leadership behavior. These were personality, role, organization, task, values, and setting. In the remainder of this chapter methods will be explored by which these variables might be operationalized in empirical research. Furthermore, some promising subjects for research associated with each variable will be suggested.

FIGURE 7. Yee's Operationalization of the Leites-George Operational Code Approach

A. PHILOSOPHICAL BELIEFS

1. What is the essential nature of politics? (George, 1969: 201-203)

   *Moral principles precede
   power politics*   / / / / / / / /   *Power politics*
                      8 7 6 5 4 3 2 1

2. Is the international system essentially one of harmony or conflict? (George, 1969: 201-203)

   Harmony is attainable   / / / / / / / /   *Continuous conflict is
                              8 7 6 5 4 3 2 1   inevitable*

3. What is the fundamental character of your political opponents? (George, 1969: 201-203)

   Friendly   / / / / / / / /   *Hostile*
                 8 7 6 5 4 3 2 1

4. Do you think the fundamental character of your opponents (e.g., hostility) can be changed? (Holsti, 1970: 129-131; McClellan, 1971: 59)

   Yes, it is flexible   / / / / / / / /   *No, it is inflexible*
                            8 7 6 5 4 3 2 1

5. Are your allies cooperative? (McClellan, 1971: 60)

   Cooperative   / / / / / / / /   *Uncooperative*
                    8 7 6 5 4 3 2 1

6. Are you optimistic or pessimistic regarding the prospects for the eventual realization of your fundamental political values and aspirations? (George, 1969: 203)

   Pessimistic   / / / / / / / /   *Optimistic*
                    8 7 6 5 4 3 2 1

7. Are historical developments (e.g., from capitalism to communism or vice versa) predictable? (George, 1969: 204)

   Unpredictable   / / / / / / / /   *Predictable*
                      8 7 6 5 4 3 2 1

8. What is a political leader's role in "moving" and shaping history in the desired direction? Can one have some "control" over historical developments? (George, 1969: 204)

   No control   / / / / / / / /   *Complete control*
                   8 7 6 5 4 3 2 1

9. What is the role of "chance" in historical developments? Can a political leader make decisions by hunch or intuition? (George, 1969: 204-205)

   *Decisions by hunch or
   intuition*   / / / / / / / /   *One "correct" policy in
                 8 7 6 5 4 3 2 1   every situation*

B. INSTRUMENTAL BELIEFS

10. What is the best strategy for selecting goals for political action? (George, 1969: 205-211)

    Satisfying strategy   / / / / / / / /   *Optimizing strategy*
                             8 7 6 5 4 3 2 1

Personality Research

Three principal tasks face students of political leadership in the still early stages of exploring personality variables in leadership behavior. *The first is to widen the range of personality theories, concepts, and measures that are being employed.*[20] To this end, psychologists and psychiatrists should be enlisted in cooperative interdisciplinary research and political scientists encouraged to become more expert in personality psychology.[21]

The second task is to view the personalities of individual leaders or of members of leadership groups in long-range developmental perspective. That is, we need to view leaders at any given time of research as being at a stage of the life cycle, where past influences, present influences, and future anticipations characteristic of that stage converge. This may be especially important for understanding the role performance of single incumbents over a long period of

FIGURE 7 (Continued)

11. How are the goals of action pursued most effectively? (George, 1969: 211-212; McClellan, 1971: 69-70)

    Negotiation or appeasement   / / / / / / / /   *Gun Boat diplomacy or containment*

    8 7 6 5 4 3 2 1

12. Do you consider "national interests" first or "world interests" first in pursuing foreign policy? (McClellan, 1971: 71)

    World interests / / / / / / / / *National interests*

    8 7 6 5 4 3 2 1

13. How often do you accept risks in political action? (George, 1969: 212-215)

    Never take risks / / / / / / / / *Frequently take risks*

    8 7 6 5 4 3 2 1

14. What is the best "timing" of action to advance one's interest? (George, 1969: 215-216)

    Wait and see / / / / / / / / *Take the initiative*

    8 7 6 5 4 3 2 1

15. What is the utility and role of different means for advancing one's interests? (George, 1969: 216)

    Means must be consistent with one's ideals / / / / / / / / *Ends justify means*

    8 7 6 5 4 3 2 1

Source: Herbert Yee, "A Leadership Approach to Foreign Policy Decision Making," (University of Hawaii, Department of Political Science, October 1974). Printed with permission of the author. References are to Alexander L. George, "The 'Operational Code': A Neglected Approach to the Study of Political Leaders and Decision-making," *International Studies Quarterly* 13, 2 (June 1969), 190-222; David S. McClellan, "The 'Operational Code' Approach to the Study of Political Leaders: Dean Acheson's Philosophical and Instrumental Beliefs," *Canadian Journal of Political Science* 4, 1 (March 1971), 52-75; and Ole Holsti, "Operational Code Approach to the Study of Political Leaders: John Foster Dulles' Philosophical and Instrumental Beliefs," *Canadian Journal of Political Science* 3, 1 (March 1970), 123-157.

time, as well as the motivations, potentials, and limitations of persons who seek intermittent role engagement. For a given group in a specific culture or subculture, we will wish to understand the effects of its characteristics distribution of life-cycle stages. Among life-cycle perspectives that deserve exploration are those of Lidz,[22] Erikson,[23] and Buhler.[24]

The third need is to challenge personality theorists with problems or puzzles arising out of the direct observation of political leader behavior.[25] As an experienced electoral campaign worker observed, "Have you noticed how some candidates just about a week before the election seem to do something stupid, as if to bring about their own defeat or at least to give them an excuse for it?" Thus, students of political leadership need to view themselves as creators of personality insights and measures as well as scientific colleagues who seek to apply the concepts, methods, and findings of personality specialists.

The most important thing now to be said about research on personality variables in political leadership behavior is that the initial results of the borrowing of concepts and methods from personality psychology are so promising that something like a quantum jump in understanding is taking place. A solid demonstration of the enormous potential inherent in the application of theories and methods of personality research in political leadership studies recently has been presented by Margaret G. Hermann and others in *A Psychological Examination of Political Leaders,*[26] representing a breakthrough in a long line of development to which Harold D. Lasswell[27] and many other political scientists and psychologists have contributed.[28]

Among the truly exciting demonstrations of methods and findings in the Hermann volume are that content analyses of first inaugural addresses of American presidents can produce personality profiles of the incumbents in terms of the Atkinson and McClelland variables of need-Power, need-Achievement, and need-Affiliation that are consistent with independent interpretations by historians who study presidential character;[29] that observational content analysis of a videotaped debate between two political leaders can produce nonverbal indicators of anxiety levels in attack and defense that can be correlated with substantive matters at issue;[30] that a Q-sort of 100 standardized personality items drawn from the psychiatric assessment literature, conducted by experts on a given political leader, can produce a profile that seems useful in describing and predicting other aspects of leader behavior;[31] that Rokeach's dogmatism scale reveals significant modal differences in open-mindedness and closed-mindedness between politicians and citizen control groups in two different political cultures—the United States and Italy;[32] that two dichotomized variables, "self-esteem" and "complexity of the self," permit additional understanding of electoral success, performance of freshmen legislators, and responses to experimental stimuli in a laboratory;[33] and that birth order and theorizing about associated political leadership styles offer insight into patterns of American presidential and British prime ministerial success over two centuries.[34] In terms of techniques the volume illustrates what can be learned from direct observation, indirect observation by expert informants, case study, content analysis of documents, films, and sound recordings, survey research, interviews with open-ended questions or numerical scales and other measures, stimuli calling for nonverbal responses, and simulation and experimentation.

Having identified "personality," "personal characteristics," or "persona," as a significant variable, and having noted some applicable theories and operational measures, we can further identify some subjects for personality research that now seem to promise increased understanding of political leadership behavior. These include inquiry into the political leadership correlates of sex, aging, creativity, family identifications, emulative modeling, and affective mapping (e.g., love, loyalty, respect, disdain, fear, and hatred). Also, inquiry into the effects of sensory deprivation and physical abuse (e.g., exile, imprisonment, and torture), modes of self-presentation, humor, courage,[35] sensitivity to criticism, and reference sources for self-evaluation. Additionally, we need to know more about the interactions of different kinds of personalities in varying political leadership roles, qualities likely to be functional for future roles (or roles likely to be functional for future personalities), and personality needs for different degrees of organizational control. Furthermore, we need to understand better the personality correlates of attachment to nonviolent versus violent values, to deprived group interests versus those of the advantaged, of voluntary versus forced relinquishment of power, and of emotional attachments to objectively given physical settings (e.g., "sea persons" versus "mountain persons"),[36] from the immediate environment through global identifications to the universe.[37]

In identifying subjects for personality research it will be helpful to ask questions about how personality relates to emerging paradigms of a political system; to specific polities, institutions, and processes; to conservative, reformist, or revolutionary patterns of leadership behavior; to role, organization, task, value, and setting characteristics; and to analytical dimensions of political and societal behavior.

Role Research

In much of contemporary leadership research, role[38] is not a variable but a constant.[39] The usual procedure is to select a single role—such as executive, legislator, party leader, or revolutionary—and then to examine variations in performance of personalities incumbent in such a role type. Since role, sometimes called "position," has not usually been treated as a variable, not much effort has been devoted to creating and validating measures of *any-political-leadership-role* that can be operationalized for comparative purposes across different types of concrete leadership position. By contrast, the general personality variables of need-Power, need-Achievement, and need-Affiliation, are capable of operational application across roles. What we now require is a concept of political leadership "role" that can be applied across different types and configurations of personal characteristics. Therefore, a prime need in the early development of political leadership studies from the present perspective will be to create and validate an operational measure of role that is independent of, even though possibly causally influenced by, the other variables. That such operational role measures can be created and applied is illustrated by Ross and Millsap's development of a position power index to compare mayoral roles in mayor-council cities. Their proposed index is composed of weights given to five socially defined dimensions of incumbent rights and obligations, as shown in Figure 8.

Reviewing the five dimensions employed in the Ross-Millsap index we find that they call attention to temporal limits on role tenure (I), task-related engagement and decision potential (II and III), organizational control (IV), and control over resource distribution (V). Among additional matters of interest not treated are control over coercive agents (e.g., police), relative material compensation, and the degree to which the mayor's behavior is subject to control or veto by external authorities (whether local, state, or national; executive, legislative, or judicial).

**FIGURE 8. Ross-Millsap Power Index for a Mayoral Role in
an American Mayor-Council City**

I.   Mayor's Term of Office
       4: 4-year term
       3: 3-year term
       2: 2-year term
       1: 1-year term

II.   Mayor's Voting Power
       3: May vote on all issues with vote being equal to that of a councilman
       2: May vote only in case of tie on substantive matters
       1: May vote only on procedural matters in case of tie

III.   Mayor's Veto Power
       6: May veto measures with three-fourths majority needed to overrule veto
       4: May veto all measures with two-thirds majority needed to overrule veto
       2: May veto selected items but can be overruled by a simple majority vote

IV.   Mayor's Appointive Power
       6: May appoint and remove department heads without approval of council
       4: May appoint and remove department heads with approval of council
       2: May appoint department heads but only with approval of council

V.   Mayor's Budgetary Power
       6: Has full control over budget preparation
       4: Shares preparation with one or more individuals
       2: Prepares budget as a member of a committee of councilmen

Source: Combined data from Russell M. Ross and Kenneth F. Millsap, "The Relative Power Position of Mayors in Mayor-Council Cities, " mimeo. (Iowa City: University of Iowa, Department of Political Science, Laboratory for Political Research, November 1971).

The Ross-Millsap index suggests that it may eventually be possible to develop general purpose leadership role measures that usefully describe theoretically relevant properties related to any one of the eighteen analytical dimensions suggested in Chapter 6, from violence to morality. Thomas W. Milburn suggested to me, for example, that it might be possible to develop for versatile role analysis a set of descriptive statements that can be "sorted" by incumbents or other experts to describe the objective characteristics of political leadership positions. This "role sort" would be the role equivalent of the "Q-sort" created by Jack Block for study of personality, with which it could usefully be combined in research.[40] A theoretically productive role measurement strategy might be to follow through on Mitchell's suggestive effort to conceptualize political leadership roles ("administrative, executive, partisan, judicial") in terms of Parsonian pattern variables ("specific-diffuse, affective-affectively neutral, universalistic-particularistic, collectivity—self-orientation, and achievement-ascription") by creating appropriate Q-sort or other measures for them.[41]

Some role studies that seem especially promising for the advancement of political leadership inquiry at the present time include comparative historical and future-oriented studies within and across societies of the development of political leadership roles in preindustrial, industrial, and postindustrial settings; description and mapping of formal political leadership roles and role-set relations in any concrete institutional setting or in any abstract model of a political system; studies that examine the compatibilities-incompatibilities of role properties and other elements of the suggested conceptual framework (personalities, organizations, tasks, values, and settings) as judged by alternative evaluative criteria; and studies that experimentally vary role prescriptions in the design of alternative political futures. For example, what would be the effects of the introduction of a leadership role specifically devoted to the advocacy of nonviolence (peace) within existing political institutions?

Paralleling concentration upon the role aspects of persons in salient leadership positions, attention needs also to be given to describing, explaining, predicting, evaluating, and designing the roles of "followers," or, more broadly, other citizens or political participants. Such roles, just as those of leaders, need not be designed to be merely supportive or compatible with equilibrium-maintaining political institutions. If violence as a means of task accomplishment is rejected, for example, then leader-follower roles of nonviolent revolutionary, nonviolent counterrevolutionary, and nonviolent neutral followers and leaders can be designed. Among follower roles of interest are those of adviser, staff assistant, general supporter, critic, general opponent, negotiator, communicator, apathetic, spy, and, regrettably and avoidably, "assassin."

Organizational Research

The main task of organizational research will be to show how direct or mediated personal interactions centered upon role incumbents influence leader behavior—and in turn are influenced by it. For this purpose, research techniques especially appropriate for various organizational contexts will have to be invented, adapted, and comparatively evaluated. Among such contexts are the dyad, triad, small groups, ad hoc assemblages, formal organizations, classes, or whole human communities. Organizational memberships may be sampled or enumerated completely within or across levels or other structural configurations. From an organizational perspective, political leaders need not be viewed only hierarchically at the top, middle, or bottom of a pyramidal structure. More generally, they can be envisioned at the intersections of multidimensional organizational influences of varying population, structure, and syntality characteristics that define the relative centrality of any given leader in relation to others in a cooperative, competitive, or conflictful cluster. Leader-leader relations, as well as leader-follower relationships, within and across levels and boundaries need constantly to be appreciated as actual or potential sources of organizational influences.

Three examples of operationally relevant organizational research methods may be suggestive of useful lines for future development. These are the social-actor-sort, interactive survey research, and the small-world mapping technique for large-scale social systems. Sources of additional insight and operational research methods may come from such fields as dyadic and group relations in psychiatry, ethnographic kinship mapping, sociometry as developed by J. L. Moreno[42] and others, industrial relations production and bargaining research, military sociology, research on communications and persuasion, and research on the diffusion of innovations,[43] as well as research upon the organizational behavior aspects of voting behavior, public opinion, executive behavior, public administration, legislatures, parties, judicial behavior, and political socialization.

The *social-actor-sort* is a highly versatile device for judgmentally identifying clusters of persons or organizations having similar characteristics. The technique is deceptively simple and provides initial judgmental groupings of actors from which a wide variety of secondary, tertiary, and further analyses may be accomplished. Riedel employed this device in a study of political factions.[44] The basic procedures are as follows: place the names of all the actors to be studied into a common pool; ask a "judge," who may be an insider or an outsider, "expert" or "layman," depending on purpose, to sort the actors into groups according to given criteria; recategorize all dimensions of interest; estimate systematic biases of judges and compare interjudge reliabilities; proceed to secondary analyses, such as examining the causal antecedents of the groupings or the intensity of attempted or effective influence of category members upon leadership behavior.

Consider how this sorting technique might be adapted to describe the organizational influences upon elected political leaders in America. After a pool of politically relevant persons and organizations was identified, leaders might be asked to sort them into categories of high, moderate, or low perceived attempted or actual influence for or against a given issue or set of issues as felt by themselves or by the leadership body as a whole. Experienced observers such as reporters who cover city halls, legislatures, executives, and elections (or diplomats who observe national leaders) might be asked to do the same with respect to individual leaders or leadership groups. Finally, members of various community groups might be asked to rank the intensity and effectiveness of their own effort to affect the issue, as well as to rate the effectiveness and intensity of the efforts of elected leaders to influence them in return. Further analysis would describe, explain, and predict the relative mutual influences of leaders and organizational pressures on given types of issues. In such analyses we may discover patterns of interaction between clusters of automatic partisan (pro or con), persuadable, and neutral leaders versus clusters of automatic partisan, persuadable, neutral, and uninformed followers. Both leaders and followers may be given responsiveness scores as well as influence scores.

Interactive survey research is merely an effort to adapt the methods of sample survey research to describing and explaining leader-follower interaction patterns over time. For example, at election time and thereafter we need to know not only the social backgrounds and attitudes of voters and citizens but also those of incumbents and candidates for elected office *in interaction*. Furthermore, we need to understand how each group influences the other, in terms of both widening and narrowing response variation over long periods of time. The design of a theoretically relevant general model for interactive survey research on political leadership in American society will require the following: specification of candidates for elected office, successful and unsuccessful, as a primary research target; specification of leaders of other societal sectors (business, labor, communications, military, religious, criminal, etc.) as potential political influentials comprising either pluralistic or monistic "power-elite" structures; specification of registered voters as the formal political validation group; and specification of a sample of persons and groups characteristic of the demographic composition of the entire political community as representative of those who are influenced by, but less directly influence, political leadership behavior. Then, using a questionnaire supplemented by other measures, we must begin to ask both leaders and the members of the other three groups: "On this particular issue, who, when, in what way, and with what effect attempted to influence your behavior?" "If no one, why?" In order to probe potentials for system variation we should ask, hypothetically, "Suppose it were known publicly that you were contemplating X, Y, or Z behavior. Who do you think might support or oppose it? How? And with what likely effect? Who might be relatively indifferent?" The four-group interactive survey research model can be adapted to any society by identifying functional equivalents so as to attempt to understand the mutually causal organizational interactions among incumbent-aspirants (conventional or revolutionary), proximate leaders in other societal sectors, principal large-scale validating groups, and the general population.

Among pioneering studies that hold promise for the development of interactive leader-follower research designs are McCloskey and associates' efforts—

they found that party leaders tend to be more ideologically committed than followers;[45] Katz and Eldersveld's work—they wrote that "the strength of [minority] Republican leadership was significantly correlated with voting behavior, the strength of Democratic leadership was not;[46] and Sartori's analysis of European political parties—he discovered the need for a map of Communist party "organizational pressure" (purposive leadership behavior) to explain Communist voting patterns in Italy, which he found could not be interpreted in terms of socioeconomic data alone.[47]

The *small world* research technique devised by Stanley Milgram will be of special interest to students of political leadership.[48] As applied in the United States, the procedure involves examining the number and social attributes of persons who serve as links in transmitting a message on a first-name acquaintance basis from randomly chosen "starting persons" to a designated "target person." Surprisingly, Milgram showed that an average of only 5.5 intermediary acquaintances are required to link any two persons in the United States. More precisely, he suggested that these represent not just 5.5 persons, but 5.5 "acquaintanceship structures," each comprising approximately 500 persons. A hypothetical example would be to show how a hermit in the Maine woods, as a "starting person," might contact a hermit living on the Hawaiian island of Maui as a "target person": the Maine hermit might know a merchant or doctor, who in turn might know a Maine local or national political figure with Hawaiian acquaintances, who might reach the Maui target person in a reverse way.

This simple technique opens up some fascinating possibilities for exploring the chains and circles of interpersonal acquaintances that link political leaders, either as starting persons or as target persons, with other members of society. Among variables to be investigated that may influence the length and quality of such chains are occupation, sex, ethnicity, community size, and levels of political participation. As Linton Freeman suggested, we will want to ask how these chains are formed as well as describe them and explore their social consequences.[49]

The problem of studying large-scale organizational behavior implies the potential usefulness of creating a large-scale scientific research effort. Following the example of the nationwide system of air defense watchers established in Great Britain during World War II, political scientists may need to organize large-scale scientific networks to observe, describe, and analyze political leader and follower behavior throughout a given society. In the United States, for example, this would imply a scientific consortium, with computer and telecommunication links, of at least fifty-two universities (one each in the fifty states, one in the District of Columbia, and one devoted to nationwide survey research) that could share timely knowledge of American leader-follower interactive behavior at national, state, and local levels.

Among important subjects for organizational research on political leadership are the leadership of leaders (i.e., organizations composed of leaders); cross-organizational, cross-cultural, and cross-national leadership; the effects of predecessor-based organizational expectations upon successor leadership style; organizational effects of leader deprivation; the effects upon leaders of varying styles of followership; leadership requirements at different stages of organizational development;[50] comparative leader-follower cognitive maps; and emotional aspects of leader-follower relationships, including political leader influences upon societal mental health. Also, we need to know more about organizational diffusion of political leadership styles; personality interactions and mutual leader-follower responsiveness; functions and dysfunctions of cross-organizational generalization of learned leadership skills; and comparative leadership problems of clandestine versus open political organizations. And we need to test the hypothesis that overt political leadership behavior is largely the product of covert manipulation by hidden influentials.[51] Moreover, we need to study leader interactions with selected age, sex, occupational, technical, income, educational, and ethnic groups; political leader attitudes, "benevolent" or "malevolent," toward children and other societal segments; political leader efforts to create holistic versus partial organizational identifications; leader relations with revolutionary versus counterrevolutionary organizations; processes of encapsulation, isolation, and manipulation of political leaders by immediately proximate staff and supporters; leadership of dominant (monopolistic) versus minority (pluralistic) organizations; and perceptions of enemies *and friends.*[52] Research is needed also to clarify the origins and effects upon leadership of factionalism and organizational schism; perceptions of ideal followership compared with those of ideal leadership[53] by both leaders and followers; leadership identifications with deprived or advantaged groups; political leader perceptions of community political influentials; political leaders' influences upon leadership recruitment; interactions between political leaders and creative thinkers;[54] and chains of organizational relationships among political leaders and other members of society.[55]

The multivariate, multidimensional approach that has been presented can further serve as a source for the systematic derivation of organizational research ideas.

Task Research

The creation of operational indicators for the concept of task constitutes a major problem for the study of political leadership. We can include, but must necessarily add to, Fiedler's dichotomy of tasks as high or low in "ambiguity,"[56] Simon's similar categorization of tasks as "routine" or "innovative,"[57] Korten's conception of task in terms of high or low "stress,"[58] and Hermann's trivariate conception of a crisis task as "surprise, short decision time, and high threat to values."[59]

One of the most promising methods for identifying the substantive tasks of political leaders as a basis for subsequent analysis will be through extended semi-structured interviews and observations of leaders and their close associates. Thus, we need to ask questions that outline the structure of leader activities on daily, weekly, monthly, yearly, or longer bases; to identify the kinds of decisions that must be made or problems that must be solved by a given role incumbent in every task sector; and to proceed to what might be called "metatask" analysis, that is, to try to understand the effects of sequencing and clustering of tasks,[60] both harmonious and discordant, upon leader behavior. A suggestive prototype for this kind of analysis that might be adapted for political leadership research was reported by Morsh, who described how the task requirements of roles in a large formal organization are periodically studied by questionnaires administered to present jobholders so as to provide up-to-date job requirement information for training schools that prepare potential role incumbents.[61] The same procedure could be applied to the study of the task requirements of the principal political leadership roles throughout a political system, with similar educational feedback as well as with greater attention to theoretical, role engineering, and normative concerns.

An example of task definition by factor analysis of documentary materials was provided by Kessel[62] in a study of foreign and domestic issues discussed in twenty-six state of the union messages presented by Truman, Eisenhower, Kennedy, and Johnson from 1946 through 1969. By means of a factor analysis of seven attributes with thirty-nine magnitudes Kessel identified "six distinctive policy areas [or task clusters] —international involvement, social benefits, economic management, natural resources, civil rights, and agriculture—characterized by unique behavior patterns and different sets of actors."[63] International involvement and economic management were identified as "imperative policy areas," in which presidents must take action. Interestingly, Kessel found that "no meaningful time dimension (such as a line along which past, present and future could be arrayed) emerged from the verbal analysis. There were more indications of a preoccupation with present alternatives than with any long-range development of future policies."[64]

Another method for task research was suggested by Bennis, Thomas, and Fulenwider in what they termed a *problem analysis diagram*.[65] An adaption of their ideas is presented in Figure 9. Assuming that a problem is "a product of forces working in opposite directions," they started with a general statement of a dependent variable to be explained, increased, decreased, or maintained at a constant level and then proceeded to identify and give weights on a five-point scale to two types of "forces" ("restraining forces" and "increasing forces") perceived as affecting dependent variable outcomes. A "task" from this point of view is thus a statement of a problem-solving, decision-making, or response requirement, plus a statement of factors that facilitate or restrain a leader's responses. Task analysis of this kind involves both qualitative and quantitative aspects. After the two kinds of forces are identified and given weights, they must be categorized in such terms as time orientation (past, present, future), locus (self, others, environment), and number of forces and people involved. Then,

FIGURE 9. Task Analysis Diagram

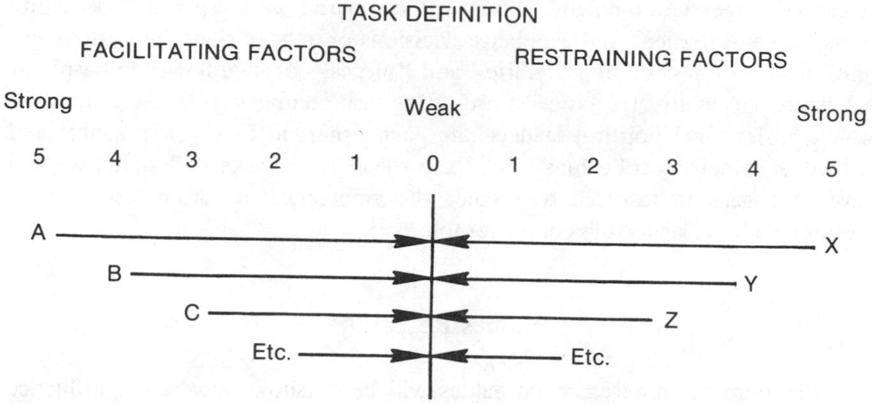

TASK DEFINITION

FACILITATING FACTORS		RESTRAINING FACTORS

Strong		Weak		Strong

5	4	3	2	1	0	1	2	3	4	5

A ————————————————→←———————————————— X

B ——————————————→←————————————— Y

C ————————————→←———————— Z

Etc. ————————→←———— Etc.

Note: Different diagrams need to be drawn, compared, and linked for past, present, and anticipated future tasks.

total weights and ratios of the forces that have been identified must be calculated. Finally, possible prescriptive strategies for changing relative weights to affect outcomes need to be examined preliminary to laboratory or field experimentation.

A fourth promising method for task research in political leadership studies is the *critical incident* technique developed by John C. Flanagan[66] and others for describing, evaluating, and improving leadership behavior. Basically, this method asks leaders and other knowledgeable persons to describe the factors most contributive to success or failure in attempts to solve a given problem. Political leadership applications might include asking leaders and followers to identify most-least successful leadership behaviors related to revolution, counterrevolution, electoral campaigning, legislating, promoting distributively just economic development, resolving conflict, and conducting intersocietal relations. By examining the experiences of different leaders confronted with substantively unique but sometimes structurally similar problems, it is possible to discover a set of behaviors that are more, rather than less, likely to ensure problem-solving "success." Thus, the leader's task is to identify the nature of the problem, to select from the repertoire of experientially tested behaviors those that are likely to facilitate solution—or to redefine the problem and invent a more appropriate solution for it. In either case, the idea of identifying problem properties, goals to be realized, and effective problem-solving behavior implies a way to obtain a sense of task structure that is independent of, although related to, the personalities of role incumbents and their organizational contexts.[67]

Among subjects of interest in political leadership task research will be to identify the nature and relative importance of tasks as associated with leadership roles in different concrete political institutions, as derived from different analytical conceptions of a political system, or as related to the dimensions of political behavior. Also we will need to study task clusters characteristic of different stages of career development; incumbent compared with aspirant task definitions; task engagement and avoidance decisions or nondecisions; definitions and implications of task-coping "failure" and "success" of incumbent and aspirant behavior; personality responses to escalating task complexity;[68] the criteria by which professional political leaders rate each other on task performance; and individual leader contributions to collective leadership tasks.[69] Finally, we will have to engage in research to predict the emergence of future tasks and to monitor political leadership coping responses.[70]

Values Research

The purpose of research on values will be to show how values influence determinants, patterns, and effects of political leadership behavior. Among basic research objectives will be to identify values of special significance for leadership behavior, to develop measures that permit analysis of the relative importance and interaction effects of value system components, to analyze the explicit or implicit empirical correlates of values, to measure the intensity and variability of value commitments of leaders and followers, to examine the effects of these values upon other aspects of leadership behavior, and to examine experimentally the effects of new values or of restructured value systems upon leader and follower behavior. Through value analysis students of political leadership will be able to link their own findings with the knowledge, insights, and methods of such fields as philosophy, religion, cultural anthropology, economics, and the arts, as well as with legal studies.[71]

Value research[72] of special interest includes the Lo Sciuto–Hartley demonstration of the binocular resolution phenomenon, the Kilpatrick-Cantril self-anchoring scale of individual values, and Osgood's semantic differential. All students of political leadership should become familiar with the still incompletely explained *binocular resolution* phenomenon that has long puzzled psychologists because it provides a dramatic demonstration of the influence of values upon perception. Once having appreciated this phenomenon, we can better understand and attempt to control for its effects upon leaders, followers, and ourselves as scientific researchers. Social psychologists Lo Sciuto and Hartley[73] reported, for example, an intriguing study in which ten Jewish and ten Catholic college students took a paper and pencil test of open-mindedness based on Rokeach's "dogmatism scale."[74] Subsequently the students were presented visually in a stereoscope with conflicting pairs of Catholic and Jewish words and pictorial symbols and required to report what they "saw." Although all students objectively had a Catholic symbol in front of one eye and a Jewish symbol in front of the other—and could objectively report "seeing" either one or both—both groups of students tended to see their own religious symbols more frequently than those of the other religion. Moreover, those scoring high on open-mindedness tended to see more symbols of the other religion. Further investigation of this intriguing phenomenon, the discovery of discriminating political symbols, and the specification of predictable leader and follower behavior correlates remain a fascinating challenge for political leadership studies.[75]

The objective of the *self-anchoring scale of individual values* developed by Kilpatrick and Cantril is to reduce the imposition by social scientists of their own or others' values upon respondents in value inquiries.[76] Such imposition occurs, for example, when respondents are asked to rate their commitment to a value such as "freedom" or "equality" on a five-point scale of intensity or to respond to a series of value statements, although both approaches are useful. By contrast, however, the self-anchoring scale method first asks the respondent an open-ended question of the form "As you think about past, present, or future condition X, what is the "best possible" (or "worst possible") state of affairs?" Having established the respondent's own qualitative conceptions of "best/ heaven" and "worst/hell" and the desirable or conceivable paths to each, the analyst can then proceed quantitatively to establish such things as the person's perceptions of past, present, and future positions on a ten-step ladder with "best" (10) at the top and "worst" (1) at the bottom. In cultures in which ladders are not meaningful symbols, other symbols can be used. Supplemental questions can be added to obtain understanding of the person's perceptions of the most valued and most effective actors and behaviors that are likely to increase the desirable and decrease the undesirable. Qualitative and quantitative value analysis can then proceed across individuals and groups within and across societies.

Among some initial findings from employment of the self-anchoring scale were those indicating that a sample of American blacks feared most "poverty, deprivation; dependency, insecurity; and illness" while aspiring most for "sufficient income for needs; moral-religious standard; and good health." By contrast "college professors thought worst "curtailment of freedom; poverty, deprivation; and illness," and best "satisfaction with occupation; sufficient income for needs; and inner well-being.""[77]

Once values are identified and perhaps rank-ordered by such means as binocular resolution, self-anchoring scaling, and other techniques, the problem still remains of seeking further clarification of the social meaning and political significance of the values. A promising research method for future development along these lines is the *semantic differential* approach developed by Osgood[78] and many other researchers. Basically, this method requires that one or more objects of judgment (e.g., certain values) be rated against a set of seven-step, bipolar scales. For example, an effort might be made to measure the cross-cultural meaning of values such as "freedom," "revolution," "nonviolence," "democracy," "equality," and "national independence" in terms of such basic physical dimensions as "hard-soft," "hot-cold," "light-dark," and "up-down." The technique of seeking basic physical measurements of abstract human values offers many possibilities for understanding the meaning of political leadership values within and across cultures. Leaders might then be evaluated in terms of the resultant value scales.

An example of a political application of the semantic differential is provided by a voter study of the 1960 television debate images of presidential candidates Kennedy and Nixon in terms of ideal and actual ratings on dimensions of "foolish-wise, unfair-fair, inexperienced-experienced, strong-weak, active-passive, deep-shallow, calm-agitated, virile-sterile, colorful-colorless, liberal-conservative, and warm-cool."[79] Such a study could be reversed to investigate leader ratings of followers on similar or other dimensions. Understanding the value dimensions of why leaders attempt to lead and the role of values in their subsequent behavior is as important as seeking insight into why followers "follow."

In addition to conducting analyses of values that influence the multidimensional aspects of personality-role-organization-task-setting interactions, students of political leadership will want to examine the origins and processes of value attachment and change;[80] to create a value and affective map of a leadership position, including both "nice" and "dirty" values, loves and hates; to explore the idea that there is a "moral equilibrium" by which leaders tend to compensate for inadequate realization in one area by exceptional value striving in another;[81] to conduct case studies of critical incidents in which values appear to be important determinants of outcomes, including apparently abrupt value reversals;[82] and to study imperatives and taboos associated with given tasks. Also of concern to the discipline will be studies of values affecting competition,[83] compromise, and peaceful or violent modes of conflict resolution; experimental studies of the effects of value congruence and dissonance between leaders and followers; studies of value diffusion;[84] leader-follower cross-cultural inquiry into the nature and importance of "loyalty" in leader-follower relations;[85] studies of culturally provided rationales for "success" or "failure" in leadership behavior;[86] and cross-cultural studies of the ways in which political leaders define and evaluate "power" as a value. Of interest, too, will be studies of the value criteria by which political leaders evaluate their own behavior, that of other leaders,[87] and that of followers, both within and across political cultures; plus studies of ideal conceptions of past, present, and especially future political leadership.[88]

In short, through sharply focused value research we shall seek ever more precise understanding of how values affect and are affected by political leadership behavior.

Setting Research

Since setting research involves the study of geographic environments, economic systems, social structures, cultural systems, technological systems, and event patterns—all at micro, mezo, and macrosocietal levels—a wide range of research techniques appropriate to these complexes must be employed. As with the other variables of the suggested framework, many opportunities for interdisciplinary inquiry and linkages are necessarily implied. Among several approaches of special interest are the general systems insights of Bertalanffy,[89] the extraordinary effort by Miller to discover regularities in overall system functioning from the organic cell to the global human community,[90] industrial and military efforts to develop large-scale quantitative models with capabilities for projecting alternative futures as aids to policy making,[91] and the multivariate "world model" developed by Meadows and others.[92]

Four research approaches will be discussed here as illustrative of attempts to devise empirical measures of setting variables. The first is the method for the study of *behavior settings* developed over a twenty-year period by Barker.[93] From this perspective, "the environment is seen to consist of highly structured, improbable arrangements of objects and events which coerce behavior in accordance with their own dynamic patterning."[94] Thus, the task of the behavioral ecologist is "to discover how the properties of the person and the properties of the ecological environment are related, *in situ.*"[95] Because "the physical sciences have avoided phenomena with behavior as a component, and the behavioral sciences have avoided phenomena with physical things and conditions as essential elements . . . we lack a science of things and occurrences that have both physical and behavioral attributes."[96] Although Barker's methods of identifying and quantifying behavior settings do not lend themselves to succinct summary here, they clearly pose a promising challenge to adapt them more specifically for inquiry into political leadership behavior in communities both smaller and larger than the small midwestern town that served as Barker's principal research site. Somewhat greater emphasis upon economic and technological variables than Barker gave also will be necessary.

A second method of setting research is *factor analysis of aggregate data* as illustrated in a study by Jonassen and Peres[97] of eighty-two community variables across eighty-eight Ohio counties, with a 1960 population of 8 million persons. Their purpose was "to discover the underlying unities which operate to produce the observed characteristics of communities, and to describe individual communities in terms of these unities of factors. This is done by expressing a great number of measures in terms of a relatively small number of linearly independent factors."[98] By this method Jonassen and Peres discovered seven clusters of correlated variables that they named by the terms listed in Table 7 (p. 176).

In further development of aggregate data and factor analytic approaches to linking setting characteristics with political leadership behavior at international, national, subnational, and local levels, a large number of pioneering aggregate data studies in political science can be drawn upon and extended.[99]

Setting research can be conducted with a future orientation as well as with emphasis upon the past or present. An illustration of *qualitative future-oriented research based upon documentary materials* is provided by John Naisbitt's continuing study in the early 1970s of 200 daily newspapers covering 105 cities in the 50 American states, for the purpose of forecasting probable future political-social-economic changes at an early stage. By this means, for example, he predicted in 1972 that ten major changes in American urban life would take place by 1980. These were that automobiles would be banned from core urban centers and public transportation would be free; fiscal crises would provoke great educational reform and experimentation; "volunteer civilian patrols" would become a major force in fighting inner city crime; "the environment would not again be a social issue of any great importance until the 1980's"; the housing shortage would become so severe that it would force "widespread adoption of prefabricated and modular building techniques"; new patterns of health care would appear in which neighborhood clinics would replace hospitals and doctors would be prepaid to keep patients well; the concept of "city" would be replaced by the idea of an "urban region"; prisons would be virtually eliminated; "the 200-year trend to big and centralized government [would] be

TABLE 7. Jonassen-Peres Factor Analysis of Community Dimensions

Factor Name	*Two Highest Loading Variables*	
"Urbanism"	Clerical and sales workers	.95
	Socioeconomic status	.93
	Plus forty-nine others	
"Welfare"	Community efficiency	.78
	Craftsmen	.72
	Plus fifteen others	
"Influx"	Population stability	-.76
	Migration population change (1950-1956)	.67
	Plus seven others	
"Poverty"	Poverty	.63
	Population change (1950-1956)	.62
	Plus six others	
"Magni-complexity"	Economic base	.83
	Population density	.79
	Plus eight others	
"Educational effort"	Educational effort	.74
	Educational sacrifice	.62
	Plus three others	
"Proletarianism"	Wealth differential	-.78[*]
	Unskilled workers	.55
	Plus educational expenditure	-.38

[*]This means that as the factor of "proletarianism" increased, the proportion of families with incomes over $5,000 decreased.

Source: Combined data from Christen T. Jonassen and Sherwood H. Peres, *Interrelationships of Dimensions of Community Systems: A Factor Analysis of Eighty-two Variables* (Columbus: Ohio State University Press, 1960), pp. 16ff.

dramatically reversed"; and "the movement for women's rights [would] achieve full equality for women in the labor force."[100]

Another future-oriented research method that can be adapted to setting research, as well as to research on the other variables of the suggested conceptual framework, is the *Delphi method,* named after the Greek oracle at Delphi. This technique for polling expert predictive opinion was first developed by Olaf Helmer.[101] The basic principles of this technique are to specify aspects of the future that are of research interest, to identify panels of experts presently knowledgeable about these subjects, to ask them to forecast the future occurrence of events and conditions in such terms as 50 percent or 90 percent probability, to report back successively to the participating panel members the distribution of judgments rendered, to seek explanations for consensual and dissenting opinions, to probe for suggested actions that might raise or lower the probability of the anticipated events, and thus to gain a clearer idea of the nature and probabilities of likely future states of affairs.[102] In an early exploration of ten- to fifty-year future foresight in six areas (science, population, automation, space, war, and weapons systems)—but not "political leadership"—for example, Helmer and his associates found that in science four trends would be likely to occur: "(1) reform of present modes of scientific communication through the use of automated information-retrieval systems; (2) reorientation of scientific methodology toward greater interdisciplinary cooperation; (3) increased emphasis on basic research in government-supported research and development; [and] (4) reformation of educational processes toward increased interdisciplinary understanding of science."[103]

Further inspiration for the development of future-oriented setting research with political leadership relevance may come from examining the logic as well as the substance of scientific demographic projections as well as the variables involved in the preparation of actuarial tables for life insurance purposes.

Although futures research methods often are used mainly for forecasting setting characteristics, they can be used to probe the futures of the other variables in the conceptual framework suggested here and can help creatively to anticipate research, teaching, and application experiences.[104] Among setting research tasks will be to probe the multidimensional implications for leadership of geographical, technological, economic, social, and cultural factors. We will eventually wish to test the hypothesis that variation in political leadership styles within economic systems is greater than that across such systems. We will wish also to understand reciprocal influences between political leadership behavior and such setting variables as poverty, affluence, food, energy, population composition, communications, transportation, increases or reductions in military armaments, housing, physical and mental health conditions, education, the arts, the nonhuman animal and the physical environment, and unexpected natural or manmade "disasters."

The logic of past-present or present-future setting change studies will be (1) to measure changes in setting variables from a base time to a forecasted time and

(2) to ask to what extent the changes observed are a product, determinant, or both of leadership behavior.

Multivariate Research Methods

We need, of course, not merely to appreciate research capabilities as applied individually to the six independent variables but also to portray them in dynamic interaction. For example, given profiles of leaders in terms of the Leites-George operational code, we should seek to analyze leadership behavior in terms of interactions among scores on measures such as the Atkinson-McClelland personality needs scale, the Ross-Millsap position-power index (role), the aggregative Milgram small-world influence matrix (organization), the Bennis and associates problem analysis technique (task), the modified Rokeach equality-freedom-violence scale (value), and the Jonassen-Peres factorial dimensions of objective environmental characteristics (setting). Assuredly, this is a complex scientific task, requiring a great deal of collaboration. And although these particular measures may not turn out to be the ones most appropriate for future political leadership inquiry, the objective characteristics to which they call attention and the problem of analyzing relationships among them continue to stand as challenges to research imagination in this field.

Among methods currently available that may be employed for multivariate research are Blalock's causal modeling approach,[105] matrix algebra,[106] factor analysis,[107] and multivariate statistical inference techniques such as multiple regression and partial correlation analyses.[108] In terms of the present approach, these and other multivariate methods can be used to describe or confirm expected relationships among the six anticipatory variables and patterns of leadership behavior. As theoretical efforts proceed beyond linkage statements to hypothesis formulation, multivariate analysis will assist in testing the predictive capability of the six anticipatory variables, taken singly and in various combinations. The application of these multivariate methods of analysis will both undergird and interact with multidimensional analysis as well as with constant efforts to improve verbal theory construction.

Multidimensional Research Methods

The posited multidimensionality of political leadership behavior also challenges the creation and application of appropriate research methods. That is, we need to find ways appropriate for measuring variation within and across the dimensions of violent coercion, nonviolent influence, control, responsiveness, conflict, compromise, consensus, positive affect, negative affect, distribution, association, space, time, communication, technicity, activeness, creativity, and morality.

Current research techniques that seem particularly appropriate for this type of inquiry include factor analysis and canonical correlation analysis.[109] Factor analysis, for example, can assist in exploring hypotheses such as (1) that political leadership behavior does exhibit the asserted dimensions; (2) that a simpler set of dimensions underlies those that have been identified; (3) that there are additional dimensions that should be investigated; and (4) that there are rank orders among the dimensions in terms of influence by and upon given patterns of political leadership behavior.

Overall there should be a constant interplay between hypothetical expectation and empirical discovery of factorial dimensions. Ideally, as Guilford has explained, theoretical efforts should continually seek to anticipate empirical factorial discoveries.[110] As further discussed by Armstrong, "Factor analysis may provide a means for evaluating theory or of suggesting revisions in theory. This requires, however, that the theory be explicitly specified prior to analysis of the data. Otherwise, there will be insufficient criteria for the evaluation of the results."[111]

Taking a multidimensional viewpoint, therefore, students of political leadership will be especially interested in the theoretical antecedents and consequences of factorial findings in leadership studies in the social sciences. These include the twenty-six factors reported by Stogdill as having appeared in more than three experimental studies of leadership in social psychology:

> (1) social and interpersonal skills, (2) technical skills, (3) administrative skills, (4) leadership effectiveness and achievement, (5) social nearness and friendliness, (6) intellectual skills, (7) maintaining cohesive work group, (8) maintaining coordination and teamwork, (9) task motivation and application, (10) general impression—halo, (11) group task supportiveness, (12) maintaining standards of performance, (13) willingness to assume responsibility, (14) emotional balance and control, (15) informal group control, (16) nurturant behavior, (17) ethical conduct, personal integrity, (18) communication, verbality, (19) ascendance, dominance, decisiveness, (20) physical energy, (21) experience and activity, (22) mature, cultured, (23) courage, daring, (24) aloof, distant, (25) creative, independent, (26) conforming.[112]

Also of interest will be political science studies such as Parker's four-factor description of motivations to run for elected office in terms of a "material factor," a "solidarity factor," a "purposive factor," and an "asked-to-run factor."[113]

The promise of canonical correlation analysis is that we may eventually be able to describe and predict relationships among clusters of political leadership dimensions (or variables). This approach challenges us to seek theoretically meaningful grounds for dividing the set of eighteen dimensions (or some subset thereof) into two subsets such that one anticipates or predicts the other.[114] Then we would proceed to analyze patterns of intersubset relationships in terms of relative magnitude of mutually predictive capabilities and in terms of the relative contributions to these patterns of intrasubset dimensional components. Additionally, the logic of this analysis is likely in the future to be of special interest in examining patterns of interaction between leader behavior on the one hand and follower behavior on the other, from any given theoretical perspective.

Five Major Modes of Inquiry

In addition to research methods that may be employed to explore the approach that has been suggested here, five classical modes of inquiry should be employed to mutual benefit in order to advance the scientific study of political leadership. These are the biographical single case, comparative analysis, aggregative analysis, experimentation, and ethnographic immersion. These major modes of research may be pursued by a combination of social science techniques in which substantial advances recently have been made. These include field observation,[115] content analysis, interviewing, and aggregate data analysis.

1. *Biography.* Following on the work of Plutarch,[116] Merriam,[117] Burns,[118] the Georges,[119] Wolfenstein,[120] Gottfried,[121] Edinger,[122] and Tucker;[123] drawing upon analytical frameworks and single case rationales such as those suggested by Edinger,[124] Garraty,[125] Bolgar,[126] and Glad;[127] and employing reference works such as the *Biography Index;*[128] students of political leadership will wish to extend the art and science of biographical research as a major tool of inquiry.

A biographical approach to political leadership studies, pursued with the triple intent of achieving single case empirical richness, aggregative potential, and theoretical-educational-operational relevance, will mean that the human basis of such studies will not be forgotten. Additionally, empirically rich single cases will both challenge and stimulate the creation of the more widely applicable abstractions of an emerging science of political leadership behavior. In such research, the biographies of "minor" leaders at every level, from the village to the international system, may be as productive of multipurpose insight as the studies of major national figures that are now customary. Furthermore, biography will provide a promising focus for mutually instructive interdisciplinary convergence: consider, for example, the insights that might follow from subjecting a carefully prepared initial leadership biography by a political scientist to a series of constructive critical suggestions for cumulative reanalysis by a research group consisting of a psychiatrist or clinical psychologist, a social psychologist, a sociologist, and a cultural anthropologist as well as a historian.[129] Autobiographical reflections by social scientists with experience as political leaders may also have extraordinary theoretical potential. It should not be forgotten that Freud made a very important discovery, the Oedipal complex, partly on the basis of a *single case: his own.*[130]

Both in creating and utilizing biographies prepared by others, as in other research matters, students of political leadership should be sensitive to the possibility of viewing political leaders themselves (aspiring, incumbent, or disengaged) as research colleagues. Proceeding from Garraty's suggestion that the best biographer may be a person with life experience similar to that of the subject, a condition conducive to empathy and comprehensibility in technical matters, we may take a special interest in such works as Woodrow Wilson's little-known biography of George Washington,[131] Stalin's essay on Lenin,[132] Trotsky's biography of Stalin,[133] Churchill's life of Marlborough,[134] and Kennedy's essays on courageous American elected leaders.[135] Through such works, scientific students of political leadership can learn from the special sensitivities of actual or potential leaders.

2. *Comparison.* Comparison provides a way of proceeding beyond the "unique" qualities of single case analysis, whether of biography or of any other aspect of leadership, toward more general insight and understanding. Paradoxically, comparison also enriches appreciation of the unique, or at least the nonshared, attributes of the subjects of comparison.

The most prominent early contributor to comparative research in political leadership studies, at least in the Western tradition,[136] is the Greek writer Plutarch,[137] who interestingly spent the last twenty-four or so years of his life as a priest at Delphi, suggesting an affinity between thought about leadership and prognostication. Fifty biographical sketches of Greek and Roman leaders by Plutarch are extant. Of these, thirty-four are the subject of seventeen short comparative analyses that juxtapose one Greek and one Roman leader; one essay in dual comparison examines two Greeks against two Romans; comparative essays on four pairs of leaders are missing; and the remaining four lives are neither paired nor compared.

Plutarch's biographies have been of great influence, especially in Renaissance Europe, where they were known to Montaigne, Shakespeare, Dryden, Rousseau, and others and affected the intellectual climate of revolutionary France.[138] Historians, preoccupied with questions of the methods and validity of Plutarch's sketches, have been little interested in his brief comparative essays, in which the logic and purpose of his juxtapositions remain somewhat of a mystery. But these very sketches are of surpassing methodological and substantive interest to the contemporary comparative social scientist. It is likely that students of political leadership eventually will master Plutarch's comparative insights and creatively adapt them for the advancement of knowledge in this field.

Central to Plutarch's analysis seems to have been a basic concern with the relationship between "virtue" and "power" in two cultural settings, as influenced by factors that can be analyzed partly in terms of the present conceptual framework: "character" (personality); nature of the kingship or military command position (role); the demands and supports of followers and opponents (organization); task difficulty and relative performance in civil and military affairs (tasks); relative degrees of corruption and adherence to principle (values); and the effects of "fortune," as well as the socioeconomic and cultural antecedents and consequences of leadership performance (setting). Furthermore, Plutarch inquired into the enduring or transitory effects of the leader's behavior upon political institutions. In these comparisons, he showed himself to be both an idealist and an empiricist, echoing Plato and Aristotle, while somewhat foretelling Machiavelli. In Plutarch, empirical description and normative judgement are artfully combined, forecasting the eventual emergence of the modern political scientist as both empirical social scientist and humane critic. Without question, Plutarch deserves rediscovery and reinterpretation, and the rise of interest in the study of political leadership undoubtedly will bring this about.

Although Plutarch emphasized paired individuals, it is also possible to make paired collective comparisons of multileader units or of leader-follower aggregates. An excellent example of this approach, combining arrays of aggregate data with contextual and historical interpretation, is provided by Brzezinski and Huntington's comparison of political leadership in the Soviet Union and in the United States.[139] Other examples include a comparative study of the social backgrounds of Chinese and Kuomintang leaders by North and Pool,[140] DiRenzo's analysis of the personal dogmatism scores of Italian and American legislators and citizens,[141] and Putman's book on the democratic belief systems of British and Italian legislators.[142]

Comparative imagination needs to be nurtured in political leadership studies, as in any area of social or behavioral science.[143] A striking reminder of this is provided by the most-similar context research design by Palmer,[144] who compared fifty-one convicted male murderers and their nearest-age brothers, in part by interviews with parents. Palmer discovered that the murderers had been viewed as congenitally "bad" as compared with their "good" brothers and tended to have been subjected to sometimes horrible beatings and torture at an early age. This finding suggests the importance of comparing political leaders not only with other leaders but also with nonleaders and leading figures in other fields.

Most comparative political leadership studies have been accomplished without reference to Plutarch—e.g., Wicker's comparison of John F. Kennedy and Lyndon B. Johnson,[145] and the comparison of Martin Luther King, Jr., and Malcolm X by Lomax.[146] Some comparisons of great potential significance need to be made somewhat after the manner of Plutarch: Chiang Kai-shek and Mao Tse-tung, Walter Ulbricht and Konrad Adenauer, Ho Chi Minh and Ngo Dinh Diem, Syngman Rhee and Kim Il Sung.

Research on these and other comparisons is important for citizenship education as well as for theory construction. Customary requirements for comparative citizen evaluation of two or more political leaders include the following: *successional* comparison of a replacement with a predecessor; *dual* comparison of two competing leaders; *multiple* comparison of more than two competing leaders; *prognostic* comparison of actually or potentially competing leaders in terms of anticipated conditions; and *ideal-type* comparison of one or more leaders with an ideal-type image of leadership. This is true of the one-party systems as well as the competitive democracies. Americans, for example, have been faced with the task of comparing two major candidates for the presidency every four years for two centuries—curiously, without a prominent place for the study and application of "Plutarchian" comparative method in their continuing education for citizenship.

Doubtlessly, some future political scientists will explore the potentials of cross-species comparison for the purpose of gaining insight into human political leadership, following the experience of some ethologists. As Tinbergen observed:

> In ethology comparison is too powerful a tool to be neglected. The bird student may acquire a better insight in his birds by studying a fish or even an insect; conversely, the study of bird behaviour may help us in studying the behaviour of other creatures, man included. As a matter of fact, the student of animal behaviour finds himself continuously applying his findings to his own species, and, without entering into details, I must confess that much of what little understanding I have of human nature has been derived not only from man-watching, but from bird-watching, and fish-watching as well. It is as if the animals are continuously holding a mirror in front of the observer, and it must be said that the reflection, if properly understood, is often rather embarrassing.[147]

3. *Aggregation.* For two principal reasons, the study of political leadership should seek progressive illumination of emerging conceptual frameworks through aggregative analysis. The first is the obvious reason that aggregative analysis facilitates appreciation of the range of empirical variation and thus not only provides "tests" of singly, comparatively, or aggregatively derived empirical hypotheses but also promotes expansion of temporarily nonempirical theoretical imagination. The second reason is that aggregation is the best approach to appreciating more fully the collective impact of political leaders from "top to bottom" and from "side to side" upon a society and for understanding the reciprocal influence of societal elements upon that collective.

Thus, we can think of political leadership studies as comprising not only single personalities but also variable clusters of personalities, roles, organizations, tasks, values, and setting elements that interact in a grand process of purposive (and often cross-purposive) collective behavior that affects and is affected by political institutions, the complex referents of a political system, and dimensions of leadership that relate to the structure and functioning of total societies.

Units of aggregative political leadership analysis may be the unique mega-universe (all political leaders in the world), macro-universes (e.g., all leaders of a single nation), mezo-universes (e.g., all leaders at any subnational level, from republics, states, and provinces through cities, towns, counties, and regions to villages and communes), or micro-universes (all leaders in face-to-face settings; e.g., politburos, legislatures, councils, committees, conventions, and cells). Aggregate samples of leaders within and across such levels, identified in terms of conceptual and theoretical interest and necessitated by both the economics of inquiry and scientific aspirations for parsimonious elegance, also will be essential and practical collective subjects of inquiry.[148] Furthermore, the extraordinary capabilities for data analysis of the computer, plus fragile but steadily growing national and transnational scholarly networks for the advancement of social science, make even global research on political leadership not unthinkable within the next half century.

Given the present conceptual framework, both universes and samples of leaders imply corresponding universes and samples of "followers," or persons who interact directly or indirectly with leaders. This leader-follower dichotomy is, it should be appreciated, a temporary natural language analytical distinction and is not intended to suggest a perpetual division of humankind into two unequal classes.

The aggregative research mode provides the main point of convergence between the study of political leadership and what have hitherto been termed studies of "political elites" or the "social backgrounds of decision makers." A vast literature of potential relevance exists,[149] and the principal conclusions of recent methodological reviews of this literature suggest that something like the idea of "political leadership" will help to link the sociological imagination of elite studies to images of politics as purposive organizational behavior. As Searing explained, standard social background categories (e.g., age, sex, occupation, religion, education) are not good predictors of specific elite attitudes (e.g., on nuclear testing), which are themselves questionable predictors of other forms of elite behavior.[150] Searing thus prescribed that standard sociological variables should be supplemented by, or redefined in terms of, theoretically relevant psychological attitude research, based partly on interviews, that would permit analysis of manifest and latent attitude structures. The logic of this critique transposed to political leadership studies would suggest that greater precision in specifying the nature of "political leadership" should lead *both* to reanalysis and redefinition of relevant social background characteristics *and* to clarification of the contributions made by political leaders to political system behavior.

4. *Experimentation.* The study of political leadership can benefit from and extend the experimental studies of leadership that have been contributed by social psychologists and most recently reviewed in Stogdill's definitive *Handbook of Leadership.*[151] Efforts to develop the experimental study of political leadership will take place within a context of rising interest in experimental methods in political science[152] and the creation of political simulations[153] stimulated by the pioneering cross-disciplinary contributions of Harold Guetzkow and his students, especially in international relations[154] but gradually spreading to other specialties[155] in a trend likely to transform political science partly into an experimental social science. James D. Barber has made a pioneering contribution to the experimental study of political leadership by securing the cooperation of six school boards to meet in a university social psychological laboratory setting, to grapple with the realistic but inventive experimental task of cutting their most recent budget to austere extremity, and by studying the

associated levels of activeness of the board leaders, measured in part by the techniques of interaction process analysis developed by Robert F. Bales.[156]

The two basic tasks facing the experimental development of political leadership studies seem incompatible but are in fact complementary imperatives for future scientific purposes. They are, first, to infuse experiments with more specific problems and content that reflect the "realities" of political leadership in natural field conditions and, second, to pursue in an imaginatively unfettered a way as possible questions of basic theory that extend beyond the present capacities for observation and measurement. This will be especially true of future-oriented experimental studies that will seek to examine the pressures, resistances, technohuman resource requirements, and learning processes that might be expected to accompany changes from existing patterns of political leadership toward alternative future states of affairs.

In conducting experiments, as in other research endeavors, it will be helpful if at least some common conceptual categories are applied across investigations so as to facilitate comparison and cumulative understanding. In this regard it is noteworthy that Fred E. Fiedler[157] has shown in two decades of experiments the operationalizability of five of the six elements of the present conceptual framework: personality ("least preferred coworker" score), role ("position power"), organization ("group relations"), task, and setting ("situation"). Following Fiedler it remains only to operationalize these five concepts in terms of political leadership, to add a concern with values after the manner of Rokeach, explicitly to add the multiple dimensions of the present framework, and persistently to view outcomes in relation to both concrete political institutions and emerging analytical conceptions of political systems. Barber's conceptions of active-passive and positive-negative leadership styles, for example, as well as all other descriptions of leader personality and their consequences, can usefully be explored by extending the Fiedler experimental method.[158]

We will wish also to explore the possibilities of experiments within the natural political community. A model for such experimentation, especially valuable for future situations in which incremental introduction of new political prototypes is attempted, was presented by Fairweather, in *Methods for Experimental Social Innovation*.[159] Political campaigns and their aftermaths in electoral democracies undoubtedly offer many possibilities for the introduction of experimental stimuli into natural settings—not only from the viewpoint of leader initiatives to influence follower behavior but also from that of follower initiatives to probable leader responses through face-to-face interaction, indirect societal linkages, and the mass media. Gosnell's classic nonpartisan experiment to stimulate voting participation provides an example.[160] Functional equivalents in less formally competitive politics may be found. Political campaigns, both conventional and revolutionary, in a sense can be viewed as applied political leadership experiments. Overall, the methodological guidance of Campbell and Stanley in *Experimental and Quasi-experimental Designs for Re-*

search[161] will be indispensable to political leadership experimentation in both laboratory and field settings.

5. *Political Ethnography.* The introduction of what might be called ethnographic methods into political leadership research will offer further possibilities for enrichment of insight. Here we can expect a natural convergence of interests with the rising field of political anthropology[162] and with growing interests of anthropologists in the nature of leadership.[163]

Some students of leadership need to prepare themselves for significant political leadership research in villages, in which the vast majority of humankind still live, and in urban settings, in which the ethnographic aspiration for holistic understanding challenges scientific imagination. Not only might we take an essentially "ethnographic"[164] approach to the study of political leadership in urban microcommunities but also we might approach the study of city halls and state legislatures as if they were "villages." For such research, documentary analyses, questionnaires, sample surveys, aggregative data analyses, and experiments may be hypothetically helpful but practically inadequate or impossible. Here the techniques of oral history,[165] documentary film,[166] still photography, participant observation,[167] sound recordings, cross-cultural learning, and long-term development of sensitive insight will be essential. As Naroll cautioned, the social scientist need not remain in a community for long to be aware of the incidence of "drunken-brawling," but it usually takes much longer to discover the presence of the practice of "witchcraft."[168] Political scientists will need to get up close and be patient in order to penetrate the myths of political leadership.[169]

Multimethod Research Strategy

The scientific development of political leadership studies—ranging from initial conceptualization through creation, operationalization, and testing of hypotheses to rigorous theoretical integration at the highest reaches of mathematical imagination—will be promoted by pursuit of a multimodal research strategy. Some of the major components of such a strategy are summarized in Figure 10. While no single inquiry need employ all these methods, it will be important for students of political leadership as a whole to explore all of them in a progressive, constructive, critical, and integrative way. Combined multimethod research will be of special interest. Figure 10 can serve as a checklist for future efforts to take stock of political leadership research progress. An early need, for example, is an inventory of linkages, hypotheses, and propositions.

Additionally, while we have been discussing research mainly in terms of methods, an alternative problem-solving approach is possible. We can begin with a given political leadership problem and create, borrow, or adapt modes of inquiry or combinations of them to facilitate problem definition and solution. In creating a problem-oriented research approach, we should find useful the scientific resources to which Figure 10 calls attention.

FIGURE 10. Multimethod Research Strategy for Political Leadership Studies

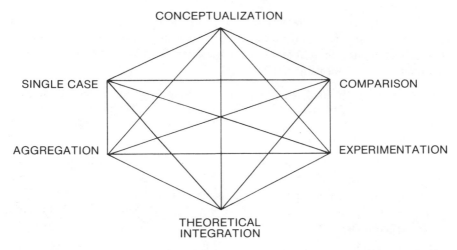

Note: Conceptualization includes seeking ideas from the natural language concepts of leaders and followers, the animal sciences, the social sciences, the humanities, the natural sciences, and the professions. *Single case* studies include biographies, critical incidents, and single-context aggregations. *Comparison* includes biographies, critical incidents, and aggregations. *Experimentation* includes laboratory, field, and simulation studies. *Theoretical integration* includes efforts to create and combine verbal theories, propositional inventories, and mathematical models.

Researchers as Subjects of Inquiry

It will markedly assist the development of scientific political leadership studies if those who study leaders take themselves as subjects of inquiry as they affect the knowledge creation process. For example, if we understand the personalities, roles, organizations, tasks, values, and settings of the scientific researchers we can expect to understand better the kinds of knowledge they are producing about political leaders and followers. Furthermore, we need to study the patterns of interaction, mutual influences, and reactive effects of relations between scientists who study political leaders and political leaders themselves. Among existing analogs for such research are the Kothari-Roy study of politician-administrator interactions,[170] the Powell-Nelson study of businessman-politician relationships,[171] and the Spaulding-Hetrick-Turner study of the political activism of sociologists as compared with political scientists and other scholars.[172] Additionally, Eiduson has given us a model of comparative psychological studies in her writings on scientists, artists, and businessmen that someday surely should be applied to the comparative study of political scientists and political leaders.[173]

Through greater self-knowledge we will better be able to educate ourselves and our research apprentices to become more valid, reliable and humane scientists studying political leadership.

Potential for Humor

In conclusion, lest the seriousness of the intellectual effort required to create a truly significant, long-term, multifaceted program of political leadership research dull our other human sensitivities, let us recall some of Charles E. Merriam's foresightful wisdom:

> It sometimes seems that we political scientists take ourselves and our subject too soberly, although I grant that we have never been called the dismal science. . . . No one of us has ever written a dissertation on the important function of humor in politics.[174]

As in other matters, political leaders themselves often provide perspectives upon the profession of political science. That political leaders, at least in some cultures, are indeed not humorless is illustrated by these examples of puns that were famous, or infamous, among the seventy-six members of the 1974 Hawaii state legislature:[175]

Bill	*Legislators' Comment*
To regulate massage parlors	"This bill rubs me the wrong way."
To promote marine life conservation	"You sure there's nothing fishy about this bill"
To provide control of pigeons	"I think this bill is for the birds, but I'll vote for it anyway."
To license acupuncturists	"Let's pinpoint the problem."

But then again, research on political leadership humor may sometimes be no laughing matter.[176]

CHAPTER 8

FIELD FOUNDATIONS: EDUCATION

*Do political science professors make any
attempt to discover, develop, train, test
potential political leaders? If not, whose job
do they think this is?*[1]

RUSSELL H. EWING
1949

THE RISE OF INTEREST in the scientific study of political leadership challenges
us to become more explicit than ever before about political leadership education. It is a question not only of focusing attention upon the concept of
leadership in theory and research but also of creating linkages between emerging
scientific knowledge and education *for* and *about* political leadership throughout
a total society. This will be a subject for continuing societal debate, to which
this chapter seeks to make a contribution.

Need for Educational Attention

The need for more focused attention is illustrated by *Careers and the Study
of Political Science,*[2] a pamphlet prepared by the staff of the American Political
Science Association to advise undergraduates. The principal sections of this
pamphlet are devoted to suggesting the relevance of a political science education
for careers in law, the federal government, state and local government, public
and private interest groups, business, journalism, precollegiate education, and
professional political science—in that order, probably determined by an estimate
of declining job opportunities. At the end of a concluding section on "the
avocational uses of political science," the following advice is given:

Finally, it should be noted that there are a variety of elected and appointed
political offices, particularly at the local level, which are not full-time

189

occupations. Many city councilmen, school board members, aldermen, and members of reform commissions are persons who have other occupations in business, the law or the home. People who are interested in political science often prove to be those who are desirous of serving in these types of positions. Although these jobs are usually low-paying and part-time, they do provide an individual with direct access to the political system, and give a person an opportunity to directly affect policy decisions.[3]

The low-keyed tone of this advice is, of course, partly the practical product of American culture and institutions, but it is also reflective of the disciplinary diffuseness in the treatment of political leadership.

A dramatically different approach, with broad implications for societal functioning, would be to stress the importance of a political science education for performing the full range of political leadership roles in American society, the massive pool of potential leaders and staff associates required, the broad range of other occupations for which political leadership knowledge could be useful, and the possibility for creating, not just fitting into, leadership-related careers. This kind of political science education would seek to prepare all citizens for the performance of political leadership functions in American society.

To achieve this kind of educational perspective, a full-scale disciplinary reorientation is required. Some will argue that even if we could educate for and about political leadership in a more explicit way, we should not do so. Among grounds for objection would be that such education would violate the egalitarian norms of American political democracy or at least aggravate already inegalitarian tendencies. Others will argue that even if we should do so, we are ignorant of what is required; too, most studies have shown political science education to be largely ineffectual, at least in terms of influencing values and attitudes.[4] There are many more objections that might be raised. Each society will have its own culturally specific sources of discontent on this issue.

Thesis: We Can and We Should

The position taken here is that *political science, cooperating with other disciplines and professions, can and should educate explicitly for and about political leadership.* We should because it is incongruous that we should so readily accept purposive education for persons to whom we entrust our personal survival (medical education), our combat survival (military education), our economic survival (business education), and our legal survival (legal education) but not education for persons whose behavior is critical for creating conditions that markedly affect the emergence of, and responses to, the crises with which these other specialists are expected to deal.

That we can educate for leadership in completely novel situations is illustrated by the selection and training of astronauts. It is also illustrated by the results of purposive educational efforts that have been reported in other social sciences and professional disciplines in which the concept of leadership has been more salient than it has in political science.[5] Such studies characteristically have compared alternative educational modes, measured their effects upon persons of known characteristics as compared with control groups, and increasingly sought to measure the posteducational effects upon performance in natural social settings. By contrast, political science understanding of the effects and consequences of education is on a much less firm footing.

This is not to argue that all such education or training is effective, or that dysfunctional consequences do not sometimes occur, but that the human capacity to learn can be engaged successfully in the subject matter of leadership. Furthermore, there is some striking evidence that education can have an effect upon at least some values and attitudes, even in the context of the amorphous American college. This is presented by Dabelko and Caywood in a comparison of "conservatism," "dogmatism," and "authoritarianism" measured among freshmen and seniors in four curriculum areas: engineering, business, education, and the arts and sciences.[6] The results are summarized as plots of means in Figures 11, 12, and 13 (pp. 192–193).

These findings, although we are unable to differentiate political science and other arts and sciences disciplines, have many intriguing implications. For example, they suggest that the value orientations of arts and sciences students may be inhibiting and skewing engagement with the subject of political leadership: avoiding something perceived as conservative, dogmatic, and authoritarian and favoring their opposite. They suggest further that the study of political leadership in American universities might not be best based mainly in the arts and sciences but rather in a position midway between business and education. At least they suggest the importance of university-wide involvement, as well as broad community participation, in political leadership education, whatever its primary institutional location.

But to be able to decide more confidently about such matters it will be necessary to extend the Dabelko and Caywood inquiry to include cognition and action skills as well as values; to differentiate among the disciplines; to include graduate training; to compare institutional contexts; and to study nonstudent control groups. The main point here is that students of different curricula tend to differ in their initial mean value positions and to change in relation to their subsequent educational experiences.

To argue that we should and can educate for political leadership does not mean that we can leap confidently into full-scale curriculum development. It also does not imply that traditional educational institutions need be the principal or only locus of educational involvement. But it does mean that we should begin to explore the kinds of things that will make intelligent experimentation with the creation of appropriate learning experiences possible. One such approach is to explore the natural process of education that is experienced by political leaders without explicit political science or other focused education.

FIGURE 11. Conservatism, a Plot of Means

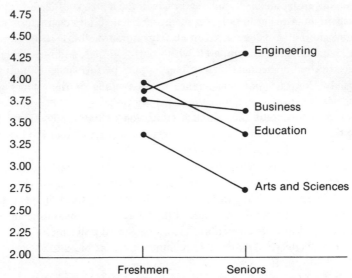

Source: David D. Dabelko and Craig P. Caywood, "Higher Education as a Political Socializing Agent," *Experimental Study of Politics*
2, 2 (March 1973), 11. Copyright, 1973, Experimental Study of Politics. Reprinted by permission.

FIGURE 12. Dogmatism, a Plot of Means

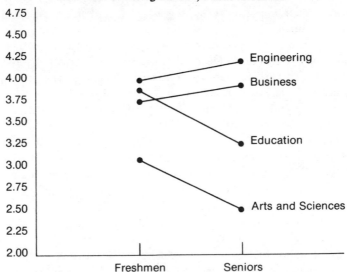

Source: David D. Dabelko and Craig P. Caywood, "Higher Education as a Political Socializing Agent," *Experimental Study of Politics*
2, 2 (March 1973), 14. Copyright, 1973, Experimental Study of Politics. Reprinted by permission.

Through research on how political leaders naturally learn to lead—as well as how other persons learn to "follow" them—we may identify the useful, deleterious, and missing effects such experience has on leader performance, thereby establishing a basis for deciding upon appropriate educational interventions.

Natural Leadership Learning

Natural learning for political leadership may be considered to occur in at least five stages related to a political life cycle: general political socialization, role recruitment, role performance, role disengagement, and retirement. Such learning includes influences from admired and detested models; making decisions and experiencing their consequences; the effects of contemporary events; vicarious learning; direct tutelage; self-education through reading, writing, asking questions, and travel; and subjection to the persuasive initiatives of others.

General Political Socialization. In this stage early positive and negative leadership models, and early experiences with initiatives and follower responses, are encountered via the family, peer groups, formal educational settings, the oral folk culture, and the audiovisual mass media.[7] Natural leaders emerge in student groups and in social, economic, and cultural groups throughout a society. In

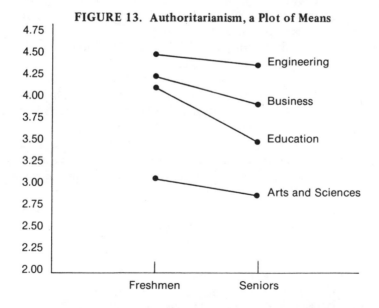

FIGURE 13. Authoritarianism, a Plot of Means

Source: David D. Dabelko and Craig P. Caywood, "Higher Education as a Political Socializing Agent," *Experimental Study of Politics* 2, 2 (March 1973), 14. Copyright, 1973, Experimental Study of Politics. Reprinted by permission.

some societies there may be relatively undifferentiated mass education for "citizenship"; in others there may be more focused socialization for potential leadership through youth organizations or through the tutelage of princes.[8]

Role Recruitment. During this stage images become more explicitly focused upon political authority figures, who aid, inspire, oppose, threaten, outrage, or ignore potential leaders. There is intense concern with finding and testing successful strategies and tactics to achieve political objectives. There may be recruitment substages of varying durations that involve a variety of apprenticeship experiences. Recruitment into salient leadership positions may come through inheritance, cooptation, self-selection, electoral competition, narrow-based coup, or broad-based revolution. As Barber has suggested, learning associated with the primary mode of achieving a person's first independent political success ("rhetoric," "business," or "interpersonal relations"—we might add "violence") may be an important predictor of the subsequent political leadership style of that person.[9] The role of more experienced, or perhaps just more confident, tutors, advisers, and mentors at this stage is important. These include family members, friends, campaign managers, consultants, revolutionary comrades, and incumbent, aspiring, or retired political leaders themselves. Internships, apprenticeships, party schools for leadership training, cell or precinct meetings, and campaign technique seminars for candidates are examples of semi-contrived natural leadership training at the recruitment stage. Leadership learning linked to recruitment may also take place in institutions outside the formal political framework; e.g., in the military, in a bureaucracy, in business, in labor unions, in student government, and in social or cultural organizations. Leadership responses thus learned are carried into political leadership role performance with varying degrees of congruent adaptation.

Role Performance. Learning continues during the period of actual political leadership performance within and across roles. Trial-and-error learning assumes high importance and critical incidents of exceptional success and failure create propensities for future styles of performance. Tutors are engaged in substantive areas of needed knowledge. Core advisers, staffs, supplicants, media commentators, and others teach, inform, advise, and persuade. Both positive and negative peer learning takes place in direct contact with other political leaders in decisional conferences, legislatures, campaign rallies, professional associations (e.g., for county officials, mayors, governors, and legislators), party conventions and congresses, and in cross-national meetings with leaders of other societies. In addition, images of actual or fictional leaders and accounts of their actions are encountered in the printed media and in audiovisual materials (e.g., intelligence reports, books, radio, newspapers, magazines, television, and film).

Role Disengagement. Political leadership learning continues in the process of role disengagement, which can occur through resignation, electoral defeat, coerced withdrawal, impeachment, imprisonment, illness, execution, or assassination. Learning may be influenced by knowledge of precedent or contemporary models of disengagement as well as by associated trial-and-error learning.

Opponents and supporters exhort, pressure, persuade, and coerce. The more reflective leadership personalities begin to ponder the meanings of their past careers and weigh the significance of alternative futures.

Retirement. Significant political leadership learning continues also in the stage following disengagement from formal authority, if the person is physically and mentally able. For some this is merely a prelude to reengagement; for others, it is the postgraduate course of their political career. The past is reflected upon, memoirs are written, experiences sifted, and positions defended or attacked. Current events may be keenly followed with an experienced eye. The leader in retirement, exile, or defeat may be reported to, and looked to for guidance, by incumbents and aspirants. As all teachers know, to teach means to learn more about oneself and others as well as about the subject matter involved. Thus, students of political leadership should be as interested in the reflective and projective learning of experienced leaders in the disengagement or retirement stages as they are in preengagement, recruitment, and role performance learning.

Parallel Educational Potentials

A major question for political leadership studies is whether science-based educational interventions can be designed at these various natural stages that will improve the quality of political leadership in a society. An adequate answer will eventually require creative convergence of the fields of political socialization and of education, focused upon political leadership development, expressed through a wide variety of innovative experiments, and monitored for effects including societywide follower satisfaction. Some possible points of parallel intervention are listed in Table 8 (p. 196). Educational intervention at any stage needs to be informed by the needs of at least four types of person: those who are political leaders; those who are likely to become or should become political leaders; all others for whom knowledge of political leadership is essential for human fulfillment; and those likely to advance scientific and human understanding of leadership in politics.

Suppose political science were to accept responsibility for societywide education for and about political leadership along the lines suggested above. What would be a responsible core curriculum that would not depart radically from past human experience and would treat equally the needs of leaders, potential leaders, other followers, and scholars? In considering this question, the importance of political biography thrusts itself upon our attention.

Significance of Political Biography

A salient feature of natural learning for political leadership at all stages is how important the study or creation of political biography seems to be. Actual

TABLE 8. Parallel Potentials for Political Leadership Education

Natural Socialization	*Educational Potentials*
General political socialization	Mass media Family counseling Preschool Primary school Intermediate school Secondary school
Role recruitment	Higher education Graduate education Professional schools Extension education "Open" universities
Role performance	Advanced professional training Adult education Consulting tutorials Sabbaticals
Disengagement	Consulting tutorials Sabbaticals
Retirement	Leaders and followers as teachers and consultants for all the preceding

or aspiring leaders may read about the lives of former leaders, actually create biographies or sketches of them, and finally may end their careers presenting their own lives in memoirs and autobiographies. This is but one indication, of course, of the importance of models for social learning and a hint that leadership itself may be viewed in part as the presentation of models to elicit or inhibit follower emulation. Thus, we note with interest that Napoleon was reputed to carry a copy of Plutarch's *Parallel Lives*,[10] that Mao Tse-tung recalled from his youth reading not only about Chinese heroes but also about "Washington . . . Napoleon, Catherine of Russia, Peter the Great, Gladstone, Rousseau, Montesquieu and Lincoln,"[11] that Woodrow Wilson wrote a biography of George Washington,[12] that Stalin wrote a laudatory essay on Lenin,[13] that Trotsky wrote a critical evaluation of Stalin,[14] that John F. Kennedy sought to discover the sources of political independence in *Profiles in Courage*,[15] that Churchill between the wars chronicled the life of his ancestor Marlborough,[16] and that the writing of memoirs by American presidents and other national leaders seems to be spreading—e.g., the memoirs of Charles de Gaulle[17] and Khrushchev.[18] Not all leaders are students of political biography nor are all as explicit in their interest as Prince Ito of Japan, who wrote:

> In reading the lives of great men I have a secret. This secret is that I first discover the genius of the man and study what deed was accomplished by this genius or what difficulty was the cause of one's failure. Then the

inference thus gained is applied as the mirror of my own political life. As I have no born genius, I always try to learn it from others.[19]

If we look to natural experience for hints about leadership learning that might guide more deliberate education for and about leadership, we cannot but note the suggestion that experimental teaching with political biographies might be a practical beginning.

Biographies need not be in written form. Autobiographical talks by active leaders or narrations by followers who know them well also can serve. So can biographical films and sound recordings.[20] In content they may range far and wide across human experience. Students as well as teachers may be engaged in creating them. They may be studied in a group or in quiet personal reflection. With all their limitations, biographies give promise of viewing leaders as whole human beings in total societal contexts—the basis to which all social science knowledge and all implied usefulness of such knowledge ultimately return.

Three fundamental limitations of biographies as educational materials may be recognized and compensated for. They tend to be distorted; then we must learn to be critical. They may only glorify dominant oppressors;[21] then we must seek out or create the biographies of the champions of the oppressed. They are history-bound and no guide to radically different expectable futures; then we must argue the ways that futures will differ from a given biographical base. Overall, to check biases, we must seek diversity, both across leaders and among biographies of a single leader. It is here also that the ancient comparative skills of Plutarch need to be revived and perfected.

Sources of Educational Insight

In addition to biographies, at least three other sources of insight may be drawn upon in creating political leadership learning experiences. These include the results of scientific research, the views of experienced leaders, and the views of other citizens whose lives are affected by political leadership behavior. Figure 14 (p. 228) suggests a university research center for political leadership studies the products of which, when combined with those of the social sciences, humanities, and other professions, could provide a sound knowledge base.

The educational advice of experienced leaders also can be sought. I once asked the prime minister of Singapore what advice he would give about the educational preparation of potential political leaders. "If things go well," he said, "they should study economics and public administration. If things go badly, they should study military science." Many leaders will argue that not much can be done—either because "leaders are born, not made," as a future prime minister of Korea told me or because of the unique complexity of political leadership roles. As John F. Kennedy observed, "There's no experience that you can get that can possibly prepare you adequately for the presidency."[22] But these views still leave open the possibility that the naturally gifted can be assisted to make better use of their talents and that there can be relative degrees of adequacy in preparation for role performance. [23]

The political educational advice of American party politicians to college students usually takes the form of urging them to get involved in precinct politics. Elected officials advise students to get involved in campaign activity, helping others and presenting themselves as candidates. American radicals give essentially the same pragmatic advice: get involved in any issue and eventually you will become radicalized by the injustices of "the system." Some experienced politicians urge studies they personally have found useful: political science, theater, or communications.[24]

A unique source, as yet systematically unexplored, is the advice of political scientists who, like Merriam, have combined careers as teacher-scholars with political action. In 1973, for example, the biographical directory records of the American Political Science Association indicated that about 500 of its members had held elected political office.[25] Most of these were teacher-scholars. Their insights into practical politics and the educational process provide a valuable resource that needs to be explored in the effort to create more adequate education for and about political leadership.

The views of persons not themselves political leaders need also to be considered. The advice of persons able to express the views of the most disadvantaged segments of society deserve special attention. The educator Paulo Freire, for example, from the perspective of the poor and illiterate, has force-fully argued that customary "leadership training" merely leads to social aliena-tion and to the improvement of manipulative skills that favor only dominant political, social, and economic interests.[26] The alternative he has proposed, however, itself constitutes a valuable pedagogy for leadership education.

Once a purposive educational program is set up, a career-long advisory system needs to be established whereby the subsequent experiences of leaders and followers are fed back into the educational process. At the same time, active leaders and followers should receive from the science-based educational effort a continuing inventory of action-related leadership propositions.

Leadership Educational Principles

Beyond achieving the holistic overviews contained in political biographies, there are five other basic principles that should be applied in the design of political leadership learning experiences. The first is the *need for omni-relevant understanding*. Political leaders, more than any other persons in a society, need to know as much as possible about every aspect of life. As Doman has explained, "If a man knows everything of something, he might be a brilliant expert but be a failure in politics. If he knows something of everything, he will be a miserable expert but a good politician."[27] Curricula design at every level should seek this kind of outreach; again, this means omni-sensitivity, not omniscience. While we are seeking general understanding, however, the importance of specialization should not be disvalued.[28]

The second principle is *value clarification,* both of one's own values—personal, group, institutional, community, and polity—and of those of others. The clarification, creation, and testing of value guides to action and evaluation should become as familiar as the creation and testing of empirical propositions in scientific research. Skills in recognizing and changing discrepancies between values and other forms of reality should be taught.

A third principle is *understanding people,* all kinds of people, in every walk of life. This is the kind of education that politicians get in door-to-door campaigning; such knowledge needs to be deepened as well as broadened in regard to unfamiliar segments of one's own society and other societies.

A fourth principle is *developing the capacity for innovation,* both by personal creativity and by intelligent support of the creativity of others. The most successfully innovative leaders are undoubtedly also the best followers, knowing how to evaluate and support the creative abilities of others. Education should provide experience in confronting novel situations leading to awareness of effective and ineffective styles of response. The proposal by Tarcher to base leadership education and action upon the scientific model of discovery and verification deserves full-scale political science attention. [29]

The fifth principle is taken from the advice of experienced leaders: *seek engagement in practical problem-solving efforts*—not this approach alone but in combination with other forms of educational experience. For the nurturing of political leadership we need to create dynamic combinations of education in action and action in education.

It will be appreciated that these principles will hold true for political followership as well as for leadership.

Focuses: Variables and Dimensions

In addition to these general principles, the components of a multivariate, multidimensional linkage approach suggest an approach to leadership education that is relatively comprehensive and capable of response to new research findings.

Leaders need to become aware of their own concepts of leadership. They need to learn as much as possible about their personalities and those of others. They need to experience the "fit" of established roles and to design and experience the consequences of different ones. They need to understand the processes of small groups, the ways in which formal organizations work, and the ways in which their behavior relates to the functioning of large human collectivities. They need awareness of values and their consequences, their own and those of others. They need task and problem-solving competence along all eighteen of the dimensions of political behavior to which attention has been called and to others not herein identified—gaining, performing in, and disengaging from leadership roles. They need awareness of the economic, social, cultural, technological, and physical aspects of the environment of political behavior and awareness of how leadership both shapes and responds to these factors. And, undoubtedly, they need education in areas not yet identified.

This is a large order for leaders, for followers, who must be nurtured in similar understandings, and for educators. But it is not an impossible task. All these processes have been occurring to some extent, recognized or not, throughout human history. What is required now is to undergird them explicitly with scientific and humane imagination and research. We need to perceive political leadership as a moral and applied social science with enormous potential for contributing to the welfare of mankind—and to think more clearly about how to educate for and about leadership.

The analytical components suggested need not be the subject of cognitive understanding alone but may also be appreciated by direct or mediated emotional involvement. For example, the concept of *personality* may lead to the discovery of the educational potential of a film in which a master sculptor, Merrill Gage, tells the life story of Abraham Lincoln, while transforming a mass of clay from the face of youth into the gaunt wrinkles of old age.[30] The idea of *role* may enhance the meaningfulness of a television presentation of the views of five experienced incumbents on the powers and limitations of the American presidency.[31] The concept of *organization* may enhance appreciation of the disciplined orderliness of a political army as portrayed in a Nazi propaganda film [32] as well as the remarkable image of what Adlai Stevenson termed the "discordant symphony of a free society"[33] in a film depicting raucous campaign heckling of British politicians.[34] With the idea of *task* in mind one listens to the recorded speeches of Franklin Roosevelt in the 1930s American Depression,[35] Winston Churchill in the Second World War,[36] and Lenin in the Bolshevik Revolution,[37] with a keener sense of the independent force of problems to be solved. For an illustration of the force of human *values* one can ponder the eloquent affirmation of "equality" and "freedom" voiced by Martin Luther King, Jr., in a recording of his remarkable speech "I Have a Dream."[38] Or we may better appreciate the lucid argument for the existence of a "God of light, truth and love" on a taped recording by Gandhi. We hear him as he argues that to deny the existence of a Supreme Being because of asserted lack of evidence is no more persuasive than the ignorance he discovered among the peasants of Mysore who did not know the name of their secular ruler.[39] Or we can be moved by the love of land and people expressed in the recorded last will and testament of Jawaharlal Nehru as spoken by his sister. She voices his moving wish that one handful of his ashes be thrown into the Ganges at Allahabad while another be thrown from an airplane to scatter over hills and fields as a symbol of his love for the traditions, people, and land of India.[40] The idea of *setting* enhances appreciation of a Canadian film depicting small town mayors in three local environments: a mayor-doctor in Brazil, a mayor-trader in Nigeria, and a mayor-farmer in Canada.[41]

Modes

In accepting the challenge of political leadership education, political science, in cooperation with other disciplines and professions, should experiment with a wide range of modes of learning. Such approaches need to be created for persons who are not yet leaders, for persons in leadership roles, and for other persons who need to know about leadership.

Existing modes of learning include the study of biography, field observation, internships, simulations, case studies, practical problem-solving experiences, and tutelage by experienced persons. The American political system of two-, four-, and six-year electoral cycles, plus relatively open city council and legislative committee deliberations, provides unusual observational opportunities. The study of media imagery, supplemented by the insights of investigative reporting, provides another mode of leadership learning that is close to the natural political environment. The wide variety of educational simulations being developed in American political science offers many suggestions for political leadership education,[42] while the remarkable success of Whitaker's students in simulating the voting behavior of Supreme Court justices offers promise of their potential validity.[43] Joint case studies by the Harvard medical and law schools of ethical crises in medical practice provide a suggestive model for the moral education of aspiring political leaders based upon actual critical incidents.

In all these modes, and in others that may be created, the multivariate, multidimensional linkage approach can serve as a learning grid to identify and relate needed experiences. In turn, feedback from educational experiences can lead to modifications in this suggested framework, just as can research and applied experience.

One mode of education suggested by natural leadership learning experience requires no external intervention but only the provision of an opportunity for solitary reflection. As explained by the American radical organizer Saul Alinsky:

> The one problem that the revolutionary cannot cope with by himself is that he must now and then have an opportunity to reflect and synthesize his thoughts. To gain that privacy in which he can try to make sense out of what he is doing, why he is doing it, where he is going, what has been wrong with what he has done, what he should have done and above all to see the relationships of all the episodes and acts as they tie in to a general pattern, the most convenient and accessible solution is jail. It is here that he begins to develop a philosophy. It is here that he begins to shape long-term goals, intermediate goals, and a self-analysis of tactics as tied to his own person-

ality. It is here that he is emancipated from the slavery of action wherein he was compelled to think from act to act. Now he can look at the totality of his actions and the reactions of the enemy from a fairly detached position.[44]

Education, as we know, does not always mean doing something *to* or *for* someone else; it may mean creating the conditions for something to happen that otherwise might not occur. This is not to suggest that students of political leadership need go to jail, but for some of us, as for many historical leaders, this can be an important learning experience. A better approach would be for educational institutions to create conditions of relative sensory deprivation that provide reflective learning opportunities for experienced political leaders.

The style of political leadership education may be conservative, reformist, or revolutionary—but it need not be limited in aspiration to any of these. Rather, it might try to respond to the educational needs of persons of all three orientations and further might aspire over a long period to educate leaders who creatively transcend these contemporary stereotypes. Such persons should be expert in applying the laws of leader-follower interaction behavior in such a way as to achieve steadily, with lessening trauma, age-old human aspirations for material and psychological well-being.

Prevocational Education

Consideration should be given to the establishment in American colleges and universities of a prevocational curriculum for preparing potential political leaders. Existing analogs can be found in colleges of business, education, and engineering. Perhaps political leadership could be combined with policy science, planning, and public administration orientations in a college of public leadership. The creation of universitywide prevocational education for prospective political leaders, including education of leader associates and provision for meeting the needs of nonleader citizens, presents a genuine innovative challenge to American higher education.

At the very least, courses in political leadership need to be established within departments of political science. Such courses should orient students to the subject of political leadership and provide introductions to the various modes of vocationally relating to it. They should draw upon the insights of all existing political science specialties, as outlined in Figure 1, and should direct student interest to these specialties as resources for meeting leadership needs.

A political science subcurriculum focusing upon political leadership might have the following three core components. Perhaps an undergraduate course in political biography would be the best introduction, providing early empirical resources for decision making in the creation of a personal identity. Such a course, aside from direct action, might also be the best serious final examination, testing skills in analysis and evaluation that had been developed throughout the person's college career. Next there would be a need for a wide-ranging exploration of alternative conceptual approaches to leadership as suggested in Chapter 4. Here a review of alternative concepts of political leadership in the history of political thought could make an enormous contribution to critical awareness and historical perspective. A third major component, after biography and conceptual exploration, would be a systematic review of emergent scientific findings based upon a constantly updated propositional inventory. A graduate seminar could address itself to reviewing the literature for propositions to be employed in undergraduate education and teaching the propositions thus discovered. Undergraduates could be taught proposition-building skills and engaged also in the inventory effort.

On this basis, undergraduate students of political leadership subsequently could be provided with four parallel and mutually reinforcing learning opportunities: research, education, application, and evaluation. These might be envisioned as four workshops, with related course offerings, that could serve as a focus for faculty, graduate student, undergraduate, and community involvement. The first workshop would be devoted mainly to theory building and research. The second would be devoted to examining formal and informal educational experiences related to leadership at all levels and to seeking modes of improvement. A third workshop would be devoted to applied politics, seeking to make knowledge useful in relation to the performance of leaders, aspirants, individual citizens, and community groups attempting to influence leadership behavior. The fourth workshop would be devoted primarily to developing skills in the critical evaluation of political leadership behavior, combining perspectives from the humanities, sciences, and professions, and reaching out to understand the criteria being employed in the natural political community from the most to the least advantaged perspective.

These prevocational workshops could lead to careers in scientific or applied research, in political education, in political leadership and in the multitude of leader-related occupations, and in the critical evaluation of leader behavior as in political journalism, the arts, and the humanities.

Graduate Education

These four undergraduate orientations could be coordinated with graduate training. Students working toward a master's degree could specialize in one or more research, educational, applied, or evaluative skills. Their experience could provide materials for undergraduate teaching, just as it could provide a bridge to professional community involvement to develop political leadership along the lines of one or more of the four modes of action orientation.

Education at the doctoral level would prepare persons to advance political leadership research, teaching, and action programs as a contribution to achieving the goals of the discipline of political science.

Initially, of course, departments may begin by adding but single courses on political leadership at the undergraduate and graduate levels. Yet they should begin now to think further ahead about the potential contributions that political leadership studies can make to departmental and community development.

Schools of Political Leadership

It is not unthinkable that one or more universities will pioneer in the establishment of a professional school of political leadership. Such a school would provide a focus for universitywide and communitywide interest in political leadership. In the United States, for example, there should be at least one of these in every state, with some major universities accepting responsibility for national' leadership development. The United Nations University eventually might come to accept responsibility for explicitly educating international and world leaders.

In an American university, a graduate school of political leadership should learn from, and maintain mutually stimulating relationships with, existing professional schools such as law, medicine, business, agriculture, education, social work, and engineering—but it should develop a unique, omni-relevant creative identity along the lines of the educational principles suggested above. Grasping scientific research, on the one hand, firmly engaged in the affairs of actual and aspiring political leaders, on the other, standing solidly on the needs of the people, and with head and heart tempered by the arts and humanities, such a school should make a clear commitment to the improvement of political leadership in its society. The most distinguished political leaders can be drawn upon as deans and faculty members, mobilizing the talents of concerned faculty in all disciplines and engaging community wisdom from all quarters. Attracting the most public-spirited and dedicated students, seeking outreach into all sources of societal vitality, such a school eventually would heighten the quality of political leadership in a society.

It is premature to specify a curriculum for a school of political leadership. Each society has its own requirements. In the United States, the plan for such a school should emerge out of a combination of academic imagination, including the advice of existing professional school participants; the counsel of experienced executive, legislative, judicial, and party leaders and aspirants; the views of leaders of citizen groups concerned with political leadership performance; and the felt needs of prospective students. A unique challenge to the design of such a school would be to find ways in which "followers," persons not themselves likely to be political leaders, might be engaged in the educational experiences of the professional leaders. This is unlike the usual practice of professional schools or military leadership training institutions.

It is likely that the Kotter and Lawrence[45] tripartite model of agenda setting, network building, and task implementation would provide a useful framework for professional political leadership education. So would concern with the power, affect, and instrumental aspects of leadership. Among likely areas of interest would be living among the unfamiliar sectors of society, campaign design, ethical role performance, leader responsiveness and citizen participation, decision making, economics and public finance, communication, ethnicity and cultural diversity, and health and career management. Again, the multivariate, multidimensional approach that has been suggested can serve as a matrix for identifying possible educational needs.

A National Institute

Beyond university schools, consideration should be given eventually to the establishment of a national institute for political leadership development. Examples of institutions in the United States whose experience could contribute to the creation and operation of such an institute include the Federal Executive Institute, the Brookings Institution, the National Academy of Sciences, the National Science Foundation, and the National Endowment for the Humanities, as well as national parties and professional associations. Through a nationwide linkage with departments of political science, this institute could have a locally sensitive yet solid scientific base.

Such an institute would be devoted to meeting the special educational needs of incumbents and aspirants at the national level. Eventually, an opportunity for educational advancement under its auspices might be provided to all successful candidates for national public office and to other leaders and citizens of national political prominence or promise. Through research, seminars, tutorials, lectures, and travel-study, engaging the best of national and transnational talent, the institute would seek constantly to improve the quality of the nation's elected leadership.

Until institutions for purposive political leadership education are established, departments of political science, and other university components, can take the lead in creating preservice, in-service, and postservice educational opportunities for political leaders and those most concerned with improving their performance. Such opportunities, based upon the innovativeness of which faculties are capable, will markedly contribute to the quality of eventual schools of political leadership at the local and national levels.

Some Implications

The quality and success of these educational efforts, however, will depend largely upon the scientific theory and research that result from the emergence of political leadership studies as a field of political science. Thus, the challenges of basic research and education, as well as that of application, are inextricably entwined.

Education of political leaders inevitably raises questions about the quality of educators. One solution will be to engage the best of leaders as teachers. Another will be to improve the political leadership education of the best of teachers. The challenge of education for and about political leadership may be expected to lead to new kinds of teacher education. All teachers are familiar with the clash of authoritarian and democratic personalities in the classroom, so well analyzed by Golembiewski,[46] and these difficulties can be expected to be magnified in the intense leader-teacher-follower interactions that will be involved in the treatment of critical political issues. The teachers of leaders will themselves have to be taught and provided with appropriate consulting assistance.

One implication is that both leaders and followers need to be engaged at all educational levels as teachers of the subject of political leadership. Professional teachers and scientists may acquire extraordinary expertise, but the best of them are always in the role of student with respect to their chosen vocation.

Quite possibly, the suggestions made in this chapter may greatly offend the egalitarian and antiauthoritarian spirit of Americans. The position taken here is that this spirit should not impede our trying to think through the educational implications of an emerging scientific interest in the study of political leadership. A solution that might still provide room for needed educational imagination would be to delay all purposive efforts to educate leaders until after their election. They might then be offered preservice or in-service educational assistance. From this viewpoint, pre-election educational intervention might not unduly advantage persons already favored by other inegalitarian forces in American society.

On the other hand, it can be argued that it is a major educational responsibility in a country founded upon the ideals of political egalitarianism to seek out and prepare for political leadership all persons with the talent and desire thus to serve society. From this viewpoint, the scientific study of political leadership, and the universal education of citizens in knowledge needed for and about political leadership becomes a major social responsibility. Furthermore, in a relatively open polity, no formal advantage would be exercised by purposively educated political leaders. They would have to compete in elections like everyone else.

Time to Respond

The time has come to respond to the provocative challenge posed by Professor Ewing in 1949: "Do political science professors make any attempt to discover, ·develop, train, test potential political leaders? If not, whose job do they think this is?" At least one major university administrator has implied that the university should take up this challenge. "In the past the great professional schools have been in law, business, and medicine," declared Harvard president Derek C. Bok in his June 12, 1975, commencement address: "In the future, education for public service must come to play an equal role."[47] While seeking to work out an appropriate response to Ewing's challenge, however, we need to keep in mind the advice of politically wise Honolulu real estate broker Fusao Taniguchi: "Watch out you don't produce a bunch of intelligent crooks up there on campus!"[48]

"A time may come," forecast William E. Mosler in 1944, "when the success of a college and particularly of a political science department will be measured by the proportion of its graduates who have become active politicians."[49] To meet this challenge will require changes in academic institutions themselves,[50] changes in their relationships with the societies of which they are a part, and ultimately changes in the communities which they serve. It may seem pretentious for political scientists to claim a role in the education of political leaders, but it is less pretentious than to perform political leadership roles without educational preparation and continuing assistance.

The time to begin to meet this educational challenge directly is now, in the context of rising interest in the scientific study of political leadership and of critical problems that demand efforts to make scientific knowledge socially useful.

CHAPTER 9

FIELD FOUNDATIONS: APPLICATION

*Science itself is not a liberator. It creates means,
not goals. . . . We should remember that the fate of
mankind hinges entirely upon man's moral
development.* [1]

ALBERT EINSTEIN
1940

THE STUDY OF POLITICAL LEADERSHIP will benefit if it is explicitly conceived
at an early stage of development as having the *potential* for becoming an area of
applied social science. Explicit acceptance of this potential will mean that
conceptualization, theorization, empirical research, and teaching will be conducted with—although not limited to—a sense of social usefulness.

Sources of Controversy

The suggestion that a part of political leadership studies can eventually
contribute to the development of political science as an applied social science
will evoke a useful controversy partly because neither the idea of science nor the
idea of an applied science are fully accepted within the discipline. In the crude,
initial stages of emergence as a social science it is natural that the more
comfortable and penetrating antiscience critical faculties associated with our
philosophical and historial tradition should be strongly with us. But note that
even those who regard the study and practice of politics as an "art" accept the
assumption that citizens can act upon artful insights, which this approach seeks
to nurture. Politics may be viewed as an applied art or as potentially a social
science applied with artistic imagination. In either case, the usefulness of seeking
to clarify the objectives, techniques, and problems of "application" seems
inescapable.

209

Another source of expected controversy is ethical. A position of complete denial is that application of knowledge in relation to political leadership is unethical. "Leadership even at its purest is unethical" is the way Baldelli summarized it.[2] From this position, efforts to apply knowledge on behalf of leaders, or on behalf of followers in relation to leaders, are immoral. This is because political institutions themselves, based upon violence and inequality, are unethical. The application of knowledge based upon the assumption of the continuation of politics as it is known and has been known in the past is indefensible.

An intermediate position is one in which the revolutionary application of knowledge on behalf of the oppressed, but not on behalf of the oppressors, is justified. The counterrevolutionary counterpart is that assistance may be given to established authorities, sometimes to conventional competitors, but never to revolutionary contestants.

An encompassing position is that the scientist should seek to apply knowledge whenever and wherever it would promise to promote valued means and ends, for and by persons ranging from individuals through classes and collectivities to the global human community. Given these complex understandings, the values of social scientists themselves may be seen as an obstacle to more dynamic and effective applied science activity.[3] These value sensitivities, varying with cultural and institutional context, can be expected to become even more acute when focused directly upon the subject of political leadership. Given the antiauthoritarian direction of values among arts and sciences students as noted in Chapter 8, it is probable that applied efforts in the United States may be skewed more to influencing followers to challenge leaders rather than to helping leaders influence followers. A balanced approach to political leadership would seek to help both leaders and followers to realize humane values. Where this is impossible, collective applications reflecting diverse value commitments can be expected and should be evaluated for overall effects upon the community as well as applied science contributors.

Applied Science Inexperience

In comparison with other social sciences, political science has not yet achieved a high degree of application orientation, despite pioneering exploratory efforts[4] and the growth of the programs in "policy science." Explicit interest in "applied anthropology," "applied sociology," and "applied psychology" is much better developed, as evidenced by contemporary graduate and undergraduate courses in these areas. The *Journal of Social Issues* manifestly seeks to encourage the development of an applied social psychology, and there are journals devoted to *applied* "behavioral science," "ecology," "economics," "psychology," "social psychology," "sociology," and so forth. A journal with this sort of orientation has not yet appeared in political science. One historical and contextual explanation for this lack may be that political science is of such obviously high application potential—dealing as it does with the ideas, institutions, and techniques of effective social power—that it must "pretend" to be *application irrelevant* in order to insure its social survival. In contrast, the other social and behavioral sciences may be more free in their claims to social usefulness, as well as more needful of making them.

Explicit interest in the study of political leadership is being voiced at a time, however, in which the ideas of "policy science" and "planning" are being better articulated and in which the scientific bases of the discipline of political science are, in fact, being strengthened despite often well founded criticism. Against such a background attention is directed to the possible future development of political leadership studies as an applied science. When the *Journal of Applied Political Science* appears, I hope it will have a section on applied political leadership, including follower initiatives to secure leader responsiveness.

In appreciating the potential for future development in this direction, we might examine the experience of other paradigms of applied science for possible insights. Consider, for example, agriculture, medicine, and business administration. Agricultural science provides a paradigm for the creation and application of knowledge from the basic scientific experiments of its component subfields through formal and extension education to actual use by the farmer. Medicine provides a somewhat similar paradigm: scientific findings are experimentally validated and then socially applied in the education of doctors and in a continuing process of postgraduate medical education that has been accompanied by increasing specialization. Business management is much less firmly based on science than is either agriculture or medicine, but it provides an example whereby theory and research on management problems are reflected in business school curricula and in such journals as the *Harvard Business Review*, in-service training seminars, and in the consulting activities of faculty members. Although none of these deal exactly with the problems that might be expected to accompany a deliberate effort to apply scientific knowledge of political leadership, they do suggest the outlines of likely future activity of this nature.

Components of an Applied Science Activity

Several necessary components for the successful and acceptable application of scientific political leadership knowledge are clear. The first is the existence of basic scientific knowledge and a continuing inventory, update, and refinement of that knowledge. Successive propositional inventories of theory and research findings in political leadership studies are essential for this purpose. Second, the basic scientific knowledge will have to be translated into forms that can be applied in political action. Knowing that leaders have personalities marked by active-positive, low esteem—high complexity, high need-Power, closed-minded, or field dependent-independent characteristics, for example, we will have to create prescriptions for actions that can be followed by both leaders and followers in making use of this knowledge. This implies a third basic requirement: experimentation in an action mode. We will have to seek validation of the results of application just as we originally sought to validate the hypothesis on which action was predicated. Next we need to transfer the application from the experimental conditions of a controlled environment into the natural society. Accompanying all of these processes we need deliberately contrived evaluations of both a scientific and a humanist nature. These will include professional self-evaluation, peer evaluation, evaluation by external consultants of varied methodological and value persuasions, and the critical responses of political leaders and other members of society.

Although mentioned last, a problem-solving approach is essential for all applied efforts, including the creation of needed scientific knowledge. To ensure that this approach guides all aspects of application activities, deliberate efforts must be made to create continuing channels of problem related feedback from leaders, followers, and other persons affected by efforts to apply knowledge or confronted by especially difficult leadership problems.

Truly significant problem-solving exchanges will occur not only when social scientists seek out or are invited to sites of social action but also when other social actors, both leaders and followers, initiate or respond to opportunities to define problems and suggest solutions for them in an academic setting. They need to question and consult social scientists as much as the latter need to question and consult them.

It is not to be assumed, however, that a simple approach will long suffice wherein social scientists become more knowledgeable about political leaders and leaders and followers become more aware of the methods and findings of social science. At primitive stages of development, this may be possible, but over the long run, the complexities of both leadership and social science may contribute, if not to a growing gap, at least to conditions in which possibly destructive lags and gains between knowledge and action will occur.[5] To lessen the gap, and to make knowledge and action mutually responsive, something new is needed in political science.

As Lundberg aptly pointed out, the successful application of scientific knowledge has been accompanied by the emergence of "conversion roles" performed by persons specifically trained to convert basic knowledge into action.

> The present stage of thought about [the effective utilization of scientific knowledge] has gone beyond the earlier simple views where either the scientist was charged with the responsibility of translating his findings, methods, skills, and so on, or where the practitioner was charged with the responsibility for acquiring this translation capacity and using it. Today, the *roles* whose central function is *the conversion of scientific resources into practice* are many and varied.[6]

To bridge the gap between the complexities of leadership and the complexities of leadership-related scientific resources, it may therefore be necessary to establish a chain, or a nonlinear group, of application-oriented role relationships.

This provides a new challenge to conventional political science education and research. We need to educate very explicitly for applied roles and for evaluative research to judge the effects of applied efforts. The general requirements have been acutely summarized by Boehringer in a critique of an enormously instructive, although painful, effort by social scientists to intervene in the violent Protestant-Catholic conflict in Northern Ireland. Boehringer advised:

> A social scientist intervening into a situation of social conflict should be required to specify carefully his goals, evaluate the costs and dangers to the participants of the techniques he proposes to use, and weigh them against his desired end, in both personal and political terms. And finally, he should devise rigorous research methodology so that he can, as scientifically as possible under the circumstances, evaluate the impact of his intervention upon the participants.[7]

The full Irish-American case experience, from which this advice emerged, should be made part of the basic education of all political scientists with applied science aspirations.[8] Other models of applied science activity need to be defined and critically evaluated in terms of participants, ends, means, and outcomes. Models of varying degrees of directness, from face-to-face exchanges to mass media communication, also need to be examined.

Sources of Applied Knowledge

Explicit concern for the potential application of political leadership knowledge will require catalytic efforts to draw upon the insights of otherwise frequently fragmented political science specialties. Political leadership studies are not all of political science but they are related to every aspect of the discipline. Thus, when contemplating the application of political leadership knowledge, we must not only translate into social action the core insights that will emerge but also do so in relation to knowledge produced by other subdisciplinary specialties. That is, specialists in applied political leadership knowledge must regard all other specialties as sources of insight. The applied scientist will need to seek the counsel of colleagues in disciplinary specialties such as parties, legislatures, public administration, judicial behavior, voting behavior, public opinion, local politics, national politics, comparative politics, international relations, political philosophy, and evaluative research methodology.

It is clear also that applied scientific efforts require formulation in relation to the broad paradigms that are emerging for the overall understanding of politics since interventions directed at crucial integrative or disintegrative figures undoubtedly offer potential for widespread system aftereffects. Thus, applied interventions usefully can be approached from the perspectives of power analysis, decision making, communications theory, structural-functional analysis, political economy, Marxism-Leninism, or others that may arise. For most of these analytical frameworks, the addition of an explicit concern with applying scientific knowledge about political leadership may mean simply providing a principal missing element whose absence has prevented their operational usefulness.

Concern with application also requires more explicit conceptualization of political leaders as social actors, with extraordinary potential for applying knowledge in action. It also requires that leaders be viewed collectively in aggregative interaction with other members of society who exert influence upon them. This greater explicitness about leaders in interaction raises questions about the appropriate educational preparation for performance by persons who influence them. Among social actors capable of acting upon a given applied theoretical proposition can be included political leaders themselves, close staff associates, opposing politicians, other professional contacts, including administrators and diplomats, social critics such as journalists, and any other members of a society who wish to influence political leadership behavior. The question is not whether political leaders, followers, and intermediary professionals can influence each other. They already do so in natural processes of political action. Rather, the question is whether addition to, or modification of, these processes in terms of scientific knowledge can improve political leadership performance for the enhancement of human welfare.

The prospect of relatively direct social intervention, even more acutely than less immediate educational preparation for political leadership, raises questions about the valued ends and means of scholarly action. Is knowledge to be applied for peace, justice, and freedom in peaceful, just, and free ways or is it to contribute to perpetuating the violence, inequities, and coercive conformity that has characterized most past political leadership domination? One thing is sure, refusal to think through the problems of applied knowledge to the point at which some form of effective action becomes possible means that these questions will be settled by default. On the other hand, merely to employ the academic base as a springboard for political action to realize preferred political values without explicit concern for applied science is laudable but not more laudable than direct professional political action—and not more promising as a way of breaking out of past or present disvalued states of affairs than would be a careful long-term effort to develop *part* of political leadership studies as an applied sociobehavioral science.

Developing an applied science of political leadership behavior is asserted to be worth exploration by specialists in this subject regardless of type of political institution, character of economy, or state of civil liberties. If scholars inside certain political communities are prevented from trying to create and apply new knowledge about leadership, then scholars outside them can at least experimentally simulate the action implications of hypotheses suggested by their more constrained colleagues. For example, rather than determine the societal adequacy of the introduction of monarchical, democratic-republican, or communist political leadership institutions for a society, these three systems can be simulated by role playing, and decisions on concrete issues of importance can be reached. Such decisions can then be evaluated for their feasibility and moral acceptability by expert judges of the culture concerned. In this way, laboratory simulation might eventually come to replace the social experimentation that now usually takes place through bloodshed in the streets or worse.[9]

Applied Science Roles

In deciding upon an appropriate applied knowledge role, the scientific specialist in political leadership also needs to define alternative modes of engagement and to seek societal acceptance of them. One such role is that of the *applied public service scientist.* Such a scientist seeks to assist both leaders and followers of all persuasions to improve their leadership-related behavior. No permanently secret contract consultancy is done and all experience in efforts to apply scientific knowledge about leadership eventually is made part of the public informational domain. Obviously, the emergence and societal acceptance of such a role will require an extraordinarily high degree of social science freedom and political tolerance. An intermediate and possibly transitional role is that of the *confidential scientific consultant.* Such a person can attempt to apply scientific knowledge on behalf of leaders, followers, or both, but on a confidential basis. This applied scientist would be in an ethical position somewhat analogous to that of the physician, psychiatrist, or lawyer serving a patient or client. Such a person will be forced to seek solutions to conflicts that arise between professional obligations and leader-follower interests. Furthermore, operating in a confidential manner, such an applied scientist will have an extraordinary responsibility for not misrepresenting the validity of scientific knowledge to persons who are being persuaded to act upon it. Quite a few American political scientists now seem to serve in this kind of capacity in the area of electoral campaign design, wherein their skills in survey research on voter attitudes are rather highly valued. Another possibility is the *indirect applied scientific consultant.* Such a scientist does not directly engage in applied political action but informally consults with those who do. This is an extension of the traditional scholar's role as a concerned citizen and sometimes lifelong counselor, especially in the case of former students. Finally, it is possible to envisage two polar types that bracket the preceding images. The first is the *scientist as political leader*—the scholar directly enters a political leadership role that may be conservative, reformist, or revolutionary. The second is the *scientist as a nonapplied basic researcher* dedicated to the discovery and publication of research findings on political leadership yet having no explicit concern for their practical application. If others would see practical relevance in such research, then let them search the scientific literature and devise their own ways to make research findings useful.

These five styles of scientific application have their own strengths, weaknesses, and difficulties of implementation. Undoubtedly, the near future of political leadership studies will see contributions to applied knowledge being made from all of these perspectives. Eventually, most political leadership specialists will probably wish to see their application efforts move in the direction of an applied public service, helping both leaders and followers solve problems in an increasingly open atmosphere of shared information. In reaching this stage, however, we may witness suffering of social science martyrs in trials before leaders or the led that is as severe, significant, and perhaps tragically inevitable as that which accompanied the search for religious truths.

Applied Implications: Variables and Dimensions

Just as a conceptual framework for scientific inquiry can assist efforts to posit and test linkages, hypotheses, and propositions leading toward more reliable theory—to devise more appropriate research methods—and to create more meaningful educational experiences—so can such a framework help stimulate thinking about potentially useful social applications of emergent knowledge.

In seeking to employ the suggested conceptual framework as a device to aid societal problem solving, it is important to understand that it can be used not only conservatively to discover and remove pathologies in existing states of affairs but also innovatively to generate alternatives for the future. For example, the number of political leaders at every level may be usefully increased or decreased, and new organizational bases for their selection may be contemplated (e.g., representation on the basis of age, sex, ethnicity, or occupation). Urgency and task complexity may suggest the idea of several successive teams of political leaders working around the clock, rather than the present system of single political executives working a one-shift day. Overall we can think of the applied aspects of political leadership studies as involving the design and implementation of alternative leadership futures as well as the solution of historically given present problems.

The idea of *personality* suggests that both leaders and followers should become more aware of alternative scientific interpretations of their own personal characteristics than is now customary. If we know more about ourselves, as well as more about each other, we may be able to devise more humane forms of social interaction. In the pioneering efforts by Barber to provide American voters with predictive personality profiles of candidates Nixon and McGovern just prior to the 1972 American presidential election,[10] and in that of Winter to provide comparative information on candidate needs for power, achievement, and affiliation in the election of 1976,[11] we have examples of attempts not only to analyze personalities but also to make such knowledge useful in assisting followers to choose leaders. Many more such efforts can be expected. We might add that greater self-knowledge by leaders might also bring them to control the more harmful effects of their personalities and to accent the more desirable. Appreciation of the clear scientific potential for achieving this goal underlies persistent suggestions for providing psychiatric consultation services to political leaders.[12] An example of the extraordinary effectiveness with which measures of personal qualities can be employed to select salient actors when role, task, organizational, value, and setting characteristics are relatively well defined is the selection of American astronauts.

The concept of *role* has a number of engineering implications. Take, for example, the simple idea of varying periods of acceptable role incumbency. This means that if we conceive a political system as a set of political leadership roles we can contemplate creating different turnover rates for each role that will affect the independence from, or responsiveness to, persons who validate role incumbency. This is, of course, an ancient idea that underlies the engineering of monarchical, parliamentary, presidential, and other systems. But we can explore very deliberately the desirability of differentially increasing turnover and respon- siveness at high, middle, or low leadership levels. In this manner, political leadership systems can be made more or less stable or responsive to the center, middle, or periphery. These turnover rates might be preprogrammed to accel- erate or decelerate in accordance with assessments of the qualities of incumbents and the tasks they face.

Consider also the possibility of creating a political leadership role set in which some roles are predominantly future oriented, others are equally future and present oriented, while others are predominantly present or past oriented.[13] Other attributes of leadership roles can also be deliberately engineered for the purpose of improving political system responsiveness, humaneness, effectiveness, and so forth; for example, prerequisites for incumbency, rights, obligations, and attached resources.

The necessity for applied experimentation with *organizational* variables that affect political leadership seems clear at all levels. In all societies, for example, the quality and organization of the staff immediately surrounding a given leader seems to be a crucial variable. This leads in virtually all cases to the "human curtain" phenomenon, in which the leader is screened from potentially valuable interactions and information, while staff members tend to aggrandize themselves at the leader's expense and often without her or his knowledge. These staff activities are both a product and a creator of leader personality. They require sharp experimental innovations to reduce their monotonously recurring deleteri- ous effects. Other organizational variables that seem extraordinarily needful of applied experimentation are leader relations with technical experts, journalists, diplomats, party members, and ordinary citizens. The conditions and techniques of effective mutual initiatives and responsiveness need gradually to be brought to awareness and added to the common repertoire of applied knowledge in politics.

One engineering application of the organizational variable would be to experiment with leadership representation based upon stratified income levels of validating followers to create a leadership body explicitly based upon low, middle, and upper income interests.

Very serious and urgent applied attention needs to be given to the concept of *task*. We are now faced with two very contradictory images with respect to leadership tasks at top levels and we need, first, research to clarify which is true in a given case and, second, action to experiment with alternatives. Probably the most prevalent task image we have of political leaders at all levels throughout the world is that the best and most important of them are incredibly overloaded with a bewildering variety of urgent problems to solve and decisions to make. They are simply overloaded with imperative tasks; consequently, they fail to decide in timely ways. Furthermore, the decisions they do make are considered only superficially; present emergencies drive out long-range foresight. At the same time they are portrayed in some areas as having extraordinary detailed knowledge and effective, even jealous, outreach in problem solving that para-lyze the efforts of others to intervene. A second prevalent image is just the opposite; top political leaders, despite the impression they like to convey, are really not that overloaded.[14] In fact, their decisions are largely the affirmation of those already determined by technical experts or pressed upon them by societal influentials.

For effective action on task variables we need to have an accurate inventory of tasks as actually experienced by incumbent and aspiring leaders at all levels. Then we need to ask, for example, whether the tasks could or should be redistributed and whether or not political scientists have substantive contribu-tions to make toward more effective and humane task accomplishment. In order to achieve this kind of task-related usefulness, scientific specialists on political leadership will have to penetrate the existing social images of political leaders as task-omnipotent, task-incompetent, or task-irrelevant persons, whether quan-titatively overloaded or underutilized. Follower task orientations and styles of task-related demands and supports directed toward leaders also require attention.

Moreover, we may eventually employ task requirements as explicit criteria for leadership recruitment. For example, rather than being asked to vote in terms of role, party, and personality, as at present, American voters of the future might be asked to choose persons in relation to ballot-defined task priorities.

From a *values* perspective, applied efforts will probably be most usefully directed initially toward increasing leader awareness of their own values and those of other people. Once values are clarified it becomes possible to examine objective conditions in relation to them, with the result that efforts subse-quently may be made to change either the values or the conditions, depending partly upon the intensity with which belief in each is held. A university president, for example, apparently acting upon a suggestion by Harold Lasswell, once carried out a "self-observation" study to find out whether his interactions were mainly "external" or "internal." Surprisingly, he discovered that more than half were with persons outside the university and that most of his "internal" relationships were with the trustees and a single dean. This new awareness of his internal isolation subsequently led the president to modify his behavior so as to associate more with faculty and students. Thus, a social scientist's research suggestion led to a social actor's awareness of a value-fact discrepancy apparently followed by behavioral change.[15] Such interventions by political scientists in relation to both leaders and followers require critical evaluation in endless chains of reduction and counterargument. But these criticisms need not be paralyzing. They need to be applied to interventions made under other concepts of the conceptual framework and to any effort by political scientists to exercise social influence.

Like values, *setting* variables may be affected directly or indirectly. One indirect technique may be simply for the applied social scientist to conduct guided tours of society for leaders in areas in which the former is especially knowledgeable. In contrary fashion, applied specialists may introduce "followers" to these same aspects as well as to political leaders in their own natural setting. Mutual understanding of, if not agreement upon, the nature of setting characteristics that influence political behavior can thus be enhanced. A direct, if unintended, example is provided by the movement of the Hawaii state legislature in 1968 from the crowded quarters of nineteenth-century Iolani Palace into a spacious new building. Legislators experienced in both settings have commented that there was greater interaction, conflict, and interpersonal knowledge in the old, cramped conditions than in the new roomy, and more impersonal environment.

Both science and art, however, have another capability for intervening in setting variables that is not entirely dependent on existing characteristics. Science can simulate plausible alternatives and art can invent them, although neither can realize them alone. Both can confront leaders and followers with the question, "What would you do if X, Y, and Z characteristics of this society were of this nature?"

Beyond enhancing awareness of actual and hypothetical alternative setting conditions, it is possible also that political leadership specialists themselves might invent a new setting technology, such as a new mode of citizen participation or a social science–based decisional checklist for political leaders that would be as functional for societal well-being as is the preflight evaluative criteria that airplane pilots employ to improve human safety aloft.

The dimensions of political leadership behavior that have been identified also suggest areas for significant applied science efforts. From an applied perspective, political leadership behavior may be conceived as affecting variation in each dimension both directly and indirectly: by what leaders do themselves and by what their behavior permits others to do. For example, national political leaders can increase the level of global violence in two ways: by preparing and employing armed forces in battle and by encouraging and tolerating the violence of others through arms aid and avoidance of violence-inhibiting alternatives.

The predictor variables may serve as focuses for applied efforts to influence dimensional variation. For example, levels of violence may be affected by efforts to change leader personalities, their violence-related role responsibilities, the violence-promoting organizational influences that are brought to bear upon them, the tasks related to violence with which they deal, violence-related value sensitivities, and the objective setting characteristics that promote violence. This assumes, of course, that applied science efforts are based upon progressively greater understanding of causal relationships among all the variables of the model.

Applied science interventions need to be approached from the perspectives of leaders, followers, and of both in interaction. If we wish to decrease levels of violence, then we need to think not only about changing directly the personality, role, organizational, task, value, and setting characteristics of leader behavior but also about the same characteristics of followers and of leaders and followers in interaction.

Analogously, applied efforts may be directed at affecting variation in other dimensions of political behavior. Nonviolence influence processes may be enhanced.[16] Control may be expanded or contracted. Mutual responsiveness may be increased or lessened. Conflict may be heightened or diminished; compromise, promoted or inhibited; and consensus, strengthened or weakened. Positive and negative emotions may be evoked;[17] distribution varied; and associational networks, extended or interrupted. Spatial orientations may be expanded or contracted and time consciousness altered. Communications may be intensified or reduced.[18] The technical aspects of problem-solving efforts may be complicated or simplified.[19] Finally, the activeness, creativity, and moral sensitivity of both leaders and followers may be deliberately enhanced or dulled. Constantly, applied scientists will need to be aware of the possibility that unintended noxious consequences may accompany their attempts at ameliorative intervention.

Despite task complexity, unintended outcomes, difficulties of moral choice, and temporarily inadequate knowledge, applied science activities in political leadership studies need not be paralyzed. These problems must be solved progressively and collaboratively under careful evaluative research controls. The rise of modern medicine provides, at least in part, an example: primitive applied efforts based upon relative ignorance became gradually transformed into high levels of applied science activity through a combination of basic multidisciplinary research, science-based education, and clinical practice.

Applied Linkages: Research and Education

In thinking about opportunities for applying knowledge in political leadership studies, it will be noted how closely linked these tasks are with basic research and education. We first identify where we are and where we would like to be. Then we attempt by quasi-educational processes to achieve self-critical and creatively adaptive movement from the one to the other. This can be done without a sense of science or without explicit reliance upon theoretically relevant empirical propositions—but it will be done less reliably over the long run in this way. The past record of human achievement in political leadership is not entirely dismal but there is almost universal acceptance of the present need for improvement. In seeking it, research, education, and applied efforts are necessarily linked: research on the results of application efforts is needed; education for both research and application is essential.

The societal usefulness of political science and the advancement of the scientific study of politics are also inextricably linked. The more applied scientific efforts can produce or test solutions to political problems that are not probable in natural social processes, the greater the social support for science and the higher the morale of those who devote their lives to its creative realization. Efforts to solve practical problems may be as evocative of scientific imagination as philosophical contemplation, and perhaps even more so on the part of those favored with the opportunity for both, as are most scholarly political scientists.

Applied Contributions: Information and Evaluation

Overall there are two major areas in which the deliberately focused scientific study of political leadership may make especially important contributions to society. The first is simply to make available to leaders and followers more accurate information about each other and about their interactions. This potential achievement, of course, is based on the assumptions that political scientists will gain social acceptance for producing such knowledge and that once available it will improve leader-follower relations in valued directions. The mutual provision of information will differ markedly from the operational mode of the secret intelligence systems (including confidential campaign polls) now employed by political leaders to manipulate each other and the public. Not only will public attitudes be polled, as in present commercial and government surveys, but also personality-, role-, organization-, task-, value-, and setting-relevant information about *both leaders and followers in interaction* will be available to all as a guide to intelligent political action. As in scientific research on human sexuality, efforts must be made to preserve confidentiality so as to avoid damage to individuals. This will be extraordinarily difficult to achieve in politics because of the small number, high visibility, and ready identifiability of political leaders, especially those few at the top, and because of citizen fear—virtually worldwide—of retribution for honest expressions of political views. This implies, paradoxically, that while we are making extraordinary efforts now and in the near future to preserve confidentiality, a long-range goal of applied political leadership studies should be to create conditions in leader-follower relations in which needs for confidentiality are minimized. That is, we need to work for a society in which access to communications facilities and to needed information is more readily available, namely, a more open informational society.

A second major applied role for political scientists in political leadership studies is to gain acceptance as *scientific critics* of political leader and follower behavior. The idea of criticism as a useful stimulus to improved performance has been accepted in such fields as sports, art, music, theater, literature, poetry, and architecture and needs to be examined in relation to political leadership performance. This does not mean only the witty, sometimes cynical, comments of persons who are taunting the political leader as surrogate father or mother figure—or their sycophantic opposite. Rather, it means sustained, principled, research-based, in-depth commentary on the origins, processes, and outcomes of political leadership behavior as influenced by the behavior of other persons in a society. It will require not only the courage to point out what is "wrong" but also the courage to recognize what is "right," as well as the courage to affirm when such judgment is not helpful. Critics of political leadership may eventually devise a way of recognizing excellence in leadership that is at least as respected, coveted, and inspiring of effort as is the present Nobel Prize for contributions to peace. The critical evaluation of political leadership behavior by no means needs to be a political science monopoly. Critics of all persuasions, from the arts to journalism, may be engaged in efforts to improve upon political leadership. Undoubtedly, the greater competence of a future science of political leadership behavior will mean the advancement of such efforts.

Critical social science commentary on political leadership behavior may eventually be possible through newspapers, television, radio, and other media, sometimes conducted in an interdisciplinary social science context and at especially significant periods of societal stocktaking; e.g., at the beginning of a new year.

In their applied and critical efforts, students of political leadership cannot themselves escape critical evaluation. They can expect rightly critical reactions from three sources: their colleagues, political leaders, and other members of society whose lives are affected. Such critics will wish to question assumptions underlying the formulation of problems to be solved, the extent of scanning for relevant knowledge, the quality of knowledge employed, the adequacy of preparation for the tasks undertaken, the extent of the results as compared with control conditions, the appropriateness of criteria employed to judge outcomes, and the ignorance thus revealed.

The intent here has been to focus this kind of discussion upon opportunities and problems in applying knowledge, both existing and potentially achievable, in the scientific study of political leadership. As Merriam illustrated by refusing to share his research-derived insights into techniques of "grafting" with a Chicago politician he regarded as being "acquisitive,"[20] we need to devote professional attention to problems of applying knowledge as well as creating, critically evaluating, and communicating it to apprentice scholars.

A sign of the professional coming of age of an applied science of political leadership studies will be a social scientist's invitation to be a research observer in the campaigns of candidates competing for elected office. Or the same scientist's acceptance as a leadership process adviser to the leaders of competing political parties. Or a political leadership specialist's invitation to observe both revolutionary and counterrevolutionary leadership behavior in the same society. The seeming absurdity of this suggestion is a measure of the distance we must travel in creating a science of political leadership studies with an applied science component. Yet such aspirations are not unreasonable since some journalists and diplomatic negotiators, for example, already have gained somewhat similar acceptance from competing leaders. Furthermore, political scientists working as interview researchers in multiparty systems or across polities have begun to pioneer the acceptance of scientific inquiry across competing value preferences from "left" to "right."[21] The continuing long-range disciplinary challenge will be not only to create but also to apply scientific knowledge in the same way that a battlefield physician might apply the results of medical research for humane ends, regardless of the uniforms of the victims or the banners under which they fought. I believe that a commitment to the value of nonviolence will serve as a moral basis for liberating political science energies for applied science action in political leadership studies.

CHAPTER 10

TOWARD GLOBAL SCIENTIFIC COOPERATION

To leap beyond yet nearer bring.[1]

WALT WHITMAN
1855

HOWEVER PERSUASIVE THE CASE may be for the scientific study of political leadership on theoretical, research, educational, and public service grounds, little progress is likely to be made—except for the remarkable achievements of isolated individuals—without skillful administration. This means the organization of support for individual and group efforts and the establishment of communication patterns that enhance the creative development of all. The purpose of this chapter is to begin a collegial discussion of these matters.

We begin with two assumptions: (1) it is essential for political leadership studies to develop "from the bottom up"; and (2) nothing short of completely global sensitivity will be satisfactory. Thus, while we begin with scientists scattered unevenly throughout the globe in institutions in which scientific research is possible, we envision a worldwide scientific community of scholars in political leadership studies that both creates and works in stimulating relationship to a world center for the scientific study of political leadership.

Bottom-up Development

In bottom-up development we begin typically with individual faculty members or graduate students in departments of political science who become aware that their past work and present concerns evoke a special interest in the study of political leadership. At this point it is essential that faculty tutors, department colleagues, chairpersons, curriculum committees, administrators, and financial sponsors provide support so that these individuals can develop their talents as contributors to this field. At a minimum, departments of political science should establish both undergraduate and graduate courses specifically devoted to "political leadership" that will provide a focus for insights into this subject from all other political science specialities and give specialists a chance to explore its core potentials. The study of political leadership is a subject par excellence for team teaching and research. At the same time, it requires specialized concern lest it escape explicit scientific attention.

It is assumed that in developing political leadership studies, individual scientists and departments of political science will be sensitive to the need for developing scientifically productive professional relationships with political leaders of all persuasions in the immediate or distant societal environment insofar as this is possible. The development of these kinds of scientifically useful relationships will demand extraordinarily high degrees of independent integrity on the part of the political leadership specialist and high degrees of tolerance from colleagues who may be suspicious that such relationships are being cultivated for personal aggrandizement or counterrevolutionary or revolutionary purposes. Even if they can obtain the understanding and support of colleagues and students, specialists in political leadership must still solve the extraordinary problem of defining their scientific roles acceptably to active incumbent and aspiring political leaders. Leaders most value the quality of loyalty in those members of society whom they permit an intimate understanding of their work. Furthermore, they generally tend to view scholars as either troublemakers or sycophants, and presently have few analogs upon which to base acceptance of the role of social scientist. Therefore specialists in political leadership must take special care to define their scientific relationship to each leader and follower. We will all benefit from sharing our experience in the establishment of such relations. Scientific specialists in political leadership must demonstrate that they are not campaign advisers, journalists, or political intelligence agents, but that they must have more reliable information than any of these. Leadership specialists must argue plausibly that the results of their efforts eventually will assist in improving the lives of political leaders and those of other members of the community whom they universally profess to serve. Although the short-range usefulness of this may not be readily apparent, the self-interested or socially oriented professional interests of the political scientists are apt to be fully appreciated by political leaders if articulated frankly and may serve as the basis for a future relationship of increased scientific significance. Given the complexity of the relationship, it is striking how successful political scientists already have been in gaining the research cooperation of active and aspiring leaders. Examples of refusal to cooperate in serious research efforts are few, but there is much tacit avoidance of efforts estimated to have a low probability of success. What is required is a steady increase in such scientifically useful relationships accompanied by more detailed and penetrating inquiries.

Multidisciplinary Scientific Base

To strengthen the scientific basis of political leadership studies in a local university context interdisciplinary teaching and research teams of social scientists should be created. For example, an interdisciplinary course on "human leadership" might be offered in an interdisciplinary program of a college of arts and sciences. In this course, political science would contribute its own perspective upon a universal social phenomenon. Another possibility is that departments of political science, or individual scientists where no departments existed, might invite other social scientists, ethologists, and humanists to focus their attention explicitly upon political leadership. Even to raise such possibilities illustrates how important is the understanding and support of deans, department chairmen, political scientists, social science colleagues, and adventurous students. Among social scientists who have much to contribute to strengthening a scientific community of teacher-scholar specialists in political leadership studies are anthropologists, ethologists, sociologists, psychologists, social psychologists, historians, and economists with interests in entrepreneurship. Their involvement in research as well as in teaching programs will help to check biases by providing the multiple perspectives of scholars who seek to achieve scientific understanding of human society. In addition, natural scientists and mathematicians can be engaged as consultants in scientific development on the one hand, while historians and humanists can contribute their skeptical critiques of science on the other. In applied science activities, colleagues in agricultural extension services, medical schools, social work, and other professional schools can be called upon for advice and shared experience.

Additionally, although it is not customary in most normal political science activities, there is nothing to prevent the establishment of community advisory groups on scientific teaching and research activities. These may be composed of local party chairpersons, active or retired leaders, and concerned citizens from groups ranging from the least to the most advantaged. Where the collegial social science base is strong, the scientific study of political leadership need not fear strong community involvement. Some will reject this scientific model and demand that it be placed in the service of a leader, a party, or a group. The scientific response in some societies and institutions must be to insist upon high degrees of scientific autonomy with the hope that eventually the benefits of such an approach will lead to global acceptance of this kind of institutional arrangement. The university has no monopoly of political leadership research, training, or application, but it has a possibly unique truth-based claim to independent involvement that needs to be articulated and defended.

Overall it is hoped that at least several universities will be willing to make a strong commitment to the scientific study of political leadership, attempting to pioneer a comprehensive set of teaching, research, and service activities—benefiting from the local community as a learning environment, extending the Gosnell-

Merriam Chicago tradition and that of Dahl in New Haven—and facilitating interdisciplinary, interprofessional, community involvement.

University Research Centers

One type of multidisciplinary research center linked to educational and applied activities is shown in Figure 14. Such a center might be related to or developed further into a science-based school of political leadership studies.

The core of the center would be a multidisciplinary *innovative workshop* that would seek creative integration of theory and action in all center activities. A constant review of emerging theory and research findings useful for all center activities would be provided by a *propositional inventory*. A *biographical research* program would seek theoretical integration by study of the lives of individual leaders, by comparisons among leaders, and by aggregate inquiry. An *audiovisual media* program would assist research, teaching, and applied activities through film, videotape, sound recordings, photography, and graphic arts. A *case*

FIGURE 14. A University Center for Political Leadership Research

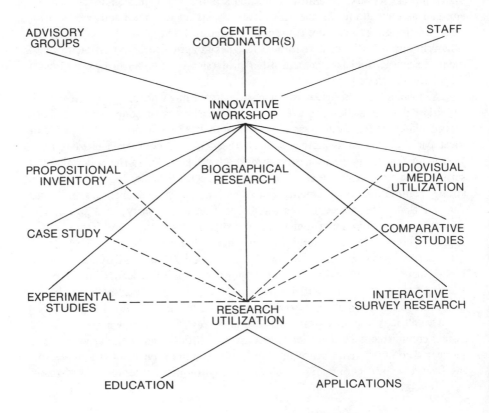

study program would take political leadership in the surrounding community as a subject for full-scale field investigation. More specific problem-oriented case studies also would be conducted. A *comparative studies* program would seek to make large-scale comparisons between two or more complete political leadership communities, including preferably the local community and one selected for highly contrasting characteristics. A laboratory and field *experimental studies* program would concentrate upon exploring critical problems of leader-follower interactions related to research, teaching, and applied activities. An *interactive survey research* program would study leaders and followers in interaction as a contribution to theoretical, teaching, and applied objectives. A *research utilization* program would concentrate upon transforming knowledge and experience gained in the foregoing inquiries into forms useful for educational and applied activities. In addition, the research utilization program would be charged with challenging all the basic research programs with educational and applied problems that arise out of field experience. As operational subcomponents of research utilization activities, an *educational* program would seek to improve leadership-related content and methods at all educational levels, while an *applied* program would seek to make emergent knowledge useful in solving local, national, international, and transnational problems. An example of a cooperative applied science activity to which political leadership studies could contribute would be a common effort by a political science department to foster the "political development" of its surrounding local community, along at least one mutually agreed upon criterion; e.g., increased participation.

The activities of the center would be guided by advisory groups with special competence in science, the humanities, academic administration, and professional application. It would also be essential to engage the advice of experienced political leaders and critical followers of varied persuasions. A constructive staff of high quality would be indispensable for the successful pursuit of center objectives. Overall scientific leadership would be sought by one or more political leadership studies *coordinators,* the improvement of whose behavior should be viewed comparatively as the academic analog of the improvement of political leadership behavior, which is the subject of research, teaching, and applied effort.

National Scientific Cooperation

At supralocal, regional, and national levels it is hoped that scientifically based scholarly activities focused upon the subject of political leadership can be created. This means at least the organization within regional and national political science associations, where they exist, of scholarly groups specializing in creating and sharing research, teaching, and applied experience beyond the bounds of local academic communities. Additionally it is hoped that other professional associations of social scientists—for example, those in anthropology, sociology, and psychology—also will form study groups that will give special attention to political leadership from the village to the world polity. Moreover, it is hoped that regional and national academies of science or the Social Science Research Council, as in the United States, will form interdisciplinary professional groups to promote the scientific study of political leadership (or at least the general study of human leadership) and to develop capabilities for research, teaching, and service activities on a larger scale. Liaison with national parties and associations of political leaders, other professionals, and citizen groups will be essential in developing adequate national overviews.

Transnational Scientific Cooperation

Beyond the nation state, it is hoped that international social science groups such as the International Political Science Association or the emerging World Future Studies Federation will be receptive to requests to establish special groups to advance the scientific study of political leadership. Through such means transnational scientific cooperation can be sought and efforts can be made to establish mutually beneficial relationships with international associations of political leaders, such as international party conferences, international meetings of legislators, international conferences of mayors, and the emergent political leadership in the United Nations. Similar linkages can be sought with transnational citizens groups that are especially concerned with international political leadership performance, such as those concerned with peace, population limitation, environmental conservation, and human rights; for example, Amnesty International. Regional consortia of university centers for political leadership studies may additionally be established in Asia, Africa, Europe, Latin America, the Middle East, North America, and the Pacific Islands.

Toward a World Center for the
Scientific Study of Political Leadership

As an expression of explicit concern for the scientific description, explanation, prediction, evaluation, and nurturing of global political leadership, it will be important to establish a World Center for the Scientific Study of Political Leadership. This center would be based upon and grow out of the scientific activities of a worldwide community of individual scholars who specialize in political leadership studies. Scientists active in national and international political leadership studies naturally will be engaged, and liaison with all subglobal scientific research programs at regional and university centers would be maintained. Communication among members of the world scientific community especially interested in this subject would first be established by private correspondence, then proceed through relatively informal newsletters, and finally achieve full scientific expression in conferences, symposia, workshops, journals, books, joint research projects, and other scientific activities.

Scientific Activities

Some important scientific activities might usefully be undertaken by a global center for political leadership studies. First, it might conduct research on political leadership problems of special interest for the world community, problems that may not be treated adequately by nationally based scientific communities. Top priority could be given to the study of leadership variables affecting performance of the U.N. secretary-general and to studies of the performance of the world political leadership collective as it affects solution of global problems. Other priority research would focus upon world leadership networks, upon cross-national and subnational comparisons, and upon evaluation of world-oriented educational and applied science efforts.

Second, the center could issue periodic reports, perhaps annually, on "the state of world political leadership." Such reports would contain demographic statistics on the changing patterns of world political leadership and could eventually include short-range forecasts based partly upon past experience. Such reports would focus upon the secretary-general of the United Nations, national leaders, party leaders, members of national legislatures, governors of large subnational units, mayors of large urban centers, leaders of counties and towns, chiefs of villages, and commune chairpersons. At some levels complete enumeration will be possible; at others, appropriate methods of sampling and statistical inference will have to be employed. As a result of such studies, it will be possible to appreciate on a cumulative basis changes that are occurring in the characteristics that define political leaders worldwide: age, sex, ethnicity, occupational background, religion, education, modes of accession, modes of removal, career mobility, international experience, value orientations, and significant leadership innovations. Assuming that political leaders at all levels play extraordinarily significant roles in relation to world problems, such a continuing inventory should supplement and be correlated with efforts to gain statistical overviews of world population trends, food production, energy resources, military capabilities, and health. The state of world political leadership should be of as much scientific and general interest as are world population, food and energy resources, and weather.

An important scientific service that could be provided by such a center would be simply to help specialists in political leadership studies find and communicate with each other. In part, this will occur naturally, through normal processes of scientific communication, but contact can be enormously improved through purposive correspondence and through translation. We need, for example, to ask colleagues in representative world universities periodically to select the best short essay they know that contributes to scientific analysis of political leadership; to translate these essays into major world languages; and to arrange for their distribution to the world scientific community as a stimulus, for, and a baseline from which to measure, the development of political leadership studies.

Another helpful activity would be to publish a journal or yearbook, *World Political Leadership,* that would cumulatively seek to advance scientific knowledge, its problem-solving relevance, and its contribution to the human development of both political leaders and followers. Such a journal might have sections that summarized scientific research findings; described new research methods; evaluated educational innovations; presented critical incident studies of successful and unsuccessful problem-solving efforts; contained evaluations of political leadership performance by scientists, humanists, leaders, and followers; and presented essays on current problems written by political leaders, scientists, and other concerned global citizens.

In connection with its constant efforts to promote scientific excellence, the center might sponsor an annual prize for exemplary scientific accomplishment in political leadership studies.

A significant activity for the center would be to carry out a long-range program on a world scale to establish the intellectual foundation for the scientific study of political leadership in a context that is sensitive to humanistic insight and to the needs of persons who are not themselves political leaders. This program should seek to summarize and stimulate multidisciplinary, multiprofessional, multicultural understanding. Such an effort might take several decades, unless support could be found for virtually simultaneous accomplishment of several necessary tasks. At least ten are clearly essential. Most are conceived as being the products of specially qualified scholarly coordinators, supplemented by diversely constituted advisory groups who identify contributors; arrange symposia in which ideas can be presented, enriched, and reformulated; and insure that the results are communicated to the world community in printed and audiovisual expressions of high quality.

1. *World Classics of Political Leadership.* Under the general editorship of a political leadership scholar, we need to create, with the support of a university press or consortium of presses, a series of "world classics" in political leadership that would provide integrated insight into the full range of human thinking on this subject. The series should include representative examples of works in the Chinese, Indian, Islamic, Greco-Roman, Judeo-Christian, and other traditions and should seek to recreate the oral traditions of Africa, Oceania, and other world areas. Folk and counterelite traditions should be sought as well as dominant traditions. With fresh translations and annotations to make them fully intelligible to modern readers, the entire series should be made available at least to readers of the official languages of the United Nations: Arabic, Chinese, English, French, Russian, and Spanish. Audiovisual presentations, radio or video dramas, for example, should be prepared to communicate the main similarities and differences among these traditions to persons who do not normally learn by reading.

2. *Political Science and Political Leadership.* This volume would seek to focus the insights of the various specialties of contemporary political science upon the subject of political leadership. Leading scholars in subfields of the discipline would be asked to write thoughtful overview essays to answer the question, "What understanding of the nature of political leadership, its potentials and limitations, emerges from the field in which you are an expert, and what do you believe the next steps in research, teaching, and service activities should be?" Insights of this kind are needed from scholars in such fields as political philosophy, empirical political theory, national politics, comparative politics, international politics, local politics, law and judicial behavior, legislatures, parties, public administration, and voting behavior.

3. *Social Science Perspectives upon Political Leadership.* In this volume, contributors from the various social and behavioral sciences would address the question, "What has our discipline learned about the nature of human leadership and what implications might this have for understanding the potentialities and limitations of leadership in politics?" Contributions would be sought from scholars in ethology, anthropology, economics, history, sociology, psychology, social psychology, and psychiatry. Contributors to this volume would be assisted to focus more sharply upon political leadership problems if they could have available in advance the results of the political science survey mentioned above.

4. *The Humanities and Political Leadership.* Leading scholars in the humanities also need to be asked to contribute the insights of their specialties into the nature of political leadership. Here we would seek to learn from scholarly imagination in such fields as art, architecture, drama, literature, history, poetry, music, philosophy, and religion. Again, it would be useful if the scholars in the humanities could have available the overviews by political scientists and other social scientists as stimuli for creating their own unique contributions to understanding.

5. *Occupational Perspectives upon Political Leadership.* The intent of this volume would be to create awareness of the significance of political leadership from the point of view of persons other than political scientists, social scientists, or scholars in the humanities. Contributions to the volume may be made by scholars in professional schools or by laymen. Perspectives would be sought from persons involved with agriculture, industry, trade, communications media, diplomacy, education, labor unions, medicine, the military, public administration, religion, and social work. Through this volume insight into the importance of political leadership for other professions would be sought in answer to the question, "How do political leaders facilitate or constrain the work of persons in your occupation? What principal problems in your relations with them need to be solved? What suggestions do you have for changes?"

6. *Political Leaders on Political Leadership.* Here is needed a volume in which experienced and insightful political leaders would have an opportunity to express their own conceptions of political leadership, identify major past problems they have solved or failed to solve and the character of present problems in

being a political leader, and explain their thinking about more desirable future alternatives. Major spokesmen should be sought from conservative, liberal, socialist, communist, and authoritarian traditions, as should revolutionary critics of any one of these, in societies that rank both high and low on indices of material well being.

7. *Alternative Futures for Political Leadership.* This volume would seek to direct the imagination of some of the world's most creative thinkers toward the subject of political leadership. Essays would be sought from a wide variety of people, including experienced leaders, social scientists, humanists, natural scientists, philosophers, and leaders in the emerging world intellectual discipline of futures studies. Such a volume would be enriched by the past- and present-oriented stocktaking efforts that have been suggested above. Its intent would be to envision more desirable forms of political leadership at local, subnational, national, regional, and world levels and to suggest ways in which progress toward them from present conditions might be made.

8. *Societal Problems and Political Leadership.* This volume, or set of volumes, would seek to examine the capabilities and limitations of political leaders in coping with a selected set of important problems. Such problems would include, for example, peace, food, population limitation, energy, human rights, and environmental protection. Toward each problem would be directed a characteristic set of contributions: a problem-defining analysis by a world expert that also included awareness of alternative problem definitions; then, responses from political leaders with experience at the international, the national, or the local level. Comments on these presentations by other political leaders, social scientists, and other discussants would then be made. The intent of these presentations would be to define more clearly the limitations and potentials of political leaders at all levels in relation to the solution of pressing world problems.

9. *Education and Political Leadership.* Partly in response to the normative forecast of desirable political leadership futures, and partly against the background of past experience, a major effort needs to be made on a world scale to share ideas about education for and about political leadership. A symposium on this problem would include reports on the experience of ad hoc learning and party schools, as well as comparative suggestions emerging from experience in purposive education for business management, public administration, and military leadership. One question to be asked is, "Insofar as the idea of purposive education for political leadership is accepted, should there be some elements shared by all leaders across the world polity, in addition to unique local cultural understanding?" To explore such a question a lively conference of political leaders of varied value persuasions, educators, social scientists, and critics of education should be convened.

10. *Research Methods for the Study of Political Leadership.* Realizing that all the foregoing endeavors and all efforts to create more desirable alternative futures are deeply dependent upon our modes of knowing, it is necessary that

there be periodic stocktaking of the methods of research available to us. Thus, this volume would attempt to inventory the most promising present methods of inquiry to use for advancing scientific understanding of political leadership. Cultural criticisms of current social science practices and orientations should be made and alternatives suggested.

If the world center were to sponsor these projects, symposia, and associated publications for two decades, for example, a very substantial contribution to world thinking about political leadership would have been made. The classical heritage would have been reviewed, and alternative futures would have been projected in a way that would make the behavior of political leaders at all levels the focus of attention of political science, the other social sciences, the humanities, political leaders themselves, other occupations, societal problem solving, education, and scientific research.

There are other services that a center might provide to political leaders and scientists concerned with political leadership studies, much as was suggested in Chapters 7, 8, and 9, including assistance with the political leadership content of world educational curricula, a periodic propositional inventory of action-relevant research findings, a world biographical book service, a world-oriented "sabbatical" educational program for leaders at various turning points in their careers, catalytic cross-national and cross-party communications conferences under scientific sponsorship,[2] and possibly eventually the provision of scientific consulting services to political leaders and followers in crisis situations. Such activities would not be designed to preempt natural activities of a similar nature but to supplement them from a specifically scientific, pluralistic, and global point of view.

Institutional Context

As yet, nothing has been said about the institutional location of a World Center for the Scientific Study of Political Leadership. One possibility is that it might become one of the research centers associated with the emerging United Nations University. As such it would be directly in touch with all member nations of the United Nations, the programs of UNESCO, the United Nations Institute for Training and Research, and the problem-solving efforts of the specialized agencies. Alternatively, the center might be endowed privately as an international nongovernmental scientific institution with principal ties to major world universities and the international social science community. Or some beneficial combination of both be created.

The center should be small in scale but exemplary in activity and responsiveness. An advisory committee composed mainly of political leaders from the principal world political traditions and natural and social scientists, combined with humanists, communications specialists, and concerned laymen, should oversee its activities.

The ideas we have been exploring at a global scale are translatable back to the activities of individual scholars and groups of scholars at the local college or university level or to national activities. Every activity that is meaningful and useful at one of these levels is potentially applicable to the other. The scale of activity and the character of participants may vary but the basic endeavors can be pioneered, shared, and made scientifically productive across levels.

Whatever the scientific activities, and whatever the institutional context, the future promise of political leadership studies will be enhanced by commitment to the values of scientific and humane intent; peace; economic, social, and political justice; creativity; a research orientation toward the future, as well as toward the past and the present; cooperation across disciplines, nations, ethnic communities, and ideologies; and concern for "followers," without whom there would be no leadership. For the scientific study of political followership is the natural complement to, and an essential component of, the study of leadership.

Conclusion: Challenge to Scientific Imagination

We end where we began: with a challenge to scientific imagination. Can we gain enough understanding of the creative potential of political leadership that will enable us purposively not only to avoid barbarous conditions of global poverty, violence, and repression but also to proceed intelligently toward economic justice, nonviolence, and the further liberation of human potential? It will depend in part upon how the scholarly discipline of political science responds.

In this book we have noted the surprising lack of disciplinary focus upon political leadership; the multiplying signs of growing interest in it; the wide range of available conceptual resources; the promising possibility of pursuing a multivariate, multidimensional linkage approach; the research, teaching, and applied foundations that are required for field development; and the need for institutionalization ranging from the work of individual scholars to the global scientific community. No single scholar can solve all the problems that are explicit or implicit in what has been attempted here. Only a community of scholars dedicated to the scientific study of political leadership can do so. But within this broad perspective, perhaps the accomplishments of the past, present, and future can be better appreciated and needed next steps more clearly seen.

APPENDIX A

DOCTORAL DISSERTATIONS
ON LEADERSHIP, 1925-1975

LISTED HERE ARE 250 doctoral dissertations accepted by American universities from 1925 to 1975 that have title references to any form of the base word "leader" coupled with any of the following keywords: "follower," "followers," "following," "politics," "political," "professional," "public," "role," "social," and "studies." These dissertations were identified through the computerized Datrix II information retrieval service of Xerox University Microfilms. (Gibbons's 1967 and Nazaar's 1972 dissertations are exceptions. I would like to learn of others not retrievable through the keyword combinations employed here.) They were drawn from a total of more than 430,000 dissertations accepted since 1861 in which the title keyword "political" appeared 3,458 times and "leadership," 990 times.

This multidisciplinary list of titles is of interest in terms of intellectual history, as a knowledge resource, and as a base from which to measure future doctoral research interest in leadership. Salient past interest in the concept of "leadership" in schools of education, for example, is striking and is consistent with the publication since 1943 of the professional journal *Educational Leadership*. By contrast, political science interest in leadership has been much less explicit, although a number of pioneering political science inquiries are readily apparent such as the three political biographies written at the University of Chicago in 1926 and 1927. Among political scientists, explicit attention to leadership in the dissertation research of scholars such as Kalaw, Shannon, Cornwell, Gottfried, Matthews, Mendel, Schlesinger, Nehring, Verba, Frey, Hoffman, Andrain, Ladd, Miller, Han, and others, with increasing frequency and with more varied analytical interests, is noteworthy.

1925

Kalaw, Maximo M. *The Development of Philippine Politics (1872-1920): An Account of the Part Played by the Filipino Leaders and Parties in the Political Development of the Philippines.* Ph.D., University of Michigan.

1926

Stevenson, Marietta. *William Jennings Bryan as a Political Leader.* Ph.D., University of Chicago.

1927

Johnson, Claudius O. *Carter Henry Harrison I: A Study in Political Leadership.* Ph.D., University of Chicago.

Peel, Roy V. *James Gillespie Blaine: A Study in Political Leadership.* Ph.D., University of Chicago.

1929

Parten, Mildred B. *An Analysis of Social Participation, Leadership, and Other Factors in Pre-school Play Groups.* Ph.D., University of Minnesota.

1930

Ramsower, H. C. *Studies in Leadership Applied to County Agricultural Agents.* Ph.D., Harvard University.

1933

Woelfel, Norman. *A Critical Review of the Social Attitudes of Seventeen Leaders in American Education.* Ph.D., Columbia University.

1934

Shannon, Jasper B. *Henry Clay as a Political Leader.* Ph.D., University of Wisconsin.

1935

Bauer, Richard H. *Ludwig Windthorst as a Political Leader.* Ph.D., University of Chicago.

Eichler, George A. *Studies in Student Leadership: Controlled Experiments in the Teaching of Leadership with a Quantitative Analysis of the Components of Leadership.* Ph.D., Pennsylvania State University.

1937

Kern, Alexander C. *The Economic Thought of Some Southern Democratic Political Leaders, 1800–1860.* Ph.D., University of Wisconsin.

Robertson, Pearl L. *Grover Cleveland as a Political Leader.* Ph.D., University of Chicago.

1939

Watson, Richard L., Jr. *Thurlow Weed, Political Leader, 1848-*1855. Ph.D., Yale University.

1940

Lahman, Carroll P. *Robert Marion La Follette as Public Speaker and Political Leader, 1855-1905.* Ph.D., University of Wisconsin.

1941

Anderson, James J. *The President's Supreme Court Proposal—A Study in Presidential Leadership and Public Opinion.* Ph.D., Cornell University.

Plummer, Leonard N. *Political Leadership of Henry Watterson.* Ph.D., University of Wisconsin.

Wicks, Rollo E. *A Survey of Political Leadership in the South with Reference to Federal Economic and Social Legislation, 1933-1940.* Ph.D., Cornell University.

1942

Nixon, Raymond B. *Henry Woodfin Grady: Journalistic Leader in Public Affairs.* Ph.D., University of Minnesota.

1943

Butler, Lonis C. *The Evaluation of Professional Preparation for Leadership in Physical Education in the Secondary Schools of New Mexico.* Ph.D., New York University.

Fisher, Luke. *Social Leadership According to Thomistic Principles.* Ph.D., Catholic University of America.

Manske, Armin A. *The Concepts of Early American Educational Leaders Pertaining to Public School Administration.* Ph.D., University of Chicago.

1947

Greenberg, Bernard. *Some Relations between Territory, Social Hierarchy, and Leadership in the Green Sunfish.* Ph.D., University of Chicago.

1949

Maas, Henry S. *Community Youth Group Leadership in Teacher Training: A Study of Changes in Social Perception and Attitudes of Youth Group Leaders.* Ph.D., University of Chicago.

White, James E. *Leadership and Social Structure in a New York Rural Community.* Ph.D., Cornell University.

1950

Bryan, George C. *Concepts of Leadership in American Political Thought: The Puritan Period.* Ph.D., Harvard University.

Fox, M. Harrita. *Peter E. Dietz and the American Catholic Social Movement—A Quarter-Century of Leadership, 1900–1925.* Ph.D., University of Notre Dame.

Telschow, Earl F. *The Role of the Leader in Nondirective Group Psychotherapy.* Ph.D., Columbia University.

1951

Edgren, Carl H. *The Concept of the Political Leader in the Romantic Period.* Ph.D., Northwestern University.

Giffin, Kim Q. *The Role of Leadership in Four Network Radio and Television Discussion Programs.* Ph.D., University of Iowa.

Kirksey, Howard G. *State Department Leadership and Public Secondary Education in Tennessee.* Ph.D., George Peabody College for Teachers.

McCunn, Drummond J. *A Study of Pasadena and Its Public Schools: Analysis of the Factors Contributing to Educational Leadership in a Community.* Ph.D., University of California, Los Angeles.

Valenti, Jasper J. *Development and Evaluation of a Leadership Attitude Scale around the Social Role of the Teacher.* Ph.D., University of Chicago.

1952

Conrad, Richard. *The Administrative Role: A Sociological Study of Leadership in a Public School System.* Ph.D., Stanford University.

Sisson, Francis W. *The Role of State Leadership in Helping Local Schools Improve Instruction Better to Meet the Needs of Youth in Virginia.* Ph.D., Columbia University.

Sutker, Solomon. *The Jews of Atlanta: Their Social Structure and Leadership Patterns.* Ph.D., University of North Carolina at Chapel Hill.

Teel, Dwight. *Aiding Elementary Principals to Assume Curriculum Leadership: The Role of the Central Office Curriculum Personnel.* Ph.D., Cornell University.

1953

Cornwell, Elmer E., Jr. *Lloyd George: A Study in Political Leadership.* Ph.D., Harvard University.

Gottfried, Alex. *A. J. Cermak, Chicago Politician: A Study in Political Leadership.* Ph.D., University of Chicago.

Hitt, Harold H. *A Rating Scale for the Measurement of Teacher Readiness for the Role of Administrative Leadership.* Ed.D., North Texas State University.

Jones, Edward E. *The Role of Authoritarianism in the Perception and Evaluation of a Prospective Leader.* Ph.D., Harvard University.

Lowe, Francis E. *The Measurement of the Influence of Formal and Informal Leaders of Public Opinion during the 1950 Senatorial Election Campaign in Madison, Wisconsin.* Ph.D., University of Wisconsin.

Matthews, Donald R. *United States Senators: A Study of the Recruitment of Political Leaders.* Ph.D., Princeton University.

Matthews, Thomas J. *The Lawyer as a Community Leader: One Dimension of a Professional Role.* Ph.D., Cornell University.

Pringle, Bruce M. *The Relationship between Elements in the Social Situation and Combat Leadership Behavior in the United States Air Force.* Ph.D., University of Southern California.

1954

Beimfohr, Herman N. *Types of Leadership as Found in the Practice of Professional Workers in the Wesley Foundations of the Methodist Church.* Ph.D., University of Southern California.

Goldstein, Norman and Ralph G. Semon. *The Group Therapy Process and Its Effectiveness with Chronic Schizophrenic Patients as a Function of the Role of the Leader.* Ph.D., Boston University.

Seidler, Murray B. *A Situational Analysis of the Political Leadership of Norman Thomas.* D.S.S., Syracuse University.

Svenson, Elwin V. *A Study of Professional Preparation Programs for Leaders in Adult Education Offered by Schools of Education.* Ph.D., University of California, Los Angeles.

Williamson, Edward C. *The Era of the Democratic County Leader: Florida Politics, 1877-1893.* Ph.D., University of Pennsylvania.

1955

Clark, Milton J. *Leadership and Political Allocation in Sinkiang Kazak Society.* Ph.D., Harvard University.

Hodges, Harold M. *Social Factors Associated with Leadership among a Selected Group of High School Boys.* Ph.D., University of Southern California.

Mendel, Douglas H., Jr. *Political Behavior in Post-treaty Japan: A Survey of Constituents and Leaders in Two Selected Areas.* Ph.D., University of Michigan.

Patterson, Franklin K. *Organized Criticism of Public Schools Viewed by Educational Leaders: A Study of Opinion.* Ph.D., Claremont Graduate School.

Schlesinger, Joseph A. *The Emergence of Political Leadership: A Case Study of American Governors.* Ph.D., Yale University.

Sharpe, Russell T. *Differences between Perceived Administrative Behavior and Role-Norms as Factors in Leadership Evaluation and Group Morale.* Ph.D., Stanford University.

1956

Brantley, Mabel R. *Assumptions Made about Teachers by Professional Leaders.* Ph.D., Columbia University.

Hafner, James L. *Social Leadership as Related to the Minnesota Multiphasic Personality Inventory.* Ph.D., Oklahoma State University.

1957

Crawford, Evans E., Jr. *The Leadership Role of the Urban Negro Minister.* Ph.D., Boston University.

English, Grace I. *The Role of the Senior High School Teacher of Academic Subjects in the Promotion of Student Leadership in the Classroom.* Ed.D., Temple University.

Eriksen, John G. *The Political Role of Church Leadership Resistance to the Rise of National Socialism in Germany, 1930–1933.* Ph.D., University of Minnesota.

Flint, Helen M. *Preparation of Public School Administrators for Instructional Leadership with Specific Reference to Course Offerings.* Ph.D., George Washington University.

Miller, Wayne V. *The Emergence of William Henry Seward as a National Political Leader, 1847–1859.* Ph.D., University of Southern California.

Orenstein, Henry. *Caste, Leadership, and Social Change in a Bombay Village.* Ph.D., University of California, Berkeley.

Schlotfeldt, Rozella M. *The Educational Leadership Role in Nursing Schools and Satisfaction of Faculty.* Ph.D., University of Chicago.

Shunk, William R. *The Role of the Christian College in Training Lay Leadership.* Ph.D., Southern Baptist Theological Seminary.

Stewart, Charles E. *A Study of Teacher Perceptions of Selected School Developments and Their Implications for the Leadership Role of the Principal in the Grant School, Ferndale, Michigan.* Ed.D., Wayne State University.

Vollmer, Joseph H. *The Role of the Leader in Curriculum Improvement in Leonia (N.J.) High School.* Ph.D., Columbia University.

Weckwerth, Charles F. *A Guide to the Planning of Curriculum for the Pre-professional Preparation of Recreation Leadership.* Ed.D., New York University.

1958

Bair, Donn E. *An Identification of Some Philosophical Beliefs Held by Influential Professional Leaders in American Physical Education.* Ph.D., University of Southern California.

Coolidge, Franklin E. *A Study of the College Grades, Leadership Roles and*

Entrance Examination Scores of Employed and Non-employed Students at Cortland State Teachers College. Ed.D., Syracuse University.

Foster, Barbara R. *Some Interrelationships between Religious Values, Leadership Concepts, and Perception of Group Process of Professional Church Workers.* Ph.D., University of Michigan.

Lambertson, Eleanor C. *Professional Education for Leadership in Nursing Practice.* Ph.D., Columbia University.

Milligan, Robert G. *A Study of the Motivation of Leaders, Followers, and Isolates in a Group of Delinquent Boys.* Ph.D., Loyola University of Chicago.

Moore, David C. *Politics of Deference: A Study of the Political Structure, Leadership, and Organization of English County Constituencies in the Nineteenth Century.* Ph.D., Columbia University.

Nehring, Earl A. *Local Political Leadership: A Study of Decision-making in a Council-Manager City.* Ph.D., University of California, Los Angeles.

1959

Bailey, Jackson H. *Prince Saionji: A Study in Modern Japanese Political Leadership.* Ph.D., Harvard University.

Bush, William T. *Behavior Requirements of School Administrators in the Task Areas of Instruction and Curriculum Development, Community-School Leadership, and Organization and Structure Based on an Analysis of Incidents Reported by Public School Administrators.* Ph.D., University of Mississippi.

Campbell, Merton V. *Self-Role Conflict among Teachers and Its Relationship to Satisfaction, Effectiveness, and Confidence in Leadership.* Ph.D., University of Chicago.

Cooper, Kenneth J. *Leadership Role Expectations in Mexican Rural and Urban Environments.* Ph.D., Stanford University.

Danzig, Martin Z. *The Motivations of Community Leaders: An Exploratory and Descriptive Study of the Deviations between the Motivations of People Who Assume Leadership Roles in the Community, and Those Motivations Which Are Used as Criteria for the Selection of Leaders.* Ph.D., New York University.

Miller, Howard L. *Procedures for Improving the Use of Publications in the Communications Process by Professional Leaders in Agricultural Education.* Ph.D., Ohio State University.

Schlutt, Edward F. *The District Extension Leaders' and the Beginning County Extension Agents' Perception of the Beginning Agents' Role Definition and Role Fulfillment.* Ph.D., University of Wisconsin.

Sissoms, Hanson D. *An Analysis of the Leadership Functions Performed within Various Recreation Agencies and Their Effect upon the Development of Recreation as a Profession: A Comparative and Factor Analysis of the Job Components of Selected Recreation Personnel with Inferences for a Plan of Certification and Professional Education of Recreators.* Ph.D., New York University.

Swafford, George E. *A Study of the Leadership Role of School Principals.* Ed.D., University of Northern Colorado.

Verba, Sidney. *The Experimental Study of Politics: The Contribution of Small Group Experiments in Leadership to the Understanding of Political Leadership.* Ph.D., Princeton University.

1960

Berman, Louise M. *The Development of the Professional Self-image in Preservice Teacher Education: Implications for Instructional Leaders.* Ph.D., Columbia University.

Binion, Rudolph. *Defeated Leaders: The Political Fate of Caillaux, Jouvenel, and Tardieu.* Ph.D., Columbia University.

Brown, William P. *Vol. I: The Political and Administrative Leadership of Fiorello H. La Guardia as Mayor of the City of New York, 1934-1941. Vol. II: An Administrative Study of Some Aspects of the 1934-1941 Mayoralty of Fiorello H. La Guardia.* Ph.D., New York University.

Burgess, Margaret E. *The Role of the Minority Community in Desegregation: A Study of Leadership and Power in a Biracial Setting.* Ph.D., University of North Carolina at Chapel Hill.

Dinardo, Vincent J. *The Development and Evaluation of a Leadership Attitude Scale around the Interpersonal Relations Role of the Elementary School Principal.* Ed.D., Boston University.

Lazer, Harry. *Balfourian Conservatism: A Study in Political Ideas and Political Leadership.* Ph.D., Columbia University.

Oniki, Shozi G. *An Exploration of the Role of the Executive in Exercising Democratic Leadership with the Board of Directors of a Voluntary Agency.* Ph.D., Columbia University.

Sawyer, Robert L., Jr. *The Democratic State Central Committee in Michigan, 1949-1959: A Study in the Rise of the New Politics and the New Political Leadership.* Ph.D., University of Michigan.

Soffen, Joseph. *Training of Non-professional Leadership in Adult Education.* Ph.D., University of Chicago.

Sohal, Takhat S. *The Role and Development of Voluntary Village Leaders in Programs of Community Development in the Punjab, India.* Ed.D., Cornell University.

1961

Armilla, José. *Leader-Follower Frame of Reference in Political Behavior.* Ph.D., University of Michigan.

Backner, Burton L. *"Attraction-to-Group," as a Function of Style of Leadership, Follower Personality, and Group Composition.* Ph.D., State University of New York at Buffalo.

Johnson, Clarence D. *Priest, Prophet, and Professional Man: A Study of Religious Leadership in a Small Community.* Ph.D., University of Minnesota.

Rosenthal, Alan. *Community Leadership and Public School Politics: Two Case Studies.* Ph.D., Princeton University.

Trent, Curtis. *The Administrative Role of the State 4-H Club Leader in Selected States—A Study in Role Perception.* Ph.D., University of Wisconsin.

1962

Beyer, Barry K. *Thomas E. Dewey, 1937-1947: A Study in Political Leadership.* Ph.D., University of Rochester.

Evans, Frank B. *Pennsylvania Politics, 1872-1877: A Study in Leadership without Responsibility.* Ph.D., Pennsylvania State University.

Feeley, Ardell L. *Administrative Leadership: A Study of Role Expectations and Perceptions in the Areas of Public Relations and Curriculum Development by Secondary School Principals and Staff Members.* Ed.D., University of Pittsburgh.

Johnson, Hubert C. *Politics of Discord: The Domestic Leadership of Frederick II of Prussia, 1740-1756.* Ph.D., University of California, Berkeley.

Papanek, Hanna K. *Leadership and Social Change in the Khoja Ismaili Community.* Ph.D., Radcliffe College, Harvard University.

Peterson, Phyllis J. *Brazilian Political Parties; Formation, Organization, and Leadership, 1945-1959.* Ph.D., University of Michigan.

1963

Burke, Wyatt W. *Leadership Behavior as a Function of the Leader, the Follower, and the Situation.* Ph.D., University of Texas at Austin.

Czajkowski, Janina M. *Differences in Perceptions of Needs for Nutrition Education as Seen by Homemakers from Different Age Groups and by Lay and Professional Leaders.* Ed.D., Boston University.

Frey, Frederick W. *Political Leadership in Turkey: The Social Backgrounds of Deputies to the Grand National Assembly, 1920-1957.* Ph.D., Princeton University.

Frey, Milton W., II. *An Experimental Study of the Influence of Disruptive Interaction Induced by Authoritarian-Equalitarian, Leader-Follower Combinations upon the Decision-making Effectiveness of Small Groups.* Ph.D., Pennsylvania State University.

Hellenga, Robert D. *A Study of Professional and Community Leadership Roles as They Are Assumed by Public School Teachers in Selected School Districts in Michigan.* Ph.D., Michigan State University.

Hoffman, Paul J. *Party Responsibility and Political Experience: An Inquiry into the Attitudes of American Political Leaders.* Ph.D., University of Minnesota.

Hopkins, Howard P. *Professional Relations of State Leaders in Vocational Agricultural Education.* Ph.D., George Washington University.

Stenzel, Anne K. *A Study of Girl Scout Leadership Training: Non-professional Leaders of Adults as Continuous Learners.* Ph.D., University of California, Berkeley.

Walker, Jack L., Jr. *Protest and Negotiation: A Study of Negro Political Leaders in a Southern City.* Ph.D., University of Iowa.

1964

Andrain, Charles F. *Political Concepts of African Leaders.* Ph.D., University of California, Berkeley.

Bartlett, Alton C. *The Attitudes of Local Union Rank-and-File Leaders about the Political Activities of Their Union: A Comparison and Contrast.* Ph.D., University of Wisconsin.

Bigler, Robert M. *The Political Leaders of the Protestant Clergy in Prussia, 1815–1847.* Ph.D., University of California, Berkeley.

Bircher, Jack L. *An Analysis of Selected Educational, Social, Economic, and Political Opinions Held by Business Leaders.* Ed.D., Indiana University.

Ibok-Ete, Isong-Uyo N. *Education and Politics in Nigeria, 1945–1960: A Comparative Study of the Educational Concepts of Selected Nigerian Political Leaders and Their Impact on Education.* Ed.D., University of California, Los Angeles.

Ladd, Everett C., Jr. *Negro Political Leadership in the Urban South.* Ph.D., Cornell University.

Morris, John E. *The Catholic High School and Education for Leadership and Active Participation in Government, Politics, and Civic Life.* Ph.D., Catholic University of America.

Nayar, Baldev R. *Contemporary Political Leadership in the Punjab.* Ph.D., University of Chicago.

Ziegenhagen, Eduard A. *Perceived Inconsistencies Regarding Self and Ethnocentric Political Leadership.* Ph.D., University of Illinois at Urbana-Champaign.

1965

Boen, Sharon E. *The Leadership Role of the Secretary-General in Times of International Crisis.* Ph.D., University of Virginia.

Busset, Glenn M. *A Comparison of Knowledge Gained by Adults When Presentations Are Followed by Discussion Led by Local Volunteer and Professional Leaders with a Positive or a Negative Attitude toward the Discussion Task.* Ph.D., University of Wisconsin.

Cobun, Frank. *Educational Concomitants of Political Leadership in Five States of the Ante-bellum North and South.* Ph.D., University of Chicago.

Grotpeter, John J. *Political Leadership and Political Development in the High Commission Territories.* Ph.D., Washington University.

Holloman, Charles R. *The Leadership Role of Military and Civilian Supervisors in a Military Setting as Perceived by Superiors and Subordinates.* D.B.A., University of Washington.

Luttbeg, Norman R. *Belief Conflict in the Community: Leader and Follower Differences in Policy Preferences.* Ph.D., Michigan State University.

McAllister, Vernon F. *A Study of Leadership Role Percepts as Viewed by Teachers, School Administrators, and School Board Members.* Ed.D., University of Oklahoma.

McLeod, John T. *The Political Thought of Sir Wilfrid Laurier: A Study in Canadian Party Leadership.* Ph.D., University of Toronto.

Nance, Jack L. *A Study of the Leadership Role of the Superintendent and High School Principal within Selected Communities of Oklahoma.* Ph.D., University of Oklahoma.

1966

Nag, Uma. *A Study of the Role of Professional Leaders in Educational Programs for Parents Handicapped by Socio-economic Status Differences.* Ed.D., University of Missouri at Columbia.

Parker, Adah D. *Projections for the Selection, Training and Retention of Sub-professional Recreation Leaders Based on an Analysis of Personality, Interest, Aptitude, and Preference Data.* Ph.D., University of Illinois at Urbana-Champaign.

Vibhatakarasa, Jin. *The Military in Politics: A Study of Military Leadership in Thailand.* Ph.D., University of Oregon.

Withers, Richard E. *Roger Williams and the Rhode Island Colony: A Study in Leadership Roles.* Ph.D., Boston University.

1967

Austin, Theodore A. *The Perceptions of Key Hospital Leaders as to the Competencies Required for Hospital Administration and Their Implications for Professional Education.* Ed.D., Boston University.

Hays, Bob B. *Student-Teacher Expectations of the Leadership Role of the Principal.* Ed.D., North Texas State University.

Gibbons, David S. *Dominant Political Leadership and Political Integration in a Transitional Society: China, Chiang Kai-shek and Mao Tse-tung, 1935–1949.* Ph.D., Princeton University.

Hohol, Albert E. *Leadership Role Conflicts of School Superintendents.* Ed.D., University of Oregon.

Kachel, Harold S. *An Identification of Philosophical Beliefs of Professional Leaders and Industrial Arts Teachers.* Ed.D., University of Northern Colorado.

Lippert, Frederick G., II. *Authoritarianism and Role Pressure as Determinants of Participative Leadership Style.* Ph.D., New York University.

Miller, Norman N. *Village Leadership and Modernization in Tanzania: Rural Politics among the Nyamwezi People of Tabora Region.* Ph.D., Indiana University.

Vidmar, Neil J. *Leadership and Role Structure in Negotiation and Other Decision-making Groups.* Ph.D., University of Illinois at Urbana-Champaign.

1968

Chweh, Christopher Y. *Factors Related to Varying Conceptions of the Modern Overseas Missionary Task Held by Professional Leaders and Laymen of the Lutheran Church-Missouri Synod.* Ph.D., University of Pittsburgh.

Greer, Clyde H. *An Analysis of the Leadership Role in Professional Negotiations in Selected Texas Schools.* Ph.D., University of Texas at Austin.

Ortell, Edward C. *Perceptions of Junior College Leaders with Respect to Selected Issues in Professional Negotiations.* Ph.D., United States International University.

Reza, Rosalio W. *Occupational Background of Political Leaders.* Ph.D., University of Iowa.

Schneider, Frank A., Sr. *A Study of the Leadership Role of Directors of Public Libraries as Reported by Selected Public Library Directors.* Ed.D., Arizona State University.

Spring, Evelyn L. *Professional Preparation in Recreation: Undergraduate Education Pertinent to Leadership with Older Adults.* Ph.D., University of Southern California.

1969

Black, Chester D. *Professional Leadership Behavior: Its Effects and Associated Factors.* Ed.D., North Carolina State University at Raleigh.

Findlay, Edward W. *Curriculum Development for Professional Leaders in Extension Education.* Ph.D., Cornell University.

Garner, Warren K. *Leader Behavior Following Executive Succession in Selected California School Districts.* Ph.D., Claremont Graduate School.

Ham, Elton W. *Political Leadership: A Case Study of Policy Formation in Kalamazoo, Michigan.* Ph.D., University of Chicago.

Johnson, Thomas A. *A Study of Characteristics of Fifth and Sixth Grade Student Leaders and Followers in Contrasting Socio-economic Settings.* Ed.D., Oklahoma State University.

Leone, Richard C. *The Politics of Gubernatorial Leadership: Tax and Education Reform in New Jersey.* Ph.D., Princeton University.

McGregor, David R. *Leadership Roles in New York Democratic State Nominating Conventions, 1952–1966.* Ph.D., Columbia University.

Sheeley, Vernon L. *Leaders in Professional Organizations in the Guidance and Counseling Movement: Some Implications of Their Personal and Professional Backgrounds.* Ph.D., University of Wyoming.

Wilbur, William A. *Crisis in Leadership: Alexander Hamilton, Timothy Pickering and the Politics of Federalism, 1795–1804.* Ph.D., Syracuse University.

1970

Berchuck, Irving. *A Study of the Relative Effect of the Method of Selecting Elementary School Teachers and the Dogmatism of the Teachers on the*

Executive Professional Leadership Rating of the Elementary School Principal. Ed.D., New York University.

Collins, Alvin L. *A Study of the Relationship of the Leadership Rating of Elementary School Principals and the Role They Play as Problem-Solvers or Information-givers at Faculty Meetings (Based on the COPED Survey).* Ed.D., Boston University.

Fuhr, Milton J. *Leadership Role of Principals Related to Innovative Practices in Selected Elementary Schools of Michigan and Ohio.* Ed.D., Wayne State University.

Hill, Richard E. *The Leadership Role as a Factor in Commitment and Satisfaction among Registered Nurses.* Ph.D., Purdue University.

Mozier, Richard F. *An Analysis of the Instructional Leadership Role of Elementary Superintendents in Small, Medium and Large School Districts in Northern Suburban Cook County.* Ph.D., Loyola University of Chicago.

Sashkin, Marshall. *Supervisory Leadership in Problem Solving Groups: Experimental Tests of Fred Fiedler's Theory of Leadership Effectiveness in the Laboratory Using Role Play Methods.* Ph.D., University of Michigan.

Snider, Joseph L. *A Study of the Leadership Role of the Secondary Science Teacher as This Role Relates to the Science Program.* Ed.D., Ball State University.

Suran, Mary E. *The Role of Trainer Personality and the Social Intelligence Factor in Effective Sensitivity Group Leadership.* Ph.D., Loyola University of Chicago.

Titus, David A. *Palace and Politics in Pre-war Japan: The Context of Imperial Involvement in Politics and Palace Leadership in the Showa Period, 1929-1941.* Ph.D., Columbia University.

1971

Brown, Martha A. *Investigation toward Development of a Model for Relating the Self-perceived Role of Professors to Leadership Styles: Limited to Public Universities and Colleges in Selected Southwestern States.* Ph.D., University of Texas at Austin.

Burg, Maclyn P. *The Careers of 109 Southern Whig Congressional Leaders in the Years Following Their Party's Collapse.* Ph.D., University of Washington.

Dandler-Hanhart, Jorge E. *Politics of Leadership, Brokerage and Patronage in the Campesino Movement of Cochabamba, Bolivia (1935-54).* Ph.D., University of Wisconsin.

De Angelis, Louis. *A Study of the Relationship between the Executive Professional Leadership of the Elementary School Principal and School Learning Atmosphere.* Ed.D., Boston University.

Dow, John, Jr. *A Comparative Study of Inner-City Elementary Teachers' and Principals' Perceptions of and Role Expectations for the Leadership Behavior of Selected Inner-City Elementary Principals.* Ph.D., Michigan State University.

Fiedler, John C. *The Student's Role in Junior College Governance: A Study of Attitudes of Administrators, Faculty Leaders, Student Leaders, and Trustees.* Ph.D., University of California, Berkeley.

Kuehl, Charles R. *Small Group Productivity as Related to Leadership Style, Role Differentiation, Status Differentiation and Organizational Backgrounds of Members.* Ph.D., University of Iowa.

Lynch, Jean M. *Development of a Field Center for the Advanced Professional Training of Instructional Leaders.* Ed.D., Columbia University.

Mann, Kenneth E. *Black Leaders in National Politics, 1873-1943: A Study of Legislative Persuasion.* Ph.D., Indiana University.

Marks, Reita J. *A Comparison of the Effectiveness of Group Camping Experiences on Change of Self-concept for Campers with Professional and Nonprofessional Group Leaders.* Ed.D., West Virginia University.

Merriam, Kathleen H. *The Role of Leadership in Nation-building: Egypt, 1922.* Ph.D., Indiana University.

Robertson, Raymond G. *The Effects of Professional Negotiations on the Leadership Role of the Elementary Principal as Perceived by Elementary Principals in Selected Schools in Texas.* Ed.D., Texas Tech University.

Siemens, Robert W. *A Study of Executive Professional Leadership in Selected Schools Holding Membership in the National Association of Christian Schools.* Ed.D., Boston University.

Simpson, Douglas B. *Leadership Behavior, Need Satisfactions, and Role Perceptions of Labor Leaders: A Behavioral Analysis.* D.B.A., University of Washington.

Singh, Raghu N. *Levels of Involvement of Local Actors in Watershed Development Leadership Roles.* Ph.D., Mississippi State University.

Tubbs, Nathan G. *A Study of the Relationship between the Professional-Employee Orientations and Selected Social and Professional Characteristics of Formal Leaders of Professional Education Associations in Virginia.* Ed.D., University of Virginia.

Wasdyke, Raymond G. *Self Role Perception and Leadership Behavior of Area Vocational School Principals in New Jersey.* Ed.D., Rutgers University-State University of New Jersey.

Wilson, Andrea. *Leadership Styles and Leaders' Perceptions of the Decentralization Law: A Study of New York City District Superintendents' Perceptions of the Anticipated Impact of the Decentralization Law of 1969 on the Role of the New Community Superintendents.* Ph.D., New York University.

1972

Baltimore, Jimmy R. *A Study of Professional Education Competencies of Public School District Vocational Education Leaders.* Ed.D., Oregon State University.

Bedrosian, Oscar T. *Community Pressures and Their Implications for the Leadership Role of Certain Superintendents in Lake County, Illinois.* Ed.D., Loyola University of Chicago.

Borowiec, Walter A. *The Ethnic Politician: The Political Leadership of a Contemporary Ethnic Community.* Ph.D., State University of New York at Buffalo.

Carvajal-Herrera, Mario. *Political Attitudes and Political Change in Costa Rica: A Comparison of the Attitudes of Leaders and Followers with Respect to Regime Values and Party Identification.* Ph.D., University of Kansas.

Chasteen, Fletcher O. *The Effect of Professional Negotiation on the Leadership Activities of Elementary Principals in the St. Louis Suburban Elementary Principals' Association.* Ph.D., Southern Illinois University.

Combs, Arthur W. *The Leadership Role of Department Chairmen as Perceived by Chairmen and Faculty with Whom They Work in Selected Florida Junior Colleges.* Ph.D., Miami University.

Franssen, Herman T. *The Issue of the "Technological Gap" between Western Europe and the United States: Causes and Effects, Myths and Realities— Opinions of Dutch Political, Academic and Business Leaders.* Ph.D., Fletcher School of Law and Diplomacy (Tufts University).

Gates, Philip E. *The Secondary Principal's Leadership Role in Organizational Problem-solving.* Ed.D., University of Massachusetts.

Hammock, Allan S. *The Leadership Factor in Black Politics: The Case of Richmond, Virginia.* Ph.D., University of Virginia.

Han, Ki-Shik. *Political Leadership and Development in Postwar Korea: Continuity and Change between the Rhee and Park Regimes.* Ph.D., University of California, Berkeley.

Hartsock, Nancy C. M. *Philosophy, Ideology, and Ordinary Language: The Political Thought of Black Community Leaders.* Ph.D., University of Chicago.

Hildebrand, Ronald W. *Emerging and Potential State Leadership Roles in Environmental Education.* Ph.D., University of Colorado.

Johnson, Josephine L. *Women Leaders in National Guidance and Counseling Associations: Some Implications of Their Backgrounds and Leadership Roles.* Ed.D., University of Wyoming.

Kantor, Paul. *Educational Reform and English Urban Politics: Leadership, Democracy, and Public Policy in Three London Communities.* Ph.D., University of Chicago.

Machado, Kit G. *Leadership and Organization in Philippine Local Politics.* Ph.D., University of Washington.

Nazaar, Fahzil M. *Development, Modernization and Leadership Styles in Afghanistan: A Human Simulation in Politics.* Ph.D., University of Hawaii.

Sanders, Charles L. *A Comparative Study of Black Professional Leaders: Their Perceptions of Institutional Racism and Strategies for Dealing with Racism.* D.P.A., New York University.

Villarreal, John J. *A Study of the Influence Relationship between Opinion Leaders and Followers.* Ph.D., City University of New York.

Whitis, Jessie D. *A Study of the Leadership Role of Financial Aid Officers of the Western Association of Financial Aid Officers.* Ph.D., Arizona State University.

1973

Call, Melvyn D. *Role-Expectations, Leader Behavior and Leadership Ideology of Academic Deans.* Ed.D., West Virginia University.

Casello, Joseph H. *The Superintendent's Leadership Style as It Affects His Role in the Collective Negotiation Process.* Ed.D., Rutgers University–State University of New Jersey.

Cronin, Jean T. *Minority Leadership in the United States Senate: The Role and Style of Everett Dirksen.* Ph.D., Johns Hopkins University.

Espiritu, Tecla A. *Teacher Perception of Professional Leadership of Public Elementary School Principals in Cebu: Its Relationship to Teacher Morale, Teacher Performance, and Pupil Learning.* Ed.D., Fordham University.

Finnessy, John A. *The Relationship between Selected Personality Traits and Leadership Expectations of the Follower.* Ed.D., Indiana University.

Harris, Johnie E. *An Investigation of Teachers' Perceptions of the Principal's Leadership Role and Parental Attitudes in Respect to School-Community Conflict.* Ed.D., George Washington University.

Healey, James S. *The Emergence of National Political Leadership for Library Development: The Case of Representative John E. Fogarty.* D.L.S., Columbia University.

Jolt, Harvey A. *The Optometric Center of New York: Its History, Organization, Development—A Case Study of the Impact of a Leadership Role and Analysis of Its Effects upon a Segment of the Health Community.* Ph.D., New York University.

Josselyn, Louis S., Jr. *A Study of the Effectiveness of Secondary School Administrators in Massachusetts and Its Relationship to the Leader Behavior of Principals Who Are Active in Professional and Non-professional Roles.* Ed.D., Boston University.

Joyner, Betty C. *The Influence of Instruction in Organizational Behavior on Some Aspects of Leadership Role Perception.* D.B.A., Louisiana Tech University.

Kracke, Waud H. *Emotions and Personality in Parintintin Politics: A Study of Political Structure and Commotive Leadership in an Amazon Indian Tribe.* Ph.D., University of Chicago.

McNelly, Frederick W., Jr. *Development of the Self-concept in Childhood: A Brief Historical Review and an Investigation of the Effects of Manipulating Leadership Position within a Structured Role System upon Self-concept, Perception of Locus-of-Control, and Performance.* Ph.D., University of Michigan.

Metz, Marie H. *The Leadership Role of the Principal in Implementing a PPBS Model.* Ed.D., University of Denver.

Natto, Ibrahim A. *An Analysis of Leadership Role Perceptions and Ethnic Membership of Elementary School Principals in Texas.* Ph.D., University of Texas at Austin.

Oliver, Mary J. *Relationships among Leadership Roles, Attitude toward Physical*

Activity, and Physical Activity Skill Success. Ed.D., Oklahoma State University.

Podemski, Richard S. *Leadership Behavior, Role-Conflict, and Role-Ambiguity: The University Department Chairman.* Ph.D., State University of New York at Buffalo.

Ralph, George S. *The T-Group Trainer in Task and Socio-emotional Leadership Roles.* Ph.D., University of Oregon.

Renaud, Albert J. *The Effects of Professional Negotiations upon the Leadership Role of the Elementary School Principal.* Ph.D., United States International University.

Ronning, Rolf O. *A Study of the Leadership Role Behaviors of the College Presidents at Selected Institutions of Higher Education in New York State.* Ed.D., State University of New York at Albany.

Suvanachot, Chareonpol. *A Study of the Leadership and Managerial Roles of the Director of Student-Teaching in Michigan Colleges and Universities.* Ph.D., Michigan State University.

Vanko, John G. *Implications for the Leadership Role of Secondary School Department Chairmen Included in the Teachers' Bargaining Unit.* Ed.D., Loyola University of Chicago.

Ward, William D. *The Role of Teacher Organizations in Professional Development and Instructional Improvement as Perceived by Selected Teacher Organization Leaders.* Ph.D., Michigan State University.

Westefield, Louis P. *Party Leaders and Followers in the House of Representatives.* Ph.D., Washington University.

Yamada, Peter S. *Teachers' and Principals' Perceptions of the Leadership Role of the Catholic Parochial Elementary School Principal in Schools with and without a Negotiated Contract.* Ph.D., Fordham University.

1974

Fletcher, Robert K. *A Study of the Role and Leadership Status of Elementary Principals in Selected Schools of Allegheny County, Pennsylvania.* Ph.D., University of Pittsburgh.

Herold, David M. *Mutual Influence Processes in Leader-Follower Relationships.* Ph.D., Yale University.

Knox, John W. *An Analysis of the Role of Selected Colorado Middle and Junior High School Assistant Principals in Curriculum and Instruction Leadership.* Ph.D., University of Northern Colorado.

Lynn, Mary A. *Task-Role Ambiguity in Teachers and Its Relationship to an Index of Professional Leadership in Selected Elementary Schools.* Ed.D., Illinois State University.

McKenney, Melvin D. *A Survey of the Leadership Role Being Played by State Education Agencies in Sex Education.* Ed.D., University of South Dakota.

Michaletz, James E. *A Comparison of the Perspectives of Two Groups of*

Elementary School Principals Concerning the Exercise of the Leadership Role in Effecting Change. Ph.D., Loyola University of Chicago.

Richards, Charlotte J. *Role Conflict Concerning Teachers of the Mentally Retarded and Its Relationship to Confidence in Leadership, Effectiveness, and Satisfaction.* Ph.D., University of Wisconsin.

Waters, Elizabeth M. *A Construct for the Conceptualization of the Leadership Role of the Cooperating Teacher.* Ph.D., Ohio State University.

1975

Bethel, Leonard L. *The Role of Lincoln University (Pennsylvania) in the Education of African Leadership, 1854–1970.* Ed.D., Rutgers University–State University of New Jersey.

Brown, Kenneth R. *The Leadership Role of the Elementary School Supervisor as Perceived by Elementary Teachers and Supervisors in Selected School Systems in Northeast Louisiana.* Ed.D., Northeast Louisiana University.

Dunn, Israel R., Jr. *A Reflection of Black Cultural and Historical Philosophical Assumptions: A Prelude to Interpreting Black Leadership Roles.* Ph.D., California School of Professional Psychology, San Francisco.

Harris, Howard L. *Curriculum Leadership Behavior and Job Satisfaction: Their Relationship to Structural Instability within the Role-Set.* Ed.D., Columbia University.

Higgs, Zana R. *Expectations and Perceptions of the Curricular Leadership Role of Administrators of Nursing Education Units.* Ed.D., Columbia University.

Logsdon, Martha G. *Leaders and Followers in Urban Neighborhoods: An Exploratory Study of Djakarta, Indonesia.* Ph.D., Yale University.

Moore, Loren I. *Towards the Determination of Follower Maturity: An Operationalization of Life Cycle Leadership.* Ed.D., University of Massachusetts.

Peterson, Robert J. *The Effect Collective Negotiations Have on the Leadership Role of the Local School Attendance Area Manager.* Ed.D., Wayne State University.

Quinn, Robert E. *Participative Leadership: Its Variation across Four Role Relationships.* Ph.D., University of Cincinnati.

Reale, Louis D., Jr. *Relationship between Role-Personality Conflict in Teacher-Board Negotiations and the Leadership Behavior of Elementary School Principals in the School Districts of the State of New Jersey.* Ph.D., Fordham University.

Reilly, Bernard J. *Societal Leadership: Toward a Theory of Roles, Resources, and Power.* Ph.D., Georgia State University.

Smith, Mary E. *Effectiveness in Urban Elementary Schools as a Function of the Interaction between Leadership Behavior of Principals and Maturity of Followers.* Ed.D., University of Massachusetts.

APPENDIX B

SELECTED MULTIDISCIPLINARY BIBLIOGRAPHY

INCLUDED HERE IS a multidisciplinary selection of more than 1100 books and articles on leadership that have appeared in English in the United States from 1920 through 1975. These citations were drawn from a pool of some 5,000 items gathered from standard social science reference works and in the course of curious browsing. Among contemporary bibliographic reference works of extreme importance for the future development of political leadership is the weekly information service *Current Contents: Social and Behavioral Sciences,* which is indexed with the keywords "leader" and "leadership" and which provides coverage of articles that appear in over 1,000 journals.

This bibliography is intended to serve two purposes: to illustrate the wide range of social science resources that can be drawn upon for the creation of a political leadership subfield in political science and to show that these resources can undergird efforts to solve the problems of field development that have been presented in this book, ranging from initial conceptualization to application of knowledge. Except for major bibliographical sources, works already cited in the text and the notes have been omitted.

Groups of citations begin on the following pages:

Three abbreviations have been employed: (1) *APSR* for the *American Political Science Review;* (2) *IESS* for David L. Sills, ed., *International Encyclopedia of the Social Sciences,* 17 vols. (New York: Macmillan and Free Press, 1968); and (3) *Annals* for the *Annals of the American Academy of Political and Social Science.*

Bibliographies and Overviews

Bass, Bernard M. *Leadership, Psychology, and Organizational Behavior.* New York: Harper, 1960. Bibliography, pp. 463–529.

Beck, Carl, and J. Thomas McKechnie. *Political Elites: A Select Computerized Bibliography.* Cambridge: MIT Press, 1968. "Leadership," pp. 193–201.

Bell, Wendell, Richard J. Hill, and Charles R. Wright. *Public Leadership: A Critical Review with Special Reference to Public Education.* San Francisco: Chandler, 1961. Bibliography, pp. 196–228.

Browne, Clarence G., and Thomas S. Cohn, eds. *The Study of Leadership.* Danville; Interstate Printers & Publishers, 1958.

Current Perspectives in Leadership. Entire issue of *Journal of Contemporary Business* 3, 4 (Autumn 1974). With essays by Stogdill, Hollander, Tannenbaum and Cooke, Vroom, Fiedler, and House.

Edinger, Lewis J., ed. *Political Leadership in Industrialized Societies.* New York: Wiley, 1967. "Leadership: An Interdisciplinary Bibliography," pp. 348–366.

Fleishman, Edwin A., and James G. Hunt, eds. *Current Developments in the Study of Leadership.* Carbondale: Southern Illinois University Press, 1973. Bibliography, pp. 195–207.

Force George T., Jack R. Van Der Slik, and Charles Dewitt Dunn. *Theory and Research in the Study of Political Leadership: An Annotated Bibliography.* Carbondale: Southern Illinois University, Public Affairs Research Bureau, 1972.

Gibb, Cecil, ed. *Leadership: Selected Readings.* Harmondsworth: Penguin, 1969. Bibliography, pp. 417–418.

Gouldner, Alvin W., ed. *Studies in Leadership: Leadership and Democratic Action.* New York: Harper, 1950.

Hunt, James G., and Lars L. Larson, eds. *Contingency Approaches to Leadership.* Carbondale: Southern Illinois University Press, 1974. Bibliography, pp. 199–215.

Hunt, James G., and Lars L. Larsen, eds. *Leadership Frontiers.* Kent: Kent State University Press, 1975.

Kymissis, Effie, and David G. Stang. "Leadership: An Index to References in Thirty-six Social Psychology Texts." *Catalog of Selected Documents in Psychology* 5 (Summer 1975), 282.

Lasswell, Harold D., Daniel Lerner, and C. Easton Rothwell. *The Comparative Study of Elites: An Introduction and Bibliography.* Hoover Institute Elite Studies. Stanford: Stanford University Press, 1952.

Leadership: The Psychology of Public Men. Entire issue of *Journal of International Affairs* 24, 1 (1970). With essays by Kelman, Mead, McClelland, and others.

Marvick, Dwaine, ed. *Political Decision Makers: Recruitment and Performance.* New York: Free Press, 1961. Bibliography, pp. 334–343.

Matthews, Donald R. *The Social Background of Political Decision-makers.* Garden City: Doubleday, 1954. Bibliography, pp. 65–71.

Putnam, Robert D. *The Comparative Study of Political Elites.* Englewood Cliffs: Prentice-Hall, 1976.

Quandt, William B. *The Comparative Study of Political Elites.* Beverly Hills: Sage, 1970. Bibliography, pp. 217–238.

Rustow, Dankwart A., ed. *Philosophers and Kings: Studies in Leadership.* New York: Braziller, 1970.

Stogdill, Ralph M. *Handbook of Leadership.* New York: Free Press, 1974. Bibliography, pp. 430–581.

Stogdill, Ralph M. *Leadership Abstracts and Bibliography, 1904–1974.* Columbus: Ohio State University, College of Administrative Science, 1975.

Concepts of Leadership

Allee, W. C. *Cooperation among Animals.* New York: Schuman, 1951. The faster or stronger animal is not always the leader.

Bass, Bernard M. "Some Observations about a General Theory of Leadership and Interpersonal Behavior." *Leadership and Interpersonal Behavior,* ed. Luigi Petrullo and Bernard M. Bass, pp. 3–9. New York: Holt, Rinehart & Winston, 1961.

Bendix, Reinhard. "Charismatic Leadership." *Scholarship and Partisanship: Essays on Max Weber,* ed. R. Bendix and Gunther Roth, pp. 170–187. Berkeley: University of California Press, 1971.

Bennis, Warren G. "Leadership Theory and Administrative Behavior: The Problem of Authority." *Administrative Science Quarterly* 4, 3 (December 1959), 259–301. Major review concluding with a typology based on a concept of leadership as "a process by which an agent induces a subordinate to behave in a desired manner" (p. 295).

Bernard, Jessie. "Political Leadership among North American Indians." *American Journal of Sociology* 34, 2 (September 1928), 296–315. Moral qualities differ from "savage" stereotype.

Binder, Arnold. "Leadership in Small Groups: A Mathematical Approach." *Journal of Experimental Psychology* 69, 2 (February 1965), 126–134. Along with Govindarajan, Rashevsky, and Wolin (op. cit., this section) and Cattell (op. cit. under "Role") challenges imagination of mathematical political scientists.

Bogardus, E. S. *Leaders and Leadership.* New York: Appleton Century, 1934.

Borgatta, Edgar F., Robert F. Bales, and Arthur S. Couch. "Some Findings Relevant to the Great Man Theory of Leadership." *American Sociological*

Review 19, 6 (December 1954), 755–759. Experimental evidence for the positive influence upon group productivity and satisfaction of leaders who have "great man" characteristics (task ability, assertiveness, and social acceptability).

Bowers, David G., and Stanley E. Seashore. "Predicting Organizational Effectiveness with a Four-Factor Theory of Leadership." *Administrative Science Quarterly* 11, 2 (September 1966), 238–263. Support, interaction facilitation, goal emphasis, and work facilitation.

Burke, Warner. "Leadership Behavior as a Function of the Leader, the Follower, and the Situation." *Journal of Personality* 33, 1 (March 1965), 60–81.

Carlyle, Thomas. *On Heroes, Hero Worship, and the Heroic in History.* London: Oxford University Press, 1946.

Cartwright, Dorwin, and Alvin Zander. "Leadership and Performance of Group Functions: Introduction." *Group Dynamics: Research and Theory,* 3d ed., pp. 301–317. New York: Harper & Row, 1968.

Chapin, F. Stuart. "Socialized Leadership." *Social Forces* 3, 1 (November 1924), 57–60. Socialized leaders are group centered: overcentralization calls for more of them.

Clague, Monique. "Conceptions of Leadership: Charles de Gaulle and Max Weber." *Political Theory* 3, 4 (November 1975), 423–440. Suggests potential for comparing ideas of experienced leaders and social scientists.

Clark, Joseph S. "Notes on Political Leadership." *Harpers,* 216 (June 1958), 23–30. View of experienced senator and mayor.

Coffin, Thomas E. "A Three-Component Theory of Leadership." *Journal of Abnormal and Social Psychology* 29, 1 (January 1944), 63–83. Planning, organizing, and persuading.

Cohen, D. L. "The Concept of Charisma and the Analysis of Leadership." *Political Studies* 20, 3 (September 1972), 299–305.

Delbecq, Andre L., and Sidney J. Kaplan. "The Myth of the Indigenous Community Leader." *Academy of Management Journal* 11, 1 (1968), 11–25.

Doshi, S. L. "On the Concept and Theory of Leadership." *Indian Journal of Social Research* 10, 3 (December 1969), 189–197. Constructs ideal types.

Fesler, James W. "Leadership and Its Context." *Public Administration Review* 20, 2 (September 1960), 122. No single concept of leadership is adequate for all task needs.

Fiedler, Fred E. *A Theory of Leadership Effectiveness.* New York: McGraw-Hill, 1967. Seminal work.

Friedrich, Carl J. "The Theory of Political Leadership and the Issue of Totalitarianism." *Political Leadership in Eastern Europe and the Soviet Union,* ed. R. Barry Farrell, pp. 17–27. Chicago: Aldine, 1970. Leaders initiate, maintain, protect; followers imitate, obey, acclaim.

Frohlich, Norman, Joe A. Oppenheimer, and Oran R. Young. *Political Leadership and Collective Goods.* Princeton: Princeton University Press, 1971. Deductive approach to what Marion J. Levy, Jr., has termed "a profit-making theory of political leadership and political following" (p. viii).

Gamson, William A. "Reputation and Resources in Community Politics." *American Journal of Sociology* 72, 2 (September 1966), 121–131. Reputation is an efficacious leadership attribute.

Gellner, Ernest. "The Great Patron: A Reinterpretation of Tribal Rebellions." *Archives Européennes de Sociologie* 10, 1 (1969), 27–40. Enhanced appreciation of the influence of the king in contemporary Morocco.

Gibb, Cecil A. "Leadership." *Handbook of Social Psychology*, 5 vols., ed. Gardner Lindzey and Elliot Aronson, 4:205–282. Reading: Addison-Wesley, 1968.

Gordon, Thomas. *Group-Centered Leadership*. Boston: Houghton Mifflin, 1955.

Govindarajan, T. N. "World Leadership: A Formula." *Journal of Psychological Researches* 11, 1 (January 1967), 38–40. Mathematical formulas expressing collective world leadership as a function of the representativeness of national leaders.

Grundstein, Nathan D. "What Is Meant by Leadership." *Public Management* 44, 11 (November 1962), 242–246.

Halal, William E. "Toward a General Theory of Leadership." *Human Relations* 27, 4 (April 1974), 401–416. Using three variables (leadership style, task technology, and subordinate motivation) derives five models of leadership (autocracy, bureaucracy, human relations, participation, and autonomy).

Hemphill, John K. "Why People Attempt to Lead." *Leadership and Interpersonal Behavior*, ed. Luigi Petrullo and Bernard M. Bass, pp. 201–215. New York: Holt, Rinehart & Winston, 1961.

Hinde, Robert A. *Biological Bases of Human Social Behavior*. New York: McGraw-Hill, 1974. "Leadership," pp. 350–353.

Hofstetter, C. Richard. "The Amateur Politician: A Problem in Construct Validation." *Midwest Journal of Political Science* 15, 1 (February 1971), 31–56.

Hollander, E. P. "Style, Structure, and Setting in Organizational Leadership." *Administrative Science Quarterly* 16, 1 (March 1971), 1–7. Reviews eleven papers in this issue.

Hollander, E. P., and J. W. Julian. "Contemporary Trends in the Analysis of Leadership Process." *Psychological Bulletin* 71, 5 (May 1969), 387–397.

Holmes, Roger. "Freud, Piaget and Democratic Leadership." *British Journal of Sociology* 16, 2 (June 1965), 123–129. From a concept of externally legitimated authority to situationally legitimated authority in the emotional development of children.

House, Robert J. "A Path-Goal Theory of Leadership Effectiveness." *Administrative Science Quarterly* 16, 3 (September 1971), 321–338. Seminal work.

House, Robert J., and Terence R. Mitchell, "Path-Goal Theory of Leadership." *Journal of Contemporary Business* 3, 4 (Autumn 1974), 81–97.

Hunt, Winslow, and Amnon Issacharoff. "History and Analysis of a Leaderless Group of Professional Therapists." *American Journal of Psychiatry* 132, 11 (November 1975), 1164–1167.

Jacoby, Jacob. "The Construct Validity of Opinion Leadership." *Public Opinion Quarterly* 38, 1 (Spring 1974), 81–89.

Jennings, Eugene E. *An Anatomy of Leadership: Princes, Heroes and Supermen.* New York: Harper & Row, 1961.

Jennings, Helen H. "Leadership—A Dynamic Redefinition." *Journal of Educational Sociology* 17, 7 (March 1944), 431–433. Leaders defined as "creative improvers of others' situations," providing "psychological comfort." Isolates repel choice, earn rejection, and cause "psychological discomfort."

Kaufman, Robert P. "The Patron-Client Concept and Macro-Politics: Prospects and Problems." *Comparative Studies in Society and History* 16, 3 (June 1974), 284–308. A critique of patronage theory.

Keesing, Felix M., and Marie M. Keesing. *Elite Communication in Samoa: A Study of Leadership.* Stanford: Stanford University Press, 1956. Broad-gauged social science approach with nine images: communicator, innovator, traditionalist, literalist, power seeker, career servant, reformer, zealot, reversionist.

Keller, Suzanne I. *Beyond the Ruling Class: Strategic Elites in Modern Society.* New York: Random House, 1963.

Kern, Robert, ed. *The Caciques: Oligarchical Politics and the System of Caciquismo in the Luso-Hispanic World.* Albuquerque: University of New Mexico Press, 1973.

Kincade, Kathleen. "Power and the Utopian Assumption." *Journal of Applied Behavioral Science* 10, 3 (July–September 1974), 402–414. Reflections of experienced American commune leader.

King, Stanley. "In Praise of Politicians." *American Scholar* 3, 1 (Winter 1934), 78–84. Politicians as peacemakers.

Klapp, Orrin E. *Symbolic Leaders: Public Drama and Public Men.* Chicago: Aldine, 1964.

Knickerbocker, Irving R. "Leadership: A Conception and Some Implications." *Journal of Social Issues* 4, 3 (Summer 1948), 23–40.

Kochan, Thomas A., Stuart M. Schmidt, and Thomas A. De Cotiis. "Superior-Subordinate Relations: Leadership and Headship." *Human Relations* 28, 3 (April 1975), 279–294. Important critique. Distinguishes among concepts of leadership, authority, and power.

Laitin, David, and Ian Lustick. "Leadership: A Comparative Perspective." *International Organization* 28, 1 (Winter 1974), 89–117. Reply by Robert W. Cox, pp. 141–144. Emphasizes leadership skills.

Lupsha, Peter A. "Constraints on Urban Leadership, or Why Cities Cannot Be Creatively Governed." *Improving the Quality of Urban Management,* ed. Willis D. Hawley and David Rogers, pp. 607–623. Beverly Hills: Sage, 1974. Seventeen constraint propositions, implying a theory of mayoral leadership.

Massey, Joseph A. "The Missing Leader: Japanese Youths' View of Political Authority." *APSR,* 69, 1 (March 1975), 31–48.

Meyer, Alfred G. "Historical Development of the Communist Theory of Leadership." *Political Leadership in Eastern Europe and the Soviet Union,* ed. R. Barry Farrell, pp. 5–16. Chicago: Aldine, 1970.

Middleton, John, and David Tait, eds. *Tribes without Rulers.* London: Routledge & Kegan Paul, 1958.

Miles, Raymond E. "Human Relations or Human Resources? Theories of Participative Leadership." *Harvard Business Review* 43 (July–August 1965), 148–163.

Miller, Walter B. "Two Concepts of Authority." *American Anthropologist* 57, 2 (April 1955), 271–289. Contrasts European concepts of vertical authority with radically different ideas of Fox Indians.

Morris, Richard T., and Melvin Seeman. "The Problem of Leadership: An Interdisciplinary Approach." *American Journal of Sociology* 56, 2 (September 1950), 149–155. Base for future interdisciplinary reformulations.

Nakane, Chie. "Traditional Pattern of Authority and Leadership in Japan." *Leadership and Authority: A Symposium,* ed. Gehan Wijeyewardene, pp. 74–82. Singapore: University of Malaya Press, 1968.

Neumann, Sigmund. "Leadership: Institutional and Personal." *Journal of Politics* 3, 2 (May 1941), 133–153.

Nix, Harold L. "Concepts of Community and Community Leadership." *Sociology and Social Research* 53, 4 (July 1969), 500–510. Leaders typed by level and function, scope of influence, and basic orientation; community power described as focused, split, multifaction, or amorphous.

Nydegger, Rudy V. "Leadership in Small Groups: A Rewards-Costs Analysis." *Small Group Behavior* 6, 3 (August 1975), 353–368.

Perinbanayagam, R. S. "Dialectics of Charisma." *Sociological Quarterly* 12, 3 (Summer 1971), 387–402. Compares Hitler and Gandhi.

Pigors, Paul. *Leadership or Domination.* Boston: Houghton Mifflin, 1935. Legitimacy versus power.

Pitkin, Hanna, ed. *Representation.* New York: Atherton, 1969.

Rashevsky, Nicholas. "Outline of a Mathematical Biology of Leadership." *Bulletin of Mathematical Biophysics* 12 (1950), 343–351.

Ratnam, K. J. "Charisma and Political Leadership." *Political Studies* 12, 3 (October 1964), 341–354.

Read, K. E. "Leadership and Consensus in a New Guinea Society." *American Anthropologist* 61, 3 (June 1959), 425–436.

Rustow, Dankwart A. "Study of Elites: Who's Who, When, and How." *World Politics* 18, 4 (July 1966), 690–717.

Salter, J. T. "The Pattern of Politics: I. The Politician." *Journal of Politics* 1, 2 (May 1939), 129–145. Democratic politician as specialist in nonviolent consensus building through public discussion.

Salter, J. T. "The Pattern of Politics: II. The Politician and the People." *Journal of Politics* 1, 3 (August 1939), 258–277. "The politician is as he is because we are as we are" (pp. 263–264).

Sarachek, Bernard. "Greek Concepts of Leadership." *Academy of Management Journal* 11, 1 (March 1968), 39–48. Challenges review of leadership concepts in the history of political theory.

Schmidt, Richard. "Leadership." *Encyclopedia of the Social Sciences,* ed. Edwin R. A. Seligman, 9:282–287. New York: Macmillan, 1933.

Schutz, William C. "The Ego, FIRO Theory and the Leader as Completer." *Leadership and Interpersonal Behavior,* ed. Luigi Petrullo and Bernard M. Bass, pp. 48–65. New York: Holt, Rinehart & Winston, 1961.

Seligman, Lester G. "Political Elites Reconsidered: Process, Consequences, and Values." *Comparative Politics* 6, 2 (January 1974), 299–314.

Shiflett, Samuel C. "The Contingency Model of Leadership Effectiveness: Some Implications of Its Statistical and Methodological Properties." *Behavioral Science* 18, 6 (November 1973), 429–440.

Sills, David L., ed. *IESS.* See articles on charisma; Chinese political thought; entrepreneurship; Ibn Khaldūn; Kautilya; kingship; leadership–political, psychological, and sociological aspects; Machiavelli; and monarchy.

Simmel, Georg. "Superiority and Subordination as Subject Matter of Sociology." *American Journal of Sociology* 2, 2 (September 1896), 167–187; 2, 3 (November 1896), 392–415.

Small, Norman J. *Some Presidential Interpretations of the Presidency.* Baltimore: Johns Hopkins Press, 1932.

Smith, Mapheus. "Leadership: The Management of Social Differentials." *Journal of Abnormal and Social Psychology* 30 (October 1935), 348–358.

Stephenson, T. E. "The Leader-Follower Relationship." *Sociological Review* 7, 2 (December 1959), 179–195.

Stinson, John E., and Thomas W. Johnson. "The Path-Goal Theory of Leadership: A Partial Test and Suggested Refinement." *Academy of Management Journal* 18, 2 (June 1975), 242–252.

Stogdill, Ralph M. "Historical Trends in Leadership Theory and Research." *Journal of Contemporary Business* 3, 4 (Autumn 1974), 1–18.

Strauss, Leo. *On Tyranny.* New York: Free Press, 1963.

Tiffany, Sharon W. "Giving and Receiving: Participation in Chiefly Redistribution Activities in Samoa." *Ethnology* 14, 3 (July 1975), 267–286.

Toynbee, A. J. "Seventeen Great Men, or Great Forces? Do Outstanding Leaders Make History, or Vice Versa?" *New York Times Magazine,* November 8, 1959, pp. 16 ff.

Tucker, Robert C. "The Dictator and Totalitarianism." *World Politics* 17, 4 (1965), 555–583.

Vroom, Victor H., and Philip W. Yetton. *Leadership and Decision Making.* Pittsburgh: Pittsburgh University Press, 1973. Of major, long-range significance.

Wiatr, Jerzy J. "Political Elites and Political Leadership: Conceptual Problems and Selected Hypotheses for Comparative Research." *Indian Journal of Politics* 17, 2 (December 1973), 137–149. Pioneering comparative conceptual discussion.

Wisse, Ruth R. *The Schlemiel as Modern Hero.* Chicago: University of Chicago Press, 1971. Reminds us not to forget our sense of humor.

Wolin, Burton R. "Leadership in Small Groups: A Mathematical Approach." *Journal of Experimental Psychology* 69, 2 (February 1965), 126–134.

Zander, Alvin. "The Nature and Consequences of Leadership." *Michigan Business Review* 13, 1 (January 1961), 29–32.

Anticipatory Variables

PERSONALITY

Adams, Bert N. "Birth Order: A Critical Review. *Sociometry* 35, 3 (September 1972), 411–439.

Anderson, Walt. "The Self-actualization of Richard Nixon." *Journal of Humanistic Psychology* 15, 1 (Winter 1975), 27–34.

Bartol, Kathryn M. "The Effect of Male versus Female Leaders on Follower Satisfaction and Performance." *Journal of Business Research* 3, 1 (January 1975), 33–42.

Berrington, Hugh. "Review Article: The Fiery Chariot: British Prime Ministers, and the Search for Love." *British Journal of Political Science* 4, 3 (July 1974), 345–369. Superb review of book by Iremonger (op. cit., this section) with a striking composite personality profile (p. 369).

Bluemel, C. S. *War, Politics, and Insanity: In Which the Psychiatrist Looks at the Politician.* Denver: World, 1950.

Bronfenbrenner, Urie. "Personality and Participation: The Case of the Vanishing Variables." *Journal of Social Issues* 16, 4 (1960), 54–63. Emphasizes class variables but presents intriguing finding that both leaders and nonparticipants ranked higher in psychosomatic complaints than ordinary participants.

Bowers, David G. "Self-esteem and the Diffusion of Leadership Style." *Journal of Applied Psychology* 48, 2 (April 1963), 135–140.

Campbell, Donald T. "An Error in Some Demonstrations of the Superior Social Perceptiveness of Leaders." *Journal of Abnormal and Social Psychology* 51, 3 (November 1955), 694–695.

Cattell, Raymond B., and Glen F. Stice. "Four Formulae for Selecting Leaders on the Basis of Personality." *Human Relations* 7, 4 (1954), 493–507.

Chapman, J. Brad. "Comparison of Male and Female Leadership Styles." *Academy of Management Journal* 18, 3 (September 1975), 645 ff.

Chapman, J. Brad, and F. Luthans. "Female Leadership Dilemma." *Public Personnel Management* 4, 3 (May–June 1975), 173–179. Reviews literature and prescribes organizational development measures to provide greater supportiveness.

Chemers, Martin M. "The Relationship between Birth Order and Leadership Style." *Journal of Social Psychology* 80, 2 (April 1970), 243–244.

Christie, Richard, and Florence L. Geis. *Studies in Machiavellianism.* New York: Academic Press, 1970.

Clifford, Clare, and Thomas E. Cohn. "The Relationship of Leadership and Personality Attributes Perceived by Followers." *Journal of Social Psychology* 64, 1 (1964), 57–64.

Constantine, Edmond, and Kenneth H. Craik. "Women as Politicians: The Social Background, Personality, and Political Careers of Female Party Leaders." *Journal of Social Issues* 28, 2 (1972), 217–236.

DiRenzo, Gordon J. "Professional Politicians and Personality Structures." *American Journal of Sociology* 73, 2 (September 1967), 217–225.

Dymally, Mervyn M., ed. *The Black Politician: His Struggle for Power*. Belmont: Duxbury, 1971.

Erikson, Erik H. "The Legend of Hitler's Childhood." *Childhood and Society* pp. 326–358. New York: Norton, 1963.

Erikson, Erik H. "Gandhi's Autobiography: The Leader as a Child." *American Scholar* 35, 4 (Autumn 1966), 632–646. With rules for interpreting life-cycle data.

Erikson, Erik H. "Life Cycle." *IESS*, 9:286–292.

Fiedler, Fred E. "Leadership Experience and Leader Performance—Another Hypothesis Shot to Hell." *Organizational Behavior and Human Performance* 5, 1 (January 1970), 1–14.

Friedlander, Saul, and Raymond Cohen. "The Personality Correlates of Bellig-erence in International Conflict." *Comparative Politics* 7, 2 (January 1975), 155–186.

Froman, Lewis A. Jr. "The Importance of Individuality in the Voting of Congress." *Journal of Politics* 25, 2 (May 1963), 324–332.

Gandhi, Madan G. "Charismatic Leadership and Mao Tse-tung." *Indian Political Science Review* 9, 1 (January 1975), 38–49.

Gaudet, Frederick J., and A. Ralph Carli. "Why Executives Fail." *Personnel Psychology* 10, 1 (Spring 1957), 7–22. Personality factors rather than lack of technical knowledge; 300 executives served as informants on persons whom they had appointed.

Gilbert, G. M. *The Psychology of Dictatorship*. New York: Ronald, 1950.

Gitter, A. George, Harvey Black, and Janet E. Fishman. "Effect of Race, Sex, Nonverbal Communication and Verbal Communication on Perception of Leadership." *Sociology and Social Research* 60, 1 (October 1975), 46–57. Nonverbal variables explained 52 percent of variance in follower responses to televised "leader" images in college student experiment.

Gordon, Leonard V., and Francis F. Medland. "Leadership Aspiration and Leadership Ability." *Psychological Reports* 17, 2 (October 1965), 338–390.

Govindarajan, T. N. "Executive Leadership and Need Satisfaction." *Journal of the Indian Academy of Applied Psychology* 9, 1 (1972), 14–17. Maslow's theory.

Hain, Paul L., and James E. Piereson. "Lawyers and Politics Revisited: Structural Advantages of Lawyer Politicians." *American Journal of Political Science* 19, 1 (February 1975), 41–51.

Hanawalt, N. G. "Level of Aspiration in College Leaders and Non-leaders." *Journal of Abnormal and Social Psychology* 38, 4 (October 1943), 545–548.

Hanna, William J. "Political Recruitment and Participation: Some Suggested Areas for Research." *Psychoanalytic Review* 52, 4 (Winter 1965–1966), 67–80.

Haythorn, William, et al. "The Behavior of Authoritarian and Equalitarian Personalities in Groups." *Human Relations* 9, 1 (1956), 57–75.

Henderson, John T. "The Childhood Origins of Political Struggle: An Interpretation of the Personality and Politics of a New Zealand Radical." *Political Science* 26, 2 (December 1974), 2–19.

Hennessy, Bernard. "Politicals and Apoliticals: Some Measurements of Personality Traits." *Midwest Journal of Political Science* 3, 4 (November 1959), 336–354.

Iremonger, Lucille. *The Fiery Chariot: A Study of British Prime Ministers and the Search for Love.* London: Secker & Warburg, 1970.

Jacobson, Marsha B., and Joan Effertz. "Sex Roles and Leadership: Perceptions of Leaders and the Led." *Organizational Behavior and Human Performance* 12, 3 (December 1974), 383–396.

Janus, Sam, Barbara Bess, and Carol Saltus. *A Sexual Profile of Men in Power.* Englewood Cliffs: Prentice-Hall, 1977. Startling insights from prostitutes' reports of perverted sex preferences of politicians.

Jennings, Helen. *Leadership and Isolation: A Study of Personality in Interpersonal Relations.* 2d ed. New York: Longmans, Green, 1950.

Jennings, M. Kent, and Norman Thomas. "Men and Women in Party Elites: Social Roles and Political Resources." *Midwest Journal of Political Science* 12, 4 (November 1968), 469–492.

Johnson, H. Russell. "Some Personality Correlates of the Relationships between Individuals and Organizations." *Journal of Applied Psychology* 59, 5 (October 1974), 623–632.

Kelley, Harold H. "The Warm-Cold Variable in First Impressions of Personality." *Journal of Personality* 18, 4 (June 1950), 431–439.

Kipnis, David, and William P. Lane. "Self-confidence and Leadership." *Journal of Applied Psychology* 46, 4 (August 1962), 291–295.

Kirkpatrick, Jeane J. *Political Woman.* New York: Basic Books, 1974. Interviews with forty female state legislators.

Kirsch, John P., and Ronald C. Dillehay. *Dimensions of Authoritarianism: A Review of Research and Theory.* Lexington: University Press of Kentucky, 1967.

Knowles, Henry P., and Borje O. Saxberg. *Personality and Leadership Behavior.* Reading: Addison-Wesley, 1971.

Knutson, Jeanne. *The Human Basis of the Polity: A Psychological Study of Political Man.* Chicago: Aldine-Atherton, 1972.

Kretschmer, Ernst. *The Psychology of Men of Genius.* College Park: McGrath, 1970. Includes studies of Bismarck and Robespierre.

Kruschke, Earl R. *Female Politicals and Apoliticals: Some Measurements and Comparisons.* Ph.D. dissertation, University of Wisconsin, 1963.

Kuehl, Charles R. "Leadership Orientation as a Function of Interpersonal Need Structure." *Journal of Applied Psychology* 60, 1 (February 1975), 143–145.

Kupper, Herbert. "Some Psychological Hypotheses on Mao Tse-tung's Personality." *Studies in Comparative Communism* 7, 1–2 (Spring–Summer 1974), 50–52.

Lane, Robert E. "Personality, Political: The Study of Political Personality." *IESS*, 12:13–21.

Larson, Lars L., and Kenneth Rowland. "Leadership Style and Cognitive Complexity." *Academy of Management Journal* 17, 1 (March 1974), 37–45.

Lasswell, Harold D. "A Note on 'Types' of Political Personality: Nuclear, Co-relational and Developmental." *Journal of Social Issues* 24, 3 (July 1968), 81–92.

Lawson, Murray G. "The Foreign-Born in Congress, 1789–1949." *APSR* 51, 4 (December 1957), 1183–1189.

Leites, Nathan. "Psycho-cultural Hypotheses about Political Acts." *World Politics* 1, 1 (October 1948), 102–119.

L'Etang, Hugh. *The Pathology of Leadership.* New York: Hawthorn, 1970. Medical problems of twentieth-century leaders analyzed by a physician. Includes John F. Kennedy and Winston Churchill.

Levinson, Daniel J. "Authoritarian Personality and Foreign Policy." *Journal of Conflict Resolution* 1, 1 (March 1957), 37–47.

Levinson, Daniel J. "The Relevance of Personality for Political Participation." *Public Opinion Quarterly* 22, 1 (Spring 1958), 3–10.

Levinson, Daniel J. "Personality, Political: Conservatism and Radicalism." *IESS*, 12:21–30.

Loevinger, Jane. *Ego Development.* San Francisco: Jossey-Bass, 1976.

Luria, A. R. *The Working Brain.* New York: Basic Books, 1973. Basis for the view of creative potential in political leadership.

Mackler, Bernard, and Franklin C. Schontz. "Life Styles and Creativity: A Review." *Journal of Psychology* 58, 1 (July 1964), 205–214.

Maier, R. F., and Richard L. Hoffman. "Acceptance and Quality of Solutions as Related to Leader's Attitudes toward Disagreement in Group Problem Solving." *Journal of Applied Behavioral Science* 1, 4 (November–December 1965), 373–386. Innovation and satisfaction increase when leaders view disagreements as valuable resources rather than as disruptive problems.

Manheim, Henry L. "Personality Differences of Members of Two Political Parties." *Journal of Social Psychology* 50, 2 (November 1959), 261–268.

Maslow, Abraham H. "Liberal Leadership and Personality." *Freedom* 2 (1942), 27–30.

Maslow, Abraham H. *Motivation and Personality.* New York: Harper, 1954. Seminal statement of a need satisfaction hierarchy that will strongly influence future political leader-follower personality studies.

McClelland, David C. *Power: The Inner Experience.* New York: Irvington, 1975. Summary of need for power theory and research that will increasingly influence political leadership studies.

McConaughy, John E. "Certain Personality Factors of State Legislators in South Carolina." *APSR* 44, 4 (December 1950), 897–903.

McGregor, Douglas. *Leadership and Motivation.* Cambridge: MIT Press, 1966.

Miller, Milton J. "Emotional Factors That Bring Leaders into Power." *Psychiatric Forum* 3, 1 (Winter 1972), 1–5.

Muthayya, B. "Elected Village Leaders of India: A Psychological Analysis." *Behavioral Sciences and Community Development* 5, 1 (March 1971), 14–20.

Oleszek, W. "Age and Political Careers." *Public Opinion Quarterly* 33, 1 (Spring 1969), 100–103.

Patterson, Samuel C. "Characteristics of Party Leaders." *Western Political Quarterly* 16, 2 (June 1963), 332–352.

Pflange, Otto. "Toward a Psychoanalytic Interpretation of Bismarck." *American Historical Review* 77, 2 (April 1972), 419–444.

Pinner, Frank A., Paul Jacobs, and Philip Selznick. *Old Age and Political Behavior.* Berkeley: University of California Press, 1959.

Porterfield, Austin L. "Dramatic Insight in the Social Leader." *Sociology and Social Research* 24, (March–April 1940), 317–325.

Pramod, Kumar. "Intelligence and Student Leadership." *Journal of Psychological Researches* 11, 2 (May 1967), 45–48. No differences on intelligence found, but elected leaders scored higher on "anxiety" and "dominance need."

Pye, Lucian W. *Politics, Personality and Nation Building.* New Haven: Yale University Press, 1962.

Raiser, John R. "Personal Characteristics of Political Decision-makers: A Literature Review." La Jolla: Western Behavioral Sciences Institute, 1965.

Rees, M. E., and M. Goldman. "Some Relationships between Creativity and Personality." *Journal of General Psychology* 65, 1 (July 1961), 145–161. "Creativity is more apt to occur in individuals who are impulsive, aggressive, dominating, and characterized by a lack of deliberation, self-control, and restraint" (p. 156). Also in persons more prone to depression.

Renshon, Stanley A. *Psychological Needs and Political Behavior.* New York: Free Press, 1974. Need for personal control as a predictor of political participation.

Renshon, Stanley A. "Psychological Analysis and Presidential Personality: The Case of Richard Nixon." *History of Childhood Quarterly: Journal of Psychohistory* 2, 3 (Winter 1975), 415–450.

Robertson, P. L. "Cleveland: Personality as a Political Leader." *Psychoanalytic Review* 51, 2 (Summer 1964), 130–154.

Rosenfeld, Lawrence B., and Timothy G. Plax. "Personality Determinants of Autocratic and Democratic Leadership." *Speech Monographs* 42, 3 (August 1975), 203–208.

Rotter, J. B. "Level of Aspiration as a Method of Studying Personality." *Psychological Review* 49, 5 (September 1942), 463–474.

Rudolph, Susanne Hoeber. "The New Courage: An Essay on Gandhi's Psychology." *World Politics* 16, 1 (October 1963), 98–117.

Schiffer, Irving. *Charisma: A Psychoanalytic Look at Mass Society.* Toronto: University of Toronto Press, 1973.

Smelser, Neil J., ed. *Personality and Social Systems.* New York: Wiley, 1970.

Smith, Louis. "Aaron Burr." *Psychoanalytic Quarterly* 12, 1 (1943), 67–99.

Smith, M. Brewster. "A Map for the Analysis of Personality and Politics." *Journal of Social Issues* 24, 3 (1968), 15-28.

Soule, John W. "Future Political Ambitions and the Behavior of Incumbent State Legislators." *Midwest Journal of Political Science* 13, 3 (August 1969), 439-454.

Stogdill, Ralph M. "Personal Factors Associated with Leadership: A Survey of the Literature." *Journal of Psychology* 25, 1 (January 1948), 35-71. Fundamental stocktaking that greatly assisted subsequent research.

Swanson, G. E. "Agitation in Face-to-Face Contacts: A Study of the Personalities of Orators." *Public Opinion Quarterly* 21, 2 (June 1957), 288-294.

Templer, Andrew J. "A Study of the Relationship between Psychological Differentiation and Management Style." *Personnel Psychology,* 26, 2 (Summer 1973), 227-238.

Terman, Lewis M. "A Preliminary Study in the Psychology and Pedagogy of Leadership." *Pedagogical Seminary* 11, 4 (December 1904), 413-451.

Theophrastus. *The Character Sketches.* Translated by Warren Anderson. Kent: Kent State University Press, 1970.

Tucker, Robert C. "Stalin and the Uses of Psychology." *World Politics* 8, 4 (July 1956), 455-483.

Wexley, Kenneth N., and Peter J. Hunt. "Male and Female Leaders: Comparison of Performance and Behavior Patterns." *Psychological Reports* 35, 2 (October 1974), 867-872.

Winter, David G. *The Power Motive.* New York: Free Press, 1973. Need for power.

Winter, David G. "What Makes Candidates Run." *Psychology Today* (July 1976), 45 ff. Profiles of 1976 U.S. presidential candidates in terms of needs for power, affiliation, and achievement as compared with past presidents.

Witkin, Herman A., et al. *Psychological Differentiation.* New York: Wiley, 1962. Field dependence/independence.

Witty, Paul A., and Harvey C. Lehman. "Nervous Instability and Genius: Military and Political Leaders." *Journal of Social Psychology* 3, 2 (May 1932), 212-233. Includes Jonathan Swift, Cromwell, Lincoln, Julius Caesar, Frederick the Great, and Napoleon.

Zaleznik, Abraham. "Charismatic and Consensus Leaders: A Psychological Comparison." *Bulletin of the Menninger Clinic* 38, 3 (May 1974), 222-238. "Father" versus "brother," or "peer," imagery.

Zink, Harold. "A Case Study of a Political Boss." *Psychiatry* 1, 4 (November 1938), 527-533.

ROLE

Allen, Ivan, with Paul Hemphill. *Mayor: Notes on the Sixties.* New York: Simon & Schuster, 1971. Mayor of Atlanta.

Armilla, José. "Anxiety in Taking the Role of the Leader." *Journal of Abnormal and Social Psychology* 68, 5 (May 1964), 550-552.

Badgley, John. *Politics among Burmans: A Study of Intermediary Leaders.* Athens: Ohio University, Center for International Studies, 1970.

Bailey, Stephen K. "Leadership in Local Government." *Yale Review* 45, 4 (June 1956), 563–573. Views of political scientist and mayor of Middletown, Connecticut, 1952–1954.

Bailey, Thomas A. "Is the Presidency a Killing Job?" *Presidential Greatness,* pp. 340–343. New York: Appleton Century, 1966. Bailey answers "no."

Barker, Anthony, and Michael Rush. *The British Member of Parliament and His Information.* Toronto: University of Toronto Press, 1970.

Bedeski, Robert E. "Leadership Roles in Communist China: The Kuomintang and Communist Experiences." *Studies in Comparative Communism* 7, 1–2 (Spring–Summer 1974), 53–63.

Berkeley, Humphrey. *The Power of the Prime Minister.* London: Allen & Unwin, 1968.

Bowman, Lewis, and G. R. Boynton. "Activities and Role Definitions of Grass Roots Party Officials." *Journal of Politics* 28, 1 (February 1966), 121–143.

Breckenridge, Adam C. *The Executive Privilege: Presidential Control over Information.* Lincoln: University of Nebraska Press, 1974.

Bugental, Daphne E., and George F. J. Lehner. "Accuracy of Self-perception and Group-perception as Related to Two Leadership Roles." *Journal of Abnormal and Social Psychology* 56, 3 (May 1958), 396–398.

Cattell, Raymond B. "A Mathematical Model for the Leadership Role and Other Personality-Role Relations." *Emerging Problems in Social Psychology,* ed. Muzafer Sherif and M. O. Wilson. University of Oklahoma Lectures in Social Psychology, series III, pp. 207–227. Norman: University Book Exchange Duplicating Service, 1957.

Close, M. John. "Dogmatism and Managerial Achievement." *Journal of Applied Psychology* 60, 3 (June 1975), 395-396. First-line and lower-middle managers were found to be more dogmatic than upper-middle and top managers.

Cohen, Michael D., and James G. March. *Leadership and Ambiguity: The American College President.* New York: McGraw-Hill, 1974.

Crosby, Robert B. (Lt. Gov.). "Why I Want to Get Rid of My Job." *State Government* 20, 7 (July 1947), 193 f., 204. "Blind alley," "empty title," costly, other roles can perform its functions.

Davidson, Roger H. *The Role of the Congressman.* New York: Pegasus, 1969.

Dennis, Philip A. "The Oaxacan Village President as Political Middleman." *Ethnology* 12, 4 (October 1973), 419–427.

Eulau, Heinz, John C. Wahlke, William Buchanan, and Leroy G. Ferguson. "The Role of the Representative: Some Empirical Observations on the Theory of Edmund Burke." *APSR* 53, 3 (September 1959), 742–756. Superb example of transition from political theory to empirical research.

Fisher, Louis. *Presidential Spending Power.* Princeton: Princeton University Press, 1975.

Flango, Victor E., Lettie McSpadden Wenner, and Manfred W. Wenner. "The Concept of Judicial Role: A Methodological Note." *American Journal of Political Science* 19, 2 (May 1975), 277–290. Four types: law applier, mediator, law extender, and policy maker.

Follett, Mary P. *The Speaker of the House of Representatives.* Reprint of 1902 ed. New York: Burt Franklin, 1974. Pioneering 1896 study of the then second "most powerful" office in the United States.

Forthal, Sonya. *Cogwheels of Democracy: A Study of the Precinct Captain.* New York: William Frederick, 1946.

Galloway, George B. "Leadership in the House of Representatives." *Western Political Quarterly* 12, 2 (June 1959), 417–441.

Garner, J. F. "The Role of the Mayor in Britain." *Journal of Local Administration Overseas* 2, 1 (January 1963), 16–23.

Goodenough, Ward. "Rethinking 'Status' and 'Role': Toward a General Model of the Cultural Organization of Social Relationships." *The Relevance of Models for Social Anthropology,* ed. Michael Banton, pp. 1–24. New York: Praeger, 1965.

Goody, Jack, ed. *Succession to High Office.* Cambridge: At the University Press, 1966.

Hage, Jerald, and Gerald Marwell. "Toward the Development of an Empirically Based Theory of Role Relationships." *Sociometry* 31, 2 (June 1968), 200–212.

Henry, William. "The Business Executive: The Psychodynamics of a Social Role." *American Journal of Sociology* 54, 4 (January 1949), 286–291.

Hughes, Daniel T. "Democracy in a Traditional Society: Two Hypotheses on Role." *American Anthropologist* 71, 1 (February 1969), 36–45. New roles without traditional counterparts will be accepted more easily.

Hughes, Daniel T. "Reciprocal Influence of Traditional and Democratic Leadership Roles on Ponape." *Ethnology* 8, 3 (July 1969), 278–291.

Hughes, Daniel T. "Conflict and Harmony: Roles of Councilman and Section Chief on Ponape." *Oceania* 40, 1 (September 1969), 32–41. Intriguing role studies by a comparative political anthropologist.

Hutchison, Bruce. *Mister Prime Minister, 1867–1964.* New York: Harcourt, Brace & World, 1964.

Imse, Thomas P. "Spiritual Leadership and Organizational Leadership: The Dilemma of Being Pope." *Social Compass* 16, 2 (1969), 275–280.

Jeffreys, M. D. W. "The Average Length of an African Ruler's Reign." *Man* 45, 103–119 (1945), 135–136. Fourteen and three-tenths years.

Komarovsky, Mirra. "Some Problems in Role Analysis." *American Sociological Review* 38, 6 (December 1973), 649–662.

Kuper, Adam. "Gluckman's Village Headman." *American Anthropologist* 72, 2 (April 1970), 355–358.

Kweeder, James B. *The Role of the Manager, Mayor, and Councilman in Policy Making.* Chapel Hill: University of North Carolina, Institute of Government, 1965.

Levinson, Daniel J. "Role, Personality and Social Structure in the Organizational Setting." *Journal of Abnormal and Social Psychology* 58, 2 (March 1959), 170–180.

Lieberman, Seymour. "The Effects of Changes in Roles on the Attitudes of Role Occupants." *Human Relations* 9, 4 (November 1956), 385–402.

Life Extension Foundation. "Job Stress and the Executive: 6000 Managers Report Their Experience." *Management Review* 47 (May 1958), 13–22.

Lipson, Leslie. *The American Governor: From Figurehead to Leader.* Chicago: University of Chicago Press, 1939.

Meller, Norman. "Representational Role Types: A Research Note." *APSR* 61, 2 (June 1967), 474–477.

Michener, James A. *Report of the County Chairman.* New York: Random House, 1961.

Neuberger, Richard L., and Maurine B. Neuberger. "Are You Fit for Political Office?" *Colliers,* November 13, 1953, pp. 36–38. Role requirements described by a pair of political leaders.

Olmsted, Donald W. *Social Groups, Roles, and Leadership: An Introduction to the Concepts.* East Lansing: Institute for Community Development, Michigan State University, 1961.

Porter, Lyman W. "Perceived Trait Requirements in Bottom and Middle Management Jobs." *Journal of Applied Psychology* 45, 4 (August 1961), 232–236.

Punnett, R. M. *Front Bench Opposition: The Role of the Leader of the Opposition, the Shadow Cabinet and Shadow Government in British Politics.* New York: St. Martin's, 1973.

Ransome, Coleman B. "Political Leadership in the Governor's Office." *Journal of Politics* 26, 1 (February 1964), 197–220.

Rodgers, David A. "Personality Correlates of Successful Role Behavior." *Journal of Social Psychology* 46, 1 (August 1957), 111–117.

Rogler, Lloyd H. "The Changing Role of a Political Boss in a Puerto Rican Migrant Community." *American Sociological Review* 39, 1 (February 1974), 57–67.

Rosenzweig, Robert M. "The Politician and the Career in Politics." *Midwest Journal of Political Science* 1, 2 (August 1957), 163–172.

Ruchelman, Leonard I., ed. *Big City Mayors: Crisis in Urban Politics.* Bloomington: Indiana University Press, 1969.

Salter, J. T., ed. *The American Politician.* Chapel Hill: University of North Carolina Press, 1938. Includes essays on La Guardia, La Follette, Norman Thomas, and others. Salter's numerous writings merit rediscovery and renewed appreciation.

Schlesinger, Arthur M., Jr. *The Imperial Presidency.* Boston: Houghton Mifflin, 1973.

Schlesinger, Joseph A. "The Politics of the Executive." *Politics in the American States: A Comparative Analysis,* ed. Herbert Jacob and Kenneth Vines. Boston: Little, Brown, 1965.

Seligman, Lester G. "Developments in the Presidency and the Conception of Political Leadership." *American Sociological Review* 20, 5 (December 1955), 706–712.

Smith, T. V. "The Role of the Politician." *Public Management* 19 (December 1937), 362–365.

Southwold, Martin. "Leadership Authority and the Village Community." *The King's Men: Leadership and Status in Buganda on the Eve of Independence,* ed. Lloyd A. Fallers. London: Oxford University Press, 1964.

Stouffer, Samuel A. "Role Conflict and Personality." *American Journal of Sociology* 56, 5 (March 1951), 395–406.

Tacheron, Donald G., and Morris K. Udall. *The Job of the Congressman: An Introduction to Service in the U.S. House of Representatives.* Indianapolis: Bobbs-Merrill, 1967.

Thach, Charles C. *The Creation of the Presidency, 1775–1789: A Study in Constitutional History.* Baltimore: Johns Hopkins Press, 1970.

Tupes, Ernest C., A. Carp, and Walter R. Borg. "Performance in Role-playing as Related to Leadership and Personality Measures." *Sociometry* 21, 3 (September 1958), 165–179.

Weber, Max. "Politics as a Vocation." *From Max Weber: Essays in Sociology.* Edited and translated by H. H. Gerth and C. Wright Mills. New York: Oxford University Press, 1946.

Weller, P. M. "From Faction to Party: The Role and Authority of the Leader." *Political Science* 26, 2 (December 1974), 41–47.

Williams, G. Mennen. *A Governor's Notes.* Ann Arbor: University of Michigan, Institute of Public Administration, 1961.

Zurcher, Louis A. "Poverty Program Indigenous Leaders: A Study of Marginality." *Sociology and Social Research* 53, 2 (January 1969), 147–162.

ORGANIZATION

Abraham, Henry J. *Justices and Presidents: A Political History of Appointments to the Supreme Court.* New York: Oxford University Press, 1974.

Almond, Gabriel, and Sidney Verba. *The Civic Culture.* Princeton: Princeton University Press, 1963.

Atkins, Burton M., and William Zavoina. "Judicial Leadership on the Court of Appeals: A Probability Analysis of Panel Assignment in Race Relations Cases on the Fifth Circuit." *American Journal of Political Science* 18, 4 (November 1974), 701–711. Leader influences organization and thereby decisional outcomes.

Balutis, Alan P. "Comparative Legislative Studies." *Polity* 8, 1 (Autumn 1975), 147–155.

Barber, Bernard. "Participation and Mass Apathy in Associations." *Studies in Leadership,* ed. Alvin Gouldner, pp. 477–504. New York: Harper, 1950.

Bartol, Kathryn M. "Male versus Female Leaders: The Effect of Leader Need for Dominance on Follower Satisfaction." *Academy of Management Journal* 17, 2 (June 1974), 225–234.

Bass, Bernard M. "Some Aspects of Attempted, Successful, and Effective Leadership." *Journal of Applied Psychology* 65, 2 (April 1961), 120–122. Effects of leader's ability and discrepancies between self- and group-accorded esteem.

Beckhouse, Lawrence, et al. ". . . And Some Men Have Leadership Thrust upon Them." *Journal of Personality and Social Psychology* 31, 3 (March 1975), 557–566.

Bell, Graham B., and Harry E. Hall, Jr. "The Relationship between Leadership and Empathy." *Journal of Abnormal and Social Psychology* 49, 1 (January 1954), 156–157. Example of ambivalent social psychological empathy findings that precede, and need to be related to, emerging political science research on legislators' perceptions of constituent opinion.

Berlew, David F. "Leadership and Organizational Excitement." *California Management Review* 17, 2 (Winter 1974), 21–30.

Blake, Robert R., and Jane S. Mouton. "Perceived Characteristics of Elected Representatives." *Journal of Abnormal and Social Psychology* 62, 3 (May 1961), 693–695.

Blum, Richard H. "The Choice of American Heroes and Its Relationship to Personality Structure in an Elite." *Journal of Social Psychology* 48, 2 (November 1958), 235–246.

Boissevain, Jeremy, and J. Clyde Mitchell, eds. *Network Analysis: Studies in Human Interaction.* The Hague: Mouton, 1971.

Booth, David A. "Are Elected Mayors a Threat to Managers?" *Administrative Science Quarterly* 12, 4 (March 1968), 572–589. "No."

Boynton, G. R., and Chong Lim Kim, eds. *Legislative Systems in Developing Countries.* Durham: Duke University Press, 1975.

Bramstedt, Ernst K. *Dictatorship and Political Police.* New York: Oxford University Press, 1945.

Bullard, Peter D., and Paul E. Cook. "Sex and Workstyle of Leaders and Followers: Determinants of Productivity." *Psychological Reports* 36, 2 (April 1975), 545–547.

Burja, Janet M. "The Dynamics of Political Action: A New Look at Factionalism." *American Anthropologist* 75, 1 (February 1973), 132–152.

Burke, Peter J. "Participation and Leadership in Small Groups." *American Sociological Review* 39, 6 (December 1974), 832–843.

Burns, Tom. "The Reference of Conduct in Small Groups: Cliques and Cabals in Occupational Milieux." *Human Relations* 8, 4 (1955), 467–486.

Campbell, Donald T. *Leadership and Its Effects upon the Group.* Columbus: Ohio State University, Bureau of Business Research, 1956.

Campbell, Donald T., and Thelma H. McCormack. "Military Experience and Attitudes toward Authority." *American Journal of Sociology* 62, 5 (March 1957), 482–490.

Cantoni, Louis, and Lucile Cantoni. "Therapy for Community Leaders." *Adult Leadership* 13, 9 (March 1965), 285–286. Friends can help by contributing a sense of worthiness.

Cattell, Raymond B. "Friends and Enemies: A Psychological Study of Character and Temperament." *Character and Personality* 3, 1 (September 1934), 54–63.

Centers, Richard. *The Psychology of Social Classes: A Study of Class Consciousness.* Princeton: Princeton University Press, 1949.

Chessick, Richard D. "Was Machiavelli Right?" *American Journal of Psychotherapy* 23, 4 (1969), 633–644. Must groups be tyrannized?

Clelland, Donald A., and William H. Form. "Economic Dominants and Community Power: A Comparative Analysis." *American Journal of Sociology* 69, 5 (March 1964), 511–521.

Clifford, Clare, and Thomas S. Cohn. "The Relationship between Leadership and Personality Attributes Perceived by Followers." *Journal of Social Psychology* 64, 1 (October 1964), 57–64.

Clive, Dorothy I. "Assessing Community Groups and Group Forces: To Be Effective, the City Manager Should Be Familiar with All of the Leadership Resources and Potential in His Community." *Public Management* 46, 5 (May 1964), 108–112. By a political science professor with experience as an elected county commissioner.

Cohen, Arthur M., and W. Bennis. "Continuity of Leadership in Communication Networks." *Human Relations* 14, 4 (November 1961), 351–369.

Cohen, E. G. "Interracial Interaction Disability." *Human Relations* 25, 1 (February 1972), 9–24.

Coleman, James, Elihu Katz, and Herbert Menzel. "The Diffusion of an Innovation among Physicians." *Sociometry* 20, 4 (December 1957), 253–270.

Craig, Gordon A. "The Professional Diplomat and His Problems, 1919–1939." *World Politics* 4, 2 (January 1952), 145–158.

Crowe, Bruce J., et al. "The Effects of Subordinates' Behavior on Managerial Style." *Human Relations* 25, 3 (1972), 215–237.

Curtis, Russell L., Jr., and Louis A. Zurcher. "Social Movements: An Analytical Exploration of Organizational Forms." *Social Problems* 21, 3 (Winter 1974), 356–369.

Cutright, Phillips. "Activities of Precinct Committeemen in Partisan and Nonpartisan Communities." *Western Political Quarterly* 17, 1 (March 1964), 93–108.

Dahl, Robert A., and Edward R. Tufte. *Size and Democracy.* Stanford: Stanford University Press, 1973.

Dalton, George. "How Exactly Are Peasants Exploited?" *American Anthropologist* 76, 3 (September 1974), 553–561.

Dansereau, Fred, Jr., George Green, and William J. Haga. "A Vertical Dyad Linkage Approach to Leadership within Formal Organizations: A Longitudinal Investigation of the Role Making Process." *Organizational Behavior and Human Performance* 13, 1 (February 1975), 46–78.

David, Stephen M. "Leadership of the Poor in Poverty Programs." *Proceedings of the Academy of Political Science* 29, 1 (July 1968), 86–100. Mayors and social welfare agencies deflect poor from political organizations and action programs that they cannot control.

Dexter, Lewis A. *The Sociology and Politics of Congress.* Chicago: Rand McNally, 1969.

Durand, Richard M., and Zarrel V. Lambert. "Dogmatism and Exposure to Political Candidates." *Psychological Reports* 36, 2 (April 1975), 423–429.

Dyer, Frederick C., and John M. Dyer. *Bureaucracy vs. Creativity: The Dilemma of Modern Leadership.* Coral Gables: University of Miami Press, 1965.

Easton, David A. "A Re-assessment of the Concept of Political Support." *British Journal of Political Science* 5, 4 (October 1975), 435–458.

Erikson, Erik H. "Hitler's Imagery and German Youth." *Psychiatry* 5, 4 (November 1942), 475–493.

Etzioni, Amitai. *A Comparative Analysis of Complex Organizations.* New York: Free Press, 1975.

Farkas, Suzanne. *Urban Lobbying: Mayors in the Federal Arena.* New York: New York University Press, 1971.

Ferree, Myra Marx. "A Woman for President? Changing Responses: 1958–1972." *Public Opinion Quarterly* 28, 3 (Fall 1974), 390–399.

Fiedler, Fred E. "A Note on Leadership Theory: The Effect of Social Barriers between Leaders and Followers." *Sociometry* 20, 2 (June 1957), 87–94. Barriers help leaders make decisions uninfluenced by followers.

Fishbein, Martin. "The Perception of Non-members: A Test of Merton's Reference Group Theory." *Sociometry* 26, 3 (September 1963), 271–286.

Fitzgibbon, Russell H. "Adoption of a Collegiate Executive in Uruguay." *Journal of Politics* 14, 4 (November 1952), 616–642.

Freeman, Linton. *Patterns of Local Community Leadership.* Indianapolis: Bobbs-Merrill, 1967.

Froman, Lewis A., Jr. *Congressmen and Their Constituencies.* Chicago: Rand McNally, 1963.

Froman, Lewis A., Jr. "Organization Theory and the Explanation of Important Characteristics of Congress." *APSR* 62, 2 (June 1968), 518–526. For example, "The larger the size of the organization, the greater the number of subgroups in it; hence the greater the overall emphasis on formal and impersonal rules and specificity of roles" (p. 524).

Gallagher, James, and Peter J. Burke. "Scapegoating and Leader Behavior." *Social Forces* 52, 4 (June 1974), 481–488.

Gerth, Hans. "The Nazi Party: Its Leadership and Composition." *American Journal of Sociology* 45, 4 (January 1940), 517–541.

Glaser, Daniel. "Dynamics of Ethnic Identification." *American Sociological Review* 23, 1 (February 1958), 31–40.

Glaser, William A. "Doctors and Politics." *American Journal of Sociology* 66, 3 (November 1960), 230–245.

Goldman, Merle. "Party Policies towards the Intellectuals: The Unique Blooming and Contending of 1961–2." *Party Leadership and Revolutionary Power in*

China, ed. John W. Lewis, pp. 268–303. New York: Cambridge University Press, 1970.

Goodenough, Ward. "Rethinking 'Status' and 'Role': Toward a General Model of the Cultural Organization of Social Relationship." *The Relevance of Models for Anthropology,* ed. Michael Banton. London: Tavistock, 1965.

Gosnell, Harold F. *Boss Platt and His New York Machine.* Chicago: University of Chicago Press, 1924.

Greene, Charles N. "The Reciprocal Nature of Influence between Leader and Subordinate." *Journal of Applied Psychology* 60, 2 (April 1975), 187–193. Extremely important contribution to causal analysis.

Greene, Lee S., ed. *City Bosses and Political Machines.* Entire issue of the *Annals* 353 (May 1964). Explores declining boss rule and emerging urban political leader relationships with organized sources of community power.

Greenstein, Fred I. "Personality and Political Socialization: The Theories of Authoritarian and Democratic Character." *Annals* 361 (September 1965), 81–95.

Greenstein, Fred I., et al. "The Child's Conception of the Queen and the Prime Minister." *British Journal of Political Science* 4, 3 (July 1974), 257–287.

Greenstone, John D. *Labor in American Politics.* New York: Knopf, 1969.

Greenwald, Howard P. "Patterns of Authority in Two Herding Societies: An Ecological Approach." *Administrative Science Quarterly* 17, 2 (June 1972), 207–217.

Greenwold, Stephen M. "Kingship and Caste." *Archives Européenes de Sociologie* 16, 1 (1975), 49–75. "The development of caste was due to the influence of the secular ruler and followed from a deliberate political and social policy devised and implemented by the Malla kings [in Nepal]" (p. 57).

Gusfield, J. R. "Functional Areas of Leadership in Social Movements." *Sociological Quarterly* 7, 2 (Spring 1966), 137–156.

Guttentag, Marcia, ed. "The Poor: Impact Research and Theory." *Journal of Social Issues* 26, 2 (Spring 1970), 1–192.

Hahn, Harlan. "Leadership Perceptions and Voting Behavior in a One-Party Legislative Body." *Journal of Politics* 32, 1 (February 1970), 140–155. Calls for further research on the hypothesis that "leaders may actually have some influence on the decisions and votes of legislators" (p. 155).

Haigh, Roger M. "The Creation and Control of a Caudillo." *Hispanic American Historical Review* 44, 4 (November 1964), 481–490. Case study of how a "kinship elite" created and controlled a military leader, concluding that he was more an "instrument" than a "tyrant."

Hale, Oron. "Adolf Hitler as Feldherr." *Virginia Quarterly Review* 24, 2 (Spring 1948), 198–213.

Hall, Gus. "On Collective Leadership." *Political Affairs* 30, 7 (July 1951), 43–49. Problems in political group relations portrayed by the national secretary of the American Communist party.

Hassel, Conrad V. "The Political Assassin." *Journal of Police Science and Administration* 2, 4 (December 1974), 399–403.

Hawver, Carl F. *The Congressman's Conception of His Role: A Study of the Use of Public Opinion Polls by Members of the United States House of Representatives.* Ph.D. dissertation, American University, 1963.

Haythorn, William, et al. "The Effects of Varying Combinations of Authoritarian and Equalitarian Leaders and Followers." *Journal of Abnormal and Social Psychology* 53, 2 (September 1956), 210–219.

Heath, Jim F. *John F. Kennedy and the Business Community.* Chicago: University of Chicago Press, 1969.

Helmich, Donald T. "Predecessor Turnover and Successor Characteristics." *Cornell Journal of Social Relations* 9, 2 (Fall 1974), 249–260. Frequent prior turnover is associated with task orientation; low turnover is related to employee orientation.

Henderson Lenneal J., Jr., ed. *Black Political Life in the United States.* San Francisco: Chandler, 1972. Includes valuable bibliographical essay by the editor.

Hicks, Jack M. "The Influence of Group Flattery on Self Evaluation." *Journal of Social Psychology* 58, 1 (October 1962), 147–151.

Hinckley, Barbara. "Congressional Leadership Selection and Support: A Comparative Analysis." *Journal of Politics* 32, 2 (May 1970), 268–287.

Hocart, Arthur M. *Kings and Councillors.* Chicago: University of Chicago Press, 1970. A classic.

Hollander, Edwin P. "Processes of Leadership Emergence." *Journal of Contemporary Business* 3, 4 (Autumn 1974), 19–34.

Hollingsworth, A. Thomas. "Perceptual Accuracy of the Informal Organization as a Determinant of the Effectiveness of Formal Leaders." *Journal of Economics and Business* 27, 1 (Fall 1974), 75–78.

Hoskin, Gary, and Gerald Swanson. "Political Party Leadership in Columbia: A Spatial Analysis." *Comparative Politics* 6, 3 (April 1974), 395–423. Organizational position as a predictor of perceptions of nine top party leaders by 412 persons in high, middle, and low ranks.

Hsu, Chris Ching-Yang, and Richard R. Newton. "Relation between Foremen's Leadership Attitudes and the Skill Level of Their Work Groups." *Journal of Applied Psychology* 59, 6 (December 1974), 771–772.

Hunt, A. Lee, Jr., and Robert E. Pendley. "Community Gatekeepers: An Examination of Political Recruiters." *Midwest Journal of Political Science* 16, 3 (August 1972), 411–438.

Ilgen, Daniel R., and Gordon Obrien. "Leader-Member Relations in Small Groups." *Organizational Behavior and Human Performance* 12, 3 (December 1974), 335–350.

Ionescu, Ghita, and Isabel de Madariaga. *Opposition: Past and Present of a Political Institution.* London: Watts, 1968.

Jackson, John E. *Constituencies and Leaders in Congress: Their Effects on Senate Voting Behavior.* Cambridge: Harvard University Press, 1974.

Janis, Irving L. *Victims of Groupthink.* Boston: Houghton Mifflin, 1972.

Jennings, Helen H. *Leadership and Isolation.* London: Longsmans, Green, 1943.

Jennings, M. Kent, Milton C. Cummings, Jr., and Franklin P. Kilpatrick. "Trusted Leaders: Perceptions of Appointed Federal Officials." *Public Opinion Quarterly* 30, 3 (Fall 1966) 368–384.

Johannsen, Dorothea. "Reactions to the Death of President Roosevelt." *Journal of Abnormal and Social Psychology* 41, 2 (April 1946), 218–222. Evidence for the affective dimension.

Jordan, Robert S., and Parley W. Newman, Jr. "The Secretary-General of NATO and Multi-national Political Leadership." *International Journal* 30, 4 (Autumn 1975), 732–757. Discusses strategies.

Kadushin, Charles, and Richard Rose. "Recent Developments in Comparative Political Sociology: Determinants of Electoral Behavior and the Structure of Elite Networks." *Current Research in Sociology*, ed. Margaret S. Archer, pp. 229–266. The Hague: Mouton, 1974.

Kahn, Si. *How People Get Power: Organizing Oppressed Communities for Action.* New York: McGraw-Hill, 1970.

Kaplow, Jeffry. *The Names of Kings: The Parisian Laboring Poor in the Eighteenth Century.* New York: Basic Books, 1972.

Katz, Daniel, and Samuel J. Eldersveld. "The Impact of Local Party Activity upon the Electorate." *Public Opinion Quarterly* 25, 1 (Spring 1961), 1–24.

Kelley, Stanley, Jr., and Thad W. Mirer. "The Simple Act of Voting." *APSR* 68, 2 (June 1974), 572–591. Implies complexity of developing an adequate model of leader-follower interaction.

Kingdon, John W. "Politicians' Beliefs about Voters." *APSR* 61, 1 (March 1967), 130–136.

Kipnis, David, and Carl Wagner. "Character Structure and Response to Leadership Power." *Journal of Experimental Research in Personality* 2, 1 (February 1967), 16–24.

Klaf, Franklin S. "The Power of the Group Leader." *Psychoanalysis and the Psychoanalytic Review* 48, 2 (Summer 1961), 41–51. Based upon reactivation of ambivalent childhood identifications with authority.

Koenig, Louis W. *The Invisible Presidency.* New York: Holt, Rinehart & Winston, 1960. Examines influence of advisers and staff.

Kornberg, Allan, ed. *Legislatures in Comparative Perspective.* New York: McKay, 1973.

Kornberg, Allan, and Lloyd D. Musolf. "Perception and Constituency Influence on Legislative Behavior." *Western Political Quarterly* 19, 2 (June 1966), 285–292.

Kornberg, Allan, and Lloyd D. Musolf, eds. *Legislatures in Developmental Perspective.* Durham: Duke University Press, 1970.

Kriesbert, Louis. "Societal Coordination by Occupational Leaders." *American Behavioral Scientist* 3, 1 (September 1959), 36–38.

Lapidus, Gail Warshovsky. "Political Mobilization, Participation and Leadership: Women in Soviet Politics." *Comparative Politics* 8, 1 (October 1975), 90–118.

Laver, Robert L. "Social Movements: An Interactionist Analysis." *Sociological Quarterly* 13, 3 (Summer 1972), 315–328.

Lawler, Edward L. "Endorsement of Formal Leaders: An Integrative Model." *Journal of Personality and Social Psychology* 31, 2 (February 1975), 216–223.

Lebeuf, Annie M. D. "The Role of Women in the Political Organization of African Societies." *Women of Tropical Africa,* ed. Pauline Denise, pp. 93–119. Berkeley: University of California Press, 1963.

Le Bon, Gustav. "The Leaders of Crowds and Their Means of Persuasion." *The Crowd,* pp. 117–140. New York: Viking, 1960.

Levitt, M. J., and E. G. Feldbaum. "Councilmembers, Lobbyists and Interest Groups: Communication and Mutual Perception in Local Politics." *Journal of Voluntary Action Research* 4, 1–2 (January–April 1975), 98–103.

Lieberson, Stanley, and James F. O'Connor. "Leadership and Organizational Performance: A Study of Large Corporations." *American Sociological Review* 37, 2 (April 1972), 117–130.

Loveridge, Ronald O. *City Managers in Legislative Politics.* Indianapolis: Bobbs-Merrill, 1971.

Lowi, Theodore J. *At the Pleasure of the Mayor: Patronage and Power in New York City, 1898–1958.* New York: Free Press, 1964.

Lowry, Richie P. "The Functions of Alienation in Leadership." *Sociology and Social Research* 46, 4 (July 1962), 426–435.

MacPherson, Myra. *The Power Lovers: An Intimate Look at Politicians and Their Marriages.* New York: Putnam, 1975. Serious, detailed inquiry supported by the Eagleton Institute of Politics.

MacRae, Duncan, Jr., and Dee M. Kilpatrick. "Collective Decision and Polarization in a 125-Man Group." *Public Opinion Quarterly* 23 (Winter 1959–1960), 505–514.

MacRae, Duncan, Jr., and Edith K. MacRae. "Legislators' Social Status and Their Votes." *American Journal of Sociology* 66, 6 (May 1961), 599–603.

Marx, Gary T. "Thoughts on a Neglected Category of Social Movement Participant: The Agent Provocateur and the Informant." *American Journal of Sociology* 80, 2 (September 1974), 402–442.

May, Ernest Richard, ed. *The Ultimate Decision: The President as Commander-in-Chief.* New York: Braziller, 1961.

May, Robert M., and Brian Martin. "Voting Models Incorporating Interaction between Voters." *Public Choice* 22 (Summer 1975), 37–53. A mathematical model.

Mayhew, Bruce R. "System Size and Ruling Elites." *American Sociological Review* 38, 4 (August 1973), 468–475. Explores Mosca's hypothesis that the larger the size, the smaller the proportion of the governing minority to the governed majority.

McClintock, C. G. "Group Support and the Behavior of Leaders and Nonleaders." *Journal of Abnormal Social Psychology* 67, 2 (August 1963), 105–113.

McKean, Dayton D. *The Boss: The Hague Machine in Action*. Boston: Houghton Mifflin, 1940.

McWorter, Gerald A., and Robert L. Crain. "Subcommunity Gladiatorial Competition: Civil Rights Leadership as a Competitive Process." *Social Forces* 46, 1 (1967), 8–21. Social structures predict patterns of leadership competition and goal achievement.

Miller, Delbert C. "Decision-making Cliques in Community Power Structures: A Comparative Study of an American and an English City." *American Journal of Sociology* 64, 3 (November 1958), 299–311.

Miller, Warren E., and Donald E. Stokes. "Constituency Influence in Congress." *APSR* 57, 1 (March 1963), 45–46.

Morgan, David R. "Political Linkage and Public Policy: Attitudinal Linkage between Citizens and Officials." *Western Political Quarterly* 26, 2 (June 1973), 209–223.

Morrow, Garry R., et al. "Perceptions of the Role of the President: A Nine-Year Follow-Up." *Perceptual and Motor Skills* 38, 3 (June 1974), 1259–1262.

Mouton, Jane S., and Robert R. Blake. "The Influence of Competitively Vested Interests on Judgments." *Journal of Conflict Resolution* 6, 2 (June 1962), 149–153.

Mueller, John E. *War, Presidents, and Public Opinion*. New York: Wiley, 1973.

Mulder, Mauk, et al. "Illegitimacy of Power and Positiveness of Attitude towards the Power Person." *Human Relations* 19, 1 (February 1966), 21–37.

Nie, Norman H., Sidney Verba, and Jae-On Kim. "Political Participation in the Life Cycle." *Comparative Politics* 6, 3 (April 1974), 319–340.

Obler, Jeffrey. "The Role of National Party Leaders in the Selection of Parliamentary Candidates: The Belgian Case." *Comparative Politics* 5, 2 (January 1973), 157–185.

Ogg, Frederick A. "Impeachment of Governor Ferguson." *APSR* 12, 1 (February 1918), 111–115.

Osborn, Richard N., and James G. Hunt. "An Empirical Investigation of Lateral and Vertical Leadership at Two Organizational Levels." *Journal of Business Research* 2, 2 (April 1974), 209–222.

Patterson, Samuel C., and G. R. Boynton. "Legislative Recruitment in a Civic Culture." *Social Science Quarterly* 50, 2 (September 1969), 243–263. Points toward understanding that political leaders themselves (both incumbent and aspiring) may influence the recruitment of other political leaders.

Peabody, Robert L. "Committees from the Leadership Perspective." *Annals* 411 (January 1974), 133–146.

Perrucci, Robert, and Mark Pilisuk. "Leaders and Ruling Elites: The Interorganizational Bases of Community Power." *American Sociological Review* 35, 6 (December 1970), 1040–1057.

Peterson, Edward N. "The Bureaucracy and the Nazi Party." *Review of Politics* 28, 2 (April 1966), 172–192.

Peterson, Edward N. *The Limits of Hitler's Power*. Princeton: Princeton University Press, 1969.

Presthus, Robert. *Elites in the Policy Process*. New York: Cambridge University Press, 1974.

Prewitt, Kenneth. "From the Many Are Chosen the Few." *American Behavioral Scientist* 13, 2 (November–December 1969), 169–188.

Price, Don K. "Professionals and Politicians." *The Scientific Estate*, pp. 208–269. Cambridge: Harvard University Press, Belknap Press, 1965.

Rice, Stuart. *Farmers and Workers in American Politics*. New York: Columbia University Press, 1924.

Riedesel, Paul. "Bales Reconsidered: A Critical Analysis of Popularity and Leadership Differentiation." *Sociometry* 37, 4 (December 1974), 557–564.

Ripley, Randall B. *Party Leaders in the House of Representatives*. Washington: Brookings Institution, 1967.

Rokkan, Stein, et al. *Citizens, Elections, Parties: Approaches to the Comparative Study of the Processes of Development*. New York: McKay, 1970.

Rose, Arnold M. "Alienation and Participation: A Comparison of Group Leaders and the 'Mass.' " *American Sociological Review* 27, 6 (December 1962), 834–838.

Sanford, Fillmore H. *Authoritarianism and Leadership: A Study of the Follower's Orientation to Authority*. Philadelphia: Institute for Research in Human Relations, 1950.

Sanford, Fillmore H. "Leadership Identification and Acceptance." *Groups, Leadership and Men*, ed. Harold Guetzkow. Pittsburgh: Carnegie Press, 1951. Urban survey research to probe citizens' orientations toward leaders and readiness to accept them.

Sayles, Leonard R., and Margaret K. Chandler. *Managing Large Systems: Organizations for the Future*. New York: Harper & Row, 1971. NASA experience.

Schulze, Robert O. "Role of Economic Dominants in Community Power Structure." *American Sociological Review* 23, 1 (February 1958), 3–9.

Scott, James. "Exploitation in Rural Class Relations." *Comparative Politics* 7, 4 (July 1975), 489–532.

Seligman, Lester G. "Presidential Leadership: The Inner Circle and Institutionalization." *Journal of Politics* 18, 3 (August 1956), 410–426.

Seligman, Lester G., and Elmer E. Cornwell, Jr., eds. *New Deal Mosaic: Roosevelt Confers with His National Emergency Council, 1933–1936*. Eugene: University of Oregon Press, 1965.

Shaw, Marvin E. "A Comparison of Two Types of Leadership in Various Communication Nets." *Journal of Abnormal and Social Psychology* 50, 1 (January 1955), 127–134.

Shaw, Marvin E. "Communication Networks." *Advances in Experimental Social Psychology*, ed. Leonard Berkowitz, pp. 111–147. New York: Academic Press, 1969.

Sheingold, Carl A. "Social Networks and Voting Behavior: The Resurrection of a Research Agenda." *American Journal of Sociology* 38, 6 (December 1973), 712–720.

Shepherd, Robert. "Leadership, Public Opinion and the Referendum." *Political Quarterly* 46, 1 (January–March 1975), 25–35.

Sherif, Muzafer, ed. *Intergroup Relations and Leadership: Approaches and Research in Industrial, Ethnic, Cultural, and Political Areas.* New York: Wiley, 1962.

Shils, Edward. "The Intellectuals and the Powers: Some Perspectives for Comparative Analysis." *Comparative Studies in Society and History* 1, 1 (October 1958), 5–22.

Sickels, Robert J. *Presidential Transactions.* Englewood Cliffs: Prentice-Hall, 1974. Precisely in the right direction: party, advisers, bureaucracy, Supreme Court, Congress, and public.

Siegel, Bernard J., and Alan R. Beals. "Pervasive Factionalism." *American Anthropologist* 62, 3 (June 1960), 394–417.

Sinha, Jai B. P., and J. Pandey. "The Processes of Decision Making in Dependence Prone Persons." *Journal of Psychological Researches* 16, 1 (January 1972), 35–37.

Sommer, Robert. "Leadership and Group Geography." *Sociometry* 24, 1 (March 1961), 99–110.

Spadaro, Robert N. "Role Perceptions of Politicians vis-a-vis Public Administrators: Parameters for Public Policy." *Western Political Quarterly* 26, 4 (December 1973), 717–725. Politicians compared with administrators take shorter range views; both distrust each other; politicians see administrators as interested in security; administrators credit politicians with wide civic consciousness.

Spearman, Diana. "Psychological Background of Dictatorship." *Sociological Review* 26, 2 (April 1934), 158–174.

Stagner, Ross. "Prestige Value of Different Types of Leadership." *Sociology and Social Research* 25 (May–June 1941), 403–413.

Stinston, John E., and John H. Robertson. "Follower Maturity and Preference for Leader-Behavior Style." *Psychological Reports* 32, 1 (February 1973), 247–250. Inexperienced prefer consideration; more experienced prefer structure.

Sullivan, William E. "Criteria for Selecting Party Leadership in Congress: An Empirical Test." *American Politics* 3, 1 (January 1975), 25–44.

Svalastoga, Kaare. "Note on Leaders' Estimates of Public Opinion." *Public Opinion Quarterly* 24 (Winter 1950–1951), 767–769.

Tannenbaum, Robert, Irving R. Weschler, and Fred Massarik. *Leadership and Organization: A Behavioral Science Approach.* New York: McGraw-Hill, 1961.

Thomas, William C., Jr. *The Politics of Bureaucracy: Ninety-one New York City Bureau Chiefs.* Ph.D. dissertation, Columbia University, 1962.

Tidmarch, Charles M., and Charles M. Sabbatt. "Presidential Leadership Change and Foreign Policy Roll-Call Voting in the Senate." *Western Political Quarterly* 25, 4 (December 1972), 613–625.

Toffler, Alvin. "A Future for Parliaments." *Futures* 7, 3 (June 1975), 182–183.

Tolley, Howard, Jr. "Private Approaches to Urban Leadership: Community Organizations, Non-profit Foundations, and Corporate Elite." *Intellect* 103, 2361 (December 1974), 152–157.

Wahlke, John C. "Policy Demands and System Support: The Role of the Represented." *British Journal of Political Science* 1, 3 (July 1974), 271–290. Suggestive contribution to the reanalysis of follower behavior that a leadership emphasis will require.

Watson, James B., and Julian Samora. "Subordinate Leadership in a Bi-cultural Community: An Analysis." *American Sociological Review* 19, 4 (August 1954), 413–421.

Weinstein, Edwin A., and Olga G. Lyerly. "Symbolic Aspects of Presidential Assassination." *Psychiatry* 1, 32 (February 1969), 1–11. Content analysis of threats and interviews with potential assassins.

Wellhofer, E. Spencer, and Timothy M. Hennessey. "Political Party Development: Institutionalization, Leadership Recruitment and Behavior." *American Journal of Political Science* 18, 1 (February 1974), 135–166. Recruitment and turnover of "novice-ideologues," "transitionals," and "statesmen" are linked to characteristics of parties at different stages of development.

Wells, Richard S. "The Legal Profession and Politics." *Midwest Journal of Political Science* 8, 2 (May 1964), 166–190.

Wells, William D., Guy Weinert, and Marilyn Rubel. "Conformity Pressure and Authoritarian Personality." *Journal of Psychology* 42, 1 (July 1956), 133–136.

Westefield, Louis P. "Majority Party Leadership and the Committee System in the House of Representatives." *APSR* 68, 4 (December 1974), 1593–1604.

Whitehorn, John C. "Alienation and Leadership." *Psychiatry* 24, 2 (supp.) (May 1961), 1–6. Prescribes a "consultative and evocative" leadership style to involve alienated patients in normal social relationships of "lead-and-be-led."

Wilkinson, A. M. *Followers All: A Book about Leadership.* London: Livingstone, 1958.

Wilson, James Q. *Negro Politics: The Search for Leadership.* New York: Free Press, 1973.

Wright, C. R. "Social Structure and Mass Communications Behavior: Exploring Patterns through Constructional Analysis." *The Idea of Social Structure: Papers in Honor of Robert K. Merton,* ed. Lewis A. Coser, pp. 379–416. New York: Harcourt Brace Jovanovich, 1975.

Yerby, Janet. "Attitude, Task, and Sex Composition as Variables Affecting Female Leadership in Small Problem-solving Groups." *Speech Monographs* 42, 2 (June 1975), 160–168.

Young, Kenneth. *Churchill and Beaverbrook: A Study in Friendship and Politics.* London: Eyre & Spottiswoode, 1966.

Zdep, S. M. "Intra Group Reinforcements and Its Effects on Leadership Behavior." *Organization Behavior and Human Performance* 4, 3 (August 1969), 284–298.

Zeigler, Harmon, and Michael A. Baer. *Lobbying: Interaction and Influence in American State Legislatures.* Belmont: Wadsworth, 1969.

Ziller, Robert C. "The Leader's Perception of the Marginal Member." *Personnel Administration* 28, 2 (1965), 6-11.

TASK

Alexander, Herbert E. *Political Financing.* Minneapolis: Burgess, 1973.

Allyn, Paul, and Joseph Green. *See How They Run: The Making of a Congressman.* Philadelphia: Chilton, 1964. Composite fictionalized account by insiders, emphasizing recruitment intrigue by "Congressman-makers."

Baus, Herbert M., and William B. Ross. *Politics Battle Plan.* New York: Macmillan, 1968. Military analog for electoral campaigning.

Bernstein, Thomas P. "Keeping the Revolution Going: Problems of Village Leadership after Land Reform." *Party Leadership and Revolutionary Power in China,* ed. John W. Lewis, pp. 239-267. New York: Cambridge University Press, 1970.

Bosch, Juan. *The Unfinished Experiment: Democracy in the Dominican Republic.* New York: Praeger, 1965. By former head of state.

Brinton, Crane. *The Anatomy of Revolution.* New York: Random House, Vintage, 1965.

Brown, David S. "The Ultimate Managerial Challenge—Creative Change." *Public Management* 45, 12 (December 1963), 271-276.

Bruning, James L. "Leadership in Disaster." *Psychology* 1, 4 (November 1964), 19-23. Effective leaders at first are decisive and action oriented; later they are more intellectually oriented.

Burke, Peter J. "Task and Socio-emotional Leadership Role Performance." *Sociometry* 34, 1 (March 1971), 22-40.

Burling, Robbins. *The Passage of Power: Studies in Political Succession.* New York: Academic Press, 1974. Supports concept of collective leadership.

Butterfield, Herbert. *Statecraft of Machiavelli.* London: Bell, 1940.

Cantril, Hadley. "Effective Democratic Leadership: A Psychological Interpretation." *Journal of Individual Psychology* 14, 2 (November 1958), 128-138.

Carter, Launor F., and Mary Nixon. "An Investigation of the Relationship between Four Criteria of Leadership Ability for Three Different Tasks." *Journal of Psychology* 27, 1 (January 1949), 245-261.

Cheng, J. Chester. "Problems of Chinese Communist Leadership as Seen in the Secret Military Papers." *Asian Survey* 4, 6 (June 1964), 861-872.

Christian, George E. *The President Steps Down: A Personal Memoir of the Transfer of Power.* New York: Macmillan, 1970. Observations on task disengagement by aide to President Lyndon B. Johnson.

Clausen, Aage R. *How Congressmen Decide: A Policy Focus.* New York: St. Martin's, 1973. Essential basis for eventual system-wide decision-making analysis, comparing leaders and interactions among them on selected tasks.

Cooper, Robert. "Leader's Task Relevance and Subordinate Behaviour in Industrial Work Groups." *Human Relations* 19, 1 (February 1966), 57-84.

Curtis, Gerald L. *Election Campaigning Japanese Style.* New York: Columbia University Press, 1971. Based upon direct observation.

Dahl, Robert A., and Charles E. Lindblom. *Politics, Economics and Welfare: Planning and Politico-economic Systems Resolved into Basic Social Processes.* New York: Harper, 1953.

Devall, W. B., and J. Harry. "Community Leaders and Urban Housing Problems: Leadership Roles, Organizational Goals and Effectiveness in 7 New York City Planning Districts." *Journal of Voluntary Action Research* 4, 1-2 (January-April 1975), 75-84.

Dexter, Lewis A. "Some Strategic Considerations in Innovating Leadership." *Studies in Leadership,* ed. Alvin Gouldner, pp. 592-640. New York: Harper, 1950.

Dill, William R., Thomas L. Hilton, and Walter R. Reitman. "How Aspiring Managers Promote Their Own Careers." *California Management Review* 2, 4 (Summer 1960), 9-15.

Dubin, Robert, et al., eds. *Leadership and Productivity.* San Francisco: Chandler, 1965.

Dubno, Peter. "Decision Time Characteristics of Leaders and Group Problem Solving Behavior." *Journal of Social Psychology* 59, 2 (April 1963), 259-282.

Erikson, Robert S., Norman R. Luttberg, and William V. Holloway. "Knowing One's District: How Legislators Predict Referendum Voting." *American Journal of Political Science* 19, 2 (May 1975), 231-246. "We are left with the irony that the legislators who claim to pay the greatest attention to constituency preferences appear to be the least able to determine what their constituents want" (p. 241).

Etzioni, Amitai. *Political Unification: A Comparative Study of Leaders and Forces.* New York: Holt, Rinehart & Winston, 1965.

Farley, James A., and Leonard W. Hall. "Two Political Pros Analyze Their Art." *New York Times Magazine,* August 10, 1958, pp. 13 ff. Task portrayal by national party chairmen.

Firestone, Ira J. "Leader Effectiveness and Leadership Conferral as Determinants of Helping in a Medical Emergency." *Journal of Personality and Social Psychology* 31, 2 (February 1975), 343-348. Crisis task.

Firth, Raymond. "Introduction: Leadership and Economic Growth." *International Social Science Journal* 16, 2 (1964), 186-191. "Leadership cannot be created to order. The problem, as Belshaw suggests, is rather to identify the principles of co-operation and co-adaptation operating in a society and to identify such persons who can best mobilize such forces for economic advance" (p. 188).

Fisher, Andrew A. "Leadership Concept for Family Planning Programs." *Health Education Monographs* 3, 2 (Summer 1975), 168-180.

Fogelman, Edwin, ed. *Hiroshima: The Decision to Use the A-Bomb.* New York: Scribner's, 1964.

Gaby, Daniel M., and Merle H. Treusch. *Election Campaign Handbook.* Englewood Cliffs: Prentice-Hall, 1976. Detailed operating manual for American campaigns.

Galtung, Johan. "Peace." *IESS*, 11:487–496. Major unfinished world task.

Gibson, James J. "The Concept of the Stimulus in Psychology." *American Psychologist* 15, 11 (November 1960), 694–703. Reviews conceptual history and posits five types of stimuli that may assist clarification of the concept of "task."

Goodspeed, David J. *The Conspirators*. New York: Viking, 1961. Principles for a successful coup d'etat; drawn from six case studies.

Gore, William. *Administrative Decision-making: A Heuristic Model*. New York: Wiley, 1964.

Gourevitch, Peter. "Political Skill: A Case Study." *Public Policy*, ed. John D. Montgomery and Arthur Smithies, pp. 239–276. Cambridge: Harvard University Press.

Gross, Feliks. *The Seizure of Political Power in a Century of Revolutions*. New York: Philosophical Library, 1958.

Hamblin, Robert L. "Leadership and Crisis." *Sociometry* 21, 4 (December 1958), 322–335.

Harris, Leon A. *The Fine Art of Political Wit*. New York: Dutton, 1964.

Hatanaka, Sachiko. *Leadership and Socio-economic Change in Sinasina, New Guinea Highlands*. Port Moresby: Australian National University, New Guinea Research Unit, 1972.

Havens, Murray C., Carl Leiden, and Karl M. Schmitt. *The Politics of Assassination*. Englewood Cliffs: Prentice-Hall, 1970.

Hebb, Donald O. "On the Nature of Fear." *Psychological Review* 53, 5 (September 1946), 259–276. Biological bases of key political leader task: coping with fear in self and others.

Hedlund, Ronald D., and H. Paul Friesma. "Representatives' Perceptions of Constituency Opinion." *Journal of Politics* 34, 3 (August 1972), 730–752. Example of growing literature with mixed findings on degrees of perceptual inaccuracy and with controversy over implications for theories of representative democracy.

Heidenheimer, Arnold J., ed. *Comparative Political Finance: The Financing of Party Organizations and Election Campaigns*. Lexington: Heath, 1970.

Heidenheimer, Arnold J., ed. *Political Corruption*. New York: Holt, Rinehart & Winston, 1970.

Heller, Frank A. "Leadership, Decision Making, and Contingency Theory." *Industrial Relations* 12, 2, (May 1973), 183–199. Looks at 360 managers in thirty firms.

Hemphill, John K. *Situational Factors in Leadership*. Bureau of Educational Research Monograph no. 32. Columbus: Ohio State University, 1949.

Hemphill, John K., et al. "The Relation between Possession of Task Relevant Information and Attempts to Lead." *Psychological Monographs* 70, 7, whole no. 414 (1956), 1–24.

Henderson, Keith M. "How Executives Handle 'Hot' Questions." *American Behavioral Scientist* 5, 1 (September 1961), 5–7.

Henry, Laurin L. *Presidential Transitions*. Washington: Brookings Institution, 1960.

Hermann, Charles F., Margaret G. Hermann, and Robert A. Canto. "Counterattack or Delay: Characteristics Influencing Decision Makers' Responses to the Simulation of an Unidentified Attack." *Journal of Conflict Resolution* 18, 1 (March 1974), 75-106.

Hill, Walter A., and D. Hughes. "Leader Behavior as a Function of Task Type." *Organizational Behavior and Human Performance* 11, 1 (February 1974), 83-96.

Hills, R. Jean. "The Representative Function: Neglected Dimension of Leadership Behavior." *Administrative Science Quarterly* 8, 1 (June 1963), 83-101.

Jenkins, William O. "A Review of Leadership Studies with Particular Reference to Military Problems." *Psychological Bulletin* 44, 1 (January 1947), 54-79.

Justice, Robert T. "Leadership Effectiveness: A Contingency Approach." *Academy of Management Journal* 18, 1 (March 1975), 160-166.

Katz, Elihu, et al. "Leadership Stability and Social Change: An Experiment with Small Groups." *Sociometry* 20, 1 (March 1957), 36-50. Leadership is more stable when tasks are chosen by the group rather than when externally imposed, but prior history of leader-follower relations may modify this pattern.

Kavanagh, Michael J. "Leadership Behavior as a Function of Subordinate Competence and Task Complexity." *Administrative Science Quarterly* 17, 4 (December 1972), 591-600.

Kelly, Stanley, Jr. *Political Campaigning: Problems in Creating an Informed Electorate*. Washington: Brookings Institution, 1960.

Kennedy, Edward M. *In Critical Condition: The Crisis in America's Health Care*. New York: Simon & Schuster, 1972.

Kipnis, David. "The Effects of Leadership Style and Leadership Power upon the Inducement of an Attitude Change." *Journal of Abnormal and Social Psychology* 57, 2 (September 1958), 173-180.

Knutson, Thomas J., and William E. Holdridge. "Orientation Behavior, Leadership, and Consensus: A Possible Functional Relationship." *Speech Monographs* 42, 2 (June 1975), 107-114.

Kushner, Gilbert, et al. *What Accounts for Socio-cultural Change? A Propositional Inventory*. Chapel Hill: University of North Carolina, Institute for Research in Social Science, 1962.

Lamb, Robert K. "Political Elites and the Process of Economic Development." *The Progress of Underdeveloped Areas*, ed. Bert F. Hoselitz, pp. 130-153. Chicago: University of Chicago Press, 1952. "You cannot any longer get ahead by pushing the other fellow behind" (p. 153).

Lee, Jong R. "Presidential Vetoes from Washington to Nixon." *Journal of Politics* 37, 2 (May 1975), 522-547.

Levin, Murray B. *Kennedy Campaigning*. Boston: Beacon, 1966.

Lilienthal, David E. *Management: A Humanist Art*. New York: Carnegie Institute of Technology and Columbia University Press, 1967.

Lingenfelter, Sherwood G. "Leadership and Decision Making." *Yap: Political Leadership and Culture Change in an Island Society*, pp. 217-257. Honolulu: University of Hawaii Press, 1975.

Longworth, Philip. "Peasant Leadership and the Pugachev Revolt." *Journal of Peasant Studies* 2, 2 (January 1975), 183-205.

Lumsden, Gay. "An Experimental Study of the Effect of Verbal Agreement on Leadership Maintenance in Problem-solving Discussion." *Central States Speech Journal* 25, 4 (Winter 1974), 270-276.

Malone, Dumas. "Presidential Leadership and National Unity: The Jeffersonian Example." *Journal of Southern History* 35, 1 (February 1969), 3-17.

Mao, Tse-tung. *Some Questions Concerning Methods of Leadership*. Peking: Foreign Languages Press, 1962.

Marak, George E. "The Evolution of Leadership Structure." *Sociometry* 27, 2 (June 1964), 174-182. Task ability brings rewards and power over others.

Mason, Joseph G. *How to Be a More Creative Executive*. New York: McGraw-Hill, 1961.

May, Ernest R., and Janet Fraser, eds. *Campaign '72: The Managers Speak*. Cambridge: Harvard University Press, 1973.

Mayhew, David R. *Congress: The Electoral Connection*. New Haven: Yale University Press, 1974. Excellent example of the interaction of task and organizational variables.

McClelland, W. G. "Mathematics in Management: How It Looks to the Manager." *Omega* 3, 2 (April 1975), 147-156.

Megargee, Edwin I., Patricia Bogart, and Betty J. Anderson. "Prediction of Leadership in a Simulated Industrial Task." *Journal of Applied Psychology* 50, 4 (1966), 292-295. Task effects upon leader-follower relations of personalities high and low in dominance.

Meisel, James H. *Counterrevolution: How Revolutions Die*. New York: Atherton, 1966.

Metcalf, George R. "How to Be a Politician." *National Civic Review* 48, 9 (October 1959), 454-457, 474. Be sensitive, gregarious, educated, inquisitive, and public-spirited.

Micaud, Charles A. "Leadership and Development: The Case of Tunisia." *Comparative Politics* 1, 4 (July 1969), 468-484.

Miller, James G. "Information Input Overload and Psychopathology." *American Journal of Psychiatry* 116, 8 (February 1960), 695-704. Reviews effects on cell, organ system, individual, group, and social institution and presents current experiments. Reports that a review of more than 1,000 articles yielded only one reference to possible cross-level similarities.

Mills, Warner E., Jr., and Harry R. Davis. *Small City Government: Seven Cases of Decision Making*. New York: Random House, 1962.

Moore, Barrington, Jr. "Notes on the Process of Acquiring Power." *World Politics* 8, 1 (October 1955), 1-19.

Morris, Norval, and Gordon Hawkins. *The Honest Politician's Guide to Crime Control*. Chicago: University of Chicago Press, 1970.

National Opinion Research Center. *Human Reactions in Disaster Situations*. Chicago: University of Chicago, 1954. Includes reference to organization and effective leadership.

Otterbein, Keith F. *The Evolution of War: A Cross-cultural Study*. New Haven: Human Relations Area File Press, 1971.

Owusu, Maxwell. *Uses and Abuses of Political Power: A Case Study of Continuity and Change in the Politics of Ghana*. Chicago: University of Chicago Press, 1970.

Palmer, George J., Jr. "Task Ability and Successful and Effective Leadership." *Psychological Reports* 11, 3 (December 1962), 813–816.

Pareek, Udai, et al. "Behavioural Characteristics of Effective Village Leaders as Reported by Non-leader Farmers." *Manas* 12, 2 (1965), 157–170. Employs Flanagan's critical incident method.

Quandt, William B. *Revolution and Political Leadership: Algeria 1954–1958*. Cambridge: MIT Press, 1969.

Rokkan, Stein. "Elections: Electoral Systems." *IESS*, 5:6–21.

Rosenau, James N. *National Leadership and Foreign Policy*. Princeton: Princeton University Press, 1963.

Rossel, Robert D. "Instrumental and Expressive Leadership in Complex Organizations." *Administrative Science Quarterly* 15, 3 (September 1970), 306–317. As tasks vary, supervisors and managers diverge in their leadership orientations.

Salter, J. T. "Personal Attention in Politics." *APSR* 34, 1 (February 1940), 54–66. Stresses importance of personal concern for others.

Shadegg, Stephen C. *How to Win an Election: The Art of Political Victory*. New York: Taplinger, 1964.

Shannon, Jasper B. *Money and Politics*. New York: Random House, 1959.

Sharp, Gene. *The Politics of Nonviolent Action*. Boston: Porter Sargent, 1973. Unique survey of nonviolent methods for political task accomplishment.

Shaw Marvin E. "Some Effects of Problem Complexity upon Problem Solution Efficiency in Different Communication Nets." *Journal of Experimental Psychology* 48, 3 (September 1954), 211–217.

Shaw, Marvin E., and J. Michael Blum. "Effects of Leadership Style upon Group Performance as a Function of Task Structure." *Journal of Personality and Social Psychology* 3, 2 (February 1966), 238–242.

Short, James F., Jr., and Fred L. Strodtbeck. "The Response of Gang Leaders to Status Threats: An Observation on Group Process and Delinquent Behavior." *American Journal of Sociology* 68, 5 (March 1963), 571–579. Direct hostility to external targets.

Sivers, Peter von. "Insurrection and Accommodation: Indigenous Leadership in Eastern Algeria: 1840–1900." *International Journal of Middle East Studies* 6, 3 (July 1975), 259–275.

Springer, Philip B., and Marcello Truzzi, eds. *Revolutionaries on·Revolution.* Pacific Palisades: Goodyear, 1973. Primarily violent perspectives on revolutionary tasks; neglects revolutionary nonviolence.

Streufert, Siegfried, Susan C. Streufert, and Earl H. Castore. "Leadership in Negotiations and the Complexity of Conceptual Structure." *Journal of Applied Psychology* 52, 3 (June 1968), 218‒223. Complex leaders were rated higher on consideration and simple leaders scored higher on initiation of structure in a simulated international conflict resolution task.

Strom, Sharon Hartman. "Leadership and Tactics in the Woman Suffrage Movement." *Journal of American History* 62, 2 (September 1975), 296‒315.

Sun-Tzu. *The Art of War.* Translated by Samuel B. Griffith. New York: Oxford University Press, 1971. "To subdue the enemy without fighting is the acme of skill" (p. 77).

Tannenbaum, Arnold S. "An Event-Structure Approach to Social Power and to the Problem of Power Accountability." *Behavioral Science* 7, 3 (July 1962), 315‒331.

Tannenbaum, Robert, and Warren H. Schmidt. "How to Choose a Leadership Pattern." *Harvard Business Review* 36, 2 (March‒April 1958), 95‒101. Classic prescriptions for varying style in accordance with task analysis. Like acting, assumes the human personality is not an invariant machine.

Taylor, Donald W. "Problem Solving." *IESS,* 12:505‒511.

Thorndike, R. L. "On What Type of Task Will a Group Do Well?" *Journal of Abnormal and Social Psychology* 33 (1938), 409‒413. Structured tasks requiring consideration of a wide range of alternatives versus ambiguous tasks; e.g., solving versus creating a crossword puzzle.

Tinker, Jerry M. "The Political Power of Non-violent Resistance: The Gandhian Technique." *Western Political Quarterly* 24, 4 (December 1971), 775‒788.

Tokuda, Kisaburo, and Gordon D. Jensen. "The Leader's Role in Controlling Aggression in a Monkey Group." *Primates* 9, 4 (December 1968), 319‒322. When members of a monkey group who ranked highest in aggression were removed, intragroup aggression *increased.*

Torrance, E. Paul. "A Theory of Leadership and Interpersonal Behavior under Stress." *Leadership and Interpersonal Behavior,* ed. Luigi Petrullo and Bernard M. Bass, pp. 100‒117. New York: Holt, Rinehart & Winston, 1961.

Tugwell, Rexford G. *How They Became President.* New York: Simon & Schuster, 1964.

Vo Nguyen Giap. *The Military Art of People's War,* ed. Russell Stetler. New York: Monthly Review Press, 1970.

Vroom, Victor H. "Decision Making and the Leadership Process." *Journal of Contemporary Business* 3, 4 (Autumn 1974), 47‒64.

Wheeler, Ladd S. "Information Seeking as a Power Strategy." *Journal of Social Psychology* 62, 2 (February 1964), 125‒130. Experimental evidence that the greater the power discrepancy in a dyad, the more the information seeking by the less powerful member.

Wiatr, Jerzy J., and Adam Przeworski. "Control without Opposition." *Studies in Polish Political System,* ed. Jerzy J. Wiatr, pp. 124–139. Wroclaw: Polish Academy of Sciences Press, 1967.

Wildavsky, Aaron. *The Politics of the Budgetary Process.* Boston: Little, Brown, 1964. Generic allocative task analysis.

Williams, Virgil. "Leadership Types, Role Differentiation, and System Problems." *Social Forces* 43, 3 (March 1965), 380–389. Functional analysis of a rural community that groups leaders in accordance with the performance of instrumental or expressive functions but finds *no* "power-mobilizing subsystem."

Ziller, Robert C. "Leader Acceptance of Responsibility for Group Action under Conditions of Uncertainty and Risk." *American Psychologist* 10, 8 (August 1955), 475–476.

VALUES

Albert, Ethel M. "Values: Value Systems." *IESS,* 16:287–291.

Archibald, Samuel A., ed. *Pollution of Politics: A Research/Reporting Team Investigates Campaign Ethics.* Washington: Public Affairs Press, 1971.

Ashcraft, Richard. "Marx and Weber on Liberalism as Bourgeois Ideology." *Comparative Studies in Society and History* 14, 2 (March 1972), 130–168.

Bailey, Thomas A. "Forty-three Yardsticks." *Presidential Greatness,* pp. 262–266. New York: Appleton Century, 1966. Criteria for evaluation of presidential leadership.

Barton, Allen H. "Consensus and Conflict among American Leaders." *Public Opinion Quarterly* 38, 4 (Winter 1974–1975), 507–530. Survey of 500 powerful leaders shows attitudes vary with issue. Formal political leaders did not lead policy change in the Vietnam War.

Boétie, Etienne de la. *Anti-dictator.* Translated by Harry Kurz. New York: Columbia University Press, 1942.

Cahn, Edmund. *The Moral Decision.* Bloomington: Indiana University Press, 1966.

Cohen, Burton, and Joseph J. Schwab. "Practical Logic: Problems of Ethical Decision." *American Behavioral Scientist* 8, 8 (April 1965), 23–27.

Conner, Patrick E., and Boris W. Becker. "Values and the Organization: Suggestions for Research." *Academy of Management Journal.* 18, 3 (September 1975), 550–661.

Costantini, Edmond, and Kenneth H. Craik. "Competing Elites within a Political Party: A Study of Republican Leadership." *Western Political Quarterly* 22, 4 (December 1969), 879–903. Finds differences in conservatism, party commitment, and public service motivation.

Crain, William C., and Ellen F. Crain. "The Growth of Political Ideas and Their Expression among Young Activists." *Journal of Youth and Adolescence* 3, 2 (June 1974), 105–134.

Dicks, Henry V. "Personality Traits and National Socialist Ideology." *Human Relations* 3, 2 (1950), 111–153. Psychiatric analysis of interviews with 138 German prisoners of war in 1942–1944. Fanatics (11 percent) were high-F; rebels (9 percent) had "cathected" Catholicism or Communism.

Donninson, David. "Ideologies and Policies." *Journal of Social Policy* 1, 2 (April 1972), 97–117.

Dumézil, Georges. *Destiny of the Warrior.* Chicago: University of Chicago Press, 1971. Indo-European ideologies of violence.

Eckhardt, William. "The Values of Fascism." *Journal of Social Issues* 24, 1 (January 1968), 89–104.

Emmett, Dorothy. "Ethics: Ethical Systems and Social Structures." *IESS*, 5:157–160.

England, George W., et al. "Union Leaders and Managers: A Comparison of Value Systems." *Industrial Relations* 10, 2 (May 1971), 211–226. Moralistic versus pragmatic value orientations.

Flathman, Richard E. *Leadership and Constitutionalism.* Ph.D. dissertation, University of California, Berkeley, 1962.

Flinn, Thomas A., and Frederick M. Wirt. "Local Party Leaders: Groups of Like-Minded Men." *Midwest Journal of Political Science* 9, 1 (February 1965), 77–98.

Forehand, Garlie A. "Assessment of Innovative Behavior: Partial Criteria for the Assessment of Executive Performance." *Journal of Applied Psychology* 47, 3 (June 1963), 206–213.

Fowler, R. B. "The Anarchist Tradition of Political Thought." *Western Political Quarterly* 25, 4 (December 1972), 738–752.

Fraser, Douglas, and Herbert M. Cole, eds. *African Art and Leadership.* Madison: University of Wisconsin Press, 1972.

Freehling, William H. "The Founding Fathers and Slavery." *American Historical Review* 77, 1 (February 1972), 81–93. Antislavery ideals and ambiguous pragmatism as precursors of the Civil War.

Gibbs, Jack P. "The Study of Norms." *IESS*, 11:208–213.

Gluckman, Max. *Politics, Law and Religion in Tribal Society.* Chicago: Aldine, 1965.

Goldman, Eric F. "Presidency as Moral Leadership." *Annals* 280 (March 1952), 37–45.

Goode, William J. "Norm Commitment and Conformity to Role Status Obligations." *American Journal of Sociology* 66, 3 (November 1960), 246–258.

Gouldner, Alvin W. "The Norms of Reciprocity: A Preliminary Statement." *American Sociological Review* 25, 2 (April 1960), 161–178.

Graubard, Stephen R., and Gerald Holton, eds. *Excellence and Leadership in a Democracy.* New York: Columbia University Press, 1962. Includes James M. Burns, "Excellence and Leadership in President and Congress" (pp. 155–170), and Don K. Price, "Administrative Leadership" (pp. 171–185).

Greene, Theodore P. *America's Heroes: The Changing Models of Success in American Magazines.* New York: Oxford University Press, 1970. Covers mass magazine imagery from 1757 to 1918. From Plutarchian models of Greece and Rome (1787–1820), through captains of commerce in the image of Napoleon (1894–1903), followed by publishers and progressive politicians (1904–1913), to idols of organization and military heroes

(1914–1918). Summarized as three main models of success: the neoclassic gentleman, the forceful individualist, and the organization man.

Gustafson, Merlin. "The Religious Role of the President." *Midwest Journal of Political Science* 14, 4 (November 1970), 708–727.

Haerle, Rudolf K., Jr. "The Athlete as 'Moral' Leader: Heroes, Success Themes and Cultural Values in Selected Baseball Autobiographies, 1900–1970." *Journal of Popular Culture* 8, 2 (Fall 1974), 392–401.

Halpin, A. W. "The Leader Behavior and Leadership Ideology of Educational Leaders and Aircraft Commanders." *Harvard Educational Review* 25, 1 (Winter 1955), 18–32.

Hanks, L. M., Jr. "Merit and Power in the Thai Social Order." *American Anthropologist* 64, 6 (December 1962), 1247–1261.

Hart, H. L. A. *The Concept of Law*. Oxford: Claredon, 1963.

Hoge, Dean R., and Irving E. Bender. "Factors Affecting Value Change among College Graduates in Adult Life." *Journal of Personality and Social Psychology* 29, 4 (April 1974), 572–586. Exceptional longitudinal study of Dartmouth students and graduates, 1931–1969, showing least change in mean political values as compared with theoretical, economic, aesthetic, social, and religious values.

Hughes, Daniel T. "Democracy in the Philippines and on Ponape: A Comparison of Two Political Systems Structured on the U.S. Model." *Micronesica* 9, 1 (July 1973), 1–10. Patron-client values versus commitment to common good as inhibitors of this kind of political development.

Jacob, Philip E. "The Influence of Values in Political Integration." *The Integration of Political Communities,* ed. Philip E. Jacob and James V. Toscano, pp. 209–246. Philadelphia: Lippincott, 1964.

Jacob, Philip E., James J. Flink, and Hedrah L. Schuman. "Values and Their Functions in Decision-making: Toward an Operational Definition for Use in Public Affairs Research." *American Behavioral Scientist* 5 (spec. supp.) (May 1962), 1–40.

Johnson, Harry M. "Ideology: Ideology and the Social System." *IESS,* 7:76–85.

Khare, Harish. "Restructuring of Values: Princes in 1971 Elections." *Comparative Studies in Society and History* 15, 4 (October 1973), 405–415. More lost than won; secular politicians gain in India.

Kynerd, Tom. "An Analysis of Presidential Greatness and 'President Rating.' " *Southern Quarterly* 9, 3 (April 1971), 309–329. Criticizes rankings as without systematic, objective, or scientific basis.

Landsberger, Henry A. "Do Ideological Differences Have Personal Correlates? A Study of Chilean Labor Leaders at the Local Level." *Economic Development and Cultural Change* 16, 2 (January 1968), 219–243. Evidence for value differences among leaders similar in socioeconomic status and other characteristics.

Lane, Robert E. *Political Ideology: Why the American Common Man Believes What He Does*. New York: Free Press, 1962.

Lerner, Melvin J. "The Justice Motive: 'Equity' and 'Parity' among Children." *Journal of Personality and Social Psychology* 29, 4 (April 1974), 539–550.

Longaker, Richard P. *The Presidency and Individual Liberties.* Ithaca: Cornell University Press, 1962.

Mazrui, Ali A. "Islam, Political Leadership and Economic Radicalism in Africa." *Comparative Studies in Society and History* 9, 3 (April 1967), 274-291. Islam is an inadequate explanation alone, but explanation is inadequate without it.

Merelman, Richard M. "Learning and Legitimacy." *APSR* 60, 3 (September 1966), 548-561. A learning theory and cognitive dissonance interpretation from the perspective of leader manipulation. Follower manipulations of leaders are recognized but not explored.

Merenda, Peter F., Jitendra Mohan, and Brian J. Shaw. "Indian Students' Perceptions of the Ideal Self, the Ideal Leader, the Ideal Teacher, Indira Gandhi and the Business Executive." *Perceptual and Motor Skills* 40, 2 (April 1975), 611-615.

Meyer, William J. "Political Ethics and Political Authority." *Ethics* 86, 1 (October 1975), 61-69.

Monsma, Stephen V. "Potential Leaders and Democratic Values." *Public Opinion Quarterly* 35, 3 (Fall 1971), 350-357. Persons who contemplate running for elected office rank higher in education, knowledge, status, and liberal values than those who do not.

Moskos, Charles C., Jr., and Wendell Bell. "Attitudes toward Democracy among Leaders in Four Emergent Nations." *British Journal of Sociology* 15, 4 (December 1964), 317-337.

Naess, Arne, et al. *Democracy, Ideology and Objectivity.* Oxford: Blackwell, 1956.

Negley, Glenn R. *Political Authority and Moral Judgment.* Durham: Duke University Press, 1965.

Negley, Glenn R., and J. Max Patrick, eds. *The Quest for Utopia.* New York: Schuman, 1952.

Okanes, Marvin, and John E. Stinson. "Machiavellianism and Emergent Leadership in a Management Simulation." *Psychological Reports* 35, 1 (August 1974), 255-259.

Ostergaard, Geoffrey, and Melville Currell. *The Gentle Anarchists: A Study of the Leaders of the Sarvodaya Movement for Non-violent Revolution in India.* Oxford: Clarendon, 1971.

Palley, Marian L., et al. "Subcommunity Leadership in a Black Ghetto: A Study of Newark, New Jersey." *Urban Affairs Quarterly* 5, 3 (March 1970), 291-312.

Pennock, J. Roland, and John W. Chapman, eds. *Equality.* New York: Atherton, 1967.

Pennock, J. Roland, and John W. Chapman, eds. *Political and Legal Obligation.* New York: Atherton, 1970.

Perrow, Charles. "Organizations: Organizational Goals." *IESS,* 11:305-311

Putnam, Robert D. "Studying Elite Political Culture: The Case of Ideology." *APSR* 65, 3 (September 1971), 651-681.

Rabow, Jerome, et al. "The Role of Social Norms and Leadership in Risk Taking." *Sociometry* 29, 1 (March 1966), 16–27. The most influential group members tend to support the normatively stronger position.

Rae, Douglas W. *The Political Consequences of Electoral Laws.* New Haven: Yale University Press, 1967.

Read, Peter B. "Source of Authority and the Legitimation of Leadership in Small Groups." *Sociometry* 37, 2 (June 1974), 189–204. Experiment shows legitimacy is more important than task competence in role tenure.

Reid, John Phillip. *A Law of Blood: The Primitive Law of the Cherokee Nation.* New York: New York University Press, 1970.

Roff, Merrill. "A Study of Combat Leadership in the Air Force by Means of a Rating Scale for Group Preferences." *Journal of Psychology* 30, 1 (July 1950), 229–239.

Rogow, Arnold A., and Harold D. Lasswell. *Power, Corruption and Rectitude.* Englewood Cliffs: Prentice-Hall, 1963. Essential.

Rokeach, Milton. *Beliefs, Attitudes, and Values.* San Francisco: Jossey-Bass, 1969.

Rokeach, Milton. *The Nature of Human Values.* New York: Free Press, 1973. Both Rokeach works are of major scientific significance.

Salter, J. T. "Smile Is the Best Argument." *National Municipal Review* 29, 2 (February 1940), 89–97.

Schaff, Adam. *A Philosophy of Man.* New York: Monthly Review Press, 1963. Existentialism and Marxism.

Schofield, Norman. "Ethical Decision Rules for Uncertain Voters." *British Journal of Political Science* 2, 2 (April 1972), 193–208. Too complicated to be of much help to voters.

Schubert, Glendon. *The Judicial Mind.* Evanston: Northwestern University Press, 1965. Provides a basic paradigm for political leadership value inquiry.

Schurmann, Franz. *Ideology and Organization in Communist China.* Berkeley: University of California Press, 1966.

Seider, Maynard S. "American Big Business Ideology: A Content Analysis of Executive Speeches." *American Sociological Review* 39, 6 (December 1974), 802–815. Comparative potential.

Seligman, Lester G. "Political Leaders and Liberalism." *Polity* 8, 1 (Autumn 1975), 117–122.

Senghor, Leopold S. "Elegy for Martin Luther King." *Phylon* 36, 3 (September 1975), 352–358. A "poem for jazz orchestra" by the president of Senegal: "I sing a paradise of peace" (p. 358).

Silvert, K. H. "National Values, Development, and Leaders and Followers." *International Social Science Journal* 15, 4 (1963), 560–570.

Singh, S. N., and H. P. Arya. "Value Orientations of Local Village Leaders." *Manas* 12, 2 (1965), 145–159. Identifies six types of leader (authoritarian, nonauthoritarian, task oriented, interpersonal oriented, self-oriented, and community oriented) in relation to three value scales (liberalism-conservatism, scientism-fatalism, nonauthoritarian-authoritarian).

Smith, M. Brewster. "Personal Values in the Study of Lives." *The Study of Lives: Essays on Personality in Honor of Henry A. Murray*, ed. Robert W. White, pp. 324–347. New York: Atherton, 1963.

Spadaro, Robert N. "Some Folkways of Political Leaders: The Rules of the Game." *Journal of Applied Psychology* 59, 1 (February 1974), 125–126.

Spitz, David. *Patterns of Anti-democratic Thought.* New York: Free Press, 1965.

Struve, Walter. *Elites against Democracy: Leadership Ideals in Bourgeois Political Thought in Germany, 1890–1933.* Princeton: Princeton University Press, 1973.

Thorndike, Edward L. "The Relation between Intellect and Morality in Rulers." *American Journal of Sociology* 42, 3 (November 1936), 321–334. Methodological refinement raises the correlation found by Frederick Adams Woods of .40 to .60. Explores implications of this finding (p. 329).

Tumin, Melvin, and Robert Rotberg. "Leaders, the Led, and the Law: A Case Study in Social Change." *Public Opinion Quarterly* 21, 3 (Fall 1957), 355–370.

Unnithan, T. K. N., and Yogendra Singh. *Traditions of Non-Violence.* New Delhi and London: Arnold-Heinemann, 1973. Introduces and attempts to compare nonviolent aspects of the Hindu, Buddhist, Chinese, Islamic, and Judaeo-Christian traditions. A flawed but pioneering effort of great potential significance. Challenges rectification and extension by experts in every culture of the world.

White, Ralph K. "Hitler, Roosevelt, and the Nature of War Propaganda." *Journal of Abnormal and Social Psychology* 44, 2 (April 1949), 157–174. Shows Hitler and Roosevelt made remarkably similar appeals.

White, Ralph K. "Value Analysis: A Quantitative Method for Describing Qualitative Data." *Journal of Social Psychology*, SPSSI Bulletin, 19 (1944), 351–358. Presents 125 value words.

Williams, Robin M., Jr. "Norms: The Concept of Norms." *IESS* 11:204–208.

Williams, Robin M., Jr. "Values: The Concept of Values." *IESS* 16:283–287.

Wilson, James Q., and Edward C. Banfield. "Political Ethos Revisited." *APSR* 65, 4 (December 1971), 1048–1062. "Unitarist" (holistic, community serving) versus "individualist" (localistic, people serving) orientations in a sample of Boston citizens.

SETTING

Arango, Jorge. *Urbanization of the Earth.* Boston: Beacon, 1970.

Bauer, Raymond A., ed. *Social Indicators.* Cambridge: MIT Press, 1966. Pioneering call for research that would markedly heighten the setting awareness of political leaders and followers if made available to them.

Bell, Wendell, and Walter E. Freeman, eds. *Ethnicity and Nation-Building.* Beverly Hills: Sage, 1974.

Bell, Wendell, and James A. Mau, eds. *The Sociology of the Future.* New York: Russell Sage, 1971.

Clark, Kenneth B. *Dark Ghetto.* New York: Harper & Row, 1965.

Clark, Terry N. *Community Power and Policy Outputs: A Review of Urban Research*. Beverly Hills: Sage, 1973.

Coleman, James S. *Power and the Structure of Society*. New York: Norton, 1974.

Coulborn, Ruston, ed. *Feudalism in History*. Princeton: Princeton University Press, 1956.

Dettman, Paul R. "Leaders and Structures in 'Third World' Politics." *Comparative Politics* 6, 2 (January 1974), 245–269. Riggsian structures (fuzed, prismatic, diffracted) as predictors of success or failure of Weberian leadership styles (traditional, charismatic, rational-legal).

Downes, Bryan T. "Municipal Social Rank and the Characteristics of Local Political Leaders." *Midwest Journal of Political Science* 12, 4 (November 1968), 514–537. The higher the municipal social ranks, the higher the education and occupational status of elected leaders.

Dunn, Edgar S., Jr. *Economic and Social Development: A Process of Social Learning*. Baltimore: Johns Hopkins Press, 1971.

Easton, David A. "Political Anthropology." *Biennial Review of Anthropology*, ed. Bernard J. Siegel, pp. 210–262. Stanford: Stanford University Press, 1959.

Ferkiss, Victor C. *Future of Technological Civilization*. New York: Braziller, 1974. Forecasts emergence of an "ecological humanist" revolution.

Foltz, William J. "Social Structure and Political Behavior of Senegalese Elites." *Behavior Science Notes* 4, 2 (1969), 145–163.

George, Alexander L. "Political Leadership and Social Change in American Cities." *Daedalus* 97, 4 (Fall 1958), 1194–1217. Setting change, task requirements, role limitations, and personal styles of mayoral leaders, comparing Daley of Chicago and Lee of New Haven.

Gottman, Jan. *The Significance of Territory*. Charlottesville: University Press of Virginia, 1973.

Hallen, G. C. "People's Reactions to Leadership in a Small Village." *Manas* 12, 2 (1965), 119–126.

Harding, Edward C., Jr., Urie Bronfenbrenner, and John Harding, eds. "Leadership and Participation in a Changing Rural Community." *Journal of Social Issues* 16, 4 (1960), 1–84. Entire issue devoted to report on an unusual five-year interdisciplinary study of a small village and its surrounding trade area.

Hayward, Fred M. "The Development of a Radical Political Organization in the Bush: A Case Study of Sierra Leone." *Canadian Journal of African Studies* 6, 1 (1972), 1–28.

Heilbroner, Robert. *An Inquiry into the Human Prospect*. New York: Norton, 1974. Argues that population pressures, diffusion of nuclear weapons, industrial resources limitations, and dangers of ecological catastrophe will produce "military-socialist" governments and a drift toward global authoritarianism. "Paradoxically it is only through leadership that authoritarian rule can be minimized, if not wholly avoided" (p. 164).

Hirschman, Albert O. "Underdevelopment, Obstacles to the Perception of Change, and Leadership." *Daedalus* 97, 3 (Summer 1968), 925–937.

Howells, Lloyd T., and S. W. Becker. "Seating Arrangement and Leadership Emergence." *Journal of Abnormal and Social Psychology* 64, 2 (February 1962), 148–150. "Seating position, by influencing the flow of communication, is a determiner of leadership emergence" (p. 148).

Hughes, J. R. T. "Industrialization: Economic Aspects." *IESS,* 7:252–263.

Huntington, Samuel P. *Political Order in Changing Societies.* New Haven: Yale University Press, 1968. Socioeconomic bases of "civic' and "praetorian" polities defined in terms of participation and institutionalization.

Kaplan, Morton A. "Systems Analysis: International Systems." *IESS,* 15:479–486.

Kirkpatrick, Jeane J. *Leader and Vanguard in Mass Society: A Study of Peronist Argentina.* Cambridge: MIT Press, 1971.

Klaussner, Samuel Z., ed. *The Study of Total Societies.* New York: Praeger, 1967. An enormous challenge to disciplinary, interdisciplinary, and transdisciplinary imagination.

Kornhauser, William. *The Politics of Mass Society.* New York: Free Press, 1959.

Kroeber, Alfred L., and Talcott Parsons. "The Concepts of Culture and the Social System." *American Sociological Review* 23, 5 (October 1958), 582–583. Defines culture as "the transmitted and created content and' patterns of values, ideas, and other symbolic-meaningful systems." The social system is taken to be "the specifically relational system of interaction among individuals and collectivities" (p. 583).

Larson, Calvin J. "Leadership in Three Black Neighborhoods." *Phylon* 36, 3 (September 1975), 260–268.

Leach, Edmund R. "Social Structure: The History of the Concept." *IESS,* 14:482–489.

Levine, Charles H., and Clifford Kaufman. "Urban Conflict as a Constraint on Mayoral Leadership: Lessons from Gary and Cleveland." *American Politics Quarterly* 2, 4 (July 1974), 78–106.

Levine, Victor T. *Political Leadership in Africa.* Stanford: Stanford University Press, 1967. Contrasts older and younger "elite" members; based on sixty-eight interviews in five states.

Maier, Henry W. *Challenge to the Cities: An Approach to the Theory of Urban Leadership.* New York: Random House, 1966.

Marien, Michael. "The Banners of Babel." *The Next Twenty-five Years: Crisis and Opportunity,* ed. Andrew A. Spekke, pp. 191–194. Washington: World Future Society, 1975. Superb review of images of alternative future societies.

Marshall, Harvey, and Deborah Meyer. "Assimilation and the Election of Minority Candidates: The Case of Black Mayors." *Sociology and Social Research* 60, 1 (October 1975), 1–21. The more the socioeconomic assimilation of urban blacks, the greater the probability of election. Employs data on seventeen cities for six independent variables (income, occupational and educational assimilation, residential segregation, region, and percentage black).

Mehta, Shiv Rattan. *Emerging Patterns of Rural Leadership*. New Delhi: Wiley Eastern, 1972. Example of vigorous interest in local leadership studies in India.

Mitchell, William C. "Systems Analysis: Political Systems." *IESS*, 15:573-579.

Modrzhinskaya, Y. D., et al. *Future of Society: Marxist and Non-Marxist Forecasts of Scientific and Social Developments*. New York: Beekman, 1975.

Moore, Barrington, Jr. *Social Origins of Dictatorship and Democracy: Lord and Peasant in the Modern World*. Boston: Beacon, 1966.

Moore, Wilbert E. "Global Sociology: The World as a Singular System." *American Journal of Sociology* 71, 5 (March 1966), 475-482.

Moore, Wilbert E. "Industrialization: Social Aspects." *IESS*, 7:263-270.

Morrill, Richard L. *The Spatial Organization of Society*. Belmont: Wadsworth, 1970.

Mumford, Lewis. *The Cultures of Cities*. New York: Harcourt, Brace & World, 1970.

Namier, Lewis B. *The Structure of Politics at the Accession of George III*. London: Macmillan, 1957. Classic on constituency bases of the parliamentary "ant heap."

Ogburn, William R. "The Great Man versus Social Forces." *Social Forces* 5, 2 (September 1926), 225-231.

O'Laughlin, Bridget. "Marxist Approaches in Anthropology." *Annual Review of Anthropology: 1975,* ed. Bernard J. Siegel et al., pp. 341-370. Palo Alto: Annual Reviews, 1975.

Ottenberg, Simon. "Leadership and Change in a Coastal Georgia Negro Community." *Phylon Quarterly* 20, 1 (Spring 1959), 7-18. Examines leadership as an overlooked factor.

Paddock, William, and Paul Paddock. *Famine 1975*. Boston: Little, Brown, 1967.

Parkin, Frank. *Class Inequality and Political Order: Social Stratification in Capitalist and Communist Societies*. New York: Praeger, 1971.

Parsons, James B. *The Peasant Rebellions of the Late Ming Dynasty*. Tucson: University of Arizona Press, 1970.

Parsons, Talcott. "Systems Analysis: Social Systems." *IESS*, 15:458-473.

Prescott, J. R. V. *Political Geography*. New York: St. Martin's, 1972. Contains suggestive chart of the influence of geographic factors on politics (p. 5).

Prewitt, Kenneth, and Heinz Eulau. "Social Bias in Leadership Selection, Political Recruitment, and Electoral Context. *Journal of Politics* 33, 2 (May 1971), 293-315.

Rapoport, Anatol. "Systems Analysis: General Systems Theory." *IESS*, 15:452-458.

Rogers, Marvin L. "Patterns of Leadership in a Rural Malay Community." *Asian Survey* 3, 2 (May 1975), 407–421.

Salamon, Lester M. "Leadership and Modernization: The Emerging Black Political Elite in the American South." *Journal of Politics* 35, 3 (August 1973), 615–681. Successful blacks tend to be from the "traditional elite." Electoral process screens out less established leaders. Asks who is coopting whom: "traditional elite" or "movement"?

Sayre, Wallace, and Herbert Kaufman. *Governing New York City.* New York: Norton, 1965.

Schapera, I. *Government and Politics in Tribal Societies.* London: Watts, 1956.

Schneider, Joseph. "Social Class, Historical Circumstances and Fame." *American Journal of Sociology* 43, 1 (July 1937), 37–56. Explains decline of English men of genius of working class background since 1800 as a function of decreased opportunity for class mobility.

Seagraves, B. Abbott. "Ecological Generalization and Structural Transformation of Sociocultural Systems." *American Anthropologist* 76, 3 (September 1974), 530–552.

Sharma, Ranbir. "The Changing Patterns of Leadership in a Hill Society of India." *Indian Political Science Review* 9, 1 (January 1975), 68–75.

Showers, Victor. *The World in Figures.* New York: Wiley, 1973. Demographic, geographic, and cultural features of countries and cities.

Singer, Milton. "Culture: The Concept of Culture." *IESS,* 3:527–543.

Sjoberg, Gideon. *The Preindustrial City.* New York: Free Press, 1960.

Skinner, G. William. *Leadership and Power in the Chinese Community of Thailand.* Ithaca: Cornell University Press, 1958.

Smelser, Neil J. "Economy and Society." *IESS,* 4:500–506.

Smelser, Neil J. "Personality and the Explanation of Political Phenomena at the Social-System Level: A Methodological Statement." *Journal of Social Issues* 24, 3 (July 1968), 111–127.

Sprout, Harold H. "Geography: Political Geography." *IESS,* 6:116–123.

Stauffer, Robert B. "Philippine Legislators and Their Changing Universe." *Journal of Politics* 28, 3 (August 1966), 556–597. Unusual longitudinal study correlating changes in the social backgrounds of leaders with changes in the socioeconomic characteristics of their society.

Suh, Dae-Sook, and Chae-Jin Lee, eds. *Political Leadership in Korea.* Seattle: University of Washington Press, 1976.

Thompson, George C. "The Emergence of Political Leadership in the Change from Colonialism to Nationalism." *Leadership and Authority: A Symposium,* ed. Gehan Wijeyewardene, pp. 17–38. Singapore: University of Malaya Press, 1968.

Twentieth Century Fund. Task Force on Governance of New Towns. *New Towns: Laboratories for Democracy.* Millwood: Kraus Reprint, 1975.

Urwick, Luther F. *Leadership in the Twentieth Century.* New York: Pitman, 1957.

Warren, Donald I., and Rochelle B. Warren. "A Community Leader's Handbook: Different Strokes for Different Neighborhoods." *Psychology Today* 9, 1 (June 1975), 76–83.

Waterbury, John. *Commanders of the Faithful: Political Leadership in Morocco.* London: Weidenfeld & Nicolson, 1970.

Watson, James B., and Julian Samora. "Subordinate Leadership in a Bicultural Community: An Analysis." *American Sociological Review* 19, 4 (August 1954), 413–421. "Hypothetical leaders are unable to lead and hypothetical followers are unable to accept followership" (p. 420).

Weaver, Thomas, and Alvin Magid, eds. *Poverty: New Interdisciplinary Perspectives.* San Francisco: Chandler, 1969.

White, Leslie A. "Iknaton: The Great Man vs. the Culture Process." *The Science of Culture,* pp. 233–281. New York: Farrar, Straus & Giroux, 1970. Sharp argument against treating leader personality as an independent variable. "In the process of cultural development a Great Man is but the neural medium through which an important synthesis of cultural elements takes place" (p. 280).

Wilbur, C. Martin. "The Influence of the Past: How the Early Years Helped to Shape the Future of the Chinese Communist Party." *Party Leadership and Revolutionary Power in China,* ed. John W. Lewis, pp. 35–68. New York: Cambridge University Press, 1970.

Wildavsky, Aaron. *Leadership in a Small Town.* Totowa: Bedminster, 1964.

Zimmerman, Carle C. "Changes in Social Leadership." *Indian Journal of Social Research* 10, 3 (December 1969), 165–173. Predicts rise of the intelligentsia to leadership when the knowledge industry comes to play a key role in the economy.

Leadership Patterns, Types, and Styles

Bogardus, Emory S. "World Leadership Types." *Sociology and Social Research* 12 (July 1928), 573–579. Reflective essay, with examples of direct and indirect, national and worldcentric types.

Brzezinski, Zbigniew, and Samuel P. Huntington. "Cincinnatus and the Apparatchik." *World Politics* 16, 1 (October 1963), 52–78.

Buck, Philip W. *Amateurs and Professionals in British Politics, 1918-1959.* Chicago: University of Chicago Press, 1963.

Crozier, Brian. *The Rebels.* Boston: Beacon, 1960. Independence movement leaders since World War II.

Etzioni, Amitai. "Dual Leadership in Complex Organizations." *American Sociological Review* 30, 5 (October 1965), 688–698. Fourfold typology of leadership based upon combination of personal power and position power: formal leader (+,+), informal leader (+,−), official (−,+), and follower (−,−).

Fanelli, A. Alexander. "A Typology of Community Leadership Based on Influence and Interaction within the Leader Subsystem." *Social Forces* 34, 4

(May 1956), 332–338. Describes relations among "active influentials, prestige influentials, active sub-influentials, and lesser leaders."

Helmich, Donald L., and Paul E. Erzen. "Leadership Style and Leader Needs." *Academy of Management Journal* 18, 2 (June 1975), 397–401.

Hill, Walter A. "Leadership Style: Rigid or Flexible." *Organizational Behavior and Human Performance* 9, 1 (February 1973), 35–47.

Lowenthal, L., and N. Guterman. "Portrait of the American Agitator." *Public Opinion Quarterly* 12, 3 (Fall 1948), 417–429.

McGregor, Douglas. *The Professional Manager.* Edited by Warren G. Bennis and Caroline McGregor. New York: McGraw-Hill, 1967.

Merton, Robert K. "Patterns of Influence: Local and Cosmopolitan Intellectuals." *Social Theory and Social Structure,* pp. 387–420. New York: Free Press, 1957.

Neumann, Sigmund. "The Rule of the Demagogue." *American Sociological Review* 3, 4 (August 1938), 487–498. "The real demagogue gives [the people] faith and security because he is so sure of himself. He regards himself as God-sent, almost God-like. . . . Only a period ripe for dictatorship could produce the idea of a leaderless democracy" (pp. 1487–1489).

Powell, H. A. "Competitive Leadership in Trobriand Political Organization." *Comparative Political Systems,* ed. Ronald Cohen and John Middleton, pp. 155–192. Garden City: Natural History Press, 1967.

Pye, Lucian W. "Administrators, Agitators, and Brokers." *Public Opinion Quarterly* 22, 3 (Fall 1958), 342–348. Six types: "administrators, agitators, amalgamate, transmitters, ideological propagandists, political brokers."

Roche, John P., and Stephen Sachs. "The Bureaucrat and the Enthusiast: An Exploration of the Leadership of Social Movements." *Western Political Quarterly* 8, 2 (June 1955), 248–261.

Rose, Arnold M. "Ecological Influential: A Leadership Type." *Sociology and Social Research* 52, 2 (January 1968), 185–192. Persons whose social position makes them centers of communication networks; e.g., barbers and bartenders.

Sahlins, Marshall D. "Poor Man, Big Man, Rich Man, Chief: Political Types in Melanesia and Polynesia." *Comparative Studies in Society and History* 5, 3 (April 1963), 285–303. Classic study in political anthropology.

Salter, J. T. "Design for a Ward Politician." *National Municipal Review* 23, 3 (March 1934), 165–167.

Shapira, Zur. "A Facet Analysis of Leadership Styles." *Journal of Applied Psychology* 61, 2 (April 1976), 136–139.

Shils, Edward. "Demagogues and Cadres in the Political Development of New States." *Communication and Political Development,* ed. Lucien W. Pye. Princeton: Princeton University Press, 1963.

Singh, S. N., H. P. Arya, and S. K. Reddy. "Different Types of Local Leadership in Two North Indian Villages." *Manas,* 12, 2 (1965), 97–107. Traditional, political, opinion, caste, and decision-making types, with first two predominant.

Tsurutani, Taketsugu. "Political Leadership: Some Tentative Thoughts from Early Meiji Japan." *Journal of Political and Military Sociology* 1, 2 (Fall 1973), 201–214. Discusses innovative, consolidative, and mediative styles.

Walton, Hanes, Jr., and Leslie Burl McLemore. "Portrait of Black Political Styles." *Black Politician* 2 (Fall 1970), 9–12.

Willower, Donald J. "Leadership Styles and Leaders' Perceptions of Subordinates." *Journal of Educational Sociology* 34, 2 (October 1960), 58–64. "Nomothetic" (normative) versus "idiographic" (personal need) styles.

Dimensions

Ackoff, Russell L., and Fred E. Emory. *On Purposive Systems.* Chicago: Aldine-Atherton, 1972.

Angell, Robert C. "Social Integration." *IESS*, 7:380–386.

Back, Kurt W. "Power, Influence and Pattern of Communication." *Leadership and Interpersonal Behavior,* ed. Luigi Petrullo and Bernard Bass, pp. 137–164. New York: Holt, Rinehart & Winston, 1961. Interdimensional linkages.

Banton, Michael P., ed. *Political Systems and the Distribution of Power.* London: Tavistock, 1965.

Brown, Steven R., and John D. Ellithorp. "Emotional Experiences in Political Groups: The Case of the McCarthy Phenomenon." *APSR* 64, 2 (June 1970), 349–366.

Burton, John W. *Conflict and Communication: The Use of Controlled Communication in International Relations.* New York: Free Press, 1970. An unusual experiment that elicited the cooperation of actual parties in conflict.

Coser, Lewis A. *The Functions of Social Conflict.* New York: Free Press, 1956.

Daniels, Norman, ed. *Reading Rawls: Critical Studies on Rawls' A Theory of Justice.* New York: Basic Books, 1975. Morality dimension.

Dolbeare, Kenneth M. "The Impacts of Public Policy." *Political Science Annual, Volume Five–1974,* ed. Cornelius P. Cotter, pp. 90–130. Indianapolis: Bobbs-Merrill, 1974.

Downs, Anthony. *An Economic Theory of Democracy.* New York: Harper, 1957. Basis for an economic approach of leader-follower interactions and their social effects.

Duffy, Elizabeth. *Activation and Behavior.* New York: Wiley, 1962. "The level of activation of the organism may be defined . . . as the extent of release of potential energy, stored in the tissues of the organism, as this is shown in activity or response" (p. 16).

Duke, James T. *Conflict and Power in Social Life.* Provo: Brigham Young University Press, 1976. Presents ninety-one illustrative hypotheses for further research (pp. 268–274).

Duncan, Graeme. *Marx and Mill: Two Views of Social Conflict and Social Harmony.* Cambridge: At the University Press, 1973.

Easton, David A., ed. *Varieties of Political Theory*. Englewood Cliffs: Prentice-Hall, 1966.

Eckstein, Harry. "Authority Patterns: A Structural Basis for Political Inquiry." *APSR* 67, 4 (December 1973), 1142–1161. Major effort to construct a general political paradigm.

Edwards, J. M. B. "Creativity: Social Aspects." *IESS*, 3:442–457.

Etzioni, Amitai. *The Active Society*. New York: Free Press, 1968. "The active orientation has three major components: a self-conscious and knowing actor, one or more goals he is committed to realize, and access to levers (or power) that allow resetting of the social code" (p. 4).

Etzioni, Amitai. "Social Control: Organizational Aspects." *IESS*, 14:396–402.

Fagen, Richard R. *Politics and Communication*. Boston: Little, Brown, 1966.

Feierabend, Ivo K., and Rosalind L. Feierabend. *Anger, Violence and Politics*. Englewood Cliffs: Prentice-Hall, 1972.

Freedman, Ann E., and Philip E. Freedman. *The Psychology of Political Control*. New York: St. Martin's, 1973. Inspired by Machiavelli, and based upon recent social psychology, presented as a pedagogical dialogue with a modern "prince."

French, E. R. P., Jr. "A Formal Theory of Social Power." *Psychological Review* 63, 3 (May 1956), 181–194.

Fried, Edrita. *Active/Passive: The Critical Psychological Dimension*. New York: Grune & Stratton, 1970.

Friedrich, Carl J., ed. *Authority*. Cambridge: Harvard University Press, 1958.

Gould, Peter. *Spatial Diffusion: The Spread of Ideas and Innovations in Geographic Space*. ISA Consortium for International Studies Education, Learning Package Series no. 11. New York: Learning Resources in International Studies, 1975.

Gray, Virginia. "Innovation in the States: A Diffusion Study." *APSR* 67, 4 (December 1973), 1174–1185; with comment by Jack L. Walker (pp. 1186–1191); and rejoinder (pp. 1192–1193).

Grofman, Bernard N., and Edward V. Muller. "The Strange Case of Relative Gratification and Potential for Political Violence: The V-Curve Hypothesis." *APSR* 67, 2 (June 1973), 514–539.

Gunnell, John G. *Political Philosophy and Time*. Middletown: Wesleyan University Press, 1968.

Gurr, Ted. "A Causal Model of Civil Strife: A Comparative Analysis Using New Indices." *APSR* 62, 4 (December 1968), 1104–1124.

Hoover, Edgar M. "Spatial Economics: The Partial Equilibrium Approach." *IESS*, 15:95–100. "Spatial economics deals with *what* is *where* and *why*" (p. 95).

Lipsitz, Lewis. "Consensus: Political Aspects." *IESS*, 3:266–271. "Democracy has often been described as politics involving bargaining among political leaders through which a consensus is created. There has been little study, however, of this consensus creating process" (p. 270).

Lowie, Robert H. "Compromise in Primitive Society." *International Social Science Journal* 15, 2 (1963), 182–229. One of the relatively few social science studies on this concept.

Mack, Raymond W., and Richard C. Snyder. "The Analysis of Social Conflict: Toward an Overview and Synthesis." *Journal of Conflict Resolution* 1, 2 (June 1957), 212–248. Propositional inventory.

McClosky, Herbert. "Consensus and Ideology in American Politics." *APSR* 58, 2 (June 1964), 361–382. Leading argument that "ideological awareness and consensus are overvalued as determinants of democratic viability" (p. 379).

McDonald, Neil A. *Politics: A Study of Control Behavior.* New Brunswick: Rutgers University Press, 1965. Approach to politics as interaction between "control acts" and "response acts," with special interest in effects that are spatially, temporally, and functionally remote.

McFarland, Andrew S. *Power and Leadership in Pluralist Systems.* Stanford: Stanford University Press, 1969.

Menninger, Karl A. *Love against Hate.* New York: Harcourt Brace Jovanovich, 1959.

Merrill, Robert S. "The Study of Technology." *IESS,* 15:576–589. "Technologies are bodies of skills, knowledge, and procedures for making, using and doing useful things" (p. 576). Whereas Merrill emphasizes primarily the physical and biological, the idea of "technicity" includes the psychological, social, and cultural.

Messick, Samuel. "Response Sets." *IESS,* 13:492–496. Surrogate for an almost totally lacking scientific literature on the concept of societal responsiveness.

Mueller, Claus. *The Politics of Communication.* New York: Oxford University Press, 1973.

Parsons, Talcott. "On the Concept of Influence." *Public Opinion Quarterly* 27, 1 (Spring 1963), 37–92.

Partridge, P. H. *Consent and Consensus.* New York: Praeger, 1971. Observing that philosophers give little attention to consensus and that social scientists direct little concern to consent, engages in a bridge-building effort that is richly suggestive for future efforts to link moral and empirical dimensions of political leadership behavior.

Phillips, Warren R., and Dennis R. Hall. "The Importance of Governmental Structure as a Taxonomic Scheme for Nations." *Comparative Political Studies* 3, 1 (April 1970), 63–89. The associative dimension.

Pool, Ithiel de Sola, and Wilbur Schramm, eds. *Handbook of Communications.* Chicago: Rand McNally, 1973.

Rae, Douglas W. "The Limits of Consensual Decision." *APSR* 69, 4 (December 1975), 1270–1294; with comment by Gordon Tullock (pp. 1295–1298) and rejoinder (p. 1298).

Rawls, John. *Theory of Justice.* Cambridge: Harvard University Press, 1971. Seminal work—evoking lively critical commentary (see Daniels, op. cit., this section)—to which the study of political leadership eventually should be systematically related.

Rose, Richard. "Models of Governing." *Comparative Politics* 5, 4 (July 1973), 465–496. Six models ("liberal, authority, leadership, grand vizier, social autonomy, and social control") that "vary in significance according to policy areas" (p. 495).

Russell, Bertrand. *Power: A New Social Analysis.* London: Allen & Unwin, 1938.

Schoeck, Helmut. *Envy: A Theory of Social Behavior.* New York: Harcourt, Brace & World, 1970. Aspect of the affective dimension.

Shils, Edward. "The Concept of Consensus." *IESS,* 3:260–266. "Three elements crucial to the functioning of consensus are: (1) common acceptance of laws, rules, and norms, (2) attachment to the institutions which promulgate and apply the laws and rules, and (3) a widespread sense of identity or unity" (pp. 260–261).

Sibley, Mulford Q. *Political Theories of Modern Pacifism* New York: Garland, 1975. Aspects of the nonviolent dimension.

Simmel, Georg. *Conflict: The Web of Group Affiliations.* New York: Free Press, 1955.

Soja, Edward W. *The Political Organization of Space.* Washington: Association of American Geographers, 1971.

Steinbrunner, John. *The Cybernetic Theory of Decision.* Princeton: Princeton University Press, 1974.

Sullivan, John L. "A Note on Redistributive Politics." *APSR* 66, 4 (December 1972), 1301–1305.

Tannenbaum, Arnold S. "The Concept of Organizational Control." *Journal of Social Issues* 12, 2 (1956), 50–60.

Tannenbaum, Arnold S., and Robert A. Cooke. "Control and Participation." *Journal of Contemporary Business* 3, 4 (Autumn 1975), 35–46.

Walter, E. V. "Power and Violence." *APSR* 58, 2 (March 1964), 350–360.

Watzlawick, Paul, John Weakland, and Richard Fisch. *Change.* New York: Norton, 1974. Multidimensional metadimension.

Wiener, Philip, and John Fisher. *Violence and Aggression in the History of Ideas.* New Brunswick: Rutgers University Press, 1974.

Young, Paul Thomas. "Emotion." *IESS,* 5:35–41.

Field Foundations

RESEARCH

Allport, Gordon W., Jerome S. Bruner, and E. M. Jandorf. "Personality under Social Catastrophe: Ninety Life-Histories of the Nazi Revolution." *Character and Personality* 10, 1 (September 1941), 1–22

Allport, Gordon W., and Hadley Cantril. "Judging Personality from Voice." *Journal of Social Psychology* 5, 1 (February 1934), 37–55.

American Psychological Association. Ad Hoc Committee on Ethical Standards in Psychological Research. *Ethical Principles in the Conduct of Research with*

Human Participants. Washington: American Psychological Association, 1973.

Anderson, Charles W. "Comparative Policy Analysis: The Design of Measures." *Comparative Politics* 4, 1 (October 1971), 117–132.

Andrews, F. M., et al. *A Guide for Selecting Statistical Techniques for Analyzing Social Science Data.* Ann Arbor: University of Michigan, Survey Research Center, 1974.

Armilla, José. "Predicting Self-assessed Social Leadership in a New Culture with the MMPI." *Journal of Social Psychology* 73, 2 (December 1967), 219–225.

Bales, Robert F. *Interaction Process Analysis: A Method for the Study of Small Groups.* Reading: Addison-Wesley, 1950.

Barber, James D. "Strategies for Understanding Politicians." *American Journal of Political Science* 18, 2 (May 1974). Valuable reflections on the construction of ideal-types by a political leadership studies pioneer.

Barnowe, J. Thad. "Leadership and Performance Outcomes in Research Organizations: The Supervision of Scientists as a Source of Assistance." *Organizational Behavior and Human Performance* 14, 2 (October 1975), 264–280.

Barton, Allen H. "Organizations: Methods of Research." *IESS,* 11:334–343.

Bass, Bernard M. "An Approach to the Objective Assessment of Successful Leadership." *Objective Approaches to Personality Assessment,* ed. Bernard M. Bass and I. A. Berg. New York: Van Nostrand, 1959.

Baumgartel, Howard. "Leadership Style as a Variable in Research Administration." *Administrative Science Quarterly* 2, 3 (December 1957), 344–360.

Bavelas, Alex. "A Mathematical Model for Group Structures." *Human Organization* 7, 3 (Summer 1948), 16–30. Major contribution to network analysis.

Beck, Carl, and James M. Mallory. "Political Elites: A Mode of Analysis (2nd ed.)." Occasional Paper of the Center for International Studies, University of Pittsburgh, 1971.

Beck, Carl, and Douglas K. Stewart. "Machine Retrieval of Biographical Data." *American Behavioral Scientist* 10, 6 (February 1967), 30–32.

Bell, Daniel. "Twelve Modes of Prediction." *Daedalus* 93, 3 (Summer 1964), 845–880. Precursor of futures research methodologies.

Béteille, André, and T. N. Madan, eds. *Encounter and Experience: Personal Accounts of Fieldwork.* Honolulu: University of Hawaii Press, 1975. Anthropologists report their experiences in India.

Blake, Robert R., and Jack W. Brehm. "The Use of Tape Recording to Simulate a Group Atmosphere." *Journal of Abnormal and Social Psychology* 49, 2 (April 1954), 311–313.

Block, Jack. "Personality Measurement: Overview." *IESS,* 12:30–37.

Boek, Walter. "Field Techniques in Delineating the Structure of Community Leadership." *Human Organization* 24, 4 (Winter 1965), 358–364.

Boguslaw, Robert, and Robert H. Davis. "Social Process Modeling: A Comparison of a Live and Computerized Simulation." *Behavioral Science* 14, 3 (May 1969), 197–203.

Bonilla, Frank, and José Silva Michelena, eds. *A Strategy for Research on Social Policy.* Cambridge: Harvard University Press, 1967.

Boruch, Robert F. "Strategies for Eliciting and Merging Confidential Social Research Data." *Policy Sciences* 3, 3 (September 1972), 275-297.

Brady, David W. "Congressional Leadership and Party Voting in the McKinley Era: A Comparison to the Modern House." *Midwest Journal of Political Science* 16, 3 (August 1972), 439-459. Diachronic approach.

Brams, Steven J. "On Measuring the Concentration of Power in Political Systems." *APSR* 62, 2 (June 1968), 461-475.

Brightman, Harvey J. "Leadership Style and Worker Interpersonal Orientation: A Computer Simulation Study." *Organizational Behavior and Human Performance* 14, 1 (August 1975), 91-122.

Browning, Rufus P. "Simulation: Attempts and Possibilities." *Handbook of Political Psychology,* ed. Jeanne N. Knutson, pp. 383-412. San Francisco: Jossey-Bass, 1973.

Campbell, Angus. "Administering Research Organizations." *American Psychologist* 8, 6 (June 1953), 225-230.

Casey, Timothy J. "Development of a Leadership Orientation Scale on the SVIB for Women." *Measurement and Evaluation in Guidance* 8, 2 (July 1975), 96-100.

Caudill, William, and Bertram H. Roberts. "Pitfalls in the Organization of Interdisciplinary Research." *Human Organization* 10, 4 (Winter 1951), 12-15. Keys to success are a common body of shared knowledge and personalities who want to learn from each other.

Cell, Charles P. "Charismatic Heads of State: The Social Context." *Behavior Science Research* 9, 4 (1974), 255-305. Unusual effort to operationalize the concept of charisma in a study of thirty-four leaders.

Chassan, J. B. "Statistical Inference and the Single Case in Clinical Design." *Psychiatry* 23 (May 1960), 173-184.

Christie, R., et al. "Narrowing the Gap between Field Studies and Laboratory Experiments in Social Psychology." *SSRC Items* 8 (1954), 37-42.

Costley, D. L., and H. K. Downey. "Measurement of Three Aspects of the Theory X and Theory Y Model." Wichita: Wichita State University, School of Business Administration, 1969. Operationalization of the Douglas McGregor leadership styles.

Criswell, Joan H. "The Sociometric Study of Leadership." *Leadership and Interpersonal Behavior,* ed. Luigi Petrullo and Bernard M. Bass, pp. 10-29. New York: Holt, Rinehart & Winston, 1961.

Dexter, Lewis A. *Elite and Specialized Interviewing.* Evanston: Northwestern University Press, 1970.

Di Stefano, M. K., and Margaret W. Prior. "Comparisons of Leader and Subordinate Descriptions of Leadership Behavior." *Perceptual and Motor Skills* 37, 3 (December 1973), 714. Further evidence for non-congruence.

Dogan, Mattei, and Stein Rokkan, eds. *Quantitative Ecological Analysis in the Social Sciences.* Cambridge: MIT Press, 1969.

Easton, Joseph W. "Social Pressures of Professional Teamwork." *American Sociological Review* 16, 5 (October 1951), 707–713. "The complexity of subject matter makes it increasingly difficult to approach any significant subject, particularly in the social sciences, with the skills and experience likely to be found in any one individual" (p. 708). "But teamwork offers no guarantee of creativity" (p. 712).

Edinger, Lewis J., and Donald D. Searing. "Social Background in Elite Analysis: A Methodological Inquiry." *APSR* 61, 2 (June 1967), 428–445.

Ehle, Emily L. "Techniques for Study of Leadership." *Public Opinion Quarterly* 13, 1 (Spring 1949), 235–240.

Elkin, F., A. Cooper, and Gerald Halpern. "Leadership in a Student Mob." *Canadian Journal of Psychology* 16, 3 (September 1962), 199–201. Contrived experiment in a natural setting.

Erikson, Erik H. "On the Nature of Psycho-historical Evidence: In Search of Gandhi." *Daedalus* 97, 3 (Summer 1968), 695–730.

Evan, William M., and Morris Zelditch, Jr. "A Laboratory Experiment on Bureaucratic Authority." *American Sociological Review* 26, 6 (December 1961), 883–893.

Fitch, David J. *Predicting Votes of Senators of the 83rd Congress: A Comparison of Similarity Analysis and Factor Analysis.* Ph.D. dissertation, University of Illinois, 1958.

Floud, Roderick. *An Introduction to Quantitative Methods for Historians.* Princeton: Princeton University Press, 1973.

Forehand, Garlie A., and Harold Guetzkow. "Judgment and Decision-making Activities of Government Executives as Described by Superiors and Co-workers." *Management Science* 8, 3 (April 1962), 359–370.

Fox, Douglas M. "Methods within Methods: The Case of Community Power Studies." *Western Political Quarterly* 24, 1 (March 1971), 5–11.

Frank, Robert S. "Eyeblink Responses to Political Stimuli: A Psycho-physiological Analysis of the McGovern-Humphrey Debates." *Experimental Study of Politics* 2, 3 (October 1973), 1–15.

Freed, Stanley A. "An Objective Method for Determining the Collective Caste Hierarchy of an Indian Village." *American Anthropologist* 65, 4 (August 1963), 879–891.

Freeman, Linton C., Thomas J. Fararo, Warner Bloomberg, Jr., and Morris H. Sunshine. "Locating Leaders in Local Communities: A Comparison of Some Alternative Approaches." *American Sociological Review* 28, 5 (October 1963), 791–798.

Frutcher, Benjamin, and James A. Skinner. "Dimensions of Leadership in a Student Cooperative." *Multivariate Behavioral Research* 1, 4 (October 1966), 437–445. Operationalization of George Homans's approach to leadership in terms of activity, interaction, sentiment, and norms.

Gatzke, Hans W. "Hitler and Psychohistory." *American Historical Review* 78, 2 (April 1973), 394–401.

Gitter, A. George, Harvey Black, and Arthur Goldman. "Role of Nonverbal Communication in the Perception of Leadership." *Perceptual and Motor Skills* 40, 2 (April 1975), 463–466.

Gordon, Leonard V. *Survey of Interpersonal Values.* Chicago: Science Research Associates, 1960.

Gottfried, Alex. "The Use of Psychosomatic Categories in a Study of Political Personality." *Western Political Quarterly* 8, 2 (June 1955), 234–247.

Gullahorn, John T. "Measuring Role Conflict." *American Journal of Sociology* 61, 4 (January 1956), 299–303.

Hanhardt, Arthur M., and William A. Welsh. "The Intellectuals-Politics Nexus: Studies Using a Biographical Technique." *American Behavioral Scientist* 7, 7 (March 1964), 3–7. Suggestive but limited.

Harrison, Frank. "The Management of Scientists: Determinants of Perceived Role Performance." *Academy of Management Journal* 17, 2 (June 1974), 234–241.

Hemphill, John K. *Leader Behavior Description.* Columbus: Ohio State University, Personnel Research Board, 1950. Major contribution to the pioneering work of the Ohio State University leadership studies group.

Hollander, Edwin P., and J. P. Julian. "Studies in Leader Legitimacy, Influence and Innovation." *Advances in Experimental Social Psychology*, 6 vols., ed. Leonard Berkowitz, 5:33–69. New York: Academic Press, 1970.

Holton, Gerald. "Models for Understanding the Growth and Excellence of Scientific Research." *Excellence and Leadership in a Democracy,* ed. Stephen R. Graubard and Gerald Holton, pp. 94–131. New York: Columbia University Press, 1962.

Holtzman, Wayne H. "Adjustment and Leadership: A Study of the Rorschach Test." *Journal of Social Psychology* 36, 2 (November 1952), 179–189.

Hunt, J. G. "Leadership-Style Effects at Two Managerial Levels in a Simulated Organization." *Administrative Science Quarterly* 16, 4 (December 1971), 476–485. Important exploration of the effects of different pairings of high and low LPC (least preferred coworker score) leaders on production and satisfaction.

Hyman, Herbert H. "Surveys in the Study of Political Psychology." *Handbook of Political Psychology,* ed. Jeanne N. Knutson, pp. 322–355. San Francisco: Jossey-Bass, 1973.

Israeli, Nathan. "Group Predictions of Future Events." *Journal of Social Psychology* 4, 2 (May 1933), 201–222. Intriguing forerunner of Helmer's Delphi. Maine students predict the future.

Jacob, Philip E. "Leadership and Social Change." *Social Science Information* 10, 1 (February 1971), 155–162. Discusses cross-national research organization.

Joseph, Myron L., and Richard M. Willis. "An Experimental Analog to Two Party Bargaining." *Behavioral Science* 8, 2 (April 1963), 117–127.

Justice, Robert T. "Leadership Effectiveness: A Contingency Approach." *Academy of Management Journal* 18, 1 (March 1975), 160–167. Illustrates use of videotaped leader image.

Kadushin, Charles. "Power, Influence and Social Circles: A New Methodology for Studying Opinion Makers." *American Sociological Review* 33, 5 (October 1968), 685–699. Important rationale for a position-based, open-ended technique for identifying the social networks of "power elites."

Kelley, Harold H. "Causal Schemata and the Attribution Process." General Learning Corporation Module. Morristown: General Learning Press, 1972.

Kelley, Harold H. "Communication in Experimentally Created Hierarchies." *Human Relations* 4, 1 (1951), 39–56.

Kleinmuntz, Benjamin, ed. *Formal Representation of Human Judgment.* New York: Wiley, 1968.

Kraut, Allen I. "Some Recent Advances in Cross-national Management Research." *Academy of Management Journal* 18, 3 (September 1975), 538–549.

Lasswell, Harold D. "The Study of the Ill as a Method of Research into Political Personalities." *APSR* 23, 4 (November 1929), 996–1001.

Laumann, Edward O., and Franz Urban Pappi. "New Directions in the Study of Community Elites." *American Sociological Review* 38, 2 (April 1973), 212–229.

Lazarsveld, Paul F. "A Professional School for Training in Social Research." *Qualitative Analysis,* pp. 361–391. Boston: Allyn & Bacon, 1972. Education for applied as well as theory-oriented research.

Lazarsveld, Paul F., and W. S. Robinson. "The Quantification of Case Studies." *Journal of Applied Psychology* 24, 4 (December 1940), 817–825.

Lijphart, Arend. "Comparative Politics and the Comparative Method." *APSR* 65, 3 (September 1971), 682–893.

Likert, Rensis. "Measuring Organizational Performance." *Harvard Business Review* 36, 2 (March–April 1958), 41–50.

Lippit, Ronald. "Field Theory and Experiment in Social Psychology: Autocratic and Democratic Atmospheres." *American Journal of Sociology* 45, 1 (July 1939), 26–49.

Lofland, John. *Analyzing Social Settings: A Guide to Qualitative Observation and Analysis.* Belmont: Wadsworth, 1971.

London, Ivan D. "The Revenge of Heaven: A Brief Methodological Account." *Psychological Reports* 34 (1974), 1023–1030. Cross-cultural elicitation of biographical recall.

Luck, David. "A Psycholinguistic Approach to Leader Personality: Hitler, Stalin, Mao, and Liu Shao-ch'i." *Studies in Comparative Communism* 7, 4 (Winter 1974), 426–453.

Mandelbaum, David G. "The Study of Life History: Gandhi." *Current Anthropology* 14, 3 (June 1973), 177–206.

Marsh, Robert M. *Comparative Sociology: A Codification of Cross-societal Analysis.* New York: Harcourt, Brace & World, 1967.

McCleery, Richard. "Prison Government and Communists: The Use of Case Studies." *American Behavioral Scientist* 1, 4 (March 1958), 21–24. Argument for case study method by a pioneer in viewing the prison as a natural experimental setting.

McConahay, John B. "Experimental Research." *Handbook of Political Psychology,* ed. Jeanne N. Knutson, pp. 356–382. San Francisco: Jossey-Bass, 1973.

Meade, Robert D. "An Experimental Study of Leadership in India." *Journal of Social Psychology* 72, 1 (June 1967), 35–43. Reversal of American findings by White and Lippitt.

Menninger, Karl A. *A Manual for Psychiatric Case Study.* New York: Grune & Stratton, 1967.

Merritt, Richard L. *Systematic Approaches to Comparative Politics.* Chicago: Rand McNally, 1970.

Merritt, Richard L., and Stein Rokkan. *Comparing Nations: The Use of Quantitative Data in Cross-national Research.* New Haven: Yale University Press, 1966.

Miles, Raymond E., and J. B. Ritchie. "Leadership Attitudes among Union Officials." *Industrial Relations* 8, 1 (October 1968), 108–117. Cross-leader comparison of union leaders with managers and public officials; found essentially similar attitudes toward participation of followers in decision making. Deviance surprisingly tended to be in a nondemocratic direction.

Miller, Delbert C. *Handbook of Research Design and Social Measurement.* New York: McKay, 1970.

Miller, Delbert C., and James L. Dirksen. "The Identification of Visible, Concealed, and Symbolic Leaders in a Small Indiana City: A Replication of the Bonjean-Noland Study of Burlington, North Carolina." *Social Forces* 43, 4 (May 1965), 548–555.

Mitchell, J. Clyde. "Social Networks." *Annual Review of Anthropology: 1974,* pp. 279–299. Palo Alto: Annual Reviews, 1974.

Moore, Wilbert E., and Eleanor B. Sheldon. "Toward the Measurement of Social Change: Implications for Progress." *Economic Progress and Social Welfare,* ed. L. H. Goodman, pp. 185–212. New York: Columbia University Press, 1966.

Mulder, Mauk, and Ad Stemerding. "Threat, Attraction to Group, and Need for Strong Leadership: A Laboratory Experiment in a Natural Setting." *Human Relations* 16, 4 (November 1963), 317–334. Questionably based on deception about the research sponsor.

Oliver, Douglas, and Walter D. Miller. "Suggestions for a More Systematic Method of Comparing Political Units." *American Anthropologist* 57, 1 (February 1955), 118–120.

O'Rourke, John R. "Field and Laboratory: The Decision-making Behavior of Groups in Two Experimental Conditions." *Sociometry* 26, 4 (December 1963), 422–435.

Otterbein, Keith F. "Basic Steps in Conducting a Cross-cultural Study." *Behavior Science Notes* 4, 3 (1969), 221–231.

Overall, John E. *Applied Multivariate Analysis.* New York: McGraw-Hill, 1972.

Page, David P. "Measurement and Prediction of Leadership." *American Journal of Sociology* 41, 1 (July 1935), 31–43.

Parker, James H. "Moral Leadership in the Community." *Sociology and Social Research* 53, 1 (October 1968), 88–94. An unusual survey research study to discover moral leaders rather than the power elite.

Perloff, Harvey S., ed. *The Future of the United States Government.* New York: Braziller, 1971. Predictive essay for the United States Congress in the year 2000 by Representative John Brademas illustrates engagement of political leader as forecaster.

Pfautz, Harold W., Harry C. Huguley, and John W. McClain. "Changes in Reputed Black Community Leadership, 1962–72: A Case Study." *Social Forces* 53, 3 (March 1975), 460–467.

Polsby, Nelson W. "How to Study Community Power: The Pluralist Alternative." *Journal of Politics* 22, 3 (August 1960), 474–484.

Preston, James D. "A Comparative Methodology for Identifying Community Leaders." *Rural Sociology* 34, 4 (December 1969), 556–562.

Przeworski, Adam, and Henry Teune. *The Logic of Comparative Social Inquiry.* New York: Wiley-Interscience, 1969. Presents logic for choosing between most similar and most dissimilar research designs.

Rapoport, Anatol, and Carol Orwant. "Experimental Games: A Review." *Behavioral Science* 7, 1 (January 1962), 1–37.

Redlich, Frederick C., and E. B. Brody. "Emotional Problems of Interdisciplinary Research in Psychiatry." *Psychiatry* 18, 3 (August 1955), 233–239. Indispensable diagnosis. May also assist anticipation of problems to be encountered with research collaboration involving political leaders and followers.

Rice, George H., Jr., and Lucy E. Burnham. *A Comparison of the Results Obtained From Various Measures of Leadership Behavior.* Technical Report no. 3, Contract Nonr 225 (62). Stanford: Stanford University, 1963.

Riley, Donald A., and Charles R. Luth. "Multidimensional Psychophysics and Selective Attention in Animals." *Psychological Bulletin* 83, 1 (January 1976), 138–160. Example of a literature that suggests how multidimensional aspects of behavior may be investigated.

Riley, Matilda White, and Clarice S. Stoll. "Content Analysis." *IESS*, 3:371–377.

Rogers, Lindsay. "Reflections on Writing Biography of Public Men." *Political Science Quarterly* 88, 4 (December 1973), 725–733. Wisdom.

Rohde, Kermit J. "Theoretical and Experimental Analysis of Leadership Ability." *Psychological Reports* 4, 2 (June 1958), 243–278. Results suggest "leadership ability" may be "nothing more than a popular myth" (p. 268).

Rokkan, Stein, ed. *Comparative Research across Cultures and Nations.* The Hague: Mouton, 1968.

Rosen, Ned A. *Leadership Change and Work-Group Dynamics: An Experiment.* Ithaca: Cornell University Press, 1969.

Rudin, S. A. "Leadership as Psychophysiological Activation of Group Members: A Case Experimental Study." *Psychological Reports* 15, 2 (October 1964), 577–578. Aggressive leader obtained more efficiency on simple tasks, less on more complex ones in simulated spacecraft.

Sattler, Jerome M. "Racial 'Experimenter Effects' in Experimentation, Testing, Interviewing, and Psychotherapy." *Psychological Bulletin* 73, 2 (February 1970), 137–160.

Schriesheim, Chester A., and Ralph M. Stogdill. "Differences in Factor Structure across Three Versions of the Ohio State Leadership Scales." *Personnel Psychology* 28, 2 (Summer 1975), 189–206.

Seidler, John. "On Using Informants: A Technique for Collecting Quantitative Data and Controlling Measurement Error in Organizational Analysis." *American Sociological Review* 39, 6 (December 1974), 816–831.

Selvin, Hanan C. *The Effects of Leadership.* New York: Free Press, 1960. Important concepts and methods for studying the effects of three different "leadership climates" (persuasive, weak, and arbitrary) upon follower behavior. Can be profitably read in conjunction with Frederick Adams Woods, *The Influence of Monarchs* (New York: Macmillan, 1913), and John Kotter and Paul R. Lawrence, *Mayors in Action* (New York: Wiley, 1974).

Sertel, Ayse Kudat. "Images of Power." *American Anthropologist* 74, 3 (June 1972), 639–658. Excellent case study and mathematical model of power attribution at the village level.

Silk, Alvin J. "Response Set and Measurement of Self-designed Opinion Leadership." *Public Opinion Quarterly* 35 (Fall 1971), 383–397.

Slovic, Paul. "Analyzing the Expert Judge: A Descriptive Study of a Stockbroker's Decision Processes." *Journal of Applied Psychology* 53, 4 (August 1969), 255–263.

Smith, Robert B. "Presidential Decision-making during the Cuban Missile Crisis: A Computer Simulation." *Simulation and Games* 1, 2 (June 1970), 173-201.

Smith, Wallace J., et al. "The Prediction of Research Competence and Creativity from Personal History." *Journal of Applied Psychology* 45, 1 (February 1961), 59–62.

Sorokin, Pitrim A. "Monarchs and Rulers: A Comparative Statistical Study." *Social Forces* 4, 1 (September 1925), 22–35; 4, 3 (March 1926), 523–533.

Stark, Stanley. "Research Criteria of Executive Success." *Journal of Business* 32, 1 (January 1959), 1–14. Inadequate criteria impede scientific prediction.

Steger, Joseph A. "A Forced Choice Version of the MSCS and How It Discriminates Campus Leaders and Nonleaders." *Academy of Management Journal* 18, 3 (September 1975), 453–460.

Stein, R. Timothy. "Identifying Emergent Leaders from Verbal and Nonverbal Communications." *Journal of Personality and Social Psychology* 32, 1 (July 1975), 125–135.

Stifflre, Volney. "Simulation of People's Behavior toward New Objects and Events." *American Behavioral Scientist* 8, 9 (May 1965), 12–15. Based on the principle that responses to new things will be similar to those to familiar things encoded in the same way. Provocative teaching and research applications.

Stogdill, Ralph M., and Alvin E. Coons, eds. *Leadership Behavior: Its Description and Measurement.* Columbus: Ohio State University, Bureau of Business Research, 1957. Essential reference for the creation of methods for the study of political leadership.

Stogdill, Ralph M., and Carroll L. Shartle. *Methods in the Study of Administrative Leadership.* Columbus: Ohio State University, Bureau of Business Research, 1955.

Stone, Anthony R. "The Interdisciplinary Research Team." *Journal of Applied Behavioral Science* 5, 3 (July–September 1969), 251–365.

Streicher, Lawrence H. "On a Theory of Political Caricature." *Comparative Studies in History and Society* 9, 4 (July 1967), 427–445.

Sussman, Leila A. *Dear FDR: A Study of Political Letter Writing.* Totowa: Bedminster, 1963.

Sweney, Arthur B., et al. "An Integrative Factor Analysis of Leadership Measures and Theories." *Journal of Psychology* 90, 1 (May 1975), 75–85.

Taft, Ronald. "Some Characteristics of Good Judges of Others." *British Journal of Psychology* 47, 1 (February 1956), 19–29. Surprisingly, physical scientists are found to be more accurate than social scientists!

Tagiuri, Renato, et al. *Behavioral Science Concepts in Case Analysis.* Boston: Harvard University, Graduate School of Business Administration, Division of Research, 1968.

Vidich, Arthur J., et al., ed. *Reflections on Community Studies.* New York: Wiley, 1964.

Vroom, Victor H., ed. *Methods of Organization Research.* Pittsburgh: University of Pittsburgh Press, 1967.

Wahlke, John C. "Psychophysiological Measures of Political Attitudes and Behavior." *Midwest Journal of Political Science* 16, 4 (November 1972), 505–537. Pioneering experimental investigation of physiological versus verbal reactions to political stimuli, including slides of political leaders.

Waters, L. K., and Darrell Roach. "A Factor Analysis of Need-Fulfillment Items Designed to Measure Maslow Need Categories." *Personnel Psychology* 26, 2 (Summer 1973), 185–190.

Wayne, Francis L. "Simulation of Committee Decision-making in a State Legislative Body." *Simulation and Games* 1, 3 (September 1970), 235–262.

Weakland, John H. "Family Imagery in a Passage by Mao Tse-tung: An Essay in Psycho-cultural Method." *World Politics* 10, 3 (April 1958), 387–408.

Weisberg, Herbert F., and Jerrold G. Rusk. "Dimensions of Candidate Evaluation." *APSR* 64, 4 (December 1970), 1167–1185. Presents an affective "thermometer" for measuring "warm-cold" feelings toward presidential candidates; see p. 1175.

Welsh, William A. "Introduction: The Comparative Study of Political Leadership in Communist Systems." *Comparative Communist Political Leadership,* ed. Carl Beck et al., pp. 1–42. New York: McKay, 1973. Contains useful summary diagrams of the research approaches then being taken by Beck, Fleron, Waller, Lodge, and Zaninovich, as compared with a general framework of inquiry.

White, Ralph K. *Value Analysis: The Nature and Use of the Method.* Glen Gardner: Society for the Psychological Study of Social Issues, 1951.

White, Ralph K., and Ronald Lippitt. *Autocracy and Democracy: An Experimental Inquiry.* New York: Harper, 1960. A social psychological classic whose approach needs to be adapted for the study of political leadership.

Williams, J. Allen, Jr. "Interviewer-Respondent Interaction: A Study of Bias in the Information Interview." *Sociometry* 27, 3 (September 1964), 338-352.

Williams, M. Lee, Vincent Hazelton, and Steve Renshaw. "The Measurement of Machiavellianism: A Factor Analytic and Correlational Study of MACH IV and MACH V." *Speech Monographs* 42, 2 (June 1975), 151-159.

Wilson, John. "Interaction Analysis: A Supplementary Field Work Technique Used in the Study of Leadership in a 'New Style' Australian Aboriginal Community." *Human Organization* 21, 4 (Winter 1962-1963), 290-294.

Wolfinger, Raymond E. "Nondecisions and the Study of Local Politics." *APSR* 65, 4 (December 1971); with comment by Frederick W. Frey (pp. 1081-1101); and rejoinder (pp. 1102-1104).

Zigler, E., and L. Phillips. "Case-History Data and Psychiatric Diagnosis." *Journal of Consulting Psychology* 25, 5 (October 1961), 458.

EDUCATION

Adelson, Joseph. "The Political Imagination of the Young Adolescent." *Daedalus* 100, 4 (Fall 1971), 1013-1050.

Airan, J. W., ed. *The Nature of Leadership.* Bombay: Lalvani, 1969. Intriguing essays on problems of educating leaders.

Anderson, C. Arnold. "Education: Education and Society." *IESS,* 4:517-525.

Asher, Herbert B. "The Learning of Legislative Norms." *APSR* 57, 2 (June 1973), 499-513. Discovers little new learning among freshman members of Congress; hypothesizes prior legislative or other experiences as source of their information.

Bahou, Victor Samuel. *The Political Drama in America since 1930.* Ph.D. dissertation, Syracuse University, 1960. Political leader-follower education through drama.

Baker, John W., ed. *Member of the House.* New York: Scribner's, 1962. Self-education of Congressman Clem Miller through preparation of constituent newsletters.

Baker, Tod A., et al. "A Note on the Impact of the College Experience on Changing the Political Attitudes of Students." *Experimental Study of Politics* 3, 1 (1972-1973), 76-88. A study showing no significant change in authoritarianism, tolerance, and patriotism in the "controlled environment" of a military college.

Bass, Bernard M., and Stanley Klubeck. "Amenability to Leadership Training Related to Leadership Status." *American Psychologist* 7, 7 (July 1952),

310. "Training significantly increased the leadership behavior of girls initially high in leadership status while it had a slightly negative effect on girls initially low in status" (p. 310).

Bavelas, Alex, and Kurt Lewin. "Training in Democratic Leadership." *Journal of Abnormal and Social Psychology* 37, 1 (January 1942), 115–119. Shows possibility of training leaders in authoritarian, laissez-faire, and democratic styles.

Berger, Milton M. *Videotaped Techniques in Psychiatric Training and Treatment.* New York: Brunner-Mazel, 1970. Application in political leadership education needs to be explored.

Biddle, William W. *The Cultivation of Community Leaders: Up from the Grass Roots.* New York: Harper, 1953. Urges nonelitist teaching of social science research skills to ordinary citizens. Note the similarity to Bennis's "agricultural model" of leadership.

Bloom, Bernard, ed. *Psychological Stress in the Campus Community.* New York: Behavioral Publications, 1974. Factors to be considered in the design of leadership education in a university.

Blotner, Joseph. *The Modern American Political Novel: 1900–1960.* Austin: University of Texas Press, 1966. Another "natural" mode of education.

Boardman, William K., et al. "Life Experience Patterns and Development of College Leadership Roles." *Psychological Reports* 31, 1 (August 1972), 333–334. Attention is directed to precollegiate experience as a predictor of a pool of potential incumbents of formal campus leadership roles.

Bolton, Charles K., and Kenneth E. Corey. *A Selected Bibliography for the Training of Citizen-Agents of Planned Community Change.* Exchange Bibliography no. 206. Monticello: Council of Planning Librarians, August 1971.

Burgess, John W. *Reminiscences of an American Scholar: The Beginnings of Columbia University.* New York: Columbia University Press, 1934. Valuable institution-building experience shared by the founder of the School of Political Science, Columbia University.

Byrd, Richard E. "Training in a Non-group." *Journal of Humanistic Psychology* 7, 1 (Spring 1967), 18–27. Claims qualitative differences—comparison is to T-groups—in the direction of greater faith in own judgment, contact with social reality, and greater tolerance.

Cater, Douglass. *Developing Leadership in Government.* Washington: Brookings Institution, 1960.

Chemers, Martin M., et al. "Some Effects of Cultural Training on Leadership in Heterocultural Task Groups." *International Journal of Psychology* 1, 4 (1966), 301–314. Shows effects of cultural versus geographical leader training on group productivity and member relations in groups with American students as leaders and Arab students as followers.

Chemers, Martin M., et al. "Leader Esteem for the Least Preferred Co-worker Score, Training, and Effectiveness: An Experimental Examination." *Journal of Personality and Social Psychology* 31, 3 (March 1975), 401–409. "High intelligence leaders profited more from training than low intelligence leaders, but low intelligence leaders were more productive overall. . . . Follower satisfaction and interpersonal affect were highest for groups with high LPC[least preferred coworker]-low intelligence leaders or low LPC-high intelligence leaders" (p. 401).

Chikin, S. Ia., et al. "Ideological and Political Education in Higher Educational Institutions." *Soviet Education* 17, 7-8 (May-June 1975), 88-124.

Cleary, Robert E. *Political Education in the American Democracy.* Scranton: Intext, 1971.

Conklin, Patrick J. *A Hard Look at the Training Ground Thesis: A Study of County and Township Experience in the Backgrounds of Legislators, Selected Executive Officers, and Supreme Court Justices in Five States.* Ph.D. dissertation, University of Michigan, 1959. Prior local government experience found not to be extensive at the state level.

Corsini, Raymond J. *Role Playing in Business and Industry.* New York: Free Press, 1961. Has potential for political application.

Counts, George S., and Nucia P. Lodge, trans. *"I Want to Be Like Stalin."* New York: Day, 1946. Translation from a Russian pedagogical textbook. Note that formal texts in all world cultures need to be compared.

Department of the Army. *Military Leadership.* Field Manual no. 22-100. June 29, 1973. Military application of contemporary social psychological theory, with cartoon illustrations and extensive behavioral science and ethnic studies bibliography.

Di Marco, Nicholas, Charles Kuehl, and Earl Wims. "Leadership Style and Interpersonal Need Orientation as Moderators of Changes in Leadership Dimension Scores." *Personnel Psychology* 28, 2 (Summer 1975), 207-214.

Donham, Wallace B. "Training for Leadership in a Democracy." *Harvard Business Review* 14, 3 (Spring 1936), 261-271. Quotes Huxley: "The great end in life is not knowledge but action" (p. 261).

Downs, Cal W. "The Impact of Laboratory Training on Leadership Orientation, Values, and Self-image." *Speech Teacher* 23, 3 (September 1974), 197-205. Pretest and posttest comparison of the effects of three courses (group process laboratory, group discussion of cases, and management lecture) reveals little effect, but laboratory group changed significantly, toward showing more consideration.

Easton, David, and Jack Dennis. *Children in the Political System: Origins of Political Legitimacy.* New York: McGraw-Hill, 1969. Political orientations of 12,000 school children seven to fourteen years old.

Eaton, Joseph W. "Experiments in Testing for Leadership." *American Journal of Sociology* 52, 6 (May 1947), 523-535. Reviews military and other screening tests with awareness of the question: are we seeking persons with capacity to dominate or cooperate?

Eulau, Heinz. *Lawyers in Politics: A Study in Professional Congruence.* Indianapolis: Bobbs-Merrill, 1964. Implies need to explore the effects of legal education upon American political leadership styles.

Eulau, Heinz, and Harold Quinley. *State Officials and Higher Education: A Survey of the Opinions and Expectations of Policy Makers in Nine States.* New York: McGraw-Hill, 1970.

Fager, Robert E. "Student and Faculty Conceptions of the 'Successful Student.' " *Journal of Counseling Psychology* 5, 2 (Summer 1958), 98-103. Explores thirty-six criteria.

Fiedler, Fred E. "The Effects of Leadership Training and Experience: A Contingency Model Interpretation." *Administrative Science Quarterly* 17, 4 (December 1972), 453-470. Essential. Recommends training in ways to improve the favorableness of the leadership situation and rotation into new situations for relationship-motivated and task-motivated leaders.

Flanagan, John C. "Leadership Skills: Their Identification, Development, and Evaluation." *Leadership and Interpersonal Behavior,* ed. Luigi Petrullo and Bernard M. Bass, pp. 275-281. New York: Holt, 1961.

Frank, Lawrence K. "Dilemma of Leadership." *Psychiatry* 2, 3 (August 1939), 343-361. Acute insights into the nature of leader-follower and teacher-student relationships. "Only the leader who does not need to destroy other persons or their ideas because of his drive to go beyond the accepted and familiar in creative endeavor can achieve and even encourage successors who will explore ahead and often render his own work obsolete" (p. 359).

Froman, Lewis A., Jr. "Learning Political Attitudes." *Western Political Quarterly* 15, 2 (June 1962), 304-313. Presents hypotheses on changes in childhood values, attitudes, and beliefs.

Gage, Nathaniel L., ed. *Handbook of Research on Teaching.* Chicago: Rand McNally, 1963.

Gibb, Jack R. "Effects of Role Playing upon (a) Role Flexibility and (b) Ability to Conceptualize a New Role." *American Psychologist* 7, 7 (July 1952), 310.

Glad, Donald D., W. Lynn Smith, and Virginia M. Glad. "Behaviour Factor Reactions to Leader Emphases upon Feelings or Social Expressions." *International Journal of Social Psychiatry* 3, 2 (Autumn 1957), 129-133. Experimental study of reactions to leader comments on group member feelings versus social interactions. "High anxiety is associated with emotional warmth and friendliness, while low anxiety is associated with emotional disturbance and aggressive behavior" (p. 132).

Gordon, Leonard J. "Leadership Research and Education." *Journal of the College and University Personnel Association* 26, 2 (April-May 1975), 25-37.

Greene, Dwight L., and David G. Winter. "Motives, Involvements and Leadership among Black College Students." *Journal of Personality* 39, 3 (September 1971), 319-332. First-rate study showing importance of high need for power, but predicting avoidance of violence. Contrasts with high need for achievement of white radicals.

Greenstein, Fred I. "The Benevolent Leader Revisited: Children's Images of Leaders in Three Democracies." *APSR* 69, 4 (December 1975), 1371-1398.

Greestein, Fred I. *Children and Politics.* New Haven: Yale University Press, 1965. Pioneering inquiry.

Halsey, A. H. "The Education of Leaders and Political Development in New Nations." *Comparing Nations,* ed. Richard L. Merrit and Stein Rokkan, pp. 201-215. New Haven: Yale University Press, 1966.

Harrison, James P. "Ideological Training of Intellectuals in Communist China." *Asian Survey* 5, 10 (October 1965), 491–502

Havighurst, Robert J., ed. *Leaders in American Education.* Chicago: National Society for the Study of Education, 1971. Deliberate education for political leadership raises the question of educational leadership capabilities. Exceptional leaders examined through an unusual combination of paired autobiographical and commissioned biographical sketches.

Hendry, Charles F., ed. *Leadership in a Democracy.* Entire issue of *Journal of Educational Sociology* 17, 7 (March 1944). With contributions by Lindeman, Lewin, Lippitt, Zander, de Schweinitz, Bavelas, Jennings, French, and others. Important wartime reflections.

Herrold, Kenneth F. "Teachership as Leadership." *Teachers College Record* 48, 8 (May 1947), 515–521.

Hersey, Paul, and Kenneth H. Blanchard. "So You Want to Know Your Leadership Style." *Training and Development Journal* 28, 2 (February 1974), 22–37. An intriguing method for self-evaluation based upon task, consideration, and life-cycle theory; suggestive of many teaching and research applications.

Hoelting, Floyd B. *The Effectiveness of Leadership Training in Changing the Leadership Behavior of Emergent Student Leaders.* Ph.D. dissertation, Oklahoma State University, 1974. No significant effects found after one- and two-month intervals.

Hollingsworth, Leta S. "What We Know about the Early Selection and Training of Leaders." *Teachers College Record* 40, 7 (April 1939), 575–592. Enormously suggestive essay; based upon experience with children of extraordinary intelligence. Curriculum ideas include study of biographies and the "evolution of common things."

House, Robert J. "Leadership Training: Some Dysfunctional Consequences." *Administrative Science Quarterly* 12, 4 (March 1968), 556–571. The difficulties externally trained persons encounter when returned to their work organizations imply that such training is effective, that strategies for coping with dysfunctions should be made part of the training program, and that in situ group training should be explored.

Hyde, Douglas. *Dedication and Leadership: Learning from the Communists.* Notre Dame: University of Notre Dame Press, 1966. Cross-polity leadership learning.

Inouye, Daniel K., and Lawrence Elliott. *Journey to Washington.* Englewood Cliffs: Prentice-Hall, 1967. Illustrative of vast autobiographical literature on "natural" political leadership socialization. Also illustrates past importance of war for leader training and motivation.

Jaros, Dean, Herbert Hirsch, and Frederick J. Fleron, Jr. "The Malevolent Leader: Political Socialization in an American Sub-culture." *APSR* 62, 2 (June 1968), 564–575. Contrasts negative attitudes of children of the rural poor with more benevolent views of the president by urban children.

Johnson, Donald M., and Henry Clay Smith. "Democratic Leadership in the College Classroom." *Psychological Monographs* 67, 11, whole no. 361 (1953), 1–20.

Kahn, Harold L. "The Education of a Prince: The Emperor Learns His Role." *Approaches to Modern Chinese History,* ed. Albert Feuerwerker, Rhoads Murphy, and Mary C. Wright, pp. 15-44. Berkeley: University of California Press, 1967.

Klubeck, Stanley, and Bernard M. Bass. "Differential Effects of Training on Persons of Different Leadership Status." *Human Relations* 7, 1 (1954), 59-72. "Persons of initially higher leadership status are more likely to benefit from leadership training than those of initially lower status" (p. 59).

Kovacs, Alberta R. "Preparation for Leadership: A Philosophy." *International Nursing Review* 21, 5 (September-October 1974), 145-146. Example of explicit, normative, educational commitment by a teacher.

Krasner, William. "The Leaders and the Led." *New Society,* August 31, 1967, pp. 284-286. Cautions that conventional leadership training simply removes normal inhibitions against dominating others. More keen observations.

Larkin, Ralph W. "Contextual Influences on Teacher Leadership Styles." *Sociology of Education* 46, 4 (Fall 1973), 471-479. Shows strong ethnic and socioeconomic contextual influences upon task, power, and expressive styles.

Lasswell, Harold D., and Myres S. McDougal. "Legal Education and Public Policy: Professional Training in the Public Interest." *The Analysis of Political Behaviour,* ed. Harold D. Lasswell, pp. 21-119. New York: Oxford University Press, 1947.

Leadership in Democratic Living. Entire issue of *Teachers College Record* 40, 7 (April 1939), 561-649. Includes essays from viewpoints of women, labor, and youth.

Leavitt, H. J. "Problem-solving Projects: A Practical Approach to Management Training." *The Development of Executive Talent,* ed. M. Joseph Dooher and V. Marquis, pp. 180-190. New York: American Management Association, 1952.

Lepawsky, Albert. "Graduate Education in Public Policy." *Policy Sciences* 1, 4 (December 1970), 443-457. A curriculum design.

Lynn, R. "Brainwashing Techniques in Leadership and Child Rearing." *British Journal of Social and Clinical Psychology* 5, 4 (December 1966), 270-273. Brainwashing techniques require playing dual role of threatener (anxiety raiser) and protector (anxiety reducer). The authoritarian leader/parent emphasizes the former; the laissez-faire type, the latter. Democratic leadership/parentage involves the dual alternating signals method.

Maier, Norman R. F., and Ellen Panza McRae. "Increasing Innovation in Change Situations through Leadership Skills." *Psychological Reports* 31, 2 (October 1972), 343-354. Leadership training is shown to affect innovation and satisfaction in role-played foreman-worker groups.

Mailick, Sidney, et al. "Educating Executives: Social Science, Self-study, or Socrates?" *Public Administration Review* 18, 4 (Autumn 1958), 275-306.

Masland, John W., and Laurence I. Radway. *Soldiers and Scholars: Military Education and National Policy.* Princeton: Princeton University Press, 1957.

Mazrui, Ali A. "Ali A. Mazrui: The Making of an African Political Scientist." *International Social Science Journal* 25, 1-2 (1973), 101-116.

McClintock, Charles G., and Henry A. Turner. "The Impact of College upon Political Knowledge, Participation, and Values." *Human Relations* 15, 2 (May 1962), 163–176. "Little, if any."

Miller, Melvin D. "Externing: Route to Local Leadership." *American Vocational Leadership* 50, 4 (April 1975), 34–37. Combination of summer workshop, regular employment, weekend seminars at different sites, and provision of consulting services for student-initiated projects leading to occupational advancement.

Mudgett, William C., et al. "A Tactical Pacification Game for Leadership Development." *Psychological Reports* 36, 2 (April 1975), 439–445. Behavioral science theory and methods in a violence-related training and assessment simulation.

Nadler, Eugene B., and Stephen L. Fink. "Impact of Laboratory Training on Sociopolitical Ideology." *Journal of Applied Behavioral Science* 6, 1 (January–February 1970), 79–92. Short-range evidence that "changes in interpersonal and small group values will generalize to larger areas of social ideology" (p. 81).

Neely, Twila E. "The Sources of Political Power: A Contribution to the Sociology of Leadership." *American Journal of Sociology* 33, 5 (March 1928), 769–783. The techniques of the corrupt political boss "are based on sound sociopsychological principles" (p. 769); therefore, the social worker should adapt them for good ends. Rich with colorful examples, including George Washington Plunkitt's advice "to study human nature and act accordin' " (p. 782).

Nelson, Charles A. *Developing Responsible Public Leaders: A Report on Interviews and Correspondence with Leading Americans.* Dobbs Ferry: Oceana, 1963.

Newton, Fred B. "Development of Student Leadership on Campus." *Journal of College Student Personnel* 16, 5 (September 1975), 422–428. Suggests five modules: "preliminary analysis and training, team or organization building, understanding and use of group dynamics, skills for decision-making and task accomplishment, and evaluation and follow up."

Norr, James L., and Kathleen S. Crittendon. "Evaluating College Teaching as Leadership." *Higher Education* 4, 3 (August 1975), 317–334.

Olmstead, Joseph A., et al. "Development of Leadership Assessment Simulations." U. S. Army Research Institute for the Behavioral and Social Sciences, Technical Paper no. 257 (October 1974).

Ostrom, Vincent. "Education and Politics." *Social Forces Influencing American Education,* ed. Nelson B. Henry, pp. 8–45. Chicago: National Society for the Study of Education, 1961.

Peabody, Robert L., ed. *Education of a Congressman: Newsletters of Morris K. Udall.* Indianapolis: Bobbs-Merrill, 1972.

Petersen, Peter B., and Gordon L. Lippitt. "Comparison of Behavioral Styles between Entering and Graduating Students in Officer Candidate School." *Journal of Applied Psychology* 52, 1, pt. 1 (1968), 66–70.

Pierson, George W. *The Education of American Leaders: Comparative Contributions of U. S. Colleges and Universities.* New York: Praeger, 1969.

Plutarch. "Can Virtue Be Taught?" *Moralia,* vol. 6, trans. W. C. Helmbold, pp. 5–13. Loeb Classical Library. Cambridge: Harvard University Press, 1939. "Oh mortal men! Why do we assert that virtue is unteachable, and thus make it non-existent?" (pp. 5–6).

Prewitt, Kenneth. "Political Socialization and Leadership Selection." *Annals* 361 (September 1965), 96–111.

Rice, Albert K. *Learning for Leadership: Interpersonal and Intergroup Methods.* London: Tavistock, 1965. Explanation of Tavistock group training procedures.

Rideout, Walter B. *Radical Novel in the United States, 1900–1954: Some Interrelations of Literature and Society.* Cambridge: Harvard University Press, 1956. Nonformal education.

Riegel, John W. *Executive Development: A Survey of Experience in Fifty American Corporations.* Ann Arbor: University of Michigan Press, 1952.

Rose, Richard. "The Making of Cabinet Ministers." *British Journal of Political Science* 1, 4 (October 1971), 393–414.

Roskens, Ronald W. "Relationship between Leadership Participation in College and after College." *Personnel and Guidance Journal* 39, 2 (October 1960), 110–114. Finds correlation, but without control group. Former student leaders recall influence of outstanding teachers.

Shaftel, Fannie R., and George Shaftel. *Role-playing for Social Values.* Englewood Cliffs: Prentice-Hall, 1967.

Shingles, Richard D. "Community Action and Attitude Change: A Case of Adult Political Socialization." *Experimental Study of Politics* 4, 3 (December 1973), 38–81. Participation of the poor can lead to greater alienation and lower self-esteem in this setting rather than opposite effects among the well-to-do.

Siegel, Roberta S. *Learning about Politics: A Reader in Political Socialization.* New York: Random House, 1970. Essential overview.

Sonnino, Paul, trans. *Louis XIV: Mémoires for the Instruction of the Dauphin.* New York: Free Press, 1970. Example of voluminous literature devoted to the direct education of successors by incumbents.

Stavrianos, Leften S. "The Training and Selection of Leaders in Fascist Italy." *World Affairs Interpreter* 9, 1 (Spring 1938), 74–77.

Sunderland, John. "Ph.D. Programs in Policy Sciences: Who, When, Where, What, and Why?" *Policy Sciences* 1, 4 (December 1970), 469–482.

Suomi, S. J. "Monkey Psychiatrists." *American Journal of Psychiatry* 128, 8 (February 1972), 41–46. Less aggressive, "normal," younger monkeys are placed for two hours each day with older monkeys who exhibit social skill disabilities. After six months, the older monkeys seem "cured."

Taylor, Milton H. "Effects of a Pre-programmed, Leaderless Personal Growth Group." *Journal of College Student Personnel* 16, 3 (May 1975), 201–204.

Maybe, "the mere passage of time, a good film, or even self-reflection would be just as effective as group experience" (p. 204).

Thomas, Maurice J., comp. *Presidential Statements on Education: Excerpts from Inaugural and State of the Union Messages, 1789–1967.* Pittsburgh: University of Pittsburgh Press, 1967.

Weinberg, Ian, and Kenneth M. Walker. "Student Politics and Political Systems: Toward a Typology." *American Journal of Sociology* 75, 1 (July 1969), 77–96. Distinguishes between proximate and distant structural linkages. The more closely linked, the more the cooptation and absorption of student ideas. The more distant, the more ad hoc and ephemeral the influence.

White, Howard. "Can Legislatures Learn from City Councils?" *APSR* 21, 1 (February 1927), 95–100. Arguing legislatures should emulate more frequent council meeting patterns, article implies broad possibilities for cross-role leadership learning.

Zaleznik, Abraham. "The Human Dilemmas of Leadership." *Harvard Business Review* 41, 4 (July–August 1963), 49–55. Six suggestions for self-training to cope with anxieties associated with fears of success and failure: accept diverse motivations, establish firm sense of identity, maintain response consistency, become selective, learn to communicate, and create a rhythmic life pattern.

APPLICATION

AAAS Committee on Scientific Freedom and Responsibility. *Scientific Freedom and Responsibility.* Washington: American Association for the Advancement of Science, 1975.

Bell, Daniel. " 'Screening' Leaders in a Democracy: How Scientific Is Personnel Testing." *Commentary* 5 (April 1948), 368–375.

Bitensky, Reuben. "The Influence of Political Power in Determining the Theoretical Development of Social Work." *Journal of Social Policy* 2, 2 (April 1973), 119–130.

Blum, Richard H., and Mary Lou Funkhouser. "Legislators on Social Scientists and a Social Issue: A Report and Commentary on Some Discussions with Lawmakers about Drug Abuse." *Journal of Applied Behavioral Science* 1, 1 (January–February 1965), 84–112.

Bolling, Richard. *House Out of Order.* New York: Dutton, 1965. Reform suggestions by a Missouri congressman; illustrates large literature on problem definition by experienced leaders.

Cangemi, Joseph P. "Leadership Characteristics of Business Executives Appropriate for Leaders in Higher Education." *Education* 95, 3 (Spring 1975), 229–232. Suggests business leadership research findings should be used to improve educational leadership.

Chen, Pi-chao, with the collaboration of Ann Elizabeth Miller. "Lessons from the Chinese Experience: China's Planned Birth Program." *Studies in Family Planning* 6, 10 (October 1975), 354–366. Direct induction of applied principles from leadership experience.

Code of Ethics of the Society for Applied Anthropology." *Human Organization* 10, 2 (Summer 1951), 32.

Cohen, Joel B., ed. *Behavioral Science Foundations of Consumer Behavior.* New York: Free Press, 1972. Reviews behavioral science theory and research on persuasion. By comparison with business efforts to persuade customers, manipulation of voter behavior is primitive. Implicitly raises ethical issues.

Coleman, James S. "Legitimate and Illegitimate Use of Power." *The Idea of Social Structure: Papers in Honor of Robert K. Merton,* ed. Lewis A. Coser, pp. 221–236. New York: Harcourt Brace Jovanovich, 1975.

Costello, Timothy W. "Psychological Aspects: The Soft Side of Policy Formulation." *Policy Sciences* 1, 2 (Summer 1970), 161–168. By psychologist serving as deputy mayor of New York City.

Deutsch, Karl W. "On Political Theory and Political Action." *APSR* 65, 1 (March 1971), 11–27.

Dion, Léon. "Politique et science politique." *Canadian Journal of Political Science* 8, 3 (September 1975), 367–380.

Elliott, Arnold A., Thomas C. Hood, and Jack E. Holmes. "The Working Scientist as Political Participant." *Journal of Politics* 34, 2 (May 1972), 399–427.

Fiedler, Fred E. "The Contingency Model—New Directions for Leadership Utilization." *Journal of Contemporary Business* 3, 4 (Autumn 1974), 65–80.

Fiedler, Fred E., and Martin M. Chemers. *Leadership and Effective Management.* Glenview: Scott, Foresman, 1974.

Frank, Jerome D. "Psychiatrists and International Affairs: Pitfalls and Possibilities." *International Journal of Social Psychiatry* 18, 4 (Winter 1972–1973), 235–238. Experienced advice of great significance, with specific reference to political leaders; younger more likely to be amenable to new ideas than are older.

Gellhorn, Walter, and William Brody. "Selecting Supervisory Mediators through Trial by Combat." *Public Administration Review* 8, 4 (Autumn 1948), 259–267. Civil service selection analog to military combat simulations: group discussion and speech making.

Gemmill, Gary R. *The Relationship between the Behavioral Sciences and Management Theory and Practice: An Exploratory Investigation.* Ph.D. dissertation, Michigan State University, 1966.

Group for the Advancement of Psychiatry. Committee on Therapy. "Problems of Psychiatric Leadership." *GAP Report* 8, 90 (March 1974), 925–946. Concludes that the psychiatric "clinical executive" must have a high energy level, a quality of fatherliness, optimism, and a capacity to inspire loyalty.

Gunther, M., and K. Reshaur. "Science and Values in Political 'Science.' " *Philosophy of the Social Sciences* 1, 2 (May 1971), 113–121.

Hemphill, John K. "Leader Behavior Associated with the Administrative Reputations of College Departments." *Leader Behavior: Its Description and Measurement,* Bureau of Business Research Monograph no. 88, ed. Ralph M. Stogdill and Alvin E. Coons, pp. 74–85. Columbus: Ohio State University, 1957.

Hilbert, Raymond L. "Modern Organization Theory and Business Management Thought." *American Behavioral Scientist* 8, 2 (October 1964), 25–29.

Hobbs, Nicholas. "Ethics: Ethical Issues in the Social Sciences." *IESS*, 5:160–167.

Jantsch, Eric. "From Forecasting and Planning to Policy Sciences." *Policy Sciences* 1, 1 (Spring 1970), 31–47.

Kariel, Henry S. "Democracy Unlimited: Kurt Lewin's Field Theory." *American Journal of Sociology* 62, 3 (November 1956), 280–289. Consensus-seeking applications deny the usefulness of conflict. And, I submit, vice versa.

Laquer, Walter, and George L. Mosse, eds. *Historians in Politics*. Beverly Hills: Sage, 1974.

Lasswell, Harold D. "The Emerging Conception of the Policy Sciences." *Policy Sciences* 1, 1 (Spring 1970), 3–14.

Levitt, Theodore. "Creativity Is Not Enough." *Harvard Business Review* 41, 3 (May–June 1963), 72–83. Invaluable advice. Supposedly "creative" people do not understand how an organization must operate to get things done. Energy, know-how, initiative, and staying power are necessary to implement ideas.

Lippitt, Ronald, and Gordon Lippitt. "Consulting Process in Action." *Training and Development Journal* 29, 6 (June 1975), 38–43.

Lipset, Seymour M., and Everett C. Ladd, Jr. "The Politics of American Sociologists." *American Journal of Sociology* 78, 1 (July 1972), 67–104. Dominants are considerably to the left of the nondominants.

Mann, Dean E. "The Selection of Federal Political Executives." *APSR* 58, 1 (March 1964), 81–99.

McCracken, Daniel D. *Public Policy and the Expert*. Special Studies no. 212. New York: Council on Religion and International Affairs, 1971.

Miner, John B. "Conformity among University Professors and Business Executives." *Administrative Science Quarterly* 7, 1 (June 1962), 96–109.

Mount, Ferdinand. "The Chancellor's Mistake: The Impact of Social Science upon Politics." *Political Quarterly* 43, 2 (April–June 1972), 145–154.

O'Brien, Gordon E. "Leadership in Organizational Settings." *Journal of Applied Behavioral Science* 5, 1 (January–March 1969), 45–63. Suggestions for applied task analysis.

Office of Strategic Services Assessment Staff. *Assessment of Men*. New York: Holt, 1948. Task knowledge applied in recruitment procedures.

Plutarch. "That a Philosopher Ought to Converse Especially with Men in Power." *Moralia,* vol. 10, trans. H. N. Fowler, pp. 29–47. Loeb Classical Library. Cambridge: Harvard University Press, 1936. "Philosophers who associate with rulers do make them more just, more moderate, and more eager to do good, so that it is very likely that they are also happier" (p. 45).

Price, Don K. "Science-Government Relations." *IESS*, 14:100–107.

Ranney, Austin, ed. *Political Science and Public Policy*. Chicago: Markham, 1968.

Reid, Herbert. "Contemporary American Political Science in the Crisis of Industrial Society." *American Journal of Political Science* 16, 3 (August 1972), 339-366.

Schensul, Stephen L. "Skills Needed in Action Anthropology: Lessons from El Centro de la Causa." *Human Organization* 33, 2 (Summer 1974), 203-215. Recommendations for graduate training. One of an important cluster of applied essays in this and succeeding issues.

Solomon, Lawrence N. "Humanism and the Training of Applied Behavioral Scientists." *Journal of Applied Behavioral Science* 7, 5 (September-October 1971), 531-547. Applied behavioral scientist as an "actualizer of values" needs a humanistic training that will not end in fruitless fear of all control, anarchy, and anti-intellectualism.

Spencer, Henry R. "Pathological Problems in Politics." *APSR* 43, 1 (February 1949), 1-16. Provocative inventory by a president of the APSA who called for a courageous collective clinical orientation by the discipline. Bears the mark of humanist knowledge and imagination.

Sullivan, Michael P. "The Question of 'Relevance' in Foreign Policy Studies." *Western Political Quarterly* 26, 2 (June 1973), 314-324.

Tinbergen, Niko. "On War and Peace in Animals and Man." *Man and Animal,* ed. Heinz Friedrich, pp. 118-141. New York: St. Martin's, 1968.

Topping, C. W. "Sociological Research and Political Leadership." *Sociology and Social Research* 20 (July 1936), 543-547. Plato's failure at Syracuse suggests that social scientists should try to contribute to political leadership through research, by establishment of a School of Applied Social Science, and less tangibly by "poise" based upon "the perspective of 25,000 years."

Toynbee, Arnold J. *Science in Human Affairs.* New York: Columbia University, Institute for the Study of Science in Human Affairs, 1968.

Tsai, Loh Seng. "Peace and Cooperation among Natural Enemies: Educating a Rat-killing Cat to Cooperate with a Hooded Rat." *Acta Psychologia Taiwanica* 5 (March 1963), 1-5. Remarkably successful experiment in teaching animal enemies to cooperate peacefully to obtain food reward. Profound human implications remain to be explored: "Many think our research has laid the cornerstone of the basic biological foundation of the theoretical possibility of world peace" (p. 4).

Turner, Henry A., and Carl C. Hetrick. "Political Activities and Party Affiliations of American Political Scientists." *Western Political Quarterly* 25, 3 (September 1972), 361-374. Democrats constituted 73.4 percent of 1970 sample. Presidents reported to have influenced this party preference, in rank order, were Franklin Roosevelt, Kennedy, Truman, Eisenhower, and Nixon. Republican preferences were influenced by Eisenhower, Franklin Roosevelt, and Lyndon Johnson.

York, Herbert. *The Advisers: Oppenheimer, Teller and the Superbomb.* San Francisco: Freeman, 1976. Case study by involved scientist-administrator.

APPENDIX C

SELECTED BIOGRAPHIES

ATTENTION IS CALLED HERE to approximately seventy biographies, autobiographies, and biographical collections of political leaders that illustrate present resources for research, teaching, and application. They may be supplemented by biographical films. Biographies cited in the text have not been included. A few autobiographies have been included as examples of a vast and growing literature that presents unique scientific challenges and opportunities of its own. An attempt has been made to give examples that illustrate diversity in historical periods, cultural contexts, and political institutions. Attention is called to revolutionaries as well as established leaders, to women as well as men, and to leaders of ethnic minorities as well as those of dominant groups.

Biographies vary enormously in quality, including those cited here, and provide a major data quality control challenge for future scientific development. For historical figures, scholarly reviews in leading historical journals are indispensable. For contemporary leaders, the judgments of knowledgeable persons, friendly and hostile, are essential. Although no biography answers all the questions raised by the emergence of the scientific study of political leadership, all biographies that contain some valid information are of inescapable interest in the effort to create a body of knowledge that is sensitive to a wide range of behavioral variation.

Collected Biographical Sketches

Alexander, Robert J. *Prophets of the Revolution: Profiles of Latin American Leaders.* New York: Macmillan, 1962.

Ayling, S. E. *Portraits of Power.* New York: Barnes & Noble, 1963.

Beals, Carleton. *Great Guerrilla Warriors.* New York: Tower, 1971.

Bennett, Norman R. *Leadership in Eastern Africa: Six Political Biographies.* Boston: Boston University Press, 1968.

Dahmus, Joseph. *Seven Medieval Queens.* New York: Doubleday, 1972.

Grant, Michael. *The Twelve Caesars.* New York: Scribner's, 1975.

Hanna, Willard A. *Southeast Asia's Charismatic Statesmen.* New York: St. Martin's, 1964.

Haupt, George, and Jean-Jacques Marie. *Makers of the Russian Revolution: Biographies of Bolshevik Leaders.* Ithaca: Cornell University Press, 1974.

Hsueh, Chun-tu. *Revolutionary Leaders of Modern China.* London: Oxford University Press, 1971.

Merriam, Charles E. *Four American Party Leaders.* Freeport: Books for Libraries, 1967.

Morris, Richard B. *Seven Who Shaped Our Destiny: The Founding Fathers as Revolutionaries.* New York: Harper & Row, 1973.

Stone, Irving. *They Also Ran: The Story of the Men Who Were Defeated for the Presidency.* Garden City: Doubleday, 1943.

Swearingen, Rodger, ed. *Leaders of the Communist World.* New York: Free Press, 1970.

Thompson, James M. *Leaders of the French Revolution.* New York: Harper & Row, 1971.

Van Thal, Herbert, ed. *The Prime Ministers.* New York: Stein & Day, 1975.

Wolfe, Bertram D. *Three Who Made a Revolution.* Dial, 1948.

Biographies and Autobiographies

Abueva, José V. *Ramón Magsaysay.* Manila: Solidaridad, 1971.

Armstrong, H. C., and Emil Lengyel. *Gray Wolf: The Life of Kemal Ataturk.* New York: Putnam, 1961.

Balfour, Michael, and Julian Frisby. *Helmuth von Moltke: A Leader against Hitler.* New York: St. Martin's, 1972.

Balsdon, J. P. V. D. *Julius Caesar.* New York: Atheneum, 1967.

Berlin, Isaiah. *Karl Marx: His Life and Environment.* 3d ed. New York: Oxford University Press, 1963.

Bodde, Derk. *China's First Unifier: A Study of the Ch'in Dynasty as Seen in the Life of Li Ssu.* Leiden: Brill, 1938.

Bradford, Ernle. *Cleopatra.* New York: Harcourt Brace Jovanovich, 1972.

Butwell, Richard. *U Nu of Burma.* Stanford: Stanford University Press, 1963.

Carlyle, Thomas. *History of Friedrich II of Prussia Called Frederick the Great.* Chicago: University of Chicago Press, 1969.

Caro, Robert A. *The Power Broker: Robert Moses and the Fall of New York.* New York: Knopf, 1974.

Chisholm, Shirley. *Unbought and Unbossed.* Boston: Houghton Mifflin, 1970.

Clark, Leon P. *Lincoln: A Psycho-biography.* New York: Scribner's, 1933.

Cohen, Stephen F. *Bukharin and the Bolshevik Revolution: A Political Biography, 1888–1938.* New York: Knopf, 1973.

Connors, Richard J. *A Cycle of Power: The Career of Jersey City Mayor Frank Hague.* Metuchen: Scarecrow, 1971.

Crozier, Brian. *De Gaulle.* New York: Scribner's, 1973.

Dahm, Berhnard. *Sukarno and the Struggle for Indonesian Independence.* Ithaca: Cornell University Press, 1969.

Davis, Varina. *Jefferson Davis.* New York: Bedford, 1890.

Fiori, Giuseppe. *Antonio Gramsci: Life of a Revolutionary.* New York: Dutton, 1971.

Fitzgerald, C. P. *The Empress Wu.* London: Cresset, 1968.

Fox, Robin Lane. *Alexander the Great.* New York: Dial, 1974.

Fraser, Antonia. *Mary Queen of Scots.* New York: Delacorte, 1969.

Galíndez, Jesús de. *Era of Trujillo: Dominican Dictator.* Tucson: University of Arizona Press, 1973.

Gandhi, Mohandas K. *An Autobiography: The Story of My Experiments with Truth.* Boston: Beacon, 1957.

Ginger, Ray. *The Bending Cross: A Biography of Eugene V. Debs.* New Brunswick: Rutgers University Press, 1949.

Grousset, René. *Conqueror of the World* [Genghis Khan]. New York: Orion, 1966.

Howard, Helen A., and Dan L. McGrath. *War Chief Joseph.* Lincoln: University of Nebraska Press, 1964.

Hutt, Maurice. *Napoleon.* London: Oxford University Press, 1965.

Khaled, Leila. *My People Shall Live.* London: Hodder & Stoughton, 1973.

Kirkpatrick, Ivone. *Mussolini: A Study in Power.* New York: Hawthorn, 1964.

Koenig, Louis W. *Bryan: A Political Biography of William Jennings Bryan.* New York: Putnam, 1971.

Lacouture, Jean. *Ho Chi Minh: A Political Biography.* New York: Random House, 1967.

La Follette, Robert. *La Follette's Autobiography: A Personal Narrative of Political Experience.* Madison: University of Wisconsin Press, 1960.

Malcolm X and Alex Haley. *Autobiography of Malcolm X.* New York: Grove, 1965.

Manning, Clarence A. *Hetman of the Ukraine: Ivan Mazepa.* New York: Bookman, 1957.

Martin, John Bartlow. *Adlai Stevenson of Illinois.* Garden City: Doubleday, 1976.

Masani, Zareer. *Indira Gandhi.* New York: Crowell, 1976.

Masur, Gerhard, *Simón Bolívar.* Rev. ed. Albuquerque: University of New Mexico Press, 1969.

McNeal, Robert H. *Bride of the Revolution: Krupskaya and Lenin.* Ann Arbor: University of Michigan Press, 1972.

Meir, Golda. *My Life.* New York: Putnam, 1975.

Meyer, Michael E. *Huerta: A Political Portrait.* Lincoln: University of Nebraska Press, 1972.

Nettl, John P. *Rosa Luxemburg.* London: Oxford University Press, 1966.

Ooms, Herman. *Charismatic Bureaucrat: A Political Biography of Matsudaira Sadanobu, 1758–1829.* Chicago: University of Chicago Press, 1974.

Parkinson, Roger. *Zapata*. New York: Stein & Day, 1975.

Patterson, James T. *Mr. Republican: A Biography of Robert A. Taft*. Boston: Houghton Mifflin, 1972.

Pye, Lucian W. *Mao Tse-tung*. New York: Basic Books, 1976.

Ridley, Jasper. *Garibaldi*. New York: Viking, 1976.

Roosevelt, Theodore. *Gouverneur Morris*. Edited by John T. Morse, Jr. New York: AMS Press, 1898.

Rourke, Thomas [pseudonym of Daniel J. Clinton]. *Gomez: Tyrant of the Andes*. New York: Morrow, 1936.

Shub, David. *Lenin*. Harmondsworth: Penguin, 1976.

Sinclair, Andrew. *Ché Guevara*. New York: Viking, 1970.

Smith, John Holland. *Joan of Arc*. New York: Scribner's, 1973.

Somare, Michael. *Sana: An Autobiography*. Port Moresby: Niugini, 1975.

St. John, Robert. *The Boss: The Story of Gamal Abdel Nasser*. London: Barker, 1960.

Swanberg, W. A. *Norman Thomas: The Last Idealist*. New York: Scribner's, 1976.

Taylor, A. J. P. *Bismark*. New York: Viking, 1967.

Thomas, Benjamin. *Lincoln*. New York: Knopf, 1952.

Toland, John. *Adolf Hitler*. New York: Doubleday, 1976.

Wedgwood, C. V. *Oliver Cromwell*. London: Duckworth, 1973.

Williams, Roger L. *The Mortal Napoleon III*. Princeton: Princeton University Press, 1971.

Witke, Roxanne. *Comrade Chiang Ch'ing*. Boston: Little, Brown, 1977.

NOTES

Preface

1. Glenn D. Paige, ed., *Political Leadership: Readings for an Emerging Field* (New York: Free Press, 1972).
2. Richard C. Snyder and Hubert H. Wilson, *Roots of Political Behavior* (New York: American Book, 1949), pp. 141–145, citing an excerpt from Charles E. Merriam, *Political Power* (New York: McGraw-Hill, 1934).
3. This citizens' conference is reported in George Chaplin and Glenn D. Paige, eds., *Hawaii 2000: Continuing Experiment in Anticipatory Democracy* (Honolulu: University Press of Hawaii, 1973).

Chapter 1. Political Leadership: Challenge to Political Science

1. John W. Gardner, *Excellence* (New York: Harper & Row, 1961), p. 123.
2. Albert Salomon, "Leadership in Democracy," in Max Ascoli and Fritz Lehman, eds., *Political and Economic Democracy* (New York: Norton, 1937), p. 245.

Chapter 2. The Surprising Lack of Disciplinary Focus

1. Jasper B. Shannon, "The Study of Political Leadership," in Jasper B. Shannon, ed., *The Study of Comparative Government* (New York: Greenwood, 1949), p. 314.
2. A useful introduction to the American branch of the discipline is presented in Albert Somit and Joseph Tanenhaus, *The Development of American Political Science* (Boston: Allyn & Bacon, 1967). Interestingly, as will become clear later, Plato, Aristotle, Machiavelli, and Max Weber appear in the index of names in this volume, but Plutarch does not. Also, whereas the subject index understandably omits "leadership" since it also omits mention of "decision making" and even "power" (although it does include "functionalism" and "Posdcorb"), it does direct attention to APSA president Peter Odegard's forthright criticism of leader-related "McCarthyism" in 1951. See footnote on page 201, although the index cites page 200.

3. Kenneth F. Janda, ed. *Cumulative Index to the American Political Science Review, Volumes 1-57: 1906-1963* (Evanston: Northwestern University Press, 1964). Seven more titles appeared from 1964 through 1975. Interestingly, the new *British Journal of Political Science* contained no title reference to "leadership" in its first five volumes (1971-1975), but "elite" appeared six times.

4. This article is not indexed in the table of contents of the 1925 volume but may be found as a subsection of "Reports of the Second National Conference on the Science of Politics," *APSR* 19, 1 (February 1925), 130-135. See also the unindexed but very interesting subsection "Various Projects for the Psychological Study of Leadership" in L. L. Thurstone's report "The Round Table on Politics and Psychology" (pp. 120-121). E.g., "Professor Yoakum suggested the possibility of what would amount to a job analysis of the political leader" (p. 121).

5. The concept of "voting" is a very interesting one for students of political leadership who may be seeking to create concepts for the future that depart from past assumptions of a dichotomy between rulers and the ruled, leaders and the led, elite and mass, etc. As the *APSR* titles show, both leaders and followers "vote"; the idea is useful in different settings such as legislatures and elections; and it is readily usable in cross-polity research. The general utility of the concept of "voting" is shared, of course, by the idea of decision making, under which it may be subsumed.

6. Franklin W. Houn, "The Eighth Central Committee of the Chinese Communist Party: A Study of an Elite" (1957); Robert A. Dahl, "A Critique of the Ruling Elite Model" (1958); Lewis J. Edinger, "Post-totalitarian Leadership: Elites in the German Federal Republic" (1960); Andrew Hacker, "The Elected and the Anointed: Two American Elites" (1961).

7. Herbert McCloskey, Paul J. Hoffman, and Rosemary Ohara, "Issue Conflict and Consensus among Party Leaders and Followers," *APSR* 54, 2 (June 1960), 406-427.

8. During 1906-1963 only six *APSR* titles referred to "citizen-citizens-citizenship." Four of these focused mainly on political participation, the other two on national status.

9. Looking toward the future, it is likely that both concepts will have to be much further developed before the dichotomy implied by them can be conceptually eliminated and new forms of political relationships first articulated and then translated into social reality.

10. Against this background, the publication in 1964 of a collection of essays on American executive, legislative, and judicial leaders under the common title of "political leadership" was an important conceptual event. See James D. Barber, *Political Leadership in American Government* (Boston: Little, Brown, 1964).

11. MacMahon (1956) most closely approximated this approach.

12. Edinger (1960) is an exception.

13. Alexander Heard, "Interviewing Southern Politicians," *APSR* 44, 4 (December 1950), 886-896.

14. It took sixty-six years for an article with the word "mayor" in its title to

appear in the *APSR,* then coupled significantly with the idea of "leadership." See Jeffrey L. Pressman's insightful and directly informed case study of factors affecting mayoral leadership in Oakland, California, "Preconditions of Mayoral Leadership," *APSR* 66, 2 (June 1972), 511–524.

15. Library of Congress, Processing Department, Subject Cataloging Division, *Classification H. Social Sciences,* 3d ed. (Washington: Government Printing Office, 1967), p. 386. I wish to thank Marilyn Harris for bringing this to my attention.

16. George H. Sabine, *A History of Political Theory,* 2d ed. (New York: Holt, 1955); 3d ed. (1961), 4th ed. (1973).

17. Sabine's remarkable effort provides insight into the enormity of the task facing political philosophers who wish to gain truly global historical perspectives.

18. Sabine, op. cit. By contrast, Leo Strauss and Joseph Cropsey, *History of Political Philosophy,* 2d ed. (New York: Random House, 1972), contains no index reference to "leadership."

19. Sabine, op. cit., p. 884.

20. Ibid., p. 901.

21. I have considered a number of ways to qualify this sentence but have decided against them all. Introductory guides to the rediscovery of this remarkable classical writer by political scientists who have too long neglected him are "Plutarch," in N. G. L. Hammond and H. H. Scullard, eds., *The Oxford Classical Dictionary,* 2d. ed. (Oxford: Clarendon, 1970), pp. 848–850; D. A. Russell, *Plutarch* (London: Duckworth, 1973); and *Plutarch's Lives,* 11 vols., trans. Bernadotte Perrin, Loeb Classical Library (Cambridge: Harvard University Press, 1914–1926). Perrin's translation is better than the more commonly encountered Dryden version. Also see Plutarch's fascinating *Moralia,* 16 vols., Loeb Classical Library.

22. Robert A. Dahl, *Modern Political Analysis* (Englewood Cliffs: Prentice-Hall, 1963). Plato and Machiavelli, but not Plutarch, are cited, as well as Hitler and two dozen historical leaders from Caesar to John F. Kennedy, with most frequent reference to Abraham Lincoln.

23. Ibid., pp. 40, and see pages following.

24. This was done, of course, in one of the most highly regarded essays in the history of American political science—Robert A. Dahl, "The Concept of Power," *Behavioral Science* 2, 3 (July 1957), 201–215—which concludes: "The power of an actor, A, would seem to be adequately defined by the measure M which is the difference in the probability of an event, given certain actions by A, and the probability of the event given no such action by A."

25. Dahl, *Modern Political Analysis,* pp. 50–51. The potentialities of social learning and reinforcement theories in psychology await exploration in this type of "power analysis."

26. Ibid., pp. 55, and see pages following.

27. Ibid., pp. 63–69.

28. Ibid., pp. 69–71.

29. Ibid., p. 107.

30. Ibid., p. 109.

31. Robert A. Dahl, *Who Governs?* (New Haven: Yale University Press, 1961).

32. Ibid., pp. 184, and see pages following.

33. Ibid., pp. 305–307.

34. Ibid., pp. 308–310.

35. Ibid., p. 325.

36. Ibid.

37. In an important addition to the New Haven study, Raymond E. Wolfinger, in *The Politics of Progress* (Englewood Cliffs: Prentice-Hall, 1974), devoted even more detailed attention to the influence of Mayor Lee, based in part upon five months of direct observation in Lee's office. The final chapter is devoted to a pessimistic evaluation of "the prospects for mayoral leadership" (Lee was perhaps unique and mayors have a dead-end, rapid turnover job in American politics, with little opportunity for upward mobility) and a more optimistic appraisal of "cosmopolitan professionals as urban leaders" (incremental changes by more numerous city managers willing to engage in skilled political influence may offer more promise for solving urban problems than "heroic mayoral leadership" by popularly elected officials [pp. 401 ff.]). Note that even in proceeding beyond the rediscovery of "mayoral leadership" in American politics, Wolfinger still retains the idea of "leadership" by "cosmopolitan professionals."

38. Richard C. Snyder, "A Decision-making Approach to the Study of Political Phenomena," in Roland Young, ed., *Approaches to the Study of Politics* (Evanston: Northwestern University Press, 1958), pp. 3–38.

39. Richard C. Snyder, Henry W. Bruck, and Burton M. Sapin, *Decision-making as an Approach to the Study of International Politics,* Foreign Policy Analysis Series, no. 3 (Princeton: Princeton University, 1954). This was later published with some added material by the same authors as *Foreign Policy Decision Making* (New York: Free Press, 1962).

40. Snyder et al., *Foreign Policy Decision Making,* p. 90.

41. Richard C. Snyder and Glenn D. Paige, "The United States Decision to Resist Aggression in Korea: The Application of an Analytical Scheme," *Administrative Science Quarterly* 3, 3 (December 1958), 341–378.

42. Ibid., p. 355.

43. Karl W. Deutsch, *The Nerves of Government: Models of Political Communication and Control* (New York: Free Press, 1963).

44. Ibid., p. xxvii.

45. Ibid., p. 254.

46. Ibid., p. 36.

47. Ibid., p. 116.

48. Ibid., pp. 159–160.

49. Ibid., pp. 163–165.

50. Ibid., p. 179.

51. Ibid., p. 189.

52. Ibid., p. 190.

53. Ibid., p. 166.

54. Ibid., p. 208.

55. David A. Easton, *The Political System* (New York: Knopf, 1953).

56. Ibid., p. 143.

57. Ibid., p. 145.

58. Ibid., p. 146.

59. Harold D. Lasswell, *Power and Personality* (New York: Norton, 1948).

60. Ibid., p. 123.

61. Harold D. Lasswell, *Politics: Who Gets What, When, How* (New York: McGraw-Hill, 1936).

62. Easton, op. cit., p. 121.

63. Ibid., p. 120.

64. Ibid., p. 121.

65. Ibid., pp. 120–121.

66. Ibid., p. 140.

67. Ibid., pp. 140–141. Easton based these authority types on the work of M. Fortes and E. E. Evans-Pritchard, eds., *African Political Systems* (London: Oxford University Press, 1940).

68. David A. Easton, *A Framework for Political Analysis* (Englewood Cliffs: Prentice-Hall, 1965).

69. Ibid., p. 115.

70. Ibid., pp. 116–117.

71. David A. Easton, *A Systems Analysis of Political Life* (New York: Wiley, 1965).

72. Ibid., pp. 302–307. Two other sources of legitimacy are taken to be "ideology" and "structure."

73. Ibid., p. 303, citing Talcott Parsons, ed., *Max Weber: The Theory of Social and Economic Organization* (New York: Oxford University Press, 1947), pp. 114–115.

74. Easton, *A Systems Analysis*, p. 304.

75. This usage is also implied by the reference to "political leaders in the role of the executive" (ibid., p. 97).

76. Ibid., pp. 87, 89, 91, 93, 95.

77. Ibid., p. 97, citing Lucian W. Pye, *Politics, Personality and Nation Building* (New Haven: Yale University Press, 1967), p. 43.

78. Easton, *A Systems Analysis*, pp. 205–211.

79. Ibid., p. 206.

80. Ibid., p. 30. The same diagram appears in Easton's *Framework of Political Analysis*, p. 110. Even accepting the inadequacy of two-dimensional diagrams to express thought, the predominant view of the behavior of the authorities as dependent variable is apparent. For two separate diagrams

that contrast political leadership as a dependent and independent variable see Dahl, *Modern Political Analysis,* pp. 109–110. For a diagram that suggests more adequately the idea of the dual independent-dependent potentialities of political leadership see Warren F. Ilchman and Norman Thomas Uphoff, *The Political Economy of Change* (Berkeley: University of California Press, 1971), pp. 43, 45.

81. Gabriel A. Almond and James S. Coleman, eds., *The Politics of the Developing Areas* (Princeton: Princeton University Press, 1960). Contributors include Lucian W. Pye, Myron Weiner, Dankwart A. Rustow, and George I. Blanksten.

82. Ibid., p. 3.

83. Lucian W. Pye, ed., *Communications and Political Development* (Princeton: Princeton University Press, 1963).

84. Joseph LaPalombara, ed., *Bureaucracy and Political Development* (Princeton: Princeton University Press, 1963).

85. Robert E. Ward and Dankwart A. Rustow, eds., *Political Modernization in Japan and Turkey* (Princeton: Princeton University Press, 1964).

86. James S. Coleman, ed., *Education and Political Development* (Princeton: Princeton University Press, 1965).

87. Lucian W. Pye and Sidney Verba, eds., *Political Culture and Political Development* (Princeton: Princeton University Press, 1965).

88. Joseph LaPalombara and Myron Weiner, eds., *Political Parties and Political Development* (Princeton: Princeton University Press, 1966).

89. Leonard Binder, James S. Coleman, Joseph LaPalombara, Lucian W. Pye, Sidney Verba, and Myron Weiner, *Crises and Sequences in Political Development* (Princeton: Princeton University Press, 1971).

90. Almond and Coleman, *Politics of the Developing Areas,* p. 7.

91. Ibid., p. 11.

92. Ibid., p. 17.

93. Ibid., p. 16.

94. Ibid., pp. 16–17.

95. Ibid., p. 16.

96. Ibid., p. 55.

97. Ibid., p. 16.

98. Ibid., p. 20.

99. Ibid., p. 24.

100. Ibid., p. 58.

101. Ibid., p. 18.

102. Ibid., p. 24.

103. Ibid., p. 47.

104. Ibid., p. 61.

105. Apparently, however, this concept was not explicitly pursued in Almond's later writings.

106. Gabriel A. Almond, "A Developmental Approach to Political Systems, *World Politics* 17, 2 (January 1965), 183–214.

107. Ibid., p. 183.

108. Ibid., p. 196.

109. Ibid., pp. 192–193. Drawing partly upon David A. Easton, "An Approach to the Analysis of Political Systems," *World Politics* 9, 3 (April 1957), 383–400, Almond specified four subcategories of demands (for "goods and services, regulation of behavior, participation, and symbolic behavior"). Four "support inputs" also were identified: "material, obedience, participation, and manifestation of deference."

110. Ibid., p. 195.

111. Ibid., p. 194.

112. Ibid., p. 210.

113. Ibid., pp. 210–211.

114. Gabriel A. Almond and Sidney Verba, *The Civic Culture* (Princeton: Princeton University Press, 1963).

115. Gabriel A. Almond and G. Bingham Powell, *Comparative Politics: A Developmental Approach* (Boston: Little, Brown, 1966).

116. Ibid., p. 325.

117. Ibid., p. 326.

118. Gabriel A. Almond, "Political Development: Analytical and Normative Perspectives," *Comparative Political Studies* 1, 4, (January 1969), 447–469.

119. Ibid., p. 454.

120. Ibid., p. 456.

121. Ibid., p. 462.

122. Ibid., p. 463.

123. Ibid., p. 464.

124. Ibid., p. 466.

125. Ibid.

126. Ilchman and Uphoff, op. cit.

127. Ibid., p. 3.

128. Ibid., p. 36.

129. Ibid., p. 38.

130. Ibid., p. 20.

131. Ibid., pp. 26–27.

132. Ibid., p. 315.

133. Ibid., p. 223.

134. See "Table of Infrastructure Inputs and Outputs," ibid., pp. 254–255, containing twenty-six rows of infrastructure elements and twenty-eight columns of cost-benefit categories.

135. Clemens Dutt, ed., *Fundamentals of Marxism-Leninism* (Moscow: Foreign

Languages Publishing House, 1961); see esp. "The Role of the Individual in History" (pp. 221-230).

136. Maurice Duverger, *Introduction à la politique* (Paris: Gallimard, 1964); trans. Robert North and Ruth Murphy as *The Idea of Politics* (Indianapolis: Bobbs-Merrill, 1966); see esp. pp. ix-xiv.

137. Neil MacDonald, *Politics: The Study of Control Behavior* (New Brunswick: Rutgers University Press, 1965).

138. Jean-Paul Sartre, *Search for a Method* (New York: Knopf, 1963); Lyle A. Downing, *Existentialist Political Theory* (Ph.D. 1965, University of California, Berkeley).

139. Giovanni Baldelli, *Social Anarchism* (Chicago: Aldine-Atherton, 1971); see "Analysis of Leadership" (pp. 80-82), which concludes, "Thus leadership leads inevitably to tyranny as fear takes the place of love."

140. Bernard Crick, *The American Science of Politics: Its Origins and Conditions* (Berkeley: University of California Press, 1959). A fresh review of the whole body of materials considered by Crick from a viewpoint implied by the question "What idea of political leadership is implied?" would now seem to be an enormously helpful contribution to disciplinary self-awareness. This should be done for other world intellectual traditions as well.

141. Ibid., p. 3.

142. Roland Young, ed., *Approaches to the Study of Politics: Twenty-two Contemporary Essays Exploring the Nature of Politics and Methods by Which It Can Be Explored* (Evanston: Northwestern University Press, 1958). No index included.

143. James C. Charlesworth, ed., *Contemporary Political Analysis* (New York: Free Press, 1967). No index reference to "leadership" alone, but a single reference to "mass leadership" is included.

144. E.g., Mulford Q. Sibley, "The Place of Classical Political Theory in the Study of Politics: The Legitimate Spell of Plato," in Young, op. cit., pp. 125-148.

145. Charlesworth, op. cit., p. 375, gives six index references to Plato.

146. Heinz Eulau and James G. March, eds., *Political Science* (Englewood Cliffs: Prentice-Hall, 1969), p. 2.

147. Ibid., pp. 143-144.

148. Harold D. Lasswell, *The Future of Political Science* (New York: Atherton, 1963).

149. Especially suggestive discussions related to the idea of leadership, the behavior of leaders, political scientists as political leaders, research problems in leadership studies, and problems of relationships between political scientists and political leaders may be found in ibid., pp. 19, 22, 33 f., 36, 38, 47-64, 99 f., 127-130, 151 f., 159, 171, 175, 180, 182-185, 213 f., 233 f.

150. Ibid., p. 13.

151. An outline of Lasswell's basic conceptual framework is in ibid., p. 83.

152. Ibid., p. 36.

153. Ibid., p. 19.

154. Ibid., p. 171.

155. Harold D. Lasswell, *Power and Personality* (New York: Norton, 1948), pp. 108–147; see also chap. 8, "Leadership Principles: Reduce Provocation," and chap. 9, "Leadership Principles: Act Positively."

156. Robert H. Connery, ed., *Teaching Political Science: Challenge to Higher Education* (Durham: Duke University Press, 1965). The delightfully scathing and erudite essay by Lindsay Rogers should not be missed.

157. Paul Tillet, "Teaching and Creative Citizenship," in Donald H. Riddle and Robert E. Cleary, eds., *Political Science in the Social Studies* (Washington: National Council for the Social Studies, 1966), p. 293.

158. Bernard C. Hennessy, *Political Internships: Theory, Practice, Evaluation* (University Park: Pennsylvania State University Press, 1970).

159. Ibid., pp. 43, 44, 47.

160. E.g., Harold Zink, *City Bosses in the United States* (Durham: Duke University Press, 1930); J. T. Salter, *Boss Rule: Portraits in City Politics* (New York: McGraw-Hill, 1935).

Chapter 3. Contributions to an Emerging Field

1. Dankwart A. Rustow, ed., *Philosophers and Kings: Studies in Leadership*, entire issue of *Daedalus* 97, 3 (Summer 1968), 687.

2. Jasper B. Shannon, "The Study of Political Leadership," in Jasper B. Shannon, ed., *The Study of Comparative Government* (New York: Greenwood, 1949). Interestingly, Shannon's 1934 Ph.D. dissertation, University of Wisconsin, is entitled *Henry Clay as a Political Leader*.

3. Lester G. Seligman, "The Study of Political Leadership," *APSR* 44, 4 (December 1950), 904–915.

4. Charles E. Merriam, *Four American Party Leaders* (1926, reprint ed., Freeport: Books for Libraries, 1967), pp. 100–101. Interestingly, Merriam did not cite Plutarch even though his final chapter, "Comparisons," compares the personal qualities of Lincoln, Theodore Roosevelt, Woodrow Wilson, and William Jennings Bryan.

5. A brief autobiography can be found in Charles E. Merriam, *Systematic Politics* (Chicago: University of Chicago Press, 1966), pp. x–xi. A long-needed, full-scale biography is Barry D. Karl, *Charles E. Merriam and the Study of Politics* (Chicago: University of Chicago Press, 1974).

6. Woodrow Wilson, *Leaders of Men*, ed. T. Vail Motter (Princeton: Princeton University Press, 1952), and Wilson's little-known biography, *George Washington* (New York: Harper, 1897).

7. T. V. Smith, *A Non-existent Man: An Autobiography* (Austin: University of Texas Press, 1962); see esp. the lighthearted "A Philosopher Turns to Politics," pp. 73–99, and the more sober "What Was I Up To in Politics,

Anyhow," pp. 100-120. Remarkable reflections of a former student and a lifelong friend of Charles E. Merriam's, with much information about the University of Chicago's tradition of political involvement.

8. Stephen A. Bailey, "A Structural Interaction Pattern for Harpsichord and Kazoo," *Public Administration Review* 14, 3 (1954), 202-204. An experienced professor-mayor delightfully suggests the contrast between classroom and City Hall.

9. E.g., see the section on "leadership" in Merriam, *Systematic Politics*, pp. 107-112.

10. Shannon, op. cit., p. 314.

11. Ibid., pp. 327-328.

12. Ibid., p. 330.

13. Seligman, op. cit., p. 904.

14. Ibid., p. 907.

15. Among major contributions to this debate are William James, "Great Men, Great Thoughts, and the Environment," *Atlantic Monthly* 46, 276 (October 1880), 441-459; Thomas Carlyle, *On Heroes, Hero Worship and the Heroic in History*, ed. Carl Niemeyer (Lincoln: University of Nebraska Press, 1966); "The Role of the Individual in History," in Clemens Dutt, ed., *Fundamentals of Marxism-Leninism* (Moscow: Foreign Languages Publishing House, 1961), pp. 221-230; and Sidney Hook, *The Hero in History: A Study in Limitation and Possibility* (Boston: Beacon, 1962).

16. Seligman, op. cit., p. 914. Compare the formulation of Cecil A. Gibb, "Leadership," in Gardner Lindzey and Elliot Aronson, eds., *Handbook of Social Psychology*, 5 vols. (Reading: Addison-Wesley, 1968-1969), 4:205-282: "Leadership is an interactional phenomenon, and an interaction theory is required to provide a framework for studies of leadership" (p. 273).

17. Seligman, op. cit., p. 914. Compare Maurice Duverger's formulation in *Introduction à la politique* (Paris: Gallimard, 1964), p. 27: "Le combat politique se déroule sur deux plans: d'un côté entre des hommes, des groupes et de classes, qui luttent pout conquérir, partager ou influencer le pouvoir; de l'autre, entre le pouvoir qui commande et les citoyens qui lui résistent" (The political struggle develops on two planes: the one, among individuals, groups, and classes who compete to gain, share, or influence power; and the other, between the power that commands and the citizens who resist).

18. Seligman, op. cit., p. 915.

19. Ibid.

20. Letter from Lester G. Seligman, February 18, 1974.

21. Harold F. Gosnell, *Negro Politicians: The Rise of Negro Politics in Chicago* (Chicago: University of Chicago Press, 1935).

22. Harold F. Gosnell, *Machine Politics: Chicago Model,* 2d ed. (Chicago: University of Chicago Press, 1968).

23. Heinz Eulau, Samuel Eldersveld, and Morris Janowitz, eds., *Political Behavior: A Reader in Theory and Research* (New York: Free Press, 1956).

24. John H. Kessel, George F. Cole, and Robert G. Seddig, eds., *Micropolitics: Individual and Group Level Concepts* (New York: Holt, Rinehart & Winston, 1970).

25. Gaetano Mosca, *The Ruling Class* (New York: McGraw-Hill, 1939); first published in Italian in 1896.

26. Vilfredo Pareto, *The Rise and Fall of Elites* (Totowa: Bedminster, 1968); first published in 1901 as "Un applicazione di teorie sociologiche," *Revista Italiana di sociologia*, 402–456.

27. Robert Michels, *Political Parties: A Sociological Study of the Oligarchical Tendencies of Modern Democracy*, trans. Eden and Cedar Paul (New York: Free Press, 1966); first published in 1915.

28. C. Wright Mills, *The Power Elite* (New York: Oxford University Press, 1956).

29. Harold D. Lasswell, Daniel Lerner, and C. Easton Rothwell, *The Comparative Study of Elites: An Introduction and Bibliography* (Stanford: Stanford University Press, 1952).

30. Donald R. Matthews, *The Social Background of Political Decision Makers* (New York: Random House, 1954).

31. Dwaine Marvick, ed., *Political Decision Makers* (New York: Free Press, 1961).

32. Carl Beck and Thomas McKechnie, *Political Elites: A Select Computerized Bibliography* (Cambridge: MIT Press, 1968).

33. Geraint Parry, *Political Elites* (New York: Praeger, 1969).

34. Donald D. Searing, "The Comparative Study of Elite Socialization," *Comparative Political Studies* 1, 4 (January 1969), 471–500.

35. John Kingdon's *Candidates for Office: Beliefs and Strategies* (New York: Random House, 1966) stimulated a critical series of comparative studies about the perceived effects of party, issues, and candidates on winning and losing. For delightful essays on defeated candidates for the American presidency, see Irving Stone, *They Also Ran* (New York: Doubleday, 1966).

36. Sidney Verba, *Small Groups and Political Behavior: A Study in Leadership* (Princeton: Princeton University Press, 1961).

37. Chester I. Barnard, *The Functions of the Executive* (Cambridge: Harvard University Press, 1938).

38. Richard E. Neustadt, *Presidential Power: The Politics of Leadership* (New York: Wiley, 1960).

39. Harlan Cleveland, *The Future Executive* (New York: Harper & Row, 1972).

40. Harold D. Lasswell, *Psychopathology and Politics* (Chicago: University of Chicago Press, 1930).

41. Harold D. Lasswell, *Power and Personality* (New York: Norton, 1948).

42. Alexander L. George and Juliette L. George, *Woodrow Wilson and Colonel House* (New York: Day, 1956).

43. E. Victor Wolfenstein, *The Revolutionary Personality: Lenin, Trotsky, Gandhi* (Princeton: Princeton University Press, 1967).

44. Alex Gottfried, *Boss Cermak of Chicago* (Seattle: University of Washington Press, 1962).

45. James D. Barber, *The Lawmakers* (New Haven: Yale University Press, 1965).

46. James D. Barber, *Power in Committees* (Chicago: Rand McNally, 1966).

47. James D. Barber, *The Presidential Character: Predicting Performance in the White House* (Englewood Cliffs: Prentice-Hall, 1972).

48. Robert C. Tucker, *Stalin as Revolutionary, 1879–1929* (New York: Norton, 1973).

49. Lester G. Seligman, "Elite Recruitment and Political Development," *Journal of Politics* 26, 3 (August 1964), 612–626.

50. Lester G. Seligman, *Leadership in a New Nation: Political Development in Israel* (New York: Atherton, 1964).

51. Lester G. Seligman, *Recruiting Political Elites* (New York: General Learning Press, 1971).

52. Lester G. Seligman, Michael R. King, Chong Lim Kim, and Roland E. Smith, *Patterns of Recruitment: A State Chooses Its Lawmakers* (Chicago: Rand McNally, 1974).

53. Joseph A. Schlesinger, *Ambition and Politics: Political Careers in the United States* (Chicago: Rand McNally, 1966).

54. Kenneth Prewitt, *The Recruitment of Political Leaders* (Indianapolis: Bobbs-Merrill, 1970).

55. Fred I. Greenstein, *Children and Politics* (New Haven: Yale University Press, 1969).

56. Lester Milbrath, *Political Participation* (Chicago: Rand McNally, 1965).

57. John C. Wahlke, Heinz Eulau, William Buchanan, and Leroy C. Ferguson, *The Legislative System: Explorations in Legislative Behavior* (New York: Wiley, 1962).

58. Angus Campbell et al., *The American Voter* (New York: Wiley, 1960).

59. James MacGregor Burns, *Roosevelt: The Lion and the Fox* (New York: Harcourt, Brace, 1956).

60. Alexander L. George, *The "Operational Code": A Neglected Approach to the Study of Political Leaders and Decision Making* (Santa Monica: Rand Corporation, 1967).

61. Howard W. Wriggins, *The Ruler's Imperative: Strategies for Political Survival in Asia and Africa* (New York: Columbia University Press, 1969).

62. David A. Apter, *The Politics of Modernization* (Chicago: University of Chicago Press, 1965). This work is noteworthy for the explicit attention devoted to leadership in the various political systems that are identified.

63. Floyd Hunter, *Community Power Structure: A Study of Decision Makers* (Chapel Hill: University of North Carolina Press, 1953).

64. Robert A. Dahl, *Who Governs?* (New Haven: Yale University Press, 1961).

65. Robert A. Agger, Daniel Goodrich, and Bert E. Swanson, *The Rulers and the Ruled* (New York: Wiley, 1964).

66. Burns, op. cit., pp. 481-487.

67. Lewis J. Edinger, "Political Science and Political Biography: Reflections on the Study of Leadership (I)," *Journal of Politics* 26, 2 (May 1964), 423-439; idem, "Political Science and Political Biography (II)," *Journal of Politics* 26, 3 (August 1964), 648-676.

68. Edinger, "Political Science and Political Biography (I)," p. 428.

69. Ibid., p. 429.

70. Ibid., p. 430.

71. Ibid., p. 438.

72. Edinger, "Political Science and Political Biography (II)," p. 653.

73. Ibid., p. 653.

74. Neal Gross, Ward S. Mason, and Alexander W. McEachern, *Explorations in Role Analysis: Studies of the School Superintendency Role* (New York: Wiley, 1958).

75. Compare Clinton Rossiter, *The American Presidency* (New York: Harcourt, Brace, 1960), which examines this particular role in a way that is reminiscent of role-sector analysis but that is not, intended to be an approach to the analysis of other leadership positions.

76. Lewis J. Edinger, *Kurt Schumacher: A Study in Personality and Political Behavior* (Stanford: Stanford University Press, 1965).

77. Lewis J. Edinger, *Political Leadership in Industrialized Societies* (New York: Wiley, 1967).

78. Lewis J. Edinger, "The Comparative Analysis of Political Leadership," *Comparative Politics* 17, 2 (January 1975), 253-269.

79. Ibid., p. 267.

80. Robert A. Dahl, "The Concept of Power," *Behavioral Science* 2, 3 (July 1957), 201-215.

81. James G. March, "An Introduction to the Theory and Measurement of Influence," *APSR* 49, 2 (June 1955), 431-451; idem, "Measurement Concepts in the Theory of Influence," *Journal of Politics* 19, 2 (May 1957), 202-226.

82. Edinger, "Comparative Analysis," pp. 256, 258-260.

83. Ibid., p. 266.

84. Rustow, op. cit. Among the contributors are political scientists David E. Apter, James D. Barber, Stanley Hoffmann, Henry A. Kissinger, and Robert C. Tucker; historians Barry D. Karl, Frank E. Manuel, and Bruce Mazlish; economist Albert O. Hirschman; psychologist Inge Schneier Hoffmann; and English literature professor Cushing Stout.

85. Ibid., p. 683.

86. Karl W. Deutsch, John Platt, and Dieter Senghaas, "Conditions Favoring Major Advances in Social Science," *Science,* February 5, 1971, pp. 450-459.

87. Rustow, op. cit., p. 688.

88. Ibid., pp. 683-684. Norman Meller has suggested adding "under what circumstances or constraints."

89. Ibid., p. 685.

90. For example, see the more than 1,200 bibliographical items cited in Bernard Bass, *Leadership, Psychology, and Organizational Behavior* (New York: Harper, 1960), and the 3,000 items covered in the extraordinary survey of the experimental and theoretical literature on leadership by Ralph Stogdill, *Handbook of Leadership* (New York: Free Press, 1974).

91. Wahlke et al., op. cit.

92. Samuel Eldersveld, *Political Parties: A Behavioral Analysis* (Chicago: Rand McNally, 1964).

93. Rustow, op. cit., p. 687.

94. Edinger, "Political Science and Political Biography (I)," p. 423.

95. Rustow, op. cit., p. 687. An example of this process of "rediscovery" and progression to a focus upon political leadership can be found in Glenn D. Paige, "The Rediscovery of Politics," in John D. Montgomery and William J. Siffin, eds., *Approaches to Development: Politics, Administration and Change* (New York: McGraw-Hill, 1966), pp. 49-58; idem, "Some Implications for Political Science of the Comparative Politics of Korea," in Fred W. Riggs, ed., *Frontiers of Development Administration* (Durham: Duke University Press, 1970), pp. 139-168, reprinted from an article first published in Korea in 1966. See Asiatic Research Center, Korea University, *International Conference on the Problems of Modernization in Asia, June 28-July 7, 1965: Report* (Seoul: Asiatic Research Center, Korea University, 1966), pp. 388-411. Compare an earlier discovery of the causal significance of monarchs that arose from a study of Portuguese history as reported by Frederick Adams Woods, *The Influence of Monarchs* (New York: Macmillan, 1913), p. 87.

96. Max Weber, "Politics as a Vocation," in H. H. Gerth and C. Wright Mills, eds., *From Max Weber: Essays in Sociology* (New York: Oxford University Press, 1958), p. 77. Two paragraphs later Weber seems to imply the equation of "leadership" with "power": "Hence 'politics' for us means striving to share power or striving to influence the distribution of power, either among states or among groups within a state" (p. 78).

97. Talcott Parsons, *Sociological Theory in Modern Society* (New York: Free Press, 1967), p. 262.

98. Rustow, op. cit., p. 689.

99. Jeffrey L. Pressman, "Preconditions of Mayoral Leadership," *APSR* 66, 2 (June 1972), 511-524. Other articles with title references to "leadership" that appeared during 1963-1974 are Lewis A. Froman, Jr., and Randall B. Ripley, "Conditions for Party Leadership: The Case of the House Democrats," *APSR* 59, 1 (March 1965), 52-63; Robert L. Peabody, "Party

Leadership Change in the United States House of Representatives," *APSR* 61, 3 (September 1967), 675–693; and Dean Jaros, Herbert Hirsch, and Frederick J. Fleron, Jr., "The Malevolent Leader: Political Socialization in an American Sub-culture," *APSR* 62, 2 (June 1968), 564–575.

100. George T. Force, Jack R. Van Der Slik, and Charles Dewitt Dunn, *Theory and Research in the Study of Political Leadership* (Carbondale: Southern Illinois University, Public Affairs Research Bureau, 1972); others who assisted were Donald Gregory, Willis M. Hubbard, and Jack D. Parson. The categories employed as organizational devices for this bibliography were "the concept of leadership—theoretical orientations; the context and necessity for leadership; the scope of power, influence, and authority of leaders; role theory and the analysis of leaders; leadership styles (bureaucratic and charismatic, situations and personality variables); leadership recruitment; and studies of political leadership."

101. Participating colleagues included James D. Barber, Lewis J. Edinger, A. J. Wann, and Andrew McFarland.

102. Kenneth F. Janda, "Toward the Explication of the Concept of Leadership in Terms of the Concept of Power," *Human Relations* 13, 4 (1960), 345–363.

103. Verba, op. cit., chap. 5.

104. James C. Davies, *Human Nature in Politics* (New York: Wiley, 1963), chap. 9; among other important insights, Davies's sketch of the "charismatic follower" (p. 300) ought to be pursued further.

105. Carl J. Friedrich, *Man and His Government* (New York: McGraw-Hill, 1963), chap. 9; see also chap. 10, "Rule and Rulership."

106. Dankwart A. Rustow, *A World of Nations* (Washington: Brookings Institution, 1967), chap. 5.

107. Léon Dion, "The Concept of Political Leadership: An Analysis," *Canadian Journal of Political Science* 1 (March 1968), 1–17. Interestingly and foresightfully, the inaugural issue of this journal was devoted to the subject of political leadership. Dion called for scientific use of the "rich biographic information" provided by historians.

108. Ann Ruth Wilner, *Charismatic Political Leadership: A Theory* (Princeton: Princeton University, Center of International Studies, 1968).

109. Donald D. Searing, "Models and Images of Man and Society in Leadership Theory," *Journal of Politics* 31, 1 (February 1969), 3–31.

110. James V. Downton, Jr., *Rebel Leadership: Commitment and Charisma in the Revolutionary Process* (New York: Free Press, 1973), chaps. 1 and 2.

111. See the following papers presented at the 1973 Annual Meeting of the American Political Science Association, New Orleans: Fred I. Greenstein, "Children's Images of Political Leaders in Three Democracies: The Benevolent Leader Revisited"; Paul L. Hain and Terry B. Smith, "Congressional Challengers for the Office of Governor"; Charles S. Bullock III, "Candidate Perceptions of Causes of Election Outcome"; M. Margaret Conway and Frank B. Feigert, "Motivations and Task Performance among Party Precinct Workers"; Elizabeth Wirth Marvick, "Personality and Decision-

making: A Psychoanalytic Application to the Reign of Louis XIII and Richelieu"; and Loch Johnson, "Operational Codes and the Prediction of Leadership Behavior: Senator Frank Church at Mid-Career."

112. Daniel Katz, "Patterns of Leadership," in Jeanne N. Knutson, ed., *Handbook of Political Psychology* (San Francisco: Jossey-Bass, 1973), pp. 203–233. Arguing that "we cannot divorce the study of political leadership from the study of social structure" (p. 222), Katz called attention to "(1) degree of formal role structure; (2) relative autonomy or dependence of system in which leadership is exercised; (3) the mix of primary and secondary relationships; (4) the totalitarian versus the democratic character of the authority structure; [and] (5) position of the leader in the hierarchical structure" (p. 232). This is an important essay, to which students of political leadership repeatedly will return.

113. Comparative Research on Events of Nations (CREON) project, involving scholars from Drew University, the University of Kentucky, Ohio State University, Rutgers University, and Vanderbilt University.

114. Gabriel A. Almond, Scott C. Flanagan, and Robert J. Mundt, eds., *Crisis, Choice, and Change: Historical Studies in Development* (Boston: Little, Brown, 1973).

115. Ibid., p. 17.

116. Ibid.

117. Ibid.

118. Ibid., p. 18.

119. Ibid., pp. 18–19.

120. Ibid., p. 19. Interestingly, the idea of attempting to relate leadership to the categories of "probabilistic functionalism" was not extensively considered. This effort, however, has been begun by Downton in *Rebel Leadership.* Interestingly also, the contributions of Richard C. Snyder to a decision-making approach to political analysis, dating from 1954, are not recognized in the extensive references to "approaches to development causation."

121. Almond et al., op. cit., p. 19.

122. Ibid., p. 20.

123. Ibid., pp. 20, 26, 33.

124. Downton's *Rebel Leadership* is discussed more fully at the end of Chapter 4.

125. Taketsugu Tsurutani, *The Politics of National Development: Political Leadership in Transitional Societies* (San Francisco: Chandler, 1973); see esp. pp. 96–113.

126. See ibid., pp. 101–109, for explanation and measurement of Tsurutani's main theoretical view: $M = [(C \times 2I \times D)/S] \div 2$, where C is a "commitment" score, I is an "intelligence and skill" score, D is a "dominance" score, S is a "situational" score, and M is a "periodic index of modernization." The formula appears on page 107.

127. Paul R. Dettman, "Leaders and Structures in 'Third World' Politics," *Comparative Politics* 6, 2 (January 1974), 245–269.

128. Robert S. Byars, "Small Group Theory and Shifting Styles of Political Leadership," *Comparative Political Studies* 5, 4 (January 1973), 443–469.

129. C. L. Sulzberger, "Leadership Crisis," *Honolulu Star-Bulletin,* April 1, 1974, p. A-12. Wrote Sulzberger of Richard Nixon, "On May 19, 1969, the President told me the U.S. was suffering from a 'leadership crisis.' " Compare also the statement of Senate majority leader Mike Mansfield in a CBS radio interview on April 7, 1975: "The American people cry out for leadership."

130. Among indicators of the mood of the times later students might wish to consult Charles Reich, *The Greening of America* (New York: Random House, 1970), for the spirit of reform; William Watts and Lloyd A. Free, eds., *State of the Nation* (New York: Universe, 1973), for sample survey evidence of basic American conservatism; Robert S. Gilmour and Robert B. Lamb, *Political Alienation in Contemporary America* (New York: St. Martin's, 1975); and Alvin Toffler, *Future Shock* (New York: Random House, 1970), for an interpretation in terms of accelerating social change.

131. Bernard Crick, *The American Science of Politics: Its Origins and Conditions* (Berkeley: University of California Press, 1959), p. 36.

132. Gordon J. DiRenzo, "Politicians and Personality: A Cross-cultural Perspective," in Margaret G. Hermann, ed., *A Psychological Examination of Political Leaders* (New York: Free Press, 1977), compares Italian and American leaders and nonleaders.

133. Robert D. Putnam, *The Beliefs of Politicians: Ideology, Conflict, and Democracy in Britain and Italy* (New Haven: Yale University Press, 1973).

134. Ralph M. Stogdill, *Handbook of Leadership: A Survey of Theory and Research* (New York: Free Press, 1974).

135. Hermann, op. cit.

136. John P. Kotter and Paul R. Lawrence, *Mayors in Action* (New York: Wiley, 1975).

Chapter 4. Alternative Sources of Conceptualization

1. Charles E. Merriam, *Systematic Politics* (Chicago: University of Chicago Press, 1966), p. 107; first published in 1945.

2. Princeton sociologist Marion J. Levy, Jr., first introduced me to this very useful basic social science insight in a freshman sociology course.

3. This point has been made most elegantly in contemporary social science by Donald T. Campbell and Donald W. Fiske, "Convergent and Discriminant Validation by the Multi-trait Multi-method Matrix," *Psychological Bulletin* 56, 2 (March 1959), 81–105.

4. Maurice Duverger, *The Idea of Politics,* trans. Robert North and Ruth Murphy (Indianapolis: Bobbs-Merrill, 1966), p. 20.

5. "Every Communist must grasp the truth: 'Political power comes out of the barrel of a gun.' Our principle is that the party commands the gun, and the

gun will never be allowed to command the party" (Mao Tse-tung, "Problems of War and Strategy," *Selected Works,* 5 vols. [New York: International Publishers, 1954], 2:272. The Chinese phrase is "ch'iang-kan-tze li-mien ch'u cheng-ch'üan" (*Mao Tse-tung hsüan chi* [Peking: Jen-min ch'u-pan she, 1952], p. 535).

6. The possibility that certain technologies may profoundly affect thinking about political leadership was suggested by Marjorie Nicolson's study of the early impact of the telescope and microscope upon poetic and literary imagination: "As Milton produced a new kind of cosmic poetry, a drama of interstellar space which could not have been composed before the telescope, so *Gulliver's Travels* could not have been written before the period of the microscope nor by a man who had not felt both the fascination and the repulsion of a new Nature shown by the new instrument" (Nicolson, *Science and Imagination* [Ithaca: Cornell University Press, 1962], pp. 193–194). Possibly, the electronic computer and new capabilities for biological engineering will bring new macroscopic and microscopic perspectives to thought about political leadership.

7. Experience in first asking simply what terms different languages would use to translate the English "political leadership" and then asking for cultural interpretations of these and related terms has shown how much cross-cultural variation exists. We have done this crudely in graduate seminars in Hawaii where native speakers of a half dozen different Asian and Pacific languages participated. It is hoped that future students of comparative political linguistics will take up the study of terms related to the idea of "political leadership" in a systematic way.

8. John Kemeny has explained that the mathematics of future social science will be more complex than the mathematics of today's physics because of the greater complexity of human behavior. John G. Kemeny, "Mathematics without Numbers," in Daniel Lerner, ed., *Quantity and Quality* (New York: Free Press, 1961), p. 37. Therefore, I am not discouraged by the modest achievements of contemporary mathematical applications in political science and am hopeful that better communication and mutual support can be established between mathematical and nonmathematical political scientists so that the emergent models will be both creatively rigorous and empirically applicable.

9. Examples of wide-ranging interview methods to probe belief systems that can be applied to the concept of political leadership are Bernice Eiduson, *Scientists: Their Psychological Worlds* (New York: Basic Books, 1962); Robert E. Lane, *Political Ideology* (New York: Free Press, 1962); Robert D. Putnam, *The Beliefs of Politicians* (New Haven: Yale University Press, 1973); and Studs Terkel, *Working* (New York: Pantheon, 1974).

10. Quoted in Arthur Larson, *Eisenhower: The President Nobody Knew* (New York: Popular Library, 1968), p. 21. Larson specifies five techniques of influence: "persuasion," "patronage," "pork-barrel," "purge," and "propaganda" (p. 33).

11. "It takes a leader to put economic, military, and government forces to work so they will operate" (Harry S Truman, *Memoirs,* 2 vols. [Garden City: Doubleday, 1958], vol. 1, *Year of Decisions,* p. 139.)

12. Response to a question asking Muñoz Marín to compare being a poet and a politician; the question was asked following a lecture at Princeton University, April 21, 1965. The former governor of Puerto Rico replied that the essential quality of both is "imagination" but that the political leader has the additional quality noted above. See also a biography by Thomas Aitken, Jr., *Poet in the Fortress* (New York: New American Library, 1965).

13. Eldon H. Barlow, participating in a discussion of women's rights, as reported in the *Honolulu Star-Bulletin*, January 25, 1973.

14. *Pacific Islands Monthly*, December 1975, p. 8. Statement made by Heinrich Iriarte during the 1975 Micronesian Constitutional Convention.

15. This slogan, "Kung-jen chieh-chi ling-tao i-ch'ieh," has frequently appeared on the front page of the Peking *Jen-min jih-pao (People's Daily)*.

16. Quoted in Louis Fischer, *The Life of Lenin* (New York: Harper, 1965), p. 377.

17. Mohandas K. Gandhi, "Indian Home Rule," in Paul E. Sigmund, Jr., ed., *Ideologies of the Developing Nations* (New York: Praeger, 1963), p. 84.

18. Mohandas K. Gandhi, *Non-violent Resistance* (New York: Schocken, 1951), p. 139.

19. Quoted in Robert Scheer, ed., *The Diary of Ché Guevara* (New York: Bantam, 1968), p. 154.

20. Eric Sevareid, reporter, "Five Presidents on the Presidency," CBS Television News Special, April 26, 1973, transcript, p. 5.

21. Adolph Hitler, *Mein Kampf* (London, 1939), p. 110, quoted in Alan Bullock, *Hitler: A Study in Tyranny* (New York: Harper, Torchbooks, 1964), p. 45.

22. Hitler, speaking at Chemnitz, April 2, 1928, quoted in Bullock, op. cit., p. 36.

23. Quoted in Bullock, op. cit., p. 69, quoting *Mein Kampf*, p. 474.

24. Lenin, *"Left Wing" Communism, an Infantile Disorder* (New York, 1940), p. 35, quoted in Alfred G. Meyer, *Leninism* (New York: Praeger, 1962), p. 41.

25. The famous Chinese phrase is "wei jen-min fu-wu" (Mao Tse-tung, "Serve the People," *Selected Works*, 4:219–220). A fuller discussion of Mao's leadership principles, including the idea of "from the masses to the masses," is "On Methods of Leadership," ibid., pp. 111–117.

26. Governor John A. Burns's farewell address to the Hawaii state legislature, "Aloha and Mahalo," April 11, 1972.

27. Paul H. Nitze, "The United States in the Face of the Communist Challenge," in C. Grove Haines, ed., *The Threat of Soviet Imperialism* (Baltimore: Johns Hopkins Press, 1954), p. 377. Although not an elected leader, Nitze is quoted because of his positional proximity to American leaders.

28. Simón Bolívar, writing after a defeat and quoted in Irene Nicholson, *The Liberators* (London: Faber & Faber, 1969), p. 165.

29. Mao Tse-tung, *Selected Works,* 4 vols. (Peking: Foreign Languages Publishing House, 1960), 4:15.

30. Merriam, op. cit., p. 104, cites C. Judson Herrick, *Neurological Foundations of Animal Behavior* (New York: Holt, 1924); William M. Wheeler, *Social Life among the Insects* (New York: Harcourt, Brace, 1923); and Alfred Espinas, *Des Sociétés animales* (Paris: Alcan, 1935).

31. Albert Somit, "Biopolitics," *British Journal of Political Science* 2, 2 (April 1972), 209–238.

32. D. O. Hebb and W. R. Thompson, "The Social Significance of Animal Studies," in Gardner Lindzey and Elliot Aronson, eds., *Handbook of Social Psychology,* 5 vols. (Reading: Addison-Wesley, 1968–1969), 2:729–774. See also Ralph M. Stogdill, "Leadership in Animal Societies," *Handbook of Leadership* (New York: Free Press, 1974), pp. 252–253.

33. Lionel Tiger and Robin Fox, *The Imperial Animal* (New York: Holt, Rinehart & Winston, 1971).

34. Among leading animal studies awaiting political science discovery are C. R. Carpenter, *Naturalistic Behavior of Nonhuman Primates* (University Park: Pennsylvania State University Press, 1964); Irven Devore, ed., *Primate Behavior* (New York: Holt, Rinehart & Winston, 1963); F. Fraser Darling, *A Herd of Red Deer* (Oxford: Clarendon, 1937); Karl von Frisch, *Bees: Their Vision, Chemical Senses and Language* (Ithaca: Cornell University Press, 1950); Niko Tinbergen, *The Herring Gull's World* (London: Collins, 1953); and W. M. Wheeler, *Social Life among the Insects* (New York: Harcourt, Brace, 1923). For an example of a contemporary, thoroughly exciting field experimental study with an explicit concern for leadership from a communication perspective see E. W. Menzel, Jr., "A Group of Young Chimpanzees in a One-Acre Field," in Allan M. Schrier and Fred Stollnitz, eds., *Behavior of Nonhuman Primates,* 5 vols. (New York: Academic Press, 1974), 5:83–153.

35. For a delightful example of an animal observational approach that offers some good lessons for politician watchers see Farley Mowat, *Never Cry Wolf* (New York: Dell, 1967); see also J. P. Scott, ed., "Methodology and Techniques for the Study of Animal Societies," *Annals of the New York Academy of Sciences* 51 (1950), 1001–1122.

36. Tiger and Fox, op. cit., p. 31. This is reminiscent of the "name recognition" publicity efforts of candidates for elected office in America.

37. Ibid., p. 39.

38. Ibid., p. 29.

39. Ibid.

40. Ibid., p. 46.

41. Darling, *A Herd of Red Deer,* pp. 82–83.

42. Gina Bari Kolata, "Primate Behavior: Sex and Male Dominance," *Science,* January 9, 1976, p. 222.

43. This distinction has been made in social science by P. J. W. Pigors, *Leadership or Domination* (Boston: Houghton Mifflin, 1935), and has been

introduced into political science thinking about leadership by Kenneth Janda, "Towards the Explication of the Concept of Leadership in Terms of the Concept of Power," *Human Relations* 13, 4 (November 1960), 345–363.

44. Jeannie C. Stewart and J. P. Scott, "Lack of Correlation between Leadership and Dominance Relations in a Herd of Goats," *Journal of Comparative and Physiological Psychology* 40, 4 (August 1947), 255–264.

45. Ibid., p. 264.

46. Bernard Greenberg, "Some Relations between Territory, Social Hierarchy, and Leadership in the Green Sunfish (Lepomis cyanellus)," *Physiological Zoology* 20, 3 (July 1947), 267–299. Greenberg found additionally that "hierarchy represents distinct levels of aggressiveness, whereas territoriality arises from a balance between almost equally aggressive individuals" (p. 298). The latter was found to be established sequentially by higher ranking individuals.

47. Konrad Z. Lorenz, "The Companion in the Birds' World," *Auk* 54, 3 (July 1937), 245–273; idem, *King Solomon's Ring* (London: Methuen, 1952).

48. Howard Moltz, "Imprinting: Empirical Basis and Theoretical Significance," *Psychological Bulletin* 57, 4 (July 1960), 291–314. For a recent view of the imprinting literature that discusses contextual, ethological, information-processing, and neuronal model interpretations, see D. W. Rajecki, "Imprinting in Precocial Birds: Interpretation, Evidence, and Evaluation," *Psychological Bulletin* 79, 1 (January 1973), 48–58, who advocates paying greater attention to physiological correlates.

49. Tiger and Fox, op. cit., p. 47.

50. Menzel, op. cit., pp. 115–116. Compare the description of Bandit's reactions with these lines from an anonymous poet in the era of Genghis Khan: "The land was emptied and I was a leader without followers; and it was part of my misery that I was alone in my leadership." The poem is quoted in John Andrew Boyle, trans., *The History of the World Conqueror* (Cambridge: Harvard University Press, 1958), p. 10. I am indebted to cultural historian William E. Henthorn for bringing these lines to my attention.

51. Menzel, op. cit., p. 117.

52. Karl von Frisch, *The Dance, Language and Orientation of Bees* (Cambridge: Harvard University Press, Belknap Press, 1967); see also a film von Frisch made in 1950, *The Dances of the Bees,* Austrian State Office of Education (22 mins.).

53. Clarence Ray Carpenter, "The Howlers of Barro Colorado Island," in Devore, op. cit., p. 290.

54. Charles H. Cooley, *Human Nature and the Social Order* (New York: Schocken, 1967), p. 328.

55. John Paul Scott, *Animal Behavior* (Chicago: University of Chicago Press, 1958), p. 18.

56. Ibid., p. 170.

57. Carpenter, op. cit., pp. 279, 286.

58. See, for example, the diagram in K. R. L. Hall and Irven Devore, "Baboon Social Behavior," in Devore, op. cit., p. 70, and the excellent 1963 film *Baboon Social Organization, Psychology Cinema Register* PCR-2133K (18 mins.). Some animal leaders, however, are not centrally placed in movement, such as the female red deer who precedes the hind group, assisted by another co-leader who brings up the rear. Darling, *A Herd of Red Deer*, pp. 69–71.

59. Scott, *Animal Behavior*, pp. 180–183; includes photographs.

60. Bernard Rudofsky, *Architecture without Architects* (New York: Doubleday, 1964), p. 133.

61. Fritz Redl, "Group Emotion and Leadership," *Psychiatry* 5, 4 (November 1942), 573–596.

62. Alex Bavelas, "Communications Patterns in Task Oriented Groups," in Daniel Lerner and Harold D. Lasswell, eds., *The Policy Sciences* (Stanford: Stanford University Press, 1951), pp. 193–202; H. J. Leavitt, "Some Effects of Certain Communication Patterns on Group Performance," *Journal of Abnormal and Social Psychology* 46, 1 (January 1951), 38–50. Subsequent literature is summarized in Stogdill, op. cit., pp. 255–259.

63. Neal Gross, Ward S. Mason, and Alexander W. McEachern, *Explorations in Role Analysis: Studies of the School Superintendency Role* (New York: Wiley, 1958).

64. Lewis J. Edinger, "Political Science and Political Biography (II)," *Journal of Politics* 26, 3 (August 1964), 653.

65. Glimpses of the potential resources of the humanities, fine arts, and performing arts for research, teaching, and service uses in political leadership studies can be gained from such works as Theodore J. Shank, ed., *A Digest of 500 Plays* (New York: Collier, 1967); Henry W. Simon, ed., *100 Great Operas and Their Stories* (Garden City: Doubleday, 1960); Henry M. Holland, Jr., ed., *Politics through Literature* (Englewood Cliffs: Prentice-Hall, 1968), which has a section explicitly devoted to "leadership"; Martin Bookspan, *101 Masterpieces of Music and Their Composers* (Garden City: Doubleday, 1973); Curt Sachs, *World History of the Dance* (New York: Norton, 1963); and Georges Sadoul, *Dictionary of Films* (Berkeley: University of California Press, 1972). Potentials for tracing images of political leaders in the humanities across time are suggested by James Emerson Phillips, *Images of a Queen: Mary Stuart in Sixteenth-Century Literature* (Berkeley: University of California Press, 1964).

66. E.g., Nigerian, *Queen Mother of Benin; Statue of Kim Il Sung* (Pyongyang Revolutionary Museum).

67. E.g., Georges Rouault, *The Old King;* Ilya Repin, *Ivan the Terrible and His Son Ivan.*

68. E.g., Shah Jahan's Taj Mahal; the Kremlin.

69. E.g., Aaron Copland, *A Lincoln Portrait*; Chinese, *Long Live Chairman Mao.*

70. E.g., Eugene Loring, *Harlequin for President* (1936); Janine Charrat, *Le Leader* (1957).

71. E.g., Sophocles, *Oedipus the King;* Francis Williams, *Portrait of a Queen.*

72. E.g., Sergei Eisenstein, *Ivan the Terrible* (1944, 1946); Preston Sturges, *The Great McGinty* (1950).

73. E.g., Modest Moussorgsky, *Boris Godunov;* Henry Purcell, *Dido and Aeneas.*

74. E.g., Oscar Brand, *How to Steal an Election: A Dirty Politics Musical;* Irving Berlin, *Fiorello!*

75. E.g., Yevgeny Yevtushenko, "Stalin's Heirs"; Walt Whitman, "O Captain! My Captain!"

76. Vaughn Meader, *The First Family,* Cadence Record CLP3060.

77. George Orwell, *Animal Farm* and *1984;* Edwin O'Connor, *The Last Hurrah.*

78. Henry W. Simon, op. cit., pp. 405-406.

79. E.g., Ward Just, *The Congressman Who Loved Flaubert* (Boston: Atlantic-Little, Brown, 1973); Tom Wicker, *Facing the Lions* (New York: Viking, 1973); Edward Stewart, *They've Shot the President's Daughter!* (Garden City: Doubleday, 1973).

80. E.g., John V. Lindsay, *The Edge* (New York: Norton, 1976); Spiro T. Agnew, *The Canfield Decision* (Chicago: Playboy Press, 1976).

81. Christopher Frayling, ed., *Napoleon Wrote Fiction* (New York: St. Martin's, 1973).

82. Benjamin Disraeli Beaconsfield, *Coningsby* (New York: Century, 1904).

83. José Rizal, *The Lost Eden* (original title, *Noli Me Tangere*), trans. Léon Ma. Guerrero (New York: Norton, 1968); idem, *The Subversive* (original title, *El Filibusterismo*), trans. Léon Ma. Guerrero (Bloomington: Indiana University Press, 1962). Rizal was also a poet. See José Rizal, *Where Slaves There Are None,* trans. Alfredo S. Veloso (Manila: Asvel, 1961).

84. Winston S. Churchill, *Painting as Pastime* (New York: Cornerstone, 1965); Paul Scofield, narrator, "The Other World of Winston Churchill," Mercury Records SR-61033.

85. A forty-item exhibit of Hitler's architectural drawings was held at the New York Cultural Center in October 1970, including visions of future Germania, monuments, stadia, Berchtesgaden, and his bunker.

86. Mao Tse-tung, *Nineteen Poems* (Peking: Foreign Languages Press, 1958).

87. E.g., "Prayer for Peace," and Sebastian O. Mezu, *The Poetry of Leopold Sedar Senghor* (London: Heinemann, 1973).

88. E.g., King Kalakaua's "Hawaii Pono'i" (1874), anthem of the Hawaiian monarchy, written with the cooperation of Captain Henry Berger, bandmaster of the Royal Hawaiian Band. Some twentieth-century Hawaiian politicians campaigned by singing and dancing; e.g., Kauai's Alfred Alohikea, composer of "Hanohano Hanalei." See Samuel H. Elbert and Noelani Mahoe, eds., *Na Mele o Hawai'i Nei* (Honolulu: University Press of Hawaii, 1970), p. 41.

89. E.g., Prince Sihanouk's "Monique," "Phnom Penh," "Séduction," and "Amour sans espoir." From a tape recording provided to me by the Cambodian Ministry of Information in 1969.

90. In 1971 Heath, an organist and amateur conductor, conducted the London Symphony Orchestra in Sir Edward Elgar's *Cockraigne* Overture. "He's a real romantic extrovert," one violinist said; "there are a lot of directors better known than he whose direction is not so good" (*Honolulu Advertiser,* November 26, 1971, p. A-9).

91. The world premiere of Manglapus's *Manifest Destiny* was performed by a faculty-student group at the University of Hawaii on July 6, 1974, with political science department chairman Robert Cahill in the role of Theodore Roosevelt.

92. Stephen W. Roskill, *The Art of Leadership* (London: Collins, 1964), p. 92.

93. Quoted in Herbert L. Matthews, *Fidel Castro* (New York: Simon & Schuster, Clarion, 1970), p. 341.

94. "On Reading 'Anthology of a Thousand Poets,' " in Ho Chi Minh, *Prison Diary,* trans. Aileen Palmer (Hanoi: Foreign Languages Publishing House, 1967), p. 100.

95. Quoted in Bernard B. Fall, ed., *Ho Chi Minh on Revolution* (New York: New American Library, Signet, 1967), p. 169.

96. A potential vocabulary for a concept of political leadership as art is contained in Mervyn Levy, ed., *The Pocket Dictionary of Art Terms* (Greenwich: New York Graphic Society, 1964).

97. During an informal discussion at the Center for Advanced Studies in the Behavioral Sciences, Palo Alto, California, in the mid-1950s, Herman Finer was asked how he defined the core concern of politics after a lifetime of study. He replied, as I recall, "I study the death-dealing power of the state."

98. T'ung-tsu Ch'ü, *Law and Society in Ancient China* (Paris: Mouton, 1961).

99. Laurence Olivier, quoted from *On the Death of King George,* Caedmon Record TC 1003. The text quoted was transcribed from the record and should be heard rather than read.

100. Robert Hazel, "Light at Arlington," in *Of Poetry and Power: Poems Occasioned by the Presidency and by the Death of John F. Kennedy,* Folkways Record FL9721.

101. The psychiatrist Fritz Redl, op. cit., pp. 576-583 has suggested ten images of the emotional significance of leaders for groups: "patriarchal sovereign, teacher, tyrant, love object, object of aggression, organizer, seducer, hero, bad example, and good example."

102. Interestingly, the English word "leader" seems to have entered the French language in about 1829; the term "leadership" entered much later, in 1878. This raises a host of conceptual and cultural diffusion questions that should be pursued in the future conceptual elaboration of political leadership studies. For the dates and definitions see Paul Robert, *Dictionnaire française alphabétique 'et analogique de la langue (Le Petit Robert)* (Paris: Société du Nouveau Littré, 1972), p. 979.

103. Personal letter from Mme Charrat, March 4, 1975.

104. Plato, *Statesman,* ed. Martin Ostwald and trans. J. B. Skemp (Indianapolis: Bobbs-Merrill, 1957), p. 39.

105. Stogdill, op. cit.; Cecil A. Gibb, "Leadership," in Lindzey and Aronson, op. cit., 4:205–282; Bernard M. Bass, *Leadership, Psychology and Organizational Behavior* (New York: Harper, 1960), with a bibliography of 1,155 items; Fred E. Fiedler, "Leadership," General Learning Corporation Module (Morristown: General Learning Press, 1971).

106. Herbert S. Lewis, "Leaders and Followers: Some Anthropological Perspectives," Addison-Wesley Module in Anthropology no. 50 (Reading: Addison-Wesley, 1974).

107. Arnold S. Tannenbaum, "Leadership: Sociological Aspects," in David L. Sills, ed., *International Encyclopedia of the Social Sciences,* 17 vols. (New York: Macmillan and Free Press, 1968), 9:101–107; Wendell Bell et al., *Public Leadership* (San Francisco: Chandler, 1961).

108. Peter Kilby, comp., *Entrepreneurship and Economic Development* (New York: Free Press, 1971).

109. Charles H. Cooley, *Social Organization* (New York: Scribner's, 1909), p. 135.

110. W. H. Cowley, "Three Distinctions in the Study of Leaders," *Journal of Abnormal and Social Psychology* 23 (July–September 1928): 145. By Cowley's distinction between "leaders/leadership" and "headmen/ headship," Lincoln, Theodore Roosevelt, and Wilson were "leaders," but Buchanan, Coolidge, and Harding were not.

111. Quoted in Gibb, op. cit., p. 215.

112. John K. Hemphill, "Why People Attempt to Lead," in Luigi Petrullo and Bernard M. Bass, eds., *Leadership and Interpersonal Behavior* (New York: Holt, Rinehart & Winston, 1961), pp. 201–202.

113. See Stogdill, op. cit., esp. "Leadership Behavior: Consideration and Initiating Structure" (pp. 128–141) and "New Scales for Leader Behavior Description" (pp. 142–155).

114. Lewis, op. cit., p. 3.

115. Ibid., p. 4.

116. Lucy Mair, *Primitive Government* (Baltimore: Penguin, 1964), p. 65.

117. A succinct review of these approaches, with stress upon the importance of "social and cultural values," is given in Randall G. Stokes, "The Afrikaner Industrial Entrepreneur and Africaner Nationalism," *Economic Development and Cultural Change* 22, 4 (July 1974), 557–579. Stokes's thesis is that "whether or not industrial entrepreneurs are forthcoming from a developing society is a direct product of the way in which the entrepreneurial role is defined, and comes to be defined by collectivities which are meaningful to the prospective entrepreneur" (p. 557).

118. David Winter, *Motivating Economic Achievement* (New York: Free Press, 1969).

119. John Carroll, *The Filipino Manufacturing Entrepreneur* (Ithaca: Cornell University Press, 1965).

120. Everett E. Hagen, *On the Theory of Social Change* (Homewood: Dorsey, 1962).

121. Gustav F. Papanek, "The Development of Entrepreneurship," *Commission Economic Review* 52, 2 (May 1962), 55–58.

122. M. Dean Havron and Joseph E. McGrath, "The Contribution of the Leader to the Effectiveness of Small Military Groups," in Petrullo and Bass, op. cit., pp. 167–178, esp. pp. 173–175.

123. Ibid., p. 175.

124. Raymond B. Cattell, "New Concepts for Measuring Leadership in Terms of Group Syntality," *Human Relations* 4, 2 (1951), 161–184, see also idem, "A Mathematical Model for the Leadership Role and Other Personality-Role Relations," in Muzafer Sherif and W. O. Wilson, *Emerging Problems in Social Psychology* (Norman: University Book Exchange Duplicating Service, 1957), pp. 207–227.

125. Quoted in Greenberg, op. cit., p. 268.

126. Fiedler, op. cit.; idem, *A Theory of Leadership Effectiveness* (New York: McGraw-Hill, 1967).

127. Quoted in Meyer, op. cit., p. 78.

128. Gabriel Tarde, *The Laws of Imitation* (New York: Holt, 1903).

129. Neal E. Miller and John Dollard, *Social Learning and Imitation* (New Haven: Yale University Press, 1941).

130. Albert Bandura and Richard K. Walters, *Social Learning and Personality Development* (New York: Holt, Rinehart & Winston, 1963).

131. Generally, higher prestige models are imitated by lower prestige imitators, but there may be caste, class, or ethnic taboos against this (Leonard Bloomfield, *Language* [New York: Holt, 1933], pp. 444, 461, 476).

132. E.g., Everett M. Rogers, *Communication of Innovations: A Cross-cultural Approach* (New York: Free Press, 1971); Torsten Hägerstrand, *Innovation Diffusion as a Spatial Process* (Chicago: University of Chicago Press, 1967); Jack L. Walker, "The Diffusion of Innovations among the American States," *APSR* 63, 3 (September 1969), 880–889.

133. André Siegfried, *Routes of Contagion* (New York: Harcourt, Brace & World, 1960).

134. Stogdill, op. cit., pp. 260–271.

135. Miller and Dollard, op. cit., pp. 13–36.

136. Ernst Kris, *Psychoanalytic Explorations in Art* (New York: International Universities Press, 1951), p. 179.

137. Willard A. Hanna, *Eight Nation Makers* (New York: St. Martin's, 1964), p. 182.

138. Quoted in Joseph C. Bailey, "Clues for Success in the President's Job," in Edward C. Bursk and Timothy B. Blodgett, eds., *Developing Executive Leaders* (Cambridge: Harvard University Press, 1971), pp. 69–70.

139. Hsiang-sheng Liang, "My Experience as Chairman of a Large Co-operative," in Central Committee of the Communist Party of China, *Socialist Upsurge in China's Countryside* (Peking: Foreign Languages Press, 1957), p. 190.

140. For a very useful discussion see Barry E. Collins and Harold Guetzkow, *A Social Psychology of Group Processes for Decision-making* (New York: Wiley, 1964), pp. 214–222.

141. Gibb, op. cit., p. 273.

142. Robert F. Bales, "Interaction Process Analysis," in Sills, op. cit., 7:465–471.

143. For a recent overview of developments in this field, see David C. McClelland and Robert S. Steele, eds., *Human Motivation: A Book of Readings* (Morristown: General Learning Press, 1973). An exciting application to analysis of the motives of political leaders has been suggested by Richard E. Donley and David G. Winter, "Measuring the Motives of Public Officials at a Distance: An Exploratory Study of American Presidents," *Behavioral Science* 15, 3 (May 1970), 227–236.

144. Bass, op. cit., pp. 148–150.

145. Amitai Etzioni, "Organizational Control Structure," in James G. March, ed., *Handbook of Organizations* (Chicago: Rand McNally, 1965), p. 652.

146. Effective language aims at producing a desired response in a listener; cognitive language seeks to communicate a maximally objective message; affective language communicates the subjective state of the speaker (Francis P. Dineen, "Linguistics and the Social Sciences," in Muzafer Sherif and Carolyn W. Sherif, eds., *Interdisciplinary Relationships in the Social Sciences* [Chicago: Aldine, 1969], p. 263).

147. Gerry Keir, *Honolulu Advertiser,* June 28, 1974, p. A-3. Fasi was subsequently defeated in the Democratic primary by a former state senator, Lieutenant Governor George R. Ariyoshi, who went on to become the first American governor of Japanese-American ancestry, with the tacit support of former Governor John A. Burns, who remained formally aloof from the primary "fight."

148. E.g., James D. Barber, *The Lawmakers* (New Haven: Yale University Press, 1965).

149. E.g., Angus Campbell et al., *The American Voter* (New York: Wiley, 1960).

150. E.g., Rensis Likert, *New Patterns in Management* (New York: McGraw-Hill, 1961), p. 91, reports that whereas 80 percent of supervisors reported that they gave "sincere and thorough praise," only 14 percent of employees reported that their supervisors did so.

151. Some recent dissertations point the way to future needed development. E.g., José Armilla, *Leader-Follower Frame of Reference in Political Behavior* (Ph.D. 1961, University of Michigan); David M. Herold, *Mutual Influence Processes in Leader-Follower Relationships* (Ph.D. 1974, Yale University).

152. Ralph K. White and Ronald Lippitt, *Autocracy and Democracy: An Experimental Inquiry* (New York: Harper, 1960).

153. Lewis, op. cit., p. 7.

154. James C. Scott, "Patron-Client Politics and Political Change in Southeast Asia," *APSR* 46, 1 (March 1972): 92.

155. E.g., recall the discussion of Menzel (p. 69) and see the distinction made by F. G. Bailey between the affective "core" and "followers" (transactional attachment) in human organization in *Stratagems and Spoils* (New York: Schocken, 1969), pp. 45–49.

156. Robert Tannenbaum and Fred Massarik, "Leadership: A Frame of Reference," *Management Science* 4, 1 (October 1957), 3.

157. Warren G. Bennis, "Post-bureaucratic Leadership," *Trans-Action* 6, 9 (July–August 1969), 51.

158. Cecil A. Gibb, "Leadership," in Gardner Lindzey, ed., *Handbook of Social Psychology* (Reading: Addison-Wesley, 1954), p. 917.

159. Gibb, "Leadership," in Lindzey and Aaronson, op. cit., 4:268.

160. For excellent statements of this basic question, see William James, "Great Men, Great Thoughts, and the Environment," *Atlantic Monthly* 46, 276 (October 1880), 441–459; Elizabeth Hagen and Luverne Wolff, *Nursing Leadership Behavior in General Hospitals* (New York: Teachers College Press, Columbia University, 1961), chap. 1, "Leaders and Leadership."

161. Fiedler, "Leadership."

162. Clare Clifford and Thomas S. Cohn, "The Relationship between Leadership and Personality Traits Perceived By Followers," *Journal of Social Psychology* 64, 1st half (October 1964), 57-64.

163. Robert Tannenbaum and Warren H. Schmidt, "How to Choose a Leadership Pattern," *Harvard Business Review* 36, 2 (March–April 1958), 95–101; e.g., the more long range the task, the more effective is subordinate-centered leadership behavior.

164. Fiedler, "Leadership," p. 9.

165. Lewis, op. cit., p. 14.

166. Edwin S. Shneidman, "Comparison of Nixon and Kennedy: The Logic of Politics," in Glenn D. Paige, ed., *Political Leadership: Readings for an Emerging Field* (New York: Free Press, 1972), p. 241. The efforts of Hermann and others to clarify the concept of a "crisis" decision represents an effort at more precise specification of task variables in political science. See Charles F. Hermann, ed., *International Crises: Insights from Behavioral Research* (New York: Free Press, 1972), esp. its important propositional inventory (pp. 304–320).

167. Thomas S. Kuhn, *The Structure of Scientific Revolutions* (Chicago: University of Chicago Press, 1962).

168. Kenneth E. Boulding, *The Image* (Ann Arbor: University of Michigan Press, 1961).

169. Paul Shorey, *What Plato Said* (Chicago: University of Chicago Press, 1933), pp. 238–243.

170. Plato, op. cit., p. 79.

171. Ibid., p. 56.

172. Niccolò Machiavelli, *The Prince* (New York: New American Library, Mentor, 1962).

173. E.g., Arthur Waley, *Three Ways of Thought in Ancient China* (London: Allen & Unwin, 1939).

174. Arthur Waley, *The Way and Its Power* (London: Allen and Unwin, 1949), p. 227. There are many similarities between Taoist thought and the ideas of Gandhi in *Non-violent Resistance* (New York: Schocken, 1967).

175. Muhammad Mahmoud Rabi, *The Political Theory of Ibn Khaldun* (Leiden: Brill, 1967); see esp. chap. 5, "The Concept of *Mulk* (Kingship)."

176. John E. Tashjean, "On Theory of Statecraft" (Manuscript, n.d.).

177. Examples of such works include Kautilya, *Arthashastra* (Mysore: Mysore Printing and Publishing House, 1960); Nizam al-Mulk, *The Book of Government or Rules for Kings* (New Haven: Yale University Press, 1960); and Alexander L. George, *The "Operational Code": A Neglected Approach to the Study of Political Leaders and Decision Making* (Santa Monica: Rand Corporation, 1967).

178. E.g., Leon Trotsky, *Stalin* (New York: Stein & Day, 1967); Andreas Papandreou, *Democracy at Gunpoint: The Greek Front* (Garden City: Doubleday, 1970).

179. E.g. Monsieur de Callières, *On the Manner of Negotiating with Princes,* trans. A. F. Whyte (Notre Dame: University of Notre Dame Press, 1963), can be read from the point of view of what kind of behavior would be required by a leader to cope with the strategies advocated by de Callières. In reverse fashion, one can read Machiavelli to devise follower strategies for coping with such a "prince."

180. Introduction to the translation of Erasmus, *The Education of a Christian Prince,* trans. Lester K. Born (New York: Columbia University Press, 1936), p. 127.

181. Stogdill, op. cit.

182. Max Weber, *The Theory of Social and Economic Organization,* Talcott Parsons (New York: Free Press, 1947).

183. Ibid., p. 324.

184. Ibid., p. 358.

185. Ibid., p. 328.

186. Ann Ruth Wilner, *Charismatic Political Leadership: A Theory* (Princeton: Princeton University, Center of International Studies, 1968), p. 9.

187. Ibid., p. 6.

188. In terming these three forms of "leadership," some damage is being done to the original Weberian framework as outlined above. Strictly speaking, they are grounds for belief in the legitimacy of authority. "Leadership" still needs to be explicated in terms of the entire Weberian concept of authority.

189. Weber, op. cit., p. 328.

190. Ibid.

191. Immanuel Wallerstein, *Africa: The Politics of Independence* (New York: Random House, Vintage, 1961), p. 99.

192. Wiatr and Ostrowski, for example, have written that "while in the past charismatic leaders constituted the center of political power in socialist countries (or, to be more exact, in some of them), this is no longer the case. It may even be predicted that, with the stabilization of post-revolutionary society with its economic growth and social modernization the opportunities for charismatic leadership will become more and more limited while the rational (legal) authority will become the established pattern" (Jerzy J. Wiatr and Kryzysztof Ostrowski, "Political Leadership: What Kind of Professionalism?" in Jerzy J. Wiatr, ed., *Studies in Polish Political System* [Wroclaw: Polish Academy of Sciences Press, 1967], p. 141).

193. Harold D. Lasswell, Daniel Lerner, and C. Easton Rothwell, *The Comparative Study of Elites: An Introduction and Bibliography* (Stanford: Stanford University Press, 1952).

194. John E. Tashjean has observed that "essentially [Lasswell's] design of *Politics* copies the political sociology of Pareto." See Tashjean's "Politics: Lasswell and Pareto," *Cahiers Vilfredo Pareto* 22, 33 (1970), 268–272.

195. Frederick W. Frey, *The Turkish Political Elite* (Cambridge: MIT Press, 1965).

196. Zbigniew Brzezinski and Samuel P. Huntington III, *Political Power: USA/USSR* (New York: Viking, 1972); see esp. pp. 129–190.

197. Donald D. Searing, "The Comparative Study of Elite Socialization," *Comparative Political Studies* 1, 1 (January 1969), 471–500; William B. Quandt, *The Comparative Study of Political Elites,* Comparative Politics Series 01-004 (Beverly Hills: Sage, 1970).

198. Geraint Parry, *Political Elites* (New York: Praeger, 1969).

199. The "elite" titles for the period 1969–1975 are Robert D. Putnam, "Studying Elite Political Culture: The Case of Ideology," *APSR* 65, 3 (September 1971), 651–681; Michael W. Suleiman, "Attitudes of the Arab Elite toward Palestine and Israel," *APSR* 67, 2 (June 1973), 482–489; and Fred W. Grupp, Jr., and Alan R. Richards, "Variations in Elite Perceptions of American States as Referents for Public Policy," *APSR* 69, 3 (September 1975), 850–858. Five "leadership" titles also appeared during 1969–1975: Ilya F. Harik, "Opinion Leaders and Mass Media in Egypt," *APSR* 65, 3 (September 1971), 731–740; Jeffrey L. Pressman, "Preconditions for Mayoral Leadership," *APSR* 66, 2 (June 1972), 511–524; Louis P. Westefield, "Majority Party Leadership and the Committee System in the House of Representatives," *APSR* 68, 4 (December 1974), 1593–1604; Joseph A. Massey, "The Missing Leader: Japanese Youths' View of Political Authority," *APSR* 69, 1 (March 1975), 31–48; and Fred I. Greenstein, "The Benevolent Leader Revisited: Children's Images of Political Leaders in Three Democracies," *APSR* 69, 4 (December 1975), 1371–1378.

200. Carl Beck and J. T. McKechnie, *Political Elites: A Select Computerized Bibliography* (Cambridge: MIT Press, 1967).

201. Kenneth Janda, ed., *Cumulative Index to the American Political Science Review, Volumes 1–62: 1906–1968 (Xerox-*University Microfilms, 1969). This order was reversed at the 1974 meeting of the American Political Science Association, when a panel discussion of "political elites and political leadership" was held under the chairmanship of Robert D. Putnam.

202. Parry, op. cit., p. 13.

203. C. Wright Mills, *The Power Elite* (New York: Oxford University Press, 1956). Mills explains: "The power elite is composed of political, economic, and military men. . . . We must be always historically specific and open to complexities. The simple Marxian view makes the big economic man the *real* holder of power; the simple liberal view makes the big political man the chief of the power system; and there are some who would view the warlords as virtual dictators. It is to avoid them that we use the term 'power elite' rather than, for example, the 'ruling class' " (pp. 276–277). Mills further differentiates the "political directorate" into three types of politician: the "party politician," the "political bureaucrat," and the "political outsider" (p. 227).

204. Polybius, *The Histories,* excerpted in William Ebenstein, ed., *Great Political Thinkers* (New York: Rinehart, 1953), pp. 112–120.

205. J. O. Hertzler, "The Typical Life Cycle of Dictatorships," *Social Forces* 17, 3 (March 1939), 303–309.

206. Jerzy J. Wiatr, "Political Elites and Political Leadership: Conceptual Problems and Selected Hypotheses for Comparative Research," *Indian Journal of Politics* 7, 2 (December 1973), 139.

207. Mills has rightly cautioned, however, that "such a simple view of 'economic determinism' must be elaborated by 'political determinism' and 'military determinism' " (Mills, op. cit., p. 277).

208. Wiatr, op. cit., p. 139.

209. Lewis, op. cit., p. 4.

210. As is frequently the case, however, Harold D. Lasswell pioneered the use of the term; e.g., "It appears that the problem of democratic leadership and eliteship is equivalent to the development of social health rather than disease" (Lasswell, *Power and Personality* [New York: Viking, 1963], p. 146).

211. Robert A. Dahl, *Who Governs* (New Haven: Yale University Press, 1961), pp. 13–14.

212. Ibid., pp. 64, 67–68.

213. Ibid., p. 170.

214. Robert A. Agger, Daniel Goodrich, and Bert E. Swanson, *The Rulers and the Ruled* (New York: Wiley, 1964), p. 63; see also p. 51. A decision process is described as having six stages plus a decisional "event": "(1) Policy formulation, (2) Policy deliberation, (3) Organization of political support, (4) Authoritative consideration—event: decisional outcome—(5) Promulgation of the decisional outcome, and (6) Policy effectuation" (p. 40).

215. Ibid., p. 70.

216. Ibid., p. 71.

217. Ibid., p. 72.

218. Ibid., pp. 78–79, p. 117, n. 16.

219. Ibid., p. 707.

220. Ibid., p. 711.

221. Ibid., pp. 381–383, 387.

222. Ibid., p. 717.

223. Dahl, op. cit., p. 115.

224. Agger et al., op. cit., p. 326.

225. Ibid., p. 346.

226. Dahl, op. cit., p. 11. Dahl also has referred to the occasional appearance of a "semi-dictatorship" in some American communities (p. 311).

227. Agger et al., op. cit., p. 472.

228. Ibid., p. 653.

229. Douglas M. Fox, "The Identification of Community Leaders by the Reputational and Decisional Methods: Three Case Studies and an Empirical Analysis of the Literature," *Sociology and Social Research* 54, 1 (October 1969), 99.

230. See index references in Dahl, op. cit., p. 354; the profile sketched in Agger et al., op. cit., p. 762; the insightful portrayals by Stimson Bullitt, "Politics as a Calling," in Glenn D. Paige, ed., *Political Leadership: Readings for an Emerging Field* (New York: Free Press, 1972), pp. 317–327, and Gary Willis, "Hurrah for Politicians," *Harpers,* September 1975, pp. 45–54.

231. This despite the urging of some social scientists in societies dominated by professional party politicians who are urging the merits of a more open, less narrowly "professional" political leadership structure. See Wiatr and Ostrowski, op. cit.

232. Clinton Rossiter, *The American Presidency* (New York: Harcourt, Brace & World, 1960), chap. 1.

233. Richard Neustadt, *Presidential Power* (New York: Wiley, 1960), chap. 3. By comparison, the experienced "activist" President Theodore Roosevelt reportedly told the English historian George M. Trevelyan that "the nature of the presidency was not conducive to the championship of unpopular causes and that it tended to put a premium upon a man's staying out of trouble rather than upon the accomplishments of results" (George Sinkler, *The Racial Attitudes of American Presidents* [Garden City: Doubleday, 1972], p. 421).

234. Erwin C. Hargrove, *Presidential Leadership: Personality and Political Style* (New York: Macmillan, 1966).

235. James D. Barber, *The Presidential Character* (Englewood Cliffs: Prentice-Hall, 1972).

236. James D. Barber, "Classifying and Predicting Presidential Styles: Two Weak Presidents," *Journal of Social Issues* 24, 3 (July 1968), 51–80.

237. Donald R. Matthews, *U.S. Senators and Their World* (New York: Random House, Vintage, 1960), pp. 61–67.

238. Charles L. Clapp, *The Congressman: His Work as He Sees It* (Washington, D.C.: Brookings Institution, 1964).

239. James D. Barber, *The Lawmakers*.

240. James D. Barber, "Leadership Strategies for Legislative Party Cohesion," *Journal of Politics* 28, 2 (May 1966), 347–367.

241. John C. Wahlke, Heinz Eulau, William Buchanan, and Leroy C. Ferguson, *The Legislative System: Explorations in Legislative Behavior* (New York: Wiley, 1962).

242. Samuel J. Eldersveld, *Political Parties: A Behavioral Analysis* (Chicago: Rand McNally, 1964), p. 254.

243. James Q. Wilson, *The Amateur Democrat* (Chicago: University of Chicago Press, 1966). Wilson draws also upon the images of the "cosmopolitan" and the "local" described in Robert K. Merton, "Patterns of Influence: Local and Cosmopolitan Influentials," *Social Theory and Social Structure* (New York: Free Press, 1957), pp. 387–420.

244. Wilson, *The Amateur Democrat*, pp. 315–316.

245. A discussion of these three types can be found in Arthur F. Bentley, *The Process of Government* (Bloomington: Principia, 1949), pp. 231–235; first published in 1908.

246. Joseph A. Schlesinger, *Ambition in Politics* (Chicago: Rand McNally, 1966), p. 10.

247. Everett Carl Ladd, Jr. *Negro Political Leadership in the South* (New York: Atheneum, 1969); see esp. chap. 4, "Styles of Race Leadership."

248. For an overview see Luther Gulick, "Political and Administrative Leadership," *Public Management* 45, 11 (November 1963), 243–247; and articles by Gladys M. Kammerer, "Is the Manager a Political Leader?— Yes," and H. G. Pope, "Is the Manager a Political Leader?—No," both in *Public Management* 44 (February 1962), 26–29 and 30–33. Other important perspectives are provided by Chester I. Barnard, *The Functions of the Executive* (Cambridge: Harvard University Press, 1938); Philip O. Selznik, *Leadership in Administration* (Evanston: Row, Peterson, 1957).

249. Gulick, op. cit., p. 244.

250. Ibid., p. 246.

251. Ibid., p. 247. Eight "political" functions listed by Gulick include policy making, mobilizing support, strengthening or altering a power structure, engaging in efforts to increase strength by concerted action, influencing voters, manipulating public opinion, building a political organization to control nominations and elections, and engaging in personal or party patronage (p. 245).

252. Kenneth F. Janda, "Towards the Explication of the Concept of Leadership in Terms of the Concept of Power," in Paige, op. cit., p. 56.

253. Ibid., p. 62.

254. Stewart and Scott, op. cit.

255. Pigors, op. cit.
256. Polybius, *The Histories,* ed. E. Badian and trans. Mortimer Chambers (New York: Washington Square, 1966), p. 214.
257. Plato, op. cit., p. 35.
258. Carl J. Friedrich, *Man and His Government* (New York: McGraw-Hill, 1963), chap. 9, "Power and Leadership."
259. Ibid., p. 161.
260. Ibid., p. 170.
261. Ibid., p. 171.
262. Ibid., p. 180.
263. Ibid., p. 181.
264. Ibid., pp. 188-189.
265. Donald D. Searing, "Models and Images of Man and Society in Leadership Theory," *Journal of Politics* 31, 1 (February 1969), 3-31; reprinted in Paige, op. cit., pp. 19-44; see p. 33.
266. Sidney Hook, *The Hero in History* (Boston: Beacon, 1962), pp. 151-183.
267. Ibid., pp. 172-173, 184 ff.
268. James V. Downton, *Rebel Leadership: Commitment and Charisma in the Revolutionary Process* (New York: Free Press, 1973).
269. Ibid., p. 12.
270. Ibid.
271. Ibid., p. 14.
272. Ibid., p. 21.
273. Ibid., p. 8.
274. Ibid., pp. 13, 52.

Chapter 5. Multivariate, Multidimensional Linkage Approach: Variables

1. See p. 81.
2. Emile Durkheim, *The Rules of Sociological Method* (New York: Free Press, 1964), p. 46.
3. Charles H. Cooley, *Social Organization* (New York: Scribner's, 1909), p. 135.
4. This will be recognized as a paraphrase of Watzlawick and associates' "meta-communication axiom" that *"one cannot not communicate"* (Paul Watzlawick, Janet H. Beaven, and Don D. Jackson, *Pragmatics of Human Communication* [New York: Norton, 1967], p. 51).
5. Robert Michels, *Political Parties* (New York: Dover, 1959), p. 400.
6. Arthur F. Bentley, *The Process of Government* (Bloomington: Principia, 1949), p. 225. For Bentley, American political parties should be viewed as creatures of outside interests, the conventions as products of the parties,

the executive committees as creatures of the conventions, and the chairpersons as products of the committees.

7. Former Indonesian vice-president Mohammad Hatta remarked to me on a visit to Hawaii in the late 1960s, "I have always believed that leaders create their own followings."

8. F. G. Bailey, *Stratagems and Spoils* (New York: Schocken, 1969), p. 50.

9. Here should be recalled the interstitial field relevance suggested for political leadership studies in Figure 1.

10. John Kotter and Paul R. Lawrence, *Mayors in Action* (New York: Wiley, 1974).

11. Compare Coffin's insight thirty-one years earlier: "As a conceptualization for empirical investigation, we offer the hypothesis that a '*job* analysis' of leaders' functions might disclose them as falling into three categories: planning, organizing and persuading" (Thomas E. Coffin, "A Three-Component Theory of Leadership," *Journal of Abnormal and Social Psychology* 39, 1 [January 1944], 82). Note that both these formulations seem to be calling attention to the instrumental, affective, and power aspects of social behavior.

12. Edward G. Bennion, "Econometrics for Management," in Edward C. Bursk and John F. Chapman, eds., *New Decision-making Tools for Managers* (New York: New American Library, Mentor, 1965), pp. 149–150.

13. A useful introduction is Hubert M. Blalock, Jr., *Theory Construction: From Verbal to Mathematical Formulations* (Englewood Cliffs: Prentice-Hall, 1969).

14. E.g., Harold D. Lasswell, *Power and Personality* (New York: Norton, 1948); Fred I. Greenstein, *Personality and Politics* (Chicago: Markham, 1969). A useful recent compilation of political personality studies is Gordon DiRenzo, ed., *Personality and Politics* (Garden City: Doubleday, 1974).

15. Harold D. Lasswell, *Psychopathology and Politics* (Chicago: University of Chicago Press, 1930).

16. Alexander L. George, "Power as a Compensatory Value for Political Leaders," *Journal of Social Issues* 24, 3 (July 1968), 29–50.

17. James D. Barber, "Classifying and Predicting Presidential Styles: Two Weak Presidents," *Journal of Social Issues* 24, 3 (July 1968), 51–80.

18. Rufus P. Browning and Herbert E. Jacob, "Power Motivation and the Political Personality," *Public Opinion Quarterly* 28, 1 (Spring 1964), 75–90.

19. E. Victor Wolfenstein, *The Revolutionary Personality: Lenin, Trotsky, Gandhi* (Princeton: Princeton University Press, 1967), p. 307.

20. Edmond Constantini and Kenneth H. Craik, "Women as Politicians: The Social Background, Personality and Political Careers of Female Party Leaders," *Journal of Social Issues* 28, 2 (1972), 217–236.

21. I have stated this hypothesis rather more crudely than the very careful comparative exploration of it in Louis H. Stewart, "Birth Order and

Political Leadership," in Margaret G. Hermann, ed., *A Psychological Examination of Political Leaders* (New York: Free Press, 1977), pp. 206-236.

22. Theodore Sorensen, *Kennedy* (New York: Bantam, 1966), p. 436.

23. W. W. Tarn, *Alexander the Great* (Boston: Beacon, 1956), p. 142.

24. Louis Fischer, *The Life of Lenin* (New York: Harper, 1965), p. 51.

25. Sorensen, op. cit., p. 201.

26. Ithiel de Sola Pool, Robert P. Abelson, and Samuel L. Popkin, *Candidates, Issues, and Strategies* (Cambridge: MIT Press, 1964), pp. 20-21.

27. Quoted in Herbert L. Matthews, *Fidel Castro* (New York: Clarion, 1970), p. 186.

28. Charles F. Gallagher, "Tunisia," in Gwendolyn M. Carter, ed., *African One-Party States* (Ithaca: Cornell University Press, 1962), p. 66. The propensity for personalities to alter physical settings as a means of self-expression and of influence upon others has been well analyzed in Erving Goffman, *The Presentation of Self in Everyday Life* (Garden City: Doubleday, 1959).

29. Norman Thomas, *The Minority Party in America*, Folkways Record FH5512.

30. Sorensen, op. cit., p. 208.

31. Lionel Tiger, "The 1970 Unesco Conference on Aggression and Recent Research" (Paper presented to the UNESCO International Symposium on Human Aggression, Brussels, September 11-15, 1972), p. 4.

32. Cecil A. Gibb, "Leadership" (Draft manuscript, August 1965), p. 127.

33. V. O. Key, Jr., *Politics, Parties and Pressure Groups* (New York: Crowell, 1942), p. 202.

34. Quoted in Kenneth P. O'Donnell and David F. Powers, with Joe McCarthy, *Johnny, We Hardly Knew Ye* (Boston: Little, Brown, 1972), p. 293.

35. Erwin C. Hargrove, *Personality and Political Leadership* (New York: Macmillan, 1966), p. 97.

36. Ibid., p. 132.

37. Quoted in ibid., p. 50.

38. Leon Festinger, *A Theory of Cognitive Dissonance* (Stanford: Stanford University Press, 1957).

39. Alan Bullock, *Hitler: A Study in Tyranny* (New York: Harper, Torchbooks, 1964), p. 650.

40. "Only an armed struggle can bring about the freedom of India." Bose is quoted in Richard L. Park and Irene Tinker, eds., *Leadership and Political Institutions in India* (Princeton: Princeton University Press, 1959), p. 81.

41. Thomas Aitken, Jr., *Poet in the Fortress* (New York: New American Library, 1965).

42. Ralph Linton, *The Cultural Background of Personality* (New York: Appleton Century, 1945), p. 77.

43. Neal Gross, Ward S. Mason, and Alexander W. McEachern, *Explorations in Role Analysis: Studies of the School Superintendency Role* (New York: Wiley, 1958), p. 67.

44. Michael P. Banton, *Roles: An Introduction to the Study of Social Relations* (London: Tavistock, 1965), p. 29.

45. Peter H. Rossi, "Community Decision-making," in Roland Young, ed., *Approaches to the Study of Politics* (Evanston: Northwestern University Press, 1958), p. 380.

46. James G. March, "Measurement Concepts in the Theory of Influence," *Journal of Politics* 19, 2 (May 1957), 203 ff.

47. Quoted in Donald R. Matthews, *U.S. Senators and Their World* (New York: Random House, Vintage, 1960), p. 103.

48. On a visit by Mayor Lindsay to Princeton University in the mid-1960s.

49. Quoted in Sorensen, op. cit., p. 315.

50. Quoted in Fischer, op. cit., p. 143.

51. E.g., Robert Rienow and Leona Train Rienow, *The Lonely Quest: The Evolution of Presidential Leadership* (Chicago: Follet, 1966); Booth Mooney, *Mr. Speaker* (Chicago: Follet, 1964).

52. Rufus P. Browning and Herbert E. Jacob, "Power Motivation and the Political Personality," *Public Opinion Quarterly* 28, 1 (Spring 1964), 90.

53. Mooney, op. cit., pp. 89–128.

54. Talcott Parsons, *Sociological Theory and Modern Society* (New York: Free Press, 1967), p. 227.

55. Clinton Rossiter, *The American Presidency* (New York: Harcourt, Brace, 1960).

56. D. R. Matthews, op. cit., pp. 109 f.

57. Quoted in Harriet J. Kupferer, "Impotency and Power: A Cross-cultural Comparison of the Effect of Alien Rule," in Marc J. Swartz, ed., *Political Anthropology* (Chicago: Aldine, 1966), p. 63.

58. Few presidents since Jefferson have expressed interest in using their role potential to influence design, but President Kennedy's concern with the design of Pennsylvania Avenue and Lafayette Square seemed especially promising (Edward J. Logue, "The Impact of Political and Social Forces on Design in America," in Laurance B. Holland, ed., *Who Designs America?* [Garden City: Doubleday, 1966], p. 245).

59. "Through his direct or indirect control over the selection of architects, he has a decisive voice on how the image of his state will be shaped during his term of office. Not only public office buildings, but state universities, colleges, hospitals, even highway design, can be executed with mediocrity or distinction, depending upon the whim of the governor. More often than not, governors seem unaware of the importance of this power" (ibid., p. 246).

60. Ibid., p. 247.

61. William S. White, *The Professional: Lyndon B. Johnson* (Greenwich: Fawcett World Library, Crest, 1964), p. 41.

62. Quoted in Eric Sevareid, reporter, "Five Presidents on the Presidency," CBS Television News Special, April 26, 1973, transcript, p. 15. This is not to imply that this kind of high-level task assignment is "good" or unchangeable.

63. Arthur Larson, *Eisenhower: The President Nobody Knew* (New York: Popular Library, 1968), p. 21.

64. Georgie Anne Geyer, Chicago Daily News Service, quoted in the *Honolulu Star-Bulletin*, April 17, 1973, p. B-6.

65. An excellent contemporary overview of the first three contexts is contained in Michael Argyle, *Social Interaction* (London: Methuen, 1969); it needs to be extended to cover the broader types of social interaction that are characteristic of political leaders.

66. Important studies include James G. March and Herbert A. Simon, *Organizations* (New York: Wiley, 1958); Amitai Etzioni, *A Comparative Analysis of Complex Organizations* (New York: Free Press, 1961); Peter M. Blau and W. R. Scott, *Formal Organizations* (San Francisco: Chandler, 1962); and James G. March, ed., *Handbook of Organizations* (Chicago: Rand McNally, 1965).

67. Alexander L. George and Juliette L. George, *Woodrow Wilson and Colonel House* (New York: Day, 1956); see esp. chap. 7, "Formula for Success," which describes House's techniques of ingratiation and influence.

68. Richard Fenno, Jr., *The President's Cabinet* (New York: Random House, Vintage, 1959).

69. Thomas E. Cronin and Sanford E. Greenberg, *The Presidential Advisory System* (New York: Harper, 1969).

70. Kenneth Janda, *A Conceptual Framework for the Comparative Analysis of Political Parties*, Comparative Politics Series, vol. 1, no. 01002 (Beverly Hills: Sage, 1970).

71. John C. Wahlke, Heinz Eulau, William Buchanan, and Leroy C. Ferguson, *The Legislative System: Explorations in Legislative Behavior* (New York: Wiley, 1962).

72. Shanti Kothari and Ramashray Roy, *Relations between Politicians and Administrators at the District Level* (New Delhi: Indian Institute of Public Administration and the Centre of Applied Politics, 1969). Compare Reed M. Powell and Dalmas H. Nelson, "Business Executives View the Politician: Negative Feelings Block Cooperative Efforts," *Business Horizons* 11, 5 (October 1968), 41–51.

73. Lester Milbrath, *The Washington Lobbyists* (Chicago: Rand McNally, 1963).

74. Angus Campbell et al., *The American Voter* (New York: Wiley, 1965).

75. Elmer E. Cornwell, *Presidential Leadership of Public Opinion* (Bloomington: Indiana University Press, 1965).

76. Seymour Martin Lipset, Martin A. Trow, and James S. Coleman, *Union Democracy: The Internal Politics of the International Typographical Union* (New York: Free Press, 1956).

77. E. P. Hollander, *Leaders, Groups and Influence* (New York: Oxford University Press, 1964), pp. 161 ff.

78. Stanley Milgram, "Interdisciplinary Thinking and the Small World Problem," in Muzafer Sherif and Carolyn W. Sherif, eds., *Interdisciplinary*

Relationships in the Social Sciences (Chicago: Aldine, 1969), p. 118. The social linkage functions of elected American officials remain to be explicitly explored.

79. Vasili Kluchevsky, *Peter the Great*, trans. Liliana Archibald (New York: Random House, Vintage, 1958), p. 218.

80. Paul Pigors, "Types of Followers," *Journal of Social Psychology* 5, 3 (August 1934), 378–383.

81. James D. Barber, "Leadership Strategies for Legislative Party Cohesion," *Journal of Politics* 28, 2 (May 1966), 347–367.

82. James C. Davies, *Human Nature in Politics* (New York: Wiley, 1963), p. 280.

83. Bullock, op. cit., p. 465. A few days later, after the Munich Agreement, Hitler was "annoyed" when the citizens of Munich gave Chamberlain an ovation as he drove through the streets (p. 471).

84. An enlightening exercise is to analyze the emotional terms contained in the memoirs of intimate associates of leaders; e.g., O'Donnell, and Powers, with McCarthy, op. cit., which contains such frequent terms as "loved, admired, happy, cheerful, merry, cherished, liked, contented" versus "hated, dreaded, furious, angry, mad, irritated, affronted, horrified, grim, disgusted, gloomy, bitter" and "cool nonchalance." The contrast with the relatively emotionless content of most professional political science analysis suggests that the emotional dimension of politics deserves special future attention.

85. E. Paul Torrance and Nicholas C. Aliotti, "Accuracy, Task Effectiveness and Emergence of a Social-emotional Resolver as a Function of One- and Two-Expert Groups," *Journal of Psychology* 61, 2 (November 1965), 161–170.

86. John F. Kennedy, *Profiles in Courage* (New York: Harper & Row, 1964), pp. 4–18.

87. Glenn D. Paige, "North Korea and the Emulation of Russian and Chinese Behavior," in A. Doak Barnett, ed., *Communist Strategies in Asia* (New York: Praeger, 1963), pp. 228–261.

88. Larson, op. cit., pp. 27–28. A similar organizational pattern, but not decisional style, seems to have characterized President (former general) de Gaulle's staff relationships (Aidan Crawley, *De Gaulle* [Indianapolis: Bobbs-Merrill, 1969], pp. 281–282).

89. Sorensen, op. cit., p. 294.

90. "Indeed, the way a senator staffs and organizes his office is a kind of political Rohrschach test which, when studied with some care, tells a great deal about him as a man, what his problems and preoccupations are and how he defines his role" (D. R. Matthews, op. cit., p. 83). Two assumptions here, of course, are not necessarily true: that leaders are male and that they have freedom of choice in staffing decisions.

91. Quoted in Sorensen, op. cit., p. 320.

92. Bullock, op. cit., p. 141.

93. D. R. Matthews, op. cit., chap. 5.

94. Fischer, op. cit., p. 237.

95. John V. Lindsay, *The City* (New York: New American Library, 1970), p. 84.

96. Harold Wilson, *A Personal Record: The Labour Government, 1964–1970* (Boston: Little, Brown, 1971), p. 5.

97. Fred E. Fiedler, "Leadership," General Learning Corporation Module (Morristown: General Learning Press, 1971), p. 12.

98. Charles F. Hermann, *Crises and Foreign Policy: A Simulation Analysis* (Indianapolis: Bobbs-Merrill, 1969).

99. Sorensen, op. cit., p. 116.

100. Robert Scheer, ed., *The Diary of Ché Guevara* (New York: Bantam, 1968), pp. 155, 159.

101. Rossiter, op. cit., p. 86.

102. Herbert S. Lewis, "Leaders and Followers: Some Anthropological Perspectives," Addison-Wesley Module in Anthropology no. 50 (Reading: Addison-Wesley, 1974), p. 13.

103. Quoted in Grace Lichtenstein, "Running for Mayor on a Garbage Truck," *New York Times Magazine*, April 25, 1971, p. 31. By 1977 Kretchmer had not taken the trip.

104. Quoted in Elie Abel, *The Missile Crisis* (New York: Bantam, 1966), p. 51.

105. Quoted in Bullock, op. cit., p. 529.

106. Quoted in Scheer, op. cit., pp. 125–126.

107. Quoted in D. R. Matthews, op. cit., p. 96.

108. The effects of role tenure on patterns of task engagement, holding personality and other influencing variables constant, deserve substantial inquiry. I was surprised to find, for example, that among a self-selected sample of twenty-nine of a total of seventy-six Hawaii state legislators in 1970, eleven indicated that they thought that practical governmental planning and action should be conducted at least more than a decade ahead (Glenn D. Paige, "Hawaii's 1970 State Legislators View Hawaii 2000," mimeo. [Honolulu: University of Hawaii, Department of Political Science and Social Science Research Institute, January 21, 1970]).

109. Joseph Napolitan, *The Election Game and How to Win It* (Garden City: Doubleday, 1972).

110. Cecil Woodham-Smith, *The Great Hunger* (New York: Harper, 1962), pp. 410–411, as quoted in Allen H. Barton, *Communities in Disaster* (Garden City: Doubleday, 1970), p. 21. Barton's book deserves special attention by students of political leadership because it presents a paradigm for crisis management at the community level and because it represents an unusual example of what Robert K. Merton has termed "middle-range" theory construction. See Merton's foreword to *Communities in Disaster*, esp. pp. xxvii–xxxvii.

111. Mike Royko, *Boss* (New York: Dutton, 1971), p. 135.

112. Alfred G. Meyer, *Leninism* (New York: Praeger, 1957), p. 287.

113. Milton Rokeach, "A Theory of Organization and Change within Value-Attitude Systems," in Glenn D. Paige, ed., *Political Leadership: Readings for an Emerging Field* (New York: Free Press, 1972), p. 168.

114. Ibid.

115. Ibid., p. 177.

116. Ibid., p. 174.

117. Quoted in H. L. Matthews, op. cit., p. 65.

118. Quoted in Bernard Fall, ed., *Ho Chi Minh on Revolution* (New York: New American Library, Signet, 1968), p. 145.

119. Herbert McCloskey, Paul J. Hoffman, and Rosemary Ohara, "Issue Conflict and Consensus among Party Leaders and Followers," *APSR* 54, 2 (June 1960), 406-427.

120. Philip E. Jacob, ed., for The International Studies of Values in Politics, *Values and the Active Community: A Cross-national Study of the Influence of Local Leadership* (New York: Free Press, 1971).

121. Robert D. Putnam, *The Beliefs of Politicians* (New Haven: Yale University Press, 1973).

122. It is realized, of course, that there is an important analytical distinction to be made between values conceived as ends-means standards to guide behavior and values defined as scarce material or psychic resources. A dual approach will be useful for political analysis.

123. Sorensen, op. cit., p. 21.

124. Herbert L. Matthews, *Fidel Castro* (New York: Simon & Schuster, Clarion, 1970), p. 18, quoting a paraphrase by Lee Lockwood of Castro's own account of his family origins.

125. Nobutaka Ike, "Political Leadership and Political Parties: Japan," in Robert E. Ward and Dankwart A. Rustow, eds., *Political Modernization in Japan and Turkey* (Princeton: Princeton University Press, 1964), p. 392.

126. Bullock, op. cit., p. 403.

127. Ibid., p. 675.

128. Sorensen, op. cit., p. 55.

129. Ibid., p. 310.

130. Fischer, op. cit., p. 39.

131. Ibid., p. 364.

132. Ibid., p. 490.

133. Quoted in ibid., pp. 120-121.

134. Ibid., p. 435.

135. H. L. Matthews, op. cit., p. 103.

136. Fischer, op. cit., p. 213.

137. Ibid., pp. 489 ff.

138. Quoted in Bullock, op. cit., p. 527.

139. Quoted in Fischer, op. cit., p. 241.

140. Quoted in Royko, op. cit., p. 71.

141. Fischer, op. cit., p. 21.

142. Mao Tse-tung, *Selected Works,* 5 vols. (New York: International Publishers, 1954), 1:21–59.

143. Jomo Kenyatta, *Facing Mount Kenya* (London: Secker & Warburg, 1966).

144. Arnold J. Toynbee, *A Study of History,* rev. and abr. ed. (London: Oxford University Press, 1972).

145. Ludwig von Bertalanffy, *General System Theory* (New York: Braziller, 1968).

146. Samuel Klausner, ed., *The Study of Total Societies* (New York: Praeger, 1967).

147. A. F. K. Organski, *The Stages of Political Development* (New York: Knopf, 1965).

148. Kazuma Tateisi, Mititaka Yamamoto, and Isao Kon, "Ten Developmental Stages of Society," in Paige, *Political Leadership,* pp. 185–192.

149. Donella H. Meadows, Dennis L. Meadows Jørgen Randers, and William W. Behrens III, *The Limits to Growth* (New York: Universe, 1972). For a critical perspective, see Michael H. Rothkopf, "World Models Won't Work," *Simulation* 21, 2 (August 1973), 60–61.

150. One place to begin will be to create a propositional inventory of setting-leadership relationships contained in works like Clemens Dutt, ed., *Fundamentals of Marxism-Leninism* (Moscow: Foreign Languages Publishing House, (1961) and Andreas Hegedus, "Marxist Theories of Leadership: A Marxist Approach," in R. Barry Farrell, ed., *Political Leadership in Eastern Europe and the Soviet Union* (Chicago: Aldine, 1970), pp. 28–56.

151. Quoted in Norman Gall, "Teodoro Petkoff: The Crisis of the Professional Revolutionary, Part II: A New Party," American Universities Field Staff, East Coast South American Series, 17, 9 (Venezuela), p. 6.

152. Lucy Mair, *Primitive Government* (Baltimore: Penguin, 1964), p. 218.

153. Erasmus, *The Education of a Christian Prince,* trans. Lester K. Born (New York: Columbia University Press, 1936), p. 205.

154. Among Casal's twenty "constants" of revolution, summarized in John E. Tashjean, "Twentieth Century Concepts of Revolution and Casal's Constants," *Cahiers Vilfredo Pareto* 12, 33 (1974), 192.

155. Toshiyuki Nishikawa, *The Newcomers to the House of Representatives of the Japanese Diet: 1946–1969 Patterns of Turnover, Recruitment, and Career Development* (Ph.D. 1974, University of Hawaii), p. 96.

156. Rienow and Rienow, op. cit., pp. 133 f.

157. Ibid., p. 149.

158. Ibid., p. 184.

159. Senator La Follette, waving from the capitol steps, appeared in one of the first campaign films made for showing in theaters in 1924 (ibid., p. 185). The film *Triumph of the Will,* produced for Hitler in 1934 by Leni Riefenstahl, is considered the propaganda film masterpiece of the Nazi era.

160. T. Harry Williams, *Huey Long* (New York: Bantam, 1970), p. 128. In the gubernatorial campaign of 1927 Long drove some 15,000 miles, making 600 speeches before 300,000 people (p. 279).
161. Bullock, op. cit., p. 201.
162. Rienow and Rienow, op. cit., p. 188.
163. Ibid., pp. 204 f.
164. Ibid., pp. 297 f.
165. Quoted in Fischer, op. cit., p. 428.
166. Ibid., p. 512.
167. Quoted in H. L. Matthews, op. cit., p. 262.
168. The recent discovery and incipient exploitation of one of the world's richest sources of diamonds in this area represents striking change in a setting variable the consequences of which for societal values and political leadership behavior remain to be explored (*New York Times,* November 23, 1973, p. 10).
169. H. L. Matthews, op. cit., p. 150.
170. Oral report by an Indonesian family planning worker at an East-West Center Population Institute Conference, Honolulu, 1972.
171. Pi-chao Chen, *The Politics of Population in Communist China: A Case Study of Birth Control Policy* (Ph.D. 1966, Princeton University).
172. Television debate among Honolulu mayor Frank F. Fasi, former lieutenant governor Thomas P. Gill, and former Senate president David C. McClung on "Crossfire," KGMB-TV, Honolulu, September 22, 1974.
173. Don Pirie Cass, *How to Win Votes and Influence Elections* (Chicago: Public Administration Service, 1962).
174. Quoted in H. L. Matthews, op. cit., p. 118.
175. Alvin Toffler, *Future Shock* (New York: Random House, 1970).
176. Two important works that suggest general contexts for change analysis are Wilbert E. Moore, *Social Change* (Englewood Cliffs: Prentice-Hall, 1963), and Gordon L. Lippitt, *Visualizing Change* (Fairfax: NTL Learning Resources Corporation, 1973).
177. Polybius, *The Histories,* ed. E. Badian and trans. Mortimer Chambers (New York: Washington Square, 1966).
178. J. O. Hertzler, "The Typical Life Cycle of Dictatorships," *Social Forces* 17 (March 1939), 303-309.
179. Vilfredo Pareto, *The Rise and Fall of Elites* (Totowa: Bedminster, 1968).
180. Dutt, op. cit.

Chapter 6: Multivariate, Multidimensional Linkage Approach: Dimensions

1. Mohandas K. Gandhi, *An Autobiography: The Story of My Experiments with Truth* (Boston: Beacon, 1968), p. 271.

2. Or, as some would prefer it, Leninist-Marxism.

3. Dov Eden and Uri Leviatan, "Implicit Leadership Theory as a Determinant of the Factor Structures Underlying Supervisory Behavior Scores," *Journal of Applied Psychology* 60, 6 (December 1975), 736–741.

4. J. P. Guilford, *Psychometric Methods* (New York: McGraw-Hill, 1954), p. 532.

5. Ibid.

6. Ithiel de Sola Pool, "Political Communication: Introduction," in David L. Sills, ed., *International Encyclopedia of the Social Sciences,* 17 vols. (New York: Macmillan and Free Press, 1968), 3:90–91.

7. Joachim C. Fest, *Hitler* (New York: Random House, Vintage, 1975), p. 157.

8. Quoted in ibid., p. 608.

9. Quoted in Gopinath Dhawan, *The Political Philosophy of Mahatma Gandhi* (Ahmedabad: Navajivan, 1962), p. 308.

10. Ibid., p. 270.

11. Adolf Hitler, *Mein Kampf,* trans. Ralph Mannheim (Boston: Houghton Mifflin, 1971), p. 684.

12. Fest, op. cit., p. 206.

13. Hitler, op. cit., p. 450.

14. Quoted in Dhawan, op. cit., p. 282. As Dhawan explained, "Gandhiji was a philosophical anarchist. He aimed at reducing state action to a minimum and believed in reform from within through private, i.e., non-governmental activities" (p. 190).

15. Ibid., p. 120.

16. Fest, op. cit., p. 283.

17. Hitler, op. cit., p. 676.

18. Quoted in Fest, op. cit., p. 607.

19. Quoted in Dhawan, op. cit., p. 286.

20. Ibid., p. 136.

21. Ibid., p. 137.

22. Quoted in Fest, op. cit., p. 594.

23. Ibid., p. 610.

24. Ibid., p. 621.

25. Quoted in Dhawan, op. cit., p. 304.

26. Hitler, op. cit., p. 393.

27. Quoted in Dhawan, op. cit., p. 63.

28. Hitler, op. cit., p. 441.

29. Ibid., p. 351.

30. Quoted in Dhawan, op. cit., p. 326.

31. Ibid., p. 92.

32. Hitler, op. cit., p. 443.

33. Quoted in Dhawan, op. cit., p. 283.

34. Ibid., p. 129.
35. Hitler, op. cit., p. 346.
36. Fest, op. cit., p. 674.
37. Quoted in ibid., p. 218.
38. Quoted in Dhawan, op. cit., p. 286.
39. Ibid., p. 93.
40. Ibid., p. 280.
41. Fest, op. cit., p. 612.
42. Hitler, op. cit., p. 384.
43. Ibid., p. 342.
44. Quoted in Dhawan, op. cit., p. 185.
45. Ibid., pp. 189–190.
46. Ibid., p. 303.
47. Ibid., p. 314.
48. Albert Speer, *Inside the Third Reich* (New York: Avon, 1970), p. 653.
49. Ibid., p. 401.
50. Ibid., pp. 464–466.
51. Ibid., p. 653.
52. Hitler, op. cit., p. 398.
53. Ibid., p. 674.
54. Quoted in Dhawan, op. cit., p. 233.
55. Hitler, op. cit., p. 293.
56. Quoted in Dhawan, op. cit., p. 115.
57. Quoted in David Shub, *Lenin* (Harmondsworth: Penguin, 1976), p. 263.
58. Quoted in Dhawan, op. cit., p. 282.
59. Ibid., p. 196.
60. Ibid., p. 285.
61. Ibid., p. 284.
62. Ibid., p. 277.
63. Ibid., p. 201.
64. Ibid., p. 325.
65. Ibid., p. 140.
66. Ibid., p. 118.
67. Ibid., p. 309.
68. Ibid., p. 115.

Chapter 7: Field Foundations: Research

1. Niko Tinbergen, *The Herring Gull's World* (London: Collins, 1953).
2. Frederick Adams Woods, *The Influence of Monarchs: Steps in a New Science of History* (New York: Macmillan, 1913). Unfortunately, this

book is out of print; it should be reprinted for widespread reexamination among scientists who study political leadership. Woods, who held an M.D., was a lecturer in biology at the Massachusetts Institute of Technology.

3. Ibid., p. 87.

4. Ibid., chaps. 1, 2, and 3.

5. Ibid., p. 2.

6. Ibid., p. 9.

7. John P. Kotter and Paul R. Lawrence, *Mayors in Action* (New York: Wiley, 1974).

8. Students of political leadership with special interests in futures perspectives will wish to keep informed of the activities of the World Future Studies Federation (WFSF), led by Johan Galtung, president, and a cross-national, interdisciplinary scientific council of some forty members. Consult the *Newsletter,* published by the WFSF Secretariat, Casella Postale 6203, Roma-Prati, Italy.

9. Michael J. Shapiro and G. Matthew Bonham, "Cognitive Processes and Foreign Policy Decision Making," *International Studies Quarterly* 17, 2 (June 1973), 147-174.

10. Robert Axelrod, "Psycho-algebra: A Mathematical Theory of Cognition and Choice with an Application to the British Eastern Committee of 1918," *Peace Research Society Papers* 18 (1972), 113-131.

11. Frank Harary and Robert Z. Norman, *Graph Theory as a Mathematical Model in Social Science* (Ann Arbor: University of Michigan Research Center for Group Dynamics, Publication Series No. 2, 1953); Frank Harary, ed., *New Directions in the Theory of Graphs* (New York: Academic Press, 1973).

12. O. J. Harvey, David E. Hunt, and Harold M. Schroder, *Conceptual Systems and Personality Organization* (New York: Wiley, 1961).

13. For a review of behavioral science resources for social persuasion that goes far beyond the contemporary literature of either political scientists or experienced politicians see Joel B. Cohen, ed., *Behavioral Science Foundations of Consumer Behavior* (New York: Free Press, 1972). Compare the relative "crudity" of Joseph Napolitan, *The Election Game and How to Win It* (New York: Free Press, 1972).

14. Nathan Leites, *The Operational Code of the Politburo* (New York: McGraw-Hill, 1951).

15. Alexander L. George, "The 'Operational Code': A Neglected Approach to the Study of Political Leaders and Decision-making," *International Studies Quarterly* 13, 2 (June 1969), 190-222.

16. Loch K. Johnson, "Operational Codes and the Prediction of Leadership Behavior: Senator Frank Church at Midcareer," in Margaret G. Hermann, ed., *A Psychological Examination of Political Leaders* (New York: Free Press, 1977), pp. 82-119.

17. Ralph M. Stogdill, *Manual for the Leader Behavior Description Questionnaire, Form XII* (Columbus: Ohio State University, Bureau of Business Research, 1963).

18. John K. Hemphill and Alvin E. Coons, "Development of the Leader Behavior Description Questionnaire," in Ralph M. Stogdill and A. E. Coons, eds., *Leader Behavior: Its Description and Measurement* (Columbus: Ohio State University, Bureau of Business Research, 1957), pp. 6-38.

19. Ralph M. Stogdill, Omar S. Goode, and David R. Day, "New Leader Behavior Description Subscale," *Journal of Psychology* 54, 2d half (October 1962), 259-269.

20. Potentials for doing this are suggested by a comparative review of the personality development theories of Freud, ego analysts Dollard and Miller, Wolpe, Adler, Rank, and Rogers, existentialists Horney, Sullivan, and others by Donald H. Ford and Hugh B. Urban, *Systems of Psychotherapy: A Comparative Study* (New York: Wiley, 1963). This review is of interest because it employs a common framework for comparison (e.g., distinctive features; normal course of behavior development, innate and learned characteristics; the development of disordered behavior; the goals, conditions, and principles of behavior change; and the behaviors expected of patients and therapists) and because it implies that the personalities of leaders are indeed variables (or clusters of variables) subject to change. See also Arthur Burton, ed., *Operational Theories of Personality* (New York: Brunner-Mazel, 1974).

21. The postdoctoral program in psychology and politics of Yale University provides a pioneering illustration of what can be done.

22. Theodore Lidz, *The Person: His Development through the Life Cycle* (New York: Basic Books, 1968).

23. Erik H. Erikson, "Eight Stages of Man," in *Childhood and Society* (New York: Norton, 1963), pp. 247-274.

24. Charlotte Buhler, "The Curve of Life as Studied in Biographies," *Journal of Applied Psychology* 19 (1935), 405-409.

25. Growing interest among psychologists in "implicit personality theory" may provide a basis for intellectual community. Political leaders already have been studied as "stimulus persons" in implicit personality research. See David J. Schneider, "Implicit Personality Theory: A Review," *Psychological Bulletin* 79, 5 (May 1973), 294-309.

26. Hermann, op. cit.

27. See Harold D. Lasswell, *Power and Personality* (New York: Norton, 1948); idem *Psychopathology and Politics* (Chicago: University of Chicago Press, 1930).

28. E.g., see bibliographical notes by Michael Lerner in Fred I. Greenstein, *Personality and Politics* (Chicago: Markham, 1969), pp. 154-184, and overviews such as Jeanne N. Knutson, ed., *Handbook of Political Psychology* (San Francisco: Jossey-Bass, 1973).

29. David G. Winter and Abigail J. Stewart, "Content Analysis as a Technique for Assessing Political Leaders," in Hermann, op. cit., pp. 28-61.

30. Robert S. Frank, "Nonverbal and Paralinguistic Analysis of Political Behavior," in Hermann, op. cit., pp. 64-79.

31. Thomas W. Milburn, "The Q-sort and the Study of Political Personality," in Hermann, op. cit., pp. 131-243.

32. Gordon J. DiRenzo, "Politicians and Personality: A Cross-cultural Perspective," in Hermann, op. cit., pp. 149–173.

33. Robert C. Ziller, William F. Stone, Robert M. Jackson, and Natalie J. Terbovic, "Self-Other Orientations and Political Behavior," in Hermann, op. cit., pp. 176–204.

34. Louis H. Stewart, "Birth Order and Political Leadership," in Hermann, op. cit., pp. 206–236.

35. A challenge to political scientists as well as to social psychologists is Morton Deutsch, "Courage as a Concept in Social Psychology," *Journal of Social Psychology* 55, 1 (October 1961), 49–58.

36. Some insightful characterizations of personality-setting linkages are given in the introduction to Bertel Bager's delightful photographic essay, *Nature as Designer* (New York: Van Nostrand, 1966).

37. Although not a political leader, Buckminster Fuller can be cited as an example of a person with marked identification with the universe as a setting for immediate human behavior.

38. Among "role" studies in political science that contain operational indicators for broadly based study of political leadership are Raymond F. Hopkins, "The Role of the M.P. in Tanzania," *APSR* 64, 3 (September 1970), 754–771; Rae Sherwood, "The Bantu Clerk: A Study of Role Expectations," *Journal of Social Psychology* 47, 2 (May 1958), 285–316.

39. Outstanding exceptions are the studies by Browning and Jacob of the apparent attracting and repelling effects of roles differently weighted by power, policy, mobility, or social status potentials upon political candidates whose personalities can be measured in terms of needs for power, achievement, and affiliation. Generally speaking, the more the power, mobility, and policy potential of the role, the more likely that candidates high in need for power and achievement will strive for it. See Rufus P. Browning and Herbert Jacob, "Power Motivation and the Political Personality," *Public Opinion Quarterly* 28 (1964), 75–90; Rufus P. Browning, "The Interaction of Personality and Political System in Decisions to Run for Office: Some Data and a Simulation Technique," *Journal of Social Issues* 24, 3 (July 1968), 93–109.

40. Jack Block, *The Q-sort Method in Personality Assessment and Psychiatric Research* (Springfield: Thomas, 1961).

41. William C. Mitchell, "Occupational Role Strains: The American Elective Official," *Administrative Science Quarterly* 3, 2 (September 1958), 216.

42. For an early statement of this method with explicit political implications, see Jacob L. Moreno, *Sociometry, Experimental Method and the Science of Society: An Approach to a New Political Orientation* (Beacon: Beacon House, 1951).

43. James S. Coleman, Elihu Katz, and Herbert Menzel, *Medical Innovation: A Diffusion Study* (Indianapolis: Bobbs-Merrill, 1966).

44. J. A. Riedel, "Boss and Faction," *Annals of the American Academy of Political and Social Science* 353 (May 1964), 14–26.

45. Herbert McCloskey, Paul J. Hoffman, and Rosemary Ohara, "Issue Conflict and Consensus among Party Leaders and Followers," *APSR* 54, 2 (June 1960), 406–407.

46. Daniel Katz and Samuel J. Eldersveld, "The Impact of Local Party Activity upon the Electorate," *Public Opinion Quarterly* 25 (Spring 1961), 15.

47. Giovanni Sartori, "European Political Parties: The Case of Polarized Pluralism," in Joseph LaPalombara and Myron Weiner, eds., *Political Parties and Political Development* (Princeton: Princeton University Press, 1966), pp. 144–145.

48. Stanley Milgram, "Interdisciplinary Thinking and the Small World Problem," in Muzafer Sherif and Carolyn W. Sherif, eds., *Interdisciplinary Relationships in the Social Sciences* (Chicago: Aldine, 1969), pp. 103–120.

49. Personal communication, fall 1974.

50. As pioneered by E. Spencer Wellhofer and Timothy M. Hennessey, "Political Party Development: Institutionalization, Leadership Recruitment, and Behavior," *American Journal of Political Science* 18, 1 (February 1974), 135–166.

51. Extending the work of Dahl, especially in terms of more detailed descriptions of elected leader associates. In testing·such a hypothesis, we will wish to understand conditions under which the opposite direction of influence may be true.

52. Following upon David Finlay, Ole R. Holsti, and Richard R. Fagen, *Enemies in Politics* (Chicago: Rand McNally, 1967), who have called for more systematic data to isolate "the impact of individual leaders on political practices" (p. 235), more inquiry into the conditions that provide varying degrees of freedom in the choice of enemies and friends (p. 237), and further inquiry into the functionality or dysfunctionality of enemies (or friends) for political systems (pp. 242 ff.).

53. This is suggested by Peter F. Merenda and Mohan Jitendra, "Perceptions of Nehru and the Ideal Self in the Indian Culture," *Perceptual and Motor Skills* 12, 3 (June 1966), 865–866.

54. Carrying one step further the insight of Dankwart A. Rustow, ed., *Philosophers and Kings: Studies in Leadership,* entire issue of *Daedalus* 97, 3 (Summer 1968).

55. E.g., the leader-administrator-citizen chain suggested by Samuel J. Eldersveld, V. Jagannadham, and A. P. Barnabas, *The Citizen and Administrator in a Developing Democracy* (Glenview: Scott, Foresman, 1968).

56. Fred E. Fiedler, "Leadership," General Learning Corporation Module (Morristown: General Learning Press, 1971), pp. 11–13.

57. Herbert A. Simon, "The Decision Maker as Innovator," in Sidney Mailick, ed., *Concepts and Issues in Administrative Behavior* (Englewood Cliffs: Prentice-Hall, 1962), pp. 66–69.

58. David C. Korten, "Situational Determinants of Leadership Structure," in Glenn D. Paige, ed., *Political Leadership: Readings for an Emerging Field* (New York: Free Press, 1972), pp. 146–164.

59. Charles F. Hermann, *Crises in Foreign Policy* (Indianapolis: Bobbs-Merrill, 1969), p. 29, and see following pages.

60. "One of the most crucial powers of the Chief Justice is the placement of cases on the calendar. For example, combining two or more slightly dissimilar cases can cause quite different results than if the cases were heard separately' (Steve Whitaker, "A Role Playing Simulation of the United States Supreme Court," *Teaching Political Science* 1, 1 [October 1973], 53).

61. Joseph E. Morsh, "Job Analysis in the United States Air Force," *Personnel Psychology* 17, 1 (Spring 1964), 7–17.

62. John H. Kessel, "The Parameters of Presidential Politics," Paper prepared for the 1972 Annual Meeting of the APSA, Washington. Kessel reported that he found useful Lewis A. Froman, "The Categorization of Policy Contents," in Austin Ranney, ed., *Political Science and Public Policy* (Chicago: Markham, 1968), pp. 41–52.

63. Kessel, op. cit., abstract preceding page 1.

64. Ibid., p. 10.

65. W. G. Bennis, J. W. Thomas, and M. C. Fulenwider, "Problem Analysis Diagram," in mimeo. materials related to MIT Bennis Projects No. 1 and No. 2, n.d., probably 1966. See also the similar diagram, "Force Field Analysis," based on ideas of Kurt Lewin, in Gordon L. Lippitt, *Visualizing Change: Model Building and the Change Process* (Fairfax: NTL Learning Resources Corporation, 1973), p. 29.

66. A basic statement of this technique can be found in John C. Flanagan, "The Critical Incident Technique," *Psychological Bulletin* 51, 3 (July 1954), 335–358. An application to improve training of village development leaders in India is K. N. Singh and T. Sen Gupta, "Measuring Effectiveness of Village Level Workers," *Indian Journal of Public Administration* 11, 1 (January–March 1965), 42–55. A military application giving case studies of combat and administrative stress situations is United States Air Force Academy, Department of Behavioral Sciences, *Critical Incidents in Combat*, USAFA/3-1211, 1962. An effort to define leadership in terms of critical incidents confronting administrators is presented in David D. Van Fleet, "Toward Identifying Critical Elements in a Behavioral Description of Leadership," *Public Personnel Management* 3, 1 (January 1974), 70–82.

67. In "How to Choose a Leadership Pattern," *Harvard Business Review*, 36, 2 (March–April 1958), pp. 95–101, Robert Tannenbaum and Warren H. Schmidt argued that the choice of an appropriate task-coping behavior should be made on the basis of an assessment by the leader of his or her own capabilities, the nature of the organization, and the specific requirements of the problem to be solved. In terms of the present framework this suggests that part of the definition of a "task" involves aspects of the other five variables: personality, role, organization, values, and setting.

68. For a delightful reminder that real-life problem solving involves multiple task engagement, despite our analytical and experimental simplifications,

see the remarkable series of "Judge Dee" murder mysteries written by the sinologist Robert H. van Gulik. In these mysteries the sagacious Chinese magistrate of the Ming dynasty is portrayed as solving simultaneously at least three seemingly unrelated murders, not just one. E.g., Robert H. van Gulick, *The Chinese Maze Murders* (The Hague: W. van Hoeve, 1956).

69. A most interesting example of this approach, using ideas proposed and accepted, is Frank H. Garver, "Leadership in the Constitutional Convention of 1787," *Sociology and Social Research* 21 (July–August 1937), 544–553.

70. Albert D. Biderman, "Anticipatory Studies and Stand-by Research Capabilities," in Raymond A. Bauer, ed., *Social Indicators* (Cambridge: MIT Press, 1966), pp. 272–301; see esp. pp. 275–276.

71. For example, it should be possible to link political leadership with the legal prescriptions provided by a comparative study of national constitutions by Ivo D. Duchacek, *Power Maps* (Santa Barbara: ABC-Clio, 1973). We need to ask how leaders contribute to the creation of value "maps" and what effects these maps have upon leaders in return. See G. S. Sharma, "Concept of Leadership Implicit in the Directive Principles of State Policy in the Indian Constitution," in Gehan Wijeyewardene, ed., *Leadership and Authority* (Singapore: University of Malaya Press, 1968), pp. 294–308.

72. An early example, still of interest, is Ralph K. White, "Value Analysis: A Quantitative Method for Describing Qualitative Data," *Journal of Social Psychology* 19, 2 (May 1944), 351–358; White applied his later method in "Hitler, Roosevelt and the Nature of War Propaganda," *Journal of Abnormal and Social Psychology* 44, 2 (April 1949), 157–174.

73. Leonard A. Lo Sciuto and Eugene L. Hartley, "Religious Affiliation and Open-mindedness in Binocular Resolution," *Perceptual and Motor Skills* 17, 2 (October 1963), 427–430.

74. Milton K. Rokeach, *The Open and Closed Mind* (New York: Basic Books, 1960), pp. 72 ff. A shortened, ten-item version of the original, forty-item scale was developed by Rolf Schulze, "A Shortened Version of the Rokeach Dogmatism Scale," *Journal of Psychological Studies* 13 (1962), 93–97.

75. The binocular resolution phenomenon may be experienced by most readers. Prior knowledge of the nature of the conflicting symbols does not seem to be a biasing factor, although some persons seem to be left- or right-eye dominant, seeing only symbols in front of that eye regardless of value content. Simply obtain a stereoscope and adjust the slide to the point where the convergent three-dimensional effect occurs. Then confront the eyes with pairs of previously prepared affect-laden conflicting value symbols—first closing the eyes to insert the pairs in the apparatus and then opening them briefly to report perception. Some experimentation with discriminating words and picture symbols (e.g., swastika versus hammer and sickle; words "democracy" versus "fascism") may be required. Even this kind of crude method can produce startling results, suggesting the potential of more controlled conditions such as those provided in an optometrist's office.

76. For an early statement, see F. P. Kilpatrick and Hadley Cantril, "Self-anchoring Scaling: A Measure of Individuals' Unique Reality Worlds," *Journal of Individual Psychology* 16, 2 (November 1960), 1-16. Some subsequent applications are Lloyd A. Free, *Six Allies and a Neutral* (New York: Free Press, 1959); Hadley Cantril, *The Pattern of Human Concerns* (New Brunswick: Rutgers University Press, 1966); and Glenn D. Paige and Doo-Bum Shin, "Aspirations and Obstacles in Korean Development Administration: An Application of Self-anchoring Scaling," *Public Policy* 16 (1967), 3-28.

77. Kilpatrick and Cantril, op. cit., p. 6.

78. Charles E. Osgood, George J. Suci, and Percy H. Tannenbaum, *The Measurement of Meaning* (Urbana: University of Illinois Press, 1957); James G. Snider and Charles E. Osgood, *Semantic Differential Technique: A Sourcebook* (Chicago: Aldine, 1969).

79. Percy H. Tannenbaum, Bradley S. Greenberg, and Fred R. Silverman, "Candidate Images," in Sidney Kraus, ed., *The Great Debates* (Bloomington: Indiana University Press, 1962), pp. 277-278. See also Dan Nimmo and Robert L. Savage, *Candidates and Their Images* (Pacific Palisades: Goodyear, 1976).

80. E.g., note the search for meaningful political values in childhood, adolescence, and early adulthood revealed in Mao Tse-tung's biographical recollections as told to Edgar Snow, *Red Star over China* (New York: Modern Library, 1944), esp. pp. 121-163. Among values progressively explored by the young Mao were monarchism, republicanism, idealism, liberalism, utopian socialism, anarchism, and Marxism.

81. That is, what might be called "washing hands" behavior to compensate for disesteem associated with what Walzer, following Sartre, analyzed as "dirty hands" political engagement. This would extend the Lasswell-George compensatory-striving hypothesis by identifying both sources of disesteem and compensatory potentials in terms of situationally given political leadership role demands and opportunities. Compare Alexander L. George, "Power as a Compensatory Value for Political Leaders," *Journal of Social Issues* 24, 3 (July 1968), 29-49, and Michael Walzer, "Political Action: The Problem of Dirty Hands," in Marshall Cohen et al., eds., *War and Moral Responsibility* (Princeton: Princeton University Press, 1974), pp. 62-68.

82. E.g., Gandhi's statement in 1920: "I do believe that where there is only a choice between cowardice and violence, I would advise violence" (Mohandas K. Gandhi, *Non-violent Resistance* [New York: Schocken, 1951], p. 132). Also Ho Chi Minh's observation: "Lenin said that even if a compromise with bandits was advantageous to the revolution he would do it" (Quoted in Bernard B. Fall, ed., *Ho Chi Minh on Revolution* [New York: New American Library, 1968], p. 196).

83. E.g., Gandhi's advice: "We must patiently try to convert our opponents. If we wish to evolve the spirit of democracy out of slavery, we must be scrupulously exact in our dealings with opponents" (Gandhi, *Non-violent Resistance,* p. 147).

84. E.g., how did Gandhian values of nonviolence spread among members of the Satyagraha movement?

85. Harold Guetzkow, *Multiple Loyalties,* Center for Research on World Political Institutions in the Woodrow Wilson School, Publication no. 4 (Princeton: Princeton University, 1955).

86. Among suggestive early studies that probed the meaning of success-failure in American elected politics are John Kingdon, *Candidates for Office: Beliefs and Strategies* (New York: Random House, 1968), and Robert J. Huckshorn and Robert C. Spencer, *The Politics of Defeat* (Amherst: University of Massachusetts Press, 1971).

87. E.g., see the fourteen-item criticism of the leadership of Nikita Khrushchev pieced together from discussions in "responsible circles" by the Moscow correspondent of the Italian Communist party newspaper *L'Unità* in *New York Times,* November 1, 1964, p. 4.

88. One past or present source may be the study of obituaries and eulogies to dead leaders.

89. Ludwig von Bertalanffy, *General System Theory* (New York: Braziller, 1968).

90. James G. Miller, "Living Systems: Basic Concepts," *Behavioral Science* 10, 3 (July 1965), 193–237; idem, "Living Systems: Structure and Process," *Behavioral Science* 10, 4 (October 1965), 337–379; idem, "Living Systems: Cross-level Hypotheses," *Behavioral Science* 10, 4 (October 1965), 380–411.

91. E.g., Walter Buckley, ed., *Modern Systems Research for the Behavioral Scientist* (Chicago: Aldine, 1968).

92. Donella H. Meadows, Dennis L. Meadows, Jørgen Randers, and William W. Behrens III, *The Limits to Growth* (New York: Universe, 1972).

93. Roger G. Barker, *Ecological Psychology: Concepts and Methods for Studying the Environment of Human Behavior* (Stanford: Stanford University Press, 1968).

94. Ibid., p. 4.

95. Ibid., p. 158.

96. Ibid., p. 19.

97. Christen T. Jonassen and Sherwood H. Peres, *Interrelationships of Dimensions of Community Systems: A Factor Analysis of Eighty-two Variables* (Columbus: Ohio State University Press, 1960).

98. Ibid., p. 5.

99. E.g., Charles L. Taylor, *Aggregate Data Analysis: Political and Social Indicators in Cross-national Research* (The Hague: Mouton, 1968); Arthur F. Banks, *Cross-polity Time Series Data* (Cambridge: MIT Press, 1971); and Charles L. Taylor et al., *World Handbook of Social and Economic Indicators* (New Haven: Yale University Press, 1972).

100. John Naisbitt, "Ten Major Changes to Expect in the Decade of the 1970's" (Speech given at the Tenth Annual Management Seminar for Women Executives, Southern Methodist University, Dallas, May 18, 1972), transcript, pp. 1–7 passim.

101. For an early statement, see Olaf Helmer, *Social Forecasting* (New York: Basic Books, 1966). A recent review of rapidly spreading usage is contained in Howard A. Linstone and Murray Turoff, eds., *The Delphi Method: Techniques and Applications* (Reading: Addison-Wesley, 1975).

102. Helmer also discusses the difficulties and limitations of such a method: "its insufficient reliability; its tendency to produce self-fulfilling or self-defeating prophecies . . . ; the sensitivity of results to ambiguity of questions; the difficulty of assessing and utilizing the degree of expertise; and the impossibility of taking into account the unexpected" (Helmer, *Social Forecasting,* p. 45).

103. Ibid., p. 55.

104. An excellent presentation of alternative futures research methods, together with suggested criteria for comparing and applying them, is Steven C. Wheelwright and Spyros Makridakis, *Forecasting Methods for Management* (New York: Wiley, 1973); an overview is contained in tables 12-1 and 12-2 (pp. 198-201).

105. Hubert M. Blalock, Jr., *Causal Inferences in Non-experimental Research* (Chapel Hill: University of North Carolina Press, 1964).

106. Paul Horst, *Matrix Algebra for Social Scientists* (New York: Holt, Rinehart & Winston, 1963).

107. E.g., Rudolf J. Rummel, *Applied Factor Analysis* (Evanston: Northwestern University Press, 1970).

108. F. M. Andrews et al., *A Guide for Selecting Statistical Techniques for Analyzing Social Science Data* (Ann Arbor: University of Michigan, Survey Research Center, 1974).

109. Jae-On Kim, "Factor Analysis," and Paul Vincent Warwick, "Canonical Variation Analysis," in Norman H. Nie et al., *SPSS* (New York: McGraw-Hill, 1975), pp. 468-514, 515-527.

110. J. P. Guilford, *Psychometric Methods* (New York: McGraw-Hill, 1954), p. 532.

111. J. S. Armstrong, "Derivation of Theory by Means of Factor Analysis, or Tom Swift and His Electric Factor Analysis Machine," *American Statistician* 21 (December 1967), 21.

112. Ralph M. Stogdill, *Handbook of Leadership: A Survey of Theory and Research* (New York: Free Press, 1974).

113. John D. Parker, "Classification of Candidates' Motivations for First Seeking Office," *Journal of Politics* 34, 1 (February 1972), 268-271.

114. Note that Lasswell divided his values into two subsets: "welfare values" (well-being, wealth, skill, and enlightenment) and "deference values" (power, respect, rectitude, and affection). See Harold D. Lasswell and Abraham Kaplan, *Power and Society* (New Haven: Yale University Press, 1965), pp. 55 ff.

115. An extraordinary observational experience has been reported in *The Politics of Progress* (Englewood Cliffs: Prentice-Hall, 1974) by Raymond E. Wolfinger, who spent seven months as a research assistant in New Haven

observing Edward J. Logue, urban renewal director, and five months in the office of the mayor, Richard C. Lee. The frankness with which Wolfinger shares the difficulties that later arose over Mayor Lee's objections to what he considered damaging revelations in Wolfinger's 1961 Yale Ph.D. dissertation will greatly aid future students of political leadership to prepare, design, and carry out research of this nature.

116. Plutarch, *Lives of the Noble Greeks and Romans.* A standard edition is *Plutarch's Lives,* 11 vols., trans. Bernadotte Perrin, Loeb Classical Library (Cambridge: Harvard University Press, 1914–1926).

117. Charles E. Merriam, *Four American Party Leaders* (1926, reprint ed., Freeport: Books for Libraries Press, 1967).

118. James MacGregor Burns, *Roosevelt: The Lion and the Fox* (New York: Harcourt, Brace, 1956).

119. Alexander L. George and Juliette L. George, *Woodrow Wilson and Colonel House* (New York: Day, 1956).

120. E. Victor Wolfenstein, *The Revolutionary Personality* (Princeton: Princeton University Press, 1967).

121. Alex Gottfried, *Boss Cermak of Chicago* (Seattle: University of Washington Press, 1962).

122. Lewis J. Edinger, *Kurt Schumacher: A Study in Personality and Political Behavior* (Stanford: Stanford University Press, 1965).

123. Robert C. Tucker, *Stalin as Revolutionary, 1879–1929* (New York: Norton, 1973).

124. Lewis J. Edinger, "Political Science and Political Biography: Reflections on the Study of Leadership (I)," *Journal of Politics* 26, 2 (May 1964), 423–439; idem, "Political Science and Political Biography (II)," *Journal of Politics* 26, 3 (August 1964), 648–676.

125. John A. Garraty, *The Nature of Biography* (New York: Random House, Vintage, 1964).

126. Hedda Bolgar, "The Case Study Method," in Benjamin Wolman, ed., *Handbook of Clinical Psychology* (New York: McGraw-Hill, 1965), pp. 28–39.

127. Betty Glad, "Contributions to Psychobiography," in Jeanne K. Knutson, ed., *Handbook of Political Psychology* (San Francisco: Jossey-Bass, 1973), pp. 296–321.

128. *Biography Index* (New York: Wilson, 1946–); a cumulative index of biographical material published in books and magazines.

129. A paradigm for multiperspective or multidisciplinary convergence upon a single case is provided by Norman L. Faberow and Edwin S. Shneidman, eds., *The Cry for Help* (New York: McGraw-Hill, 1961). See also Clemens A. Loew et al., eds., *Three Psychotherapies: A Clinical Comparison* (New York: Brunner-Mazel, 1975).

130. Bolgar, op. cit., pp. 31 ff; Marthe Robert, *The Psychoanalytic Revolution: Sigmund Freud's Life and Achievement,* trans. Kenneth Morgan (New York: Harcourt, Brace, 1966), pp. 108 ff.

131. Woodrow Wilson, *George Washington* (New York: Harper, 1897).

132. I. V. Stalin, "Lenin," *Works*, 13 vols. (Moscow: Foreign Languages Publishing House, 1952–1955), 6:54–56.

133. Leon Trotsky, *Stalin,* ed. and trans. Charles Malamuth (New York: Stein & Day, 1967).

134. Winston S. Churchill, *Marlborough,* 4 vols., abr. ed. (New York: Scribner's, 1968).

135. John F. Kennedy, *Profiles in Courage* (New York: Harper, 1956).

136. Although the practice of writing biographical sketches of moral exemplars was common to Chinese tradition, apparently the method of paired comparison was unique to Plutarch and possible predecessors. Modern social science students of political leadership will need the cooperation of classicists, historians, and other humanists in seeking an answer to the still open question of whether or not there were Plutarch-like efforts in the Chinese, Islamic, and other civilizations.

137. For a general introduction to the remarkably scanty literature in English on Plutarch, see D. A. Russell, *Plutarch* (London: Duckworth, 1973); C. P. Jones, *Plutarch and Rome* (Oxford: Clarendon, 1971); Reginald H. Barrows, *Plutarch and His Times* (Bloomington: Indiana University Press, 1967); and the entry on Plutarch in N. G. L. Hammond and H. H. Scullard, eds. *The Oxford Classical Dictionary,* 2d ed. (Oxford: Clarendon, 1970), pp. 848–850.

138. Martha Howard, *The Influence of Plutarch in the Major European Literatures of the Eighteenth Century* (Chapel Hill: University of North Carolina Press, 1970).

139. Zbigniew Brzezinski and Samuel P. Huntington III, *Political Power: USA/USSR* (New York: Viking, 1972), pp. 129–190.

140. Robert C. North, with the collaboration of Ithiel de Sola Pool, *Kuomintang and Chinese Communist Elites* (Stanford: Stanford University Press, 1952).

141. DiRenzo, op. cit., pp. 149–173.

142. Robert D. Putnam, *The Beliefs of Politicians* (New Haven: Yale University Press, 1973).

143. The logic of most similar versus most dissimilar systems designs for comparative research is presented in Adam Przeworski and Henry Teune, *The Logic of Comparative Social Inquiry* (New York: Wiley, 1970).

144. Stuart H. Palmer, *A Study of Murder* (New York: Crowell, 1960).

145. Tom Wicker, *JFK and LBJ* (Baltimore: Penguin, 1969).

146. Louis-E. Lomax, *To Kill a Black Man* (Los Angeles: Holloway, 1968).

147. Tinbergen, op. cit., pp. 72–73.

148. An example is the study of business, labor, government, political party, and voluntary association leaders described in Allen H. Barton, "The American Leadership Study: Issues and Methods," mimeo. (New York: Columbia University, Bureau of Applied Social Research, August 1972).

149. Carl Beck and J. T. McKechnie, *Political Elites: A Select Computerized Bibliography* (Cambridge: MIT Press, 1967). Two pioneering efforts to establish computerized data banks for aggregate data analysis have been the Berkeley Elites Automated Retrieval System (BEARS) at the University of California, Berkeley, developed by David Nasatir and Charles Yarborough, and the Archive on Political Elites in Eastern Europe, created by Carl Beck and associates at the University of Pittsburgh.

150. Donald D. Searing, "The Comparative Study of Elite Socialization," *Comparative Political Studies* 1, 4 (January 1949), 471–500.

151. Stogdill, op. cit.

152. E.g., see *Experimental Study of Politics,* a journal that began publication in 1971. As of 1975, no article in this journal had a title reference to "leadership" or "followership," although, of course, many of the articles on voting behavior, coalition formation, attitude change, etc., are highly relevant for a more explicit leader-follower interaction approach: Gary L. Reback, "The Effects of Precinct-Level Voter Contact Activities on Voting Behavior," 1, 3 (December 1971), 65, 97; Meredith W. Watts and Ronald D. Hedlund, "An Experiment in Modifying Affect toward Socio-political Authority Figures," 4, 3 (December 1975), 82-98.

153. Although "leadership" itself seems not to be a salient subject of interest in the simulation literature as compared with the social psychological experimental literature, several political roles of related interest are being explored through this technique; e.g., legislators, mayors, councils, and politicians.

154. E.g., Harold Guetzkow, Philip Kotler, and Randall L. Schultz, eds., *Simulation in Social and Administrative Science* (Englewood Cliffs: Prentice-Hall, 1972), esp. Paul Smoker, "International Relations Simulations" (pp. 296–339); J. A. Laponce and Paul Smoker, *Experimentation and Simulation in Political Science* (Toronto: University of Toronto Press, 1972).

155. E.g., Andrew M. Scott et al., *Simulation and National Development* (New York: Wiley, 1966).

156. E.g., James D. Barber, *Power in Committees* (Chicago: Rand McNally, 1966); Robert F. Bales, "Interaction Process Analysis," in David L. Sills, ed. *International Encyclopedia of the Social Sciences,* 17 vols. (New York: Macmillan and Free Press, 1968), 7:465–471. A modification of the Bales approach is contained in Richard P. Butler and Edward F. Cureton, "Factor Analysis of Small Group Behavior," *Journal of Social Psychology* 89, 1 (February 1973), 85–89.

157. Fiedler, op. cit.

158. James D. Barber, *The Presidential Character: Predicting Performance in the White House* (Englewood Cliffs: Prentice-Hall, 1972).

159. George W. Fairweather, *Methods for Experimental Social Innovation* (New York: Wiley, 1968).

160. Harold F. Gosnell, *Getting Out the Vote* (Chicago: University of Chicago Press, 1927), employing successive mailed appeals based upon prior research into reasons given for nonvoting.

161. Donald T. Campbell and Julian T. Stanley, *Experimental and Quasi-experimental Designs for Research* (Chicago: Rand McNally, 1963).

162. E.g., Marc J. Swartz, ed., *Political Anthropology* (Chicago: Aldine, 1966). See also *Political Anthropology*, a journal begun in 1975.

163. Herbert S. Lewis, "Leaders and Followers: Some Anthropological Perspectives," Addison-Wesley Module in Anthropology no. 50 (Reading: Addison-Wesley, 1974).

164. A basic guide to contemporary ethnographic research methods of interest to political scientists is Raoull Naroll and Ronald Cohen, eds., *A Handbook of Method in Cultural Anthropology* (New York: Columbia University Press, 1973).

165. E.g., Jan Vansina, "Once upon a Time: Oral Traditions as History in Africa," in Felix Gilbert and Stephen R. Graubard, eds., *Historical Studies Today* (New York: Norton, 1972), pp. 413–435: "A chiefdom whose traditions acknowledge it lost a battle is a rare thing" (p. 419).

166. Ellen M. McGrath, "Uses of Film in the Study of Human Behavior: The Social Scientist as Film-maker and Analyst—An Annotated Bibliography" (Paper presented to the Research Film Committee, African Studies Association, Philadelphia, 1972).

167. Eugene J. Webb, Donald T. Campbell, Richard B. Swartz, and Lee Sechrest, *Unobtrusive Measures: Nonreactive Research in Social Science* (Chicago: Rand McNally, 1966).

168. Raoull Naroll, *Data Quality Control* (New York: Free Press, 1962).

169. A delightful analog for this in the study of animal behavior is Farley Mowat, *Never Cry Wolf* (New York: Dell, 1963), which, like Plutarch, ought to become part of the essential training for every student of political leadership.

170. Shanti Kothari and Ramashray Roy, *Relations between Politicians and Administrators at the District Level* (New Delhi: Indian Institute of Public Administration and the Centre of Applied Politics, 1969).

171. Reed M. Powell and Dalmas H. Nelson, "Business Executives View Politicians: Negative Feelings Block Cooperative Efforts," *Business Horizons* 11, 5 (October 1968), 41–51.

172. Charles B. Spaulding, Carl C. Hetrick, and Henry A. Turner, "Political Activism and Attitudes of Academically Affiliated Sociologists," *Sociology and Social Research* 57, 4 (July 1973), 413–428.

173. Bernice T. Eiduson, *Scientists: Their Psychological Worlds* (New York: Basic Books, 1962).

174. Charles E. Merriam, "Progress in Political Research," *APSR* 20, 1 (February 1926), 5. My colleagues Robert Cahill and Henry Kariel have impressed upon me similar insights. An example of political leader humor at one time in American culture is *The Kennedy Wit*, RCA Victor Record VDM-101, which is introduced by Adlai E. Stevenson, a fan of Lincoln's humor.

175. Among puns reported by State Representative Robert Kimura at a Democratic party public legislative briefing session, State Capitol, Honolulu, February 23, 1974, crediting many to Representative Hiroshi Kato.

176. Consider William C. Mitchell's insightful observation: "The role of humor ought not to be underestimated as a means for handling the strains. of politics, including that of status insecurity. . . . The politician . . . is quite capable of laughing at himself. The fact that he can and does may constitute an effort to minimize the difficulties of political life" (Mitchell, op. cit., p. 227).

Chapter 8. Field Foundations: Education

1. Question 225 in Russell H. Ewing, "A Manual for Ten Types of Leaders: 1000 Questions, Answers and References," mimeo. (Clinton: Hamilton College Bookstore, 1949); copy in Firestone Library, Princeton University.

2. Mary H. Curzan, ed., *Careers and the Study of Political Science,* 2d ed. (Washington: American Political Science Association, 1976).

3. Ibid., p. 24.

4. For some negative findings see Marvin Shick and Albert Somit, "The Failure to Teach Political Activity," *American Behavioral Scientist* 6, 5 (January 1963), 5–8; Dean Jaros and R. Darcy, "The Elusive Impact of Political Science: More Negative Findings," *Experimental Study of Politics* 2, 1 (1972–1973), 1–13; Tod A. Baker et al., "A Note on the Impact of College Experience on Changing the Political Attitudes of Students," *Experimental Study of Politics* 2, 1 (1972–1973), 76–88. Baker and associates found no significant change in authoritarianism, tolerance, or patriotism across classes in the "controlled environment" of a military college.

5. E.g., John R. P. French, Jr., "Retraining an Autocratic Leader," *Journal of Abnormal and Social Psychology* 39, 2 (April 1944), 224–237; Fred E. Fiedler, "The Effects of Leadership Training and Experience: A Contingency Model Interpretation," *Administrative Science Quarterly* 17, 4 (December 1972), 453–470.

6. Measures employed were those of McClosky, Rokeach, and Adorno. For details of design and data analysis see David D. Dabelko and Craig P. Caywood, "Higher Education as a Political Socializing Agent," *Experimental Study of Politics* 2,2 (March 1973), 1–24.

7. The pioneering research now being accomplished on the political socialization of children needs to be supplemented by asking not only how children think *about* political leaders but also what children are learning *for* political leadership.

8. A survey of several approaches to elite education can be found in Rupert Wilkinson, ed., *Governing Elites: Studies in Training and Selection* (New York: Oxford University Press, 1969). The essay by anthropologist Henry

Selby, contrasting education for leadership in caste versus mobile societies, is of special interest (pp. 3–22).

9. James D. Barber, "Classifying and Predicting Presidential Styles: Two 'Weak' Presidents," *Journal of Social Issues* 24, 3 (July 1968), pp. 51–80; reprinted in Glenn D. Paige, ed. *Political Leadership: Readings for an Emerging Field* (New York: Free Press, 1972), pp. 85–114.

10. Martha W. Howard, *The Influence of Plutarch in the Major European Literatures of the Eighteenth Century* (Chapel Hill: University of North Carolina Press, 1970), p. 111.

11. Edgar Snow, *Red Star over China* (New York: Modern Library, 1944), p. 134.

12. Woodrow Wilson, *George Washington* (New York: Harper, 1897).

13. I. V. Stalin, "Lenin," *Works*, 13 vols. (Moscow: Foreign Languages Publishing House, 1952–1955), 6:54–56.

14. Leon Trotsky, *Stalin,* ed. and trans. Charles Malamuth (New York: Stein & Day, 1967).

15. John F. Kennedy, *Profiles in Courage* (New York: Harper, 1956).

16. Winston S. Churchill, *Marlborough,* 4 vols., abr. ed. (New York: Scribner's, 1968).

17. Charles de Gaulle, *Memoirs of Hope,* trans. Terence Kilmartin (New York: Simon & Schuster, 1971).

18. Strobe Talbott, ed. and trans., *Khrushchev Remembers* (Boston: Little, Brown, 1970).

19. Quoted in Kaju Nakamura, *Prince Ito* (Tokyo: Anraku, 1910), pp. 80–81.

20. Present multimedia technologies need to be combined to create biographical modules for individual and group study. Computer-assisted retrieval of multimedia materials desired by students reading traditional printed biographies offers enormous possibilities.

21. "No pedagogy which is truly liberating can remain distant from the oppressed by treating them as unfortunate and by presenting for their imitation models from among the oppressors. The oppressed must be their own model in the struggle for redemption" (Paulo Freire, *Pedagogy of the Oppressed* [New York: Seabury, 1974], p. 39).

22. Quoted in Eric Sevareid, reporter, "Five Presidents on the Presidency," CBS Television News Special, April 26, 1973, transcript, p. 15.

23. In Kennedy's case, it undoubtedly would have been helpful if he had been assisted to know more of the United States before becoming a senator and more of the world before becoming president. As Sorensen observed, before his presidential campaign Kennedy had quite limited knowledge about economics, blacks, poverty, and the world outside the East Coast, Europe, and the South Pacific (Theodore Sorensen, *Kennedy* [New York: Bantam, 1966], pp. 18, 28, 444).

24. This paragraph is based upon advice given by local leaders to students at the University of Hawaii in an undergraduate course on political leadership.

25. Appreciation is expressed to Thomas E. Mann, APSA staff associate, for help in determining this.

26. Freire, op. cit., pp. 138 f.

27. Nicholas Doman, "Politics for Politicians," *South Atlantic Quarterly* 42, 4 (October 1943), 337.

28. For an excellent discussion of the problem of political generalization that itself can become a kind of narrow specialization, see Jerzy J. Wiatr, "Political Leadership: What Kind of Professionalism?" in Jerzy J. Wiatr, ed., *Studies in Polish Political System* (Wroclaw: Polish Academy of Sciences Press, 1967), pp. 140–145.

29. Martin Tarcher, *Leadership and the Power of Ideas* (New York: Harper & Row, 1966).

30. *The Face of Lincoln,* University of Southern California, Department of Cinema (22 min.).

31. CBS Television News Special, April 26, 1973; the views of Truman, Eisenhower, Kennedy, Johnson, and Nixon.

32. *Triumph of the Will* (120 min.); produced in 1934 by Leni Riefenstahl.

33. *Portrait of Adlai Stevenson,* Spoken Arts Record 770; Stevenson in conversation with Arnold Michaelis.

34. *The Hecklers,* Time-Life Films (35 min.); made for BBC-TV.

35. Henry Steele Commager, ed., *F.D.R. Speaks,* Washington Record M-2243 (6 LPs); the authorized edition of Roosevelt's 1943–1945 speeches.

36. E.g., *Sir Winston Churchill: A Selection from His Famous Wartime Speeches,* Capitol Record TBO 2192.

37. *Lenin's Speeches,* Melodiya Record D-16693-4; in Russian, recorded in 1919 and 1920.

38. *I Have a Dream: The Rev. Dr. Martin Luther King, Jr., 1929-1968,* Twentieth Century–Fox Record TFS-3201.

39. "On the Existence of God," tape recording provided by the Indian Ministry of Information, New Delhi.

40. "His Last Will and Testament," *Jawaharlal Nehru,* Odeon Record MOCE 1020.

41. *The Head Men,* Canadian Film Board (28 min.).

42. E.g., Marvin G. Weinbaum and Louis H. Gold, *Presidential Election: A Simulation with Readings* (New York: Holt, Rinehart & Winston, 1970); Leonard Stitleman and William D. Copland, *The Congressman at Work* (Chicago: Science Research Associates, 1969); Andrew M. Scott et al., *Simulation and National Development* (New York: Wiley, 1966).

43. Steve Whitaker, "A Role Playing Simulation of the United States Supreme Court," *Teaching Political Science* 1, 1 (October 1973), 47–58. Students achieved never less than 96 percent accuracy.

44. Saul D. Alinsky, *Rules for Radicals* (New York: Random House, 1971), p. 156.

45. John Kotter and Paul R. Lawrence, *Mayors in Action* (New York: Wiley, 1974).

46. Robert T. Golembiewski, "The Assignment Problem: Managing a Management Course," *Journal of the Academy of Management* 6, 1 (March 1963), 18–35. This may be compared with psychiatric research findings that some therapists actually systematically lower the heart beat of their patients.

47. Derek C. Bok, "Harvard: Then, Now and in the Future," *Harvard Today,* Spring 1975, p. 5.

48. Personal communication, April 1, 1975; quoted with permission.

49. William E. Mosler, "Wanted: New Type Politician," *National Municipal Review,* 33 (May 1944), 237.

50. This is suggested in a brilliant and compelling way by Catherine V. Richards and Norman A. Polansky, "Reaching Working Class Youth Leaders," *Social Work* 4, 4 (October 1959), 31–39.

Chapter 9. Field Foundations: Application

1. Quoted in Otto Nathan and Heinz Norden, eds., *Einstein on Peace* (New York: Simon & Schuster, 1960), p. 312.

2. Giovanni Baldelli, *Social Anarchism* (Chicago: Aldine-Atherton, 1971), p. 187.

3. For a more complete analysis of similar obstacles in social psychology and a set of recommendations for overcoming them see Morton Deutsch, "On Making Social Psychology More Useful," *SSRC Items* 30, 1 (March 1976), 1–6.

4. E.g., Austin Ranney, ed., *Political Science and Public Policy* (Chicago: Markham, 1968); Harold D. Lasswell, *The Future of Political Science* (New York: Atherton, 1963). Compare, however, Paul F. Lazarsfeld, William H. Sewell, and Harold L. Wilensky, eds., *The Uses of Sociology* (New York: Basic Books, 1967), and Benjamin B. Wolman, ed., *Handbook of Clinical Psychology* (New York: McGraw-Hill, 1965).

5. This is not to imply that all such discrepancies are dysfunctional but only that some can be, and that neither positive nor deleterious effects can be appreciated without some kind of monitoring effort.

6. Craig C. Lundberg, "Middlemen in Science Utilization: Some Notes toward Clarifying Conversion Roles," *American Behavioral Scientist* 11, 6 (February 1966), 11.

7. G. H. Boehringer et al., "Stirling: The Destructive Application of Group Techniques to a Conflict," *Journal of Conflict Resolution* 18, 2 (June 1974), 258–259.

8. See Leonard W. Doob and William J. Foltz, "The Impact of a Workshop upon Grass-roots Leaders in Belfast," *Journal of Conflict Resolution* 18, 2 (June 1974), 237–256 and its bibliography; Daniel I. Alevy et al., "Rationale, Research and Role Relations in the Stirling Workshop," *Journal of Conflict Resolution* 18, 2 (June 1974), 267–284.

9. A pioneering political science effort to simulate and evaluate three alternative political institutions (monarchical, republican, and communist) is represented by Fazil M. Nazaar, *Development, Modernization and Leadership Styles in Afghanistan: A Human Simulation in Politics* (Ph.D. 1972, University of Hawaii). Nazaar tried by human "laboratory" simulation to forecast alternative empirical and normative conditions that often are explored only through coups and revolutions accompanied by bloodshed.

10. James D. Barber, "Question of Presidential Character," *Saturday Review,* September 23, 1972, pp. 62–66.

11. David G. Winter, "What Makes a Candidate Run," *Psychology Today,* July 1976, pp. 45–49, 92.

12. E.g., Group for the Advancement of Psychiatry, *The VIP with Psychiatric Impairment* (New York: Scribner's, 1973). This book includes also brief case studies of George III, Ludwig II, Paul von Hindenburg, Woodrow Wilson, Franklin D. Roosevelt, Mussolini, Earl K. Long, and James V. Forrestal.

13. For a business application of this approach in terms of top (80 percent future versus 20 percent present), middle (50-50), and lower (20-80) management positions, see Paul Mali, *Managing by Objectives* (New York: Wiley-Interscience, 1972), pp. 41–42.

14. George E. Reedy, *The Twilight of the Presidency* (New York: World, 1970).

15. Harold D. Lasswell, "Self-observation: Recording the Focus of Attention," *The Analysis of Political Behavior* (New York: Oxford University Press, 1947), pp. 279–286; esp. p. 281.

16. E.g., in electoral systems, both candidates *and voters* may be assisted in campaign design.

17. Both leaders and followers will need to be assisted in the management of emotional blocks to effective cooperative action.

18. A key future task will be to design more adequate information systems to assist both leaders and followers in making political decisions.

19. An important applied as well as educational area will be to assist both leaders and followers to identify persons with the competencies they need to solve problems.

20. Charles E. Merriam, "Progress in Political Research," *ASPR* 20, 1 (February 1926), 1–13. "We do not teach all that we have learned and are driven to teach sometimes what we are not so sure of" (p. 6).

21. E.g., see the studies of Italian and American politicians by Gordon DiRenzo, "Politicians and Personality: A Cross-cultural Perspective," in Margaret G. Hermann, ed., *A Psychological Examination of Political Leaders* (New York: Free Press, 1977), pp. 149–173, and of British and Italian politicians by Robert D. Putnam, *The Beliefs of Politicians: Ideology, Conflict, and Democracy in Britain and Italy* (New Haven: Yale University Press, 1973).

Chapter 10. Toward Global Scientific Cooperation

1. Walt Whitman, *Leaves of Grass,* "Song of Myself," line 1087.
2. The cross-national success of the Stanley Foundation in organizing ten conferences on the future of the United Nations from 1965 to 1975 suggests that this format might be extended from diplomatic and administrative personnel to political leaders at various levels.

NAME INDEX

397

G

Gage, Merrill, 200
Gall, Norman, 374
Gallagher, Charles F., 108, 368
Galtung, Johan, 378
Gandhi, Mohandas K., 16, 47, 50, 56, 65,
    109, 133, 151–152, 200, 351, 361,
    375–377, 384
Gardner, John W., 1, 333
Garraty, John A., 180, 181, 387
Garver, Frank H., 383
George III, 38, 395
George VI, 72
George, Alexander L., 47, 48, 59, 113, 159,
    160–161, 178, 180, 344, 361, 367, 370,
    378, 387
George, Juliette L., 47, 59, 113, 180, 344,
    370, 387
Gerth, H. H., 346
Geyer, Georgie Anne, 370
Gibb, Cecil A., 78, 80–81, 97, 109, 342,
    357, 360
Gilbert, Felix, 390
Gill, Thomas P., 375
Gilmour, Robert S., 349
Glad, Betty, 53, 180, 387
Gladstone, William E., 196
Goffman, Erving, 388
Gold, Louis H., 393
Goldwater, Barry M., 57, 120, 121
Golembiewski, Robert T., 206, 394
Goode, Omar S., 379
Goodrich, Daniel, 363
Gosnell, Harold F., 45, 227–228, 342, 389
Gottfried, Alex, 47, 180, 344, 387
Graubard, Stephen R., 390
Greenberg, Bernard, 68, 353
Greenberg, Bradley S., 384
Greenberg, Sanford E., 113, 370
Greenstein, Fred I., 12, 47, 344, 347, 362,
    367, 379
Gregory, Donald, 347
Gross, Neal, 49, 70, 110, 345, 354, 368
Grumm, John G., 34
Grupp, Fred W., Jr., 362
Guerrero, Léon Ma., 355
Guetzkow, Harold, 184, 359, 385, 389
Guevara, Ché, 65, 118, 119
Guilford, J. P., 139, 179, 376, 386
Gulick, Luther H., 93, 365
Gulik, Robert H. van, 383
Gupta, T. Sen, 382
Guyot, Dorothy, 54

H

Hacker, Andrew, 334
Hagen, Elizabeth, 360
Hagen, Everett E., 357
Hägerstrand, Torsten, 358
Hain, Paul L., 347
Haines, C. Grove, 351
Hall, Arnold B., 12
Hall, K. R. L., 354
Hammond, N. G. L., 335, 388
Hanna, Willard A., 358
Harary, Frank, 378
Harding, Warren G., 128
Hargrove, Erwin C., 109, 364, 368
Harik, Ilya F., 362
Harris, Marilyn, 335
Harvey, O. J., 378
Hartley, Eugene L., 172, 383
Hatta, Mohammad, 367
Havron, M. Dean, 75, 358
Hazel, Robert, 73, 356
Heard, Alexander, 334
Heath, Edward, 71, 356
Hebb, D. O., 352
Hedlund, Ronald D., 389
Hegedus, Andreas, 374
Helmer, Olaf, 177, 386
Hemphill, John K., 74, 159, 357, 379
Henderson, Nevile, 119
Hennessey, Bernard C., 36, 341
Hennessey, Timothy M., 381
Henthorn, William E., 353
Hermann, Charles F., 54, 117, 169, 360,
    372, 382, 395
Hermann, Margaret G., 60, 162, 349, 378,
    379
Herold, David M., 359
Herrick, C. Judson, 352
Hertzler, J. O., 86, 131, 363, 375
Hetrick, Carl C., 187, 390
Hindenburg, Paul von, 395
Hirsch, Herbert, 347
Hirschman, Albert O., 345
Hitler, Adolf, 2, 15, 16, 38, 42, 50, 52, 56,
    71, 109, 113, 116, 119, 120, 122, 123,
    124, 128, 139–149 (compared with
    Gandhi), 351, 355
Hobbes, Thomas, 14, 34
Ho Chi Minh, 5, 52, 57, 72, 121, 182, 356,
    384
Hoffman, Paul J., 12, 334, 373, 381
Hoffmann, Inge Schneier, 345
Hoffmann, Stanley, 345

SUBJECT INDEX

409